A Community of Writers

A Community of Writers
A Workshop Course in Writing

Peter Elbow
University of Massachusetts at Amherst

Pat Belanoff
State University of New York at Stony Brook

Random House

New York

First Edition
98765432
Copyright © 1989 by Peter Elbow and Pat Belanoff

Library of Congress Cataloging-in-Publication Data

Elbow, Peter.
    A community of writers : a workshop course in
  writing / Peter Elbow, Pat Belanoff.—1st ed.
        p.   cm.
    Bibliography: p.
    ISBN 0-394-35488-5
    1. English language—Rhetoric.   2. College
  readers.   I. Belanoff, Pat.   II. Title.
  PE1408.E38   1989
  808'.0427—dc19   88-26785
                                              CIP

Manufactured in the United States of America

Cover design: Lawrence R. Didona

A Community of Writers
A Workshop Course in Writing

Peter Elbow
University of Massachusetts at Amherst

Pat Belanoff
State University of New York at Stony Brook

Random House

New York

First Edition
98765432
Copyright © 1989 by Peter Elbow and Pat Belanoff

Library of Congress Cataloging-in-Publication Data

Elbow, Peter.
    A community of writers : a workshop course in
writing / Peter Elbow, Pat Belanoff.—1st ed.
        p.   cm.
    Bibliography: p.
    ISBN 0-394-35488-5
    1. English language—Rhetoric.   2. College
readers.   I. Belanoff, Pat.   II. Title.
PE1408.E38   1989
808'.0427—dc19   88-26785
                                             CIP

Manufactured in the United States of America

Cover design: Lawrence R. Didona

Preface

We have written *A Community of Writers* for college freshmen and women in a one-semester writing course.* We've made our book as practical as we can, with lots of hands-on workshop activities. But we don't hide our interest in theory. We push students to become thoughtful about their writing process through regular entries in a writing process diary. Our book reflects much recent scholarship in composition.

We have structured our book into nineteen *units*—each consisting of a set of activities and ☆ a writing assignment designed to illustrate an important feature of the writing process (and designed to take up one to two weeks). The units are arranged in a coherent order that provides plenty of direction for teachers who want to follow our lead. (And we've written an extensive instructor's manual for teachers to consult.) But we've also given teachers great latitude by including far too many units for one semester and by making each unit self-contained—so that teachers can completely rearrange the order of the units to suit their own approach or priorities.

In addition to the main units, there are ten *mini-units*—short pieces each devoted to a smaller feature of writing or usage and suitable to be assigned as outside reading or used for a single class meeting.

The third part of the book is an unusual feature we're particularly proud of: a separate booklet called *Sharing and Responding,* which helps students learn to respond usefully to each other's writing. We've met many teachers who say, "Peer feedback doesn't work," but it's really a matter of giving students more guidance.

We've tried above all to make a book that is *writerly.* Our overriding principle is that we all learn writing best by writing: writing a great deal, in various modes, to various audiences, and with lots of feedback from diverse readers. The book is not a handbook that lays out rules of grammar or guidelines for good usage—nor even principles of good writing. It is a book of writing activities.

Yet in taking this writerly—even idealistic—approach we have been mindful of the constraints of the classroom setting: grading; time cut up artificially into fifty-minute blocks and into semesters or quarters; and the sometimes vexed authority relationships that come from teachers having to teach large groups rather than individuals in a course that is required rather than freely chosen.

We have been writing this book for more than three years. We and a number of our colleagues have tried out various drafts of the text in our own classrooms, and we have been able to include samples of student writing derived from these trials in the "Readings" section of each unit. We do not intend these samples as models of excellence to imitate or illustrations of pitfalls to avoid, but simply as *examples:* a range of what students have written in response to these tasks. We like these pieces—just as we also like the examples of professional writing that we include with them in the readings. We have purposely mingled the student and professional writing together without differentiation in order to emphasize that we don't think there is anything *different in kind* that distinguishes student writing from professional writing.

For it is a point of principle with us to treat students as writers: people who deserve to be in charge of what they write, who already know a lot about discourse (even when it doesn't

---

*It is also appropriate for a one- or two-quarter course—and perhaps for a full-year course if supplemented with readings. The book will also be useful for high school seniors or college sophomores or juniors—for we haven't much differentiated our audience in terms of age or skill level: we're talking equally to strong and weak students. That is, when we work with unskilled or reluctant students, we find they benefit from working on the same interesting, substantive, and sometimes difficult writing tasks we ask of our most skilled students—so long as we explain clearly what we are asking and why we are asking it, and give lots of support. On the other hand, even when we are working with very skilled and experienced students, we give lots of encouragement and take the informal, nontechnical stance you see here. The core of our book is a series of writing activities that we have found appropriate whether we're working with young children or college faculty.

look like it)—and whose greatest need is *readers*. Feeling ourselves speaking to students as other writers, we have tried to speak honestly about our own writing in a series of boxes scattered throughout the book—excerpts from our own process writing diaries.

Although each unit is self-contained, we have created a network of flexible links between them. In particular, because we want to emphasize revision (and because most writers can wait a few weeks or months before revising something they care about), we have designed many units in such a way that students can fulfill the assignment by revising or transforming a piece they did for an earlier unit. For example:

- Unit 5 (narration) can build on 4 (description);
- Unit 7 (public writing) can build on 6 (private writing);
- Unit 8 (exposition) can build on many units;
- Unit 9 (focusing on revising) can build on any unit;
- Unit 11 (argument) can build on 10 (persuasion);
- Unit 13 (analysis of audience and purpose) can build on any unit;
- Unit 14 (library research) can build on any unit;
- Unit 15 (case study of self) can build on Unit 1 (and on all the process writing from the whole semester);
- Unit 18 (writing in the disciplines) can build on 8 (exposition).

Also, many of the readings in one unit link to the readings in another. For example, in Unit 5 we see the image Eudora Welty wrote as the germ of a story; in Unit 6 we get the full story; and in Unit 13 we read her own reflections on what she had in mind in writing the story. There are many similar links in the text, where a student or professional builds or comments in one unit's readings on a piece included in a different unit.*

We are grateful for help in what (like all writing tasks) has proved to be a bigger job than we expected. We thank our numerous friends and colleagues who have tried out drafts of the text—and to the students in their classes and our own. These students and teachers gave us many good comments that have improved our book. We particularly thank those students and professionals who have allowed us to use their pieces in the readings. We feel lucky to have worked with Steve Pensinger, Jennifer Sutherland, and Barbara Hale at Random House, and to have gotten such helpful and detailed feedback from our reviewers: Richard L. Larson, Lehman College of the City University of New York; Carol Singley, Brown University; Michael Steinberg, Michigan State University; and John Trimbur, Boston University.

We also thank Doris Alkon, Paul Connolly, Cami Elbow, Claire Frost, Roni Keane, Laurie Kutchins, Glen Klopfenstein, Irene Papoulis, Marlene Perl, Pat Perry, Debrah Raschke, Valerie Reimers, John Trimbur, John Wright, and Fran Zak.

---

*There are other kinds of linking too: Units 12, 13, and 19 (and Mini-unit C) all take different approaches to textual interpretation; 14 and 16 take different approaches to research; 8 and 17 take different approaches to exposition; and 10 and 11 take different approaches to persuasion.

Contents

Expanded Table of Contents

Units

- Understanding the importance of learning to write within your chosen discipline.

- Becoming a better and more critical reader of texts in various disciplines.

- Connecting what you learn in a writing class to what you learn in other classes, and getting help with your writing from teachers of other courses.

- Thinking about the relationship between writing and the creation of knowledge.

UNIT 19: Text Analysis through Examining Figurative Language

- Writing an analysis of a text based on its figurative language; finding more to say when you're analyzing a text by paying attention to figurative language in the analysis of discourse.

- Understanding the main kinds of figurative language.

- Assessing the ways texts affect readers.

Mini-Units

MINI-UNIT A: Writing Skills Questionnaire

- A questionnaire to help you understand your attitude toward writing and see more specifically what you can already do and what you need to work on; to help you monitor your learning at the middle and the end of the course.

MINI-UNIT B: Double-Entry or Dialectical Notebooks

- A simple and practical way to take notes on what you're reading.

MINI-UNIT C: Breathing Life into Words: Text Rendering and Reading Out Loud

- Suggestions for reading out loud in order to interpret and/or enjoy a text.

MINI-UNIT D: Writing with a Word Processor

- The effects of word processing on writing: advantages and disadvantages.

- Learning to master your word processor.

MINI-UNIT E: Midterm and End-Term Responses to a Writing Course

- Suggestions and formats for writing evaluations of your writing course.

MINI-UNIT F: The Sentence and End-Stop Punctuation

- Practice with identifying sentences, run-ons, and fragments.

A Community of Writers

Introduction

OUR VIEW OF WRITING

This book has two main messages: Writing is hard. Writing is easy. It is obvious that writing is hard—or at least that writing *well* is hard. But it helps to understand where the difficulty comes from.

Imagine you are having a relaxed, interesting conversation with your best friend. You're in a comfortable room where you both feel right at home. You are both talking away and having a wonderful time. You find you have lots to say because you like talking to this person who likes you and is interested in what you have to say.

Then someone else comes into the room and starts listening to the conversation. A friend. But quickly you feel that something is peculiar because this friend doesn't say anything, doesn't join in, only listens. It makes you feel a little funny, but you keep up the conversation.

Then more people start coming in. Some of them are strangers, and they don't say anything either: they just listen.

Then your friend stops talking altogether and asks you to do all the talking yourself.

Then someone pulls out a tape recorder and starts recording what you say.

Finally your friend, even though she won't join in the conversation, starts quizzing you as you are talking and asks:

- Are you really sure that what you are saying is interesting?

- Are you sure that what you are saying is right?

- Are you really sure you understand what you are saying?

And she doesn't just ask questions, she gives "helpful suggestions":

- Make sure that what you say is well organized.

- Think carefully about who is listening. Are you speaking in a way that suits these listeners?

- Watch your language. Don't make any mistakes in grammar. Don't sound dumb.

This is an allegory of writing. In writing you must keep on putting out words, but no one answers or responds. You are putting out words for an audience, but you don't know how they are reacting. You may know who the intended reader is (probably someone who will *grade* it), but you don't really know who else *might* read it: whom the reader might show it to or who might find it lying around. You are trying to get your thinking right, your organization right, and your language right—all at the same time. And there are spelling and punctuation to worry about too.

No wonder writing is hard.

But we have another message: writing is easy. Writing is easier than talking because it's safer than talking. You can "say" something on paper and no one has to see it. If you've ever blurted something wrong to the wrong person and wanted to bite your tongue off as soon as the words came out of your mouth, you know that you can never undo what you've spoken. But in writing you can blurt out anything and see what it looks like on paper, and no one need ever see it. You can even keep yourself from ever seeing it again. In short, writing is much more flexible and private than talking.

People expect you to make some sort of sense when you talk—otherwise they'll stop listening or think you're odd or give you a hard time. But you don't *have* to make any sense when you write. You can go on and on forever when you write; you can't do that in speech because people will stop listening after a while no matter how much they like you.

Writing lets you "talk" about any topic at all, even if you don't know anyone who is interested enough to listen. And there are certain things it's hard to talk to anyone about. Writing lets you "talk" to anyone and tell them anything—and you can decide later whether to show it to them.

Admittedly, in describing how easy writing is, we're talking about writing in itself, not about *good* writing, and not about writing that will be read by someone else, particularly a someone else who will judge it. But even when your goal is to produce good writing for a harsh judge, you can start out this way, just writing for yourself. Afterwards it turns out to be much easier to make it good than you thought. For one thing, when you do all that easy writing, surprising amounts of it are in fact already pretty good. Those parts that are potentially good but badly written are surprisingly easy to fix

2

up once you've got them down in one form or another. What's really hard about writing is unnecessary: trying to get it right the *first time.*

Behind what we've just said is the fact that writing requires two mental abilities that are so different that they usually conflict with each other: the ability to *create* an abundance of words and ideas and the ability to *criticize* and discard words and ideas. To write well we need to be both generative and cutthroat. We all know the awful feeling of trying to use both "muscles" at once: trying to come up with words and ideas and at the same time seeing how nothing is good enough. We get stuck. But we can get unstuck by separating the mental processes: we can think of more words and ideas if we hold off all criticism (as in brainstorming), and we can be more critical and tough-minded if we have already piled up more material than we need.

In short, even though writing gets most of us into the pickle of trying to use two muscles that get in each other's way, it is writing that is ideal for using those muscles one at a time.

ABOUT THE STRUCTURE OF THIS BOOK

Our textbook is in two separate parts: this book (made up of units and mini-units) and a separate booklet, *Sharing and Responding.*

Units. These make up the main part of the book. They contain the main activities and writing assignments (one major assignment per unit). We believe that most of the learning will come from these activities and assignments, not from any ideas or information we give. We assume that most teachers will spend a week on each unit (though longer would make sense too). There are too many units for one semester, so teachers will have to leave some out. Many of the units ask you to write something that builds upon what you wrote for a previous unit, so in a sense there are a number of two-unit cycles. Despite these potential sequences, all the units stand on their own, and thus teachers can use the units in whatever order suits them. However your teacher arranges the units, you'll want to keep all your writing for possible later use.

At the end of most units, we have included a section titled "Ruminations and Theory." To "ruminate" is, literally, to "chew the cud." In this section we share some of the thinking we've done that lies behind the unit. We are wrapped up in these explorations, and so we think the issues are important. But we have no doubt that the main way you learn is by doing the unit's activities, not by reading theory. So if you don't feel that our explorations are helping you do the activities of the unit, feel free to skip them (unless your teacher says otherwise).

Mini-units. These short sections can be read or studied on your own or be used as the basis of single class sessions. Mini-units don't involve writing assignments.

3

Sharing and Responding. We've put into this booklet all the good methods we know for getting feedback from classmates on your writing. You can do this in pairs or in small groups. The ability to give responses to your classmates' writing and to get their responses to your own writing may be the most important thing you learn from this book. Learning to do it well takes time and practice. We want you to try out many methods; we ask you to be rather disciplined in following our directions. Our goal is for you, as writer, finally to be able to choose whatever kinds of feedback you think will help you most for any given piece of writing. But you can't make good choices until you've learned about the feedback options that are available to you. We're almost sure that you do not already know most of these methods for responding to writing.

We've put all these sharing and responding activities and suggestions in a separate booklet so you can carry it around easily. Although the booklet is intimately connected to the textbook, you can use it for all writing tasks, in school and out. Actually, we hope it's the part you'll find most useful for later writing; thus we have bound it separately to make it easier for you to continue to use after you've finished this particular course.

KEY WORDS IN THE TITLE: COMMUNITY, WORKSHOP, WRITER

Community. Language is social and socializing. We talked before about writing just for yourself and throwing it away. But if we never had anyone to talk to, we would never develop any language at all—and therefore wouldn't be able to talk or write even to ourselves. And the benefits of social language continue throughout our lives. The more we experience the pleasure that comes from communication—listening to others, reading to them, writing for them, talking to them—the better we get at all these skills.

Workshop. A workshop is a place where people *do* things, usually under the guidance of a master craftsperson. Our text suggests a classroom where students do things under the guidance of a teacher who is a master at writing because she has done more of it and thought more about it than students. But she isn't a person who does it in some special, magical way any more than a master carpenter works in a magical way. The only way to learn to write is by writing. No one can teach you how to write; others can only create a situation in which you learn for yourself from what you're doing.

This book can't really teach you how to write either, though we can in certain sections explain key ideas or principles involved in writing. You learn from *writing*—if you go about it right. Thus the heart of this book is a series of writing situations and assignments. If you enter into them, you will teach yourself writing. Thus perhaps the most important piece you'll write is the long case study of yourself-as-writer at the end of the course. It should contain *what* you've learned and *how* you've learned it. It will be a useful document, particularly if you include advice for yourself for future writing: sort of a little individualized textbook.

Writer. You may not think of yourself as a writer, but we do. We are going to treat you like a writer. A writer isn't some peculiar absent-minded genius who goes into a trance and magically produces good writing. A writer is someone who writes a lot and who cares a lot about it. The best writers struggle. You may well already be a writer. If not, we can help you become one in this nonmagical sense of the word—someone who enjoys writing, cares about writing, and struggles but gets satisfaction from the struggle. Our first step is to start right off *treating* you like a writer.

Here are the things we assume when we treat you like a writer:

- Like all writers, you have lots of words and ideas in you. If it feels as though you don't, that's just a sign that you haven't put down enough words and ideas yet. Paradoxically, the more you put down, the more you'll have left. We'll get you started.

- Like all writers, you own your writing. Only you can know when the words you put on paper fulfill the intentions toward meaning you started with. Others—your classmates, friends, teacher, tutors in your school's writing center—can help you see how your words work for them, but it is you who must decide what suggestions are important and what changes to make (if any). Some pieces you won't want to revise; others, once you try them out on readers, you will have a greater incentive to work on.

- Like all writers, you need others to write to. Real writers write things they care about for real readers. The problem in schools and colleges is that you often write only for a teacher and you usually write about topics the teacher knows more about than you do. We can't totally eliminate this twofold problem, but we can get you to write for more people than your teacher. After all, writers don't write for just one person. Thus they learn that different people have different reactions to the same piece. That's something you'll discover too from listening to various classmates' reactions to your writing. Also, we encourage teachers to exchange papers with other teachers so that students can benefit from the responses of more than one experienced reader. The more you feel in touch with a broader audience, the more you'll feel like a writer.

- Like all writers, you need to share your writing with others. Only by sharing your writing, getting the feeling of what it's like to have an audience by actually reading to one—only in this way will you begin to know what it means to communicate through writing. Perhaps in the past you've felt that you wrote pieces which disappeared into a black hole, only to reappear several days or even weeks later with grades added. Such experiences don't give you any sense of communicating with readers. To be a writer, you need that sense.

5

- Like all writers, you're already a sophisticated user of your native language. When you speak, you don't consciously think about words; you think about meaning, and the words tend to come out correctly. Unless you are scared, subjects and verbs usually agree, sentence structures work, vocabulary is appropriate. In addition to that, you also react almost intuitively to your social situation—where you are and whom you're talking to. Therefore when you concentrate on your meaning as you write, all these natural language abilities will function in the same way to produce mostly correct language. This natural language ability will also help you make judgments about your writing and the writing of your classmates. You may need to learn to trust these natural abilities more and to think consciously about them so as to learn from them.

But it's just as well to acknowledge a difficulty on this score. We say we want you to *own* your writing and to take responsibility for your own choices. But here is a book full of "orders" for you to follow—used in a course where your teacher will also give you "orders." It's easy to feel like you are just doing "our" writing or "your teacher's" writing.

It might seem as though the definition of a good student is someone who's good at following orders. But that's not quite right. The definition of a good student is someone who can learn the most, and what makes you learn the most is the ability to *own* even what you are stuck with—to take over or internalize what comes from outside. This is a difficult and paradoxical skill. Sometimes in order to learn to internalize, you need to be able to resist. Thus it might happen that we tell you to do x, and your teacher compounds it by requiring y in addition, but you realize that you will learn the most if you do z; and if you get a lower mark for it, well, you decide that's worth the price—because it's your learning.

UNITS

UNIT

1

An Introduction to the Variety of Writing Processes

We have a couple of related goals for this first unit. First, we will show you how to get words on paper quickly, easily, and productively—and try to prove to you that there are always lots more where they came from. We can help you build a foundation of confidence in the face of a blank page, confidence you can draw on later when writing tasks get harder. Our emphasis here is on the process of *generating* words and ideas.

Second, we want to introduce you to a wide *variety* of kinds of writing to show you that there is no one thing, "writing," but rather different kinds of writing for different situations. The heart of this unit is a series of short writing tasks that are very different in process (though similar in content since they will all explore your memories of writing). Some of the pieces will be for others to read and some only for yourself; some pieces will have a specified topic and some will not. Your teacher will ask you to do some of this writing in class and some of it at home.

Through these short writing assignments, we are introducing a major goal: for you to become more aware of what is going on as you write so that you can take more control of your writing process. By trying out different kinds of writing and reflecting on what you've just done, you will not be so likely to assume that "writing is writing" and to fall into just one way of writing—one "writing gear"—for every writing task.

We won't work much with revising in this unit, but we'll introduce "cut-and-paste revising" to help you end up with a final assignment: a "collage" of good passages that will be a mini-portrait of yourself as a writer at this point. This will be a piece of finished writing that you can be proud to share with others and with your teacher.

A SPECTRUM OF WRITING TASKS

Your teacher may select which of these to do for class, but we hope you'll find time to do all of them.

1. *Careful writing to be evaluated by a teacher.* Many students have never written except for a teacher; their writing has always been evaluated or graded. Have you, like many students, fallen into assuming that writing *means* writing for evaluation by a teacher? We will try to convince you that this is *not* the most useful way to think about writing. Yet, of course, much of your school writing will be evaluated by your teacher. Now is probably such an occasion, since, at the beginning of the course, your teacher may need to evaluate a piece of every student's writing to help plan her teaching and to see whether any students belong in a different course. Possible topics:

- Tell about a time when writing went particularly well. What was the topic and audience? Try to tell the story in detail: how you went about writing, what happened, what feelings you had, and so forth. What can you learn from this example?

- Write a short summary of the process writing by Pat Belanoff that appears in a box on page 12. This is a test of careful reading as well as of careful writing.

2. *Public writing.* This is writing you share with others (in this case with your classmates), but not for evaluation, only for the sake of communicating with them. This sharing will help everyone in the class learn about the writing process and about each other. Possible topics:

- An introduction of yourself to others in this course. You choose the form and the length: don't tell more than you feel comfortable telling.

- Your strengths as a writer and learner. What are you proud of? What do you need as a student and writer? What do you most want to learn? What can you contribute to a learning community?

3. *Freewriting.* This is private, nonstop writing where you write about whatever you want to write about or put down whatever comes to mind. Your teacher will not ask you to hand this in or share it. Don't worry about whether your writing is any good or even whether it makes sense. Don't worry about spelling or grammar. If you can't think of the word you want, just put in a squiggle. Just keep writing and see what comes. Changing topics is fine. Try to follow the writing where it wants to go. If you seem to run out

of something to say, just write that you have nothing to say or write about how you feel at the moment or keep repeating the last word or the last sentence. More will come. If *too* much comes to mind, don't worry about trying to keep up or get it all down. There is an example of a student's freewriting (voluntarily submitted) in the readings at the end of the unit. (We talk some more about why freewriting is important to us in the final optional section of the unit, "Ruminations and Theory.")

4. *Focused freewriting.* This is freewriting where you stay on one topic. It harnesses the "freewriting muscle"—the ability to produce and put down words quickly without planning or worrying about quality—for the sake of exploring one subject. It's a useful skill for the hardest stage in any writing assignment: getting started. Try ten minutes on one of these:

- Tell about someone who was important to your writing—helpful or harmful, a teacher or someone else.

- Do you think of yourself as a writer? What does it mean for someone to be a writer?

5. *Public freewriting.* This is freewriting that you share with a reader. You may find it hard to write without stopping when you know you will show it to others, particularly to others you don't yet know: your teacher and other students in the class, who will probably read this freewriting. But, while writing, try to resist the need to pause and ponder what to say and how to say it. After you've finished this and before you hand it in, your teacher will give you time to look over what you've written and see whether you want to cross out or change anything.

Try ten minutes of this kind of writing on one of the following topics. (Staying on one topic makes it not only public freewriting but also focused.) There's an example of a student's public focused freewriting in the readings section at the end of this unit.

PROCESS BOX

There seems to be a sort of fatality in my mind leading me to put at first my statement and proposition in a wrong or awkward form. Formerly I used to think about my sentences before writing them down; but for several years I have found that it saves time to scribble in a vile hand whole pages as quickly as I possibly can, contracting half the words; and then correct deliberately. Sentences thus scribbled down are often better ones than I could have written deliberately.

CHARLES DARWIN, *THE AUTOBIOGRAPHY*

- Tell about a time when writing went particularly badly. What was the topic and audience? Try to tell in detail how you went about writing and what happened. What can you learn from this example?

- What is hardest and easiest about writing for you? ☆

6. *Invisible writing.* If you write on a word processor and turn down the screen (or if you write with an empty ballpoint pen on a sheet of paper on top of carbon paper and another sheet), you won't be able to see what you are writing. This is invisible writing (Blau). It seems odd, but most people get used to it after a few trials and then find it a surprisingly useful exercise. For one thing, you can't pause in your writing or else you'll lose track of what you're saying. Thus the exercise makes you write *more.* What's more important, invisible writing increases your concentration on the *emerging meaning inside your head:* it forces you to focus better on what you have in mind. Invisible writing makes most people realize how often in their normal writing they lose track of what they are writing about by stopping to look back at what they have on paper. Try invisible writing, especially if you write on a word processor. Possible topic:

- Write about the *physical conditions* for your writing. Where and when do you like to write? What implements (pen, pencil, typewriter, computer, kind of pad or paper) do you use and why? Do you need silence and solitude, or do you prefer to have music on or other people around?

7. *Letters.* Letters are partly public and partly private. That is, they go ☆ to a reader, but usually to only one or two readers. ("Open" letters or "letters to the editor" in a newspaper feel different from most letters precisely because they are so much more public.) Letters to friends or family are often very informal, even casual; sometimes we don't even look them over before mailing. But letters can be just as formal as any writing when they are for business or to someone with authority whom one doesn't know. But even in the most formal letter, we usually write directly *to* the receiver—addressing him in the second person—which is rare in any other kind of writing.

- Try using the letter form in a way that is probably new to you. Write a letter to your present teacher introducing yourself. Say as much or as little as you want. We suggest that you talk about your hopes, goals, or needs for this class: what you would like to get out of it, what you can contribute, what you hope will not happen, and what makes you nervous or anxious about the class. This will not be graded; its purpose is to communicate information. Teachers can teach better if they know more about what their students want and need from the course.

8. *Revising.* We are not asking for what may be the hardest task in writing: to revise a long piece of writing. But try revising one of the shorter

pieces you have written so far. For now we won't talk about techniques for revising (we will in some later units). Just pick a short piece that interests but dissatisfies you—perhaps one that you have read out loud. Wade in and make some significant changes, not just a word here and there. See if you can make it work better—please you better.

✮ 9. *Process writing.* Process writing means writing to explore what was going on as you were writing: writing *about* your writing process. What works best is simply to record what actually happened, with as much honesty and detail as possible—and with a spirit of calm, benign acceptance of yourself. That is, you aren't trying to *judge* yourself or prove anything or reach big conclusions—just to find out what actually goes on when you

---

PROCESS BOX

I've just written and revised a paper about freewriting I was writing for a conference.

I procrastinated, as I always do, waiting for special inspiration— it didn't come (usually it doesn't). So I forced it, felt like I was stammering on paper. After ten minutes, though, I was rolling.

After about thirty minutes of this nonstop writing, I had a good amount of stuff on paper, although I still wasn't particularly pleased with what I had come up with. Still, I had to get it done, so I started working with it. As I did that, more and more came out. Soon I had a rough draft of my paper. But I didn't particularly like it, so I fiddled with it some more. Since I had agreed to read it at a get-together of a group of us who meet about once a month to work on our writing, I had to get it in some sort of presentable form.

I told everyone before I started reading it that it sort of did what I wanted it to do; I just didn't think it did it very well. After I finished reading, the members of the group started talking about the ideas in it—not criticizing anything and not giving me many suggestions, just talking about it.

As I drove home that night, it came to me—I knew what I had to do. I had to reorganize, present what I wanted to say as a story of an intellectual quest, what started me on the quest, what I found along the way, and what I concluded when I finished the quest. I don't know why I hadn't seen this before, but I hadn't. Something about sitting in the group and reading it, hearing it discussed a bit, made it (my text) into an object I could look at from a greater distance and shape in a more logical way. The next day I made these revisions with very little effort.

---

write. You can be sure that if you do process writing regularly (and we will try to make that happen!), you will reach plenty of interesting conclusions. You don't have to *try* for them. But you probably will have to work at trying to capture the steps you went through, the feelings and thoughts that occurred, and so forth. It's usually easier to remember and write down what happened if you write it in the form of a story. For example:

> First I thought of so-and-so and the words came tumbling along as fast as I could write. Time went faster than I expected. I came up with some thoughts that were new to me. Then when I wrote about such-and-such I began to feel mixed up and I slowed down and I couldn't figure out what I wanted to say. Then I stopped for a long time and walked around feeling stuck. Then [and so forth].

Sometimes process writing is easier if you do it after *two* writing sessions and compare what happened in the two. Remember that process writing is not just about the act of writing itself, but also about everything that goes into writing: thoughts about your topic when you are not actually writing, collecting material to use, talk with others, feedback, daydreaming, false starts.

Do a few ten-minute process writings about what was happening as you wrote some of the preceding tasks or assignments. Look for the details or specifics of what you did or what happened.

At the end of this unit is a piece of process writing by Regina Olmeyer. Also, you'll see bits of process writing (mostly ours) in "Process Boxes" scattered throughout the whole text—as well as some examples of other people's process writing in some of the "Readings" sections. As you read this process writing, you'll see how much else besides the physical act of writing is actually involved.

MAIN ASSIGNMENT FOR THE UNIT: A COLLAGE ABOUT YOU AS WRITER AND HOW YOU WRITE

A *collage* in the original sense, as used by artists, is a picture produced not by painting or drawing but by pasting objects on the canvas—objects such as theater tickets, bits of cardboard or tin or colored paper. A written collage consists of separate, disconnected bits of writing rather than of one continuous piece. Usually there are spaces or asterisks at the "joints" between the pieces of writing.

A collage can serve as a "quick and dirty" way to produce a finished piece of writing. That is, you can just pick out the passages of writing that work best or that you like most and put them together in whatever order strikes you as interesting or best. Don't agonize over the order; it is traditional in collages to call on your intuition.

In effect a collage allows you simply to *skip* what are often the hardest parts of the writing process: revising passages that don't work, struggling with organization, and writing explicit connections or transitions between sections. And yet the finished collage is often a remarkably satisfying and effective piece of writing. In the readings following this unit there are three sample collages: one by a student, one by an editor at *The New Yorker,* and one by Donald Murray. Also, in the "Ruminations and Theory" section at the end of the unit, there is a collage that explains collages.

Since the collage you produce is a portrait of yourself and your experiences in writing, think of your audience for this assignment as your teacher and your classmates: you are introducing that side of yourself to these relative strangers—and also helping them learn about what writing is for other people. But think also of your audience as yourself: you will manage to tell yourself things about yourself that you didn't know before.

Perhaps the best way to explain a collage further is simply to give you the minimal directions you need for doing this unit's main assignment.

- Look through all the pieces you have written so far and choose the ones that seem best for giving a picture of how you write.

- Spread them out so you can see them all and then arrange them in what seems the best order.

- Feel free to make all these decisions by instinct or intuition.

- Next, revise it all, but in a minimal and purely "negative" way. That is, don't rewrite (unless there's some particular section you really want to rework). Just *leave out* words, phrases, sentences, or passages that don't work. And instead of trying to make nice connections or transitions between the remaining passages, leave spaces or put in asterisks.

- Type your collage and proofread and copyedit it carefully. Since your collage will be distributed to some or all of your classmates, you'll want to present a finished piece you can be proud of. You may need help from a classmate, family member, or roommate. You can return the favor by carefully copyediting and proofing something of theirs, since most of us see usage problems and mistakes in typing more quickly in someone else's writing than in our own.

KEEPING A PROCESS JOURNAL

We ask you to keep a process journal for this course. It might be a handy separate notebook or a section of a larger notebook, or it might be a folder where you keep separate pieces of paper on which you do process writing. Your teacher may make this notebook a requirement for the course, and perhaps even end the course with Unit 15 for which the major assignment is a full case study of your writing and writing process throughout the semester. For this case study, you can draw heavily on your process journal.

The best time to do process writing is right after you have been writing. The goal is to find out what *really* happened—the facts of what occurred on that particular occasion. Don't struggle for conclusions; trust that they'll come.

We spoke earlier of doing process writing in the form of a story of your writing session. Another good approach is to plunge into an exploration of what was most difficult or frustrating for you in that session. Explore what happened: what led to this difficulty? What did you do while in it? How did you get out? Tell everything you can. Interesting insights often come. In short, you can use process writing as a way to try to move against what is giving you trouble. As you do this over a number of sessions, you will begin to figure out how to avoid trouble.

Try to make at least one short entry in your process journal whenever you do a significant piece of writing, keeping an eye out for clues about what helps you and what hinders you in your writing. Remember that "writing" doesn't just mean "school writing." You are also writing when you leave someone a note or write a letter or fill out an application—even when you make a list of things to buy or do. What do you notice when you do these usually unnoticed kinds of writing?

(The term "process writing" is sometimes used—especially in the field of scientific and technical writing—to mean writing that describes some particular and often technical process, for example, how blood samples are analyzed in a lab or how to construct a piece of equipment. This is a completely different kind of process writing from the one we are talking about.)

PROCESS JOURNAL QUESTIONS

In each unit we'll give you a few questions for your process journal. If you find yourself able to relive the experience of writing a particular piece and able to record it on paper, you will not need our questions. They are here *only* to help you if your mind goes blank. So feel free to ignore the following questions (unless your teacher asks for entries on specific ones).

- Freewriting. How did the process differ from your usual writing? Could you continue writing without pause? What were the effects of trying not to stop? How much did you worry about whether your private writing was "good"?

- In which piece(s) did you write things that surprised you—things you didn't know you were thinking or feeling? In which piece(s) did you write mostly what you already knew?

- Audience. What did you notice about writing to different audiences? no audience? classmates as audience? teacher as audience? Do you experience your private writing as being to yourself or to no one?

- What did you notice about making a collage? About how you chose the passages to keep, how you decided on the order for those passages, and how you pruned for your final version?

- Sharing. What was it like reading your words to others—and listening to theirs? Having your collage distributed? What did that process make you notice?

RUMINATIONS AND THEORY

We have no doubt that the main way you learn is by doing the activities of the unit, not by reading some of our background thinking in these ruminatory sections. So if you don't feel that these explorations at the end of each unit are helping you do the activities of the unit (and if your teacher doesn't say otherwise), feel free to skip them. There are three subsections that follow:

A. Why We Think Freewriting Is Important

B. Why We Think Process Writing Is Important

C. A Collage about Collages.

A. Why We Think Freewriting Is Important

Freewriting is obviously important, but it's perplexing. For most people it's the easiest exercise and yet the most powerful and versatile. It leads naturally to some of the worst writing and also to some of the best. Why should that be?

Freewriting teaches us to "say on paper" anything we have in mind. It helps us take our mind off the *medium* of writing, off the fact that we are engaged in an odd, artificial way to express our thoughts—artificial, that is, in comparison to speaking. Freewriting helps us put all our attention on what we have in mind, so we can, as it were, just wiggle our pens without paying attention to it—and trust the words will come out making sense. That's what we do when we speak: we put all our attention on what we have in mind and just wiggle our mouths without paying any attention to it. Thus freewriting can make writing as natural as speaking.

To analyze freewriting is to understand why regular writing is so difficult.

- Writing is usually judged or even graded. Freewriting isn't.

- Writing is supposed to make sense, but freewriting can be incoherent or nonsensical.

- Writing is supposed to stay on one topic and be organized, but freewriting can jump all over the place.

- Writing usually means thinking about spelling and grammar. But you skip all that in freewriting.

- Writing is usually for an audience, while freewriting is private. Thus freewriting is even *safer* than speaking, since we almost never speak except when someone's listening.

- Writing is usually supposed to be more important and dignified and "better" than speech. (Why take the time to write something out unless you are going to try to get it right?) But freewriting is an invitation to let the written word be *less* important and careful than the spoken word—and to see what you can learn from it.

Thus freewriting removes all the difficulties of regular writing except one— the brutal necessity of putting words down on paper.

Sometimes a skilled student objects, "But freewriting is for blocked beginners, and I'm a fluent, skilled writer already." It's true that freewriting is good for unskilled students, but we find that *skilled, experienced* writers get the most out of freewriting. It's an exercise whose payoff increases with the expertise of the writer.

You can't predict how freewriting will work for someone. Some people start off with coherent freewriting but gradually, as they use it, drift into freewriting that's more jumpy and surprising. Some people start off jumpy. It seems as though better writers allow more shifts and jumps into their freewriting—and more talking to themselves. We sense that people go through stages, perhaps even a stage where they write only "Nothing today, nothing, nothing" over and over—or some other kind of refusal to make meaning. It is important to give yourself permission to do this and not measure the usefulness of freewriting by the *quality* of what you turn out. We sense that freewriting "works" in an underground way on what the writer needs to work on—but obviously that's a statement of faith. (We first heard of freewriting from an important pioneer teacher of writing, Ken Macrorie. We've listed a couple of good books by him in the *Works Cited.*)

A Few Thoughts about Freewriting and Bad Writing

We think of writing as getting from the chaos inside our head to coherence on paper. But this is too hard for most of us to do in one step. Freewriting provides a helpful middle step: getting the chaos in our head onto paper. This frightens some people at first, but it turns out to be helpful to discover that in fact it's not so hard to get down on paper what's going on in your head. By doing so, you can get a helpful perspective on it. What's hard about writing is trying to *improve* what's in your head. Once it's on paper, *then* you can improve it. Thus you have *two* steps to produce coherence instead of struggling to do it all in one.

When you try to avoid bad writing you write careful, planned sentences. In doing so, almost inevitably—despite your best efforts—you produce some sentences that are tangled, unclear, wooden, or hard to read. This happens because in careful writing you keep stopping, being bothered by something, thinking about what's wrong, and trying to make some change or adjustment. In all this stopping you often lose the thread of your thought, even the connections of your syntax—and certainly you lose concentration and energy. But when you freewrite, you almost *never* produce a wooden, tangled sentence; virtually every sentence is lively and energetic and easy to understand.

It's not that freewriting is always good. Far from it. (Though some of it is good.) But interestingly enough, it's easier to tighten and clarify bad freewriting than bad careful writing. Try it. Find a long stretch of bad freewriting, and also a piece of careful writing—writing you struggled over—which is still weak or problematic. Now try to clean up both passages. You'll discover that the careless writing is easier to fix. The careful writing is delicately glued together and therefore hard to reglue.

Freewriting is full of "wrong words." You are writing along and get to a word and have a feeling it's the wrong one but you haven't got time to find a better one, so you put it down. But because freewriting follows your thinking, putting down the wrong word often leads you naturally to the right word. ("And I said it because I dislike him. No, it's not that I *dislike* him, it's that I'm always uncomfortable around him.") Stopping, not writing, pausing to search your mind for the right word—as in careful writing—often leads to the almost-right or sort-of-right word. Not stopping and therefore blurting out the wrong word leads you to the really right word.

B. Why We Think Process Writing Is Important

The most important kind of learning in school is learning about learning. The most important thinking is thinking about thinking. (Psychologists call these activities "metacognition.") Without good learning about learning you are stuck knowing only what you've already learned in school. Metacognition gives you power over your future learning and over yourself.

By the same token, the most important writing you do in this course may be writing about writing. Process writing is what gives you the most control over your future writing and over yourself. It's simple—just telling what happened—yet because it consists of self-reflective thinking, it is also the most cognitively sophisticated writing.

Writing usually seems a mystery: sometimes you slave over something and it comes out awful; sometimes you dash something off and it comes out good. And yet, of course, dashing things off is no answer either. Thus it is common to feel frustrated and even helpless about writing. But regular process writing can give you power and control over yourself as a writer. You can figure out what specific procedures work for you—under what kinds of conditions and for what kinds of tasks—and what kinds of procedures undermine your thinking or tend to get you stuck.

If someone asks you out of the blue to tell how you usually write, you may tell lies:

- "It always helps me to write an outline first." But what about that assignment when you didn't have time and produced a well-organized piece without an outline? Or that time when you got stuck trying to keep to an outline which you eventually abandoned anyway?

- "Words always come slowly and with effort, and writing discourages me." But what about those moments when a whole train of thought bubbled up into your mind as you were writing, and you felt completely confident of it as you were writing? How could you make that happen more often?

Your memory is apt to play tricks on you and make you think there is one pattern to your writing. But if you do regular process writing, you'll discover that the truth is more complicated and usually much more interesting—and more useful.

It feels odd to some students to write about their writing. It makes them feel self-conscious. "It's hard enough trying to think about what I'm writing about without also trying to think about how I'm writing." (What would happen to the centipede if he had to think about all his legs as he walked?) But process writing doesn't require you to watch yourself writing *while* you write, only to think back *afterward* to what happened.

Think of process writing as doing an "instant TV replay" of your writing. (The sports metaphor is instructive here.) Videotaping is crucial for tennis, football, and baseball players. In every sport serious players and coaches carefully watch tapes of themselves in order to reflect at leisure on matters of technique they cannot give full attention to while playing. Teachers and psychiatrists watch tapes of themselves on the job to try to see what works and what doesn't.

Peter Elbow got interested in writing by going through a period of not being able to write (and having to quit school). The way he got himself going again was by doing process writing about almost every writing session—and discovering what was getting in his way. But neither of us thought about what now seems obvious—using this kind of writing as a teaching tool—till we learned about it from Sondra Perl in the New York City Writing Project.

C. A Collage about Collages

I sit here with seven short pieces of writing scattered around me on the sofa and the floor. Some are in pen, some in pencil. A couple of the "pieces" consist of two smaller pieces taped together. The shortest is only two sen-

tences long; the longest is three paragraphs. The miracle is that I *like* it all.
I want to show all these blips to readers. But how am I going to put them
all together?

ooooo

How could I like all this writing when I didn't feel I was doing anything
particularly good this week—just churning stuff out, writing fast, producing
assorted blips and pieces? And I didn't make *any* changes in what I wrote—
or hardly any. (I changed six words, two phrases, and I more or less rewrote
one short paragraph.)

The secret weapon was simply to choose bits I liked and cross out and
throw away everything I didn't like—and not feel bad that I wrote lots that
I didn't like. On the one hand I didn't change a word. On the other hand
my pile of writing feels completely different because of all that I left out.

ooooo

The collage is cheating but it works. That's why so many professionals
write collages. I see them everywhere now that I've got my eye cocked for
them. It stresses what is easy and finesses what is hard.

What makes good writing good? Details. Lively, human, clear language—words that sound like someone talking. Surprises. The sense that the
writer cared and was involved. Not hitting the reader over the head. If I
write fast and with confidence or in a good mood I get plenty of details and
lively language—so long as I pick out the good pieces and throw the rest
away. Thus I get good writing. (Or at least writing that's better than most of
my labored writing.)

What makes good writing difficult? Sitting down and planning and then
producing a complete piece of writing; trying to know where I'm going and
trying to get it right as I go; getting the connections or transitions right; figuring out the right organization; working out my train of thought fully and
avoiding contradictions. If I just pick out the good pieces and make a collage
I get to skip all those difficulties—and still get good writing.

ooooo

Surprise. I am surprised by what I find in the words I've already written.
Here's that experience again: finding something rolling off my pen that I
hadn't planned on writing or couldn't have planned on writing. This is perhaps the most important writing experience for me. I'll bet not many people
write by choice unless they have tasted this pleasure of surprise and are hungry for more of it.

ooooo

A TV documentary on cancer. It's really a collage. It opens with shots
of a funeral—people standing around the side of a grave: close-up of a
widow and then down to the coffin being lowered. Cut to a sequence of cells
under a high-powered microscope—time-lapse so that we see the cells mul-
tiplying and going crazy; a voice is telling us about how cancer cells behave.
Then a sequence of a man in the doctor's office—getting the verdict. Then
Ronald Reagan making a joke about his cancer. Then a young medical stu-

dent talking about wanting to go into cancer research—why she finds it exciting and all the progress that's being made. We cut from her, bursting with enthusiasm and health, back to the victim, balding and emaciated from the therapy, but walking in the woods—obviously drinking in the scene as though he can't get enough. Then a sequence of someone earnestly giving us statistics. How many cases of this and that, how much more than in the past, but also how there are more successful treatments and cures. Back now to Reagan going about his work. Then the victim trying to explain things to his child. Finally a sequence of advice about how to avoid cancer.

It's all a hodgepodge—completely "disorganized"—no connectives. But it works.

ooooo

Advice:

- Write on only one side of the paper—so you can cut your pieces out with scissors.

- You can even write a collage without knowing what it's going to be about. Just do a lot of pieces of writing about what comes up. Use all kinds of prompts for writing: hunches, instinct, snippets of overheard conversation, street signs—anything at all. Then look through it for what seems to be the main thing on your mind and make a collage.

- Try to make the writing experimental and alive, not expository or conceptual. Try for little stories, moments, snapshots, portraits, dialogues—perhaps even a bit of ranting. Try to make the writing *convey* experience, not explain it. (See the prompts for kinds of writing listed in Unit 3, "The Loop Writing Process.")

- After a while, look for the good passages. Don't just trust your own silent reading here; read lots of raw writing to listeners you trust and see how it sounds and what they respond to.

- Save those pieces. Don't revise or change—just cross out and carve away what isn't so good.

- Put all the pieces you come up with on the floor and live with them a bit, contemplate them, and see what they are about. (If it seems obvious, wait and see whether perhaps they're not really about something else.) If there's time, go away and try to forget about them for a while. Then intuitively put them in an order that pleases you: no transitions or connections. In the final copy, just mark transitions with spaces or asterisks.

- Cleaning up: try if possible to make *no* changes at all except for fixing mistakes in spelling and grammar and figuring out punctuation marks for the words you have. Perhaps you'll see a few words or phrases you need to change, even a few phrases or sentences to add. Perhaps you need to write one new piece now to put near the end, the beginning, or somewhere else—to make things hang together more. Perhaps you'll want to add a title. But try to work entirely by cutting and as little as possible by adding or changing, so you don't lose the life that comes from writing without a "grand plan." That is, keep it from being "careful," "self-conscious" prose.

○○○○○

I've been working for a long time on a difficult essay. I'm writing to readers who will disagree with me, and I've spent hours and hours trying to strengthen and refine these ideas. I care about them. My early rough writing was exciting to me. I know I'm going in a direction that's important to me, yet it's rough, incomplete, and at times downright wrong. Thus I'm trying to revise and revise.

As I've revised, I've added and then cut and then added and then cut—all this going on over a long period. I'm very invested in this piece; it's very important. I finally feel I'm getting it right, but I must put it aside for a few days while I do other things. I finally come back to it with excitement—it's the fruit of so much work and caring. But when I read it through I discover it is *terrible:* muddy, tangled, badly disorganized, frustrating to read, unconvincing. How can it be that my best efforts lead to terrible writing? My first raw writing was better—and yet it was no good either.

It's at times like this that I need to remember collages—and how I can produce clear and lively language and interesting ideas without ever having to agonize. It's *not* that I don't have good language in me or can't think; it's just that in my efforts to work on *these* thoughts (which are hard) and for *this* audience (which is hard), everything turned to sludge. But I can fix it. My collages and freewriting are there to prove that I *can* find lively, clear language and good ideas—naturally.

○○○○○

The principle of negativity: absence. What makes writing good is not what you put in but what you take out. The mark of old timers and seasoned professionals. The old tennis pro who never moves. Line drawings by Picasso as an old man. If everything there is strong, the reader will put in what's not there. Silence is what's most powerful in music; space in art.

○○○○○

I read my collage out loud to a friend. He ended up thinking I had the opposite opinion from the opinion I really have. Is it because I wrote so badly? No, it's not badly written. It's because, as a collage, it doesn't try to *say* anything: it just *presents* material. Yes. And I like that about collages. They can settle for throwing lots of material at readers and asking them to *experience* it and make up their *own* mind.

But his "misreading" leads to a subversive thought. Perhaps he's right. Perhaps, now that I look at my collage again, I don't think what I thought I thought. Perhaps my collage allowed me to find words for what I didn't know. My collage—and my reading it out loud to my friend—are making me start to disagree with my old self.

READINGS

EXAMPLE OF A STUDENT'S FREEWRITING

There we go again—am I back in Ms. Wendell's class? freewritg, freewritg, freewritg—freewriting up to my ears—never did learn how to write an essay. I should really learn to write out my ings—I feel like I write like John Madden talks—slow at first, then speeding up the end to a point that one can't even understand what he's says, or with me, what I'm writg. I dont do this as well as I used to. Forget that. I do this better than I used to. I have such a cold—if I dare get any sicker I'll die. I weighed myself today & almost fainted!!! I'll be eatg oranges for months! There is this cute middle-aged woman sittg next to me who looks at us all as if we are in a ecological study—look at this speciment, semi shaved heard—North Edgewick's only punk—but wait—she wears wool sweaters and skirts—ala Princeton Prep! But that must be the influence of livg so near there. Princeton means Bruce—that little park by the Nassau Inn—getting lost in the campus—could always find my way in, could never get out. PRB—Owen's radio show—fallg asleep on this filthy vinyl couch in that creepy dank cellar—listeng to the death of Suzzy Rocke.—Of course Martini. There is no fall in New York City—There were no leaves to kick around like there are in Princeton!! I missed fall. At least I don't sneeze anymore like I used to when the two oak trees would drop leaves in great big piles in my back yard & I'd fall asleep in them & the dust and dirt would make me sneeze until my mother forbade me to romp in the leaves—we used to play that spider game in Elinor's backyard—she had little skinny trees—I had great big oak trees—Sam is sittg next to me as usual—I can't decide whether or not I should put him on my roster. I miss the cats. I know they must be so adorable by now—so fat & stupid—they surely did take my place—when I left. My poor guilty mother over Thanksgiving battling over her love for the cats & her love for me—would she let me die from my allergy from them—or let them all freeze to death out in the cold! didn't the air filter work? Finally the stupid cat had more kittens in the cellar—three more—longhairs too— the father wooed her away for three weeks—what a romance—she finally came back and then had them. I saw him once, he was huge & longhaired, pale yellow—sort of champagne.

EXAMPLE OF A STUDENT'S PUBLIC FOCUSED FREEWRITING

(This is focused *freewriting because the student is staying on topic—i.e., answering questions supplied by the teacher for an end-of-semester evaluation of the course. It is public because the student knows it will be read by the director of the writing program and by the teacher after grades are given. It is only an excerpt from the whole evaluation.)*

23

"Has Your Attitude Toward Writing Changed?"

My whole outlook on writing has improved. I feel better about my writing. I had previously felt that my ability to communicate through writing was minimal, at best. Now I feel I have learned about a whole new world of skill I didn't even know I had. I know this sounds obnoxious, but I'm writing quickly. The biggest problem I had with this course is that now I'm very seldom happy with a work as 'completed'. I find myself revising over and over, which is not necessarily bad, but I'm going to have to learn how to take a timed essay exam all over again (this I learned from in-class essays). I'll do it, though. Overall I think I benefited from this class a great deal (that from one who resented it more than most, I think).

"Specific Things the Instructor Might Do to Improve Her Teaching."

I think the biggest problem (and perhaps the most serious) I have with———is his grading. He grades much too hard, effort seems to have little to do with his grading, which is ok at times, but this is a freshman course. The work load is tremendous (a lot more than any of us expected). I'm working harder in this course than I am in chemistry, a four credit weed-out course. Well, that's neither here nor there, but I think ———should try (at least in the beginning) to be more gentle, and objective. This is a freshman writing course. We all come from different backgrounds, and our first essays may often be disasters through very little fault of our own. It's possible that our beginning essays are counted less heavily than our last, but still, it's discouraging to know that you made your very best possible effort, and that it was only worth a 'C'. I sometimes got the feeling that I would not be given a better than X grade because it is only the second essay, and I can't have improved that much. Also maybe I wouldn't keep working. If early essays count less in grade averaging, we need to know that. I am much more likely to give up if I have cruddy grades for a lot of work than if I have reasonable ones, or at least know my grade is not a straight average (I'm assuming it isn't, if it is the grading system stinks!).

ROBERT BINGHAM (1925–82)

He was a tall man of swift humor whose generally instant responses reached far into memory and wide for analogy. Not much missed the attention of his remarkably luminous and steady eyes. He carried with him an education from the Boston Latin School, Phillips Exeter Academy, Harvard College—and a full year under the sky with no shelter as an infantryman in France in the Second World War. Arriving there, he left his rifle on the boat.

One of his lifelong friends, a popular novelist, once asked him why he had given up work as a reporter in order to become an editor.

"I decided that I would rather be a first-rate editor than a second-rate writer," he answered.

The novelist, drawing himself up indignantly, said, "And what is the matter with being a second-rate writer?"

Nothing, of course. But it is given to few people to be a Robert Bingham.

To our considerable good fortune, for nearly twenty years he was a part of *The New Yorker,* primarily as an editor of factual writing. In that time, he addressed millions of words with individual attention, giving each a whisk on the shoulders before sending it into print. He worked closely with many writers and, by their testimony, he may have been the most resonant sounding board any sounder ever had. Adroit as he was in reacting to sentences before him, most of his practice was a subtle form of catalysis done before he saw a manuscript.

Talking on the telephone with a writer in the slough of despond, he would say, "Come, now, it can't be that bad. Nothing could be *that* bad. Why don't you try it on me?"

"But you don't have time to listen to it."

"We'll make time. I'll call you back after I finish this proof."

"Will you?"

"Certainly."

ooooo

"In the winter and spring of 1970, I read sixty thousand words to him over the telephone."

ooooo

"If you were in his presence, he could edit with the corners of his mouth. Just by angling them down a bit, he could erase something upon which you might otherwise try to insist. If you saw that look, you would be in a hurry to delete the cause of his disdain. In some years, he had a mustache. When he had a mustache, he was a little less effective with that method of editing, but effective nonetheless."

ooooo

"I turned in a story that contained a fetid pun. He said we should take that out. He said it was a terrible line. I said, 'A person has a right to make a pun once in a while, and even to be a little coarse.' He said, 'The line is not on the level of the rest of the piece and therefore seems out of place.' I said, 'That may be, but I want it in there.' He said, 'Very well. It's your piece.' Next day, he said, 'I think I ought to tell you I haven't changed my mind about that. It's an unfortunate line.' I said, 'Listen, Bobby. We discussed that. It's funny. I want to use it. If I'm embarrassing anybody, I'm embarrassing myself.' He said, 'O.K. I just work here.' The day after that, I came in and said to him, 'That joke. Let's take that out. I think that ought to come out.' 'Very well,' he said, with no hint of triumph in his eye."

ooooo

"As an editor, he wanted to keep his tabula rasa. He was mindful of his presence between writer and reader, and he wished to remain invisible while representing each. He deliberately made no move to join the journeys of research. His writers travelled to interesting places. He might have gone, too. But he never did, because he would not have been able to see the written story from a reader's point of view."

ooooo

"Frequently, he wrote me the same note. The note said, 'Mr. ———, my patience is not inexhaustible.' But his patience *was* inexhaustible. When a piece was going to press, he stayed long into the evening while I fumbled with prose under correction. He had pointed out some unarguable flaw. The fabric of the writing needed invisible mending, and I was trying to do it with him in a way satisfactory to him and to the over-all story. He waited because he respected the fact that the writing had taken as much as five months, or even five years, and now he was giving this or that part of it just another five minutes."

ooooo

"Edmund Wilson once said that a writer can sometimes be made effective 'only by the intervention of one who is guileless enough and human enough to treat him, not as a monster, nor yet as a mere magical property which is wanted for accomplishing some end, but simply as another man, whose sufferings elicit his sympathy and whose courage and pride he admires.' When writers are said to be gifted, possibly such intervention has been the foremost of the gifts."

COLLAGE ABOUT ME AND MY WRITING
Regina Olmeyer

No matter what others may think of writing, for me, this future pediatrician, pen and paper are two of the best sources of relaxation and comfort a person can find.

ooooo

Both my parents are immigrants, yet from totally different parts of the world. Because I have such a diverse heritage, I have grown up learning and experiencing different lifestyles—which shaped my personality. My mother was a fairly fresh immigrant so she taught me German as a child so it became my first language. I grew up in New York as a German girl.

ooooo

I write stories about my background. I love doing it—and writing so detailed that people get a feeling and idea for the culture. I love writing poems and short stories when I am inspired. Even if it is scribble, by just writing what I am thinking or feeling, I love it. Writing gives me something to look back upon to recall aspects of my life that have passed. Some works are good and others aren't but I keep at it. One poem won a prize in New York City.

ooooo

It gives me great pleasure when I can write, whether it is a poem, short story, or just something concerning my thoughts, feelings, and inspirations—and when people are enthusiastic about it.

My cousin is an exceptional force for me. If I lose the desire to write, I think of him and his appreciation and support for me, and the desire to write flows right back, and soon onto the paper. I love writing and sending him my works, knowing he is so appreciative and receptive to what I create. Out of everyone, he was the only one who openly reacted to the feeling I put into the poem.

ooooo

I never read my work right away though. I look forward to reading it a little later, and think about what I have written.

ooooo

They (two teachers) helped me create my technique and build on my own style.

For this other teacher, I had to write a whole new made-up way, which I developed just for her class, and so I did well. This teacher was a creative writer, but she was too closed-minded to other people's styles and creativity. To change someone's thoughts, creativity, and ideas so that they correspond to her own is wrong.

If I submitted a poem or short story which I enjoyed writing, she usually would make so many corrections and changes that the piece wasn't my work at all. My lines were crossed out and rewritten so that it didn't sound like what I wanted to write at all. I thought, why should I write my real thoughts and feelings if she changes it or asks me to change it anyway? I was never happy writing for her. Once I left her class I was relieved that I could write free again.

ooooo

Since everyone else is asleep, I don't have to worry about being disturbed or interrupted in my trains of thought. I am so relaxed that my head is clear and free to write.

PROCESS WRITING FOR "COLLAGE ABOUT ME AND MY WRITING"
Regina Olmeyer

I had a hard time starting the collage. From each writing assignment I picked out a few sentences or passages. I tended to pick out more of the same passages from my different works. The picking out of the bits and pieces was pretty easy. After I cut out each slip of paper I was able to make a group for the four or five different areas.

Once I got the groupings I was stuck. When I first looked at each group I couldn't see how I could form it all so that the collage would make some sense, so I came up with the idea of putting each group into an order and then putting it all together. That didn't work because it was too choppy. It turns out I had to arrange and rearrange a few times before I was happy. When I was finally done, I was pleased with most everything, except the ending was difficult.

THE FEEL OF WRITING—AND TEACHING WRITING ✱
Donald Murray

Emptiness. There will be no more words. Blackness. No, white without color. Silence.

I have not put down any words all day. It is late, and I am tired in the bone. I sit on the edge of the bed, open the notebook, uncap the pen. Nothing.

Or.

Everything has gone well this morning. I wake from sleep, not dreams, the car does not have a flat tire, I do not spill the coffee grounds, I do not turn the shower to cold instead of hot. The telephone does not ring, and I sit at the typewriter with a clean piece of white paper twirled into the machine. Nothing.

If I can make myself wait, remain calm, ready to write but not forcing writing, then words come out of silence. Out of nothing comes writing.

Now it is hard to keep up with the words which write what I did not intend, do not expect. Often this is the best writing, and I know it, but I never welcome that emptiness, that terrible feeling that there will be no more words.

ooooo

The student sits in my conference chair, a Van Gogh miner, his hands clasped and hanging down between his legs near the floor, his head slumped forward. He mumbles. "I didn't write nothing." His head rolls up, his face defiant, and then angry when he sees me smiling at him. "What's the matter?" he snarls.

"You look like me, sound like me this morning. Nothing happened."

"What d'ya do?"

"I wanted to kick the cat, but I don't have a cat, and I couldn't pick a fight with my wife. She was out shopping. So I had to sit there and wait."

"And?"

"The words came. Not what I expected. But words. You want to read them?"

I wait while he reads my uneven, early morning draft. I can see him getting interested and suspect he's saying to himself that he could do as good, or perhaps a bit better.

"You just wait?"

"Yes, it isn't easy though."

"Will it work for me?"

"I don't know. Sometimes it works for me and sometimes it doesn't."

○○○○○

The writing is going well. Everything is connecting. I need a word, and it is in my ear; I need a fact, and it flows out of my fingers; I need a more effective order, and my eye watches sentences as they rearrange themselves on the page. I think this is what writing should be like, and then I stop. I go for another mug of coffee, visit the bathroom, check the mail.

I wonder about this compulsion to interrupt writing which is going well. I see my students do it in the writing workshop. It's so much of a pattern there must be a reason for it. Sometimes I think it is the workman's need to stand back to get distance; other times I think it is simple Calvinist distrust—when everything's going well something must be wrong.

○○○○○

My students arrive in class just at the bell, as if they were hurled there by some gleeful giant. They are rushed, harried, driven. They remind me of me. I barely made it myself. How am I going to create a quiet space around us within which we can listen to writing trying to find its voice?

This is the writer's problem: take all the energy you have to fight your way to the writing desk: reject wife, child, friend, colleague, neighbor; refuse to carry out the trash, take the car to the garage, transplant the blueberry bush; leave the mail unopened and the opened mail unanswered; let the telephone ring; do not answer the knock on the door or prepare for class; ignore the message on your desk to call somebody back; do not rehearse the speech that will impress at the afternoon meeting; do not remember, do not plan; use all your energy to get to your desk, and then try to sit there, calmly, serenely, listening for writing.

I hear a teacher asking a student who has just begun to write, "What is your purpose?"

I hope the teacher will not come to my door when I have just begun to write. What, indeed, is my purpose? To make it through the day? To get tenure? (I already have tenure.) To become rich? (I will not eat on this article.) To impress my parents? (That sounds more like it, but they are dead, and would not read what I wrote when they were alive because, true Scots, they knew they would be disappointed.)

I hear more of the teacher's questions. "What is your purpose in this piece? What do you intend to say in the piece you are writing? Who is your audience?" They may be good questions but it's the first week of the semester and the student has passed in his first tentative draft.

He'd better not ask me. If I knew all those things—my purpose, my content, my reader—I wouldn't have to write this. Well, that's not really true. Perhaps I know my audience in a sort of general way, and perhaps I know what I'm going to say. And that worries me, because I want to write to surprise myself. It would be terrible if I knew my purpose, if I knew what I was doing, how it would all come out. That's when I'll know I'm finished. There are few things more dangerous in writing than too much purpose. . . .

○○○○○

My father died with a machine plugged into his chest and a small smile on his face. The police found my mother on the floor of her apartment in a nest of covers tugged from the bed. My daughter, Lee, stands always at the corner of my eye, but at twenty she lay in a hospital bed, a beautiful woman without brainwaves. I made the decision to kill my father, to kill my mother, to kill my daughter, to let them go. I hope they have found more peace than I.

I have never said these words until this moment. I did not know I would say these words. They came out of silence. I heard them and I believe them.

Facing their own silences, my students write of death, of hate, of love, of living, of loss. They put down words which reveal a mother plunging a knife into a father while a girl looks on; a student tells of a failure—to kill herself; another student carries her father in her arms, rocking him, trying to comfort him against the pain of cancer in the night.

I tell them that they do not have to write of these things. I tell them they should write of such matters if it bothers them. They tell me it feels good, and then look guilty. I tell them I know. It helps, somehow, to put words on paper. I tell them it gives me distance, in a way, it makes what cannot be believed, a fact. I tell them I cannot understand why it feels good to write of such terrible things, but I confess it does feel good; that is my way of achieving a kind of sanity.

ooooo

A student comes to conference and shows me her new notebook. We marvel over it—a looseleaf notebook has a third arm with a clipboard on it which folds over the notebook. We share our wonder at it, for we share the thrill of writing and know the importance of tools. We are always trying out each other's pens or feeling the texture of a new kind of paper between our fingers. We are writers and we know that there is writing in the paper if we know how to let it out.

ooooo

Often I write by not writing. I assign a task to my subconscious, then take a nap or go for a walk, do errands, and let my mind work on the problem. It doesn't do much good for me to think thinking.

I tell my students to write every day, for a short time, going away from it and coming back. The going away is as important as coming back. Read, stare out the window, jog, watch a ballgame, eat, go to bed. Sometimes I feel I have to make a note. It's too bad; for what can be forgotten usually should be forgotten. Writing surfaces from my subconscious, but I push it away, the way I shove an over-friendly puppy from my knee. Go away and work by yourself, writing, and come back when I'm at my desk.

ooooo

I can recognize my students' papers without looking at their names. I hope they hear their own voices as clearly as I do, for writing is mostly a matter of listening. I sit at my desk listening to hear what my voice says within my head. Sometimes it speaks so clearly I feel I am taking down dictation while I write.

Voice gives writing the sense of an individual speaking to an individual. The reader wants to hear a voice. Voice carries the piece of writing forward; it glues the piece of writing together. Voice gives writing intensity and rhythm and humor and anger and sincerity and sadness. It is often the voice of a piece of writing that tells the writer what the writing means.

ooooo

The experience I imagine, the one I have dreamt by writing, is often more real than the experience I have lived. I hope my students feel the twice-lived life of the writer, know the double experience of this kind of living.

ooooo

Dictating this I pace the floor. I have just moved one chair and two rugs. Writing gives me so much energy it is hard for me to sit still. I move from one part of the room to the other, sit in this chair, leap up and move over to the couch. I stretch while I type, swing around in the chair, get up to pace and return. If I write by hand I work at the desk, then in the Morris chair on a lap desk, then over the rocker, then back to the desk, over to the couch. I encourage my students to move around in the writing workshop, to pace, twitch, mutter to themselves, hurl paper into the waste-basket. I can't write in libraries. My ideal work place is a bustling lunchroom in a town where no one knows me.

ooooo

I don't want to know the rules of language. My problem is that my words dis-cover rules all the time. My sentences obey rules I don't even know. One problem in writing is that my students and I can't seem to avoid the conventions of language, and what we write is so very conventional. Of course, I have students who don't know the rules, but nobody ever stands up to denounce goody-goody students who follow the rules right over the cliff, taking their writing with them.

ooooo

My wife cannot seem to understand that when I dictate to her at the typewriter I am trying to hear a voice within my skull that she cannot hear and that I can barely hear. There's nothing on paper, yet, nothing in memory, yet, just a hint of a voice which may speak and may say something which may not disappear under my own editorial pen.

Listening for that voice I do not want to hear her voice, or any voice. I must concentrate when there is an interruption and hold myself intensely empty so that the voice can, that voice that is not yet heard, stay where it is in the dark cave until the interruption is over and I can listen for it.

I fear that I ask my students too many questions, suggest too much, praise too much, make educational noise, and get in the way of their hearing what they have to say. . . .

ooooo

I used to be on newspaper rewrite, and I respond to deadlines the way a punch-drunk fighter staggers from an imaginary corner when he hears a bell. And yet I've learned not to force the writings. I have to keep the writing muscles exercised and the motto, "nulla dies sine linea"—never a day without a line—hangs over my writ-ing desk. I start the day by turning on a timer and writing for fifteen minutes; I dis-cipline myself to get to the writing desk and hope for two hours a day, five days a week. And if I am not at the writing desk, I am never far from my canvas office which is filled with pen refills, ink, notebook, clipboard, staples, scissors, paperclips—any-thing I might need to capture writing if it comes. But waiting for writing to be cap-tured I have to make myself relax. The more at rest I am at my writing desk, the less busy I am, the more productive I become.

ooooo

Often I have to write badly to write well. My students want to write too well, too early. I have to get them to put something down on the page, no matter how bad it is, so they can see and hear what they have to work with.

There's something marvelously satisfying with finishing a draft, no matter how bad it is. Now I can go to work. Before the piece of writing was all idea and vision, hope and possibility, a mist. Now it is ink on paper, and I can work it.

ooooo

It's wonderful fun to invade a piece of student writing. The better the writing is the more tempted I am to get inside it, to manipulate it, to make it mine. And sometimes in conference I will tell a student, "This is a really good piece of writing. Do you mind if I mess with it?"

She looks apprehensive but she is a student. She nods okay.

Gleefully, I mess around for a few lines or a few paragraphs. I sharpen, I cut, I develop; I add my words for hers, my rhythm, my meaning.

"That isn't right at all. That doesn't sound like me," she says. "That isn't the way it was. Give me back my writing."

She grabs it from my desk and charges out of the office.

Good. She has the feel of writing.

Writing in the World:
An Interview about Writing

In this unit you will be asked to conduct and write up an interview with someone about how they write. Our goal is for you to learn the great diversity of kinds of writing and ways of writing in the world so that you'll see more options when you approach a writing task. As you hear the interviews written by your classmates, you will get much more perspective and awareness about the writing process.

But we also have other goals in this unit:

- School writing and academic essay writing are always in danger of going dead. The interview is good for helping you get lively speech qualities and "voice" into your writing because you will use so much quoted speech.

- As you work through this unit, you'll also begin to learn how to find or carve out a theme or develop a conclusion from a mass of diverse material.

- You'll also learn to conduct interviews: to hear what another person is saying but also "hear" what's behind what she is saying.

MAIN ASSIGNMENT

Your main assignment, then, is to write up an interview with someone about his or her writing. Choose someone who does a significant amount of writing and who takes writing seriously. Make sure your interview includes three things:

1. The *kinds* of writing the person does.

2. The *ways* in which the person writes.

3. Most important, something *you* conclude. That is, don't just give a portrait of your writer; make your interview an occasion for explaining a *conclusion you have reached about writing or thinking* on the basis of the interview: in effect, a "moral to the story" or a "so what?" for the interview. Perhaps it will be a conclusion about why the person writes well or with satisfaction—or why she has difficulty—or about the nature of writing or language or readers. Perhaps it will be something you conclude about *your* writing on the basis of interviewing the person. Figure out something that is interesting to you, and it will probably be interesting to readers.

In the "Readings" section after the unit, we have included drafts of interviews written by students and a piece of a published interview of a professional writer.

Choosing Someone to Interview

Pick someone who writes a significant amount and cares about writing. Four possibilities suggest themselves:

- An adult professional: either a professional writer or someone who has to write for her job. You might even want to use this assignment as an opportunity to talk to someone in a field you are considering for yourself. (You may be surprised how much people have to write in fields that seem distant from writing. Recent research shows that engineers, for example, spend an average of 25 percent of their week writing.)

- An adult who is devoted to writing though it is not part of her job. This might be someone who writes fiction or poetry or does research in her free time.

- A junior, senior, or graduate student who is in a field you would like to explore.

- A member of your writing class. (Probably you'll want to pick someone who is particularly interested in writing, though it could also be useful to interview someone who particularly hates writing in order to learn how that can happen to people and what the effects are.)

We suggest that groups of four work together and that each member choose a different kind of person to interview. Adult subjects make the most sense for students who live at home or nearby, since they can pick an adult from their home environment. But of course there are adults on any campus—not just faculty—who write either for their job or for themselves.

It's best to have *two* interviews with your subject (about three hours in all). Set up these interviews early and follow through to make them happen. (Busy people sometimes have to change appointments, so you may need to push to get your interviews.) The important thing is to make sure the person has enough interest and sympathy to give you the time you need.

A PRACTICE INTERVIEW WITH A CLASSMATE

Some of you may have done some interviewing in the past, perhaps as a reporter for a school newspaper, perhaps as part of an assignment for a particular class. If so, you can help others in the class who haven't had this experience. Interviews *can* be fun, but they do take some practice and skill, especially if the process makes you nervous. We've set things up so you can have a quick practice session with a classmate.

Before your interview, you need to have some questions to ask. Either in class (if your teacher provides time) or prior to class, jot down some things you would like to know about how other people write. Shape these into questions, but beware of making the questions too abstract or general. Otherwise you'll learn only people's *theories* about writing, not how they actually go about writing. You can't trust people's theories. For example, a person might say, "I always start with an outline" or "I always use 3 × 5 cards," but if you can get them to tell important stories and incidents from memory in detail, they will often realize (perhaps for the first time) that some of their best writing *didn't* involve outlines or 3 × 5 cards. Or sometimes people say that writing is always agony for them, but if you can get them to ramble honestly, they'll come upon times when they were genuinely enjoying themselves. (As your subject speaks, you can intervene with clarifying questions, e.g., "What were you writing with? How were you feeling at that point? Did that take a long time? Were you thinking about your audience at that point or just steaming along suiting yourself?")

Together with your classmates, you'll probably come up with questions useful for both your in-class practice interview and your "real" interview. Here are some questions we've found useful:

- Kinds. Would you tell me all the kinds of writing that you do: not just "important writing," but also informal letter writing, note taking, list making, diary keeping—whatever.

- Good, bad, perplexing moments. Tell me the story of some of the important writing times or incidents in your life.
  —Times when things went well—when you were pleased or proud of how things came out.

—Would you be willing to tell me about some disasters—when things went badly or you felt depressed about your writing?

—How about some writing experiences which were somehow unusual or perplexing for you? Perhaps an occasion sticks in mind when something unexpected happened, but you don't know why. Perhaps you were forced to write in a completely different way from the way you are used to writing (for example, using different materials, writing to a different audience, or following a different assignment).

—What I find hardest in writing is ————; is that hard for you too?

- Mini–case study. Please show me something you wrote and just tell me the whole story of how it got written: all the thoughts, feelings, and stages you went through in writing it. Point to one or two specific passages in the piece that seem important to you and tell me why they are important and what thinking and writing processes led up to them.

- Conditions. Tell me something about where and when you usually write and what you usually use: pencil, pen, paper, computer. Do you think any of this makes a difference in your writing?

Suggestions for Your Practice Interview

Interview your classmate for ten minutes. Take notes, and don't be nervous or furtive or self-conscious about doing so either now or in your longer interviews. Be proud of it. Most people are flattered that you care enough about what they are saying to get it right.

For this practice interview, it's best not to use a tape recorder; you'll benefit from being forced to attend closely to all the spoken words. Some interviewers take full notes; some take sparse notes, but obviously you can't take down all the words. Instead of trying for everything, try to jot down a running list of interesting key words and phrases. You need words that *sound* like the person talking—words that will help you recapture full phrases and whole sentences when you go over your notes right after the interview.

For that's the crucial thing: going over your notes right after the interview. Treat your notes as temporary memory jogs, not attempts at a full record. Thus you can put your main energy during the interview into listening, being interested, asking questions out of your genuine curiosity, and jotting down that rich list of words and phrases as you listen.

Stop after ten minutes. Go over your notes immediately, using them to make additional notes of the most important and interesting things your subject said—trying wherever possible to reconstruct the person's actual words, phrases, and sentences.

If this were your longer interview, you would be going over your notes alone, writing these things out. But for this exercise, do this reconstructing aloud in front of your subject. As you go through your notes repeating and

PROCESS BOX

Feelings when getting together a complete manuscript? Well, I certainly didn't really want to look at it closely for fear of not liking it or finding bad things or typos or ideas which could be improved. I knew that if I stopped to do those things I'd never get it together and off to the publisher. So I tried deliberately not to read anything—just look at page numbers and succession of chapters. But couldn't help feeling somewhat awed that we'd actually written so much, that somehow seeing it there I forgot about all the hard work and was just sort of pleased at the sheer size of it.

PAT BELANOFF

reconstructing, she can help by making corrections of wording. And after you finish, she can mention things that *she* thought important or interesting that you didn't mention—just to give you another perspective on what you recorded.

If this were your longer interview, you would also be jotting down some of *your* thoughts and observations and trains of thought as you reconstruct the interview. But for this quick in-class exercise simply *say* some of these observations after you have reconstructed your subject's words. After this interview-and-reporting-back, switch places and give your classmate a chance to practice interviewing-and-reporting-back.

You and your partner will also find it valuable to talk about what it was like being interviewed—what approaches made you feel most comfortable and which questions proved to be the most effective prompts for stimulating memory and thoughts.

Option in threes. This same interviewing exercise can be rich and interesting in groups of three. One person interviews another for ten minutes, as before, but with the third person as onlooker, either just listening or also taking notes (for practice). Then when the interviewer reconstructs his notes, the onlooker can chime in to help capture the words actually spoken or to comment on things he would have tried to record that the interviewer omitted. Or they can both reconstruct notes, compare them, and learn from each other—with, of course, the help of the interviewee.

YOUR REAL INTERVIEW

What we've said about your practice interview applies to your real interview. You may be nervous as you start, but once you relax you'll enjoy the process. Remember to be open about taking notes—your interviewee will probably be disappointed if you don't—but don't get so caught up in note taking that you can't get involved in the conversation. Jot down key words, words that capture your subject's way of talking. When you get involved and listen attentively, your natural curiosity will begin to direct the questions you ask. And the fact that you become genuinely engaged in what your subject says will increase your ability to remember it.

Try to give your subject enough freedom to get involved in what she's saying. If she doesn't seem to want to talk and just gives short answers—if you feel your interview falling into a lifeless question-and-answer pattern—try to use more open-ended questions such as "Tell me a story about a time when you were really pleased (disappointed) with . . ." or "Tell me more about that," or "How did you feel about that?" and so forth. And don't be afraid to wait a bit at the end of an answer: be willing to leave some silence hanging there in the air. People often give their best answers after a long pause for reflection. Remember that one of the best things you can say is simply, "That sounds interesting; talk some more about that."

Tape recorder. You might use one for your interview if you prefer, and if you have one available. It lets you quote your subject's words exactly. Most people don't mind being recorded and soon get over being self-conscious. You won't have to take notes during the interview (except perhaps to record your own thoughts and reactions). But a tape recorder doesn't solve your interviewing problems. You'll still probably have to take notes *as you listen to the tape.* And taping can deceive you into becoming a lazy listener. You can capture much more in notes than you might expect, and note taking is an important skill to develop.

The First Interview

For your first interview, you can use the original questions you developed with classmates or the ones we suggested for your practice interview—or the questions that seemed most valuable to you and your partner or your group as you interviewed each other. Or perhaps you'll decide to use the questions you formulated afterwards as you were discussing the interviewing process. You'll want to write out these questions for yourself—perhaps put each one on a large index card to take to the interview. But remember not to stick slavishly to these questions; let your interviewee guide the direction of the conversation. Use your prepared questions when you seem to have reached the end of a line of thought. And remember, as you are deciding what to ask, that open-ended questions give your subject freedom to explore whatever comes to mind. As a result your subject will enjoy being interviewed; she too will have a chance to come to new observations and insights.

Reconstructing Your Notes after the Interview

It is crucial to make time right after the interview to go over your sketchy notes.

- Reconstruct and write out in more detail your subject's most interesting or striking words.

- Write out some of your *own* observations, reactions, questions, and trains of thought about what the person has said.

- If you had to decide now on a "moral of the story," what would it be? You don't have to settle it yet, but what's the most interesting conclusion you could draw at this point?

- Don't forget to include some *physical* details about the setting (the room and the atmosphere), the person's appearance (how she was dressed, how she spoke and moved), what her pieces of writing actually looked like (whether drafts or final copies). Such details don't just "add color"; they often help tell the story and convey ideas you want to get across.

If you delay going over your notes for even three or four hours, you will lose many crucial details. Remember that for right now you are not trying even for a draft of your interview; all you're doing is going over and adding to your notes, drawing some conclusions, and capturing some of the physical setting.

Questions for Your Thinking and for the Second Interview

Here are questions to keep in mind as you go over and add to the notes from your first interview—trying to get straight what you have already found out and what you still need to ask at a second interview. These questions may also be helpful in writing the essay itself.

- Kinds. What are the different kinds of writing the person does? Be a bit suspicious if she says she does only one kind. If she says she writes nothing but news stories for a newspaper, ask her to explore differences between *kinds* of news stories. And more important, don't let her ignore the other kinds of writing she does even if they don't feel so much like "writing" to her: such things as taking notes for stories, keeping lists of stories to write, making lists for the grocery store, keeping a diary, and writing memos, notes, or letters to friends.

- Processes. Get her writing process for at least a couple of pieces of writing—as different as possible. In detail. What happened in her mind before she did any writing—during the hours or days *before* she put a word on paper? What were her first words on paper? notes? outline? or just random jottings? Or did she go right to written-out drafts or perhaps even directly to final drafts? What was the process of getting to a final draft? Were there events from final draft to finished piece (e.g., typing, copyediting, checking with someone)? What were the succession of feelings throughout the whole process? What about the role of other people? Discussing ideas with them beforehand or reading them drafts? What kind of feedback? In other words, don't settle for a "general story of how I *always* or *usually* write." Probe for differences and exceptions.

- Incidents. What past experiences have been helpful and harmful to how she writes now? What helped her most in learning? What was the role of instruction versus learning by experience or seat-of-the-pants?

- Conditions. Where and when does she write? What's the atmosphere? What implements does she use? What kind of paper? How important are these factors to her? Again, if she says it's always the same, probe for exceptions.

- Audience. Who have been important readers, past and present: former teachers, present friends, supervisors? What makes an audience helpful or not helpful for her? (Audience is a complicated issue because often, especially on the job, there is more than one audience. The news story may be for people who buy the paper, but the editor sees it first and has to like it; the memo may be for the clients or buyers, but it has to work for the writer's immediate supervisor too.) Does she think a lot or not so much about audience when writing? At which points in the writing process does she think about audience most?

- Changes. What important changes have there been in how she writes and feels about writing?

- Future. What seem to be your subject's goals, hopes, and fears about future writing?

Before you go to the second interview, try sharing things with a class partner or small group (or friend or parent). Share your rough write-up of the first interview, your questions, and the tentative conclusions you've drawn. You'll particularly want to ask others if they see implications in the material which you haven't noted, or if there are certain issues which they think you need to follow up on during the second interview. In this way everyone gets practice looking through rough material and speculating about conclusions or inferences: practice with "So what?" or "What's interesting here?" or "What bears pursuing here?" Besides helping you see and do more with your material, there is another goal in this sharing: to help you learn more about interviewing and what kinds of questions to ask. You will be a bit more skilled when you come to your second interview.

The Second Interview

You may want to start off the second interview by asking whether the person herself thought of things she'd like to add to the previous interview. You'll probably also want and need to clarify some points from the first interview, things you realized weren't clear to you while reconstructing your first interview. You may find it helpful to use the questions we've just listed.

Before the interview is over, try out a few of your conclusions and see what her response is. You can state these as only tentative: "As I was looking over my notes, it struck me that you seem to get the ideas that matter to you when you are *not* writing. Am I right?" Or, "I got the idea that your writing process is changing—that you now take more chances. Do you feel that's so?" Your subject should do most of the *talking,* but you should probably give more *direction* this time than with the first interview; there are things you need to find out, and this is your last chance. You should probably come prepared with questions important to your own understanding and try to get your subject to reflect on them a bit.

WRITING YOUR PAPER

The easiest way to get a draft is to make a collage. Using your intuition, simply choose the most interesting bits from both interviews: quotations that best recall the person's voice to you, pieces from your own reflections and explanations, and observations that capture essential points particularly well. Don't start out with some preconceived organization; pick the bits and let *them* guide you toward structure. How do they seem to fit together? chronologically? by kinds of writing? by her ideas? by your ideas? or perhaps more randomly for now? This is only rough.

Perhaps you don't yet have any conclusions or thoughts of your own— any "so what's?" But this is the time to dream some up, even if they are very speculative or uncertain. It will hasten your thinking process and stimulate more useful feedback on your draft. (Someone in disagreeing with your crazy idea may give you a genuinely good one.)

For now let your collage be a bit too long: in effect you're leaving too much there, allowing it to be a bit of an everything-but-the-kitchen-sink collage. This will give you a chance to let it settle, putting off for a while the decision about what it's really about and where to cut further.

Moving to a Draft of an Essay

Put your rough draft aside for a day or two if possible. Then read it aloud to yourself first and then to your partner, group, or some friends. Don't ask them for a critique but rather for collaborative help. If you do this after only one interview, you'll probably need even more help from others in seeing the implications of what your subject has said.

You've set the draft aside, read it over yourself, gotten feedback from readers—perhaps gotten reactions during the second interview from the person you interviewed. Now take the plunge into creating a strong, coherent, and more definite draft. At this stage, you have to be firmer about cutting and figuring out what you are really trying to show and say.

Audience. You might assume your audience to be your classmates and your teacher. Admittedly this is a "school assignment" and may even be graded. But remember that you are the expert on your topic: you are telling your audience things that they don't know, things that will be helpful to them. And your classmates and teacher are not the only likely audience. This kind of interview is frequently published in local newspapers, campus newspapers, and magazines—especially magazines that writers read. You might choose this piece to revise during one of the later revising units—and then send it off to see if it could be published.

You will need to make some important decisions.

- What will your main thought be? You may only *now,* on the basis of feedback and rethinking, figure out what you really want to *say* in this piece. It's usually a good sign when your "point" arrives late in this way.

- Which bits will you keep and which leave out?

- Make sure you have the three ingredients asked for in the assignment: *kinds* of writing, *ways* of writing, and *your* conclusions.

- How will you structure your piece so it doesn't seem too jumpy or collage-like (unless, of course, your teacher has asked for a collage)? Find some way to connect all the parts into a coherent sequence—with a sense of beginning, middle, and end. You could structure it as a narrative, simply reporting the most interesting things that were said in the actual order they occurred and putting your conclusions at the end or interspersed throughout. But this is dangerous since a good interview is likely to be *un*structured or wandering because the interviewer invites the subject to follow her digressions. Therefore you'll probably have to figure out a focus and arrange your material to fit it. You could structure your piece around the three requirements for the assignment. Or you may find a more interesting or pleasing or dramatic structure—perhaps starting off with a theme you saw or a conclusion you drew and supporting that theme or conclusion with words from your subject.

It's a struggle to take a lot of rough writing and turn it into something organized, coherent, and effective for readers. You will have to work at standing back, choosing the best parts, and figuring out the best order—and then tightening sentences and polishing grammar, punctuation, and usage. Most teachers ask that even mid-process drafts be typed. This is a way of emphasizing that they are not just "rough manuscript"—they are genuinely revised and meant for readers.

As a step toward revising either now or later in the semester, you can send your good draft to the person you interviewed. Ask her to correct quotations and respond to the portrait you have written and to the observations and conclusions you have made. This response will be particularly important if you had only one interview. You may even be able to incorporate parts of her response in a final version if you revise several weeks later.

Your Words and the Words of the Person You Interview

Some interviewers go so far as to omit any words of their own, presenting only the words of the subject interviewed. Though these "modest" interviewers do not say anything explicitly, they may imply a great deal by means of how they select and arrange the words spoken by the person interviewed. Other interviewers include many of their own words but none of their own ideas or conclusions—just summaries and explanations of what was said by the person interviewed.

In this assignment, however, we are asking you not just to portray the person you are interviewing but also to "say" something in your own right: to figure out some conclusion of your own and say it instead of just implying it. Notice how both the student samples at the end of the unit say something that they have concluded about their interviewees. Nevertheless, interview essays are intriguingly different from most other writing in that you can get the person you interview to do much of your "writing" for you. If you interview thoughtfully, take good notes, and choose from them well, a substantial part of "your" piece will consist of your subject's words.

About accuracy in quotation. If you used a tape recorder, you can note somewhere that you did so and that your quoted passages are the actual words spoken by your subject. Even so, however, it is customary when transcribing someone's casual speech to do minor cleaning up: leaving out "um's," "er's," and digressive phrases and fixing grammar and the like. If you didn't use a tape recorder, do your best to find and reconstruct some actual words, phrases, and sentences and put them in quotation marks, for actual quotations are the lifeblood of an interview. But acknowledge that you were working from notes and therefore might not have gotten some of the quotations exactly right. (For help with the mechanics of quoting, see Mini-unit I.)

SUGGESTIONS FOR SHARING AND RESPONDING

If you are using this unit early in the semester, the main benefit from readers will come from just sharing (see the booklet *Sharing and Responding*, section I). We recommend staying away from judgment or advice. You could also use sections IIA and IIB (modes of descriptive responding). Here are some questions for readers that are particularly appropriate to your task of writing an interview:

- What do you hear me saying? implying but not saying? What themes or conclusions do you see in my material?

- What inferences do *you* draw about this person's writing—or about writing in general on the basis of my material? What's the moral of the story for you?

- How would you describe the "voice" you hear in my interviewee? What words and phrases sound most like her? Which seem most characteristic?

- What else do you want or need to know? What issues do you wish I could follow up on in another interview?

PROCESS JOURNAL QUESTIONS

You won't need the questions that follow if you can just write about moments in this week's writing when things went well and badly—and surprisingly. What was going on for you: in your thinking? feeling?

How did words behave for you? These stories will build a powerful foundation for growth in your writing.

If you're having trouble doing the process writing, pick the two or three most interesting questions which follow and read over this week's writing with these questions in mind. The questions will help you be a better observer of yourself as a writer.

- Why did you pick the person you chose to interview? Was there something particularly useful to you that you were hoping to learn from this person? What advice might this person give about your writing?

- Write about your note taking: How did you do it? How did it work? What did you learn from this process—not just about conducting interviews but about other matters, such as college note taking, the workings of memory, the traits of speech, and so forth?

- What was it like reconstructing your notes? How did it go? Include advice for yourself for the next time.

- In your written interview, how much language from your interviewee did you end up with and how much of your own language? What factors led to this outcome? Were you pleased, or would you rather have it different next time?

- About finding a conclusion (a "moral" or "so what?"): How did you get it? When did it first occur to you? Was it suggested by a listener or your subject? "Finding the *point* in a great mass of messy material" is one of the main cognitive skills involved in learning. What helps you do this? Give yourself advice for the future.

READINGS

⭐ PORTRAIT OF MY MOTHER AS A WRITER
Kristin Bresnan

My mother was a writer? The thought made me laugh when I first considered it, but as I sat at the kitchen table with her that Sunday evening, sharing a bottle of wine and listening to her talk, that silly thought I had quickly diminished.

I have to admit now that I wasn't very excited about doing the interview, just because I didn't think that my mother would have anything interesting to say about writing. Wrong again. My mother's always been one who loves to talk, so it turned out that I'd ask a simple question, and she'd go on supplying me with such a long, elaborate answer that I couldn't keep up with her!

I started off by asking my mother what kinds of writing she does at this point in her life. She then proceeded to tell me that most of the writing she does now is for her job; it's not private writing. She finds this unfortunate because she loves writing poetry, but she just doesn't seem to have the time for it lately. My mother develops corporate training programs, and it takes up a lot of her time. She's not afraid to admit that she doesn't find it very exciting, and she's looking for something new. At the present time she is also designing a user's manual for a hotel reservations computer software system that my father is developing. She says sarcastically that this is the only spark of excitement in her job right now.

I find it interesting that she doesn't like to write for business, because she also has her Ph.D. I asked her, "How could someone who doesn't enjoy writing for business ever desire to get their Ph.D., which requires such a great deal of writing?" Well, in her opinion, writing her doctoral dissertation was a great experience. She started with a very clear idea of what she wanted to accomplish. It was all very organized. "The fact that it was so organized made the scientific aspect of it a little easier for me to deal with." Overall it ended up being an enjoyable experience and made her learn a lot about herself. She finds that when she writes now, whether it's private writing or business writing, she has a lot of pre-organization. "I'm clear about what I'm going to write; it doesn't unfold as I write, it's already there to begin with."

Even before high school my mother was told that she had writing talent. It was this talent that won her a writing contest which made her the editor of her high-school yearbook. While in college she continued and was frequently published in the college paper.

When I asked how she felt about herself personally as a writer, she replied, "I take pride in the quality of my writing. When I write I have a whole choice of possibilities of how I'm going to write something and I like to make sure that I make the best choice. I'm gifted in that way. It's like I have an internal computer. I automatically choose what's best, and if I can't do it right away, I elaborate on it for a while until I do get it right." I then thought to myself how nice it must be to have so much self-confidence about your writing.

I then asked my mother if there was any particular person or experience that influenced her as far as her writing skills and techniques were concerned. In other words, was she born with it or did it slowly develop with the help of some outside influence? I'm always wondering why some people have it and others don't. My mother then laughed and told me that the best thing that ever happened to her as far as writing is concerned was that she was raised as a product of the Catholic school system. She says, "I never thought I'd be saying anything positive about going to Catholic school, but I do have to admit that they really helped me develop my talent. They were so scrupulous about writing skills that students would strive for perfection in their writing. To them it was a special craft. I was always told that I had talent and I was encouraged to go on further with my writing. So this was where my self-confidence first developed, and I then had the incentive to move on and write more. For this I am very thankful."

Assuming that that was enough said on that subject, I then switched the topic a little bit and asked my mother if she ever thinks about an audience when she writes. After a long pause, she decided that she doesn't think about one at all because "I have a lot of confidence in my writing ability. I feel that I'm the best one to evaluate my writing, so I usually don't even think about an audience. The only time I might is if I was going to write fiction."

This coincidentally led us into talking about her hopes and fears about writing in the future. More than anything my mother would like to write a novel. Something along the lines of a Danielle Steele novel. Well, for those of you who don't know who Danielle Steele is, she writes tasteful, classy, "trashy" novels, not cheap Harlequin Romance stories. I found this amusing simply because I could actually picture my mother, the nine-to-five business woman with the Ph.D., writing a soap-opera story!

For now she only has time to write her poetry once a month or so. "When I do get the chance to write, I get an idea and it doubles. I become the vehicle for the poem and it flows through me. The words seem to have a life of their own."

I told her that with a tacky statement like that, she ought to be writing more than once every month or so just to get it out of her system! She laughed at that, a little. I asked her if she ever felt frustrated because she didn't get the chance to write very often. She explained to me that she doesn't really get frustrated but when she does get the chance to write her poetry, it seems to "explode out onto the page."

"What's your one biggest regret about writing?" I then asked. She replied, "I mainly regret the fact that I haven't kept a steady diary over the years. Writing a diary would serve a great purpose to me because then I could see how my attitudes and opinions have changed over the years. I've never given my writing the credit that it deserves by keeping and storing it all in one place—it's all kind of spread out all over the place."

I then decided to wrap things up by asking her what her overall view was on writing. Was there any sort of moral to the story? She started off by saying that different circumstances provide different ways of writing. Obviously this is easy to agree with. My mother explained that "Sometimes writing can be emotional, as with a poet, and other times writing can be more intellectual and logical, as with a scientist. There is more of a set process with a scientist than there is with a poet."

I thought about the differences for a minute and then decided that one thing that they share is the importance of clarity. Whether it's one or the other, the message has to be clear. That's where the audience comes in. My mother agreed with me. She said, "That's why poetry is more exciting to me. I want them to understand and feel the same emotion." We both agreed that the main point is that the audience has to feel what one is saying. A person can't relate to your writing unless they feel what you're saying.

I came out of the interview with a more positive attitude than when we began.

I realized that my mother and I agreed on a lot of the same things. It's not so much your skill that matters when writing, it's the feeling and desire that you put into it.

The one thing that we didn't agree on was the audience aspect. According to my mother, the audience only matters in some kinds of writing, like fiction and poetry. For me the audience plays a large role all of the time. I find it impossible not to think about who will be reading my paper and what they will think. Can they relate to it? Do they feel what I'm trying to say? For me that's always the number one concern.

PROCESS WRITING
Kristin Bresnan

I was dreading this assignment but when I was actually writing the final draft I found myself enjoying it. I liked the way it was all fitting together. But at the end I realized that this was probably because of the fact that almost the entire thing is made up of direct quotes from my mother! It's her stuff that sounds nice, not mine! This upset me, but then I realized that it wasn't totally true—only partially. Oh well, I'm sure I'll never be 100 percent satisfied with anything I write.

I learned a lot about my mother that I didn't know to begin with. We don't get to spend much time together and this gave us a chance to sit down and have a nice talk. It turned out to be fun.

I found myself kind of turning it into a parody while I was writing the final draft. I could've stuck in a few really good one-liners but then I immediately remembered that I'd be reading it out loud to the class, so I decided not to stick them in. I *hate* reading out loud. It unfortunately influenced the way I wrote, but not much.

KATHY'S WRITING
Robert Parker and Vera Goodkin

Kathy looks and acts like a vivacious college coed rather than a young mother of teen-age children. She looks forward to classes with the enthusiasm of a high school graduate. Actually, entering college means a great deal to her. She has found key new ideas and expanded intellectual horizons. She is a busy housewife who has added a new dimension to her life, and she is eager to share her knowledge and excitement with her husband and children.

She has done considerable writing in each of her courses. She is convinced, for example, that once she writes down information, it sticks with her more than if she just reads it. "There's something about the connection with paper. It's more than just going over it." She also says,

> I write not just to remember, but to learn, to think about later. Any paper that I do, any test that I take, an essay or a report, I have to rewrite it constantly. . . . I think I use writing more than anything else to learn subject matter in the courses I'm taking now. Past courses involved reading over my notes; that's basically still writing. I was learning from my own writing, whether it was notes from class or something I took out of a book. I lose it if I don't.

Her class notes, which trigger recall of things the teacher has said, are difficult for anyone else to read. They are cast in a personal, idiosyncratic shorthand used in the process of constructing knowledge from the information presented by teacher or text.

The "Psychology of Human Relations" writing has been like a mirror for myself, to bring out feelings and sort them into a certain pattern. That's been very helpful. If I just sit and think about it, it's not as helpful as when I write it down. It's better than looking in the mirror to me. When I go back and read this spontaneous writing, it shocks me. When you write it down off the top of your head, it's surprising what you come up with.

In the other psychology class, "Psychology of Women," all the tests are essays, and there are five subjects to investigate. Kathy has to write on all of them in preparation for the one the instructor will pick, but she has to know each one before she writes an essay on it.

I was worried about the essay tests because I'm not good at spontaneity. Learning comes harder to me than to other people. I have to really concentrate on it, and I found that if I wrote it down, just the fact of putting it down on paper, and then learning it is better than any other process I could follow. Certain things stick with me, but others, like facts, experiments and technical things, I have to write down.

Different kinds of assignments have proved useful in generating thought in the various subject areas. In nutrition, Kathy enjoyed doing the research for the required reports, as well as writing the reports, even though she found the subject "kind of dry." She has learned a great deal from rereading and rewriting, "picking things out" of different readings and research projects, and putting them in her own sequence. In "Psychology of Human Relations," she wrote to learn about herself and her surroundings, and she felt she has learned a great deal by doing so. In her writing for "Psychology of Women," she became quite emotional. She enjoyed the writing because she really wanted to do it. She has remembered more from that particular semester because of the writing.

. . . because I have to sit down and actually give myself enough time to write material, think about it, and absorb it; whereas last year, it was mostly class notes and going into short answer tests; I didn't retain as much.

Kathy has always enjoyed using writing for personal purposes. "It's a tremendous means of reflection. It's there, it's permanent." She found the practice of journal writing "a marvelous outlet, a tremendous enjoyment." To give herself 10 minutes or so just to write something out freely and then to go back and read what she had written: this was exciting and helpful.

She has pragmatically developed a number of writing-to-learn strategies. She uses "whatever works." She likes to learn, and writing seems to be a natural aid in doing so. Moreover, if something seems important and she wants to remember it, she writes it down. "If I don't, it gets lost in the shuffle." In fact, by her own account Kathy was spurred on to do more writing by her participation in this project. Now not only the teacher was reading her writing, but also other interested adults.

Class notes are important to Kathy, and she takes them carefully. She also makes careful marginal notes and uses both when she studies for tests. In addition, she writes questions in her books, and in her nutrition book she writes comments she may want her son or daughter to read later or that she may use to think about food shopping. Generally speaking, these notes and questions reflect "things that I want to change as a result of the course." In "Psychology of Women," "I raised a lot of questions in writing. Some I answered myself as I did more research on them; others I asked in class."

Kathy does other writing to prepare for class discussions or, in the case of nutrition, for oral presentations. First, she makes a rather comprehensive set of notes, and then she turns the notes into a final draft. In either case, she engages in multiple encounters with the material, and writing plays a central role: getting material out, organizing it, expanding upon it, or focusing on the main point.

She describes her composing process as follows:

> I have to more or less clear my head; find a quiet and comfortable place; make sure everything is there, and I don't have to get up again. I'll think about it for about an hour before I start to work to put myself in the mood for it, I guess. Then I'll sit down and start writing. A lot of things will come out, and then I have to make some kind of an outline form to contain the thoughts that come out; then I have to rearrange them.

Her sense of the audience for her writing greatly influences how she does it. In the "Psychology of Human Relations" journal, she writes for herself. Consequently, Kathy feels free to write without constraints. In the term paper for that course, she had to discuss a specific emotional learning problem. Because the paper was not for herself alone, she tried to eliminate emotional language and confine herself to a more impersonal problem-solving approach. She reread and rewrote the paper several times

> so that the paper was [oriented] for him, but the thoughts were still mine. For the first paper, I went back to the journal. It started to show me a real pattern of what I was doing. After two years of doing nothing, I was coming back to what I wanted to do: in other words, getting my life organized again. I took all that personal material and made it more factual, more objective. It was almost like feedback, as if I had been sitting there talking to a psychiatrist and all of a sudden, I felt as if he had recorded myself and then listened to it. When you're saying or writing something, it's feeling, but when you read it, it's there in black-and-white. It's proof that you're the one that said it.

Kathy tries to allow herself enough time to rough draft her work, staying with it until she gets tired or until she begins "dragging with thoughts." Then, she leaves the writing and comes back to it later, when she is fresh, and begins rearranging it. The third time she returns to the writing, she does some further rearranging and rewriting. Each time, the writing becomes a bit more organized, more "like the finished product.". . .

[Third Draft]

Ms. Weisstein, in her article "Psychology constructs the female" very adeptly points out how our present psychology of women is truly useless and bound to the past by a lack of research on what women want or need, much less what makes a woman function in our modern society. I use the word modern loosely because I'm not sure "we have come a long way, baby."

Ms. Weisstein's view of psychology and its failure to understand the reasons people act as they do and what might change their actions is not limited to women, but includes men. Personality psychologists have been accumulating evidence that what people do and who they believe they are is, in general, a function of what people around them expect them to do or be, or what their surroundings imply they should be or do. Ms. Weisstein points out that most therapy is based on theories of Freud, Erikson, on experimenter bias, theories without evidence, experiments used to support experimenter hypothesis, such as primate behavior, reports on differences and non-reports of similarity.

In 1952 Eysenck reported on a study of "outcome of therapy" wherein there was a 44% improvement among patients in psychoanalysis, 64% improvement of those in psychotherapy and 72% improvement among patients receiving no treatment. J. B. Rotter states "research studies in psychotherapy tend to be concerned more with psychotherapeutic procedure and less with outcome . . . to some extent it reflects an interest in the psychotherapy situation as a kind of personality lab."

I agree with Ms. Weisstein's overall view of psychology and the definite lack of true research of women. However, I feel we must work with therapy limits in an effort to improve it, and bring about a new awareness of what women want and what makes women act or react as they do.

Until women are capable of feeling an equality in society, there will never be any real change in social expectations, which is precisely what appears to shape our present status as second class majority. Unless we break the negative chain of events (social expectation/self-fulfilling prophecy/confirmation of social expectations) our future women will be writing similar articles 50 years from now.

Where do we start to make changes? Since knowledge is power, we must work to bring about an awareness of what women are made of, and it isn't always "sugar and spice."

Notes:

H. J. Eysenck, "The Effects of Psychotherapy: An Evaluation." *Journal of Consulting Psychology* 16 (1952), 319–324.

J. B. Rotter, "Psychotherapy." *Annual Review of Psychology* 11 (1960), 381–414.

Kathy's analysis of Phyllis Chesler's article, while more subdued in tone, still expresses her difficulty in suppressing anger and dealing with such emotionally charged issues in a detached manner. The initial draft clarifies the issues, and the final draft shows the results of her reworking of both the ideas and the language. . . .

[Final Draft]

After reading Phyllis Chesler's article "Patient & Patriarch" I know we have not "come a long way, baby!" I realize just how far my head has been stuck in the sand for so long a time. I shudder to think how many other women are in the same sand box.

When I first started reading Ms. Chesler's study I thought perhaps the high percentage of women in therapy could possibly relate to the way most women are capable of disguising problems. It would appear this is not the case at all, but again a show of male dominance through male oriented psychology in a stereotyped role of submissive patient and doctor Patriarch. A role in which the therapist allows women to find the reasons for feeling as they do and then "adjust" to the role of being a woman as defined by a man. The role man has created for women.

Ms. Chesler's comparison between therapy and marriage as the two accepted mediums for women is excellent, one I had never considered but agree with totally. Any divergence from our prescribed role is socially labeled maladjusted.

Ms. Chesler also points out society (both male & female) feels the female therapist (with the same male oriented training) is somehow less qualified than the male therapist. Further study shows therapists themselves actually prefer to treat female patients over male patients.

It appears to me, women are, from the moment of birth molded more by men than any other so far considered factor, such as anatomy or even environment. Male oriented beliefs & ideas even form the basis of the mother that gives birth to the female child.

As Ms. Chesler asks in her article, where do women begin to make changes? I believe, we women must first develop a bond among ourselves. Women have forever been divided and conquered by man. I think Ms. Chesler's suggestion to any who are in therapy to seek guidance from women therapists who are feminists is an excellent beginning.

But what about the thousands of women who are not in therapy for one reason or another? It occurs to me that the majority? of women are not conscious of just how male oriented & dominated our lives really are.

Perhaps one "small step" for women would begin with the change of our the female image as seen by society through the media, advertising and the like.

Kathy's treatment of "women in the media," which follows, is softer in tone. Much of her anger, it would seem, has been spent on the issues raised for her by Phyllis Chesler's article. Consequently, she can handle the issues and the writing of this next paper with greater equanimity. In this case, the final draft differs little from the first draft. Kathy makes a few corrections and that's all.

[Initial Draft]

Advertising on television and in magazines is the mirror "image" of how society sees the women. Advertising doesn't create the beautiful, not too bright, floor cleaning "lady of the house" but it does perpetuate the image. Doesn't everyone become ecstatic over the smell of freshly laundered towels & underclothes? Isn't every women (under 41 that is) thankful for the turtles giving up their precious oils to keep us younger looking?

I was delighted to find Lucy Komisan's artiels

I was surprised to discover in Lucy Komisan's article that there are advertising agencies that are attempting to make changes in the stereotyped roles of women.

I think *TV has an enormous impact on a large amount of people.* I can't help often wonder what the response would be if the advertising agencies exposed the viewers to a different image of woman. Instead of the women executive behind the big desk who losing a big deal because she's worried about a run in her stocking, why not just show the logical reasons for buying the stockings, such as to give the legs a hint of color, etc.

I have seen a few attempts to show women in a better light but we have far to go. One good thing about the "not too bright" image that women see every day in advertising is that there is a new awareness of how we are seen by society. All of us must become angry enough to do something to make the changes in our image.

In her journal and in these papers, writing helps Kathy to focus on those pieces of information or those opinions or those conclusions that she finds personally telling. She uses the writing, especially the movement from first draft to final product, to understand why women are still "behind the appliances" and to pose the question of how women might begin making the changes that she feels are necessary. We see Kathy working out her point of view in relation to the readings and discussions in the course. Thus, she is not just summarizing the main points of an article to show the teacher she can do it, or repeating facts to demonstrate that she has them at hand, but she is genuinely working on the alteration of her own consciousness, and the writing is a powerful tool in this process. Whether the final products are "good" pieces of writing is not the main issue, for this is not a writing course. It is a course on the psychology of women, and the issue is for all the students to confront information and issues in ways that transform their thinking and their consciousness.

Like other students described in this volume, Kathy writes to recall things as well as to think and learn. She is perhaps as acutely aware as any that we can learn from and through our writing. The fact that she is unusually comfortable with writing essay tests is due to the multiple-draft approach and the advance preparation encouraged in McGlynn's class. In this course and in "Psychology of Human Relations," Kathy learned a great deal about herself through freewriting and journal writing. She also discovered, in Odell's (1980) words, that "writing gives thoughts permanence."

Other students in McGlynn's course confirmed Kathy's experience of writing to learn. As they said, whether one writes out answers to questions contained in course objectives or uses writing to work out ideas while reading, the results include better problem solving and greater learning by induction. By consensus, this group also confirmed the value of careful rewriting of notes, agreeing that writing "stamps information into the brain," that it builds confidence and reinforces the special vocabulary of each discipline, and that writing to think is the opposite of, and the antidote to, the practice of rote regurgitation of information.

INTERVIEW
Salvatore Bianco

I conducted my interview with my brother, Anthony Bianco. I interviewed him as a person who greatly dislikes writing. Our conversation took place in my bedroom, and it lasted about an hour and fifteen minutes. The atmosphere was a very relaxed, casual one, and, because of this, my brother's opinions were both open and honest.

Anthony is a sophomore in high school and feels that he has had his share of writing assignments. I asked him how he felt about writing, and he said that he disliked it so much to the point where he actually hated it. The main question that I wanted answered was—Why?

My brother told me many reasons for his attitude toward writing. The primary reason, according to him, is that, "I never get the grade I feel I deserve. I've put a lot of effort into some assignments, and they were given bad grades." He told me about the time he was working on a biography about Edgar Allan Poe. Anthony stayed up most of the night, dedicating a great deal of time and effort to it, but all he received for it was a C−. "I did all that work for nothing! I don't even like writing; it's just a waste of my time." He also told me that he does not like writing book reports which have to be due at a certain date because he feels they take up too much of his time, and he does not like having these things on his mind. When he does do poorly on reports that he knows he has put time and effort into, it comes back to him with comments and question marks written all over them. "That gets me annoyed because the way I wrote the sentences seemed right to me; I don't understand what the teachers want from me!"

The actual writing of an essay seems to be a problem for my brother. He finds it difficult to write proper introductions and conclusions. Also, he is unable to recognize when new paragraphs should be started. He is easily at a loss for ideas, and he feels that his vocabulary is very limited. Because of this last problem, Anthony usually cannot find the proper words to express his ideas. "I know what I want to say, but I just don't know how to say it."

I then asked my brother what thoughts run through his mind just prior to writing. He often wonders about the length of the essay, what it will be about, when he will finish it, if he will be satisfied with it, and how the teacher will grade it. When he writes, he finds that he really does not concentrate on what he is doing. This is especially true during essay exams. "When I'm being rushed, I can't think straight!"

I thought it was necessary to find out just how he goes about writing something. Anthony told me that if his grades were borderline, he would take "very short" notes on his subject. Then he would write his rough draft before actually writing the final version. If, however, his grades were not borderline, he would just write the essay straight through and only recopy it if the first one was totally illegible.

Although Anthony hates to write, he does prefer some aspects of it to others. He would rather write a composition than, for example, a biography because he feels biographies are boring, yet finds it easy to make up stories and exaggerate them when possible. He also likes writing at home more than in school because there is hardly any pressure for him to deal with at home. When at home, Anthony prefers to write in either the kitchen during the evening or in the backyard on the picnic table during the late afternoon hours. Noise does not seem to bother my brother's concentration. Yet he does feel that he writes better when there is little noise. But he does not care about writing enough to worry about finding a place to work where it is quiet. Anthony seems to write only for himself, unless grades are involved. He says he does not write for the class because "the teacher doesn't make us get involved with discussing each other's essays." And he does not write for the teacher because "no matter how much I work on my essay, it won't meet my teacher's standards anyway."

In conducting this interview on my brother, I feel that I have learned some things about him and myself as well. I never realized how much my brother was so dead set against writing. I can understand how trying one's best but failing to be rewarded for it is enough to discourage most people. I have also learned that no matter how many times he is forced to write, and no matter what grades he receives for his writing, my brother is not going to change his attitude toward writing. What I learned about myself from this interview was that I value writing more than I previously thought I did. Of course, I have had my share of disappointments. But I am glad that I have been able to push myself to do better because writing can very well be an extremely pleasurable experience.

Writing to Explore:
The Loop Writing Process

Writing is a tool for *figuring out new things to say,* not just for *expressing what you've already figured out.* The loop writing process is particularly valuable if you can't think of much to say about a topic or feel disconnected from it. (In fact it helps for any topic you want to think more about.) The loop process consists of a series of techniques or exercises to help your thinking. Whenever you are stymied during any writing task, you can stop and try one or more of these loops. (Should you use loop writing on a topic where you already know exactly what you think? Yes—so long as you are willing to rethink your thinking.)

MAIN ASSIGNMENT

The final assignment for this unit will be to produce (out of all the material generated by loop writing) a draft of an essay which you can revise later in the semester. Your teacher may invite you to choose your own topic or perplexity to explore, or she may set the topic. Here are some topics we consider useful to work on as you begin a new writing course and a new stage in your schooling:

- Explore the relationship between speaking and writing. In what ways are they similar and different?

- Explore your gender, race, religion, class, and cultural background in ☆ order to show three things:

—The strengths and virtues they have given you (i.e., what are you proud of in your inheritance?)
—The ways in which they have made people tend to stereotype you or be prejudiced against you.
—The ways in which they might have led you to stereotype or be prejudiced against other people.

- Some people think the chief purpose of education is to make one a better person; others think the chief purpose is career preparation. Explore this dispute.

These topics might seem difficult: either too large or too personal or too academic. We think they are important in themselves, but we also chose them because we want to show how the loop writing process is helpful when you are faced with a tough topic not of your own choosing. Loop writing is ideal for taking a topic that seems foreign and helping you *own* it.

The task of this unit is to produce a rich and full draft, not a finished, polished work. Our emphasis will be on generating a great deal of writing and selecting from it pieces that you can use for a draft. (In fact, you will have material for rough drafts of several essays.) Your teacher will say whether you should end up with something more like a collage or more like an essay. In either case, you will have a chance in a later unit to rework and revise this draft into a final version of an essay.

WHAT IS LOOP WRITING?

Loop writing consists of a series of writing activities to help you think more productively and write more interestingly. It is called a "loop" process because you begin writing from a focus on your topic, but you allow yourself to loop away from that focus as you continue writing. It's important while doing these loop pieces *not* to worry about the final product, *not* continually to ask, "What will I have to show for this writing?" For it to work, you need to trust that the pieces will be productive in the end.

The cognitive power in the process comes from the looping away—even the forgetting of your topic. You need to trust that no matter how distant some of your writing seems from where you began, there *is* a connection. (Otherwise you could not have gotten to it.) You often learn the most exciting things about your topic later, as you look back and reflect on the relationship between the topic and what looks at first like a digression. (If you're interested in understanding better how and why the loop process works, read our "Ruminations and Theory" at the end of the unit.)

We'll show you five loop processes:

1. First thoughts, prejudices, preconceptions

2. Moments, stories, portraits

3. Dialogue

4. Variations on the audience, the writer, the time

5. Lies, errors, sayings

You probably can't use all of the loop processes on one writing task, but it's worth learning them and being comfortable with them. That's why we're asking you to try them all out for this unit. In the readings you'll find examples of loop writing and collages made from loop writing. (By the way, when writing loops, it's best to write only on one side of the paper, so you can cut and paste and rearrange later.)

1. First Thoughts, Prejudices, Preconceptions

You have already sampled this kind of writing if you did focused freewriting in Unit 1. It is just a matter of putting down whatever first comes to your mind about your topic. Focused freewriting might have felt like a "mere exercise," but writing first thoughts is in fact a good way to start out writing a serious essay: you always know more about a topic than you realize. The important thing is to jump in and keep on writing and let yourself get past what you already "have in mind."

A helpful way to write first thoughts is to use what might be called "narrative thinking." Simply write your thoughts in the form of a story *as* you're thinking them: "When I think of this topic, what happens first is that I remember ————. Then I think of ————. Then it occurs to me that ————. And then I wonder about ————," and so on. Putting your writing in the form of a story about what's happening in your head from moment to moment takes the emphasis away from the question of whether your thinking is true or right or sensible. It puts the emphasis instead on a different kind of truth and validity: that these thoughts, feelings, images, hunches, and wishes are going on in your mind; that these are snapshots of what *you bring* to the topic. This approach adds to the sense of adventure in the process and often encourages more exploration.

You might worry that this acceptance of prejudices will lead you to wrong ideas or bad thinking. Remember that you're treating this writing not as "the answer" but as exploration. If you want to do good thinking on a topic, you need to understand your own prejudices and preconceptions. The best way to understand them—and to prevent them from infecting your *careful writing*—is to get these candid snapshots of what your mind brings to the topic and how it works.

For example, let's say you've decided to focus on the relationship between speaking and writing. Let's say further that you're sick of writing and tired of people (like us) *glorifying* it. You could call this a first thought or preconception. Take it seriously. Explore it; it may lead you somewhere useful. Why are you sick of writing? What about it has been glorified too much? What happens to you when you write? Why do teachers, textbook writers, and journalists glorify writing so much? We think you're more likely to understand writing this way—by acknowledging and exploring your first thoughts—than by either pushing those thoughts aside or defending them as gospel.

Give yourself permission to go along with your preconceptions—even to exaggerate your prejudices. You might want to start off by saying something as extreme as "There is no longer any need to teach students to write now that we have telephones." Once you've written this, you may react so strongly against its absoluteness that you'll want to cross it out. But we suggest that you follow through, push it, nurture it a bit, and protect it from your own criticism for a while. You may be surprised by the good that comes out of this. As you allow yourself to get carried away by your extreme idea, you may discover some unexpected problems with writing—or why writing *has* been so important to humankind. You'll begin to understand some of the significant differences between talking on the telephone and writing things down. Almost invariably there are good ideas and interesting insights tangled up in the worst thinking. People seldom come up with good new thinking except through some obsession or exaggeration.

(If you are doing a research project and have to do a lot of reading or research before you can write, use first thoughts and prejudices *before* you do that reading and research. By putting on paper all the ideas you already have—even writing out a quick twenty-minute fantasy of what you *hope* your research will show—you'll find that your reading and research become far more interesting and productive. You'll already have ideas of your own to compare with what the others say: you won't be reading with a blank mind. You're more likely to remember what you read and have more reactions to it.)

2. Moments, Stories, Portraits

You sampled this kind of loop writing in Unit 1 when you wrote moments, stories, and portraits from your past writing experiences. Just sketch in whatever moments, events, and people you can think of that somehow seem connected to your topic or that come to mind. At this point don't spend any time trying to connect separate pieces to one another or to elaborate on the significance of them—unless, of course, that just happens while you're writing.

The cognitive power here comes from using *experiential* writing (description and storytelling) for the sake of *expository* writing or thinking. Most of us have had more practice with describing and storytelling than with abstract and inferential writing, so we are often *smarter* when we tell stories than when we give ideas and reasons.

Try testing this idea sometime by asking someone his ideas about the differences and similarities between speaking and writing. After he has said a few things, ask him to tell you moments, incidents, and people that come to mind when he thinks about speaking and writing. After he's talked some more, ask him to reflect on these moments, stories, and portraits to find insights or implications about speaking and writing in each of them.

Usually people come up with more and better thinking by means of this roundabout loop path than by means of careful thinking. Often they'll surprise themselves with new views and realize that they now disagree with some things they'd always thought they believed. The person you tested this idea on may be surprised to discover that what he said about speaking and writing when you first questioned him is different and not as valid as the reflections he had *after* telling stories. That's why we include this loop on storytelling, portraits, and concrete moments. Loop thinking is concrete and specific thinking that cuts a path around generalities, pieties, and prejudices. Thus writing up remembered moments sometimes works *against* first thoughts in a productive way.

3. Dialogue

Describing and storytelling seem more natural than the more abstract or expository forms of discourse like *explaining, giving reasons,* and *making inferences* because all of us have been describing and telling stories since infancy. Describing lets us just close our eyes and *see* what to say; storytelling carries us along on a stream of "and then, and then, and then."

But there's an important exception here, because ever since we could talk we've engaged in *dialogue* too, and dialogue tends to consist of explaining, giving reasons, and making inferences. When someone told us that we couldn't have ice cream before lunch or that we had to go to sleep after our snack or asked us why we thought the flower was "sad," we fell naturally into giving reasons, explaining, and making inferences. We've been doing it

---

PROCESS BOX

What you finally read in the published text is what's been collaged and montaged (can one use these words like this?) from all my various improvisations. In other words, writing for me is also a way of splicing stuff together. That's real writing for me, and not that initial spontaneous flow of words. That's in the final text too, but buried inside the other levels of improvisation. It's in the various *re*-workings and *re*-writing sessions that the real elements of improvisation (and not inspiration) come, because improvisation is always something that builds on something else.

RAYMOND FEDERMAN, *ANYTHING CAN HAPPEN*

---

ever since. That is, dialogue pops us right into the kind of conceptual rather than experiential language that we need for essays. (Of course, it doesn't *organize* that conceptual language and thinking into an essay-like form.)

There are other powerful advantages to dialogue. A dialogue injects unusually strong energy into language and thinking. A dialogue makes you speak and think from your own point of view and yet forces you to imagine another point of view at the same time. (See the O'Toole dialogue in the readings for Unit 7 to get a sense of how this works in practice.) A dialogue leads you to the very stuff of essays: assertions, summings-up, reasons, arguments, examples, counter examples—and probably all in down-to-earth, clear language.

Thus one of the most powerful ways to do exploratory writing for essays is simply to write a dialogue with someone. Who, for whatever reason, seems important to the topic you want to explore? The person can be real or fictitious, live or dead, someone you know well or someone you've never met. And it turns out you don't need *persons:* you can have wonderful dialogues with a thing (such as your telephone), with an institution (such as your school), or with an abstraction (such as "learning" or "silence"). You can make writing and speech have a dialogue with each other. You don't even have to decide who to have a dialogue with: you can just start off a dialogue and get a voice to answer—and wait and see what kind of person or entity it turns out to be.

The trick in writing a dialogue is to avoid planning. Simply start by saying something *yourself,* perhaps something as simple as "Hello" or "I remembered you when I was thinking about the relationship between learning and teaching, a topic I'm working on for a writing assignment." And then just let the other person reply. Don't try to figure out what the other person would say. Don't worry about whether it's really what they would say or how they would say it. Just force yourself to give a reply for them: accept it as an act of faith that you can talk for them or that they can talk through you. The goal is not fidelity, but thought stimulation.

4. Variations on the Audience, the Writer, the Time

It is classic advice to write to someone who doesn't understand your topic, even if you are really writing something for experts. Writers have traditionally benefited from writing their technical material as though to children; Dr. Samuel Johnson, one of the most prolific and popular writers of the eighteenth century, used to read his writing to his uneducated servant and not stop revising till it was clear to her. It's not just that this process forces you to be clear. The more important effect is that you *see* your topic differently when you direct your thinking to someone different—and this process gives you new perspectives and new ideas.

But sometimes the *assignment* is to write to someone who doesn't understand the topic, and that somehow makes it hard for you to write— and you start reluctantly to put out big, fat, dull, empty sentences. ("School is an institution for educating the young.") It will usually help you get started and involved if you change the audience—but of course this time changing it in the other direction: write to someone directly involved in your topic even though your real audience is a bystander. For example, you might try writing about learning and teaching to that person who was your best teacher—or your worst teacher—or to your childhood self who is about to set out for first grade. Think of interesting or unexpected people to write to.

You can achieve comparable benefits by varying the *time*. Write about learning and teaching as though you were living in the future or during some period in the past. You will notice many things about teaching and learning that you wouldn't otherwise notice.

Varying the *writer* will even more directly change your perspective and give you new insights. Pretend *you* are that best or worst teacher of yours— step into her shoes—and then try writing from her point of view about you and your learning. How do you suppose she saw you as a student or even as a small child? See, in other words, what that teacher might write about you. Or write in the voice of some famous teacher or thinker you admire.

If you want to end up with something fair and judiciously detached, spend some time writing from the point of view of someone who is very biased and involved in the subject. Then write as someone with the opposite bias. (Obviously this category can merge into a dialogue.)

This mode is good for experimenting: start out writing to various audiences and at various times and as various people. See which are most fruitful to continue with.

5. *Lies, Errors, Sayings*

These are just sentences or phrases, not extended pieces of writing. Therefore lies, errors, and sayings have a kind of coiled up cognitive power, a lurking energy. They imply more than they state. Afterward you can explore the implications of your lies, errors, and sayings. You'll find much more meaning than you expected.

With *lies* it's fine just to write single sentences, but now and then let yourself spin one out a bit more if it intrigues you. Be bold in your lies: "I *never* remember anything I read." "All teachers are dumb."

By *errors* we mean ideas that are almost right—assertions that are wrong but tempting. Write down things that many people believe, or things you're not sure of, or things you wish were true but might not be: "Careful study always helps me remember better." "Obviously I know more than I used to." "Most students learn to read more easily than they learn to write."

Sayings tend to carry "folk wisdom"; they are worth exploring *and* questioning. They teach you to squeeze a lot of meaning into a pithy and memorable chunk of language. You can use sayings that already exist: "A little learning is a dangerous thing." "All work and no play makes Jack a dull boy." But get yourself to make up your own sayings: "When the student is big, the teacher shrinks." "A triangle is the most stable figure: teacher, student, and book. Take away the book and the figure becomes unstable." You don't always have to know exactly what you mean by sayings you make up. Playing with "proverb syntax" will lead you to formulations that are interesting to explore: "A little danger is a learning thing." "Where there's milk there's money."

If it sounds merely foolish or game playing to write lies, errors, and sayings, try pondering their implications especially in conjunction with each other. Ask yourself questions like these:

- In what respect is this lie true?
- Why do some people think this idea is true?
- Are there times when this is true and times when it's not?
- What would follow if this were true?
- What is it that makes this untrue?

Discussing lies, errors, and sayings with your partner or group is particularly fruitful. You can also make up good ones collaboratively with them.

USING THE LOOP WRITING FOR YOUR MAIN ASSIGNMENT

If you want to make a collage, it won't require many steps to produce one from your loop writing. In fact, writing loops is an ideal way to produce a collage. Read through all the pieces you've written ("blips" we sometimes call them). As you read, decide which are the best ones and keep asking yourself, "What does this passage tell me or imply about my topic?" This exploration can lead you to write a bit more—to explore or spell out some of these implications. Then arrange the pieces in whatever order seems most interesting or effective, and type and proofread it carefully.

Sometimes a collage can be a more powerful and satisfying piece than an essay. A collage doesn't have to "say" what it's saying; it can plant seeds in the reader's mind. When such seeds bear fruit, the effect on readers is usually more powerful than if you had told them what you wanted them to think. (See the collage in this unit's readings and Don Murray's collage, "The Feel of Writing—And Teaching Writing," in the readings following Unit 1.)

If you want to produce an *essay,* you will be able to use many short passages and probably some long ones, but you will have to work harder at shaping and transforming your loop writing. The loop writing process produces richer material and uses more parts of the mind than most other kinds of exploratory writing, but for that reason the raw writing usually needs a bit more focusing.

Here are steps you might follow to produce the draft of an essay:

- Turn back to your topic and get it firmly in mind. (All the loop writing may have gotten you to drift a bit. That's where some of the power comes from.) If the topic was given by your teacher, it's particularly important to get back to it. If you chose the topic, you can change it now, but even so, you need to decide what your topic *is* so your essay doesn't drift.

- Next go over all the writing and decide what each piece tells you about your topic. Sometimes what it says will be clear and obvious, but sometimes the insights will only be hinted at or implied. You can learn much if you sort loop pieces into piles that "seem to go together." New perspectives come when you see pieces together that you didn't write together.

- Get responses from your partner or your group as to what your loops are "saying"—both individually and as a whole. Readers will find implications and themes in your writing that you can't see. Your teacher may allow class time for this.

- Based on this analysis, decide what you want your essay to say.

- Figure out an order for your ideas. Perhaps write an outline.

- Choose the passages and sections you can use, rewrite what needs rewriting, and write the new material that you now need.

- Because this is rich material for an essay—full of stories and experiential writing—you may want to try out some organizational strategies that are new but promising for you. But keep in mind that you will have to *wrestle* it into some kind of shape and coherence for a reader. You'll be starting with more than usual messiness, so it'll take more than usual bravery to revise. Try to bring the same spirit of adventure to revising that you are developing for generating new material ("What the hell, take a risk"). But when you use that spirit for revising, it should lead to radical pruning and tightening rather than a timid refusal to rearrange or throw things away. The goal is to make something that's not a mess for your readers.

- Share your draft with your partner or writing group or with at least one sympathetic listener-reader.

By the time you finish—whether it's a collage or an essay draft—you may discover that you've used only half or less of your total loop writing. This doesn't mean you wasted time doing this writing; what you got as a result was choice. And we're willing to bet that what you decide to use is far richer and more interesting than what you would have come up with if you had just sat down and written a draft from beginning to end instead of doing the looping.

PROCESS BOX

I just figured out what it is I'm trying to say—found my point or asser-tion. I've been wrestling for three days and unable to figure it out—knowing that I've been saying good stuff—knowing that long passages I've been writing are good (some as long as 3-4 pages)—but unable to *say* exactly what it is I'm really trying to say.

I found it when I started to write out a slightly tangential thought. I realized this was a side thought and started writing the sentence as a parenthesis. In mid-sentence I recognized it was even more tangential than I had realized and almost just stopped and crossed the whole thing out as an unhelpful side road. And then I just said what the heck and kept going, and all of a sudden it led to a sentence that zeroed in on and specified *exactly* the precise issue that was at the heart of the 15-20 pages I'd so far written but been unable to sum up.

It's simple and clear once it's said. (And perhaps some person who reads my 15-20 pages would impatiently see my point as obvious and say, "Why don't you just *say* what you're trying to say—and say it in the beginning—instead of meandering all over the place making a mess.") But *I* couldn't see it. Or I couldn't see it till late in the game—and not till I let myself ride on this digression.

PETER ELBOW 5/81

If you learn to use the loop process and become comfortable with it, you'll learn that you can use a *bit* of it here or there when you are in the middle of a writing task and feel dry or stuck. We are teaching it as a full and extensive technique, but after you learn it, you don't always have to say, "Am I going to do this piece of writing by means of the loop process or some other process?" You can use bits and pieces of various processes as they become useful. One of the main goals of the process journal is to help you become more *aware* of how you can use various writing processes so you can end up being more flexible and efficient in your writing.

Audience. Obviously your audience is your classmates and your teacher. It's hard not to think of your teacher as the most "important" audience, espe-cially for an essay on a somewhat academic-sounding topic. But try to avoid that crippling "school writer's stance" of merely "performing for a judg-ment"—of writing in a merely obedient voice that says, "You probably know this already but I want to show you that I know it too." Insist to your-self that you are telling what you have figured out to people who care. It may help on this score to concentrate on your classmates as audience—or even to think of some other readers to whom you *want* to tell these things.

SHARING AND RESPONDING

In using loop writing for a collage or an essay, you learn most by just reading aloud what you have written to your partner or small group and by getting answers to these key questions:

- Which parts seem strongest to you?

- What do you hear these parts saying and almost saying?

- What do you hear in *everything* I've read?

- What is the main point or "center of gravity"? That is, if you cut away everything but one section, what section would seem to carry most forcefully what you hear the piece saying? (If this question is used when sharing unshaped and unpruned loops, there may well be as many as three or four centers of gravity, but having them pointed out will show you various possibilities.)

- If it were your piece, how would you organize it? (What would you start with, build up to, and end with?)

These suggestions are covered in the booklet *Sharing and Responding* in Section I (Sharing), IIA (Sayback), and IIB (Pointing). If you're working hard on organizing an essay, you'll also find Section III, Analytic Responding, useful.

PROCESS JOURNAL QUESTIONS

As always, the meat and potatoes for your process journal are simply stories of what happened on particular writing occasions. But there is also a particular issue for your process journal for this unit: how to get the most out of the loop process. How can you make it work best for *you?* Some questions to explore:

- What happened when you were invited to do the loop process itself— that is, to put aside for a moment the need to write directly on the topic and instead write obliquely about stories, and so on? Did you resist or gratefully jump in? Describe the reactions you remember having.

- Which loop processes seemed to suit you best or seemed to lead you to more new views or ideas? Why do you suppose they worked that way? Are there ones that you find uncongenial but that you think you ought to work on?

- Which loop processes do you think you'll find most useful for *which kinds of topics or writing tasks?* Do some work best for more personal topics versus more academic topics? for collages versus essays? for assigned topics versus free-choice topics?

- How far did you loop away from your original topic? Did you tend to stay close or take long digressive journeys? Are you pleased at how that works, or would you like to push yourself more one way or the other?

- How much of your loop writing were you able to use? Could you use (i.e., learn from) loops that were not suitable for your draft? Do you wish you could have used more? Can you think now of some way to do that?

RUMINATIONS AND THEORY

    A. "It's Impossible *Not* to Think of Something."
    B. Loop Writing and the Dangerous Method

"It's Impossible Not *to Think of Something."*

So wrote the poet William Stafford. Whenever we focus on the inside of our heads, we find something there that seems already to exist in the form of words. If we put these down on paper, something else takes their place inside our heads. By definition this process is infinite. But we're quite likely not to believe in it until it is proved to us; we need to record the words we find in our head and realize for ourselves that others take their place. This new set of words may or may not have an obvious connection to the old set of words. And the same may be said for each succeeding set of words. Consequently, the only limit to what we can write comes from our muscles: how long we can sit up, hold a pen, type.

When we write something down and don't stop to look back inside our heads, more words come anyway, and these words begin to appear on the page. If we continue to write, we become conscious of new sets of words only as they appear on paper. This gives us the sense that the words are writing themselves. In truth almost all writing happens this way, whether it's exploratory or not. We rarely plan any written sentence out entirely in our heads. We start off a sentence with an intention to go somewhere with it and with the faith that we can do that. And we continue the same way when we've finished that sentence.

This is not to say that we don't get stuck. We do. Think of yourself, if you will, as being in a maze. You come to a junction and are baffled. You could just sit and try to reason through the alternatives, but if you've never been in this maze before, that's hopeless. Your best chance of getting to the end is just to try every possibility. Since every piece of writing is unique, you can think of each one as a maze you've never been in—even though you may know something about mazes in general. When you're stuck, it isn't because you don't have words; it's because you're trying to figure out *in advance* whether they're the right words. But the only way to know that is to write them out.

At first they may seem as though they're "wrong" words, but if you keep writing, you may arrive at some good ideas which you would never have gotten to otherwise. And even if you come to a dead end or become irreversibly discouraged, you can always return to the point in the maze where you were stuck in the first place and go a different way. And remember: if your *aim* is to learn more about mazes themselves, you would deliberately take as many routes as possible.

This, of course, is analogous to loop writing. You start off a certain way, a way that seems to be heading where you want to go, and travel wherever that takes you. If you are blocked in some way or don't like what you're doing, you can return to your original subject and start off from it again in another way. You may well discover that there are quite a few effective approaches to your topic. Once you know that, you have choices. And— if your aim is just to learn more about writing—you can explore every approach to maximize that learning.

Loop Writing and the Dangerous Method

The loop process is most useful if you want to do a lot of thinking about your topic; if you are having trouble finding things to say; or if you feel bored, unconnected, or alienated from what you have to write about. It is probably *least* useful if you already know what you want to say or are in a hurry for a final draft. (The loop process does make a mess.)

Many teachers and textbooks say that in order to produce a "good" piece of writing, you must figure out what you want to say *before you start writing:* "Think before you write," they say. Once you've done that, they suggest that you make an outline of your whole paper. Only then are you to start actual writing in the sense of producing a connected series of sentences and paragraphs.

This advice sounds sensible. But trying to begin by getting your meaning clear in your mind—so that you can write something right the first time—is what we call "the dangerous method." It's dangerous because it leads to various writing difficulties that most of us are familiar with.

- You find yourself procrastinating: "I can't start writing yet. I haven't thought this through well enough. My outline isn't right. I've got to do more reading and studying and thinking."

- You spend hours trying to figure out what you want to say—perhaps even making a very careful outline—but you don't really come up with much that's interesting.

- Even when you *do* figure out much to say beforehand and get it neatly outlined, you find that as you try to write from your outline you feel constrained. You start to wander away from the outline, which makes you feel guilty. You think of a new idea you love, but it doesn't fit. Or worse yet, your planning starts to unravel as you write: you think of new problems or objections to something in your outline, or you can't quite explain the idea or the transition that seemed so right when it was in outline form.

- You agonize over every sentence in an effort to get it right. You constantly cross out, change, revise, start over.

- When you finally get it written, you can't bring yourself to make major revisions—or throw even a sentence away—because you've poured so much agonizing effort into writing it.

Perhaps you are not troubled by these difficulties. Perhaps you are actually *good* at the dangerous method of getting everything clear before you start writing. If so, by all means write in that way. And of course there are a few writing tasks where you must get your meaning clear before writing—such as for exams with no revising time.

But usually when we write we *need* to do more thinking about our topic. Even if we believe we understand quite well what we want to say, our thinking can benefit from exploratory writing: we find new thoughts and new ways of talking about our old thoughts. It's as though we cannot see the full implications of our thoughts until we see them concretized in writing.

Loop writing is also useful because it stimulates fluency and makes you feel freer as you write. Since the process is a bit unusual, it jogs you out of any writing rut you may be in. One of the main reasons people don't write better is that whenever they write, they unthinkingly slip into their habitual gear. Our goal in this book is to get you to experience an array of *different* processes for getting things written so that you have more options. With more options you can choose the writing process that's best for you and for the particular writing task you face.

Of course writing *does* require getting your meaning clear in your mind, often even making an outline. And writing certainly means communicating to others what you've *already* figured out. But these processes usually work best *after* you've already done enough exploratory writing to produce good raw material—and if possible after you've felt the mental click that tells you, "Ah! That's it! *Now* I see exactly what I want to say." This insight is often accompanied by some clues about organization.

READINGS

LOOP WRITING ON LEARNING
Sharon Flitterman-King

First Thoughts: I'm learning all the time. As I think about it, I learn as I teach, learn from my work, learn from others. Creating a conference was learning for me. I had to design it—identify a theme, or focus, for the day. Learn how to write an invitation that would explain the conference in an inviting way, learn how to get beyond the obstacles and roadblocks presented by different personalities.

Learn how to deal with stress—yes, that's the big thing I'm learning these days. I think of last June when things were out of control—the new job, losing the old one, dealing with ————'s deception, his unethical conduct, intellectual dishonesty. How best to confront these.

He said to me that first year, "You seem to have a fragile ego." I should have replied, "That's no problem. Yours is big enough for both of us." What I have learned is that apparent strength is often a mask for weakness inside—deep down, where it counts the most. I'm going to win this battle because at the center, where it matters, I'm made of steel.

Portrait: David. Handsome. Strong. Face with lines. Pain line at the bridge of his nose (I don't notice it any more). Moustache. Craggy face. Voice like chocolate—rich, deep. And gentle.

Quiet strength. Patience. Cheerfulness. These are qualities I love about him. Qualities that I'm learning? I'd like to think so. Cheerfulness, especially. But these days I get so harassed—cranky, grouchy. Not spiteful, really, but like a sourpuss.

It's David's humor that I love. How he manages to stay funny and warm in the face of all he endures. Polio survivors are strong people. FDR. David. Is it that polio picked strong people? Or that the ones who could cope with that affliction managed in spite of the enormous hardship?

Why did I choose David? I didn't choose—he came to me. And I let my mind play with it to see what would happen. Quiet strength and patience.

Lies about Learning: Learning stops when you get out of school.
          I don't learn from other people.
          You should always trust everybody else, never yourself, if
              you really want to learn.
          Everybody learns in the same way.

Scene or Moment: David on the hospital bed in our living room. In Washington, David not being able to go on. Beautiful moment. Sad moment. Can I write about it?

It's the foyer of the Washington Hilton. Across the entry are the registration tables, white-skirted booths with friendly NCSS hosts and hostesses. Cheerful, welcoming faces. This is Sunday; the conference is almost over. We are scheduled to fly back to Albany at 1:00 P.M. We've spent the morning in a meeting with Maggie Hennen, the new product manager, and have started a program for selling David's 11th grade American History text.

We are in that lobby after gathering up last minute flyers and folders and literature from the different booths. I come out of the washroom and see David sitting on the ledge by the potted palms. Crutches propped up by his side. Head in his hands. This is terrible. I can't look. I have never seen him dispirited like this. All I can do is hold him, hug him, help him recover his strength and his spirits which he's lost, I know, only for now.

DIALOGUE

VICKI: It's important to move toward an assertion. That's the direction this writing should head in.

PETER: But sometimes you don't know what your assertion is and if you try too hard to guide toward it you lose some interesting bits, possibilities. You have to make room for the unexpected. You have to allow for that to happen.

ME: You mean like letting David come into my loops. When he came into my mind for the portrait I thought, "Nah—too personal; this will never do for the 'assignment.'"

PETER: So what did you do?

ME: I wrote about him anyway, for the sheer pleasure of it. I thought, "It must have come from *somewhere.*" I let the impulse guide me. I guess I trusted the process.

PETER: So did you get anywhere with your portrait? Did it tell you anything about learning?

ME: Well, I haven't read it over yet, but what I felt emerging was something about strength and courage and trust. Something about patience. Maybe that these are things you need to be a good learner. Or maybe that patience is something I have been learning all my life, something I value.

What-I-Seem-to-Be-Saying Step: What am I trying to say here, and how is it involved with or connected to learning? I am learning something by living with David, seeing his courage, and his strength. Is it that patience takes courage? Yes— something there feels right. To let students rebel. Not concentrating. Want to have a better focus. Write another portrait? Scene?

Wednesday morning—a hot, August day. This is midweek, middle of the program, middle of my life. The class is restless, bored. Beth, looking sour, sitting on the floor, disappearing into the carpet, hiding behind other people's knees. Leslie scribbling with yellow marker all over the Lippman text we're supposed to be reading. "I *am* responding to his stupid argument about majority. Can't you see I'm underlining?" And Alison, head bent, writing feverishly in her journal, her own private poems about pain.

I give up—it's not working. I *know* the second week is deadly, that the excitement of the first week is over, that week three stretches interminably off into the distance. And my little group of 10—fresh out of high school, now entering the grown-up world of college, still riding high from the excitement of June's graduation—is sullen, resistant, and unwilling to give me the last summer weeks of the best year of their lives.

There's nothing for it but to go outside—down the 3 flights of stairs, out of stuffy Aspinwall, and onto the grass in front of the quad. Marcia tells me that this kind of group behavior is called "assassinate the leader." The group has taken over—its will prevails.

But what have I really given up by allowing the class to break apart this way; have I lost—*or* have I won? To my students it looks as if I've given in. Leah feels sorry for me: "I hate to see what the class is doing—that it's all fallen apart and they're blaming you." For some reason I *don't* feel sorry for myself. I'm not afraid of this new turn. I trust my students—in their desperation, in their boredom—to come to some conclusion, to make the disaster of this morning's class into an experience we can all learn from.

Patience takes courage; it takes courage to let students rebel, to let them "assassinate the leader," courage to be unthreatened by the chaos. The kind of courage I couldn't have the first year of the program. But now, 3 years stronger, I feel more able to take those risks that begin with patient strength.

Process on Composing This Draft: I was eager to read over my loops from this morning. I was excited that I'd written about David and the polio. I didn't think I could do that scene at the Washington Hilton where he broke down. But I knew there was something important there. Something about courage, and patience, and what keeps you going. (Sometimes you only see that when you let go—it's as if I wouldn't have noticed—no—it's as if his breaking down called my attention to his usual enormous strength and will and cheerfulness.)

Anyway, when I started to do the "What I seem to be saying" I was writing in circles. Repeating words. Getting nowhere. What finally happened for me is that I wrote my piece about something unrelated—or seemingly unrelated—an afternoon with my freshmen at Bard.

PROCESS WRITING ON LOOP WRITING
Sharon Flitterman-King

The topic for our morning's loops was "learning." I've done "loops on learning" so many times that I figured I'd end up with my usual stuff, but somehow because of the turmoil of the last six months other things were pushing their way to the surface. Instead of forcing myself to write about the topic ("Now what portrait comes to me in connection with learning?"), I wrote about the first person who jumped into my mind—David. I held off asking, "What has this got to do with learning?"; and I didn't let my conscious mind steer.

In the end—and I was exhilarated by it—I felt I'd gained new insight into how I define learning. I felt that, in my writing, I'd experienced what loops are all about— letting your unconscious tell you things you didn't know you knew, allowing that new knowledge to nourish and enrich your thinking.

THE HUMAN DIFFERENCES: A COLLAGE
Marichu Meyer

I can still remember the day when Jen sat next to me in Zoology class. The first words she shyly uttered asked if I could share my book with her. My first impulse was to say, "No." My manners, however, took control of my vocal chords, and I grudgingly allowed her to look on. As my curiosity took over, I gave the girl a few quick glances. These were enough to convince me that I should try not to socialize with her in any way. How could people be so careless about their weight? Not only was she chubby, but her facial structures left much to be desired. The same went for her clothes. Short, curly hair, badly applied eyeshadow on a soap-washed face, a faded jacket, seemingly found in a garage sale, stretched over a wrinkled T-shirt with a representation of an electrocuted cat imprinted on it.

I suppose these thoughts are difficult for me to admit, since, much to my sur-

prise, Jen is one of my closest friends today. I must admit she does have a few negative points: she is vulgar, has one of the loudest laughs in the world, is on school
probation, and as far as I know still has not gone on a diet. And yet I have found
few people who can be as friendly, and so easy to communicate with as this girl. The
bond of friendship was immediately established with the boredom of that Zoology
class, when I softly began to whistle "The Yellow Submarine" and she joined in the
chorus.

ooooo

Don't judge a book by its cover.

ooooo

"You what?"

"I believe the idea of true communism is fantastic."

"You're crazy. Communism is the downright violation of human rights."

"On the contrary, perhaps it's capitalism which infringes on those rights."

"Where on earth are you getting your facts from? Haven't you heard about all
the political prisoners in Russia? They aren't just sent to Siberia but to jails, concentration camps and insane asylums as well."

"But those are the criminals, the disturbers of the peace. But what I am getting
at here is the way the Soviet government works for the people. Everyone there is
provided with a job and a home. Do you realize the amount of homeless folk there
are in Massachusetts alone? And a lot of them do work, but they simply cannot afford
a home for themselves. While in Russia criminals of the state are sent to freeze in
Siberia, here innocents are left out in the bitter cold to die."

"Well, then, why don't you tell me why this nation is not prospering economically. People have to wait in endless lines to simply buy a loaf of bread, while the
leaders in the Kremlin have more than enough for themselves."

"Well, then that is one aspect that Russia has to change. The Soviet Union has
not as yet reached true communism."

"And what about the high divorce rates in communist countries, and the lack
of freedom of expression?"

"Perhaps too much freedom of expression is not the best thing. And as for
divorce rates, what have you to say about the number of divorces in the United
States. The annual statistics are becoming incredible."

"That's different."

"How?"

"I don't know. Americans seem to be degenerating as a society. Everyone seems
to be getting a divorce these days."

"So what's wrong with divorce? It gives a chance for a new start."

"Never. Marriage is forever. Until death do us part and all that."

"So what happens if your husband turns out to be a wife abuser or a crazed
killer?"

ooooo

I never get drunk. Don't be ridiculous. I've got German blood. I was brought up
on beer. Practically.

ooooo

Piece of pie . . . easy as cake?

ooooo

Do you realize the number of religions there are, splitting humanity into even
smaller sects in society? Judaism, Christianity, Hinduism, Islam, Shintoism, and so

on are simply labels of another sort. In the end, these forms of beliefs are all the same, believing in some sort of strong spiritual power who controls the universe.

If one ponders carefully about the way people see themselves and others in connection to society and different religions, one will soon realize that there are only a small handful today who are the ardent believers.

ooooo

Looking back on university life today, I am still not willing to admit the fact that I probably did not take the full opportunity of going to college in a serious manner. To me, it was more an experience of separating myself from the authoritarian rule of my parents. Instead of spending countless hours in the library, I spent most of my time in just about everyone else's dorms. It seemed at the time like I simply had to get to know a large number of students in the university. It really did not matter much how different they were from me. I did not care if they came from faraway countries, practiced different religions, or even if they listened to classical or country music. As long as they did not play their music when I stepped into their rooms. My father was always on my back, continuously reminding me that he was paying for an education. Not for a social event. Although I argued that I was studying more than enough, he refused to listen.

Today, as I accuse my daughter of the same things, I have come to realize that my father was in mostly all things, right.

ooooo

A hug a day keeps insanity away.

PROCESS WRITING ON
"THE HUMAN DIFFERENCES: A COLLAGE"
Marichu Meyer

I found writing this collage easier than the last one. Perhaps this was because there were more types of loop writing to experiment with. The subject, human differences, seemed to motivate a bit more will to write a bit more imaginatively.

The different forms of loop writing had varying degrees of difficulty to accomplish. The first thoughts, prejudices, and so on—as well as the writing portraying and bringing out moments—was the usual form of writing I am used to. I found the dialogue writing interesting and stimulating. The one with varying times, audiences, or writers was one which I found much less inspiring, as were the errors, sayings, and lies.

I might have done this wrong because I found others put more emphasis on prejudice and their own self.

ooooo

[Written after Reading Out Loud in Class]

When I was reading my collage out loud I noticed some pieces were a bit "looser" than others.

Certainly I noticed this collage as better and less jerky than the last one, possibly pointing toward more relaxation and comfort with writing.

I also found the last longer piece did not seem to have anything, or very little, to do with human differences—and seemed a bit disorganized.

71

LOOP WRITING ABOUT TEACHING WRITING
Lynn Hammond

[First Thoughts]

"I don't want to teach 75 students. I can't reach 25 in a class, I can't keep track of 75 individual progresses. In fact, I'm not sure I have enough caring in me to muster up for 75 students every 10 weeks."

"Yep. That's a problem."

[Moments; Portraits]

Henry who said he'd get his paper to my door by 6:30 am yesterday before I left for my 8:00 plane. It wasn't there. He gives great feedback but can't ask for help when he needs it, I think. I missed him in some way this quarter. Didn't know he was in trouble until his last papers didn't arrive. One of the silent lost in a crowd of 75 students.

Vincent. Tall black, very slow of speech, not a speaker much less a writer of standard English. I told him at the beginning of the quarter he would have to work very hard to pass this course.

"I'm not stupid," he said, "but I'm not a good writer."

He was right on both counts, though many would have taken his slow speech for slow brain power. Somehow I liked him from the beginning. He knew it and I knew that he knew it in the way that dogs know who isn't afraid of them. In other classes (overgeneralizing: in many other classes) I think kids would have derided him. In my class we listened supportively. His big breakthrough came after a conference in which I told him that his topic seemed to be "why he hated writing."

He wrote it, and he even shared it in class. A torrent of experiences roaring out of him in a totally new, angry, authoritative voice. He was writing about something he knew about and had strong feelings about. After that, he became a writer. He still doesn't speak a standard dialect, but we understood him, and he has a lot to say to us.

[Sayings; So What?]

Teachers should be caring. Teachers should be encouraging. Teachers shouldn't have to grade. Teaching works best in small groups. Teaching works best when there's a caring (engaged?) relationship between students and teachers. Teachers have to be generous, to give more sometimes than can be reasonably expected. Teachers can therefore burn out. I think some of this is overload with papers, etc., but I think even more it has to do with so much *giving* usually with little recognition from colleagues or superiors. Students respond enthusiastically sometimes but not always, and you can't always either predict or remedy. You can try to be a researcher in your classroom. An important way, I think, to keep yourself alive and improve your teaching, and if you can share this in a writing group with peers, so much the better.

I.e, I think we have to form communities among ourselves to help us keep writing, keep investigating and learning, and to give each other support.

A wonderful part of being a member of this Institute has been having a writing group of fellow teachers who are genuinely dedicated to helping me, each other, our students move in our thinking. People who are genuinely interested in what I have to say who have given me permission to write in my own idiosyncratic ways.

So that has been enormously empowering and has helped me want to write.

[Stories]

Janet reminded me of Donna, a little black girl in my class this fall who asked the first thing in her first conference:

"You aren't married?"

"No," I answered.

"How do you stand it?"

I don't know what I answered. It was clear that she came from a culture in which this was not an offensive question and I didn't take offense. She picked up the ball again soon.

"I'm going to be married by the time I graduate so my boy . . . husband can give me a car for graduation."

"I find it easier to buy my own cars and have the resulting freedom," I said, perhaps a little too aggressively, but I felt a need to burst her secure sense of being able to predict these things so clearly when I wasn't even sure she was going to be able to pass my course. I wondered as she left how large a role intention plays in outcome. Maybe she will be married by the time she graduates.

I'm surprised in other ways by their insularity. They thought the reason [the black writer James] Baldwin encountered racial prejudice in NJ was that when he moved from Harlem to NJ he had moved "down South."

[So What? What's the Assertion?]

What concerns me about teaching writing? With 25 students in a classroom, I simply can't keep track of them all, can't keep them all engaged. At least, not in the big group. If I break them into small groups, I can keep them mostly all engaged, but then I have so little sense of what's going on, and I don't get to know them and their writing so well.

[Stories]

Landau, tall, black, sexy, shy, towering over everyone. Hard to get him to sit down. Introduced himself as "Lazy Landau" [in an introducing game in the first class where you have to put an adjective with your name].

"Is that a warning?" I asked. No. He let me in little by little. He wouldn't come to conferences but would always see me far off on campus and stop to talk. He asked if this course was supposed to be personal, and I said he didn't want people to get to know him that well.

Eventually he finally came to a conference and said, "I probably shouldn't admit this to you, but I don't need to learn how to write. I'm going to be a naval aviator."

I struggled to keep myself from pointing out all the ways he might need writing in his adult life, from being an aviator to writing love letters. I tried to be with him, to hear what he was saying. I sensed that if I prescribed, I'd lose him. I said, "OK. Write about that. That's what's on your mind."

He did. I don't remember that paper too well, but as I recall, before it was finished, he allowed that there might be reasons to write. More importantly, he had written.

Then we read James Baldwin. He kept saying he had nothing to write about. Finally I said, "Why don't you write about being black in America today. From your experience, is Baldwin dated or not?"

"OK." he said.

Next class, nothing. "What's going on?" I asked.

"I'll write something for you, but I won't share it in my writing group."

"OK," I said.

He came in the next time and handed me 10 pages. He had grown up in a white neighborhood. He could pal around with white kids, but it was understood that he couldn't go out with white girls. His mother had warned him about that as Baldwin's father had warned him.

Then Sheri, a white girl, convinced him that she wanted to be his girlfriend and that it would be OK. He hesitated, but he got along with her family, she with his. They became very involved. One day Sheri said since he'd be going off to college soon, she wanted their relationship to cool down. After dealing with a lot of evasion he learned that her parents couldn't stand the pressure from neighbors at letting her go out with a black guy, and her grandmother had written her out of her will.

"I don't see how you can keep from smashing things," I said.

"It's hard," he said calmly, "but you learn. I play a lot of soccer."

After we talked about his experiences for a while I asked, "How can you turn this into a 'paper' about Baldwin?"

"I don't know."

"Landau, I think this is a powerful piece of writing. As a letter to me, it's finished. But I need to be moving you toward writing an essay about Baldwin. Can you compare and contrast other experiences you've had with Baldwin's and make it more a public document? Can you write something to show my all-white class? They think Baldwin is too extreme and that no prejudice exists today."

The next day I had conferences until five. At five, Landau danced in and handed me a paper. "Is this long enough?" he asked, not sitting down. "How would I know?" I ask.

I read it while he danced nervously around the room. It was full of one detail after another. All fraternities on campus—all black and all white; no mixtures. No black head basketball coaches in the US. All kinds of personal anecdotes written with voice and conviction.

"It's wonderful," I said. "Can I read it to my 9:00 class? They need to know this."

"That's why I wrote it," he said, looking down at me straight, finally standing still for the first time.

The next day I asked students who I thought had written the best papers to read theirs out loud. Then I read Landau's. They were all riveted, stunned, moved. They knew it was much more powerful than anything they had written. This was writing with a mission.

[So What?]

What am I trying to say with this story? And with Vincent, too? Kind of what I wrote last night about other teachers as an audience? That for people to see themselves as writers, they need real audiences, not graders, but people who want to hear what they *really* want to say and who have the skills to help them find out what that is and how to do it. I think anything less isn't really teaching, and trying to do it with 75 students is crazy.

Maybe I also need to acknowledge that I wrote only about my minority students.

COLLAGE ABOUT HUMAN DIFFERENCES ☆
Amy Vignali

I grew up in a fairly small town in southeastern Massachusetts; middle class is definitely a word you could use to describe it. Most of the kids I went to school with had the same basic middle-class background. But working in a jewelry factory in East Providence this past summer gave me a chance to be exposed to people very different from me in many ways such as education, home life, morals, etc.

At first, I was stared at constantly as every newcomer is, and I'm sure I was viewed as a college snob by many. But as they got to know me, I was accepted by the people I worked closely with. I was known as the little freckle-faced white girl. I didn't mind the name because I knew they didn't mean any harm by it. I became particularly friendly with a black guy named Paul. By talking to him I really began to realize a lot of misconceptions people had about me. He truly believed that my parents gave me money whenever I wanted and that all white people did this. I almost laughed in his face because this is something my parents would never do. My mother once told me she'd choke on the words if she told me not to get a job. Since leaving that job, although we still keep in touch, I haven't had a chance to see Paul again. He believes that this is because he's black and I think that makes him only good enough to talk to at work. He'll never know how mad that makes me when he says that.

ooooo

Because I've grown up in the middle class I've always believed in the American dream. I believed that everyone had the chance to be successful and there was a solution to every problem. I remember reading *Native Son* last year and not being able to believe that Bigger could not have straightened himself out. He was given a chance and he blew it, and he would blow every chance he ever had because of the circumstances of his life; he was a born loser.

One day while working at my job in the jewelry factory this summer, I found myself in a conversation with a guy named Bob. I discovered, much to my surprise, that he was well educated and had at one time shared my ambition of law school. But in his last year of school, his father became very ill and Bob was forced to quit school and get a job in order to support his family. I thought it was such a pity that he was wasting his brain doing manual labor. So a few days later I went to Bob to encourage him to finish his education and earn his law degree. But he told me that it was impossible now, he had his own family to support and could never take the time out of work. What a tragedy! Even though Bob wasn't a born loser like Bigger he had also suffered an unfortunate twist of fate and would never be able to realize his dream. I can't imagine what I would do if my life's dreams were dashed apart before my eyes.

ooooo

"Hi Bigger!"

"Hi Amy!"

"Bigger, why couldn't you behave when you got that job for the white family?"

"I did behave. It was Mary and Jan who couldn't leave me alone. I just wanted to be left alone."

"Why did you have to go and kill Mary?"

"I didn't want to, I just wanted her to be quiet so her mother wouldn't find me in her room. I did not want to get in no trouble."

"Her mother was a good woman, she would have understood."

"You're stupid if you think that way, especially when it comes to a daughter. I don't trust no white folks."

"I guess I really don't know how you feel. I've always been among mostly whites, and I don't know how it feels to be outnumbered. But I still don't understand."

"There's nothing to understand; that's just the way things are. You can't change them."

ooooo

Our similarities as human beings far outweigh our differences.

ooooo

Differences. I think they're important. I love to talk to people from different places. I mean, imagine what a boring place the world would be if we all were 5'8", had blond hair and blue eyes, played racquetball on Tuesdays, ate at 6:00 every night, etc. And if everyone would view these differences as enriching aspects rather than negative ones, I think the world would be a much better place. Furthermore, I feel that everyone has prejudices even if they keep them well hidden. Although I won't deny my own feelings against certain people and things, I must admit that I had never experienced prejudiced feelings toward me until I came to U. Mass. I think it's ironic that a place that's supposed to be teaching open-mindedness is home to some of the worst discrimination.

PROCESS WRITING
Amy Vignali

Peter,*

I had a lot of trouble with this assignment at every step. I have no idea what you wanted. Everything I write sounds terrible. I especially had trouble with the dialogue because every time I began a conversation in my head it sounded so predictable. I couldn't think of anyone I could have a conversation with naturally. I revised it as best I could. For some reason I concentrated mostly on the differences between whites and blacks, although I don't consider myself prejudiced.

I really wanted to write the story about Bob no matter what because that really bothered me. I also wanted to include Bigger from *Native Son* because the two circumstances were similar: people being trapped into a pattern they just can't break free from.

I found the stories and prejudices to be easier even though they blended together a lot. I find that I'm even having trouble writing this. I'm putting a lot of time and effort in, but I don't feel that it's showing. I wrote the two articles on the jewelry factory for Tuesday, and although they seemed bad to me, they sounded better when

---

* We sometimes ask students to put their process writing in the form of a letter addressed to us.

I read them to Karen. I was afraid they would be too boring, but Karen said they really made her think. I guess if I can't make people laugh, I can make them think. I sometimes think of things to write about my boyfriend, but I don't like to mention him too much and have you and the class saying, "Not another Jim story." All my roommate wrote about last semester in her class was her boyfriend, and that's still all she talks about. I'd hate to have my life depending on one thing. Sorry I got off the subject.

Sincerely,
Amy Vignali

ooooo

Peter,

I think it sounded better when I read my collage* out loud—I guess because I could let my voice help the words. On my second blip I had to explain a lot about what I meant concerning differences. Basically I meant that although I have the chance to go to college and succeed, not everyone else can, and therefore we are different. There are so many different factors that contribute to it. Also I had a lot of trouble deciding on how to label my town's size. I mean it's small, but not that small. About 12,000 people. It all depends on the size of the town that the person reading it comes from.

Amy Vignali

---

* Students were asked to read some or all of their collage in class and then do a bit more process writing about what they noticed.

Experience into Words: Description

Your poetry issues of its own accord when you and the object become one.

(Bashō)

Our goal in this unit is to help you make readers *experience* what you are writing about—not just understand it. We're after words that don't just *describe* the desk by the window, but make your reader *see* the desk by the window. This means producing words that somehow carry some of the life or energy of what you are writing about. This may sound special and magical (and indeed such writing is much too rare), but in fact it's not so hard to get this precious quality into your writing if you take the right approach.

The basic principle here—learning to get experience into words—applies to all kinds of writing, including essays. But it is easier to learn how to make it happen with descriptive writing. That is, it's easier to learn to get visual and sensory experience into words—and see when you have succeeded—than it is to get intellectual experience into words. But when you learn the principle, you'll be able to apply it to essays.

In a nutshell: if you want to get your reader to experience something, *you* must experience it. If you want your reader to see something, then put all your effort into *seeing it;* give all your attention to having a hallucination. Don't worry about words; worry about seeing. When you can finally see it, just open your mouth or start the pen moving and let the words take care of themselves. They may not be elegant or well-organized words; you can take care of that problem later. But if you are actually seeing what you are describing, your words will have some of that special quality that gives your experience to the reader. If you don't see what you are describing, you may find very nice words, but they are less apt to make the reader *see* what you are talking about.

MAIN ASSIGNMENT

Your final project for this unit will be to develop an image into a completed piece of writing. Your teacher will let you know whether she wants you to save this piece for revision later in the semester or do an extensive revision immediately.

LETTING WORDS GROW OUT OF SEEING

You can begin this unit's activities by using remembered or imagined objects that you look at in your mind's eye or by using actual objects right before your eyes. The main mental process is the same either way. We suggest you try both. Your teacher may illustrate the processes with the whole class before you use them in small groups.

Using a Remembered or Imagined Object

Think of some small object—for now something simple that you know well. For example, you might think of your favorite mug or coffee cup on the kitchen counter. The goal is to describe your mug in speech so as to make your listeners see it.

What's crucial is to take your time and not utter a word till *after* you close your eyes and put all your effort into *seeing* that mug on the counter. Don't try to see the whole kitchen or even the whole counter. Focus all your energy on seeing that mug—hallucinating, if you will. Don't worry about words or about classmates' listening; indeed, try to forget about them. Take your time. The important thing is to wait with your eyes closed until you can really see what you are going to describe. When you can finally see it, open your mouth and say what you see, letting the words take care of themselves. Don't worry if they are halting or broken, "not literary," not grammatical. For example, someone might say:

> I see my mug. It's white with a blue pattern of flowers. Narrow, small mug. I look inside. Dull gleam on the side of it from the fluorescent light. A few sips of cold coffee left.

Listeners should just listen: no response. Then the next person gets a turn to describe her object. Make sure the teller takes plenty of time to *see* it before talking. Later you can check with listeners to see what they saw, but for at least the first time, people need to try out the process—get warmed up—with no responses at all. And listeners need practice listening just for fun.

This procedure takes just a few minutes for each person: a minute or so for going inside your head and trying to see, a minute or so for saying what you see. Such descriptions are short, no more than four or five sentences at the most. If it starts to take longer, that probably means that the speaker is falling into one of three common traps. If so, interrupt him and remind him of three crucial rules:

1. *No people.* People are too big and complicated to describe at this point.

2. *No large scenes.* It is tempting to start describing the whole kitchen: the fluorescent lights, the stove, the toaster, the dishes in the sink, the green plants on the window sill. Block that impulse for now. Keep to one object with no more than those few things that touch it or interact with it. The point of this exercise is *real* description: transporting the thing itself inside readers' minds. (Sometimes readers say, "What a good describer she is: she told me about *fifteen* things in the kitchen." Usually, however, those things were not really transferred into the reader's head.)

3. *No stories.* Again, it's tempting to tell the story of who gave you the mug and how you knocked the mug off the counter and slopped coffee all over the floor. Of course these memories and stories *are* part of the mug for you, but skip them now. We outlaw stories here to keep you on the more important task of making your listener experience that coffee mug. Think of it this way: in this unit we ask you to stick to a photograph or to what fits in one instant of time. At the end of this unit, we will invite the germ of a narrative, and in the next unit we will invite "movies" or pictures through time, since that unit is about narrative.

Using an Actual Object before Your Eyes

Take some object out of your purse or pocket or from a nearby table and put it where you can see it but others in the class cannot. Don't deliberately seek something interesting to describe; just accept something handy. Your teacher will probably give as many students as possible the chance to describe their objects. When it's your turn, fix your eyes steadily on your object and describe it so that listeners *see* it. Don't rush and don't try to make your description dramatic. Again, limit yourself to a handful of sentences or phrases. For example:

> I see a black ballpoint pen, long and slender, with a small one-eighth-of-an-inch indentation at one end that's a bit narrower. A silver clip. A blob of ink on one side of the tip. Lots of scratches along the black plastic.

The main traps you can fall into here are storytelling, memories, and feelings: talking about when you got the pen, who gave it to you, your attach-

PROCESS BOX

My task which I am trying to achieve is, by the power of the written word to make you hear, to make you feel—it is, before all, to make you *see*. That—and no more, and it is everything. If I succeed, you shall find there according to your deserts: encouragement, consolation, fear, charm—all you demand—and, perhaps, also that glimpse of truth for which you have forgotten to ask. . . .

To arrest, for the space of a breath, the hands busy about the work of the earth, and compel men entranced by the sight of distant goals to glance for a moment at the surrounding vision of form and colour, of sunshine and shadows; to make them pause for a look, for a sigh, for a smile—such is the aim, difficult and evanescent, and reserved only for a very few to achieve. But sometimes, by the deserving and the fortunate, even that task is accomplished. And when it is accomplished—behold!—all the truth of life is there: a moment of vision, a sigh, a smile—and the return to an eternal rest.

JOSEPH CONRAD, PREFACE TO *THE NIGGER OF THE NARCISSUS*

ment to it, and so forth. Save all that for another time and keep yourself focused solely on the physical attributes of your object.

Can Listeners See It?

After everyone has had one turn at describing either imagined or present objects, go around again, but this time let listeners give some feedback. Have them tell you which parts of your description (if any) they could see (or hear or smell). This is a difficult test. Don't despair if at first listeners can't see *anything* of what you described. It happens frequently. Words that actually carry life are rare. Don't give up; don't assume you are incapable.

The main thing to remember is that if your listeners can't see what you describe, it's not a problem of wrong words or lack of words; it's a problem of *experiencing* your object. You may have interesting ideas or words about your object; you may have strong feelings about it. But these are not the point; they will not do. If listeners aren't seeing it, *you're* probably not really seeing it either—even though it may be directly in front of you. (Of course the fault may be partly with listeners too; they may be bad at experiencing. But you can't write only for ideal readers.)

Here are some reminders for when you start again:

- Wait. Stop talking. Get the image clear *for yourself.* In fact, even if you're describing an object in front of you, it's helpful to close your eyes and see if you can still see it. Don't say anything until you do.

81

- Concentrate on what's most important. What's the center of gravity, the point to which your eyes are most drawn? You may be wandering or darting around in your description, changing focus as you pause in your talking. You talked about the mug, then about the flower pattern, then the light on the surface, then the crumbs on the counter, then the half-eaten bit of toast right next to the mug. This *may be* too much to include. You will do better if you pause, look again, wait for the center of gravity to appear, and fix your eyes on it. See it before you talk.

- Having talked perhaps haltingly in bits and pieces (there's nothing wrong with that if you are experiencing the mug or pen), now pause a moment and say your description again, all in one piece, trying to get it whole.

Now ask again which parts your listeners see most.

Questions for Listeners

The next stage is to let listeners enter the game a bit more. Listeners can ask you about details you may not have thought of. For example:

- Would you help me see the coffee in the mug? color? texture?
- Help me see the handle on the mug.
- Tell me more about the clip.

Listeners can then introduce other senses:

- What do you hear?
- What does the surface of the mug (or pen) *feel* like?
- What do you smell?

While answering these questions, don't let the image slip from your mind or eye. Keep your attention on it and make *it* give you the new answers. And hold off any questions that might lead to storytelling.

The Germ of Narrative

After a while you can let a listener ask, "What happens next?"

But remember that even here your goal is not to tell a story but to enrich an image. *See* the event and make listeners see it. Avoid the temptation to sneak in a long story, especially a corny story. "A hand drops a poison tablet into the mug!" "A mysterious aura emanates from the pen!" No. The point is to let the next event be small and real—*generated by* the image rather than *imposed on* the image. The image must be in charge, not the event. This exercise is practice in standing out of the way—not steering, but letting the image steer: letting reality be generated *by reality,* not imposed by a creator.

So when someone asks you, "What happens next?" your job is easy. Whether your object is imagined or present, just close your eyes, go back inside your head, and look at the mug or the pen and just *wait*. Wait to see what *does* happen next. Don't be in a hurry. Some events may come to your mind that are fake or corny. You'll usually be able to tell that they are manipulations of your mind, not products of the mug or pen. They'll be too contrived or phony. Wait for the event that really happens or really could happen. Perhaps it will just be

> The rock song on the radio ends and a man's voice—fake cheerful—announces the time, "It's eight forty-seven now, folks. Maybe you should be leaving for work."

or

> I pick up the pen and rub my nail back and forth, hearing it click as it moves across the slight ledge where the top fits over the bottom.

For listeners the question is always, "Do you believe it? Did it really happen or was it just made up?" Again it is a matter of *experiencing*—applied this time to an event: did you give the experience of the event to the listeners? (At the end of Unit 5 you'll find two narratives that grew out of descriptions included at the end of this unit.)

Collaboration

Now your group or pair is ready to try some interaction among participants on one image.

- One person starts by suggesting a time of day.

- The next person provides an image occurring at that time of day.

- The next person adds a *detail,* but from a different sense (e.g., hearing).

- The following person tells what happens next.

- Another person gives another detail or tells what happens next.

- And so on, as far as you care to carry it.

You can, of course, vary the sequence any way you like. Remember, though, that this collaboration works only if all of you continue to hold the same image in mind even as it changes. Perhaps you could even call this a kind of group hallucination. It's good at certain points to stop talking and give everyone time to continue developing the image *in writing*. You can compare what people write and maybe even practice collaboratively producing just one version.*

IMAGES INTO WRITING

So far this has been mostly talk. But you've been working on what is perhaps the main thing in writing (and not just descriptive writing): giving experiences, not just meanings, to an audience. You should engage in writing at least a couple of times during the game.

That is, we've described all this as though it were one long game, but there is obviously too much to do in one session. Work it out so that at a couple of points—when you have at least fifteen minutes left of class—you stop talking and start a piece of writing. (Your teacher may take charge of the timing.)

Choose an image—preferably someone else's image that you've heard on at least one occasion—and start writing. Describe it, develop it, and explore it. See where it leads. Think of this fifteen minutes as a *start*. You may want (or be asked) to continue it at home. If you wish, allow it to develop into narrative. But don't *impose* events or a story on the image: stand back, respect the image, let it be in charge, let it choose or find its own events. (At the end of this unit is a student's rough draft description of an ice-cream truck written during such a pause.)

The reason we suggest writing from someone else's image is that it often liberates your own imagination to take a ride on an image that didn't come from you. It gives you practice in relinquishing control and letting the image generate material. Because it is not *your* image, you'll have less need to own it or control it, and you'll have fewer preconceptions about it. You'll probably find yourself more receptive to allowing meaning to develop from it rather than imposing meaning on it.

Always start off the *next* session of the game by hearing people's rough exploratory writing based on images from the previous session. (It needn't take much time if you quickly read in pairs or small groups with no responses.) There is a helpful cycle here. First, the game gets you in the right spirit for writing; then hearing the writing gets you in the right spirit for the game. Listen for how the images from last time have been enriched and transformed in the writing.

MAKING A DRAFT

You may want to base your draft for this unit on one of the images you've worked on in class, developing it into a completed piece of writing. Or you

---

*We are grateful for having learned about all these seeing activities from John Schultz's work—which he describes in his *Writing from Start to Finish*.

PROCESS BOX

I didn't even want to do this exercise but felt I had to. Yoon's image was Oriental, although I think I de-Orientalized it as I wrote. I saw the road going down into the woods and I knew at some level that it was only one fork of the road because I seemed to be standing just before the break—but I saw that road more and more, twisting and winding (it was dust-colored) into the trees and forest surrounding it and disappearing into the dark.

But then the leader suggested looking at different parts of the image. I did. And there was the other fork going up a sloping grass-covered hillside toward an open blue sky. Why did I see the "half-empty glass" first? That open blue beckoning sky was there all along.

I was floored by what such a sample game led me to. I certainly won't listen when someone says it's stupid. Is is possible my resistance led me into the forest and obscured the blue sky and when I stopped resisting I saw the blue sky? It was even a different bodily sensation. The tension left my bones and muscles. Wow! And that's an understatement.

PAT BELANOFF

may want to start fresh on some new image, since this is your chance to do one of the things prohibited earlier: describe a person, capture a large scene, or let a full narrative develop out of an image.

But: as you do this more ambitious writing, make sure to rely most on the techniques we've been emphasizing in this unit. Above all, don't fall back on any old ways of writing where your attention and energy go into thinking about words instead of into having experiences. As you are writing, make yourself visualize or hallucinate; forget about words. Let the *seeing* carry you along. When you feel stymied, stop, close your eyes, look inside, and listen. Or return to the real object from which you started and study it. You might call this a meditation on the object. Go through this root experience again and again, as often as you need to. There will be plenty of time afterward to clean up what may be the jumble you put down; time to rearrange words, sentences, paragraphs; time to add necessary connections.

We haven't talked much about revising yet. (We concentrate on it in Unit 8.) We're not suggesting that what you hand in at the end of this unit is the most finished piece possible; you may well have a chance to rework it if you go on to the following unit on narrative writing.

Audience. Your classmates and teachers are the readers who will definitely see this. Try to think of them as an inviting audience: people to whom you can give an *experience,* people who will enjoy having the vision in your head. No one else can see what you see unless you help them. An imaginative descriptive piece is also the kind of thing that all readers like to read; student writers can write pieces that sophisticated adults really appreciate. You might want to revise this and send it off to a campus or regional newspaper or magazine.

SHARING AND RESPONDING SUGGESTIONS

Feedback should focus on the main thing we are working on in this unit, namely, the ability to make readers *experience* what you are describing. "Sayback" will be helpful (*Sharing and Responding,* Section IIA), but perhaps the following pointed questions will be even more helpful:

- Which parts do you see most? Tell in your *own* words what you see.

- Where do you feel the most energy, voice, and life in the writing?

- Which parts are most believable?

- At which points do you feel the image in charge or steering? Are there places where you feel me trying to take the image where it doesn't want to go?

- Where would you take the image if you were working with it?

- If there's narrative development, does it seem to grow out of the image? Is it believable?

After you've gotten feedback on your draft, your teacher may ask you to revise it fully right away (or revise it partially) on the basis of feedback. Or she may ask you to set it aside for revision later in the semester.

PROCESS JOURNAL QUESTIONS

The mental process we emphasize in this unit may be new and difficult for you (trying to put all your energy into experiencing something and not into thinking about which words to use), but it's important in all writing. Therefore we think it's particularly important to try to reflect in your process writing on what happens when you engage in this activity. These questions are only here to get you started if you run up against a blank wall.

- Did you find yourself resisting this whole imagining or experiencing procedure or joining in with pleasure?

- Was it hard for you to see your object and stay focused on it? Could you get the *seeing* or *experience* to lead to words instead of your having to *look for* words? What helped? Was it different for a remembered object compared to an actual object in front of you?

- What happened when you tried to *say* to others what you were seeing? What kind of words or speech did you come up with? (halting, broken, bursting forth, coherent?) Did talking make it harder to stay with the image?

- What happened when you tried to enter into someone else's image? What did you notice happening to you in the collaborative process as you worked with others to build up an image?

- What happened in moving from speech to writing?

RUMINATIONS AND THEORY

Writing and Getting Carried Away

Here's a longer passage from which the opening quotation of this unit was taken:

> Go to the pine if you want to learn about the pine, or to the bamboo if you want to learn about the bamboo. And in doing so, you must leave your subjective preoccupation with yourself. Otherwise you impose yourself on the object and do not learn. Your poetry issues of its own accord when you and the object have become one. . . . (Bashō 33)

In this unit we bring out into the open one of the most important but often most hidden experiences at the heart of good writing: getting fully caught up in your meaning or getting carried away. Needless to say, we think it is a good thing. We suspect that few writers would continue writing unless they were granted the excitement of this experience. After all, the word *inspiration* means literally "a breathing into." We advise paying attention in your process writing to the occasions when you get carried away or inspired, so you can increase the chances of its happening more often.

Jonathan Swift (the eighteenth-century author of *Gulliver's Travels*) said that good writing is nothing but finding the right words and putting them in the right places. In a sense, of course, he's right; and it's a fine way to describe good *revising*. But for *producing* or *generating* good writing, you'll find it helpful to think of writing just the other way around (as Bashō does). Don't seek words or worry about where to put them. Put all your energy into "becoming one" with what you are writing about.

It is a relief to take this approach to writing. It means that in the early stages, when you are trying to get going and write drafts, you needn't have a fancy vocabulary or be verbally sophisticated. Plenty of words will come of their own accord, perfectly good ones, if you will just close your eyes and take yourself to the scene you want to describe: really see, hear, smell, and feel what you are describing. Writing turns out to be a richer and more interesting experience this way—less dry or tense because it isn't so much a struggle to find correct words as a struggle to have or relive or enter into experiences. In a sense writing means going inside your head and showing yourself movies.

If you are a Puritan and worry that this approach might make writing seem too easy, you can rest assured that you won't run out of difficulty. For one thing it's not so easy, especially for some people, to go inside their heads and see, taste, and smell what they want to describe. (Interestingly enough, experienced and—in a sense—skilled writers sometimes have the hardest time. They love to think about words as they write and give more attention to words than to the experience they are writing about; they find lots of smooth, elegant, or impressive words. But as we read their writing, we are more aware of their search for nice words than of what they are saying.)

In addition, being carried away brings its own kind of problems. Most of us have had the experience of getting caught up in our meaning as we were writing and becoming very excited with it, but then later discovering that it was terrible writing. This is an especially common experience with expository writing or essays, but it can happen with descriptions and narratives too.

One problem with being "carried away" is that it leads to writing that is jumbled or disorganized. The excitement we feel removes all sense of perspective and control and produces a mess—a rich mess, perhaps, but still a mess. Because of this experience, some people try to avoid getting carried away; some teachers warn against it. They conclude that you should write only when you are cool and in control.

The important thing to remember is that you don't have to choose between being carried away and being coolly controlled. You can be excited or caught up in your meaning when you are writing *drafts*—and we think you should. But when you *revise,* you need to be coolly controlled and tough. Each of these opposite moods or frames of mind helps enhance the other. That is, if you know you will be tough and controlled as you revise, you'll feel safer about letting yourself get carried away as you generate words. And if you know you'd let yourself get carried away as you generated, you'll feel tougher about revising—more willing to use a knife to prune and shape.

So the control problem is easily solved if you take the right approach. But there is a more serious problem—and a more interesting one—involved here. For being carried away can mean two very different things. It can mean getting all wrapped up in what you are writing about (which is what we advocate here); *or* it can mean getting all wrapped up in your *feelings about* what you are writing about (which is *not* what we advocate here). To make readers experience your subject, you need to "go to" or focus all your attention on the pine tree or the coffee mug. If you get too wrapped up in your *feelings about* the pine tree or the mug, readers will get your feelings, but no sense of the source of those feelings.

We're not trying to argue in general against having feelings as you write; we're not trying to insist on the idea of the artist as coolly detached and paring his fingernails as he looks down on life from a distance.* And of course it is legitimate to decide that *your feelings* are what you want the reader to experience. But this danger—the danger of sliding away from the thing itself into your feelings about the thing—highlights all the more clearly what discipline is needed in trying to give experience to readers: pouring yourself into experiencing the thing (or idea) itself. Are you one with what you are writing about? Or just excited?

READINGS

OPENING IMAGE FROM "A WORN PATH"†
Eudora Welty

It was December—a bright frozen day in the early morning. Far out in the country there was an old Negro woman with her head tied in a red rag, coming along a path through the pinewoods. Her name was Phoenix Jackson. She was very old and small and she walked slowly in the dark pine shadows, moving a little from side to side in her steps, with the balanced heaviness and lightness of a pendulum in a grandfather clock. She carried a thin, small cane made from an umbrella, and with this she kept tapping the frozen earth in front of her. This made a grave and persistent noise in the still air, that seemed meditative like the chirping of a solitary little bird.

She wore a dark striped dress reaching down to her shoe tops, and an equally long apron of bleached sugar sacks, with a full pocket: all neat and tidy, but every time she took a step she might have fallen over her shoe-laces, which dragged from her unlaced shoes. She looked straight ahead. Her eyes were blue with age. Her skin had a pattern all its own of numberless branching wrinkles and as though a whole little tree stood in the middle of her forehead, but a golden color ran underneath, and the two knobs of her cheeks were illuminated by a yellow burning under the dark. Under the red rag her hair came down on her neck in the frailest of ringlets, still black, and with an odor like copper.

Now and then there was a quivering in the thicket. Old Phoenix said, "Out of my way, all you foxes, owls, beetles, jack rabbits, coons, and wild animals! . . . Keep out from under these feet, little bob-whites. . . . Keep the big wild hogs out of my path. Don't let none of those come running my direction. I got a long way." Under her small black-freckled hand her cane, limber as a buggy whip, would switch at the brush as if to rouse up any hiding things.

On she went. The woods were deep and still. The sun made the pine needles

---

*This conception of the artist was classically expressed by Stephen Daedalus in James Joyce's *Portrait of the Artist as a Young Man.* And it is *one* good way to go at writing.

†See the readings after Unit 5 for how this image and the next one by Shack were made into stories.

almost too bright to look at, up where the wind rocked. The cones dropped as light as feathers. Down in the hollow was the mourning dove—it was not too late for him.

The path ran up a hill. "Seem like there is chains about my feet, time I get this far," she said, in the voice of argument old people keep to use with themselves. "Something always take a hold of me on this hill—pleads I should stay."

After she got to the top she turned and gave a full, severe look behind her where she had come. "Up through pines," she said at length. "Now down through oaks." . . .

IMAGE OF ICE-CREAM MAN
Mitchell Shack

My image of an ice-cream man starting as I hear the ice-cream bells ringing the next block away. As he comes closer, he puts on his blinking red lights and his sign, Watch-children, comes out on the driver's side of the truck. I go around the opposite side and find a window about 3 feet square. Around the outside of the window are pictures of bomb-pops, snow-cones, chocolate bar pops, ice-cream cones, shakes, hot fudge sundaes and a bunch of other treats. Next to each of these items is the price, usually about 20 or 30 cents higher than the same item bought in the supermarket. There is a little ledge where the ice-cream man puts down the various items and counts the pennies, dimes, and nickels the children give him. He places the change in a chrome change dispenser he wears on his waist. Inside the truck I see a metal freezer—actually it looks sort of like a refrigerator placed on its back. On shelves over the freezer are boxes of gum, candy, baseball cards and other sweets. The outside of the truck is mostly white, except for the area I mentioned earlier around the window. The shape of the truck reminds one of a modified bread delivery truck. Next to the window is a little cutout where there lies a garbage can on the other side so the kids can dispose of the wrappers. Towards the front of the truck on the passenger's side is a door similar to the kind you find on a school bus. Looking into the truck from the doorway, you can see the driver's seat—it's worn in with a jacket hanging over the chair. There's a big steering wheel and a little metal fan aimed at the seat. There are great big rear view mirrors outside of the window next to the seat and door. Above the front windshield are the big letters spelling ICE-CREAM, and next to it is the infamous bell the kids can hear for five blocks away.

PROCESS WRITING ON ICE-CREAM MAN
Mitchell Shack

I had to think of vivid images of what I see when I think of the ice-cream man. Since there was no ice-cream truck in front of me, I had to rely totally on the images I had from my memory. Since it had been awhile since my last encounter with an ice-cream truck, I had trouble remembering some of the details. I found that I could remember more when I closed my eyes and concentrated on what I saw when I looked at the ice-cream man. As I started writing down the major things, more detail popped into my head. I kept on remembering more things as I kept thinking and my picture in my mind became much more vivid. I could remember myself studying the pictures of the various ice-cream cones and figuring out what I could get with the money I had. I remember racing into the house when I heard the bells and running upstairs to get the money.

I tried to remember the most minute details like getting Italian ices with the little wooden spoon and turning over the Italian ice to get to the bottom which was the best part. It almost seemed as if the ice-cream truck was there—too bad I was getting hungry and would haved loved a hot fudge sundae. Anyway, by creating this image in my mind all the details and little things I forgot over the years came back to me as clear as ever.

MONICA'S BARREL*
Madeleine Blais

First you have to pack the heavy things, the cans of tuna fish and fruit cocktail so that you don't crush anything treasured and fragile, like the box of corn flakes clearly labeled Leonard. Long ago Monica learned to assign by name all the major items in her barrels because that keeps people from fighting about who gets what.

Monica tries to send four barrels a year to Jamaica, sturdy cardboard cylinders filled to the brim. She has been here four years, but she has not forgotten the poverty there, what her life would be like if she'd stayed. The brightest prospect would be a job at the bra and underwear factory, making $50 a week in an economy where $5 buys a pound of rice. In the United States, Monica earns about $200 a week, living-in Monday through Friday as a housekeeper for a family with three children. She says that she has a perfect boss who even lets her keep her baby Ivor with her and who pays for his Pampers, too. On weekends, she moves out to her own two-bedroom apartment in Little Haiti with a sofa set she bought on time ($80 a month) at the furniture place up the street and protects with plastic and a color television and a shelf full of carefully arranged ceramic statuettes.

Monica is always radiant. She is trim, with an easy smile and obedient hair that responds favorably to the chemicals in a curly perm. Her face is a sculpture, all planes and angles.

She likes her work as a housekeeper and calls herself a professional, pronouncing professional in that Jamaican way that combines a native lilt with hints of a British education, combines song and royalty. She prides herself on how well she takes care of her employer's possessions, the children and the crockery, shining both. There is only one thing she hates doing and that is getting on a ladder and dusting the paddle fans.

Monica's apartment costs $400 a month. The extra bedroom is generally occupied by friends who want temporary shelter before finding places of their own. Right now Abner and Velma live there and pay half the rent. Once in a while, on Sundays, everyone who has the day off gets into Abner's blue and white truck and goes to the beach to barbecue, and, if they are lucky, Monica has made meat patties or, even luckier, her famous curry goat. Monica can make anything, including wedding cake, the kind that takes weeks because of having to soak the raisins and the nuts in rum.

On Saturday nights the house comes alive: Monica and her music; she loves her tapes. But by day she is often out, on her mission, harvesting the flea markets and tag sales and discount stores for bargains and bibelots, setting them aside in a corner of her bedroom waiting for the pile to grow until it swells finally and magnificently into a bundle big enough to warrant the purchase of a barrel for $10 at the Jamaican Grocery on 79th Street. The man who sells her the barrel is friendly, but she always

*See the readings for Unit 13 for Blais's comments on this piece.

91

inspects the barrel anyway to make sure it's not warped, and tests the lid with a knowing tap before handing over the money.

Here is what is in Monica's most recent barrel:

Sunsuits and dresses from K mart, bags of clothes her boss gave her filled with things the children have outgrown: Oshkosh overalls and Lacoste shirts, some slightly stained but all usable, marked for Kerry, Andrew and Stacy. There are five brightly colored size 10 dresses for girls that cost $9.99 each. These are brand new, and whenever something is brand new, tags and hangers are pointedly included. For this barrel she was lucky enough to find for $7 a pair, four pairs of high heels, all different sizes, in pretty party colors: white and yellow, pink and peach. She packs shampoo and lotion and toothpaste and toothbrushes. She includes a few of those little soaps from hotels that she gets from her boss' husband's business trips. There is no such thing as a barrel without a 20-pound bag of rice. And you have to have red beans: Those people waiting in Jamaica, you don't want to disappoint them.

This barrel has a box of grits, some canned corn and canned peas and two boxes of macaroni and cheese. Monica always likes to include the centerpiece of the food items, ham in a tin. Processed food from America is considered something of a delicacy. The only dependably plentiful food in Jamaica is fruit—wonderful fruit with sap, with bolts of moist heavenly flavor, fruits like mangos and sapodillas and naseberry—even so, the children especially prefer the foreign and renegade taste of Del Monte's canned fruit with its thick sweet sauce. It is easy for Monica to picture them, their young eager faces, as they witness the ceremonial opening of the barrel and to hear that gasp of breath, that rushing sound that signals their joy. Usually everything in the barrel is laid out, as if in state, for everyone to look at, to circle and admire. Only after the full munificence of the bounty has registered, is the can of fruit from America opened. Monica imagines them eating it the way children who grow up in a culture in which food is not taken for granted tend to eat, not in greedy gobbles but slowly, silently, with respect.

For the children, there are also toys and trinkets, balls and pencils and hair clips and barrettes and ponytail holders and chocolate eggs (bought at half-price after Easter). There are many, many candles, and Monica laughs her quick laugh at the notion that this is because Jamaicans are romantic. Oh, they like romance, but they also live in a country in which the electricity is forever going out.

As one of the final acts before sending the barrel out, she goes through her closet for any clothes she doesn't want and asks her friends to do the same. Toward the top of the barrel Leonard, the recipient of the corn flakes, once again scores a luxury item; this time a stack of Lipton tea bags bears his name. (Who is this Leonard? What kind of king?) Clearly, it would be better to be him than to be Sonya, who upon the opening of the barrel, will surely curse her reputation for practicality, decry her drab fate. In her name, labeled for all to see, comes a huge bag of detergent plus about 20 Brillo pads.

"Leonard?" says Monica. "Oh he's just a cousin," and she laughs, but this time there is a touch of the islander in the sound. It still has heart, but it is protected too, surrounded by private waters, not quite scrutable.

Last packed are the perishables, the codfish, the garlic and the onion. It is important to keep these items as far from the clothing as possible. The codfish is meant to be combined with a vegetable called ackee to create the Jamaican national dish, and so its presence is akin to a salute.

The barrel is an abundance from an abundant land. Only milk and honey are missing.

The best barrel is the heaviest, taking at least two men to lift, sometimes three. And then off it goes, to cargo at Jamaican Air, which charges $44 for the first 100 pounds, 44 cents a pound for every one after that, and $5 for paper work. The airline tries to guarantee that within three days the barrel will have arrived in the place Monica and her friends love in a homesick travelogue way that often overcomes exiles. Oh how they miss the beaches, the view, the sun, the waterfall near Montego Bay. The excitement.

Yet she never forgets how lucky she is to be here, where she can fill barrels instead of wait for them.

And so the gifts are also an offering in the religious sense, a way of thanking the gods and appeasing them. This task, like tides, like seasons, is agreeably haunted by the endlessness of its phases. The minute one barrel is gone, another is begun.

MY GRANDMOTHER
Paul DePonte

The image I see is my grandmother lying in a hospital bed, motionless. Her hands crossed at her waist outside the covers. I notice the thumb nail of her right hand, the pink nail polish half peeled off. Two weeks ago my grandmother had a stroke and has remained in a coma.

My grandmother's hands are very wrinkled. Her skin reminds me of a crumpled-up piece of paper that was straightened out. Her skin is very pale, almost as white as this paper. In contrast to her aging features, I noticed that my grandmother has no gray hair. Her eyes are shut; however, I feel she can still see. She is motionless, except for the expanding and contracting of her chest while breathing. Her breathing seems to be perfectly synchronized with the ticking of a clock in my sister's bedroom. For the first fifteen years of my life, I fell asleep listening to the tic-tic of that clock. The clock was a red Mickey Mouse clock that I could hear through the wall of my bedroom. Now as I watch the blankets covering my grandmother's torso rise up and down I am reminded of that clock.

The room she occupies has a very institutional look to it. The color of the walls and ceiling are an antique white. Facing the bed is a television which is hung from the ceiling at such an angle that it looks like it is going to fall to the floor at any moment. The window is very small, only a little larger than a passenger-car window. The floor is made of twelve-inch by twelve-inch gray square tiles. The floor reminds me of the floor at a department store because of its worn yet polished appearance.

The room has a very pleasant smell. It does not smell like the combination of isopropyl alcohol and ammonia, as I had expected. I remember how my grandmother would smell everything. When I was younger I used to think it was her hobby. Once at the Bronx Zoo, I remember her smelling the elephant food before I could give it to the elephants. The living room of my grandmother's apartment always smelled of fresh flowers. My grandmother always had fresh-cut flowers in a ceramic vase. The vase was light green in color. It was shaped like a tennis ball can. It had a design of flower petals around the base and several vertical lines extending the length of the vase. The vase sat on a matching green plate about six inches in diameter. The plate had the same flower petal design at its edges. The vase was a wedding gift from one of my grandmother's girlfriends about sixty years ago. I have tried many times to buy a similar vase for my mother, but have never been able to find one. The vase is very special to my grandmother. I remember watching my grandmother put the flowers in the vase, and how she would smell each flower before she put it in the vase. Once all the flowers were in the vase she would again smell the entire flower arrangement. I mimic my grandmother everytime I smell flowers, but never in a derogatory sense. Everytime I see a vase I compare it to my grandmother's. I would be willing to bet the next time I go to see my grandmother in the hospital that her vase is in the room.

Sitting in the corner of the room is my father, her son. As he slumps in a chair, I notice for the first time his gray hair, the wrinkled skin of his forehead and face. I can see his facial muscles getting tense and his eyes straining to hold back tears as he reads a document from the hospital. Upon finishing the document he looks out the window. He is looking for an answer to a question he knows can't be answered.

PROCESS WRITING FOR "MY GRANDMOTHER"
Paul DePonte

The purpose of this paper is to describe an image. The image I describe is my grandmother. Primarily, I use three factors to describe my grandmother. First, I use a physical description. Secondly, I describe her appreciation for the sense of smell. And lastly, I describe my father, her son.

I have used several sources for the revision of this paper. Initially, I had the paper reviewed by my roommate. I then proceeded to copyedit the paper and submit it in my midterm portfolio. I then met with Glen and he helped me with a few structural errors. I then revised several paragraphs and submitted it back to Glen for his comments. Glen pointed out mistakes made during the revision. I then revised the paper for a third time.

This paper is based on fact. In writing this paper I was able to express my feeling of helplessness over my grandmother's condition.

UNIT
5

Experience into Words: Narrative

The larger goal in this unit is the same as for the last unit: to produce writing that readers will *experience,* not just understand. But in this unit we will emphasize narration rather than description, and we will emphasize using conscious awareness and theory rather than just intuition and instinct. Thus, we will ask you to think consciously about three important elements in narrative: (1) point of view, (2) structure, and (3) meaning or significance. ★

But we won't forget about instinct either, for it's important to "trust your story" and see that events cause or bring about other events, so you can often let the events themselves do much of the work. In addition we want to help you make better use of your memory. It holds more than you think, and the events you hold in memory often carry rich and interesting significances you are not consciously aware of.

Narrative is probably the oldest literary form there is: storytelling. All of us derive pleasure from telling stories. We tell stories even to ourselves, and stories not only about what happened but also about what *might* happen—what we hope or fear might happen or what is fun to imagine. We don't even stop at night, since dreams are usually stories. (Dream research tells us that we need to tell these stories to ourselves to stay healthy.)

Our minds sometimes settle for thoughts like, "I had a wonderful time last night," or "I wish he'd fall on his face while everyone's watching!" But often enough our minds do not stop there and go on to tell the story of last night or the fantasy of his falling on his face. It seems as though we can enter into or experience things more vividly in narrative form. It would seem as though we experience our own lives as narrative—as events ordered by time. And that's what underlies your narrative task in this unit: to reproduce experience as it is ordered by time.

MAIN ASSIGNMENT

Your final project will be to produce a narrative, a piece of writing whose basic structure relies on a sequence of events as they occur through time. You may choose to tell the story of something that actually happened (to you or to someone else) or to tell an imaginary story—or to create some mixture.

WHAT IS NARRATIVE?

As we saw in the previous unit (Description), a photograph never explicitly *tells* a story (though it may *imply* a story), for it captures only one instant of time. But when we turn on a movie camera, we set time into motion and we have narrative. "What happens next?" is the root question for narrative. You noticed this effect if you did the "Then what?" exercises in the last unit, thereby turning descriptions into mini-narratives. (You'll notice a particularly heavy reliance on the connective "then" in Bede's story of Caedmon at the end of this unit.)

Generally events within a story follow one another in the same order as they would in time. But not always. Sometimes writers deliberately take events out of their time order (in a flashback, for example) in order to give a different experience of the events. Even so, however, that difference can be achieved only if we are conscious of the fact that events are being told in the "wrong" order. So even though time is violated, time still dominates the structure.*

In a basic narrative, you can add the connective "and then" between each sentence:

> John knocks on the door. (and then) Jim opens it. (and then) John says, "Is Joe at home?" (and then) "Yes," says John.

Of course most narratives are not as bare as this. Many writers stop time, in a sense, to tell their audiences more about the event or characters or surroundings:

> John knocks at the door. He is nervous and unsure of himself. Jim opens the door, which groans ominously as it swings open. . . .

---

*Try this test. Find a piece of experimental writing or a poem that is full of *events,* which are ordered so perplexingly that you have no sense of the actual or natural sequence of these events. Would you call it a narrative? We suspect not, even if, in fact, it is a powerful piece of writing that consists of a "sequence" of events.

Many writers stop time for pages, even chapters, while they analyze the state of a character's feelings and thoughts, describe the environment in great detail, or expound upon a philosophical point.

Point of View

We tend to expect a single and consistent point of view from stories. If you tell an experience of your own, you will probably tell it from your point of view—that is, as you experienced it—and so the point of view will almost automatically be single and consistent. If you begin fictionalizing it, however, you might change the point of view or add other points of view. For example, you might tell the story from the point of view of someone else in the story (not letting this character see or know what he couldn't realistically see or know). Or you could adopt the traditional all-knowing point of view where the narrator of the story knows everything that happens and everyone's thoughts and feelings. We see this "omniscient narrator" in most fairy tales.

We tend to expect a single and consistent point of view because we experience life only from our own single perspective. We may *imagine* someone else's experience or view of life, but we usually need help in learning to do this. Or feeling some connection with a person can lead us to experience his view of life. In "real time," we live in one point of view, but through imagination we can break out of time and out of our limited point of view. The attraction of storytelling (and all literature) is that it provides this "escape" for us, a chance to widen our own consciousness, to feel and experience the thought and life events of others who live in different times and places.

Many story writers and novelists today deliberately alter or move back and forth among different characters' points of view in the course of their narratives. Because we expect consistency, the very lack of it warns us to read with particular attention to point of view. A shifting point of view can be crucial to certain stories or to particular effects on a reader. But to juggle point of view successfully you need to have your story under skilled control; otherwise you risk losing your readers. We suggest that you not try juggling until you have thorough control over single point of view. (The narratives in the "Readings" section don't use very unusual points of view, but notice how some of the narrators speak from the present but drift into conveying the point of view of their past, younger selves.)

Perhaps the best way to understand the importance of point of view is to try your hand at writing the same story from different perspectives. As examples, we'll rewrite our basic narrative in two ways:

Feeling nervous and unsure of myself, I knocked on the door. I could hear heavy footsteps approaching from inside. As the door swung open, groaning ominously, I could dimly see a man's figure in the darkness of the cavernous house.

Jim heard a loud knock. Moving cautiously toward the door, he pushed against it. As it swung open, groaning ominously, Jim could see outlined vaguely against the stormy sky a dark figure.

In the first version of this story, we are outside the house with the "I" of the story, invited by the writer to share the fears of that "I," to experience what is happening from that "I's" point of view. In the second version, we are inside the house with Jim, being invited by the writer to share Jim's fears, to experience events from his point of view.

Let's try a third way:

It was a dark and stormy night. A carriage drew up before a darkened house, and a large figure, clutching his cloak about his shoulders, climbed down to the rain-slick pavement and moved up the path to stand before the door. He knocked. The door swung open, groaning ominously. A dark figure stepped into the door frame. The two men faced one another.

Here it is the situation that is fearful. We do not know whether the two men are afraid or not. We are experiencing the story through the point of view of a narrator who is not personally involved in the impending story, or at least not so far.

Try rewriting the following passage yourself, choosing a point of view different from the one it has:

I threw on my sweater and ran down the stairs, wondering why Juanita wanted to see me again so soon. Her voice had sounded odd on the phone. "Where are you going?" my mother called to me as I opened the door. "Just up to Juanita's," I answered. At the edge of the sidewalk, I bumped into my sister. "What are you in such a rush about?" she asked, annoyed. "Nothing," I answered. As I came closer to Juanita's house, I could see her sitting on the steps. She was bent over, clutching her knees against her. She looked depressed.

Structure

In addition to expecting a narrative to give us events in a time-ordered sequence, we also expect it to have a beginning, a middle, and an end. Most novels written a century or so ago begin with long introductions to provide readers with detailed information about the characters, the setting, and even direct comments about the ideas or themes of the novel. (Notice the opening words of Charles Dickens's *A Tale of Two Cities:* "It was the best of times; it was the worst of times. . . . ") Many modern novels, on the other hand, begin with no explanations at all. Still we are not satisfied unless we understand why the writer begins as he does, unless we feel that the beginning "works" as a way to get started.

The middle section of any narrative gives the main events of the story, including whatever description or analysis the author thinks necessary. It is in this section where writers complicate events in such a way that an audience asks, "How is this going to come out?" There is usually some tension or need for resolution.

The ending of a narrative must satisfy the reader that what occurred in the middle of the story has come to an end or is in some way resolved. A good many readers and writers, particularly in recent decades, prefer stories that don't end neatly, stories which other readers complain of as "broken off" or "unresolved." People who like these stories reply that "Life's like that"—or even that "Life's *not* like that, but I like my stories that way." In either case the story may seem unresolved, but there is nevertheless a *sense* of rightness or resolution that the reader finds satisfying. Usually you know an ending has worked when you feel no need to look for more.*

Meaning or Significance

Another thing that we expect from a narrative is that we should understand why the writer chose to tell the story. In other words, after we read a narrative, we should be able to answer the question, "So what?" or "What's the point?" or "What does it mean?"—or at least not be bothered by the need to ask. We do not have to agree with other readers on the answer, nor do we even necessarily give the same answer every time we read or hear the narrative. We don't even have to be sure of an answer; we only need to feel that the question is answerable. People seem to have a basic need to seek meaning; this need does not go away when we read.

Sometimes the writer spells out explicitly why he wrote the story. Some stories (like fables) seem to have a point that can be summed up in a statement. Other stories seem to have a "theme": they don't seem to be trying to "say" something, but they do seem to be exploring some issue. Yet other stories seem to try as hard as they can to *avoid* having a moral or a meaning or a theme: merely to "be" a story pure and simple. If they are "saying" anything, they are saying only, "Things sometimes happen this way—or might—or never do—but I thought you might like to read this."

It's important to remember that you don't have to spell out for readers what your story means; often it's better not to. Indeed, when you write a narrative of any kind, fictional or based on personal experience, *you* don't even need to know what it means. Just the fact that you want to tell the story is proof that it means something to you. If you give the story a chance—and especially if you get a point of view and structure that work—your audience will understand why you wanted to tell it.

English teachers and literary critics are famous for seeing meanings in stories where other readers see nothing but a story. But recent critics are also taking pains to argue that there are no meanings at all "in" stories: it's all a question of what readers see. The point is that humans have a tendency to

---

*It's interesting to apply the same *functional* definitions of structure to the essay: the beginning must work to get us "in"; the middle complicates and enriches and makes us not satisfied until we get . . . what? . . . something that satisfies or resolves things for us, namely an ending.

In describing a scene of the past, many of the small subscenes or specifically small areas were focused on and described briefly. It was similar to taking puzzle pieces and looking at them individually and analyzing them and then fitting them together to make up the whole scene. The scene described in this case was a main street in a local area filled with several grocery and fruit stores in uptown, westside Manhattan. The puzzle pieces in this case were the old bums sitting on the benches, the cement islands in the middle of the streets, stacked fruits and vegetables, the store owner, and the bystanders and customers. The clothes and posture of the bums, the rust, littered condition of the islands, the color and quality of the fruits, the characteristics of the owner, and the facial expression of the people were focused on, respectively. The writing started out with all these puzzle pieces being placed together in written form as one large puzzle. As the writing progressed, a few feelings and emotions began to mix in, especially in describing the facial expression of the people. That was where it stopped. The lack of my emotional expression seemed to amaze my group of readers. The opinions and feelings began to arise at the end, but the general mood and feeling for the whole scene was lacking. I couldn't really explain it myself, and therefore the message that I was supposedly approaching was difficult to figure out for everyone because I hardly wrote any emotional expression, and that was one thing the group questioned. For an unclear reason, I found the memory pleasant to think of. Yet, what was more unclear was the reason why I remembered this scene the same way as I did when I was the age of 7. It was probably special because it was a new sight then. The group generally felt that the approaching message had something to do with why I've decided in my writing to be so physically descriptive of such an environment or that there was a discovery that was being made by me about life in that scene that seemed surprising and interesting. During my thought before writing up the scene, during the writing, and after writing it up, I did not realize what the group did realize except that the scene was interesting to me. I finally figured out that the real message was that people in the city seemed unconscious about each other's existence and did not appreciate or care about the individuality of everyone including themselves, and that irony of having underprivileged people suffer while most of everything they needed was literally in front of them, such as the fruits, was appalling. I had to read my writing like a story more than once in order to get the main idea. At first, I had no main idea in mind about the scene but just to describe it. Eventually, an idea was derived from what seemed abstract or separated puzzles.

A STUDENT

"see meaning." The mind seems to resist seeing anything as senseless. Where readers disagree about significance or interpretation—and they often do—things cannot be settled with certainty: it is always a matter of judgment, experience, and context.

When you write your story, you may *want* to make it "say" something to the reader; you may have a message you are trying to send. But we would warn you against this impulse. If you start out with a meaning or moral in mind, the story very often comes across heavy-handed or preachy. Almost always you do best to concentrate on what might be called "finding the story," or "letting the story tell itself," or "letting the meaning take care of itself." You always have more chances later, during revising, to spell out the meaning more clearly if necessary—or let the events hint at it more pointedly; it's almost always better not to think about this at first. Have faith in the materials you choose, in your vision, and in the power of narrative once you set it loose.

Applying the Theoretical Concepts

As you read about these theoretical concepts (point of view, structure, significance), you need to see them in relation to actual stories. Look at the narratives at the end of this unit (by both students and professionals), at some story you've written in the past, or a favorite one you've read. Or your teacher may ask you to read some specific narrative so that everyone in the class will be analyzing the same one. As you read, focus on the following questions:

- What is the point of view in this narrative? Who is seeing things and talking?

- What is the structure? Which parts function as beginning, middle, and end? Describe the shape or pattern. Does the author use flashback or distort the time sequence in some other way? Does time move fast? slow? stop?

- What is the significance? Don't get trapped into seeking the "right" answer; state what you see as the significance and be prepared to listen to the conclusions of others, which may differ.

WRITING A NARRATIVE

Short Exercises to Get Started

These can be done in or out of class, on paper or orally, in pairs or small groups.

1. Search your own mind. You can count on many stories or germs of stories being there; maybe you've been wanting to write one or tell one.

Now's the time. Just tell the story on paper as it occurred or might have occurred in time. To do this, it helps to transport yourself to the time and place of the story itself. Spend a few minutes going there before you start writing. Whenever your writing lags a bit, take time to again get yourself back into that time and place. This will keep you from writing *about* the story rather than actually telling it. If you practice some of the exercises in Unit 4 (*experiencing* the scene), you can avoid this pitfall.

2. Develop a story from an image. You may have already developed one image into a narrative during the last unit. Your teacher may want you to develop another image or go farther on the one you've already started. Suggestions: choose a spoken image or a written description from the last unit—one you produced or one you heard. Choose one that feels important to you—that resonates or feels perplexing or mysterious. It's often better if you don't even know *why* the image or description feels ripe or sticks in your mind. Write farther on it by asking, "And then what happened? And then what?" Let it develop into a story. Don't plan, don't decide where it should go. Just start by re-creating the image and events you remember. Then continually ask, "And then what?" Better yet, ask the question of your developing *story:* ask *it* "What next?" Trust it and yourself, and the answer will always come: a good story will emerge. Allow yourself to be surprised. At the end of this unit, you'll find two narratives ("An Ice-Cream Man" and "The Worn Path") which grew out of descriptions included at the end of Unit 4. (You may want to look now at Welty's comments on her story at the end of Unit 13.)

3. Use a "life line." Think back over your life to the present time. Strictly speaking, everyone's life is continuous, but lives do seem to divide up into segments like chapters in a book or acts in a play. Imagine your life as a play which you want to present in three acts. At what points would you end one act and begin another? You may want to think of the continuum of your life as a time line:

Birth ———————————————————————————————— Now

Divide this line into three or four segments; each dividing point will represent the beginning of a new act. Some people divide the line almost equally:

Birth ——————— age 6 ——————— age 12 ——————— age 19

| (moved to | (started | (now) |
| Long Island) | high school) | |

This student thought of his family's move to Long Island as causing a memorable change in his life. The second big change occurred in his life between junior high and high school. Another student's line looked like this:

Birth ————————————————— age 16——— age 17——— age 19

| (began | (began | (now) |
| senior year) | college) | |

PROCESS BOX

> When she first told us to divide our lives into three parts, right away I thought of school. But that passed quickly into people and situations. My first dividing point changed from an event into a meeting.
>
> When I was writing about the meeting of my best friend and his brother, it brought back memories of those long hot summer days following their moving in next door. The summer days where we had nothing to do, but always found a game to play. Joey's father was there at that first meeting, but he's gone now. He died at an accident at work last year.
>
> The writing of this started out making me feel happy but it ended in making me feel sad. It gave me a sense of loss all over again.
>
> A STUDENT

This student said that her closest friend for twelve years moved away after their junior year in high school and that coming to college meant she was away from her family and on her own for the first time.

Once you have divided your life into segments, sit and reflect for a while about the points where you drew the dividing lines. Why did you put them there? What occurred just at those points that makes what comes after seem like another chapter or another act in your life? People often speak of such spots in their lives as "turning points." Imagine yourself back into one of these spots. You may even want to try writing about it as you might have written at the time. Begin by freewriting, focusing (at least at first) on re-creating an actual event or events which characterized that turning point.

4. You can also get started by freewriting in response to one or several of the following questions. Time yourself so that you write for at least ten minutes.

- What event keeps coming back to your mind? Tell the story *without* analyzing or explaining—just say what happened.

- Have you ever been in a situation where you couldn't convince someone you were telling the truth?

- Tell about a time when you lied to someone.

- Tell about a time when you were mistreated or judged unfairly, *not* because of something you did but because of who you are (your religion, skin color, sex, class, age, sexual orientation, nationality).

- Do you remember a time when you tried being someone different from yourself?

- What was the most important "first time" for you?

- Can you remember an event that changed the way you think about yourself or about someone important to you?

✭ • Tell about an event which made you angrier than anything that ever happened to you before or since.

- Start story for them.

Moving toward a Draft

You may now have begun several narratives—on your own or because of our suggestions or your teacher's suggestions. You need to select one to work on more. Perhaps that choice will be easy for you: your own gut reactions as you write may point you to the narrative that appeals to you most. But if the choice is not obvious, readers can help you decide. Read them your beginnings and see which one they find most interesting or want to hear more about. (Sometimes the act of reading to listeners will tell *you* which is most important, apart from how they react.)

As you extend your beginning into a full narrative (if it isn't already full), discipline yourself not to impose meaning on the story: just tell it. While you're writing, try to keep yourself inside the events of the story so that the story itself can influence what happens.

When you've got your story told, you'll need to think consciously about details, for it's easy to leave out certain details or events that you've taken for granted. Listeners can tell you what they think is missing—what details they still need in order to visualize, experience, and understand your story better. But, of course, different readers will experience your story differently, and in the end you'll have to make up your own mind.

Once you're satisfied that you've got your story the way you want it, you can begin to revise by consciously thinking about the major points we've been making: point of view, structure, and significance. Ask yourself what you want the point of view to be. Read back over your story slowly, questioning yourself about whether you're being consistent. Others can help you here. Rewrite wherever necessary.

Next look at the structure. How would you characterize the beginning? Does it give background, make some general point, or just plunge in? Ask yourself why you've started as you have and what effect you'd like to have. You may, of course, not have an answer to this question: the beginning may just "feel" right to you. That's fine. Others may be able to tell you why it works or they may not. We consider these questions worth discussing even if the answers are elusive. You'll also want to check with others about your ending, about whether they feel you've stranded them at the end. Endings *are* difficult; if you find yourself struggling, try just stopping wherever your story itself stops. The commonest weakness in stories is not stopping soon enough—which means the writer didn't trust her story enough—or her readers.

Finally read back over your story to see if you've stated explicitly what your meaning is. If you have, think seriously about leaving it out and see what overall effect its deletion has. Again, others can help here: ask them what meanings they get from the story once you've omitted explicit statements. You may be surprised by their answers. The discussion will give you some guidance as you make final revisions either now or later in the term.

As for audience, think of your classmates and teacher as readers to whom you want to give something of yourself. And like the descriptive piece, stories are appropriate to publish in all sorts of places, from a campus paper or literary magazine to the feature department of various local papers.

SHARING AND RESPONDING

Descriptive responding (Section II in the booklet *Sharing and Responding*) is particularly appropriate for narrative writing, especially subsections IIC and IID. Perhaps imaginative writing provides a good occasion to start working on reader-based responding or Movies of the Reader's Mind (Section IV). For with imaginative writing (rather than expository writing), it's particularly clear that what you need is not so much impersonal verdicts from some Olympian critic, but rather trustworthy information about what's going on in readers as they read your story.

Here are some additional questions for readers which may be useful for this unit:

- Where do you find the story most alive?

- Which words or phrases remain most vivid in your mind?

- Where is the sense of movement-through-time most real?

- What is the point of view in the narrative? Is it consistent?

- Describe the structure: are there flashbacks, significant jumps? Describe how the beginning and ending work as beginning and ending.

- How would you answer the question "So what?" after hearing the story.

PROCESS JOURNAL QUESTIONS

Your process notebook is a place for slowly building up more and more knowledge of your writing process. Remember to ground this knowledge in *details*. Conclusions and helpful advice for yourself will naturally emerge from the details. If you just tell the full story of your experiences while writing, you won't need the following questions. But you may find them helpful for prompts.

- How did you get started? You'll have a much better time writing if you begin to understand the slippery process of getting started.

- What was going on for you as you were doing the writing? Did you feel again any of the emotions you were describing? Could you see mental pictures of people and scenes? What didn't get on paper? Did you remember things you didn't know you knew?

- Compare what happened for you in the last unit where we emphasized intuition and instinct ("Don't think about words, just *see* what you are describing") and what happened for you in this unit where we gave more emphasis to theory and conscious awareness ("Think about point of view, significance, and structure").

- Point of view. Were you conscious of choosing (or changing) point of view, or did it take care of itself? Did it change or get fuzzy? Why do you think this happened?

- Structure. Were you conscious of choosing (or changing) the structure, or did the story seem to shape itself? What aspect of structure caused you the greatest difficulty: the beginning, middle, or end? What can you learn from the structural changes you made—or would make if you were to revise?

- Significance. Did you know the "point" or meaning in the image pieces you wrote in the last unit? Did you know the point before you wrote your story for this unit? Did anyone see a meaning that you hadn't seen but which made you say, "Yes, I guess I was 'meaning' that without realizing it"?

READINGS

AN ICE-CREAM MAN*
Mitchell Shack

It was a scorching hot day in the middle of July, almost 100 degrees outside. I was playing football with a bunch of kids from my neighborhood. We were playing ball for almost an hour and I had worked up a good sweat. My throat was dry and I was in desperate need of an ice-cold glass of iced tea. We went into a huddle and I started daydreaming about jumping into a cold pool. The score was tied at twenty-one apiece and we all agreed that the next team that scores wins the game. We were about fifteen yards out from the end zone, actually the area between my friend's mail box and the pine tree across the street. Our team discussed our options and decided we were going to play on fourth down instead of kicking.

*Shack developed this story from his description included in Unit 4.

We lined up at the line of scrimmage and I was ready to start the down when I heart a faint sound. It sounded like a mixture between the fire bells in school and the bell I used to ring on my tricycle. I stepped back to throw the ball when I heard the noise again. This time it clicked in my head that what I was hearing was the ice-cream man the next block away. I dropped the ball and announced, "I forfeit! The ice-cream man is coming." I reached into my pockets in search of a few coins, but to my dismay they were empty. "Darn," I thought to myself, "I must have left my money in my pants in my room." I started to run toward my house and looked back to see my friends doing the same. The long game and the excessive heat seemed to have little effect on me, for I was running as fast as I ever had. I turned the corner and started running down my block. I could see my house at the end and it seemed as if I was never going to reach it. I ran and ran and then sprinted up the driveway. I reached out for the doorknob to open the door and tried to turn it, but it didn't budge an inch. I started banging on my door and ringing the doorbell, hoping my mom would hear.

My mom came to the door and I was halfway up the stairs before she had a chance to yell at me for almost breaking down the door. I ran into my room in search of my pants containing my allowance money. I checked my floor, under my bed, my closet, my hamper, and behind my dresser, but the pants were nowhere to be found. "Mom! Mom! Where are my pants?" I screamed down to her. "I just took the laundry from your room—check the laundry basket," she replied. So downstairs I ran and grabbed the basket from atop the washing machine. I dumped the laundry on the floor and searched for my pants. I threw socks and shirts all over the place before I found what I was looking for. I reached into my pockets, grabbed the change, and flew out the door. Again I ran down the block, huffing and puffing all the way. I turned onto the street where I was playing and saw the truck in the distance. "Oh no, I better hurry—I think he's getting ready to leave," I thought to myself. The truck from far away looked like an old bread truck, but it would not have mattered one bit if it looked like a garbage truck, just as long as it sold ice cream.

I started getting close to it, when the red blinking sign WATCH—CHILDREN went on and the truck began to move. "Stop! Stop!" I yelled as I ran holding up both my hands. I put on my afterburners and ran in hot pursuit of that beat-up white truck. "Stop! Stop!" I continued to scream, but it had no effect and the truck kept on driving. I ran past my friends who were hysterically laughing as they watched me run while they unwrapped the ice cream they had just bought. The ice-cream truck stopped at a stop sign then turned the corner without noticing me at all. I figured I had better take a short cut so I ran through my friend's back yard, hopped a fence and sprinted through a little patch of woods. I noticed that I had ripped the pocket of my pants, probably while climbing over the fence. I was too concerned about intercepting the ice-cream truck to worry about my pants and I came out of the woods and ran in the middle of the street so I could flag down the truck. I held out both hands and screamed, "Stop!" as I saw the truck approaching, but I noticed something looked different. The truck came to an abrupt halt and I ran alongside it. I looked up but instead of a window, I found a sign reading "Bob's bread delivery service." "Oh no, I stopped the wrong truck," I thought to myself as the driver stepped out and asked me what's wrong. "Oh, nothing. Forget it," I said to the driver, "I just thought you were the ice-cream man." He started laughing and pulled away. I felt like an idiot and just sat on the curb and tried to catch my breath.

I figured I had better get home and clean up the mess I made out of the laundry. I walked about two blocks, when I turned the corner and saw the ice-cream truck on the side of the road. I couldn't believe my eyes. I thought he was gone for good. I ran alongside the truck and knocked on the closed window. I looked at the pictures next to the window and wanted to buy everything he had. The man came to the window and said, "I'm sorry—we're closed. I'm just packing up a few things before I go home." "Oh please," I pleaded with him, "I ran two blocks home, my house was locked, I couldn't find my pants, I wrecked my mom's laundry, I chased after you another three blocks, ran through my friend's woods and ripped my pants, stopped the wrong truck and when I finally catch up with you, you tell me you're closed!" "You did all that just to buy an ice-cream cone—I think we can make an exception," he said as he smiled at me. I said I wanted a hot fudge sundae and he turned around and started to make it.

I watched him as he was making it, and my mouth watered just looking at all the ice cream, lollipops, bubble gum, chocolate bars, Italian ices, and other candy I saw inside the truck. He reached into the freezer to scoop out some ice cream and I started counting my change as I placed the coins on the little ledge outside of the window. He finished making the sundae and handed it to me along with a plastic spoon. I went to hand him my money when he said, "Forget about the money. This treat is on me." "Thanks a lot! Thank you, Thank you very much!" I blurted out. He closed the window and drove off. I just sat there eating my ice cream, watching the truck fade away into the distance. I was the happiest kid alive.

A WORN PATH*
Eudora Welty

It was December—a bright frozen day in the early morning. Far out in the country there was an old Negro woman with her head tied in a red rag, coming along a path through the pinewoods. Her name was Phoenix Jackson. She was very old and small and she walked slowly in the dark pine shadows, moving a little from side to side in her steps, with the balanced heaviness and lightness of a pendulum in a grandfather clock. She carried a thin, small cane made from an umbrella, and with this she kept tapping the frozen earth in front of her. This made a grave and persistent noise in the still air, that seemed meditative like the chirping of a solitary little bird.

She wore a dark striped dress reaching down to her shoe tops, and an equally long apron of bleached sugar sacks, with a full pocket: all neat and tidy, but every time she took a step she might have fallen over her shoe-laces, which dragged from her unlaced shoes. She looked straight ahead. Her eyes were blue with age. Her skin had a pattern all its own of numberless branching wrinkles and as though a whole little tree stood in the middle of her forehead, but a golden color ran underneath, and the two knobs of her cheeks were illuminated by a yellow burning under the dark. Under the red rag her hair came down on her neck in the frailest of ringlets, still black, and with an odor like copper.

Now and then there was a quivering in the thicket. Old Phoenix said, "Out of my way, all you foxes, owls, beetles, jack rabbits, coons, and wild animals! . . . Keep out from under these feet, little bob-whites. . . . Keep the big wild hogs out of my

---

*This is the complete story Welty developed from the image reprinted in Unit 4. For Welty's comments about her writing process, see the readings for Unit 13.

path. Don't let none of those come running my direction. I got a long way." Under her small black-freckled hand her cane, limber as a buggy whip, would switch at the brush as if to rouse up any hiding things.

On she went. The woods were deep and still. The sun made the pine needles almost too bright to look at, up where the wind rocked. The cones dropped as light as feathers. Down in the hollow was the mourning dove—it was not too late for him.

The path ran up a hill. "Seem like there is chains about my feet, time I get this far," she said, in the voice of argument old people keep to use with themselves. "Something always take a hold of me on this hill—pleads I should stay."

After she got to the top she turned and gave a full, severe look behind her where she had come. "Up through pines," she said at length. "Now down through oaks."

Her eyes opened their widest, and she started down gently. But before she got to the bottom of the hill a bush caught her dress.

Her fingers were busy and intent, but her skirts were full and long, so that before she could pull them free in one place they were caught in another. It was not possible to allow the dress to tear. "I in the thorny bush," she said. "Thorns, you doing your appointed work. Never want to let folks pass—no sir. Old eyes thought you was a pretty little *green* bush."

Finally, trembling all over, she stood free, and after a moment dared to stoop for her cane.

"Sun so high!" she cried, leaning back and looking, while the thick tears went over her eyes. "The time getting all gone here."

At the foot of this hill was a place where a log was laid across the creek.

"Now comes the trial," said Phoenix.

Putting her right foot out, she mounted the log and shut her eyes. Lifting her skirt, levelling her cane fiercely before her, like a festival figure in some parade, she began to march across. Then she opened her eyes and she was safe on the other side.

"I wasn't as old as I thought," she said.

But she sat down to rest. She spread her skirts on the banks around her and folded her hands over her knees. Up above her was a tree in a pearly cloud of mistletoe. She did not dare to close her eyes, and when a little boy brought her a little plate with a slice of marble-cake on it she spoke to him. "That would be acceptable," she said. But when she went to take it there was just her own hand in the air.

So she left that tree, and had to go through a barbed-wire fence. There she had to creep and crawl, spreading her knees and stretching her fingers like a baby trying to climb the steps. But she talked loudly to herself: she could not let her dress be torn now, so late in the day, and she could not pay for having her arm or her leg sawed off if she got caught fast where she was.

At last she was safe through the fence and risen up out in the clearing. Big dead trees, like black men with one arm, were standing in the purple stalks of the withered cotton field. There sat a buzzard.

"Who you watching?"

In the furrow she made her way along.

"Glad this not the season for bulls," she said, looking sideways, "and the good Lord made his snakes to curl up and sleep in the winter. A pleasure I don't see no two-headed snake coming around that tree, where it come once. It took a while to get by him, back in the summer."

She passed through the old cotton and went into a field of dead corn. It whispered and shook and was taller than her head. "Through the maze now," she said, for there was no path.

Then there was something tall, black, and skinny there, moving before her.

At first she took it for a man. It could have been a man dancing in the field. But she stood still and listened, and it did not make a sound. It was as silent as a ghost.

"Ghost," she said sharply, "who be you the ghost of? For I have heard of nary death close by."

But there was no answer—only the ragged dancing in the wind.

She shut her eyes, reached out her hand, and touched a sleeve. She found a coat and inside that an emptiness, cold as ice.

"You scarecrow," she said. Her face lighted. "I ought to be shut up for good," she said with laughter. "My senses is gone. I too old. I the oldest people I ever know. Dance, old scarecrow," she said, "while I dancing with you."

She kicked her foot over the furrow, and with mouth drawn down, shook her head once or twice in a little strutting way. Some husks blew down and whirled in streamers about her skirts.

Then she went on, parting her way from side to side with cane, through the whispering field. At last she came to the end, to a wagon track where the silver grass blew between the red ruts. The quail were walking around like pullets, seeming all dainty and unseen.

"Walk pretty," she said. "This the easy place. This the easy going."

She followed the track, swaying through the quiet bare fields, through the little strings of trees silver in their dead leaves, past cabins silver from weather, with the doors and windows boarded shut, all like old women under a spell sitting there. "I walking in their sleep," she said, nodding her head vigorously.

In a ravine she went where a spring was silently flowing through a hollow log. Old Phoenix bent and drank. "Sweet-gum makes the water sweet," she said, and drank more. "Nobody know who made this well, for it was here when I was born."

The track crossed a swampy part where the moss hung as white as lace from every limb. "Sleep on, alligators, and blow your bubbles." Then the track went into the road.

Deep, deep the road went down between the high green-colored banks. Overhead the live-oaks met, and it was as dark as a cave.

A black dog with a lolling tongue came up out of the weeds by the ditch. She was meditating, and not ready, and when he came at her she only hit him a little with her cane. Over she went in the ditch, like a little puff of milk-weed.

Down there, her senses drifted away. A dream visited her, and she reached her hand up, but nothing reached down and gave her a pull. So she lay there and presently went to talking. "Old woman," she said to herself, "that black dog come up out of the weeds to stall you off, and now there he sitting on his fine tail, smiling at you."

A white man finally came along and found her—a hunter, a young man, with his dog on a chain.

"Well, Granny!" he laughed. "What are you doing there?"

"Lying on my back like a June-bug waiting to be turned over, mister," she said, reaching up her hand.

He lifted her up, gave her a swing in the air, and set her down, "Anything broken, Granny?"

"No sir, them old dead weeds is springy enough," said Phoenix, when she had got her breath. "I thank you for your trouble."

"Where do you live, Granny?" he asked, while the two dogs were growling at each other.

"Away back yonder sir, behind the ridge. You can't even see it from here."

"On your way home?"

"No, sir, I going to town."

"Why, that's too far! That's as far as I walk when I come out myself, and I get something for my trouble." He patted the stuffed bag he carried, and there hung down a little closed claw. It was one of the bob-whites, with its beak hooked bitterly to show it was dead. "Now you go on home, Granny!"

"I bound to go to town, mister," said Phoenix. "The time come around."

He gave another laugh, filling the whole landscape. "I know you old colored people! Wouldn't miss going to town to see Santa Claus!"

But something held Old Phoenix very still. The deep lines in her face went into a fierce and different radiation. Without warning, she had seen with her own eyes a flashing nickel fall out of the man's pocket onto the ground.

"How old are you, Granny?" he was saying.

"There is no telling, mister," she said, "no telling."

Then she gave a little cry and clapped her hands and said, "Git on away from here, dog! Look! Look at that dog!" She laughed as if in admiration. "He ain't scared of nobody. He a big black dog." She whispered, "Sic him!"

"Watch me get rid of that cur," said the man. "Sic him, Pete! Sic him!"

Phoenix heard the dogs fighting, and heard the man running and throwing sticks. She even heard a gunshot. But she was slowly bending forward by that time, further and further forward, the lids stretched down over her eyes, as if she were doing this in her sleep. Her chin was lowered almost to her knees. The yellow palm of her hand came out from the fold of her apron. Her fingers slid down and along the ground under the piece of money with the grace and care they would have in lifting an egg from under a sitting hen. Then she slowly straightened up, she stood erect, and the nickel was in her apron pocket. A bird flew by. Her lips moved. "God watching me the whole time. I come to stealing."

The man came back, and his own dog panted about them. "Well, I scared him off that time," he said, and then he laughed and lifted his gun and pointed it at Phoenix.

She stood straight and faced him.

"Doesn't the gun scare you?" he said, still pointing it.

"No, sir, I seen plenty go off closer by, in my day, and for less than what I done," she said, holding utterly still.

He smiled, and shouldered the gun. "Well, Granny," he said, "you must be a hundred years old, and scared of nothing. I'd give you a dime if I had any money with me. But you take my advice and stay home, and nothing will happen to you."

"I bound to go on my way, mister," said Phoenix. She inclined her head in the red rag. Then they went in different directions, but she could hear the gun shooting again and again over the hill.

She walked on. The shadows hung from the oak trees to the road like curtains. Then she smelled wood-smoke, and smelled the river, and she saw a steeple and the cabins on their steep steps. Dozens of little black children whirled around her. There ahead was Natchez shining. Bells were ringing. She walked on.

In the paved city it was Christmas time. There were red and green electric lights strung and crisscrossed everywhere, and all turned on in the daytime. Old Phoenix would have been lost if she had not distrusted her eyesight and depended on her feet to know where to take her.

She paused quietly on the sidewalk where people were passing by. A lady came along in the crowd, carrying an armful of red-, green-, and silver-wrapped presents; she gave off perfume like the red roses in hot summer, and Phoenix stopped her.

"Please, missy, will you lace up my shoe?" She held up her foot.

"What do you want, Grandma?"

"See my shoe," said Phoenix. "Do all right for out in the country, but wouldn't look right to go in a big building."

"Stand still then, Grandma," said the lady. She put her packages down on the sidewalk beside her and laced and tied both shoes tightly.

"Can't lace 'em with a cane," said Phoenix. "Thank you, missy. I doesn't mind asking a nice lady to tie up my shoe, when I gets out on the street."

Moving slowly and from side to side, she went into the big building and into a tower of steps, where she walked up and around and around until her feet knew to stop.

She entered a door, and there she saw nailed up on the wall the document that had been stamped with the gold seal and framed in the gold frame, which matched the dream that was hung up in her head.

"Here I be," she said. There was a fixed and ceremonial stiffness over her body.

"A charity case, I suppose," said an attendant who sat at the desk before her.

But Phoenix only looked above her head. There was sweat on her face, the wrinkles in her skin shone like a bright net.

"Speak up, Grandma," the woman said. "What's your name? We must have your history, you know. Have you been here before? What seems to be the trouble with you?"

Old Phoenix only gave a twitch to her face as if a fly were bothering her.

"Are you deaf?" cried the attendant.

But then the nurse came in.

"Oh, that's just old Aunt Phoenix," she said. "She doesn't come for herself— she has a little grandson. She makes these trips just as regular as clockwork. She lives away back off the Old Natchez Trace." She bent down. "Well, Aunt Phoenix, why don't you just take a seat? We won't keep you standing after your long trip." She pointed.

The old woman sat down, bolt upright in the chair.

"Now, how is the boy?" asked the nurse.

Old Phoenix did not speak.

"I said, how is the boy?"

But Phoenix only waited and stared straight ahead, her face very solemn and withdrawn into rigidity.

"Is his throat any better?" asked the nurse. "Aunt Phoenix, don't you hear me? Is your grandson's throat any better since the last time you came for the medicine?"

With her hands on her knees, the woman waited, silent, erect and motionless, just as if she were in armour.

"You mustn't take up our time this way, Aunt Phoenix," the nurse said. "Tell us quickly about your grandson, and get it over. He isn't dead, is he?"

At last there came a flicker and then a flame of comprehension across her face, and she spoke.

"My grandson. It was my memory had left me. There I sat and forgot why I made my long trip."

"Forgot?" The nurse frowned. "After you came so far?"

Then Phoenix was like an old woman begging a dignified forgiveness for waking up frightened in the night. "I never did go to school, I was too old at the Surrender," she said in a soft voice. "I'm an old woman without an education. It was my memory fail me. My little grandson, he is just the same, and I forgot it in the coming."

"Throat never heals, does it?" said the nurse, speaking in a loud sure voice to Old Phoenix. By now she had a card with something written on it, a little list. "Yes. Swallowed lye. When was it—January—two-three years ago—"

Phoenix spoke unasked now. "No, missy, he not dead, he just the same. Every little while his throat begin to close up again, and he not able to swallow. He not get his breath. He not able to help himself. So the time come around, and I go on another trip for the soothing medicine."

"All right. The doctor said as long as you came to get it, you could have it," said the nurse. "But it's an obstinate case."

"My little grandson, he sit up there in the house all wrapped up, waiting by himself," Phoenix went on. "We is the only two left in the world. He suffer and it don't seem to put him back at all. He got a sweet look. He going to last. He wear a little patch quilt and peep out holding his mouth open like a little bird. I remembers so plain now. I not going to forget him again, no, the whole enduring time. I could tell him from all the others in creation."

"All right." The nurse was trying to hush her now. She brought her a bottle of medicine. "Charity," she said, making a check mark in a book.

Old Phoenix held the bottle close to her eyes and then carefully put it into her pocket.

"I thank you," she said.

"It's Christmas time, Grandma," said the attendant. "Could I give you a few pennies out of my purse?"

"Five pennics is a nickel," said Phoenix stiffly.

"Here's a nickel," said the attendant.

Phoenix rose carefully and held out her hand. She received the nickel and then fished the other nickel out of her pocket and laid it beside the new one. She stared at her palm closely, with her head on one side.

Then she gave a tap with her cane on the floor.

"This is what come to me to do," she said. "I going to the store and buy my child a little windmill they sells, made out of paper. He going to find it hard to believe there such a thing in the world. I'll march myself back where he waiting, holding it straight up in this hand."

She lifted her free hand, gave a little nod, turned round, and walked out of the doctor's office. Then her slow step began on the stairs, going down.

STORY
A Student

This story all started one day when my father asked my uncle and me if we wanted to go fishing. This trip was no ordinary fishing trip, it was very unusual, and this made me feel very uneasy. I could not understand what was going on because of my young age.

One Sunday morning my uncle showed up at my house. It was about 6:00 in the morning. We left right away. We did not want to be late because the boat left at 7:00. We packed my mother's station wagon and we were off. We got there at about 6:20. The captain was not letting us board until 6:50. As we were waiting on the dock, the weather struck me as being very unusual. It was very dark out. You could see the light just starting to break through in spots, but it was very foggy and misty too. I could never remember the weather being like this before, and it made me feel very uneasy about the trip. The wind was gusting also. This made it very cold and eerie out.

We were finally able to board the boat. I remember the smell as I first came aboard. It was a terrible fish smell, worse than I had ever smelled before. I could hear the killies that they used for bait jumping around in the pails on the deck. Everyone shuffled into the cabin to keep warm. As I walked in, I noticed that there were no seats. It was all open except for the beams that held the roof up. Life preservers were scattered all over the floor of the cabin. I noticed my father falling asleep while on the other hand, my uncle was very excited about the trip. It took almost half an hour to reach the inlet. Once we arrived, we started to fish.

My father and uncle went into the cabin to see if they could get something to drink. All they had was beer. They bought two beers, but the boat hand had no change for a five. My father said, "Do not worry about the change. We will just drink five dollars' worth." I could not remember ever seeing my father and uncle drink beer before. They gave me a taste and I did not like it. I could not understand why they kept drinking it when it tasted so terrible to me. The fish were not biting, but my father and uncle sure were drinking. They polished off five dollars' worth in no time. This also struck me as very unusual because my father and uncle really are not heavy drinkers. In fact, they even frown upon people who drink because they feel it is no good for them.

Then my uncle came up with a great idea to get some free beer. When we would catch a fish on the boat, you would yell, "Net," and the boat hands would run over with nets to help bring the fish up on the boat. My uncle told my father to yell, "Net" even if he did not have a fish. When he did, my uncle ran around the other side of the cabin and grabbed a couple of beers. They were drinking and having a great afternoon.

Suddenly the captain said that we were going in because of the bad weather. We had only caught three fish. It was getting colder, and everyone went into the cabin. My uncle laid down on some life preservers and fell asleep. As for my father, he just leaned against a beam in the cabin with his eyes wide open. His lower jaw hung down so his mouth was wide open. He still had a glass of beer in his hand. The glass was tilted so the little bit of beer that was in it almost spilled out. I just stood there in amazement. Never before had I seen my father or uncle in this kind of condition. It was so unusual because now it was my uncle who was tired and my father who was wide awake.

It took so long to get back to the dock. When we arrived the boat hands cleaned and bagged our three fish. As we walked to the car, I noticed that my father was not walking the way he usually did. He was swaying back and forth and kept leaning on my uncle's shoulder. I could not figure out why he was doing this and it made me feel uneasy. After reaching the car, we threw the bag of fish and the poles in the back of the station wagon. My uncle was feeling better because of his nap so he drove home.

Once we arrived at my house, we unloaded the gear from the car. My father grabbed the poles when I noticed the bag of fish had ripped open. All of the smelly fish water ran into the crevices of the back of the station wagon. Months after that, the car still smelled terrible. It was so disgusting. Each time I would get in the car to go somewhere, I could not help but remember that unusual fishing trip and how uneasy I had felt because I was too young to understand what was going on.

THE STORY OF CAEDMON'S HYMN*
Translated from Bede's *Ecclesiastical History*

In this abbess's monastery was a brother especially distinguished and honoured by divine favour, for he was wont to make agreeable songs which befitted religion and piety, so that whatsoever he learnt from divine writings through bookmen, that he after a little space adorned in poetical language with the greatest sweetness and feeling, and brought it forth, for the most part, in the English tongue; and by his songs the minds of many men were often fired with a contempt of the world and desire of the heavenly life. And likewise many others after him, in the English nation, have begun to make religious songs, but none however could do it like him: for he not only was not taught by men, nor through man, that he should not learn the song-craft, but he was divinely assisted, and through God's gift received the art of poetry. And therefore he never could compose anything of leasing, or of idle song, but even those only which belonged to religion, and became his pious tongue to sing.

This man was set in worldly condition until the time that he was of advanced age, and he never learned any poetry, and therefore, at entertainments, when it had been deemed [proper] for the sake of mirth, that they all in turn should sing to the harp, when he saw the harp approach him, then rose he for shame from the banquet, and went home to his house. One time when he had done that, he left the house of the entertainment, and went to a neat-stall, the care of which was committed to him that night; when he there then at the proper time had set his limbs to rest, and fallen a-sleep; then a man stood by him in a dream, and hailed and greeted him, and named him by his name. "Kedmon, sing me some what": then answered he, and said, "I cannot sing any thing, and I therefore went out from the entertainment, and came hither, for I could not sing." Again he who was speaking with him said, "However thou canst sing to me." Quoth he, "What shall I sing?" Quoth he, "Sing me Creation." When he then had received this answer, then began he at once to sing, in praise of God the Creator, the verses and the words, which he had never heard. Of which the order is this:—

"Now we owe to praise the Warden of heaven's kingdom, the Maker's might, and his mood-thought, the works of the glorious Father; how of all wonders the eternal Lord installed the beginning. The holy Creator first shaped heaven for a roof to earth's children; then the Warden of mankind, Eternal Lord, Almighty Master, afterwards made the earth, a fold for men."

Then arose he from sleep, and all that he sleeping had sung he held fast in memory, and soon added to those words many words, after the manner of a song worthy of God. Then came he on the morrow to the town-reeve, who was his alderman; and told him what gift he had received; and he led him to the abbess, and shewed and told it her; then she ordered to assemble all the most learned men, and the learners,

---

*You'll notice that the language here is archaic, an attempt to capture the feel of the original Old English language. You probably noticed the double negative and a few obsolete words: "leasing," meaning *lying;* "neat," meaning *cattle;* and "tined," meaning *closed.*

and bade him in their presence tell the dream and sing the song, that by the doom of them all it might be proved what [it was], or whence it came. Then it seemed to all, as it was, that a heavenly gift had been given him by the Lord himself. Then they related and said to him a holy speech, and words of divine lore; and then bade him, if he could, turn that into the melody of song. When he then had received the matter, then went he home to his house, and came again on the morrow, and sang and gave them what had been committed to him, composed in the best poetry.

Then began the abbess to cherish and love the grace of God in the man; and she then admonished and taught him, that he should forsake the worldly condition, and enter the monastic order. And he readily granted that; and she received him into the monastery with his goods, and joined him to the congregation of God's servants, and bade [them] teach him the number of the holy story and spell [that is, the whole course of sacred history]. And all that he learnt by hearing, he remembered by himself, and, as a clean beast chewing the cud, converted it into the sweetest verse, and his song and his verse were so winsome to hear, that his teachers themselves wrote and learnt them from his mouth. He sang first of the creation of the world, and of the origin of mankind, and all history of Genesis, which is the first book of Moses; and again of the outgoing of Israel's folk from the land of the Egyptians, and of the ingoing of the land of promise, and of many other spells of holy writ—the book of the Canon; and of Christ's incarnation, and of his suffering, and of his ascension into [the] heavens; and of the coming of the Holy Ghost, and the lore of the Apostles; and again he made many a lay of the awe of the future doom, and of the fear of hell's torment, and of the sweetness of the heavenly kingdom; and he likewise made many others of the divine kindnesses and dooms. In all these he earnestly cared that he might draw men off from the love of sins, and from misdeeds, and awaken them to the love and carefulness of good deeds; for he was a most pious man, and humbly subject to regular discipline, and was fired with the heat of great jealousy against those who would do otherwise; and therefore he tined and ended his life by a good end.

Private Writing: Finding What You Have to Say

In this unit we want to teach you that you always have lots to write about and that you can always get it on paper without much agony. We will show you two processes for using private writing to find what you have to say: Sondra Perl's guidelines for composing and the open-ended writing process. Most important of all, we want to convince you that your best writing may consist of material you didn't know you had in mind.

We think of this unit as a kind of beginning—in fact we sometimes start off the semester with it. For surely the experience of looking inside and finding out what *you* have to say makes an ideal starting point in any writing course. But sometimes when we start courses with this unit, students get nervous about the emphasis on "making everything up out of your head": nothing but a blank page and no topic to write about. Thus we started our sequence of units with ones that students usually feel more comfortable about at first—units where there is plenty *outside you* to write about.

We invite you to think of this unit as a presentation of the basic *foundation* for writing: learning how to keep on writing after you run out of things "in mind." Once you learn to do this, you'll realize that you can always keep going even when you feel stuck. You can apply this basic ability to all writing occasions.

Just as important, we hope you will discover the benefits of *private writing.* If you're interested in reading more about the theory behind these practices, you can turn to the exploration of private writing in "Ruminations and Theory" at the end of this unit.

MAIN ASSIGNMENT

1. At least ten pages of private writing produced by using the Perl guidelines and/or the open-ended process. Thus we're asking for a considerable amount of writing with no assigned topic: you work with whatever topics are most important for you. No one but you will see this writing (though your teacher might insist that you flash an impressive wad of pages to show that you have done this exploratory writing at home as well as in class). You can emphasize one method or the other in your private writing, depending on which one is more helpful to you. There are samples of both kinds of writing at the end of the unit.

2. Two to three pages of process writing about what happens when you work on the Perl guidelines and the open-ended process. Your teacher may ask you to build a genuine essay or draft out of your process writing—unified and reaching some definite conclusions. Or she may ask that this writing be rough, just a couple of pages of the best bits of your process writing slightly cleaned up but not fully shaped into a unified, connected essay. At the end of this unit, you'll find some samples of process writing that deal with the ten pages of private writing. Remember that there are many different, equally valid ways of making an essay from process writing.

SONDRA PERL'S COMPOSING GUIDELINES

These writing guidelines will help you discover more of what is on your mind and *almost* on your mind. If they seem artificial, think of them as "exercises." But they are exercises that will help you to perform certain subtle but crucial mental operations that most skilled and experienced writers do naturally:

- Continue writing, even when you don't know where you're going.

- Periodically pause and ask, "What's this all about?"

- Periodically check what you have written against your internal sense of where you're going or what you wanted to say—your "felt sense."

Your teacher may guide you through the Perl guidelines in class. If it feels too mechanical to follow them in a group setting, remember that the goal is to teach you a procedure you can use on your own. But we can teach it best by giving you a taste of it in practice—which means trying it out in class. It's hard to learn the guidelines alone because your old writing habits are so strong.

After some practice with each of the directives or questions that follow, you'll be able to sense how to distribute your time yourself.*

---

*We thank Perl for permission to copy these guidelines. We have made tiny modifications—mostly just some cutting. Sondra Perl is a professor of English at Herbert Lehmann College and founder of the New York City Writing Project.

1. Find a way to get comfortable. Shake out your hands, take a deep breath, settle into your chair. Close your eyes if you'd like to; relax. Find a way to be quietly and comfortably aware of your inner state.

2. Ask yourself, "What's going on with me right now? Is there anything in the way of my writing today?" When you hear yourself answering, take a minute to jot down a list of any distractions or impediments that come to mind.

3. Now ask yourself, "What's on my mind? Of all the things I know about, what might I like to write about now?" When you hear yourself answering, jot down what comes. Maybe you get one thing, maybe a list. If you feel totally blocked, you may write down "Nothing." Even this can be taken further by asking yourself, "What is this 'Nothing' all about?"

4. Ask yourself, "Now that I have a list—long or short—is there anything else I've left out, any other piece I'm overlooking, maybe even a word I like, something else I might want to write about sometime that I can add to this list?" Add anything that comes to mind.

5. Whether you have one definite idea or a whole list of things, look over what you have and ask, "What here draws my attention right now? What could I begin to write about, even if I'm not certain where it will lead?" Take the idea, word, or item and put it at the top of a new page. (Save the first page for another time.)

6. Now—taking a deep breath and settling comfortably into your chair—ask yourself, "What are all the associations and parts I know about this topic? What can I say about it now?" Spend as long as you need writing down these responses. Perhaps it will be a sustained piece of freewriting or stream of consciousness, or perhaps separate bits, a long list, or notes to yourself.

7. Now having written for a while, interrupt yourself, set aside all the writing you've done, and take a fresh look at this topic or issue. Grab hold of the *whole* topic—not the bits and pieces—and ask yourself, "What makes this topic interesting to me? What's *important* about this that I haven't said yet? What's the *heart* of this issue?" Wait quietly for a *word, image,* or *phrase* to arise from your "felt sense" of the topic. Write whatever comes. (For more on "felt sense," see "Ruminations and Theory" at the end of this unit.)

8. Take this word or image and use it. Ask yourself, "What's this all about?" Describe the feeling, image, or word. As you write, let the "felt sense" deepen. Where do you feel that "felt sense"? In your head, stomach, forearms? Where in your body does it seem centered? Continue to ask yourself, "Is this right? Am I getting closer? Am I saying it?" See if you can feel when you're on the right track. See if you can feel the shift or click inside when you get close, "Oh yes, this says it."

9. If you're at a dead end, you can ask yourself, "What makes this topic so hard for me?" or "What's so difficult about this?" Again pause and see if a word, image, or phrase comes to you that captures this difficulty in a fresh way—and if it will lead you to some more writing.

10. When you find yourself stopping, ask, "What's missing? what hasn't yet gotten down on paper?" and again look to your "felt sense" for a word or an image. Write what comes to mind.

11. When again you find yourself stopping, ask yourself, "Where is this leading? What's the point I'm trying to make?" Again write down whatever comes to mind.

12. Once you feel you're near or at the end, ask yourself, "Does this feel complete?" Look to your "felt sense," your gut reaction, even to your body, for the answer. Again write down whatever answer comes to you. If the answer is "No," pause and ask yourself, "What's missing?" and continue writing.

About the Perl Guidelines

These guidelines sometimes work differently for different people—and even differently for you on different occasions. The main thing to remember is that they are meant for you to use on your own, flexibly, in your own way. There is nothing sacred about the exact format or wording. They are not meant to be a strait jacket. To help you in adapting them to your own needs, here is a list of what are probably the four pivotal moments:

- Relax, stretch, clear your mind, try to attend quietly to what's inside—and note any distractions or feelings that may be preventing you from writing.

- Start with a list of things you *could* write about. Often we can't find what we really want to write about till the third or fourth item—or not till that subtle after-question, "Is there something else I might have forgotten?"

- As you are writing, periodically pause and look to that felt sense somewhere inside you—that feeling, image, or word that somehow represents what you are trying to get at—and ask whether your writing is really getting at it. This comparing or checking back ("Is this it?") will often lead to a productive "shift" in your mind ("Oh *now* I see what it is I want to say").

- Finally, toward the end, ask, "What's this all about? Where does this writing seem to be trying to go?" And especially ask, "What's missing? What *haven't* I written about?"

The specific details of the procedure are much less important than the charitable, supportive, and generative spirit behind the whole thing. (In the readings at the end of the unit, we have printed Peter Elbow's Perl guidelines writing—writing that formed the basis of his mini-unit, "Writing with a Word Processor.")

PROCESS BOX

On Writing When Using Perl Guidelines

Didn't write what I intended to write—intended to be pragmatic—write out what I *needed* to write out. But someway the other topic forced itself on me and became too exciting to ignore. Topic appeared on paper when I searched my head for something I really wanted to write about. Found all the prompts helpful except one.

The nonhelpful one was, "Use image, idea, phrase, and keep trying to get it right"—because it felt right to me already. The spot when I started on metaphor metonomy. Don't know why I got on that. Doesn't connect in very well—and yet I know there's a connection, and I guess I saw it as relevant. But I did drop it when Peter said, "Where is this going?"

While writing, I found pleasant revealings coming forth and thought, "Gee! These are good ideas!" Thought of typing it up and giving copies to Peter and Don for comment—not sure I was thinking of them as audiences. Didn't really feel I was writing for them as I wrote—they came to mind because I know they have thoughts on these subjects. I'd like them both to think I'm on to something good—but I'm really wanting this idea worked out for myself. Believe they could help me do that.

I did have some feeling of going around in circles, not putting things together into one Bingo result—but I do think there's stuff there to explore. I'm glad I wrote this.

PAT BELANOFF

THE OPEN-ENDED WRITING PROCESS

The open-ended process is another way to encourage exploratory writing. Where the guidelines help you find words for what is sort of in your mind but not in words, the open-ended process pushes you to figure out entirely *new* thoughts and ideas that are as yet nowhere near your mind.

The open-ended process consists of a simple movement back and forth between two basic activities: *freewriting* and *summing-up.*

Start by freewriting. (Or, if you prefer, you can first list things you *might* write about and then start freewriting.) Simply explore whatever topics emerge for you *while* you're doing this unfocused freewriting.

After ten or fifteen minutes of freewriting, stop and look back or think over what you've written. (Pause, take a deep breath, stretch, look around.) Then write down a sentence, phrase, or image to summarize the most interesting or important thing you find in your freewriting. Look for a center of gravity: that piece of your writing that seems to pull on you most strongly. It's important to note that you don't have to try for an accurate or objective summary of your freewriting. You might focus on some small detail from your freewriting if that seems most important to you now. You might even write down a thought that hasn't yet occurred in your freewriting but occurs to you now as you pause. The point of these summings-up or "pause writings" is to provide a *springboard* for your next piece of freewriting, your next dive into language.

For that's the next step: more freewriting. As you write, learn to keep on writing even if you don't know where you are going. Learn to ride waves of writing for longer and longer periods of time. When words start to run out after only five minutes, force yourself to keep going. Remember, you don't have to stay on the same subject. Write, "What else could I write about?" and "What else?" and keep on writing to see what comes. The goal is to lose yourself in language, to lose perspective.

Then stop again to sum up. And so on.

Follow this back-and-forth chain of freewriting and summing-up wherever it leads you.

The open-ended process gets its power from alternating two contrary kinds of mentality or two opposed ways of producing language. During the freewriting you are *immersed* in your words: your head is down and you are tumbling along in an underbrush of language; you tend to be working more in words than in thoughts. Indeed the *goal* is to get lost in the words and not worry about the thoughts or where they are going.

When you pause and sum up, you use a completely different mentality or way of producing language. You extricate yourself from the underbrush of words and, as it were, climb up a tall tree to see where you have gotten yourself: you seek perspective and detachment. In this process you are trying to work more in thoughts than in words. These summing-up sentences or phrases help keep your freewriting productive. For if you do nothing but freewrite for hours, you sometimes get caught in a rut or go in circles.

As you move back and forth between the two activities, sometimes your writing will change: in subject, in mode, or in style. For example, having written the story of what happened to you, your pausing and summing-up may lead you to see that you now need to write about the *person* who was involved in that event. Let these changes occur. Perhaps you've been writing to yourself, and now you realize you want to write to someone else—a letter, perhaps. You may even want to write a poem or a prayer or a dialogue. Sometimes the open-ended writing will lead you closer and closer to what you were trying to get at from the beginning; but sometimes it takes you afield to something new that surprises you.

Your teacher will probably introduce the open-ended process in class. Sitting and writing private words in a group might seem artificial at first— just as it did with the Perl guidelines. But again, we want you to practice this new procedure *once* with some direction. Otherwise you tend to drift

---

PROCESS BOX

I got out this diary, & read as one always does read one's own writing, with a kind of guilty intensity. I confess that the rough & random style of it, often so ungrammatical, & crying for a word altered, afflicted me somewhat. I am trying to tell whichever self it is that reads this here-after that I can write very much better; & take no time over this; & forbid her to let the eye of man behold it. . . . But what is more to the point is my belief that the habit of writing thus for my own eye only is good practise. It loosens the ligaments. Never mind the misses & the stumbles. Going at such a pace as I do I must make the most direct & instant shots at my object, & thus have to lay hands on words, choose them, & and shoot them with no more pause than is needed to put my pen in the ink. I believe that during the past year I can trace some increase of ease in my professional writing which I attribute to my cas-ual half hours after tea.

VIRGINIA WOOLF

---

into your usual writing habits. The goal is to learn a *new* writing process so you can then use it flexibly by yourself. (In the "Readings" section, we have included Pat Belanoff's open-ended writing.)

PROCESS WRITING ASSIGNMENT

Make sure to do process writing each time you use each method, whether in or out of class. (If you need some prompts, see the process journal ques-tions below.) Then read through it all and decide what themes seem impor-tant. Make a collage or build an essay around these themes, using the rele-vant parts of your process writing. For an essay you need to make a point or connected points—come to some conclusion.

SHARING AND RESPONDING

Of course you will not get any responses to your exploratory writing since it is all private. But you might want some feedback to your process writing, either at an early or late stage. "Sayback" (Section II A), "Pointing" (Section IIB), and "Metaphorical Descriptions" (Section IID) in the *Sharing and Responding* booklet will give you helpful methods for feedback. But here are a few additional questions that are particularly apt for this week's pro-cess writing:

123

- Which parts do you like most?

- Which parts tell you the most about the way I write?

- Which parts give you the most vivid *experience* of my writing process?

- What do you hear me *saying* in my process writing?

- What am I emphasizing most: (1) objective observations of what happened? (2) accounts of what it felt like? (3) conclusions or answers to the question "So what?"

- What did *you* learn from my process writing?

PROCESS JOURNAL QUESTIONS

- What happened in using the Perl process? In particular:
  —When finding or choosing your original topic?
  —When pausing to sum up in a phrase or image or to get yourself focused back on your chosen topic?
  —When seeking your "felt sense" and checking your writing against it?

- What happened in using the open-ended process? In particular:
  —When finding or choosing the idea you started with?
  —When summing up or finding a center of gravity?
  —What about the overall path or progression? Where did it take you?

- What did you notice about the difference between doing these processes in class and at home? In what ways did the teacher's prompts help? get in the way?

- So much of this week's writing is *private*. How (if at all) did this affect *what* you wrote and *how* you wrote?

- What did you learn about *your* writing? language? thinking? And what did you learn about writing, language, and thinking in general by comparing your experience with that of your classmates?

RUMINATIONS AND THEORY

A. Private Writing and Feeling Free to Explore

B. On Felt Sense

A. Private Writing and Feeling Free to Explore

We stress *private* writing here because it's hard to learn to explore what's really in mind if you have to share your writing immediately with others. Privacy can help you feel safer, help you explore things that readers might not like. Private writing reduces the pervasive pressure of the social context around us. A traditional form of private writing—the diary or journal—has long given people a chance to feel what they want to feel, and even *be* what they want to be, apart from how others want them to feel or be. Private writing gives *space*.

Some of you may find private writing difficult at first. You may scarcely have written anything except what you hand in to a teacher. "Why write it if she's not going to read it?" you may feel. But this is exactly the feeling we want to help you get past. You can't write well till you really *own* your writing—yet how can you really own it if you always have to check it with someone else?

But if you haven't done much private writing, you may find at first that it's hard to get "up" for private writing; you miss a kind of alertness or pressure that an audience puts on you to stay on your toes. Talking to listeners can get your juices flowing. But you can always show your writing to an audience later: we're just asking you to assume it's private *while* writing and not let yourself show it to readers except as a later separate step (and then only if you want to).

You may even find it slightly scary to be invited to write privately about "whatever comes": you may have some unpleasant thoughts or feelings—some piece of unhappiness or fear—that you know will come up but which you don't want to deal with.

It's true that these thoughts and feelings will come: anything that's important will come. But it turns out that private writing gives you a chance to *abandon* thoughts and feelings that are clogging up your head and getting in your way. Oddly enough, once you write things down, you can more easily move beyond them and not feel their pressure. Writing is a way to let something go.

For a striking example of using private writing to let go of what is unhelpful, consider Ray Knight's private writing. Here we have a successful major league baseball player who was dropped from his team. What follows is from an interview with him after a strong comeback:

RESURRECTING A CAREER

The test for him came last fall when he went home to Albany, Ga., and considered that he was standing at the crossroads of his career.

"Your physical ability gets you to the big leagues," he reasoned. . . . "Your mental ability keeps you there. And I knew I had the mental ability."

"So, I got very strong physically. I lifted weights for the first time in three or four years. I built a batting cage. . . . But the key was that I made up my mind I was going to show Davey [Johnson, coach] I could do it."

"I started writing down my thoughts in a book—my notes. If I had a positive thought, I'd write it down at once. If I had a negative thought, I'd write it down and scratch it out." (Durso S3)

We have met teachers who think that their students have nothing to write about because they are "too young" or have led "sheltered lives" or "can't think"—or have such inferior writing skills that they should not be invited to write about whatever is on their minds. It's not surprising that some students and teachers have been fooled in this way because of the following experience. The teacher says, "Okay, now you can write about whatever you want to write about." But the student, given complete choice, can't think of anything to write; she goes blank, feels empty or bored. Or else she starts off strong but runs out of things to say after only a short burst of writing. After this experience even the student may be tricked into feeling, "Oh dear, I have *nothing* to write about."

But to engage in private writing for extended stretches as in this unit is to discover that this experience is misleading. You discover that at any moment of the day or night, even if you are completely bored and out of the mood for writing, your head is nevertheless full of rich material to write about. It is this confidence in having *plenty* to say—in inner fecundity— that provides an important foundation for *all* future writing.

Here is an eloquent personal statement by a distinguished writer about private writing for exploring:

> I am following a process that leads so wildly and originally into new territory that no judgment can at the moment be made about values, significance, and so on. I am making something new, something that has not been judged before. Later others—and maybe I myself—will make judgments. Now, I am headlong to discover. Any distraction may harm the creating.
>
> So, receptive, careless of failure, I spin out things on the page. And a wonderful freedom comes. If something occurs to me, it is all right to accept it. It has one justification: it occurs to me. No one else can guide me. I must follow my own weak, wandering, diffident impulses.
>
> A strange bonus happens. At times, without my insisting on it, my writings become coherent; the successive elements that occur to me are clearly related. They lead by themselves to new connections. Sometimes the language, even the syllables that happen along, may start a trend. Sometimes the materials alert me to something waiting in my mind, ready for sustained attention. (Stafford 18–19)

We know all of you can discover what William Stafford discovered, but no one discovers it unless she gives herself the freedom to risk, and perhaps to try out new ways of writing privately (such as the Perl guidelines, the open-ended process, and the loop writing you did in Unit 3). For more perspective on private writing and its relation to writing for different kinds of audiences, see "About Audience and Writing" in "Ruminations" in Unit 7.)

B. On Felt Sense

Felt sense may seem a vague concept, but we get new leverage in our writing if we realize that there is always *something* there "in mind" before we have words for it. In one sense, of course, we *don't* know something till we have it in words. But in another sense we do indeed know quite a lot, and it's a question of learning to tap it better.

So what is it that's in mind before we find words? Is it some set of words that's farther inside our heads—fainter or in smaller print? If so, what lies behind *them* to guide or produce them? Behind our words, then, inevitably, is some nonverbal feeling or "sense."

You can easily prove this mysterious phenomenon to yourself by asking yourself, after you've been writing a while, the crucial question: "Is this what I've been wanting to say?" What's interesting is that we can almost always give an answer. Then we need to ask this: "What is the *basis* for our answer—for our being able to say, 'Yes, this really *is* what I was wanting to say,' or 'No, that's not it,' or 'Sort of, but not quite'?" We haven't got *words* for what's in mind, but we have *something* against which we can match the words we've used to see whether they are adequate to our intention. We know what we want to say well enough to realize that we have or haven't said it.

"Felt sense" is what Eugene Gendlin has named this internal awareness that we call on. And his point—which we too want to emphasize—is that we can learn to call on it better. (It may seem odd or unfashionable to suggest that our felt sense of what we're writing about might be located in a part of the body. But many people experience what's "in mind" not just "in the head" but also—as they say—in the "gut.")

The crucial operation in the Perl process is when you pause and *attend* to that felt sense—pause and say, "What's my *feeling* for what I'm getting at?" (or "What's my image or word?"). You *then* ask yourself, "Have I said it?" The most productive situation, ironically, is when you answer, "No." For in that moment of experiencing a *mis*match or *non*fit between your words and your felt sense, *you tend to experience a click or shift that moves you closer to knowing this thing that you can't yet say.* In short, pausing, checking, and saying "No" usually lead you to better words.

One reason people don't pause and check their words against their felt sense often enough is that they get too discouraged at the negative answer. They think that the question is a *test* and that the negative answer means they've failed the test. ("*Again* I've proved that I'm no good at finding words!") They don't realize that if you ask the question of yourself in the right way—in a charitable and constructive spirit—"No" is the better answer: it can always lead you to a better understanding of what you are trying to get at.

Remember, however, that when we urge you to attend more to your felt sense and then pause and check your words against it, we're *not* saying that thing that perhaps you've heard too often: "Stop! What is your *thesis?*" It's not, "What is your thesis?" but rather "What is the physical feeling or image you have that somehow *stands for* what you're wanting to say?" You haven't *got* a thesis yet—haven't got the right words yet—but you do have a genuinely available feeling for what you're trying to get at. If you check any trial set of words against that feeling, you can tell whether or not they are what you were trying to say.

For a concrete and vivid example of how this works—this recurrent process of checking your words against a felt sense in order to gradually figure out what you really mean—see the short passage written by Eugene Gendlin in the "Readings" for this unit.

READINGS

PROCESS WRITING ABOUT PRIVATE WRITING
Irene Wong

When I began my diary writing, I wrote about how I felt about writing on my problem, "Can I write ten pages about this?" But after I stated my issue, it just started to roll. Thoughts which at first came out randomly began to get thought out, and detailed discussions emerged. I found myself debating ideas and reasons that I had never before discussed at such lengths.

It surprised me when I came to realize just how much the people in my life play on the decision I make. It surprised me many a time when I wrote down things that were in the back of my mind but that I had never taken the time out to analyze. Some other times, I found out those things were points I was afraid to look at in the eye. But by writing it out, I was able to partially explain the reason why I felt that way. Seeing my hostilities or fears written out made them seem less ominous and much easier to extinguish. It also enabled me to distinguish exactly the size of this problem, and I felt a little more secure after knowing how big it was. It's ironic, but although now I realize how big this problem is, it was better than when it was an unpredictable problem lurking in the dark. I can't say I figured much out. The solution is there; it's the outcome of my solution that scares me. It's something I have to do, and I can't bear the consequences. I tried to trick my mind by writing things that are "logical," but my mind clicked right back into the "illogical" track.

I learned a lot through this assignment. As I said, it cleared up a few important things for me. The ultimate answer lies ominously in its sleep.

EXAMPLE OF WRITING USING
THE PERL GUIDELINES FOR COMPOSING
Peter Elbow

Note on this text. *This was Perl writing I did during a workshop—about an hour and a half—demonstrating the Perl process to teachers. I emphasized to everyone that the writing would be private and that they could use it for whatever kind of writing they wanted or needed to do. When I started listing things I could write about (I didn't save my list), I was hit hardest by my need to get going on the job currently staring me in the face: writing a piece for this textbook about writing on a word processor. Most of my previous Perl writing had been personal and exploratory—about some strong feelings or event in my life. Once I even tried writing a story. And usually I don't have much sense of audience during Perl writing. But on that morning I gave myself permission to work on this piece of public, pragmatic, "duty" writng for our textbook.*

Because I was leading the workshop and my mind was somewhat occupied by that role, I didn't have as much concentration for my own work as I would have had if someone else had been in charge. I didn't get so much written. I remember feeling distracted. (Also slightly guilty, for as it were, "doing my homework in class.")

I give here what I wrote that morning—as I wrote it (except for correcting some spelling and filling in some missing punctuation and making a couple of other minor corrections so it's readable). In several places I insert, in capital letters, the Perl questions that my writing is responding to (e.g., WHAT'S THIS ALL ABOUT?)

See the mini-unit on "Writing with a Word Processor" for a revision of this material.

I'm sitting here writing with my pen. About writing with a word processor. Seems odd. I normally write on my WP, but today I'm in a workshop with other teachers and we have a chance to write together about whatever we need to write.

The two main skills in writing are making a mess and cleaning up the mess.

That is, it's hard to write well unless we are inventive and fecund—open to lots of words and ideas. That means being open and accepting to the words and ideas which come. Not being too quick to reject and say no. When we do that, we make a mess. We write down (or at least consider) too much. We Too many words; we start down too many paths. Branching and complex. We need that mess.

Yet in order to write well we also need to do just the opposite: we need to say no and be skeptical and rejecting—to throw away or change everything that's not the best; to reject what looks or sounds nice but isn't really, in the end, up to snuff.

It turns out that the WP is ideal for both these mental operations. It helps

It helps in make makes it easier than with pen and paper to make more of a mess. We can throw down everything to the screen easily in more [I left a few blank lines; I think I assumed I'd come back and say more.]

Yet it also makes it easier than with pen and paper to clean up that mess. It's so easy to throw away what's discarded, fix words and spellings—and come up with neat copy.

Indeed, I would say that the main psychological danger in writing with a WP is that its fixing and cleaning up is so easy—indeed so fun—that it's tempting to stop every time you mistype or misspell a word or change your mind about a word and go back and fix it.

Learn to block that impulse. Learn to sustain your generating. Learn to keep on writing—as though it were pen and ink or typewriter and it were too hard to make a change. Otherwise you will distract yourself from your generating. Learn, in short, to make a mess.

You can let yourself write notes to yourself in your text when you're not sure. Instead of stopping and scratching your head and thinking when you become puzzled, you can keep on writing about your puzzlement. (Because it's so easy to erase them later.) I tend to put these remarks in CAPS—or indent them 5 spaces [in a block that's all indented]. So I can see later that they're not part of the text.

Why that's useful. When you keep writing

But—edit on screen/paper.

Start anywhere—cause you can move it around

WHAT'S IT ALL ABOUT?

—new power

—new relationship to words

—addiction
—my duty
—new horizons
WHERE DO YOU FEEL IT?
I feel it in my upper stomach.
WHAT'S THE PHRASE?

new power
It's scary: but it leads to addiction. It can change your relationship to writing.

click [I felt a click here; a shift of felt sense. Asking myself what it's about, what's the phrase, and where I feel it—these acts led me closer to what I seemed interesting and important. Leading to what follows.]

Screen is something half way between mind and paper.

Mind is a mess: paper is supposed to be neat. When I'm writing on screen, it feels like it's sort of—half—still in my mind. It's a second mind. It's not still partly in me.

Like my mind I can't look at all of it at once, I can only put my attention on one bit at a time. I don't yet have complete detachment from it till I print it out.

It gives me a second mind.
WHAT'S LEFT OUT?
Techniques.
   —How to adopt right attitude.
   —Not be scared. You can't hurt the machine.
   —You can get into trouble by losing text if you aren't careful to back up—but don't be worried.
   —Writing as play.
What do I love about it?
   —That it lets me get so much down.
   —When I have a new idea, I just start writing it (using a carriage return to start a new line). I don't have to worry about putting it in the right order. I can jump back from idea to idea.
   —Because you know you can correct, you have permission to write a messier way.
   —You can start anywhere, in the middle, add late idea—cause you can move things around.
   —It's so easy to revise. I suddenly see a new idea or new arrangement after I'm almost done—and I can wade in and do it—and print out clean copy.
   —I can experiment. Leave one version as it is. Copy. Start revising but leave the old one. In case I lose good aspects of the old one in the revising process.
   —I can print out 3–4 copies—at middle stage—and give 'em to someone else. And they'll be neat and easy to read.
   —Spelling and grammar checker. Handwriting and spelling have always been superficials of writing, but they've influenced readers more than anything else. Form of snobbery. If your spelling and handwriting and grammar are bad, I won't take you seriously. Now anyone can turn out professional copy.
   What's hard/Don't like
   Another mind. Sometimes I make such a mess that I feel in a swamp. Too many options. Once I remember feeling. "Oh, I wish I were writing in ink on expensive velum so that I would just choose a word and be done. Not feel like I have to keep revising and changing. I want something final (I must find that process piece I wrote when I was in that situation).

Sometimes I try to revise too much on screen. Too much chaos in the mind.

It's an enharmonic, changeable medium: it's a mind or it's paper—and it moves back and forth. If on screen, it's fluid—it's my mind; if I print it out, it stops being fluid and changing and I get it still and quiet where I can deal with it. I can take a mind scan.

Need it.

One can move back and forth.

It's like a brain photograph.

OPEN-ENDED WRITING
Pat Belanoff

Okay. What to write about. Let's see. Testing. How I think it has gotten out of hand. Everyone testing all the time—testing everything. School isn't teaching anymore. It's just testing. I don't like giving tests and I don't like grading tests. Whenever I do it, I realize how inept testing is. What can testing tell us about what anyone knows? Think about tests you've taken. Let's see. I've taken written tests and oral tests. The oral ones were a bit more frightening because you have to look the testers in the eye while you're answering questions. If you are hesitant for fear of blurting out something stupid, your questioners see you sitting there looking doubtful. When you're doubtful on a written test, you don't have to worry so much about what the testers are thinking. They aren't seeing what you're writing while you're writing it. So what am I saying? That oral tests are tougher than written tests. But what I started out with was just how awful testing of all kinds is. But if students aren't tested, how do we find out what they know? I know lots of times I walked out of a test and felt that I hadn't had the chance to say what I knew best. But then a test is supposed to find out if students know what they're *supposed* to know. The teacher is the one who's supposed to decide what students need to know. After all, we're the experts. So then students' biggest challenge should be to decide what's most important to know—with the teacher's help—and then find ways to make sure they know it. But actually this is all talk about tests given in a class where students have read texts, listened to a teacher, had the chance to ask her questions. That kind of testing has its own problems. But the kind of tests that bother me the most are the so-called standardized ones. Reading tests, writing tests, regents' tests, SATs of all kinds, entrance exams to college, all that stuff. You go in one day and that's it. If for some reason you feel lousy, or your confidence is low for some other reason, maybe you lost a contest for a parking spot or something equally stupid and unrelated and your confidence has been undermined—maybe a fight with a friend, irritation at some bureaucratic nonsense or something, or maybe the first questions throw you off, you lose confidence, then you do the rest of the test feeling weak. If some other question had come first, you would have done better on all of them. I remember reading some research somewhere that showed that on standardized tests, if you get a question or two right you go on doing well and if you get a few wrong, you keep on that way. In other words, right and wrong answers come in streaks. Unfair. And then these standardized tests are always timed tests and some people need more time. Does it matter whether Tolstoy spent two months or ten years writing *War and Peace?* It's a good book—or a bad book—no matter how long it took. Finding a cure for AIDS is a result of careful work, not fast work. Some things are just not matters of time. But standardized tests are. I had quite a few friends and classmates that I thought were really smarter than me, but they just didn't do well on standardized tests. There's a knack to it, but it doesn't mean you're smarter. And, also, I suppose I have problems with standardized tests' absoluteness. The most important things in life don't usually have right and wrong, one word or one sentence answers. They're usually more complicated than that. Standardized tests don't really show *how* you think about things and that's really important. It's important for you too to know where your thinking about something goes off—regardless of whether you get the right answer or the wrong answer. Otherwise, how can you approach such a problem more effectively the next time? But then I've heard the argument from others that life is one big competition and students have to learn how to be competitive and if there are things about it that are unfair, that's tough—since that's what life is going to be like also.

Okay. Time to stop and try to summarize or tie up. I think what I got to at the end is important to me—the difference between competition and cooperation. Maybe students should cooperate on tests. But then how could I decide about the contribution of one person—but then how do we ever know that? But the other thing about always feeling like you're on the carpet is important too. Which one of those ideas do I want to run with for the second freewrite?

I'll start with the cooperation-competition thing. Some time ago I read a book called *The Territorial Imperative*. The author's point is that creatures—animals or humans—compete until they all feel threatened and then they cooperate. It seems to me we as humans are in a threatened condition now. The economic situation seems grim worldwide. The AIDS problem makes us all feel helpless. The threat of nuclear warfare is crippling—so much suicide among young people. And all the corruption in government—city and nation. But we don't seem to be cooperating—we continue to compete. So, so much for a territorial imperative. The myth is that individuals working in isolated garrets invent new, wonderful things. But an article recently in the newspaper talked about how Edison (I think) in his diaries notes how others' ideas had contributed to his own. If that's the case (and other scientists' writing seems to support that—even that awful atomic bomb was a group effort) then why do we encourage individual effort through individual testing? And how do we know or measure the value of individual contribution in group projects? Someone may contribute only one element—one small suggestion or idea—catalytic—and yet it may be that one small thing that makes a big difference even though others may have contributed more quantitatively. That's it too. Always thinking everything can be measured quantitatively and being afraid of qualitative judgments because they *are* qualitative—because you can't assign a number to them—reminds me of the movie *10* after which it came to be quite a fad to give numbers to everything as though a number could encompass the truth, the reality. You meet someone and a friend says "What is he?" and you say "2." It's a joke. But if you had to explain that 2 in words, you'd get at what your judgment really was. But then maybe the 2 is okay because it's really a gut reaction and we have to honor those too because they usually get at something valid. We usually do make judgments like that and then back up and try to figure out why we made the judgment. It doesn't make the 2 wrong, does it? Where am I going with this? Better stop and reread and see what kind of summary statement I can make.

Let's see: the relative value of qualitative as opposed to quantitative judgments— what does that have to do with competition vs. cooperation or with standardized testing which is where I started from? Somehow I see a connection between qualitative judgments, cooperation, and non-testing and a connection between quantitative judgments, competition, and testing. Can I make those connections more solid? I'll try for one more freewrite.

Standardized testing fosters competition because the standards for the test are set on the basis of how everyone does—and my grade is really a reflection of how I rate in comparison to everyone else who has taken the test. It lessens cooperation. I certainly wouldn't want to help others do well because that would make me do less well—but if I'm in an operating room involved in a delicate surgical operation, I want everyone else on the team to do well because that way we'll all succeed. I certainly don't want to way: "Aha. He made the wrong cut and I made the right one!" Because we're both likely to fail and the patient will die. So standardized testing is a form of competition. And it's also a quantitative kind of testing because it almost always relies on multiple-choice answers—that's the only way thousands of students can be tested—otherwise teachers would be spending all their time marking essay answers. Yes, there's another thing I dislike. Multiple-choice questions assume that there's only 5 possible answers to a particular question. Maybe there's another answer that's better than the choices given. I've often felt that way when answering one of those questions. I think they've not given the best choice possible; it closes down possibilities, puts blinders on those being tested. The test makers always say, "Choose the best answer." But that's annoying. I've wandered off again. But I suppose that's what this sort of writing is supposed to encourage. Wandering off. Students who have taken so many multiple-choice tests expect us as teachers to give them a list of possible answers to everything when actually the hardest thing is to come up with that list. We shouldn't be relieving them of the most difficult part of the process. So many students want us to tell them what to write on, and I'd rather the students chose. Coming up with what *you* want to write about is hard just as coming up with possible answers may be the hardest thing about answering questions. If you have choices, you are already part of the way home. It leads us to think that life is simpler than it is. We need to be able to think of possible answers that no one has yet come up with. Going back to (forgot what I was going to say—drat!) Oh, yes, going back to the scientists' coming up with answers to tough things, like cures for AIDS or cancer. They need to come up with possible answers no one has thought of—possible answers to test out. They can't rely on possibilities that others have already come up with. One more time to solidify and then I'll stop.

What I think bothers me the most is that quantitative, standardized tests give us the feeling that there are definite answers to questions and maybe there really aren't. We need to work with the answers we have, but always with an open mind, always with the idea that there are better answers somewhere or that there are flaws in the answers we do have. Multiple-choice tests don't make that evident and competition makes us defend what we're doing, rather than trying to see the good in what our competitors are doing and seeing how that will help us and how what we've done can help others. Many years ago I read an article in *Scentific American* (wish I had kept it) that talked about the importance of variety in the ecosystem: that ecosystems which were characterized by a large variety of flora and fauna tended to be successful and places where flora and fauna were more akin often became barren and unproductive. The point is that the world needs variety, needs to encourage it in people as well as plants and animals. That way each of us has something unique to contribute and there's no point in trying to outdo someone else because you're not only hurting yourself, but diminishing variety. Let's try to get that more solid.

Life is not as simple and clear-cut as standardized tests suggest it is—and therefore it's bad for schools to use them too often because students get the wrong idea. Stop.

PROCESS WRITING ABOUT USING THE OPEN-ENDED PROCESS
Manuel Depina

As I was doing the private writing, I struggled tremendously, especially with the open-ended process. I went through the open-ended guidelines, I read them about twenty-five times, and still couldn't come up with anything. I couldn't figure out how to do the mechanics and compose it in a way which I would feel most comfortable with.

I followed everything that was in the guidelines. I shook off my hands, took a deep breath, closed my eyes, and still the paper in front of me was blank. I couldn't get myself to relax and concentrate like I usually do. This was probably due to the different method and procedure that I would normally follow.

Believe it or not, reading the guidelines for the twenty-sixth time, I finally got something down. The word *pressure* came to my mind, and I wrote it down as soon as I could, fearing I might forget it.

After I wrote the first word, it seemed like a bomb waiting to explode. Afterward my pen couldn't keep up with my brain, and the words seemed to fall into their proper places. Meanwhile I felt a pleasant feeling of relief and comfort which propelled me and made we want to write more.

The thing that contributes most to my technique is the listing process. After I had that part done, I simply followed the guidelines. And I must admit it was very helpful.

FELT SENSE
Eugene Gendlin

You say that I am tired. If you consider your statement to be phenomenological, you will consider your statement wrong if I do not feel tired.

Your statement invites me to see if I am tired. How would I do that? Not by reviewing how long I have worked, and not by looking in the mirror. I can attend to my body directly and see if I find there what is called "tired." That is direct reference. Until you asked me, I paid no attention. Now, in reaction to your words, I seek to set up such "an" experience as we call "tired." If I cannot do so (and, note, this is not a matter of choice), your statement was wrong. Let us suppose that I agree I am "sort of tired."

Let me show how much further we can go than when we first considered this example.

Now suppose I say, "I am not exactly tired, but I am getting a little weary." It is clear that here you were definitely right in some way. Your words succeeded in "directly referring." They were also close in what they conveyed; they were pointing in the right direction. (I might have said, "No, I have a slight toothache.") We do not know as yet why I prefer "weary" to "tired"—they seem to be indistinguishable. "Weary" might perhaps include along with "tired" some sense of some long, drawn-out cause for being tired, and indeed we have been working all day and all evening. (It is this sort of experiential sense of how a word is used which the linguistic analysts explicate.)

We must note that I probably did not feel tired until you said so. Your saying it made it true by leading me to create, specify, set out, distinguish (these words are equivalent here) "an" experience. Before I tried to refer to it, it wasn't there; now that I do, it is.

Yet, the feeling must be there; I do not just make it. Trying to refer to it, trying to see if I am tired, doesn't always make that feeling. Since now it did, for me, I would want to say that it was there before only I didn't notice it. Of course, as a "this feeling" it certainly was not there before. (Yet the case is different than if you had suddenly made me tired, perhaps by telling me some heavy news. There is a continuity between how I remember being before, and my direct reference now to this tired feeling: thus the tired feeling is a newly set-out aspect of the over-all experience I was attending to.)

Suppose I now continue to explicate why "weary" seems to be true for me, and "tired" doesn't. I may say next, "Well, it's sort of not tired, but tired-of. That's why I said 'weary.' I don't feel like going on to this next job we have to tackle now. It's too tough."

Having said this, which is a more exact version of how I feel (as well as an explication of the use of the word I preferred), I might say, a moment or two later, "I feel like going out and having a good time. I am not at all tired—just so we don't have to get into this next job, it's too hard to do."

Now I am actually denying flatly what seemed above to be "in the right direction," though I really feel no different. I am still talking about "the same thing," and, despite the flat denial of what I said, I hold that what I say now is what my feeling really "was."

As I continue now to say just what it is about the next job that seems so tough, I may say, "Well, it isn't exactly hard to do, but what is hard is that I know they won't like how I'll do it." And then, "The job is really easy." And, again, further, "It isn't so much that I care what they think of it; it's just this one way I care, and that's a way that they're right, really. Gee, I don't care at all what they think! But this one criticism they'll make, I know they're right about that. It's really what I think that I care about." And, further, "I could help it, but I would have to take a day off to study up on how to do it right, and I don't want to do that."

And, again, "Really, I do want to. Every time I hit this sort of thing I wish so much that I could take the time off to learn how to do it, but I just can't give myself the time off. It would seem like a whole day with nothing done. I don't feel any trust in myself if I go and do something that isn't a part of the routine we call work, just doing something because I'd like to do it." And, later, "Hell, I'll do it tomorrow."

This aspect of experience—its vast capacity to be further schematized and unitized in relation to verbalization, and thereby revealing aspects which, we now say, it most truly "was," has not been recognized at all in philosophy until now. Therefore no systematic method has been devised for the various kinds of steps involved in explication.

It is clear from the example that one's own feelings can be stated falsely by oneself, and later corrected. There can be several steps in such correcting.

After you've read this, you may want to turn to two analyses of it which we have included in the readings for Unit 12.

From Private to Public Writing: A Study of Genres

In this unit we ask you to use your private exploratory writing from Unit 6 as seeds or raw material for a piece of public writing. The main activity is a series of short exercises where you explore the possibilities in your private writing in terms of various *genres* or forms or types of writing. Indeed, we have made this unit into a study of genres in writing as a way to show you how genres constitute choices. After you choose the genre in which you want to develop your private writing, the main assignment is to write a full draft of your public piece and take it through one revision to be shared with others.

As you explore the possibilities latent in your private writing, we hope you'll get good at quickly trying out different directions or transformations—doing fifteen-minute sketches to help you decide which directions are worth pursuing further. This process should give you a better feeling for different genres and audiences—and how you can use genre and audience to take a piece of writing where you want it to go. You will come away with a better understanding of the tricky relationship between form and content.

LOOKING BACK OVER YOUR PRIVATE WRITING

Much of what's inside our heads remains private. We couldn't get it all into speech or writing, and even if we could we wouldn't want to. We need privacy. You may well not want to share much of what you wrote in the pre-

vious unit. Some theorists think that we haven't, in a sense, *finished* expressing our thought until we finally make it public in some form, but we think
that each of us can be our own audience also. We think it's perfectly natural
to keep some things to ourselves.

But much of what's inside our heads does need to be communicated to
others. That means we have to transform it in some way—turn it from
something private into something public. Part of that transformation occurs
even during private writing since writing requires us to use something public: language. But often private writing needs to be transformed even more
in order to communicate its sense to others. Depending on the audience, we
can modify it only slightly (perhaps for a good friend) or extensively (perhaps for a speech to strangers). (There's more later on audience and its effect
on writing in "Ruminations and Theory.")

The first step is to look back over the private writing you did in Unit 6
just to get it fresh in mind. As you look back, you're likely to have mixed
feelings about it. You may feel good about how much you wrote, about how
diverse it is, about your ability to use writing to record your thinking and
feeling in a way you'd never done before. As you read it over, part of it will
probably match up again with the "felt sense" of it still in your head, and
the match will feel gratifying to you. Or perhaps you'll be pleased because
this private exploratory writing is not very much of a mess at all: some of it
at least is strong, clear, and fully formed.

But you may also react negatively, at least to part of it: "Yuck. What a
mess! What drivel my mind is full of." This reaction often occurs when people first try out the kind of private exploratory writing you did in Unit 6.
But it's important to remember that you weren't trying to produce good,
well-organized writing. You were trying to give yourself the safety to produce, as it were, an accurate mind scan or brain X-ray. Of course our minds
are messy. If you produce writing that's a mess, that's probably a *good* sign.
It means not only that you were able to trust yourself enough to record what
was actually going on in your mind, but also that you have begun to learn a
powerful heuristic—that is, a powerful way to find things to write. For if
you read through that mess in the proper spirit of inquiry, you will find
many more interesting possibilities for writing than if you had carefully
written something with full attention to organization and logic.

We suspect your private writing has some or all of the following
characteristics:

- Contradictions. At one point you thought or felt *x,* but then later on
  you wandered into thinking or feeling not-*x.* If you are going to engage
  in good thinking, you *need* contradiction—you need to wrestle with
  both sides, get them to wrestle with each other. In this way you'll come
  up with *new* thinking, not just a restatement of your old thoughts.

- Changes of topic and digressions. Your writing goes in one direction
  and suddenly veers off or changes direction completely. There's cog-

nitive power in this jumpy diversity—seeds for different pieces of writing. But even more interesting than that, *there are important unstated insights implied at every point of change or digression.* Look closely at each jump or shift in your writing. Pause and ask yourself: "How did my mind make that jump? What is the connection?" Even if there is no "real" or "rational" connection (say you jumped from carburetors to cucumbers), there was always something *in your mind* that served as a bridge, and it may throw light on your topic (whether carburetors or cucumbers). The mind is never random.

- Obsessions. The writing seems to be in a rut, grinding over and over again at the same event or the same feelings. Some people who have not done this kind of private exploratory writing before say, "How childish!" or "How irrational!" The thing to remember is that if this stuff came out on paper, it's in your head: you can't get rid of it by *not* writing it down. Indeed writing it down is the best way to get rid of it or get past it. Writing gives you perspective on these thoughts and feelings and thereby decreases the likelihood of their playing over and over in your head like a broken record. Remember that everyone obsesses sometimes. Try to learn about the issue or about yourself by reading through the obsessions. You may discover that you want to talk to someone you trust about them. And there may well be something in the obsession that you would enjoy communicating even to an audience you don't know.

TRYING OUT GENRES

After you've read through your private writing, the next step is to try out various genres or forms of public writing using the private writing as source material.

Genres are publically recognized forms of writing. There are large inclusive genres such as *poetry* and *prose;* there are somewhat smaller less-inclusive genres such as *lyric poetry, essay,* and *fiction.* And there are even smaller, more specific genres or forms—which are what we will ask you to try out in this unit:

1. Description or portrait

2. Narration

3. Letter

4. Monologue or dialogue

5. Persuasive essay

6. Expository or analytic essay

7. Satire or parody

8. Meditation or prayer

9. Poetry

As you try out the various genres we suggest, don't just think of yourself as pouring *existing content* into various containers; think of yourself also as trying out containers that will bring *new content* into being. (If this seems an interesting theoretical point, you will want to read about it in "Ruminations" later on.)

In your private writing in Unit 6 we suggested that you deliberately refrain from being in control and give over the reins a bit to the pen or to the emerging words. Here, we are setting the opposite task: to *reassert control* and consciously choose how you want to transform your raw material.

To give you some idea of what these transformations might look like, we'll give you little simple transformations based on our own two pieces of private writing at the end of Unit 6.

Here are the genres we invite you to try out:

1. Description or Portrait

Read through (or think back over) your private writing to find a *scene, object,* or *person* that feels important but is not much developed. First close your eyes and try to see, hear, feel, and smell your subject; then go on to describe it in writing for at least ten minutes. Obviously time won't allow you to complete a large scene, but take a few more minutes of writing to sketch an overview or rough outline of how you'd shape or organize a full descriptive piece. The goal here is simply to get a start—to test how fruitful it might be to write a longer piece of public descriptive writing.

If your private writing is already mostly descriptive, this shows that description is the genre that your private writing led you instinctively to use. Now take a moment or two to write about what changes you would make, if any, in making your piece *public:* Would you shape it any differently? What would be the center? Are there any changes in style or approach you would want to make?

Example. In reading back over her open-ended writing in the "Readings" section in Unit 6, Pat Belanoff looked for some seed of a portrait or description. She remembered a friend who did poorly on standardized tests and began to write a description of her. Here's her beginning:

My friend Joan was quiet, a girl who rarely said anything in class. She was tall and thin, about 5'7" and 120 pounds, with straight blond hair and blue almost translucent eyes though they were hidden by thick glasses. She was a wonderful listener and when you got to know her very funny. Although she didn't say much, whenever she did speak you realized she had been listening carefully and had a very dry sense of humor. . . .

2. Narration

Where are the potential *stories* in what you wrote? Look for crucial events, turning points, moments of tension or suspense. These points might not even be *in* what you wrote—but you can find them implied. Perhaps, that is, your writing is nothing but your feelings about a certain person or your thoughts about a certain issue. Still, think of the stories that could be *found* or *made* which are important to that person or that issue. Start at an important moment in that story—not necessarily the beginning—and just begin writing for at least ten minutes to get the feel for a transformation of your material into narrative. You may find that it leads you to new material or new insights.

If your private writing is already mostly narrative, consider what adjusting or focusing you'd make to turn it into public writing. Would you work on point of view, shaping (beginning, ending), implications? You might wish to turn back to Unit 5 for guidance here.

Example. Pat Belanoff realized she could tell a story about what happened when her friend Joan did poorly on the SATs. While writing out that story, she realized it would even be possible to fictionalize it and make it into a piece that would show dramatically the often disastrous results of standardized tests. Here's a piece of what she wrote:

> Almost from the beginning of our junior year, we began to worry about taking the SATs. We had heard disaster stories from seniors about doing poorly on the tests and having to give up going to a particular college. Some people who had dreams of being doctors or lawyers didn't think they'd ever be able to do it. This talk scared us. My friend Joan and I took a special course to prepare us for the tests. Many students signed up for the course and didn't do any of the work and missed lots of classes. But not my friend Joan. . . .

3. Letter

Think of the letters that your private writing might give rise to. Does your exploratory writing tell you that there are certain people you need to communicate with or things you need to tell someone that you've never told them? Do you want to say how much they helped or hurt you? how much you admire them? or simply what has been happening to you since they last heard from you? Remember that some letters are more private (to a close friend) and others more public (to an organization or newspaper editor). You might want to spend ten minutes on each type if you find this genre productive.

It may be that your private writing already *is* a letter. Could it be that most of these words are really addressed to someone—telling them something you need to say to them? If so, just write for a moment or two about what you'd do if you were actually to revise it so you could send it.

Examples. Pat Belanoff realized she could write a letter either to Joan or to the Educational Testing Service. She started the latter as follows:

> In your public statements, you often claim that SAT results predict how well a student will do during college. You probably have some statistics to back up what you are saying, but my experiences do not support your claims. You also say that you advise colleges not to use just SAT scores when making admissions decisions. My experience again suggests that colleges usually use *only* SAT scores when admitting students. . . .

See also Mark Levensky's letter to the teachers at the Perkins Elementary School in the readings for this unit. It actually was a letter to his former teachers—and he really sent it to the school—but he found the form of a letter to be the way he wanted to publish his thoughts on spelling to a wider audience in a professional journal for teachers.

4. Monologue or Dialogue

There will be germs of dialogue or passages that imply a dialogue in your exploratory writing. Perhaps you wrote about someone who disagrees with you about something important. Have a dialogue with that person. Or perhaps there are two people in your private writing who disagree. Get them talking. But it's not necessary that people disagree. If they simply have different temperaments, any dialogue between them will be fruitful.

Don't forget that you can easily write productive dialogues with *objects* or *ideas:* with a car, a house, anything that is important in some way in your exploratory writing. The trick is simply to get one member to say something and let the conversation proceed. Just get your pen moving, and the dialogue will unfold and create new material, new ideas that are not part of your original exploratory writing. The dialogue may affect or even change the views or feelings you had when doing the exploratory writing.

Examples. In reading back over his Perl guidelines writing in Unit 6, Peter Elbow realized that he could set up a dialogue with his computer. He began the first of these dialogues like this:

PETER: Why do you always give me such trouble? Why do you so often mess me up or not do what I want you to do? I paid a lot of money for you. I got instructions. Most of all, why won't you *talk* to me when I need you?

COMPUTER: Actually, I talk to you quite often.

P: Yes, you send me messages—"bad command," "insert target disk in Drive B"—worst yet, "FATAL ERROR"—but when

I'm really in trouble, you just sit there silent and refuse to do what I want you to do.

C: Unfortunately it's you who gives me trouble—you refuse to do what's needed. But I don't hold it against you. I just wait for you to catch on. I do everything you ask me to—no matter how many times you ask me to do it. I never forget anything. I'm never bored or impatient. There's only a problem when you don't know my language or you ask me to do something that is impossible. I'm not programmed to know your language perfectly. It's your job to learn mine. As soon as you speak meaningfully to me, I'll speak meaningfully to you.

P: Don't take that superior tone with me! "I never make a mistake. I never make a mistake." Why do you keep saying that to me?

C: I didn't say that; I never have. But in fact I never do make a mistake. In our dealings I'm sorry to say that it's only you who make mistakes.

P: *SEE!* I won't put up with this arrogance. (Wait a minute, let me get hold of myself. It's only a machine. Calm myself.) Okay, I'll be more reasonable with you. I admit it. Of course I make mistakes. But I'm doing the best I can. I try to do things right, and when something doesn't work, I look at the manual. I go over my steps one at a time and try it again and again. But still it doesn't work. Sometimes I get so mad I want to hurl you across the room. And you just sit there silent, superior, condescending.

C: But that's it, don't you see? You are so irrational. Why do you give me the same order again and again when you see it's not working? And then you get so *angry* because *you're* doing something irrational.

P: But I can't help it.

C: Yes, that's what perplexes me. Why do I bring out irrationality in you? I've been watching you these months. I've never seen you as furious and fuming—as close to violence—with anyone else as with me. Not with your wife or children or students or co-workers. What do I do that brings out your irrationality?

P: That's a good question.

5. *Persuasive Essay*

What are some of the important *opinions* or *beliefs* in your exploratory writing? What if you tried to persuade everyone to agree with you? Are there certain readers you might particularly try to persuade? You'll find that the persuasive essay as a genre serves as a means of invention: it helps you think of reasons or arguments that you didn't come up with earlier when you were just exploring for yourself.

Take at least ten minutes now and start a persuasive essay, beginning perhaps with summing-up your claim as briefly as possible. Before you stop, try quickly to sketch in more reasons you could use and a possible organization for the essay. (If what you wrote was already more or less in a persuasive mode, write for a few moments about what changes you would make to shape it or make it stronger. You may want to look ahead at Unit 10 on persuasion for some suggestions.)

Example. Pat Belanoff, as she reread her open-ended writing, realized that with work the piece could be a persuasive essay on the subject of standardized tests, competition, and quantification. It was this genre that produced the strongest "click" for her. She began:

> Standardized tests are producing a generation of students who think that all questions admit of definitive answers. This being the case, everyone should always arrive at the same answer to every question. People who feel like this tend to be narrow-minded, dictatorial, and competitive. . . .

Before she continued any further, she made a list of all her reasons for disliking standardized tests and all the reasons she had heard others give for why they were valuable or necessary. She decided to begin her essay by listing briefly the reasons *for* using standardized tests, but to spend the bulk of her effort on presenting her side of the issue.

6. *Expository or Analytic Essay*

What's the most interesting *issue, question,* or *concept* in your exploratory writing? What would you like to understand better? The best way to generate this kind of essay is not to look for answers or explanations or persuasive arguments, but for *questions.* What is the point of greatest perplexity for you?

Perplexity. When students are writing and begin to feel confused, they usually *stop* writing and start thinking. If they can't clear up the confusion, they usually find a way to *avoid* the issue in their writing. They hide it; sweep it under the rug. The assumption is that writing is for *telling,* not *asking.* It's for saying what you already understand, not exploring what you don't understand. But most good expository writing comes from the writer's delving into perplexity and uncertainty. Don't drop the issue. Spell out the things that seem odd or hard to make sense of, explain why they seem this way, and work toward possible resolutions. It's this process that gives life to thinking and writing. You'll discover that you can produce much good

143

material in a condition of not yet understanding what you are trying to write about. Remember that many good published essays don't give solutions: they simply clarify or analyze a question so that others can understand it better and perhaps go to work on it.

So sniff out the issue of greatest perplexity and start writing out your uncertainties. You may find it helpful to think of certain *particular* sub-genres of the essay that could give shape to your search—and also, in that process, help you generate new material. Some sub-genres are:

- Pure analysis or exposition. What rich issues does your private writing invite you to explore more fully? (For fuller treatment, see Unit 9 on the expository essay.)

- Analysis of data. Perhaps your private writing raises the question of what someone really *meant* when they did or said or wrote something. Or the question of whether someone really *did* something or not. One of the major kinds of writing in sciences and humanities is a zeroing in on careful analysis of the evidence: words, behavior, clues. (See Unit 11 on analyzing arguments; Units 12 and 19 on analyzing texts; and Unit 13 on analyzing discourse.)

- Definition. Perhaps your private writing leads to some complex or slippery concept you want to elucidate for readers. What is selfishness? love? The classic method is "collection and division": "collecting" the concept with its cousins to see what families it belongs to, then "dividing" it from its cousins to see how it is special or different. (How is selfishness different from getting your own way? How is love different from lust?) Thus the essay of definition is closely related to the next form.

- Compare-contrast. Does your private writing suggest two people, places, or ideas that invite comparison? Considerable cognitive power comes from focusing on two comparable matters instead of just one and continually holding them up against each other to find similarities and differences.

- Process essay. In technical or scientific writing, this means writing about how to do something (e.g., how to go about making water from hydrogen and oxygen). But process essays are not limited to these disciplines. For example, you can write about the steps in cooking a particular meal, preparing a garden plot in the spring, or doing something less concrete: for example, convincing your parents to let you do something. We asked for a process essay about private exploratory writing in the last unit.

- Research essay. Since this would involve interviewing people or doing library research, it's not a feasible task for this unit. But if your private writing suggests some interesting areas you'd like to learn more about, you can now write out some of the questions you would pursue. You could then take the issue up again in one of the two later units of this book: Unit 14, *Library Research as Revising,* or Unit 16, *Personal Research.*

- Five-paragraph essay. This is a school-invented genre; some of you may not be familiar with it at all; others of you may think it is the only kind of essay there is. Unfortunately, it is often the *only* essay form students learn. In this rigid form, the first paragraph is an introduction that usually begins with some statement which is broader than the essay's topic. Succeeding sentences narrow this topic down to the end of the paragraph, whose last sentence states the thesis for the paper. The second, third, and fourth paragraphs make up the body of the essay. Each of these usually presents one reason with illustrative examples in support of the thesis statement. The final paragraph acts as a conclusion, usually restating the thesis of the paper in words somewhat different from those used in the first paragraph.

  Frankly, we think this particular genre tends to give more weight to form than to content and thus limits thinking. After you try it for yourself, you'll be in a position to agree or disagree with us—although we suspect that most of you will have had some experience with this form and thus already have some opinions about it. We do recognize that under certain circumstances, it may provide a quick solution for organization of ideas—particularly on essay exams when you need to get your writing done rapidly.

Select one or more of these essay sub-genres and write for at least ten minutes on each one you pick.

Examples. Peter Elbow used the private, exploratory Perl writing included at the end of Unit 6 as the basis for the mini-unit, "Writing with a Word Processor" p. 437 which is a mixture of expository and process essay.

Pat Belanoff realized she could use her open-ended writing on standardized testing as source material for essays comparing and contrasting competitive and cooperative people, good and bad tests, and quantitative and qualitative responses. Here's the beginning of her additional freewriting on the first of these essays:

> Competitive people are often aggressive and obnoxious, but even if they aren't, you usually can't trust them. These are the medical students who tear articles out of books and journals so other medical students won't be able to read them and will do poorly on tests. Competitive people seem always to be thinking about themselves, but basically they're insecure. They don't think they're really better than others because if they did, they wouldn't need to play dirty little tricks to stay ahead. But competitive people are often very hard workers and the world does need hard workers. . . .

7. Satire or Parody

What could your private exploratory writing lead you to *make fun of?* a person you'd like to show as silly? an opinion or view that needs puncturing? yourself? a situation or "scene" that is on the brink of the ridiculous (e.g., people who show off)?

The essence of satire is to exaggerate or distort. Thus you could satirize someone in your exploratory writing (or yourself) by simply describing him but exaggerating certain traits. Or you could put down the thoughts and feelings that run through the person's head (a monologue) but overdo it—carry the thoughts and feelings beyond the plausible and exaggerate the manner of talking. You might prefer to make your satire subtle: it's fun fooling readers by not letting them know for a while that you're satirizing—as in some good Woody Allen scenes. Or you can jump overboard into spoof and slapstick—go for the Abbott and Costello dimension.

You can make fun of a view by stating it and even arguing for it but pushing it a bit too far: a persuasive essay but in a satiric or parodic vein. (Swift's "A Modest Proposal" derives much of its force from doing just this—it all sounds so logical!) Or you can give lots of reasons and skew them slightly. Or you can create a tone or voice that is off: treat something seemingly trivial in a dignified epic tone as Chaucer does in "The Nun's Priest's Tale." You can make a satiric or parodic form of any genre. If you've never done satire, try it now and see how satisfying it can be.

Examples. Pat Belanoff decided that it might be fun to devise some comprehensive standardized tests in order to make her point that such tests cannot deal with anything really important. Here's some of what she wrote:

> As a product of public education in the United States of America, I realize now the importance of standardized tests and feel strongly that such forms should play an even larger role in our society. I plan to devise and market standardized tests to determine when people should die. Further work needs to be done on some of the questions, but here are a few of them:

> 1. Is there a God?
>   a. Yes
>   b. No
>   c. It depends on how you define "God."
>   d. None of the above
>   e. All of the above
> 2. Are you ill?
>   a. Yes
>   b. No
>   c. Only physically
>   d. Only when I think about dying
>   e. I plead the Fifth Amendment

Also, see Gertrude Stein's parodic writing on punctuation and Alan Devenish's parody of political speeches in the readings at the end of the unit.

PROCESS BOX

I'm revising the text. Already two weeks late for our second deadline. Needing to go fast. Just get *done*. It's not good enough, but we're both tired of it. Can't fiddle and revise any more.

Yet the push of the deadline makes it more real to me that this writing actually *will* be seen by readers. (At some level I didn't quite believe it before.) That makes me want to revise more. More important, it gives me a kind of *force* behind my mind that permits me to cut through some tangles that I hadn't been able to cut through before. Some combination of added courage and added clarity. I see a fog of two or three sentences that beat around the bush and I am impatient and think of some more direct way of saying it. Somehow, I *hear* it more—and make revision more with my mouth than with my eye. I experience this impatience and cutting through as a kind of clenching of my jaw as I try to clarify.

PETER ELBOW 10/87

8. Meditation or Prayer

These are particularly interesting forms of public writing because they are essentially *private* genres—turned public. That is, when we share or publish a meditation or prayer, we are in effect inviting others to overhear our transaction with ourselves or with what is holy. It might well be that your private exploratory writing—as it is, with only minimal cleaning up—could be turned into public musings, meditation, or prayer.

As you do your ten minutes of writing in this genre, you'll probably sense the presence of eavesdroppers in some way.

Examples. Peter Elbow began to write a brief meditative piece building on some of his private Perl writing, but also reflecting on ideas he generated in his dialogue. (You may find, as he did, that these genre explorations begin to interact; that's as it should be.) Following is part of what he wrote:

He's right. (Or is it she?) I do get madder at that machine than at anyone else in my life. Why should that be?

Is it because it's a machine and I *can* get mad at it? I can't let myself get so mad at people? That's a nice thought—me as sensible and rational: that I don't act irrationally toward people since it would hurt them and instead I save it for a machine which can never be hurt by my feelings. That's like the dog who moderates his roughness when playing with a tiny toddler. It's like the toddler who hits his parents as hard as he can in blissful faith that anything he does, they can deal with. Can I remember when I first realized I could *hurt* my parents? No; but it must have been an awful realization.

147

But somehow that's too pretty a story: me as purely sensible and rational. There's undeniably something disturbing about getting so heated up at a machine. Is it that I want to kick it because it's helpless? Little kids often seem to pick on the weak one.

But in a way it's not weak at all. It's so powerful, so much more powerful than I. It can do all these things I can't do. And my frustration mounts because I know what's happening is not its fault. *And* if I harm it, *I* would be the one to suffer and would have to pay to have it fixed.

But that reminds me of other occasions when I feel that way. It's true that I never seem to get as mad at people but I do get almost as mad and frustrated when I'm trying to *fix* some object or machine and cannot do it. It makes me want to cry with frustration.

Perhaps I was getting at something important in my dialogue earlier: the fact that the damn thing won't talk to me. Somehow there's nothing worse than when someone won't talk to me. I guess that's the hardest thing for me to bear—it's certainly the best way for someone to torture me—not to talk to me. I need a response from creatures around me. Without that, I find existence intolerable.

Pat Belanoff began to meditate on a world characterized by co-operation.

In a world where cooperation was valued more than competition, I wouldn't tell you that my God was better than yours. I'd find out as much as I could about your God and you'd find out as much as you could about mine; I bet we'd find that our Gods are more alike after we shared our beliefs than they were before we did. In a world where cooperation was valued more than competition, you and I could take a test together and talk over what the best answer was and then we'd both learn something and we'd both get the right answer . . . and so forth.

See also "Meditation" and Virginia Woolf's "Moments of Being" in the readings as examples of this genre.

☆ 9. Poetry

We believe that young children are naturally drawn to poetry, but that most of us become somewhat intimidated by it as we grow older and listen to teachers talk about its intricacy. We also know that some of you have probably continued to write poetry since childhood—or perhaps have come back to it in your early teenage years. We will attempt no formal definition of poetry here but say only that for us poetry is language which is unusually rich in images and connotations. We think most people can write poetry with a little encouragement and if they know that they don't have to show it to anyone unless they want to. We also believe that the very process of writing poetry brings us to a richer understanding of the potential in all language—including even the language of formal essays. That's why we have included poetry as a genre in this unit.

As you read back over your private writing, you may find language that already seems especially resonant. Perhaps you can shape it into poetry.

Remember that poetry does not have to rhyme or even have a formal design; much modern poetry has neither, at least not in a strictly patterned way. You may find that you can create poetry out of some of your private writing with minimal changes. Or you may want to extract a line or more and build a poem on it. Another way to get started is to uncover the pattern in an existing poem and imitate it. You might try this out by imitating the pattern of Nazim Hakmit's poem "Autobiography" included in this unit's readings. You will see that this is a poem which could have grown out of autobiographical narrative. Or you might prefer to use Kate Barnes's poem in Unit 19, which is built on contrast, as a model.

MAIN ASSIGNMENT

As you try out these genres one after the other, look for a "click"—a click that tells you that the genre you are trying has matched up to something latent in the writing itself or matched up with where you want to take it. But even if this does not happen, you will undoubtedly find some genre that seems more appropriate than the others. After you decide on one, read back over all your private writing from the last unit and take quick notes on what you want to include in your first draft. You may find that you can lift whole sections and use them as is or with very small changes; you may find that you'll have to do a fair amount of alteration. Using the old material and whatever new material you need, write a first draft for your assignment.

If after trying out the genres, you're still not sure which you would like to use, try reading selected pieces of your genre tryouts to friends or classmates. (Your teacher may want you to do this even if you have decided on a genre.) The "sayback" form of responding makes sense here (*Sharing and Responding,* Section IIA). This process can help you arrive at a final decision. Ask listeners to tell you which ones click or work best for them. If there's time, they can help you even more by explaining why they prefer certain ones.

Your teacher may want to make sure that you have enough expository writing in the semester and therefore ask you to restrict yourself to some form of *essay* for your main assignment. Even with that restriction, you still have a lot of choices.

Once you have a draft of your major assignment for this unit, your teacher will either give you an opportunity for more feedback or ask you to set it aside for further development in connection with another unit in this book.

PROCESS JOURNAL QUESTIONS

Again, the questions we provide here are meant to serve only if you need memory jogs.

149

- What did you notice looking back over your private writing? Did you feel encouraged, discouraged, bothered? Why?

- What do you notice about going from private to public writing? How do your reactions and feelings differ in each?

- What was it like doing all those short genre tryouts or mini-starts? Could you get yourself to jump in and do one burst of writing and then move on to another? Or did you find the process disorienting?

- Which genres were you most and least comfortable with? Why?

- How did you make the decision as to which genre to use? Did it seem as though *you* decided on the basis of what you wanted? Or did it seem as though the material itself—in combination with the genres—somehow picked itself?

- How do you feel about doing so much writing that no one may ever read or that your teacher may never see or grade?

RUMINATIONS AND THEORY

A. About Audience and Writing

B. Are Genres Form or Content?

A. *About Audience and Writing*

After a unit on private writing and another one on transforming it into public writing, this is a good time to summarize some important principles about the relationship between writing and audience. We will end up with some practical advice for how to make audience work *for* you and prevent it from working against you.

A Balance among the Three Possible Relations to an Audience

Many students have never written except in school: all their writing has been assigned, read, and evaluated or graded by a teacher. If you never write except for evaluation by teachers, you can drift into unconsciously feeling as though that's what writing *is:* performing for someone in authority in order to be judged. Many students have no sense of writing as a way to *communicate* with real readers. And they may lack any sense of writing as a way to communicate privately with themselves, to explore thoughts and feelings on paper just for the sake of exploring. It will help you to become more conscious of the three main ways of relating to or using an audience in writing:

1. Keeping your writing to yourself. This is a case of *not* using an audience—keeping readers out of your way, out of your hair. We hope you have already learned how fruitful it can be not to worry or even think about readers as you write. Many people who were blocked in their writing and learn the knack of private writing say: "I discovered that the problem wasn't *writing:* it was writing *for an audience.*" If you have kept a diary which you don't intend to share, you have participated in a venerable and traditional form of writing for no audience other than oneself. (Of course you can use private writing to help you produce material which is *eventually* intended for an audience.)

2. Giving your writing to an audience but getting no feedback or response from them: sharing. Here, too, we hope we have already shown you how much you can learn from this simple, quick, and satisfying way of relating to an audience. When you share but don't get feedback, it emphasizes writing to *communicate* rather than writing to perform or be judged. Obviously communication is the most natural way to use words—the way with which we have the most practice.

3. Giving your writing to an audience for feedback or response. We know this way of relating to an audience from being in school: getting critical comments from teachers. Therefore it's important to emphasize that it is possible also to get extensive, helpful feedback that is *not* critical—indeed not even evaluative—and that it's possible to get this feedback from readers other than your teacher: from peers, friends, parents, and others you think might be interested in what you've written. Suggestions for this sort of feedback appear in most of the "Sharing and Responding" sections of this book and in the *Sharing and Responding* booklet. After you've learned how to get noncritical feedback, you will usually make better use of evaluative and critical feedback.

Our main point, finally, is that it is important to use audience in all three ways. If you *never* write except for occasions when you submit your writing for feedback (such as from a teacher), your writing is probably suffering. You will increase your skill, your satisfaction, and your productivity if you find occasions for using the other two modes: writing just for yourself and writing just for sharing without feedback.

Audience as a Focusing Force on Our Minds

Think of audience as exerting a kind of magnetism or focusing force on our minds. The closer we are to our listeners or readers and the more we think about them, the more influence they have on our thoughts and feelings. That is, when we are with people or very aware of them in our minds, we are more likely to feel their concerns or see their point of view. When we go off by ourselves or forget them, we ignore their point of view. Both these situations have harmful and helpful aspects.

Some audiences are helpful because they make it easier to write. Such an audience usually consists of a person or a group who likes us and respects us and is interested in what we are interested in. People who want to hear what we have to say tend to make us think of more things to say and to write more fluently. Their receptivity opens our minds. And the act of writing to such readers tends to shape and focus what we are thinking about— even if we had been confused before sitting down to write.

Other audiences, in contrast, are unhelpful or problematic because they make it harder to write. This may be an audience which somehow intimidates us or makes us nervous. Most of us have had the experience of finding it harder and harder to write for a teacher because the teacher did nothing but criticize what we wrote. We may actually find ourselves *unable* to write for this type of person no matter how hard we try. (This happened to Peter Elbow; in fact it was this experience that got him interested in the writing process.) There are other kinds of problem audiences too. If an audience is completely strange, unknown (for example, a prospective employer you've never met or someone from another culture), or vague ("the general public"), you may find it hard to write for them.

The trick then is to learn when an audience is being helpful or not helpful so you can decide whether to think about them or forget about them as you write. Sometimes it's not easy to decide. Even a frightening or difficult audience is occasionally helpful to keep in mind right from the start. We decide to be brave and look them in the eye, and doing so empowers us and clears our minds: we suddenly find exactly the words and thoughts we need to say to them.

Even though audience is a tricky theoretical issue, the practical answer is simple if you think in terms of a little three-step dance with readers: first a step *toward* readers, then *away from* them, and finally *back toward* them.

- Toward your audience. Start by bringing your readers to mind. Imagine them; see them. Doing so may help you focus your thinking and your approach to your topic. By bringing readers consciously into your mind, you may well find more to say, just as you would naturally find things to say if you were standing there in front of them and they asked you what was on your mind. If things go well, you simply keep this first relationship to the audience for the whole writing process.

- Away from your audience. *If* you have any difficulty with your writing, it may be because your audience is getting in your way: because they are unknown or intimidating or because thinking about them makes you worry too much about trying to get your writing right. Try putting them out of mind and writing for yourself: get your thoughts straight in your *own* mind—even if you know that this process is leading you to write things that are not right for your intended audience. If you can once put clearly on paper what *you* think, then it's not so very hard afterward to make changes or adjustments to suit your words to the audience.

- Finally, back again *toward* readers. No matter how clear you see things for *yourself*, you must consciously bring your audience to mind again—as a central part of your revising process. In doing so you may realize that what is clear for you is *not* clear for them unless you explain something they may not know about; or you may realize that for them you need a change in approach. You may even decide you need to *hide* some of your own ideas or feelings when writing to them. This would have been hard earlier, for it's hard to hide something while you are in the act of working it out.

B. Are Genres Form or Content?

Starting with Content

In this textbook we often suggest doing freewriting or exploratory writing without worrying about organization. "Invite chaos," we say; "Worry later about organization or form." In making this suggestion we might seem to be making an interesting (and arguable) theoretical assumption: that first you create "content" (pure content-without-form, as it were) and then you give it "form."

Even though Genesis tells us that God took this approach when He created the heavens and the earth (starting out with "formless" matter), it is clearly a one-sided way to talk about the process of creation. Yet the approach is remarkably helpful to many people in their writing. Whether skilled or unskilled, many people find it a relief when they allow themselves to produce "raw content-without-form"—find it *enabling* to turn out pages and pages of writing without worrying about whether it's organized or fits a certain form.

In Units 6 and 7 we may seem even to have *exaggerated* this one-sided approach. In Unit 6 we asked you to produce, as it were, gallons of formless *content,* and now in this unit we ask you to pour those gallons into various bottles or forms.

Let us now be more careful and compensate for this one-sided way of talking. In the first place, strictly speaking *all* writing has form: there's no such thing as content-without-form. All that writing you produced in Unit 6 cannot but have *some* form. Perhaps the form is mixed or messy, but that's form too. Besides, what looks messy at first glance is often quite patterned. What you wrote may have a large coherent pattern which is obscured by local clutter, digressions, and interruptions.

For example, if you look carefully at your seemingly chaotic private, exploratory writing, you may see that it is shaped by a single narrative flow—or even by a clever flashback narrative pattern. Or perhaps your exploratory writing has a three-step pattern of moving from (1) *event* to (2) *reactions* to the event to (3) *reflective thoughts* about that event and your reactions. Or maybe you'll find the opposite pattern: a movement from reflective thoughts back to the events which originally gave rise to the thoughts. The point is that if you manage to record what's going on in your mind, you are almost certainly recording patterns. Our minds operate by patterns even when we are confused. The human mind is incapable of pure randomness or chaos. Therefore when you look at your private exploratory writing, don't just respect the chaos as useful and valid (which it is); keep an eye out also for the *order* hiding behind the seeming chaos.

This realization leads to a very practical consequence: there are always organizations and genres *already lurking* in your seemingly messy exploratory writing—organizations and genres that you can discover and prune into shape (like recovering a shapely tree that has become overgrown). Just because you weren't *aware* of writing within a particular genre doesn't mean that you wrote genreless material. When you "organize" your chaotic private writing, you probably don't have to *create* organization from scratch; you can clarify the latent organization that's already there. Or more likely you can choose and develop one of the two or three overlapping organizations that are operating—like wave patterns caused by two or three pebbles dropped in a pond.

In sum, there's no such thing as "starting with content only"; you can't have a smidgen of content that is not fully formed. But you can *pretend* to start with content—that is, you can put all your attention on following a train of words or thoughts where they lead and totally ignore consideration of form.

Starting with Form

So too, it's possible to *pretend* to start with form. And this too is a very practical approach that can help in writing. That is, it can be helpful to *start with an organization or genre* and look to content afterward. For a genre isn't just a mold to pour unformed raw writing into or a sewing pattern to lay on top of whole cloth to show us what cloth to cut away. A genre can serve as a way to *generate* or invent content: choosing a genre will make you think of words and ideas that you might not think of otherwise. For example, if you decide to use narrative as a form, you will not just *arrange* your material in terms of time; you will almost certainly *think of* certain connecting or even causal events you had forgotten. If you are vacillating between a persuasive and an analytic essay, the persuasive genre will cause you to think of reasons and arguments; the analytic genre will cause you to think of hypotheses and causal relationships.

Of course it's a common occurrence to start by choosing a genre. For example, we may decide to write a letter to someone and not be sure yet what we'll say. Or we may decide to write an essay with a certain organization (for example, a point-by-point refutation of someone else's view). Or someone may choose a genre for us: "Write a persuasive essay on any topic." In Units 4 and 5, we specified description and narration as the starting points for writing. In loop writing we started with mini-genres (portrait, narrative, letter, and so forth). In this unit, however, we ask you to think about these genres or types *after* you have done lots of writing.

Because language is inherently both form and content, we can never really have pure content or pure form. It is only *our* consciousness which tends, at any given moment, to be more aware of one than of the other. If we use process writing to study our tendencies of mind when we write, we will gradually learn when it's helpful to put more attention on form as we write, and when it's helpful to put more attention on content. In this way we can take better control of our writing process.

READINGS

MEDITATION
A Student

I enter the store and quietly take a seat, while music fills the air. Sitting in here, I can hear a piano melody drifting on by, and the screeching of a trumpet being played out of tune. Endless time passes by, and then my teacher clomps on in, venerable in wisdom if not in age. He shoots a smile, and we begin a new lesson on how to play music.

We enter a stuffy little room and talk a while about how things are going, and we tell a few jokes. Eventually we decide that it's time to play some music, so I take out my guitar. It's an electric, so we plug it into the amp and make some adjustments. We play some jazz tunes for a while, and I crack up because the B string keeps on going out of tune. All of my strings are dead as a doornail and need to be replaced badly. A little light is being reflected back from the black finish—the way the light is reflected off a car's hood. This looks really impressive, but I really wouldn't want to be caught in the glare. It is great though, and the whole thing has a lot of sentimental value for me.

My guitar in general is great—if you ignore some minor imperfections. While we're playing, I can see a clear reflection of the opposite wall in its finish. I also begin to notice the thing's general condition. There's a little bit of dust and grime accumulating on the finish, but it's nothing that a little polish couldn't take care of. I've gotten it scratched up a bit—not too badly, but just enough to notice at a certain angle. The pick guard is scratched up pretty badly too, but I can't complain, because that's what it's there for. These things don't really detract from its appearance, though; they're just my mark on the instrument. I use it on a regular basis, and if it wasn't a little worn, I'd be pretty upset.

After my teacher tells me that I have got to get new strings (ha ha), we go on to play a few more songs. We play lots of good music in the process—the fretboard action is great, and I manage to keep the thing relatively in tune. The music is a little too loud at first, but we adjust the volume a bit to fix that. First, I play harmony, and my teacher plays melody, and then after a while we switch parts. The harmony is a kind of structure to build the melody around, the melody gives definition to the music. The music has many dimensions to it, and different groups of notes change and flow, transmogrifying into new things as they move through time. Then I make a mistake, and we laugh as the whole thing falls down like a house of cards. We try again. The music floats, soars, and dives—it stops and starts again and shudders with a kind of life of its own. It becomes one big cohesive thing, a whole somehow bigger than its component parts, a kind of thing in itself. And ultimately it ends.

And when the music's over, I pack away the guitar in a black hard-shell case and say good-by. We tell a few more jokes and go our separate ways—until next week. . . .

ooooo

There won't be a "next week" for lessons, though I can't hold onto the past. I'll always remember the people, though, and what they stood for—their hopes, their dreams, and their fears. And they'll always be a part of me. Forever.

Just like my guitar.

PROCESS NOTE

In this essay, I wasn't just describing a guitar—I was describing much more. I was describing my feelings toward musicianship in general, and toward some of the most important people in my life—my guitar teachers. I think and feel very much along the lines of them, and I'll be in debt to them forever. This is a kind of tribute to them.

A LETTER
Published in *Elementary English*

Teachers
Perkins School
43 & College
Des Moines, Iowa 50311

Dear Teachers:

This morning, just as I woke up, I remembered something that I have thought about off and on for years. I remembered taking spelling tests when I was in grade school at Perkins. As I remembered this, I experienced some of the feelings that I experienced when I prepared for these tests, took them, and got them back. I experienced fear, anxiety and humiliation.

I remember the spelling books that we used. The color, size and shape of the books. How the words to be learned were grouped on the page. And I can remember how hard I tried to learn these words. Doing just what my teachers said. Printing the words over and over again. Spelling a word to myself with my eyes closed and then opening my eyes to check if I was right. Spelling the words for my parents before bed. Going over them again and again right before the test. I can also remember what it was like to take the spelling tests. A piece of wide margined paper and a pencil. The teacher saying the words aloud. Fear and anxiety. I struggled to remember how to spell each word. Erase. No matter how I spelled a word, it looked wrong. Fear. I crossed out, printed over, went back, tried again. "One minute left." Anxiety. When my spelling papers came back they were covered with red marks, blue marks, check marks, correction marks, and poor grades. It was so humiliating. And it was always the same. No matter how much I prepared or how hard I tried, I couldn't spell most of the words. And no matter how many spelling tests I took and failed, there were always more spelling tests to take and fail. We got a new book of spelling words at the beginning of each term.

At the time my teachers tried to help me. They told me what I had to do in order to improve: "Print the words over and over again. Spell a word to yourself with your eyes closed and then open your eyes to check if you are right. Spell the words for your parents before bed. Go over them again and again right before the test." My teachers also said that unless I learned to spell I would never get into high school, or out of high school, or into college, or out of college. And the last thing that they always told me was that I couldn't spell.

What I want to say to you teachers now is this. I couldn't spell very well then, and I still can't. I got into high school, and out of high school, and into college, and out of college. While my teachers at Perkins didn't teach me to spell, they did manage to have an effect on me. For example, this morning, twenty five years later, I woke up and remembered their spelling tests, and experienced the fear, anxiety and humiliation that I felt when I prepared for these tests, took them, and got them back. If you are still giving children these spelling tests, please stop doing so at once.

Sincerely yours,

Mark Levensky
Associate Professor
Department of Humanities
Massachusetts Institute of Technology
Cambridge, Massachusetts

DIALOGUE ON NUCLEAR ENERGY
Lucy O'Toole

One of the most controversial issues debated today is the matter of nuclear energy. I think the use of nuclear fission is extremely dangerous and shouldn't be experimented with without full knowledge and control. The following is a conversation between a pro-nuclear acquaintance and myself.

ME: I think "nukes" should be eliminated and shut down.

HIM: How do you expect us to fulfill our energy requirements? If today's trends continue, fossil fuel will almost all be used up in a few decades.

ME: Nuclear energy is not the only alternative source of energy we can use.

HIM: Well, we don't have much time to play around because after we run out of fuel it won't be easy to develop the technology to produce other energy sources.

ME: Although nuclear fission is a short-term solution, it creates long-term deadly effects. Radioactive wastes and fallout are lethal for thousands of years. Just because it's convenient now, we're condemning the world ecology for hundreds of generations. And they won't be able to do anything to remedy it.

157

HIM: Well, if nuclear energy is controlled and used responsibly, we won't have to worry. There are ways to safely dispose of nuclear wastes.

ME: Nuclear wastes cannot be disposed of! They remain active for thousands of years, and there's nowhere to put them. Radioactivity seeps through the storage containers, so there's no place where it can be hidden away and forgotten. Already there are some "hidden" canisters in such places as the San Andreas fault line, buried underground, under the ocean, and even in New Jersey. The earth is the only place we have, and there's nowhere to escape to.

HIM: There are plans to put wastes other places, such as on the moon or in outer space.

ME: That idea is not only ridiculous, but dangerous. If a rocket carrying those wastes crashed, it would be as catastrophic as a nuclear warhead. Other nuclear accidents are also a prevalent threat—events like Three Mile Island occur repeatedly. Just one mistake could create a nuclear disaster that would not devastate just the local environment, but a phenomenon like the China Syndrome, a complete meltdown through the earth's core, would possibly ruin the whole world. Some nuclear plants are even ingeniously located on fault lines, like Indian Point in upstate New York. Therefore if a major earthquake should occur, we're really in for it.

HIM: Nuclear reactors are very sturdy and strictly controlled, so a meltdown is highly unlikely. Three Mile Island was just an exceptional mistake, and even then nothing serious happened—everything was kept under control. Reactors are equipped with multiple backup systems so nothing like a complete meltdown would ever occur.

ME: Well, they have almost occurred numerous times. And what damage they did do should be evidence enough as to how dangerous this matter really is. It also shows that we don't know how to control it. Nuclear forces are tremendous, and what we've developed just isn't sufficient enough to control them. Just ask the people who live(d) at Three Mile Island.

HIM: Well, the whole situation was blown out of proportion.

ME: That's because citizens have a right to know and protest against apparent dangers. Many nuclear physicists are even against it. They realize how powerful and dangerous fission really is. There are other sources of energy, such as nuclear fusion, solar energy, geothermal energy, hydropower, wind power, or a combination of any of these.

I think nuclear fusion and solar energy are the best possibilities. Fusion is different from fission in that fission separates one large heavy atom into smaller radioactive elements with a consequential release of tremendous amounts of energy. Fusion, which occurs in the sun, combines two light elements, hydrogen and helium, and releases a tremendous amount of energy without any radioactivity.

HIM: Well, fusion is not yet possible and probably won't be for some time.

ME: True, but I do believe it's the answer. In the meantime we could probably use solar energy or other sources. The total power requirements of the U.S. could be met by using giant solar collectors spread out over about one-tenth the desert area of Arizona or New Mexico. Orbiting space collectors are also an idea.

HIM: Those ideas sound ridiculous. By the time we accomplished that, all our fuel would already be gone!

ME: A more feasible way to take advantage of solar power would be the use of rooftop solar collectors. The roof area of a typical house would be able to supply the occupants with their total energy needs.

HIM: What about buildings larger than a house—how will their needs be met?

ME: Solar panels in office buildings are already being used. Other potential sources of energy can be utilized more efficiently, such as wind power, which has been used for centuries, water power (hydropower) from waterfalls and tides, as well as geothermal heat from the earth's interior. We just have to learn how to operate the energy collectors to their full potential.

HIM: Yes, all these are possible, but economical use still needs to be developed.

ME: Well, we still have time. Meanwhile nuclear fission is obviously not the answer. We don't have the ability to control nuclear reactors and until we do, it's playing with fire—a highly volatile one. We only have one chance and one world. We have to understand what's going on before we attempt to use nuclear power.

HIM: Right now it's the only solution available to us. When we gain the technology we'll switch to other forms of energy production.

ME: Well it doesn't work that way. The mistakes we make now will never go away. We are responsible for the future of the Earth.

Note: This dialogue was written prior to the Chernobyl disaster.

FROM "PARTS OF SPEECH AND PUNCTUATION"
Gertrude Stein

What does a comma do.

I have refused them so often and left them out so much and did without them so continually that I have come finally to be indifferent to them. I do not now care whether you put them in or not but for a long time I felt very definitely about them and would have nothing to do with them.

As I say commas are servile and they have no life of their own, and their use is not a use, it is a way of replacing one's own interest and I do decidedly like to like my own interest my own interest in what I am doing. A comma by helping you along holding your coat for you and putting on your shoes keeps you from living your life as actively as you should lead it and to me for many years and I still do feel that way about it only now I do not pay as much attention to them, the use of them was positively degrading. Let me tell you what I feel and what I mean and what I felt and what I meant.

When I was writing those long sentences of The Making of Americans, verbs active present verbs with long dependent adverbial clauses became a passion with me. I have told you that I recognize verbs and adverbs aided by prepositions and conjunctions with pronouns as possessing the whole of the active life of writing.

Complications make eventually for simplicity and therefore I have always liked dependent adverbial clauses. I have liked dependent adverbial clauses because of their variety of dependence and independence. You can see how loving the intensity of complication of these things that commas would be degrading. Why if you want the pleasure of concentrating on the final simplicity of excessive complication would you want any artificial aid to bring about that simplicity. Do you see now why I feel about the comma as I did and as I do.

Think about anything you really like to do and you will see what I mean.

When it gets really difficult you want to disentangle rather than to cut the knot, at least so anybody feels who is working with any thread, so anybody feels who is working with any tool so anybody feels who is writing any sentence or reading it after it has been written. And what does a comma do, a comma does nothing but make easy a thing that if you like it enough is easy enough without the comma. A long complicated sentence should force itself upon you, make you know yourself knowing it and the comma, well at the most a comma is a poor period that it lets you stop and take a breath but if you want to take a breath you ought to know your-self that you want to take a breath. It is not like stopping altogether which is what a period does stopping altogether has something to do with going on, but taking a breath well you are always taking a breath and why emphasize one breath rather than another breath. Anyway that is the way I felt about it and I felt that about it very very strongly. And so I almost never used a comma. The longer, the more compli-cated the sentence the greater the number of the same kinds of words I had following one after another, the more the very many more I had of them the more I felt the passionate need of their taking care of themselves by themselves and not helping them, and thereby enfeebling them by putting in a comma.

So that is the way I felt punctuation in prose, in poetry it is a little different but more so and later I will go into that. But that is the way I felt about punctuation in prose.

ACCEPTANCE SPEECH
[*on being elected to the Bard Institute Advisory Board*]
Alan Devenish

As a recent Chinese fortune cookie assured me:

> The great pleasure in life is doing
> what people say you cannot do.

In taking office, as a freely elected official, I hope to live up to this ancient wis-dom, or at least to avoid *not* doing what people say I *can* do.

As for your part, my fellow Athenians, remember always how special you are, how your Institute is admired in the world and how it becomes you to bear adversity with honor, and how on the contrary, constant bitching and moaning will get you nowhere anyway.

Remember too, that the only thing to fear is reality itself, and the constructs we project upon it. Therefore, when times are hard and decisions are made that do not always agree with your construct, just think of something nice.

Finally, ask not what your Board can do for you but what you can do for your-self. Trust that our decisions are in your best interest or if not, bear them with the kind of dignity for which you are so justly renowned. Think twice before reaching for that phone (I'm probably not home anyway).

It is with these sentiments that I assume the mantle of office, reminding you only that I didn't ask for this job. Thank you.

MOMENTS OF BEING
Virginia Woolf

Often when I have been writing one of my so-called novels I have been baffled by this same problem: that is, how to describe what I call in my private shorthand—"non-being." Every day includes much more non-being than being. Yesterday for example, Tuesday the 18th of April, was [as] it happened a good day; above the average in "being." It was fine; I enjoyed writing these first pages; my head was relieved of the pressure of writing about Roger; I walked over Mount Misery and along the river; and save that the tide was out, the country, which I notice very closely always, was coloured and shaded as I like—there were the willows, I remem-ber, all plumy and soft green and purple against the blue. I also read Chaucer with pleasure; and began a book—the memoirs of Madame de la Fayette—which inter-ested me. These separate moments of being were however embedded in many more moments of non-being. I have already forgotten what Leonard and I talked about at lunch; and at tea; although it was a good day the goodness was embedded in a kind of nondescript cotton wool. This is always so. A great part of everyday is not lived consciously. One walks, eats, sees things, deals with what has to be done; the broken vacuum cleaner; ordering dinner; writing orders to Mabel; washing; cooking dinner; bookbinding. When it is a bad day the proportion of non-being is much larger. I had a slight temperature last week; almost the whole day was non-being. The real novelist can somehow convey both sorts of being. I think Jane Austen can; and Trollope; perhaps Thackeray and Dickens and Tolstoy. I have never been able to do both. I tried—in "Nights and Days"; and in "The Years." But I will leave the literary side alone for the moment.

As a child then, my days just as they do now, contained a large proportion of this cotton wool, this non-being. Week after week passed at St. Ives and nothing made any dint upon me. Then, for no reason that I know about, there was a sudden violent shock; something happened so violently that I have remembered it all my life. I will give a few instances. The first: I was fighting with Thoby on the lawn. We were pommelling each other with our fists. Just as I raised my fist to hit him, I felt, why hurt another person? I dropped my hand instantly, and stood there, and let him beat me. I remember the feeling. It was a feeling of hopeless sadness. It was as if I became aware of something terrible; and of my own powerlessness. I slunk off alone, feeling horribly depressed. The second instance was also in the garden at St. Ives. I was looking at the flower bed by the front door; "That is the whole," I said. I was looking at a plant with a spread of leaves; and it seemed suddenly plain that the flower itself was a part of the earth; that a ring enclosed what was the flower; and that was the real flower; part earth; part flower. It was a thought I put away as being likely to be very useful to me later. The third case was also at St. Ives. Some people called Valpy had been staying at St. Ives, and had left. We were waiting at dinner one night, when somehow I overheard my father or my mother say that Mr. Valpy had killed himself. The next thing I remember is being in the garden at night and walking on the path by the apple tree. It seemed to me that the apple tree was connected with the horror of Mr. Valpy's suicide. I could not pass it. I stood there looking at the grey-green creases of the bark—it was a moonlit night—in a trance of horror. I seemed to be dragged down, hopelessly, into some pit of absolute despair from which I could not escape. My body seemed paralysed.

These are three instances of exceptional moments. I often tell them over, or rather they come to the surface unexpectedly. But now that for the first time I have written them down, I realise something that I have never realised before. Two of these moments ended in a state of despair. The other ended, on the contrary, in a state of satisfaction. When I said about the flower "That is the whole," I felt that I had made a discovery. I felt that I had put away in my mind something that I should go back to turn over and explore. It strikes me now that this was a profound difference. It was the difference in the first place between despair and satisfaction. This difference I think arose from the fact that I was quite unable to deal with the pain of discovering that people hurt each other; that a man I had seen had killed himself. The sense of horror held me powerless. But in the case of the flower I found a reason; and was thus able to deal with the sensation. I was not powerless, I was conscious— if only at a distance—that I should in time explain it. I do not know if I was older when I saw the flower than I was when I had the other two experiences. I only know that many of these exceptional moments brought with them a peculiar horror and a physical collapse; they seemed dominant; myself passive. This suggests that as one gets older one has a greater power through reason to provide an explanation; and that this explanation blunts the sledge-hammer force of the blow. I think this is true, because though I still have the peculiarity that I receive those sudden shocks, they are now always welcome; after the first surprise, I always feel instantly that they are particularly valuable. And so I go on to suppose that the shock-receiving capacity is what makes me a writer. I hazard the explanation that a shock is at once in my case followed by the desire to explain it. I feel that I have had a blow; but it is not, as I thought as a child, simply a blow from an enemy hidden behind the cotton wool of daily life; it is or will become a revelation of some order; it is a token of some real thing behind appearances; and I make it real by putting it into words. It is only by putting it into words that I make it whole; this wholeness means that it has lost its power to hurt me; it gives me, perhaps because by doing so I take away the pain, a great delight to put the severed parts together. Perhaps this is the strongest pleasure known to me. It is the rapture I get when in writing I seem to be discovering what belongs to what; making a scene come right; making a character come together. From this I reach what I might call a philosophy; at any rate it is a constant idea of mine; that behind the cotton wool is hidden a pattern; that we—I mean all human beings— are connected with this; that the whole world is a work of art. "Hamlet" or a Beethoven quartet is the truth about this vast mass that we call the world. But there is no Shakespeare, there is no Beethoven; certainly and emphatically there is no God; we are the words; we are the music; we are the thing itself. And I see this when I have a shock.

AUTOBIOGRAPHY
Nazim Hakmit

I was born in 1902
I never once went back to my birthplace

I don't like to turn back
at three I served as a pasha's grandson in Aleppo
at nineteen as a student at Moscow Communist University
at forty-nine I was back in Moscow as a guest of the Tcheka Party
and I've been a poet since I was fourteen
some people know all about plants some about fish
                              I know separation
some people know the names of the stars by heart
                              I recite absences

I've slept in prisons and in grand hotels
I've known hunger even a hunger strike and there's almost no food
    I haven't tasted
at thirty they wanted to hang me
at forty-eight to give me the Peace Medal
                         which they did

at thirty-six I covered four square meters of concrete in half a year
at fifty-nine I flew from Prague to Havana in eighteen hours
I never saw Lenin I stood watch at his coffin in '24
in '61 the tomb that I visit is his books
they tried to tear me away from my party
                         it didn't work
nor was I crushed under falling idols
in '51 I sailed with a young friend into the teeth of death
in '52 I spent four months flat on my back with a broken heart
    waiting for death
I was jealous of the women I loved
I didn't envy Charlie Chaplin one bit
I deceived my women
I never talked behind my friends' backs
I drank but not every day
I earned my bread money honestly what happiness
out of embarrassment for another I lied
I lied so as not to hurt someone else
    but I also lied for no reason at all
I've ridden in trains planes and cars
most people don't get the chance
I went to the opera
    most people can't go they haven't even heard of the opera
and since '21 haven't been to the places that most people visit
    mosques churches temples synagogues sorcerers
    but I've had my coffee grounds read
my writings are published in thirty forty languages
    in my Turkey in my Turkish they're banned
cancer hasn't caught up with me yet
and nothing says that it has to
I'll never be a prime minister or anything like that
and I'm not interested in such a life
nor did I go to war

163

or burrow in bomb shelters in the bottom of the night
and I never had to take to the roads under diving planes
but I fell in love at close to sixty
in short comrades
even if today in Berlin I'm *croaking* of grief
     I can say that I've lived like a human being
and who knows
    how much longer I'll live
      what else will happen to me.

UNIT
8

Revising

If you did the preceding units, you've already done a lot of revising. In Unit 1 you did quick revising (but nevertheless major revising) by simply cutting heavily to make a collage. In Units 2 and 3 (interview and loop writing) you were faced with a mass of disorganized, rough, exploratory material from which to produce a coherent draft: you had to go through and choose, discard, shape, and rewrite. *All* the activity in Unit 7 was revising: a series of quick transformations of parts of your private writing to try out genres, and then a sustained transformation and rewriting as you worked on your main piece of public writing. (Even your narrative in Unit 5 probably involved a kind of revision of your descriptive writing from Unit 4.)

Thus we've already asked for lots of revising—just treating it for what it is, namely, an inherent part of the whole writing process. But at some point it's worth making revising the main focus of a whole unit's work. (Your teacher may decide to use this unit earlier or later in the sequence.) In this unit the whole assignment is to work on revising something you've written earlier.

Many people believe that good writers write something and send it off to a publisher who prints it exactly as it's written. When we read something published, we see only the words in front of us; we don't usually have any way of knowing what happened before the author wrote the version we see: what it first looked like and what changes the author made. A number of writers though have commented on their own writing processes, how often they need to revise, and what a struggle revision can be. Here are two writers talking about revision:

I am a witness to the lateness of my own vocation, the hesitations and terrors that still haunt all my beginnings, the painful slowness with which I proceed through a minimum of four drafts in both fiction and nonfiction.

—Francine du Plessix Gray

I had a difficult time revising this piece. I was never sure if my ideas made sense. I wasn't sure of what I really wanted to say. My feedback groups helped a lot by offering opinions on different directions my original paper seemed to be taking. They helped me to see where my thoughts got hidden somewhere in the words I used. After a lot of rethinking and reorganizing (and also with the help of a class-mate's "literary analysis" on my paper), I found my way through my thoughts and realized where my paper should go. The revision process was long and diffi-cult, but I feel it did a lot of good.

—Stephanie Curcio (student, process writing)

Our goals in this unit are to help you understand better the nature of revising and its importance for good writing, and most of all to be better at doing it. We will show you a number of useful revision strategies.

You will have noticed the note of pain and struggle in the preceding quotations, and you may have painful revising memories yourself. There's no way to make revising easy or fun: inherently it involves going over work again and again, evaluating, criticizing, and throwing away what sometimes seems like part of yourself. ("Having your nose rubbed in your own mess" is how some people think of it.)

Nevertheless we hope to counteract the tendency to be too grim or tense about revising and show you that, like generating, it benefits from a spirit of playfulness—a spirit that can take away some of the pain.

THREE LEVELS OF REVISING

Many students equate revision with "correcting mechanics" or copyediting; experienced writers never confuse the two. For them, revision means enter-ing into a conversation with their previous thoughts. They match what they have already written against what they *now* wish to say and create out of the two a new piece which suits their present purpose. What this implies is that revision never stops. But of course writers need to finish things for particular deadlines, and so they revise what they have and submit it—usually with the recognition that if they submitted it later, they'd make additional changes.

Since this is how revision actually works, no one can say exactly what revising is. Probably the best definition is this: revising is whatever a writer does to change a piece of writing for a particular reader or readers—whoever they may be (e.g., friends, colleagues, an editor at a publishing house, the general reading public of a particular publication, a teacher, or even oneself). But to help us talk about revision, we're going to distinguish three levels:

1. Reseeing/rethinking; changing *what* a piece says or its "bones"

2. Reworking, reshaping; changing *how* a piece says it or changing its "muscles"

3. Copyediting or proofreading for mechanics and usage; checking for deviations from standard conventions or changing the writing's "skin"

1.   Reseeing, rethinking, or changing the bones. You reread a piece and realize it doesn't say what you want it to say: you see you were wrong, you've now changed your mind (probably *because* you wrote out your earlier ideas), you need more, you left something out, you remembered something wrong (or didn't remember it at all), or you didn't understand the full implications of what you were saying. The process of writing and rereading *changes* you (changes *you*). At its most extreme, this level of revising may mean that you crumple up what you've written and aim it toward the trash basket: the cartoon image of a writer at a typewriter surrounded by wads of discarded paper is not far from the truth. Most writers feel they have to discard lots before they come up with something they can use.

2.   Reworking, reshaping, or changing the muscles. This second level of revising means that you're satisfied with *what* you are saying (or trying to say), but not with *how* you've said it. Working on "how" tends to mean thinking about readers: thinking about how your thoughts will be read or understood by people other than yourself. Thus feedback from readers is particularly useful for this level of revising. One of the most common kinds of reworking is to improve clarity. Perhaps you realize you need to change the order you present things in; or you need an introduction, conclusion, and some transitions; or you've implied ideas or suggested attitudes that you don't want there.* Most common of all, you simply need to *leave out* parts that may be okay in themselves (or even precious to you) but that don't quite belong in *this* piece of writing—having finally figured out what this piece of writing is really saying. These passages clog your piece and will distract or tire readers. (You may not believe we left out a lot of the first draft of this book, but we did.)

3.   Copyediting or proofreading. This third level of revising is usually what you do right before you hand something in. At its simplest, it means finding typographical errors. At a level slightly above that, it means fixing sentence

---

*In our reworking level of revising of this text, we found ourselves giving a good deal of attention to the subtitles scattered throughout the units: adding some and clarifying many. Having finally figured out what *we* were trying to say—where we were going—we were now trying to improve the road signs *others* would try to follow.

PROCESS BOX

Mid afternoon. I see Hugh as I'm walking back from Ludlow. I'm working on my memo about the goals of the Bard writing program. Rained *hard* all morning and suddenly now it's steamy bright sun with no trace of cloud in the sky.

We're standing in the middle of the path because I decided on the spot to ask him for feedback on the draft of my memo. I stand there with my little canvas briefcase and umbrella between my legs and read my draft outloud to him.

He nods his head at certain points and I nod inwardly: yes, he likes these places; they are strong. But when he speaks I learn they are places he *doesn't* like. He returns to an objection he'd voiced last week when I'd been talking about goals in our meeting. (An objection to my being too pushy and dogmatic in stating goals—trying to claim too much.)

After he's spoken, I know my response immediately. I'm polite, I don't argue, but I know clearly that I want to do it *my* way. I'm not threatened but I'm not in the slightest willing to back down and do it the way he suggests.

Right afterwards I discovered I was missing a crucial page of an earlier draft with a bit I wanted to use. It must be lying in a wastepaper

structure and checking spelling, punctuation, subject-verb agreement, and other features of usage.

Our language here about revising may seem to imply that you are working on an essay rather than a descriptive piece or a story. But descriptions and narrations are fine to use for revising work—often they allow you to be a bit more playful. We trust the translation will be clear throughout: Where we talk about changing what you "say," you would change what a story or description is "about." Where we talk about changing "how you say it," you would change "how you treat" the elements of the description or story.

A writer needs to do all three kinds of revising and ideally in the order we've described them. After all, there's no point in fixing the spelling of a word if you're going to cut it, and no point struggling to rework the presentation of an idea till you know you're going to keep it. But of course writing activities don't always stay in a neat order. Sometimes, while checking the spelling of a word, you realize you need to change the structure of the whole piece. Sometimes it's not until you rework the presentation of an idea that you realize that it needs to be cut. And you *can* check spelling during early stages if you wish, but most people find that it interrupts their thinking and generating.

basket on the third floor of Ludlow. I go back, scared I might have lost it. (I am still sometimes hit by feeling that if I lose a piece of writing I've worked on I'll never be able to create it again—it will be a permanent loss of something precious.)

I go back and find it, and while I'm there at my desk, I decide to work on the piece a bit more. With some quick cleaning up I can xerox a few copies and get more feedback—for my session with Hugh made me feel more settled in my mind as to how I wanted it.

I start working—cleaning up and retyping messy bits—and suddenly I realize I need to back down from my position of stubbornness. Chagrined to realize not just that I need to but *want* to. Just what Hugh suggested. For now in reading my memo I can notice a kind of tightness or restrictedness or off-balance in my writing which stemmed from my attempts in the memo to be stubborn and pushy and claim so much. For some reason, I *had* a need to make that claim; for some reason I don't need to make that claim now—and can see it's better not to.

In a nutshell. I got feedback from Hugh; I was forced to see my words through his eyes; I felt secure in rejecting that way of seeing my words; but then in going back to the text with my own eyes, I could no longer see it as I had seen it.

PETER ELBOW 8/84

FIRST-LEVEL REVISING:
GROUP WORK AND RESEEING, RETHINKING, AND CHANGING THE BONES

Choose a piece of your writing that you want to revise at all three levels. It probably makes most sense to pick something that you feel dissatisfied with so that you know you won't mind doing extensive work on it.

Share it with your group and use them to help you explore some possible major revisions: ways in which you might change your mind or disagree with your earlier draft or reach different conclusions—or discover aspects of your subject which you have neglected or have mentioned without developing. Perhaps it's a descriptive piece or story, and you want to change the whole approach. Here are two suggestions to guide that group work:

1. When you've finished reading your piece (and before oral discussion), allow a few minutes for freewriting. You can write down any additional thoughts you have on your topic or story, any doubts you now have about what you've written—anything at all about what the piece says. Those who have been listening to you should simply pretend that they've been assigned your subject and write whatever they wish about it. At the end of

this freewriting period, each group member can read what he's written. All this can serve as starters for discussion, but since this is your paper, you should guide the discussion and follow-up on what is particularly interesting to you. (The others will have this same chance to be in charge when they read their papers.) You may want to ask your group members to give you their copy of what they've written so that you can reread it at your leisure.

2. Another way to approach this level of revision is to ask each group member (including yourself) to pick out the sentences that most interest him and freewrite about why they are so interesting, what he thinks the sentences mean, and so forth. For this exercise you'll have to read your paper twice to your group—but reading twice is always a good idea. (It's best *not* to provide copies for your group since you want them to focus on your ideas, not on specific wordings.) While doing this, it isn't necessary or even advisable for any of you to try to stick to what your main idea is. Remember, you're trying to explore all aspects of a topic no matter how unrelated they might seem at first.

Assignment for First-Level Revising

On the basis of your group's discussion, decide what you *now* want to say; then rewrite your paper. Don't be surprised if you find yourself doing more revising than you expected. You may even discard the ideas you started to revise with. That's part of what should happen.

If you find you don't want to change what you've said or what the story deals with, do some experimenting anyway. Play with your ideas or story. Revision is usually done in a spirit of clenched teeth and duty, but it can be done in a spirit of play and fooling around. For example, you could pick a paragraph (or even a sentence or image) and build a whole new essay or story around it. In other words, deliberately try to write something different even if you're satisfied with what your original piece says. It helps to start with a fresh sheet of paper to free you from the original way you developed your ideas.

If you give it half a chance, you can let yourself get caught up in this kind of play. The words you produce will undoubtedly create their own complex of ideas which in turn will lead to other words, sentences, and para-graphs. Soon you'll discover that your mind-set is quite different from when you were writing the original version. You'll no longer be striving to write something different from the original version; you'll be working toward ful-filling some new goal or purpose, one that has grown out of the writing itself.

Once you've made your revision, you can decide whether you want to use it or your original for the remainder of the work in this unit. Remember: revisions aren't necessarily better—they're different. Once you understand this, you'll be willing to take risks as you revise: changing everything almost totally, exploring something which seems at first silly or trivial to you, trying new approaches, developing some ideas that you don't even agree with, and so forth. You can throw it all away if you want to. Almost invariably, though, you discover something substantial that you like—something that you'll want to incorporate into your original. Whatever happens, there's no reason to use a revision just because it's a revision. It's possible, of course, that you'll now decide you've got two pieces you want to finish up.

SECOND-LEVEL REVISING: GROUP WORK AND REWORKING, RESHAPING, AND CHANGING THE MUSCLES

When you've decided which version of your essay to use, you're ready to practice the second level of revision—reworking. For this prepare a good, legible copy of the version you've selected and write or type it with very wide left- or right-hand margins—say about three inches. Make copies for your group. Before going to class, write a brief paragraph just for yourself which states briefly your purpose for writing the paper and the reasons why you chose to accomplish your purpose in the way you did. Then, on your copy of the essay, write in the margin some notes on each paragraph. These notes should include a brief *summary* of what the paragraph says and a brief statement of its *purpose* and how it fits in where it is. Purposes can include introducing, restating, giving examples, setting a scene, building suspense, giving your opinion(s), describing, moving to another aspect of your paper, concluding, and so forth. (See *Sharing and Responding* Section IIIC, "Descriptive Outline," for more about this powerful activity.)

Here's what one student writer wrote as the purpose of a paper she planned to work more on in the way we've just described:

> I wanted to make readers see the disco scene, so I described it. But I also wanted to show how silly it is—poke fun at the people in it.

And here are the marginal comments she wrote about the first few paragraphs of her essay (you'll notice that she had already begun to think of possible changes):

Outside, the crowd waits. Guys clad in their outermost layer of skins, their pants, are nervously looking for their "Id's" within their wallets. Of course they make sure every girl sees the big wad of bills. What they don't know is that there is always a girl in the crowd who decides to light a cigarette and upon doing this sees that the big wad of bills is in fact one dollar bills. News travels fast and soon everyone is laughing at the guys. Then there are the young enticing girls. They look about twenty with their make-up caked upon their faces (you'd need a Brillo pad to scrub it all off),

I'm introducing here, setting the scene, describing the people outside the disco.

I'm also trying to set the tone—being sarcastic. I'd like readers to be thinking: what's going to happen here?

171

skin-tight Spandex and heels. These "women" are in actuality fourteen or fifteen years old; what gives them away is the way they smoke. They simply don't inhale. The drag of smoke enters and exits in the same dense cloud; they need to fan the air with their hands so as not to die of suffocation.

The tension is building, and it seems to hang in the air like a low-lying cloud. The people are moving closer and closer to the entrance as if stalking prey. The doors open and everyone pushes in. Suddenly a pink Cadillac screeches to a halt and the driver gets out. The multitude of people stop! It's as if a spell were cast upon them. "It's him!" a young girl cries.

Showing what happens right before the doors open, maybe try to get suspense going. I also want to introduce Mr. Big—be sarcastic about him too.

He is tall, dark, and rich! He is wearing a white suit (polyester of course) with a black "silk" shirt. His shirt was, of course, opened to his navel displaying the jewelry. His jewelry consisted of three rope chains, each varying in length and width, and the fourth was an inch-thick rope chain exposing the Italian phallic symbol, the horn. The crowd, still mystified, parted like the Red Sea, allowing Mr. Big to enter the disco. The two-ton bouncers who were once mountains of malice became little pups when greeting him. "Can I help you, Mr. Big?" "Your table is waiting for you, Mr. Big." "You look very nice today, Mr. Big," and so on.

Describes and makes fun of Mr. Big. Moves the story ahead a bit. Shows how people react to him and how phony everything is.

Once that awesome happening settled and passed, the crowd went back to pushing and shoving through the doors. It's really ridiculous to see people, who are supposed to be grown-ups, react like little children when they see a circus for the first time. If they only realized that the circus they're watching (Mr. Big) gets his ears boxed by his mother if he comes home too late.

Gives my opinion about all this, although I'm not sure why I put it here—maybe because I'm now going to move the scene inside.

Once inside, the eardrums shatter like a drinking glass does when a high-pitched voice is applied to it. This calamity happens because of the booming music which seems to vibrate the entire building. Ah, there's Mr. Big and his harem. All the women flock around him as if he were a mirror. He'll make his grand entrance on the dance floor later on.

Here I'm describing the scene inside, including Mr. Big. I'm making fun of the women who hang around him. I want to describe everything step by step as someone would see it when they went in.

Upon entering, the bar is to the person's left, and a few steps below is the dance floor. By the way, the steps are notorious killers since many, under the influence of alcohol, forget they exist. On the other side there is the seating area consisting of dozens of tables and

This is more description of the inside. The thing about the steps is something I always think about

black velvety, cushiony, recliner-type chairs. They are the type of chairs you lose yourself in.

when I look down at the dance floor because I fell on them once. Maybe this should all be added to the paragraph before since it's all description.

Ask your group members to write the same kind of margin notes on their copies of your essay. Also ask them to jot down a few words specifying any emotional reaction they may have to each paragraph: are they curious, bored, annoyed, offended, excited, informed, hostile or so forth, and can they pinpoint the words or phrases that cause their reaction? They can do all this at home or in class. In class you can get your paper back and get clarification of whatever you don't understand. But even if this work is done at home, your teacher will probably give you some time in class to share and get clarification.

Assignment for Second-Level Revising

Using the feedback you've gotten, decide what changes, if any, you want to make. Most of your changes will probably be aimed at making your meaning clearer. This can include restructuring your essay (reworking sentences and paragraphs, reordering them, adding transitions, providing or reworking introductions and conclusions, adding background information, and so forth), rewriting sentences or phrases to alter their emotional impact or clarify their meaning, adding sentences and phrases to emphasize important points or provide examples and illustrations, and replacing problem words. If, while doing this, you find yourself moving back to the first level of revision (altering *what* you say), don't be surprised. We told you that the three levels of revision cannot be fully compartmentalized. You need to keep in mind too that form and content are inextricably linked; changing *how* something is said almost always affects *what* is said.

One final note about this level of revising. Your paper is yours and you need to trust your own instincts about how you say something. We think that, before ideas get into words, there is always an impulse toward meaning. Once we put an idea into words, we test it against that original impulse—and when the words and the impulse match, we know it—we know that we've got the idea right for ourselves. Sometimes this felt sense of "rightness" comes immediately—sometimes we have to rewrite several times before we feel it—and sometimes we just give up and recognize that, for the moment, we can't achieve it. Our point is that only you know exactly when you've said what you want to say.

In the readings at the end of the unit, we have included drafts and revisions of two essays. As you read them, you may want to jot down a list of the changes each author makes. For another example of revising, compare

PROCESS BOX

I got the idea for the topic for this piece from something my brother said the last time I saw him. When I first wrote this piece on my brother, I truly loved the way the experience just rolled off my tongue. Yet I knew I needed to work on the grammar. When I read it to the small group in class, I realized that I didn't want to really share this experience with others. But the group had no criticism of my paper at all; they just loved it which really wasn't helpful.

So my next step was I went to the Writing Center and made an appointment with a tutor. She told me that I needed to continue the psychoanalysis of the main character and be more definite in my writing. She also suggested to change the order of the paper. Start with setting the scene of the barbecue and then lower the boom on my brother's dropping out of medical school.

So I revised the paper then making it more descriptive and analyzing the character. At this point I really disliked the whole paper. I believe this is because I enjoyed writing the paper from the point of view of a child rather than an adult. I thought for quite a long time after writing this paper about how to improve it, but I was unable to do so.

Finally after making many appointments at the Writing Center, I truly became disgusted with the paper. The appointments were canceled because of the weather, but at that point I didn't care anymore because I no longer wanted to improve a paper that in the beginning I really loved.

A STUDENT

Peter Elbow's Perl writing (Unit 6, "Readings") and his revision of it in the mini-unit "Writing with a Word Processor."

When you've finished this second level of revision, type up a final, clean copy of your paper—double or even triple spaced. It should be all ready to submit to your teacher. Make at least two copies of this final version. It is these copies which you will use for copyediting and proofreading, the final level of revision. For suggestions on this final, third level of revision, see Mini-unit K.

PROCESS JOURNAL QUESTIONS

You've probably done *some* process writing in previous units about the revising you did in those units. But since we haven't until now made revising the focus of a unit, it's important to try to learn as much as you can about what happens for you in this slippery process. Try to re-create and describe as much as you can of what you did in all the revising activities of this unit: feelings, thoughts, reactions, things you can learn. If you need help, these prompts may be of use:

- Simply gather as many memories and reactions as you can under the three stages:
  —first-level revising of "bones" or *what* you said
  —second-level revising of "muscles" or *how* you said it
  —third-level "skin-deep" copyediting or proofreading.

- After you did first-level revising, which version did you pick to work on: your new one or the original? Why?

- Freewrite about your own revision processes in the past and about how you feel about revision. Do you revise a great deal? If so, why? What writings of your own are you most reluctant to revise? Why? When you revise, which level do you most tend to work at?

- At what points in your writing do you tend to stop and fix things? Is it frequent? What triggers you to stop the flow of words and go back to change something?

- Freewrite about how you feel about the quality of your spoken and written English. What aspects of "correctness" are most difficult for you? How have you coped with the difficulty? What do you think you could do? In general how do you feel your language measures up in this area?

- Freewrite about how you feel about the value of "correctness" in language. If you were in charge of language, what changes would you make in the system? Do you think language standards should be looser? stricter?

RUMINATIONS AND THEORY

A. Putting Revision in Perspective

B. Revising and Grammar

A. Putting Revision in Perspective

Resources for Revising

The most powerful resources for good revision are time and new eyes. Obviously the best source of new eyes is other people. But if you let time go by, *you've* changed since you did your draft, and so in a sense your eyes are different. You don't see things the same way you did. This is why it's so important to try to put something aside for a while and do your serious revising after several weeks have passed. This is why we've arranged this text so that you revise something a week or more after you first explored and wrote it.

Let's say you've written a draft of a paper opposing a rise in the drinking age. If nothing occurs in your life which relates to this issue, you probably won't want to revise much what your first draft says. However, if you do research and, as a result, acquire more knowledge about the relation between drinking and auto fatalities, you may decide you want to revise your earlier drafts. Or if you or a friend of yours is involved in an accident caused by a young drinker, you're likely to change your attitudes. Even if your opinion doesn't change, it will be affected. You'll revise because you think differently on the issue. Perhaps others will point out to you some fallacies or weaknesses in your arguments, providing a new light for you to see by. Or time may change your opinion, since eventually you'll be old enough to drink. What you write, conditioned by these new perceptions, may not necessarily be better than your earlier draft—but it will be different.

Revision for the sake of revision can be a deadening chore. That's why we ask you to practice first-level revision as a game. "What would I say *if* I really saw things differently?" (Of course, you don't need the game if you discover you actually do see your subject differently.) Playing the game may lead you to new insights about your subject which you'll want to incorporate into what you're writing.

We know that much revision in the working world is probably reworking, not reseeing. If your boss tells you to write a report on a meeting of a special planning group, you can hardly revise it into suggestions for improving company management even if that's what you'd rather write. Still, if you can learn that you need not slavishly stick to what you've already written, you can free yourself to use first attempts as seeds rather than constraints. There are always deadlines, of course, and so at some point we have to stop new thinking about our subject and focus instead on refining what we've already said. We think that most students, however, get to this second step too fast; they don't even recognize the existence of a prior step. This is why, in this unit, we require you to do first-level revision even if you *are* satisfied with what you've already said.

We can't give you a handy bag of tools for revising, because your piece is unique. To revise it—if you need to—requires hard work: grunting and sweating, trial and error, putting aside and coming back, feedback from yourself, from others, from teachers, research, and so forth. There's no formula, no sure-fire series of steps that guarantees success. And finally only you know when you've said what you intended to say. Sometimes that happens immediately, sometimes it happens only after disciplining yourself to stick to it long after you'd like to chuck the whole thing.

Revising Isn't Everything

Almost everything we write needs revision of some kind, but often not much. Perhaps you knew ahead of time exactly what you needed to say and got it more or less right. Or you've written a story or description, and you know exactly what it should contain (especially if you are describing real events): you won't need any first-level revision, only work on details, clarifying, and perhaps structure. *Or*—and don't forget this—the piece is rough but not *important* enough to revise: better to start over or even to write something entirely different.

Sometimes revising can squeeze the life out of language. Something in our original impulse to communicate injects a particular and unique energy into the words we use. Revising can drive us farther and farther from that impulse and deaden what we write.

The message in all this is that revising *is* important, but you don't have to revise everything (and revising doesn't have to be a quest for perfection). Otherwise writing is too much of a chore. Choose pieces that are good or that you love; learn to let other pieces go altogether. Learn to do superficial revising when you just want to make something presentable and aren't trying to make it the greatest thing you've ever written. Some people say we learn most by revising. Perhaps. But we may learn just as much by writing and writing and writing.

Another important lesson: deep revision of *what* you say does not necessarily produce a better piece of writing. It produces a different piece of writing which you or your reader may or may not like better.

And Yet. . . .

Despite what we've said about the value of *not* revising, we end up having to say that revision is almost always necessary to produce a good piece of writing. We've revised the units of this textbook over and over: some parts of it have been changed very little from the first time we wrote them, but most have changed a lot, and some are unrecognizable. We've added much and discarded almost as much. We've struggled with ways of saying things and even more with what is necessary to say at all. And through all this revising, we've tried to keep the language alive.

Ultimately there are rewards for this hard work: the feeling that we've gotten something the way we wanted it, the feeling that by working so hard we've actually realized for the first time the fullness of some idea lurking just below words. The reward is that sense of knowing, finally and for certain, that we actually do know what we want to say.

B. *Revising and Grammar*

Many students think that learning to write means learning grammar (and it's not just students who think this way). When we ask students at the beginning of a semester what they expect from our course, many say they expect to be taught grammar. They rarely understand that "grammar mistakes" (deviations from standard usage such as subject-verb agreement, spelling, tense forms, and so forth) do not usually lead to a distortion of meaning though, of course, they can. But deviations from standard usage can be quite *distracting* for many readers. Each of us can probably tolerate a different level of deviation. Some people can read a whole paper in which the final *s* is missing from present-tense verbs and not react. Others will react to even one missing *s*.

The real problem with errors in usage is that they force the reader into giving his attention to the words instead of the meaning. If a reader is continually distracted in this way, be begins to believe that the author's meaning is unclear, the organization is poor, or the quality of thinking is mediocre. Or he'll think that the writer is not very committed to the ideas she's presenting—and if that's the case, why should he as a reader give them much attention?

There is a continuing debate in scholarly and pedagogical journals about whether to teach grammar and usage in writing courses. Here is our position:

- Instruction in grammar cannot serve as a substitute for instruction in writing.

- What students learn from doing grammar exercises rarely transfers to their writing.

- Elimination of certain usage errors (particularly the dropping of *s*—as in *she see*—and the use of nonstandard verb forms—*she done it*) is a slow process. We cannot expect students to alter very quickly something so basic to their natural language.

- Instruction in standard usage should focus on the errors students actually make and the contexts in which they make them.

- Students should be forced to articulate for themselves the reasons why they use nonstandard forms. Only in this way can they begin to build different rules into their personal language.

- Students should be required to submit final copies of their revised pieces that are free from errors in typing and usage. We believe in giving students some help in achieving this, but what's most important is making them realize that they have to find whatever help they need. Students who are poor spellers, for instance, may always have to find someone who is willing to check their papers for all misspelled words. Spelling checkers on computers are a godsend for such students. It may well be that computers will soon be supplied with easy programs for checking other aspects of usage. (Remember, however, that a checker cannot tell you that "pair" should be "pear.") In any event, we believe students must find ways to write Standard English whenever they want or need to. This does not mean we consider Standard English superior to other varieties; in fact, we encourage students to hold on to their native dialects, whatever they may be. Such dialects give language life. But we also want students to be proficient in Standard English.

READINGS

THE MALE BASHING STEREOTYPE—EARLY DRAFT
Kimberly Graham

Why did we, as a society, need to create a term such as "male bashing"? What is it? Who is guilty of it?

Many women are now feeling dissatisfied with aspects of their lives that they once accepted. They want to be more than housewives. Some want to go back to school in the pursuit of an education and a better job. Many that are in the work force want more power and prestige. Some of these women believe that men are to blame for their dissatisfaction; it was men, after all, that controlled most parts of their lives. They married men and became housewives. Most of their bosses are men. Women needing a scapegoat? Women are very demanding; they like to intimidate men, and if they do not get what they want, they do not see a future in their relationship with him. To vent their frustrations they resort to male bashing. They blame men for everything. If their car wasn't fixed right, it was because the mechanic is a man. When a crime is committed against a woman, they blame all men. If a female co-worker was sexually harassed by her boss, they assume all male bosses would do the same thing. Male bashing is an overgrown tendency to blame men for every dissatisfaction and to assume all men are alike. It's too bad that we had to come up with this term because it is dangerous and self-destructive.

The media and certain medical circles played a big part in the creation of the term "male bashing." Almost every week on either *The Oprah Winfrey Show* or *Donahue*, there is one segment on the state of male-female relationships. Most of the segments include panelists who have just written a "revolutionary" new book, or a group of women (or men) talking about their problems. Inevitably one show turns into a male bash event because of either a panelist's views or the comments from a participant in the studio audience. One *O.W.S* was originally about why women marry men that are less financially successful or intelligent than they are. The view at the end of the show turned out to be that women were sick of the games men usually play and they wanted someone they had control over. Men they were used to going out with were egotistical, selfish, cruel, stupid, immature, afraid of commitment, and the list continued. Phil Donahue presented one panel of all men that had formed a "men's club," and the women in the audience felt that they were weak and immature for wanting to be with each other instead of women. There has also been a rapid flow of books written by psychologists and therapists on the state of the sexes. *Men That Hate Women and the Women Who Love Them* was a best seller in hardcover and paperback. *Women That Men Love, Women That Men Leave* is a fairly recent one describing types of women and why men leave them. Books like these give male bashers fuel for their arguments because, as the titles suggest, they put men in a bad light.

One of the most controversial books of late is Shere Hite's new one titled: *Women and Love: A Cultural Revolution in Progress*. It presents the views of 4500 women and Hite's conclusions from those views. Critics of the book called it inaccurate and false and also think Hite is guilty of male bashing. She based her report on findings from only 4500 women when the number should have been much larger. She assumed that the views of the participating women were also those of the rest of the female population. For instance, she has concluded that about ninety-three percent of all women are unhappy with their current relationships and about seventy percent are unfaithful but believe in monogamy. It's inaccurate to judge for the many with data from only the few. The book is presented as a testament to the unhappiness of women because of men, and it should be presented more objectively.

The first draft ended here. Following, in boldface type, are questions the writer's group members asked and the writer's responses to them.

Do women have a reason to bash and holler? I have to admit—I have met some stupid, immature, egotistical men. But I don't think that all men are alike and I haven't blamed all my frustrations on them. Why do some women resort to mental violence? The media has provided many groupings for men and women. There are the "men afraid of commitment," "the older men only interested in younger women," "the men obsessed with getting ahead in their careers," and "all men in their twenties."

Many women tend to find one fault in a man and turn it into a basis for criticism of all men who have the same fault. Then they find a media grouping and conclude that all men are alike. There are also slots for women: "tired housewives and mothers not wanting sex," "women only interested in having a career," "women living off the men who marry them," and "all women in their forties." If we stopped creating these groupings maybe there would not be bashing against anybody because people would be judged as individuals.

Male bashing is dangerous because it gives men the idea that all women are out to get them. That's not true. Yes, some are, but not all of us are violent militant feminists. It gives society the impression that feminism is to blame and that things were fine before it started. Women guilty of male bashing also put down the concept of feminism. They are fighting for equality, yet they are discriminating against all men for the actions of a few of them. We seem to be going backward in our struggle.

THE GRAHAM REPORT—MIDDLE DRAFT
Kimberly Graham

What women want—recently there has been a lot of publicity on what women were not getting. And who do we point our lotioned, perfumed hands at? MEN—who else? If we are unhappy, then men, as a race in themselves, are to blame, right? We don't have anyone else to blame. The whole female population is unmistakably guiltless. Why the propensity to turn men into scapegoats?

HIM: (while watching the Minnesota Twins win the World Series): Yeah!!! GO, GO, GO!!!

HER: Let's go to a movie or something. Do you want to talk?

HIM: Umm.

HER: Was that a yes or a no?

HIM: Umm.

HER: Why don't you ever want to talk?

Now, there is a definite problem going on there. The woman (we'll call her June) obviously wanted to talk about something, and she tried to communicate her desire to the man (he's Ward). But her timing was off. Asking her husband, or boyfriend, if he wanted to talk while the World Series was on is like asking her to meet his mother-in-law while she is applying a deep-cleaning, pore-rejuvenating, look-twenty-years-younger facial mask. Neither the game nor the mask are necessarily important things, but to the person involved, they constitute a sort of livelihood. June could have waited until Ward was done watching the game to ask him to go out. It's common courtesy. Just because it was a man (inarticulately) refusing to talk does not mean that all men would do the same thing. If June had realized how she would feel if Ward did the same to her, then she might have understood his grumbling disinterest. Many frustrated women today are trying to pin the source of their dissatisfaction onto men only, when a more constructive activity would be to look inside themselves and find the core of their pain. It is a difficult thing to do when the easy way out is to blame, accuse, and complain.

A spotlight has been lit on one woman of the last few turbulent decades who has analyzed the state of relationships in the horrendous romantic environment of the eighties: Shere Hite. Her new book, entitled *Women and Love: A Cultural Revolution in Progress,* is fast on its way to becoming a very controversial bestseller. In it she explores the mentality of dissatisfied women and concludes that men play a large, if not total, role in the creation of female frustration.

I say: poop on her. Yes there are some disgusting examples of the male species, for example: men that proudly and continuously examine just how many decibels their next belch can create (and whether it will crack the tempered glass of their bathroom windows); blind dates that show up displaying their impressionist renditions of nine tattoos scattered extremely artistically upon their mud-splattered arms; college letches that, when confronted with a group of two women and seventeen inebriated fraternity brothers, suggest consuming and emptying all the bottles of Rolling Rock Beer to start a game of strip spin-the-bottle; polyester-clad barflies ambling up to a woman and, in not so much as two steps, managing to regurgitate the evening's content of alcohol consumed into her lap. . . . Need I go on? But it is very important to remember (I know . . . even I am having a hard time after the last paragraph) that not all men are responsible for women's anguish. Many people search for scapegoats because they are afraid to admit that they might have made a mistake. A lot of women find it easy to blame men because they know they will receive sympathy from many other women. Ms. Hite has perpetuated the myth of male-created frustration by presenting the views of 4500 women and applying them to the national population. She has not stated what women want—she has stated what *unhappy* women want.

Why are we bringing up the question of what women want, anyway? Why now? Don't get me wrong; it's not that I think the question is not an important one. On the contrary; I consider it crucial. But why all the clamor now?

I think I have an answer. Now that women have gone out and "done it all"—

worked, had babies, entered politics, entered space, developed an argument supporting the metaphysical qualities and the transcendental properties of the color black, drank a six-pack of Jolt—they are beginning to realize that maybe they overdid it. Stress and burnout are beginning to catch up. In their struggle to prove themselves to society, some women went too far and are now afraid to say, "Hey, I made a mistake. This isn't what I wanted." I can understand why they would be afraid to admit it. Some men would turn around and reply, "You should have stayed in the kitchen where the little woman belongs!!" They have also seen many stressed-out men continue with their struggles, and the women do not want to be the ones to quit. Women have had to prove themselves to society by going beyond what men have done, and for that reason they find a purpose to voice their unhappiness to their boyfriends, husbands, lovers, and so on.

This society would not have to wonder what women (or men) wanted if there were no sexual barriers. Just suppose that there were no physical differences between the male and female bodies. Yes folks, it would be mighty boring, but for the sake of argument, imagine. (Here comes another scenario.)

WARD: Hello Ms. Flintstone. How did the reports on juvenile penguins in the South Antarctic come out on the IBM/PC with color graphics?

WILMA: Just fine, Mr. Cleaver. but I had problems in the area of young penguin street gangs terrorizing the arctic corners.

WARD: Well, why don't you work on it some more and I will get back to you.

Neither Ward nor Wilma has any distinguishing sexual characteristics, so Ward is not wondering what color Wilma's lingerie is while he curses her feminine lack of computer literacy, and Wilma is not wondering if Ward wears boxers or jockeys as she tears apart his masculine egocentricity. Without sexual characteristics people would not be considered men and women separately, but people . . . just people. Then our society would wonder about the wants of everybody as a whole. Definition of this fantasy land: UTOPIA.

THE GRAHAM REPORT—FINAL DRAFT
Kimberly Graham

What women want—recently there has been a lot of publicity on what women were not getting. WHAT DO WE WANT?? Who has the answers?? Shere Hite? Oprah Winfrey? Ronald Reagan? My plumber? I don't know if I even understand the question.

The statement—what women want—has turned into the question: What kind of men do women want? I cannot speak for the whole female population, but I know what I want in a man; or rather, what I don't want.

I do not desire any man that proudly and continuously examines just how many decibels his next belch can create (and whether it will crack the tempered glass of his bathroom windows). So he drank sixteen cases of Ballantine Ale—big deal! He must be able to control his bodily functions among mixed company. Besides, I do not appreciate his friends' attempting to grade the intensity of the belch by holding up their calloused fingers.

Nor do I remain at my door, awaiting blind dates that show up displaying their impressionist renditions of nine tattoos scattered extremely artistically upon their mud-splattered arms. A date is an occasion for which one showers, washes, scrubs, DISINFECTS, FUMIGATES!! And I am not the least bit interested in hearing that the tattoo "artist's" name was Anthony "Michelangelo" Giancanna.

Since I am a female University of Massachusetts student, this next type of man particularly makes me ill. College letches that, when confronted with a group of two women and seventeen inebriated fraternity brothers, suggest consuming and emptying all the bottles of Rolling Rock Beer to start a game of strip spin-the-bottle. What's even more terrifying is when one of them shows up with a Twister mat and a bottle of Mazola. I'm just as fun and exciting as the next person, but hey, public displays of sweltering lust just aren't my style.

The least desirable of this lengthening list of odd personas is the pseudo-feminist pig who claims to respect Gloria Steinem's every word, while secretly wondering if there exists a small, white, cotton flower embroidered in the center of her brassiere. It is this same sad excuse for a man who, after suggesting an evening at the Four Seasons, thinks convincing a date to pay for a thirteen-course dinner with raspberry crepes and two orders of baked Alaska constitutes a feminist attitude. After all, if she wants to be equal then she should pay for his dinner, theater tickets, Brooks Brothers' suits, IBM/PC with full-color graphics, diamond-blue metallic Porsche, fifty-three-room chateau in the Swiss Alps, etc. The pseudo-feminist pig is also very articulate concerning women's issues and proves it with a phone bill of $3,975.87 to Dial-a-Porn. He is the most dangerous of the undesirables since he has the ability to con unknowing women into thinking that he is compassionate and charming, while secretly wanting to cover them with instant banana Jell-O pudding while handcuffed in the back seat of a mint-green 1974 Chevy Impala.

I do not want to dwell on the above descriptions because, as a feminist, my imagination concerning the various mutant abnormalities of the male species may . . . how can I say it subtly . . . run rampant through the hellish field of sarcastic literary discourse. I have determined what kind of men I don't want. Hopefully these caustic exaggerations will not offend any male egos. As unbelievable as it may seem, I do have a glimmer of hope in the existence of desirable men. But where are they? Do I have to travel to southwest Kansas to find an underpaid tractor salesman who loves to wear the color pink? I suppose there is an Antarctican ice fisherman who is more than willing to relax and enjoy the benefits of my making fifty times more income than he would ever make. Maybe there is a Holiday Inn pool maintenance staff person, living in Acapulco, Mexico, who knows how to cook homemade turkey soup and double German chocolate cake while diapering an infant. WHERE ARE THEY?

So what does this paper prove? I have come up with an answer to what women want. Or have I? No, the statement is too vague. Society should not generalize—it's an emotional question. I do know what qualities I like in a man: compassion, sense of humor, intelligence, sense of equality toward women, respect for the human race, the ability to read aloud the works of D. H. Lawrence while stirring instant banana Jell-O pudding. . . .

DIVISIBLE MAN—EARLY DRAFT
John Edgar Wideman

In 1968 when I first read Daniel Patrick Moynihan's *The Negro Family: The Case for National Action,* I was teaching English at the University of Pennsylvania. Nearly all my students were white, most from well to do families and they came to me, a black man, born "disadvantaged" and poor, to learn to read and write. I was an outsider. The only black associate professor in the college of Arts and Sciences, the youngest member by at least a decade of the tenured faculty, and for three years, 1963–66—the tumultuous summers of freedom rides, urban riots, voter registration drives, the march on Washington, JFK assassination—I'd been living in another country, gaining advanced training at Oxford University in the art of being an anomaly. The fiction written by my Penn students revealed their fears, ambitions and frustrations. I was positioned in an ideal place to hear the intimate histories of a generation. Because I'd been conditioned since childhood to pay close attention to the ways of white folk who held the power of life or death over me, and because my decision to be a writer obliged me to cultivate a curiosity and sensitivity to other people's lives, I listened closely to my students. Clearly, they weren't very happy. Though they were the natural inheritors of America's vast postwar prosperity and power, the prospect of stepping into their mothers' and fathers' shoes did not enthrall them. A counter culture was forming. How and why is a fascinating story but not one I want to tell here. The point here is that I understood beyond a doubt that the American Dream, the American family Mr. Moynihan was prescribing as an antidote to black family breakdown and social delinquency was itself compromised, in dire need of revitalization and redefinition.

I'd been raised in the briar patch Mr. Moynihan was attempting to describe with his statistics, categories and comparisons, so I dismissed much of what he said as inessential and misguided, the kind of response to me and mine I'd been warding off all my life, a part standing for the whole, my color or poverty or speech or hair or anger, anything different, distinctive about me used to explain me, contain me. Bits and pieces of me all my fellow Americans across the racial chasm cared to acknowledge. Hadn't black Americans always been a divisible people: Africans doomed to slavery by arguments claiming they were less than human, the slave defined by the Constitution as 3/5's of a person, and now the urban underclass perceived not as people but a threatening swarm of cripples, criminals, and misfits? So Mr. Moynihan's failure to see me whole came as less of a surprise than his acceptance of white American family life as a solid, enduring model for blacks to emulate. . . .

Blacks remain clustered at the bottom of the economic ladder so the plight of the underclass appears to have something to do with color. Look again. The exit doors are crowded and all the faces are not black. Are we in the midst of another experiment, testing with black shock troops whether in times of shrinking economic resources we can expel the poor and dependent from the social compact?

The real voodoo economics works something like this. Take a black doll. Stick a pin in its breast. See if it cringes, hollers, cries; see if anybody notices or cares. Then you know how much you can get away with. How much of the White Man's burden can be borne by the Black man, and vice versa.

There are no black people or white people in America. There are Americans of countless colors. And fear. And confusion. And a history compounded of fear, confusion, violence, lies, a past so terrible we cannot behold it without resorting to the myths of blackness and whiteness in order to explain, justify and perpetuate a way of being that denies the evidence of our eyes, our hearts and minds. . . .

A color jones rides us. We're addicted. The habit of perceiving people as black or white feeds upon itself. Consumes us. We are the junky who wakes up each morning in hell, reeking, crusty, who promises himself no more. For a clear moment he sees the terrible shape he's in and knows he must stop his death dance with the drug.

But he's so deep into his habit that he depends on it to get himself started. To move he needs a hit. And then another. He's gone again till another morning when he awakens, wallowing in his filth, stunned that things are a little worse than the last time he looked around. And so on. . . .

Because the concept of a White American is meaningless, the way White Italian or White Hungarian would be meaningless without Black Italians or Black Hungarians, the very terms of separation have become terms of mutual dependency. If we are not black or white, what are we? Though biologists and geneticists have discredited the notion of race as a significant measure of difference among the world's peoples, the world goes on punishing people for skin color, hair texture, the absence or presence of epicanthic folds in the eyes. Culture, the play of man's biological imperatives within the threshing round of space/time and physical environment, creates the evaluative frame that gives meaning to individual lives. To paraphrase an Ibo proverb, a man without a culture is like a butterfly without wings. I'm intensely proud of my Afro-American heritage. But color can also be a cage. Culture provides terms of reference for making sense of the world; color-consciousness leads to color itself becoming a terminal condition. For over 350 years Americans identified as black have been hammering away at the cage of color, using black to deny and affirm, to elaborate a culture, to refuse a culture.

> Whither shall I go from thy Spirit
> Or whither shall I flee from thy presence?

I still teach creative writing to mostly white students at the University of Massachusetts now. I remain an outsider. By choice. By necessity. The sixties are being re-invented. Mr. Moynihan's report is exhumed and vindicated as prophetic. The story of the sixties is being packaged in—surprise, surprise—black and white: good whites helping downtrodden blacks out of the darkness into the light. A noble effort that failed because a handful of evil whites and a horde of unreconstructable blacks weren't ready for the great leap forward. Old business recycled as new business as it's business as usual. An old man is fired because he trots out biological inferiority or superiority (it's not exactly clear which) to justify the status quo in professional sports: black players, white coaches, managers. CBS disassociates itself from the commentator's racist remarks, then broadcasts without apology the game between the Redskins and Vikings he was scheduled to cover. Redskins? Washington *Redskins?*

I remember a time when Americans all across this remarkable land were awakening to a sense that something drastic was wrong, that our history burdened us with failures and responsibilities, that we might hold in our hands the power to change what worried us. I remember entertaining the possibility of a better life. Really better. A life in which words like *freedom, justice, conscience* had a place. I recall Martin Luther King exhorting us to imagine ourselves as participants in the ancient drama of sacrifice, redemption and salvation. A dream of better, not more. Really better. Not more pigs slopping at the tough, not a larger bite of a rotten pie, not more but better. For everyone, and everyone meaning really everyone.

The Sunday morning of the Washington-Minnesota game I went with my son, Dan, for breakfast at the Classe Cafe in Amherst, Massachusetts, and a young guy and his lady friend sit down at the next table. As he undrapes the oversize, forties, street-person-look overcoat in which he's swaddled, the guy complains to his companion, "It's white, it's so white, everybody in here's so white. I mean white white.

Geez. They're just so white." I can't tell you for whose benefit he's speaking but I overhear him without much effort and wonder as I look at his "whiteness," what color he thinks he is and whether or not he counts Danny and me as allies or if in some way we'd been subtly incorporated into the white, white everywhere the young man found so discouraging.

We returned home for a double-header of play-off games. As a kid I always rooted for the underdog. One of the worst sounds in the world was the cavalry bugle in the Saturday matinee signalling that John Wayne was coming to kick the Indians' behinds. That Sunday Minnesota was the underdog so I couldn't help rooting for them, even though the possibility of a black quarterback in the Super Bowl squeezed me inside Doug Williams's jersey, a second heart pumping, urging him to excel. I was a divisible man. As homework for this essay, I'd promised myself I'd keep track of how and when racial issues entered into an ordinary All-American orgy of football on the tube. Very quickly I gave up the project. Race was implicated so much, in so many ways, that my choice was either watch or write and that one was easy.

Can a black in America ever be a whole person in the eyes of his countrymen? In the phrase "black man" the adjective subdivides the man before man ever arrives on the scene. Metonymy—a part signifies the whole. A black athlete may have super thighs sure enough but why should that attribute imply, as it does, the absence of dedication, practice, willpower, a brain. Doesn't everybody have a brain? Why must each part be attested, proved, explicitly cataloged again and again to guarantee a black athlete, any of us, the harmony, integrity of a human being. Consider the reams of statistics accumulated about black people. Why all the numbers and tables and graphs? What they produce are fragmentary people, abstractions, stereotypes that the media solemnly report, then transform, by way of countless TV cop shows, into a violent fantasy that has come to stand for black life in the national consciousness. Are the people who claim to be trying to put Humpty-Dumpty together again, the same ones who keep pushing him off the wall?

Redskins, Blackskins. Minstrels. Beasts in the Jungle. Superstars. Our fear of being what we could be rather than what we are causes us to invent labels, to resist as long as we're able that moment when we must stare at the Other and see ourselves. But the road home leads home, and home is where we all must live and if that road's not taken, no one ever gets there.

THE DIVISIBLE MAN—AS PUBLISHED IN *LIFE* MAGAZINE
John Edgar Wideman

Valentine's Day, 1988, sun shining, sky blue and I find myself climbing the stairs outside New Africa House, where the Afro-American Studies Department of the University of Massachusetts, Amherst, is located. Black students, outraged by racial attacks and harassment, have occupied New Africa House and sent out word they aren't leaving until changes are made. This quiet Sunday afternoon no barricades, no cop cars yet, or milling crowds, no gaggle of TV trucks, but trouble's here sure enough, trouble with explosive potential, the recurring national nightmare—restless natives, the never-ending business of pacification, reassertion of hegemony and preservation of the natural order, white over black.

Mounting those steps I begin to visualize the faces inside the building. Their youth, vulnerability, beauty, righteous anger, and I want to scream, shout, tear down that building and lots more. I've been here before. Oh, yes. Twenty years before, when I was a professor at the University of Pennsylvania, black students had taken over Penn's College Hall. Then as now most of my colleagues and students were white. Then as now I was a man in the middle, witness, victim, protester, tenured member of the establishment students were challenging. Thus I am remembering faces, anticipating faces. Not white or black, but real colors, real faces, like my children's. Yours. The inheritors of our racial confusions and hate. What hurt me in 1968 and lacerates me again is that I have much to say that will confirm and almost nothing to offer that will alleviate the problems driving these young people to the edge of despair.

Why are students still locking themselves within walls, forced by the very form of their protest to reproduce the segregated society they cannot abide? Where are the alternative institutions—educational, economic, political—we dreamed of creating in the '60s? Wouldn't this student demonstration be followed by a flood of apologies, promises, the inevitable backsliding and backlash, leaving the circle of racism unbroken? I recalled the publication nearly 25 years ago of Daniel Patrick Moynihan's *The Negro Family: The Case for National Action.* Didn't it confuse the nature of race relations? It took the view that the American Dream was not failing, it was failing only for blacks. A false description leading to false remedies: Let's determine what's wrong with blacks so we can cure them, bring them, or some of them, aboard our Good Ship Lollipop. Hadn't Mr. Moynihan heard James Baldwin's eloquent refusal to be integrated into a burning house? The plethora of Great Society social programs that perpetuated a doctor–patient, patron–client, master–slave relationship between whites and blacks remains a withering testament to a failure of vision.

I'd been raised in the briar patch Mr. Moynihan attempted to describe with his statistics, categories and comparisons, so I could dismiss many of his conclusions as nonessential and misguided, the kind of response to me and mine I'd been warding off all my life. Metonymy: a part signifies the whole. My color, poverty, hair, speech, anger, anything different about me used to explain me. In the phrase "black man," *black* subdivides *man* long before *man* ever arrives on the scene. Hadn't Afro-Americans always been a divisible people: Africans doomed to slavery by arguments claiming they were less than human, the slave defined by the Constitution as three fifths of a person, the urban poor perceived not as people but as a threatening swarm of cripples, criminals and misfits?

Conditioned to treating us as Other, the majority doesn't react to atrocities visited upon the black community as if those horrors are happening to fellow Americans and ultimately, inevitably, to themselves. We are shock troops, guinea pigs. Blacks remain clustered at the bottom of the economic ladder, so the plight of the underclass appears to have something to do with color. Check it out. The exit doors of industry are crowded with people being pushed out of jobs, and not all the faces are black.

The original voodoo economics works something like this. Take a black doll. Stick a pin in its chest. See if it cringes, hollers, cries; see if anybody notices, if anybody cares. Then you know how much you can get away with. How much of the white man's burden can be borne by the black man, and vice versa.

There are not black people or white people in America. There are Americans of countless colors. The wrong questions are always the ones we ask about ourselves. Wrong because they are framed in terms of black and white. A color jones rides us. We're addicted. The terms of separation are the terms of our dependency. If we are not black or white, what are we? Though biologists and geneticists have discredited the notion of race as a significant measure of difference among the world's peoples, the world goes on punishing people for skin color, hair texture and the absence or presence of epicanthic folds in the eyes. It is culture that creates the evaluative frame that gives meaning to individual lives. To paraphrase a Kongo proverb, a man without a culture is like a grasshopper without wings.

I am intensely proud of my Afro-American heritage and of my color. But color can also be a cage and color consciousness can become a terminal condition. For more than 350 years Americans identified as black have been using the cage of color to deny and affirm, to elaborate one culture, to refuse another.

I remember a time when Americans all across this remarkable land were awakening to a sense that something was drastically wrong, that our history burdened us with failures and responsibilities, that we might hold in our hands the power to change what it was that worried us. I remember entertaining the possibility of a better life. Really better. A life in which words like *freedom, justice, conscience* had a place. I recall Martin Luther King exhorting us to imagine ourselves as participants in the ancient drama of sacrifice, redemption and salvation. A dream of better, not more. Truly better. Not more pigs slopping at the trough, not a larger bite of a rotten pie, not more, but better. For everyone, and everyone meaning really everyone.

I reach out to the door of the New Africa House.

UNIT
9

The Expository Essay and Academic Discourse

"Expository" has come to be the term used in schools and in academic discourse for essays that *explain*. In this unit our aim is to help you become a better explainer. We'll ask you first to explain something from another course you are taking—explain it to yourself and then to two other audiences: your class partner or group members (amateurs or "general readers" who know relatively little about your subject) and the teacher of that course (an academic professional who knows a lot about the subject you are explaining). Your main assignment will be to write two versions of the same expository essay—one for each of these audiences.

By working on this assignment—and working through the unit—we hope you will make some progress on another, broader, and somewhat controversial question: to what extent do different audiences need different discourse (different kinds of language, explanation, and stance), and to what extent will the same kind of discourse work for different audiences? Or, to focus the question more directly on the school setting: to what extent is *academic discourse* different from "normal" or "general reader" discourse and to what extent is it the same?

○○○○○

We often explain something to ourselves in order to make it clear to others. But it can work the other way too, where we explain something to others in order to make it clear to ourselves. In either case, if we want to understand something fully, we have to integrate the new knowledge with what we already know. In a sense we "compose" our own knowledge by seeing new ideas in relation to old ones. We can learn or memorize facts, but knowledge is a product of our own minds—a result of "composing" a coherent something out of disparate, maybe even discordant, bits. Although in this textbook we prefer the term "writing" to "composition," here is one spot where "composition" is probably a more appropriate term. When we write we are "composing" our knowledge by putting together things in a way that makes them more understandable to ourselves and others. Writing helps us learn.

It often happens that what you learn just for a test doesn't become *really* learned unless you incorporate it into what you already know. Probably you've had an experience we've had in school: you're in a class that's very difficult for you and you're lost; then a test comes up. So you read your textbook and go over your notes and memorize lots of words and phrases. You go to the test and read the question, pick out key words that match up to some part of what you've memorized, and then just blurt out on paper everything you've memorized that seems related to the question. You aren't really answering the question; you aren't even really sure you know what the question is asking or what you're saying. Sometimes you're lucky and answer the question without knowing it. Sometimes you fool the teacher, who's impressed by how much you *seem* to know. Of course, as soon as the test is over, you forget all the memorized stuff. You never really learned it.

But at other times, we learn something in class that we remember *because* we're able to see how it fits into our lives and previous knowledge. Perhaps you learn in an introductory psychology or sociology course that the tendency for teenagers to form groups that give them a feeling of belonging is important for genuine maturation into adulthood. You are able to relate this piece of information to your own awareness of how important your own group of friends is—and so you have no problem whatsoever remembering this idea. Of course the idea won't stay in such a simple form for long; it will be modified on the basis of additional material you learn and additional experiences you have. But learning based on this idea will continue.

Exploratory Writing: Getting the Concept Clear for Yourself

We ask you now to explore two different topics or concepts: a new idea you feel confident you have learned this year and one that you are having trouble understanding. Try out both, so you'll have a choice of which to pursue further.

Also, as you do this exploratory writing, try both audience modes: address your words to yourself (trying to get your own thoughts clear before explaining them to others) and address your words to some friendly reader (trying to use an audience to help you understand something). Notice the interesting audience variation this represents: they are both private writing (since you don't have to show them to anyone), but in one case you are keeping a reader in mind and in the other you are not. Keep your eye out for how you react to the two modes.

1. Do focused freewriting about something new and exciting you've learned in school this year. (Of course you've learned much outside of school, but for this assignment we want you to concentrate on something learned in a class. We also hope you've learned lots in your writing class, but again we're asking you not to use this either. You'll see why later in the unit.)

- Perhaps as soon as you read the preceding, you knew what idea you wanted to write about. Fine. Explore it fully. What's new about it? or exciting? How does it relate to other things you know? to your personal life? Has it changed the way you think or behave? Is the idea important in the course and discipline where you learned it?

- Did you have to struggle to understand it? Did it seem to conflict with other knowledge you had? Tell the story of your thinking as you worked through the idea.

- Or was it one of those ideas which you recognized instantly: "Yes, of course, that's true!" And with this realization, did other ideas and experiences suddenly have new and different meanings for you?

- If you feel, "There's *nothing* interesting I've learned this year," start by listing *some things* you've learned in a class and then focusing on whether there might not be some new or exciting aspects for you. If nothing seems worth exploring, move to another class and write about what's been happening in it.

- After you've been freewriting for at least fifteen minutes, stop, read over what you've written, and write down some questions to follow up on—questions suggested within the freewriting.

2. Do focused freewriting about some issue, topic, or concept you are having trouble learning in some course you're taking. Focus on what the difficulties are and why you think you're having problems.

- Perhaps your puzzlement is broad and generalized: What is sociology? What is its subject matter? How does it go about doing what it does? How does it differ from political science or psychology? What are the major assumptions underlying sociology as a discipline?

- Perhaps your puzzlement is quite specific: What is the gross national product? What causes the dollar to change in value? Why are employment figures high? low? How can the value of a dollar change?

- As you freewrite, concentrate first on what you *do* know even if that may seem unproductive to you. (List all the different subjects you touch on in your sociology class and try to figure out what they have in common. Or think about *gross, national,* and *product.* Then try to figure out what they might mean when linked in a phrase.) Don't dodge the assignment by thinking you don't know anything. You do—so keep writing.

- Don't be afraid of contradictions. They can stimulate productive writing: "Sociology studies individuals in society. Sociology is unconcerned with the individual." And don't be afraid of your own reactions: "Sociology is a useless discipline; all it deals with is common sense. I don't have to go to school to learn what it teaches!"

- After at least fifteen minutes of focused freewriting, read over what you've written and add to it questions you think you need to answer in order to understand the ideas better.

Now decide which approach you want to follow up on: the one focusing on an idea or concept you *can't* understand or the one focusing on an idea or concept you *do* understand. If you choose the first, you'll be working from fuzziness toward clarity; if you choose the second, you'll be working from clarity toward further implications (which may bring new fuzziness) and then back toward clarity. If both approaches are feasible for you, we suggest working with the idea you *don't* yet understand: nothing is more valuable than learning to write your way through to understanding. And don't forget to try both audience modes: addressing your exploratory words to both self and others.

If there's time, put this all aside for at least a day (although even a few hours can provide the needed distance). Come back to the approach you want to work on, read it over again stopping to do more freewriting at points where you think you've left something unexplored or only partially explored. Be on the lookout for ideas that do not seem to fit with each other. It is just such points of conflict that may lead you to the most productive thinking as you try to work through the contradictions. If you can't figure out a particular problem, pose it for yourself as a question so you'll have some base to work from in a later version. Again, give yourself at least fifteen minutes of writing time.

When this second freewriting period is over, write out as clearly and briefly as possible what your new or puzzling concept is and why it's important to you and to the class you learned it in. We realize we may be asking you to do exactly what you can't do since you may still be having problems with the idea or its implications. Still we want you to try to state it as clearly as you can *at the moment.* At this stage you're aiming *toward* making the idea clear; this should help you see better exactly what remains *un*clear.

Using Others

Your next task is to look for help from others. We suggest three sources:

1. Read over your class notes and whatever your textbook or assigned readings say on the subject. It's good practice to write out your notes fully or paraphrase particularly troublesome sections in the reading material. When we can get something into words that make sense to us, we know we understand it. After you've done this, write some more on the basis of what you've learned.

2. Seek out others in the class you're writing about. Ask them to respond to what you've written after they read it or listen to you read it. Perhaps they'll lend you their notes. After you've done this, write out what you've learned as a result and add it to the collection of writing on your idea. (See the suggestions that follow for guiding classmates' responses.)

3. Go to see the professor of the class you've been writing about. Try to pinpoint for her exactly what you are having trouble with. Often you can do this most quickly by reading a passage or two that centers on your difficulty. She'll probably be gratified that you're taking the time to write out something and to come to see her about it. Explain to her that the assignment is for your writing class, but that you also want it to be acceptable for her. After your talk you should ask her if she'd be willing to read a final draft of the paper and perhaps give you some brief feedback. (You might show her the little form printed at the end of this unit, which will help her give comments quickly. Some teachers of other subjects feel nervous and inexperienced about commenting on essays.) As soon as possible after this appointment, do some more freewriting based on what you talked about.

Sharing Your Early Exploratory Writing

You now have a good quantity of exploratory writing to share with others in your writing group. Read most or all of it to them—and ask them these questions:

- Ask them first whether they are taking or have taken the course you are writing about or are working in the same discipline. Since for this unit's assignment we'll be asking you to decide on how to *vary* your expository writing (if at all) depending on whether readers are working in the discipline or not, you need to know whether your responders are speaking from within the discipline or from outside it. (People outside a discipline can often ask questions which get to the root of a particular issue more readily than those within the discipline. People in a discipline are sometimes unaware of the assumptions underlying their thinking because they are too close to the assumptions.)

- Ask them to "say back" to you what they hear you saying. This will help you pinpoint areas where you can work for greater clarification, both for yourself and for them.

193

- Ask them also to question you about ideas, words, theories, and so forth that you talk about but that they don't understand, either because they're not taking the same class or because they are taking it and understand your issue differently.

Since this is early exploratory writing, don't let your readers *criticize* your writing. Insist they respond as friendly allies looking over your shoulder at unfinished work, simply telling you what they hear you saying or almost saying and what they are perplexed by.

Once you've gotten this feedback, examine it carefully and try to classify it into two categories:

- Feedback that makes you realize what you *yourself* don't yet understand about your issue

- Feedback that demonstrates that your readers don't understand what you wrote because they're not familiar enough with the subject matter

MAIN ASSIGNMENT

In Units 6 and 7, we asked you to work out a private and public version of the same material. We wanted you to explore in the most concrete way the effect of audience. We ask you here to continue your exploration of the effects of audience. The assignment now is to write *two* versions of the same expository essay: the first version for members of your group who are not in your other class, and the second version for the professor who teaches the other class.

You can decide to make the two versions very different, very similar, or even the same. Making this decision will help you most in understanding the crucial but difficult issue of *academic discourse:* what kind of language, explanation, and stance is appropriate for academic writing and what should be avoided. Even if you decide to write one version for both your classmates and the teacher of the other class, you'll still need to think carefully about

---

PROCESS BOX

Anybody who finds himself in this situation of writing to a prescribed notion or to illustrate or to fill in what he already knows should stop writing. A writer has got to trust the act of writing to scan all his ideas, passions, and convictions; but these must emerge from the work, be *of* it.

E. L. DOCTOROW, *ANYTHING CAN HAPPEN*

---

what kind of language works for both audiences. It may help you to consider some other sub-purposes for one or both versions:

- to demonstrate how this concept is important within its discipline and why;

- to tell why you think the concept is important even beyond the confines of its discipline;

- to show how the idea relates to your own life and experience and how it might relate to the lives of others.

As you write these two versions of your essay, use as source material the exploratory writing you've done and any other writing added to it as a result of feedback you get. The material you've produced so far is probably not organized in a usable way. You'll need to read it over and identify parts you want to use. As you write each version, try to visualize your audience. Think of yourself as writing *for* the members of your writing group and then writing *for* the professor of the other class.

Collaborative approach. Your teacher might invite or assign you to make this a collaborative assignment: two of you working together to make the two drafts. If so, don't make the mistake of working entirely separately on either version. You will need to discuss with each other what the differences need to be between the two versions.

THE QUESTION OF ACADEMIC DISCOURSE

In this unit we are asking you to engage in research in what is now a "hot" topic. There are really three questions involved here. Teachers and research-ers in composition and specialists in various disciplines (biology, sociology, etc.) are currently very interested in the questions yet unable to reach any agreement on them.

1. The first question is obvious: What is academic discourse? The easy answer is simply that it's what academics write: the discourse faculty mem-bers, scholars, and researchers use when they publish in their professional journals. But it's not so easy to describe the *characteristics* of that discourse and to say how much it differs from discipline to discipline and differs from what we might call "regular, standard educated written English." Scholars are currently busy researching exactly this question.

2. The second question is obvious too—and it's especially obvious to most students the night before they have to hand in a history or economics paper: What kind of discourse do faculty members in various disciplines want *students* to use in their papers? For *graduate students* the answer is easy: they should write the discourse that's in those professional journals because they're being trained to publish in those journals. But do faculty

members want *undergraduate majors* in the field to use the same discourse as professional scholars? Perhaps. But how about freshmen and sophomores who aren't going to major in the discipline: what kind of discourse do faculty members want *them* to use in papers for introductory courses? There is no clear or settled answer to this question: As every student knows, "It depends on whom you get for a teacher." Different teachers have different aims and expectations—and often they haven't really thought through just *what* kind of discourse they want from their freshman and sophomore non-majors.

There's a danger in being too quick and cynical in saying "It all depends on whom you get for a teacher." For perhaps there *are* some definable features of what we might call a *subcategory* of academic discourse—that is, discourse which faculty members want students to use even though the students will not major in the field. As to finding out what characterizes this discourse, you will be on the front lines of research.

3. The third question has gotten to be the hottest one among writing teachers and researchers: What kind of discourse should we try to teach in freshman "general" *writing courses?* Since one course cannot train students in the discourse of *all* disciplines (after all writing teachers aren't qualified to say what characterizes professional writing in physics and economics and art history), can we train students in a kind of generic all-purpose academic discourse that fits—or at least can be adjusted to fit—all disciplines? Is there such a thing? And if so, how does it differ from "regular, standard educated written English"? Perhaps there should not be "general" writing courses in college but only specialized ones.

Asking all these questions in detail this way begins to make even *our* heads swim—especially because scholars in writing and in other fields cannot yet give full answers to many of them, much less agree on answers. Nevertheless you have a straightforward, concrete task ahead of you—not a simple task but one that is no different from what you are accustomed to: write an explanatory paper for your writing partners or your group, and write an explanatory paper for your subject-matter teacher. This dual task will begin to suggest answers to the hard theoretical question, but not just theoretical answers. For it will also put you in a much better position for future occasions when you must write essays for college teachers.

On the basis of your experiments—and especially the feedback you get—you can decide how different these two drafts need to be. You may even take on the challenge of trying to get one version to fit both audiences. We think it's possible and, in fact, desirable in many cases.

We've provided three readings at the end of the unit that should help you in your thinking and discussions about academic discourse. As you'll see, two are by the same two authors and based on the same material (about the use of good-luck charms). One was published in *Psychology Today* for what we can call a general educated reader who (though interested) is not expected to have special training in the field. The other was published in *Current Anthropology,* a professional journal for scholars. In a sense these two academics have already done the assignment we've set for this unit.* The third piece is also about luck, this one published in *Sports Illustrated.*

SHARING AND RESPONDING

When you have two versions of your essay which have the same purpose but different audiences, you need to test them out on their intended audiences. If you elected to compose one version suitable for both audiences, you'll be testing just one version, but two audiences.

With the Teacher of the Other Course

It's probably not fair to ask the teacher of the other course to read two versions. But perhaps she will be willing to read and respond to the version intended for her if you show her the questions in the box on page 198 and assure her they are designed to help her comment *quickly* and without having to become a "writing teacher."

If you can't get comments from the teacher of the subject-matter course perhaps you can find one or more students in that class who are willing to read your version(s) and give their reactions as people knowledgeable in the field.

With Your Partner or Group

You should be able to share *both* versions with members of your writing group. But that makes more reading and there are certain things you can do to cut down on the burden. You might find a way to mark all the passages in both versions which are the same (or different) to help readers more easily see differences between the versions.

There probably won't be time enough to read and discuss all this writing in class, so bring in copies to permit others to take them home for commenting. Everyone in the group can comment on everyone else's paper or everyone can read all the papers, but write comments on only one or two. Then when the group meets, each person's writing gets discussed, but the main comments are by the person(s) who wrote comments--and others chime in briefly based on their reading at home.

Particularly valuable as a basis for comments are descriptive responding (explained in Section IIC of *Sharing and Responding*), metaphorical re-

---

*Since you really are engaged in useful research on this complex topic of academic discourse and how it differs from standard discourse and differs in its variant forms, you may want to write up what you discover. That's precisely what the assignment is in Unit 18, *Writing in the Disciplines.* Your process writing from this unit should throw interesting light on that topic— whether you pursue it on your own or later in Unit 18. (By the way, we are grateful to Linda Peterson of Yale University for bringing these two essays to our attention.)

QUESTIONS FOR THE TEACHER OF
THE SUBJECT-MATTER COURSE

You can give me very helpful responses by just marking certain key passages in my paper:

- Please use a check mark to indicate phrases or passages where I've got the idea or concept right and a cross where I seem to be misunderstanding it or getting it wrong.

- Please use a straight line to indicate phrases and passages that are clear and effective for you and a wiggly line where it's unclear.

- Please circle words or passages where the discourse, style, language, or approach seems *inappropriate* for you as a teacher and reader in the field.

If you have time, are there any other comments you would make—either orally to me or in writing? There are two emphases to my assignment: (1) to explain a concept adequately and (2) to think about the difference between discourse needed for professionals in the field (like you—when I'm writing in a course like this one) and the discourse needed for general readers or amateurs (classmates in my writing class).

---

sponses (Section IID), and movies of the reader's mind (Section IV). You can also ask readers to compare versions on these matters:

- Which version (or passages) do you like most? Why?

- Which versions (or passages) are clearest and most unclear for you?

- Which version (or passages) seems to suit you best as someone in or not in the field? suit you least?

- Compare the tone or stance of the writer in each version and his attitude toward the reader and toward the material.

- Are there any other aspects of "discourse" or "style" you didn't talk about which you could compare? kind of language used? way of thinking?

PROCESS JOURNAL QUESTIONS

If you need some help retrieving from memory your experiences and reactions during this unit's writing, you can use the following questions:

- What was it like writing about something you did understand versus something you didn't understand?

- What was it like directing exploratory writing to yourself versus toward someone else?

- What did you learn from bringing your writing course to bear on another course? writing about that subject for this class? seeing that teacher for help and feedback?

- What did this unit's activities tell you about how you learn in that course (perhaps in comparison with how you learn in this course or other courses)?

- What did you notice about the different kinds of feedback you got from students and two different teachers?

- What did you notice about trying to write two versions of the same paper? about trying to write for two different audiences?

- What did you notice about trying to think about and write academic discourse?

READINGS

WHAT KEEPS AN AIRPLANE UP?
Gary Kolnicki

Version for teacher or for people who know a bit about physics.

Even though many people believe they understand the way an airplane flies, very few truly know the physical processes which occur.

Two dynamic effects join to supply nearly all the support, or lift, for an airplane in flight. For an airfoil or wing, dynamic lift and the kite effect provide nearly all the lift.

Instrumental in understanding dynamic lift and the kite effect is a fundamental understanding of the gas particle theory along with a concept of pressure at a microscopic level. The Bernoulli equation predicts that these two effects will bring lift but does not aid in explaining them.

Air, a gas, consists of a very large number of particles in high-speed motion which travel in straight lines in all directions. Because air is so dense, particles continually collide with one another, bouncing off into other directions, in zig-zag paths. Since there are a large number of particles in this random motion at any one time, about the same number of particles move in all directions causing no net movement of air.

Pressure of a gas on a surface is a force due to collisions of molecules of the gas with that surface. As the molecules in random motion move in a way so that they hit the wall and transfer their momentum, pressure results. Therefore, the more par-

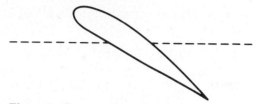

Figure 1. Cross section of a wing

ticles in the gas, the more particles that will be moving in that certain direction, colliding with the wall, and putting more pressure on it. In an air-filled box, the air exerts an equal pressure on each wall, since there are an equal number of particles bouncing off each wall.

An airfoil is shaped and oriented so that an imbalance in pressure results as the wing passes through the air. The following effect accounts for the majority of this pressure imbalance. It is called dynamic lift.

A wing's cross section appears in Figure 1. It is rounded in the front and arches to a point in the back. Figure 1 also illustrates the upward direction in which the wing points.

As the wing passes through the air, air takes two distinct paths across the wing: above and below. Since the upper stream travels a longer path than the lower stream, the lower stream reaches the back of the wing first. This is illustrated in Figure 2. Because the upper stream hasn't yet reached the back, the air above the rear of the wing has lower pressure, causing the lower stream to curl up and back rather than to continue in the same direction. The upper stream meets this curling stream and forces it into a circular flow, called a vortex. Figure 3 shows this flow. The upper stream is accelerated due to the lower pressure under the vortex. Once the upper

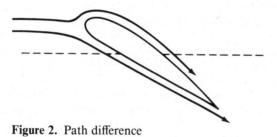

Figure 2. Path difference

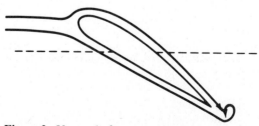

Figure 3. Vortex before constant flow

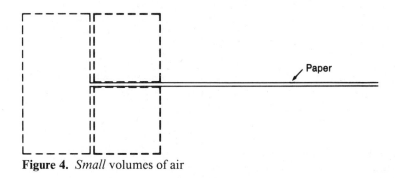

Figure 4. *Small* volumes of air

stream has reached a velocity so that the upper and lower streams simultaneously reach the trail end of the wing, a pressure difference will no longer exist to curl up and back the lower stream. The vortex then moves away and dissipates, leaving this continuous flow of air above the wing.

The Bernoulli principle predicts dynamic lift under these conditions. A higher velocity results in lower pressure, according to this principle. Above, a stream with higher velocity than the lower produces lower pressure. Therefore, a net upward force, lift, results.

Microscopically, this effect is caused by molecular collisions.

Consider a piece of paper in a horizontal position with three volumes of air: one below, one above, and one in front (see Figure 4). This picture describes a case in which no motion results. Focus now on Figure 5 with the top box now moving to the right. The force which moves the upper box must result from an imbalance in pressure between it and the larger box in front. Since the large box's pressure hasn't changed, the upper box must have a lower pressure in order to be moved to the right. It follows that the faster the motion, the lower the pressure.

Now, think of air passing across a wing in steady flight. As shown earlier, the upper stream has a higher velocity than the lower stream. Since the air in front of the wing exerts the same pressure on both these streams, similar to Figure 5, the upper stream must have a lower pressure than the lower stream. The greater velocity is the result of a larger force, or greater pressure imbalance. The lower pressure above results in a net force upward, or lift.

The kite effect is also described in a microscopic way. This effect occurs due to the upward orientation of the aircraft's wing. As the wing proceeds through the air,

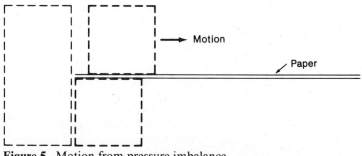

Figure 5. Motion from pressure imbalance

molecules slam with high speed into the slightly upturned bottom giving more lift to the plane.

The kite effect accounts for about one-third of total lift. Dynamic lift claims the majority of lift—almost two-thirds. Aircraft velocity is necessary for both these effects, and, therefore, thrust must be supplied. For this reason, aircrafts are designed to minimize friction. In some ways, an airplane is designed to slip through the air like a paper airplane.

Flaps, moveable deflectors at the trailing edge of the wing, control the amount of lift. If a flap is in a downward position, it increases the curvature of the wing and thus makes the path difference between upper and lower flows even greater. This results in a process similar to the one just described and lift increases. The opposite occurs if the flap is in an upward position.

Of course, more can be explained about the complicated subject of flight. Basically, however, the physical processes described above prevent an airplane's falling out of the sky. Though not magical, the effects which describe the way air alone can hold up a jumbo jet are quite fascinating, complicated, and unexpected. Even a person with basic physics knowledge may not be aware of the sources of an airplane's lift on a fundamental level.

BIBLIOGRAPHY

"Aerodynamics." *Encyclopedia Britannica*. 1970, I, 205–214.

HALLIDAY, DAVID, AND RESNICK, ROBERT. *Fundamentals of Physics*. New York: John Wiley & Sons, Inc., 1974.

"Airplane." *Compton's Encyclopedia*. 1944, I, 90–110.

WHAT KEEPS AN AIRPLANE UP?
Gary Kolnicki

Version for general readers or students in the writing class.

At least once in the course of your life while sitting in an airplane, you must have asked yourself, "What keeps this thing from falling out of the sky?" You may think you understand. You've probably studied it or had it explained to you. But ask yourself, as you sit there looking out at nothing but clouds, if you can explain it to yourself and the answer will probably be No.

Two dynamic effects supply the lift for an airplane in flight. The simplest and most obvious source is what is called "the kite effect." Because the wing of the plane is slightly tipped upwards like a kite (see Figure 1), and because the plane is moving forward through the air, molecules slam with high speed into the *bottom* surface of the wing, pushing it upwards. Clearly there would be no kite effect if the plane were not moving forward. (It's true that the kite may not seem to be moving forward, but in fact it is moving forward with respect to the air around it—for the kite only flies if there is a good breeze.)

But the kite effect supplies only about one-third of the lift in an airplane. Two-thirds of the lift comes from what is called the "dynamic lift effect." This effect also depends upon the plane moving forward very fast. (Thus planes don't try to take off till they have a good velocity.) But to understand the dynamic lift effect, the major source of support for an airplane, you need to understand how gas particles exert pressure at a microscopic level.

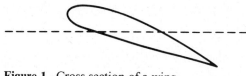

Figure 1. Cross section of a wing

Air is a gas that consists of a very large number of particles or molecules in high-speed motion. These molecules travel in straight lines in all directions. Because air is so dense, these molecules continuously collide with one another, bouncing off in all directions in zigzag paths. But because there are so *many* molecules moving randomly in this way, it turns out that at any given moment about the same number of particles are moving in all directions—with a result that there is no net movement of air. There's lots of motion, but as a whole it's getting nowhere.

But these molecules do exert pressure on any surface that they run into (and the more molecules, the more pressure). For when the randomly moving molecules hit the wall, they transfer their momentum to the wall—causing pressure. In an air-filled box, for example, an empty cigarette box on the table, the air exerts an *equal* pressure on all the walls since there are an equal number of particles bouncing off each wall. Thus the box stays where it is on the table: all those molecules are hitting on all walls equally.

An airplane wing is shaped in such a way as to make an "airfoil." It is rounded in the front, and arches to a point in the back. Because of this airfoil shape (and because it is somewhat tipped upward) there is an *imbalance* of pressure as the wing passes through the air.

As the wing passes through the air, the air takes two distinct paths across the wing: above and below (see Figure 2). Since the upper stream travels a longer path than the lower stream, the lower stream reaches the back of the wing first.

Because the upper stream hasn't yet reached the back, the air above the rear of the wing has lower pressure, causing the lower stream to curl up and back rather than to continue in the same direction. The upper stream meets this curling stream and forces it in a circular flow, called a vortex (see Figure 3). The upper stream is accelerated due to the lower pressure under the vortex.

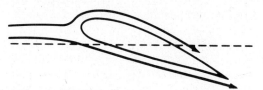

Figure 2. Path difference

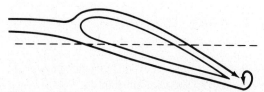

Figure 3. Vortex

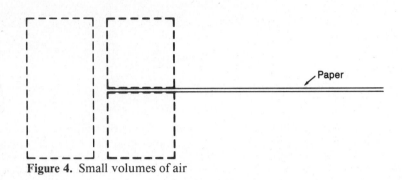

Figure 4. Small volumes of air

The Bernoulli principle predicts dynamic lift under these conditions. According to this principle, a higher speed results in lower pressure. The stream above the wing has a higher velocity and produces a lower pressure—thus a net upward force or lift. Remember that this effect is all being produced by molecular collisions at the microscopic level.

To illustrate this principle more schematically, consider a piece of paper in horizontal position with three volumes of air: one below, one above, and one in front, as shown in Figure 4.

This picture describes a case in which no motion results. Look now at Figure 5 with the top box moving to the right. The force which moves the upper box must result from an imbalance in pressure between it and the larger box in front. Since the large box's pressure hasn't changed, the upper box must have a lower pressure in order to be moved to the right. It follows that the faster the motion, the lower the pressure. The lower pressure above results in a net force upwards, or lift.

Flaps, moveable deflectors at the trailing edge of the wing, control the amount of lift. If a flap is in a downward position, it increases the curvature of the wing and thus makes the path difference between upper and lower flows even greater. This results in a process similar to the one just described and lift increases. The opposite occurs if the flap is in an upward position.

Of course, more can be explained about the complicated subject of flight. Basically, however, the physical processes described above prevent an airplane's falling out of the sky. Though not magical, the effects which describe the way air alone can hold up a jumbo jet are quite fascinating, complicated, and unexpected. Even a per-

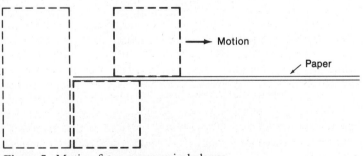

Figure 5. Motion from pressure imbalance

son with basic physics knowledge may not be aware of the sources of an airplane's lift on a fundamental level.

CAN A LUCKY CHARM GET YOU THROUGH ORGANIC CHEMISTRY?
George Gmelch and Richard Felson

[Published in *Psychology Today*]

During his stay in the South Seas in World War I, Bronislaw Malinowski observed that the Trobriand Islanders used magic in situations of danger and uncertainty, when circumstances were not fully under human control. In a classic illustration of this principle, the anthropologist compared two forms of Trobriand fishing—fishing in the inner lagoon and fishing in the open sea. In the safety of the lagoon, fish were plentiful and there was little danger; the men could rely on their knowledge and skill. On the open sea, however, fishing was dangerous and yields varied widely; to ensure safety and increase their catch, the men turned to rituals and fetishes for help. Malinowski wrote that the fishermen's magic was performed "over the canoe during its construction, carried out at the beginning and in the course of expeditions, and resorted to in moments of real danger."

Even in our technologically advanced society, we are often at the mercy of powerful, unknown forces. How do we handle this uncertainty and unpredictability in our personal lives? Some people are fatalistic—What will be will be. Others try to manipulate unknown forces. When they request a deity to intercede in their behalf, we call it prayer; when they attempt to influence unknown forces through ritual or the use of charms, we call it magic.

For example, when Gloria, a university secretary, has an outdoor activity planned for the day and the sun is shining, she is careful not to comment on the weather. "I think it's bad luck," she explains. "If I said it was a gorgeous day, the sky would fill up with clouds and it'd rain. I know, it's happened to me. So now I am careful not to pass any comment on the weather when I've got something planned." Gloria has a lucky number—7—and would never work for a company located on the 13th floor. She reads her horoscope in the newspaper every morning and sometimes makes a wish on the first star she sees at night. An amber glass piggy bank sits atop her dresser containing the 20 lucky pennies she has found over the years.

Mary Sue is a B+ student at the State University of New York at Albany. Each time she prepares for an exam, she travels 12 miles to the library of another university and sits in the same carrel to study. She once got an exceptionally high mark on a physics test after studying in that library, and ever since, she has returned.

It is perhaps surprising to some that enlightened people in an advanced society can be serious when they behave in such ways. Not long ago, we decided to investigate the use of magic among supposedly sophisticated college students. We wanted to understand why they seemed to use magic—whether their motives were similar to those of the Trobrianders and other preliterate peoples. Magic, as defined by anthropologists, refers to rituals that are meant to influence events and people but have not been proved empirically to have the desired effect. We wanted to know whether the student practitioners of magic really believed in its efficacy or were simply trying to alleviate the anxiety created by uncertain conditions by making a ritual gesture of some kind.

We distributed questionnaires on the subject to 270 students in sociology classes at the State University of New York at Albany and to 180 students at University College Dublin, in Ireland. (The choice of Irish students was a matter of convenience; one of us, Gmelch, often works in Ireland.) The students in the American sample were primarily urban and from middle-class Catholic or Jewish backgrounds. In the Irish sample, as many students came from small towns and villages as from cities; the group was predominantly Catholic and mainly middle class.

Students were asked if they did anything special to give themselves luck in each of six circumstances: when they were gambling; in a dangerous situation; taking exams; playing in a sports contest; before an important meeting, date, or interview; when they were ill. We also asked students how much they worried about each of those circumstances. In addition, we asked them how much they cared about the outcome; if using magic made them feel less anxious; and if they really believed that magic worked. We had independent judges—40 sociology students who were not included in our sample—rank the six circumstances according to how difficult it was to predict the outcome (for instance, a grade on an exam). The raters put gambling at the top of the list as entailing most uncertainty, followed by dangerous situations, exams, sports, face-to-face encounters, and, lastly, illness.

Of the 450 subjects, about 70 percent used magic. The percentage of users was about the same in the two countries: 69 percent of the Americans, 75 percent of the Irish. But larger between-nation differences were found in the circumstances under which magic was used. As the following table shows, a significantly higher proportion of the Irish employed magic in exams and face-to-face encounters, while a significantly higher percentage of Americans used it in gambling and sports.

Situation	Americans	Irish
Gambling	48%	33%
Dangerous situations	41%	49%
Exams	39%	57%
Sports	40%	26%
Face-to-face encounters	35%	48%
Illness	21%	23%

Students used both productive magic (for example, carrying a good-luck charm to an exam), to improve achievement, and protective magic (such as crossing one's fingers), to ward off danger. Several rituals were shared by subjects of both nationalities. Asked if they had a lucky number, 43 percent of the Americans and 32 percent of the Irish said yes. Other shared practices were crossing fingers (38 percent of the Americans, 44 percent of the Irish), knocking on wood (41 percent of the Americans, 47 percent of the Irish), carrying good-luck charms (19 percent of the Americans, 13 percent of the Irish), and wearing particular clothing for luck (25 percent of the Americans, 14 percent of the Irish). Not all rituals were shared. Only the Americans—23 percent—said they walked around ladders.

Overall, the difference between the Irish and American students was not large, possibly because the uncertainties of student life are similar in the two countries.

Particular kinds of rituals, such as knocking on wood, had large numbers of adherents in both countries. (It has been suggested that knocking on wood originated when men lived in huts. Supposedly, if a man was prosperous, it was important for him not to let evil gods or spirits know about it. If he knocked on the wooden walls while he spoke of his good fortune, he would cover the sound of his voice, and the gods would not hear him.)

Much student magic was associated with particular activities, for instance, exams. One young woman who was never confident that her preparation for tests was adequate believed that using a particular pen could boost her performance. "I took an economics test and afterward thought I had failed," she said. "But I got a B on the test. I knew it couldn't be me who had done that well; it must have been the pen."

In card playing, the favorite gambling activity among students, the most frequently mentioned good-luck practice was not looking at one's cards until all the cards were dealt. One student reported that he waited to look at his cards until all the other players had looked at their hands.

Athletes were among the most ardent practitioners of magic. Wearing a piece of clothing associated with a previous good performance was mentioned by both males and females. Also cited was the use of crucifixes, neck chains, and coins as good-luck charms. Some of the most elaborate personal rituals were those of male students on intercollegiate teams. Unable to attribute an exceptional performance to skill alone but hoping to repeat it in future contests, players superstitiously singled out something they had done in addition to their actual play as partially responsible for their success. That "something" might be the food they had eaten before the game, the new pair of socks or sneakers they had worn, or just about anything they had done that was out of the ordinary. Mike, a linebacker on a varsity football team, vomited and was the last player to come on the field before a game in which he made many tackles. Before each game during the remainder of the season, he forced himself to vomit and made certain he was the last to leave the locker room.

The fact that students could easily repeat the behavior they had decided was crucial to success gave them the illusion that they could influence their performance simply through repetition of that behavior. That sense of control, however groundless in reality, increased their confidence, which may have improved their performance.

To learn more about the kinds of students who practiced magic, we asked subjects whether or not, and to what degree, they believed in God, science, astrology, ESP, and the supernatural. The Irish were more likely than the Americans to believe in the supernatural (66 percent versus 50 percent), but otherwise the two student groups were similar in their beliefs.

In general, students had more doubt about God than about science. Approximately 90 percent claimed a belief, either strong or weak, in science, while about 80 percent said they had either a strong or a weak belief in God. Prayer was more frequent than the use of magic; for example, 39 percent of the Americans said they often prayed that things would turn out well for them, 51 percent said they occasionally prayed for favorable outcomes, and only 10 percent said they never did so. Students who used prayer tended also to use magic, suggesting that the two are related and that both may be responses to uncertainty.

Students who used magic were likely to believe in God, astrology, ESP, and the supernatural, although the relationships were not strong. Strong believers in science were just as likely as weak believers to use magic. Generally, the use of magic accompanied more practical, scientifically approved, actions. Exam magic, for instance, did not replace studying hard but supplemented it.

Despite their rational acceptance of the need to study, many students nevertheless do not accept the scientific fact that luck is random, that an outcome dependent on chance is independent of previous outcomes. Fully 27 percent of the Americans and 35 percent of the Irish agreed with the following statement: "If one has some good luck, one can expect some bad luck in the future." This implies a belief in what Piaget called "imminent justice," meaning that unknown forces will act in a just and equitable way to even things up, balancing a run of good fortune with some hard going.

Our findings confirm Malinowski's observation that people practice magic chiefly in uncertain situations. There was a statistically significant correlation between the uncertainty of an activity and the amount of magic the students used. (For the Irish, this relationship was apparent only when we controlled for anxiety, that is, when we held anxiety constant by comparing students with similar levels of anxiety.) The more uncertain the outcome, the more likely the student was to use magic. Thus, as the table on page 206 shows, more American students used magic in gambling, the activity rated most uncertain, than in exams and sports, activities with medium uncertainty. Magic was least common during illness, which had the lowest uncertainty rating. There were small to moderate correlations between the anxiety students experienced in various activities and the amount of magic they used. And, when we asked students if using magic ever made them feel better, more than 70 percent said it did. In short, magic *did* reduce anxiety.

This anxiety appeared to stem from the importance students attached to particular activities. As one might expect, responses to our questionnaire suggest that those students who care most about the outcome of exams, sports, or gambling feel most anxious about them and use more magic as a result.

In general, the more people care about the outcome of an activity, the more they'll use magic to "ensure" that the outcome is favorable. This leads to an interesting anomaly. As societies become more technologically advanced, people become more highly educated and, as a result, presumably less inclined to use magic. However, emphasis on achievement and success also increases with modernization. Since people seem to use more magic when they care most about the outcome of a performance, the use of magic in some activities may *increase* with modernization, not decrease.

We have left to last our most paradoxical finding. Although many of our subjects practiced magic, they didn't believe in it very strongly—at least not consciously. When we asked, "How certain are you that such things [magical rituals] can bring luck?" only 1 percent of the American users were "very certain." Another 27 percent answered "a little certain"; 54 percent answered "not at all certain"; and 18 percent said that they were "certain that they did not bring much luck." The comments of a 20-year-old senior illustrate the attitudes of many students. "I usually wear a certain ring and earrings every day, but I make doubly sure I wear them on the day of a test," she said. "It's not that I believe I will do poorly if I don't wear them; it's just that they were given to me by someone special, so I like to make sure I have them with me in tough situations. You could say they give me confidence."

In short, most students seem to be at least intellectually aware of the fact that magic does more to reduce their anxiety than it does to bring about favorable results. The psychoanalyst might say that belief in magic probably persists beneath the level of awareness. We prefer to say that students are just playing it safe when they practice magic. They are not sure it works, but they are not sure it doesn't, either. Since the cost of performing magic is small, they use it—just in case. This lack of strong belief in the efficacy of magic may be the major factor distinguishing practitioners of magic in industrialized societies from those in preliterate cultures. Put simply, the Trobriand fisherman had faith that his magic worked. The student with her "magic" pen lacked faith but wasn't taking any chances.

UNCERTAINTY AND THE USE OF MAGIC[1]
Richard B. Felson and George Gmelch

[Published in *Current Anthropology*]

Probably the most widely cited theory of magic is that of Malinowski (1948). Malinowski postulated that people resort to magic in situations of chance and uncertainty, where circumstances are not fully under human control. In what has become one of the most frequently cited examples of magic in primitive societies, he described the Trobriand Islanders' use of magic in fishing. On the open sea, where catches were uncertain and there was considerable danger, the islanders used a variety of magical practices. When fishing within the safety and plenty of the inner lagoon, they used none.

A number of other qualitative studies support the relationship between uncertainty and magic within modern, more scientifically oriented societies (e.g., Stouffer et al. 1949, Vogt 1952, MacNiece 1964, Gmelch 1978). The only previous quantitative test of this proposition, however, does not support Malinowski. Lewis (1963) found that the use of magic by American mothers with sick children depended on the mothers' knowledge of medicine and not on the uncertainty or danger of a particular illness. However, Lewis's use of length of illness as the measure of uncertainty is questionable.

According to Malinowski, people use magic to alleviate or reduce the anxiety created by conditions of uncertainty. Through the performance of the appropriate rituals, people "work off" the tensions aroused by fear. An alternative explanation would be that magic results from purely cognitive processes and represents an effort to produce favorable results. In other words, people believe that unknown forces—"good luck" and "bad luck"—play a role in the outcome of events and that these forces can be manipulated by magic.

This study examines these relationships using a sample of American and Irish college students. It considers the use of magic in six activities—gambling, athletics, exam-taking, illness, face-to-face interaction, and dangerous activities—in relation to the degree of uncertainty of each. It investigates the relationship between the use of magic and anxiety within each activity. Finally, it examines students' beliefs about the ability of magic to alleviate anxiety and produce favorable outcomes.

Questionnaires were administered to students in sociology classes in the United States (State University of New York at Albany; $N = 270$) and in the Republic of Ireland (University College, Dublin; $N = 180$). The students in the American sample were primarily urban and from middle-class and either Catholic or Jewish back-

[1]We wish to thank Marcus Felson, Sharon Gmelch, and Walter P. Zenner for their comments on an earlier draft and Don Bennett, Des McCluskey, Kevin Buckley, Debbie O'Brien, and Ruth Pasquirello for their assistance in collecting the data.

TABLE 1
CONCEPTS AND QUESTIONNAIRE ITEMS USED TO MEASURE THEM

Concept	Questions Asked	Coding and Responses
Use of magic	Do you do anything special before or during the following activities in order to give yourself luck? (*a*) when you're gambling; (*b*) when you play in a sports contest; (*c*) when taking an exam; (*d*) before an important meeting, date, or interview; (*e*) in regard to something dangerous	1. Yes 0. No Missing Data: I can't answer since I don't engage in this activity
Confidence in efficacy of magic	How certain are you that such things can bring luck?	1. Certain that they do not affect luck 2. Not at all certain 3. Somewhat certain 4. Very certain
Anxiety about activity	How much do you worry about the following? (*a*) gambling; (*b*) sports contests; (*c*) exams; (*d*) important meetings, dates, or interviews; (*e*) illness; (*f*) accidents	1. Not at all 2. A little 3. Very much Missing Data: I haven't engaged in this activity
Belief that magic reduces anxiety	Does it ever make you feel better when you do things to give yourself luck?	1. Yes 0. No Missing Data: I don't do things to give myself luck
Uncertainty	For some things it is very certain before you start how well you'll do. For other things it is pretty unpredictable and uncertain. Rank the following in terms of certainty about the outcome you would feel beforehand: when you're involved in a dangerous activity; when you're gambling; when you're ill; when you have an important meeting, date, or interview; when you play in a sports contest; when you're taking an exam	

ground. The students in the Irish sample were predominantly Catholic, of mainly middle-class background, with as many from small towns and villages as from the city. A list of concepts and the items used to measure them is presented in table 1.

Following Malinowski, we wished to compare activities known to vary in degree of uncertainty. Since it is extremely difficult to construct objective measures of uncertainty, we used independent judges—another group of sociology students ($N = 40$)—to rank the activities according to the degree of uncertainty.

The percentage of students who use magic for each activity and at each level of anxiety is presented in table 2. For the American sample, the correlation between mean uncertainty and mean use of magic over these six activities is quite strong, whether anxiety level is controlled or not. Respondents use more magic for uncertain activities like danger and gambling than they do for more certain activities like illness and exam-taking. For the Irish sample, the overall relationship between mean uncertainty and mean use of magic is slight. However, when anxiety level is controlled, the relationship between uncertainty and magic increases substantially.

For each activity, students who experience more anxiety are more likely to use

TABLE 2

PERCENTAGE OF RESPONDENTS WHO REPORT USING MAGIC IN ACTIVITIES VARYING IN UNCERTAINTY, CONTROLLING FOR ANXIETY

	Anxiety							
	U.S.A.				Ireland			
Activity	High	Medium	Low	Total	High	Medium	Low	Total
Gambling (4.8)[a]	63	57	39	48	−[b]	65	23	33
Dangerous activities (4.4)	59	40	21	41	61	47	42	49
Exams (3.3)	45	24	−[b]	39	65	48	29	57
Sports (3.1)	67	34	19	40	36	34	19	26
Face-to-face interaction (2.9)	42	27	33	35	51	50	13	48
Illness (2.5)	40	18	16	21	39	26	10	23
Correlation with uncertainty	.64	.92	.53	.82	.64	.78	.69	.21
Probability level	.08	.01	.18	.02	.12	.03	.06	.34

[a] Mean uncertainty rank; a high rank indicates high uncertainty.
[b] Only three American students had low anxiety about exam-taking, and only one Irish student had high anxiety about gambling.

211

TABLE 3

PERCENTAGE OF USERS AND NONUSERS OF MAGIC REPORTING
VARIOUS DEGREES OF CONFIDENCE IN THE EFFICACY OF MAGIC

Degree of Confidence	Americans			Irish		
	Users (N = 183)	Non-users (N = 81)	Total	Users (N = 126)	Non-users (N = 43)	Total
Very certain	1	1	2	11	2	9
Somewhat certain	27	12	23	31	12	26
Not at all certain	54	46	51	33	28	31
Certain it does not bring luck	18	41	25	25	58	34

magic. Contrary to Malinowski's hypothesis, however, the uncertainty of an activity does not have a positive relationship to the amount of anxiety experienced. In fact, this relationship is negative for both samples.

Irish students use more magic than American students in four of the six activities: exam-taking, face-to-face interactions, illness, and dangerous activities. There is also a slight tendency for Americans to use more magic in gambling and sports, although the differences between the two groups are not statistically significant. Frequency distributions for degree of confidence in the efficacy of magic for the total sample and for users and nonusers of magic are presented in table 3. The table indicates very little confidence about the efficacy of magic, even among persons who use it. On the other hand, most students who use magic indicate that it often relieves their anxiety. When asked if it ever made them feel better to use magic, 76% of the Americans and 71% of the Irish who do so answered yes.

This study supports Malinowski's basic notion that people use magic in situations of uncertainty. Students reported using more magic in activities that are relatively uncertain (e.g., gambling) and less in activities that are relatively more certain (e.g., illness). It also supports Malinowski's contention that magic is used to reduce anxiety. For a given activity, the greater the anxiety the students experience, the more magic they use. Furthermore, the students indicated that using magic reduces their anxiety. The evidence, however, does not support the notion that uncertainty results in use of magic because of the anxiety it produces. It appears instead that magic is used under conditions of uncertainty because of a belief in its ability to alter the forces of luck rather than its ability to reduce anxiety.

The fact that a significant amount of magic is used among the college students in our sample suggests that magic is not simply superstitious, irrational behavior confined to primitive peoples. Rather, magic appears to be used in various activities to produce favorable outcomes where other techniques are limited in their effectiveness. Magic is irrational, of course, if one accepts the scientific position that luck is unalterable.

Irish students reported using more magic than Americans in four of the six activities. This is not surprising, given that Ireland is a more traditional society than the United States. However, in two activities, gambling and sports, the Americans appeared to be slightly more likely to use magic than the Irish. This may be due to the fact that gambling and sports are more important and anxiety-producing for Americans.

While most students feel that magic reduces their anxiety, they do not feel as confident that it will produce favorable results. This suggests that many students are merely playing it safe. They are not sure that magic works, but they use it just in case. The cost of performing magic is small, and there is always the possibility that it may help. The lack of strong belief in the efficacy of magic may be one of the major differences between industrialized and primitive societies in the use of magic. Put simply, tribal man has faith that his magic works; modern man lacks faith but is not taking any chances.

REFERENCES CITED

GMELCH, G. 1978. Baseball magic. *Human Nature* 1(8):32–39.

LEWIS, L. S. 1963. Knowledge, change, certainty, and the theory of magic. *American Journal of Sociology* 69:7–12.

MACNIECE, L. 1964. *Astrology.* London: Aldus Books.

MALINOWSKI, B. 1954. *Magic, science, and religion and other essays.* New York: Anchor Books.

STOUFFER, S., ET AL. 1949. *The American soldier.* Princeton: Princeton University Press.

VOGT, E. 1952. Water witching: An interpretation of a ritual pattern in a rural American community. *Scientific Monthly* 75:175–86.

SUPERSTITION: GREEN CARS, BLACK CATS, AND LADY LUCK
Jack McCallum

[Published in *Sports Illustrated*]

The next time you're at a baseball game, watch the first base coach to see if he kicks the bag before he enters the coach's box each inning. Now, he may kick the bag because he has nothing else to do, a frequent problem for first base coaches. More likely, though, he kicks the bag because he feels that, if he doesn't, all sorts of bad things will happen. Runners will get picked off. Or runners will get thrown out trying to stretch a single into a double. Or runners who beat throws to first will be called out by a diabolical umpire. Or, if he's the New York Yankees' first base coach, he will get word that George Steinbrenner wants to see him after the game.

The next time you see Mario Andretti, hand him a green pen and ask for an autograph—then duck. He may throw the pen to the ground. He may throw *you* to the ground. Like many race car drivers, Andretti considers the color green more of a threat to his well-being than Turn 1 at Indy.

The next time you're around Buffalo Bills quarterback Jim Kelly before a game, you may find you want a quick change of company. Why? Because Kelly may suddenly bolt from his seat, rush to the bathroom and force himself to vomit. He has been doing this since his days at East Brady (Pa.) High, not because a physician or trainer told him it would help relieve pregame jitters, but because Kelly feels it brings him luck. "I don't eat a pregame meal," says Kelly. "I rent it." Ugh!

In the world of sports, superstition isn't all rabbit-feet and four-leaf clovers. Sometimes, in fact, it's octopuses, as it is at Detroit Red Wing hockey games. The tradition of throwing octopuses onto the ice started at the old Olympia in 1952, when

213

a seafood merchant named Peter Cusmano tossed one out, reasoning that its eight tentacles would help the Wings achieve the eight victories (in two series) they needed to win the Stanley Cup. Sure enough, Detroit won, and its fans never forgot. When the Red Wings, who now play in Joe Louis Arena, qualified for the playoffs last season for only the fourth time in the last 16 years, down came the octopuses. Some eager fans even throw them during the regular season. That's not superstition, however—it's mass hysteria.

Th.? —— Your basic, run-of-the-mill superstitions usually don't cut it with athletes. Take the case of former New York Yankee pitcher Bob Tewksbury. One of the first things Tewksbury did last season after he learned he had been demoted to Columbus was kick his lucky rabbit-foot across the locker room. However, when athletes indulge in superstition, it generally involves something stronger and more unusual than mere rabbit-feet. Marvin Johnson, three times a light heavyweight champion from 1978 to '86, for instance, never washed in the 24 hours before a fight. Now, *that* was a strong superstition.

Th.? Superstitions have been around since the dawn of man—we know this from cave drawings showing Neanderthals stepping carefully over foul lines—but athletes probably do as much as anyone to perpetuate superstitions in this enlightened age. There are several reasons for this. Superstitions tend to be passed down from one generation to the next through the strong oral tradition of the locker room—in between dirty jokes, of course. Athletes, too, seem largely unburdened by the commonly held assumption that superstition is mumbo jumbo that doesn't work. And some athletes turn to superstition for the same reasons that others turn to religion or drugs—to relieve pressure, to convince themselves that results are predetermined, to take the fear out of the unknown.

"A superstition is a way to get through a tough situation," wrote Carole Potter in *Knock on Wood,* a 1983 book about superstitions. For the athlete, superstitions are a crutch, a secret weapon, a way to get that little edge. And a superstition can't fall out of, say, Joe Niekro's pocket on the mound, the way an emery board can. ☺

Much as they might indulge their superstitions, however, athletes, coaches, team executives and other sporting types rarely admit that they are superstitious. They prefer to talk about "habits" or "routines." New York Giants coach Bill Parcells is a classic example. Each morning when he's not on the road, Parcells follows this "routine": He drives from his house in Upper Saddle River, N.J., to Elmer's Country Store for a cup of coffee and then stops by Christiana's Coffee Shop in nearby Wood-Ridge and picks up two more containers of coffee to drink in his office at Giants Stadium in East Rutherford.

def. Now, one might assume that Parcells simply likes the coffee brewed by those two establishments (which happens to be true). But a routine becomes a superstition when someone believes that he must follow it to have good luck, or that bad luck will come knocking if he doesn't. Put Parcells in that camp. He doesn't want any of his players or staff to precede him into the locker room, and he always wants to see the same three players—Phil Simms, Brad Benson and Chris Godfrey—before he sees anyone else. He'll never pick up a penny that has tails facing up. He collects brass statues of elephants—20 of them adorn his office—but only elephants whose trunks are pointing upward.

Parcells should be in baseball. Superstition envelops that game like a shroud. It's bad luck for a pitcher to strike out the first batter. Never mention a no-hitter in the dugout. Don't cross bats. Don't wash your uniform or change your sanitary socks during a winning streak. Step over the baseline, not on it. The fans get involved too, joining the seventh-inning stretch to bring good luck to their team. Let's be careful, however, to exclude from the list of venerable baseball superstitions such modern gimmicks as the Homer Hankies that were waved by Minnesota Twins fans during last year's World Series. Anything invented since 1950 and done by more than, say, 100 people at a time isn't a superstition. It's an effort to get on national TV. *judge?*

Why is baseball so rich in superstition? Probably because it's older than most *why* American sports and is so enmeshed in folklore. Many early baseball players weren't the most educated of men, and the idea of rubbing a bat with a hot towel to get out of a slump seemed more effective than, say, adjusting your stance. Remember, back then there were no videos, nor analytical batting coaches like Charley Lau to talk about "a tension-free swing." Even Christy Mathewson, a college man, wrote in his 1912 book *Pitching in a Pinch:* "[A jinx can] make a bad pitcher out of a good one and a blind batter out of a three hundred hitter."

Some superstitions are endemic to baseball, but others were simply adapted to the sport from sources lost in the murky depths of time. Stepping over the foul line *origins* is no doubt an offshoot of the old childhood superstition that says, Step on a crack, break your mother's back. That superstition, incidentally, can be traced to the belief that a crack represented the opening of a grave, and to step on that crack meant you might be walking on the grave of someone in your family. Ask a base coach about this sometime and notice how he nods his head in pensive accord before he spits tobacco juice on your shoes. ☺

The idea of not bathing during a hot streak is an offshoot of the centuries-old *origins* superstition about washing away good luck. According to Raymond Lamont Brown, author of *A Book of Superstitions,* Welsh miners never washed their backs for fear that the roof would fall in on them. Though the percentage of Welsh miners on their roster was small, the Salt Lake Trappers of the Class A Pioneer League adopted the no-wash superstition last summer during their 29-game winning streak, a professional baseball record. No player washed his socks, and some washed nothing at all. When their streak finally ended with a 7–5 loss to the Billings (Mont.) Mustangs on July 27, the rest of the league was relieved in more ways than one. . . .

Wade Boggs of the Boston Red Sox could match any of the old-timers superstition for superstition. Eating chicken every day barely scratches the superstitious surface for Boggs, whose game-day routine makes a guy like Parcells seem positively spontaneous. Here's the Boggs Log for every Red Sox home night game:

- 3 p.m.: Leave apartment for Fenway.
- 3:30: Sit in front of locker and change into uniform.
- 4:00: Go to dugout and sit down.
- 4:10: Warm up arm.
- 4:15: Take grounders for 20 to 25 minutes.
- 4:35 or 4:40: End grounder drill by stepping on third, second and first (in that order). Take two steps in first base coaching box and lope to dugout in four steps, preferably hitting the same four spots every evening. Get drink of water. Jog to centerfield for meditation.
- Just before infield practice: Stand or sit in runway between clubhouse and dugout and toss ball against wall.
- 7:17: Do wind sprints.
- While in on-deck circle: Arrange pine tar, weighted doughnut and resin in a precise way and apply them in that order.

- Upon stepping into batter's box: Draw a *chai,* the Hebrew symbol for life.
- After that: Hit the ball where it's pitched—and where they ain't—whenever possible.

"Everybody has a routine," says Boggs. "Mine just takes five hours." . . .

Th.?

Superstitions like these will always have a place in sport, if only because an athlete's life-style makes him vulnerable to them. "Athletes do the same thing day after day," says Nanne. "They practice at the same time, they eat at the same time, they play at the same time. Important parts of their lives are very ordered, and so, perhaps, they want to bring that same kind of order into every aspect of their lives. Little rituals become little obsessions. Obsessions become superstitions."

Cincinnati Reds reliever Rob Murphy has a little obsession that even a superstitious turn-of-the-century ballplayer might have looked at askance: He's convinced that wearing black silk underwear helps his pitching. (At least two other major league pitchers share Murphy's attachment to a certain undergarment: Houston Astros space cadet Charlie Kerfeld often wears a Jetsons T-shirt on the mound, while Montreal pitcher Bryn Smith wears one bearing the logo of the rock group Rush.) Murphy relies on the silk undies only while he's in action. "Right now I'm wearing an ordinary pair of J.C. Penney cottons," said Murphy during a recent interview. But, since he's a frequently used reliever who's never sure when manager Pete Rose is going to call on him, he puts on his silk skivvies at the ballpark 162 times a year.

"I look at it as my security blanket," says Murphy. "You can't see them. Nobody but me knows they're on. But they're important. I have certain things I do to get ready for the game—go over the hitters, warm up, etc.—and putting on the underwear is part of that, part of my mental preparation."

sarcasm?

What loyalty. What devotion. What faith. Bet you'd stick with the black-undies routine even if your pitching started going bad, right Rob?

"Are you kidding me?" said Murphy. "I'd take 'em off in a minute."

Purpose — inform only?
         or   judge — sarcasm?

Aud. — all?

Persuasion

The emphasis in this unit is on writing persuasively: how can *written words* cause people to change their thinking or action?

First Activity: Exploratory Freewriting on Experiences with Persuasive Words

We'd like your thinking on this subject to be grounded in your own experience—not just in theories. Therefore, please stop now and look to your own experience before reading any further. Freewrite about an occasion in your own life when someone's words played a big role in affecting how you felt or thought about something—or even changed your action. Or write about an occasion when *your* words affected someone else's thinking, feeling, or behavior. Tell the story of this event in some detail. What really happened? And then speculate about how or why these words managed to be persuasive. If something else besides logic was important, what was this something else?

PERSUASION AS INFORMAL ARGUMENT

Sometimes people are persuaded by long, formal arguments that somehow "prove" or "settle" an issue by means of conclusive reasoning and evidence. But sometimes these good arguments don't work, that is, the reader is somehow not persuaded even though the argument seems very good. (In fact there is no such thing as pure logic except in closed systems like mathematics or symbolic logic; as soon as you apply logic to real events and natural language, there is always slippage because premises are debatable.) Persuasion always boils down to what is persuasive to what listener. Worse yet, there is always the question of whether a given listener will "listen"—take *seriously* or *try on* what you say. No logic or information can be effective if a listener is fighting you or has closed her mind to what you are saying. So at the heart of persuasion is the ability to get someone to *listen* to you.

The focus for this unit then is the process of how people's minds are affected by more informal, often shorter pieces of writing. To get someone else to really *hear* an opinion that differs from his own, to feel it as "interesting," to swallow it just a bit even if not actually believing it—that is a huge accomplishment. In this unit we will consider persuasion not as the formal problem of argument and logic, but as the human problem of getting someone to *listen* to your opinion. (In Unit 11, we will focus on argument.)

At first glance it might seem discouraging that "good" arguments often don't work. It means that if you take your goal to be the complete persuasion of "the enemy," you are almost bound to fail, for people seldom change their minds all at once. Complete arguments which "prove" that our side is right and their side is wrong are usually useful only for our side: for gatherings of our team to help us clarify our thinking, to help us remember why we believe what we believe, and to make us feel better about our position. But they are seldom read by the other team (except on occasions when they are doing research about why we are wrong).

But this view is not so discouraging if you look closely at how words really affect people. After all, it would be odd if people actually changed their minds all at once. And we see that though progress in persuasion is always slow, and we may not be good at creating a perfect, airtight argument, nevertheless the *main* art in persuasion is something we *are* all good at: sensing the other person, somehow reaching out and getting the other person to *listen.* Best of all, persuasion doesn't require length. The main task is to get readers to open the door, and too many words only make resistant readers close the door tighter.

Consider the fact that more people read letters to the editor in the newspaper than read the news or editorials or even sports. What distinguishes these published letters is that they are short, and they consist of people speaking out to others. If you want the quickest and best way to affect the thinking of the community you are part of, get a good letter published in your student or city newspaper or in a magazine that publishes letters. In this way you can be *published* and *read.*

Here are some examples:

To the Editor:
    On July 3, 12 honorees will receive the Medal of Liberty. They are mostly rich and famous. I cannot see what great things they did for our country in ref-

erence to what the Statue of Liberty stands for. When my parents came to the U.S., they contributed to its growth by using the crafts they had learned in the old country. Why not give a Medal of Liberty to such immigrants? They may not be rich and famous, but they are average, proud people.

—Michael L. Levine, *New York Times,* March 20, 1986

To the Editor:

(A previous letter writer) feels women with children should be prohibited from going on spaceflights. If there is to be such a rule, it should also prohibit men with children from going on spaceflights. The loss of a father is just as bad as the loss of a mother.

—*Daily News,* March 20, 1986

To the Editor:

Your editorial on "Snow White" [a favorable editorial about the re-release of the Walt Disney movie] could have been written only by someone who has forgotten or ignored major changes as a result of the women's movement.

My memories of "Snow White" are tarnished by the distaste I felt for a (cartoon) character who was cheerful about housekeeping for seven men (including a grump) and lived for the day when her prince would come.

Without denying the appeal of finding someone to love, I also found it appealing to go back to school and find a rewarding career, just in case my prince turned out to be a frog.

Heigh-ho, it's off to work I go. When I get home, I expect my prince to do half the housework!

—Pauline Lurie, *New York Times,* August 19, 1987

To the Editor:

We have lost another dear young person this year due to speeding- and alcohol-related car accidents. Who has to die next in order for the people of this Island to open their eyes to the problems of their children and my fellow classmates? On the whole, we teenagers do not have anything to do for social activities. Our choices are to walk the streets in Oak Bluffs, go to an arcade, or maybe see a movie.

Do you want your children to walk the streets? I and my fellow high school students would rather stroll along in our cars. It is inexpensive and "the thing to do."

All we need is a place we can call our own, and the sooner the adults on the Island realize this the fewer tragic accidents, like Kenny's and Jeff's, will happen. We are not bad kids, just bored and taking risks to make life exciting.

But what many of us are doing is taking our own lives as well as placing others in jeopardy. Please give us something to look forward to on the weekends, and to keep us entertained. That way I and others to come will graduate with all our friends alive and happy.

I was not a close friend of Jeff's, but as a resident of this Island I knew of him and his friendly attitude. I will miss him, and I hope that Ethan and Chris will be all right.

—A Concerned Martha's Vineyard Regional High School Student

SECOND ACTIVITY: EVALUATING THESE SHORT PIECES OF PERSUASIVE WRITING

By yourself—or better yet with your group—answer as many of the following questions as possible. Don't fail to answer the first five or six:

1. *Most persuasive.* Which letter persuaded you most? least? Make your answer by a quick intuitive judgment. After answering the following questions, come back to this one. You may discover you've changed your mind.

2. *Listening and trust.* Which one made you *listen* most—even if it didn't change your thoughts or feelings? Was it because you trusted the writer? How would you describe the *voice* of each writer? Do you sense the writer as reasonable or reliable? Can you point to the exact features of each letter that help you make these decisions?

3. *Your position.* What was your position on the topic of the letter *before* reading it? For each letter, how much did it *change* your thinking or feeling? (You might discover that the letter you initially chose as most persuasive was trying to persuade you of what you already believed.)

4. *Claim.* For each letter, what is the claim—summarized in a short sentence?

5. *Support.* For each letter, what is the support? Try to summarize it in a sentence. What would you say the writer was relying on: logic, information, example, emotion, language, or what else?

6. *Assumptions.* What did each author seem to be assuming as true? Do you agree with these assumptions? What does that have to do with your reactions?

7. *Audience.* For each letter, do you think you're the audience the writer had in mind? How does that affect whether or not you're persuaded? If you're the wrong audience, what sort of audience do you think the writer was addressing?

8. *Language.* In each case, did the language add to or detract from the writer's presentation? Try to be specific about exactly which pieces of language had what effect on you.

9. *Conclusion.* On the basis of these examples and questions, can you reach some tentative conclusions about what is most helpful and least helpful in short informal persuasion—in trying to get readers who disagree to *listen* to you?

We hope these examples and questions will demonstrate how complex persuasion is. First, there's the whole problem of whether or not an author's issue is of any concern to you. Then there's the character of the writer to be considered: does he or she seem like the kind of person you tend to believe or like? Authors of persuasive pieces (indeed, all authors) base their writing on certain assumptions. If you don't share those assumptions, it's difficult to give credence to what the author says. If the tone or style or level of formality is alien to you, you're unlikely to be persuaded. And, finally, if you're not the audience the writer had in mind, the writing probably won't work for you—indeed you may be put off or feel (rightly, of course) that the author doesn't care to talk to you.

THIRD ACTIVITY: WRITING A LETTER
TO THE EDITOR

kinds : 1) praise
2) complain (+ recommend)

Write a short letter to the editor which attempts to persuade readers to agree with you or even to act in some particular way. Your teacher may suggest a topic or give you free choice or ask your group to agree on a topic. It could be a letter to a campus paper, to a small newspaper in the region, or to the largest and most prominent newspaper around.

There's much to recommend writing about some campus issue and addressing your letter to your campus newspaper, because it is easier for you to believe that you *have* the capacity to influence opinions on your campus and thereby influence decisions at your particular school. Perhaps you'd like to change people's minds about grading policies, about your school's food plan, about the condition of the buildings or the dorms, or about the way student government functions. (Other possible targets are scheduling, academic requirements, safety patrols, proficiency tests, size of classes, or availability of advising, counseling, or health facilities.)

If you write to a non-campus paper, you might want to suggest some way of improving the functioning of your town or city: something about transportation, education, politics, drug use. It's also interesting to write a letter that praises or blames someone: a local figure or office holder or faculty member who is doing a particularly good job or being negligent.

You'll notice that we're deliberately avoiding some of the more global issues often assigned for persuasive essays, matters such as abortion, drinking-age laws, the death penalty, draft registration, and so forth. It isn't that we don't take these issues seriously: we do. The discipline of rhetoric itself—the art of persuasive discourse—was born in ancient Greece out of the activity of citizens speaking in public meetings to influence fellow voters. (It was a pure democracy—for men and non-slaves, anyway—where almost all decisions were reached by votes of citizens, as in town meetings in many New England states.)

But these "big" topics tend to cause problems for many students because they are assigned too often, and students often feel that their opinion won't really carry any weight in public policy. It is hard to write persuasively if you don't have a sense of at least potential power. Also, it's hard to change people's minds about these issues, since it seems as though they've

---

PROCESS BOX

Again (working on doubting/believing). Had experience of feeling an objection to my argument. Bothered me: kept tickling my mind. Didn't know how to answer it. I kept trying to put it aside, not think about it—and sort of hope that readers wouldn't notice.

Then I remembered the idea (my own idea) that it's better to write these things down. (But reluctant to do so. I'm in a hurry; trying to finish this version; don't want to fiddle with it—don't want to deal with objections.)

Took out a separate sheet and wrote out the objection. Immediately it led to an answer to the objection that I'd not been able to think of before. The answer is short and will be useful for this draft—didn't waste a lot of time.

PETER ELBOW 6/82

---

already heard all the arguments and already made up their minds. The only effective essays we've read recently on these topics have been written by students who have actually had some direct personal involvement in the topic.

MAIN ASSIGNMENT

Your main assignment for this unit is to write a persuasive essay about some issue important enough to you that you'd like to get others to agree with you about it—or even act in some way you consider beneficial. This will be an informal argument that is longer than most letters to the editor. When you've written your first draft, make enough copies of it to share with the members of your group.

One possible way of approaching this assignment is to think back to when you first became aware of how you felt about the issue you want to write on. Describe the experience that led to your stance. Personal experience can be central to persuasion, for readers can easily discount your *reasons,* but they can't discount your *experience.*

The recounting of experience is often the first step toward getting someone to listen. Even if you decide not to retell the experience in your essay, just writing it out for yourself will help you get a firm grip on why *you* believe as you do. It's usually possible for a reader to tell if you really believe something or are just going through the motions of writing a persuasive essay.

Even though we asked you to think about audience when discussing the letters to the editor earlier, and even though you were probably thinking about audience as you wrote your own short letters, we still suggest that you *ignore* audience as you write your first draft. Write your essay in the way that seems—intuitively perhaps—most effective. If you let yourself pursue the writing in its own terms—or as you most want to write it—you'll probably begin to sense who would be the most likely audience for this piece. Perhaps it will be a fairly long letter to a newspaper or an article or editorial. Perhaps it will be an essay or letter to some particular person, group, or committee whom you want to influence. Allow your choice of topic and your writing process to *lead you* to your audience.

Another way to approach this assignment is to think of the possible objections to your view. After you've finished your draft, make a list of all the reasons that might keep people from accepting your assertions. See how many of these reasons you have taken into consideration in your draft. Readers can help you here. You may or may not want to incorporate additional answers to their objections into the draft. You may just want to write out your answers—what you *could* say in response to those potential objections—and then take this extra writing to class with your draft. For it's not *necessarily* a good idea to answer all opposing opinions: sometimes too much answering-of-objections can make your piece sound defensive. Sometimes you are better off with a piece that is shorter and more direct. It's all a question of what works with readers—and with *which* readers.*

SHARING AND RESPONDING

With persuasive writing in particular, we need to see how it works with readers. Thus it is important to get the kind of feedback you need using techniques from the *Sharing and Responding* booklet. The main feedback technique might be movies of readers' minds—where they start by telling you their original opinion on your topic. You can even ask readers to talk about your topic before you show them your piece, and then have them tell you what went on in their minds *as* they were listening to it. The early forms of feedback are helpful for early drafts—helping you develop your own thinking. "Believing" feedback can help you develop your argument further; "doubting" can help you see what objections readers *could* raise. Getting people to describe your voice tells you how trustworthy you sound.

---

*Notice how Lucy O'Toole ("Readings," Unit 7) used an interesting way to generate a persuasive essay by thinking of possible objections. She probably had an easier time writing that dialogue than writing a persuasive essay: for the dialogue process leads you naturally to generate reasons: You don't have to worry so much about structure in the dialogue form. Yet the dialogue form helped her to sharpen her *reasons* and *arguments* and see them more clearly—so that now she would be in a good position to shape it into a persuasive essay. (Not that she necessarily should. We're not implying that the essay is a better or more advanced form than the dialogue. Only that if you must or wish to write an essay, a dialogue is often a good way to start because it usually helps you develop reasons. We like her piece as a dialogue.)

PROCESS JOURNAL QUESTIONS

- What did you notice during the four activities of the unit: initial free-writing and discussion of times when words were persuasive, reading and discussing letters to the editor, writing a short letter to the editor, and the final assignment? How did each of these activities affect your sense of what and how words can persuade?

- How did you choose your topic for the letter—or the main assignment? Could you find a topic you felt committed to? Did you find yourself believing your assertions more and more as you wrote—or less and less? How does the task of *persuading* seem to affect how you wrote?

- About audience. You were probably very aware of audience when writing letters to actual newspapers: it's hard not to think, "What if my letter were really printed?" Then for the longer piece of persuasive writing, we suggested you start out not worrying about who your audience might be and where the piece might go—and let the audience emerge. Reflect a bit on what happened and what you came to notice about yourself and your relationship to audience.

- Explore what went on for you during the whole sharing and responding process: how you responded to the writing of others and how you reacted to their responses to you. Which remarks were the most helpful? least helpful? Did you feel as though your respondents were being honest?

- About working in pairs or groups. What did you do that was helpful to the pair or group—perhaps making the group work better? What did others do that helped? Were there things that you or others did that seemed harmful? What would it take to avoid such words or actions next time?

RUMINATIONS AND THEORY

Informal Persuasion and Formal Argument

We find it useful to lay out two opposite answers to the question of how words can persuade. At one extreme is the *extended, formal argument*—the careful, elaborated "proof"—in which you are as logical as possible and you don't resort at all to feelings or emotional "persuasive language." At the other extreme is *informal persuasion*—more intuitive and experiential. It doesn't try to mount a full argument, in fact it may not use an "argument" at all. It may just convey an important piece of information or tell a story.

Extended formal argument requires readers to read carefully and at length. They've got to be interested enough in you or in what you are saying to give you lots of time and attention. Extended, careful argument is what you might be expected to write for an audience that is *expert* or *professional*—for example, if you were writing a report for a legislative task force about the location of a highway or about a particular health-care plan. Such an audience isn't interested in emotional arguments or in being persuaded. You don't have to coax them to read and to think carefully about the matter; they're already interested in figuring out what's the best point of view. It's their job to read with care. They want good analysis and good reasons. If they find you trying to persuade them with an emotional appeal rather than reasons and evidence, they'll likely start to distrust you and say, "What is this pesky writer trying to hide? What are the 'real' reasons he's covering up?" Clever persuasion gets in their way.

Informal persuasion—at the other extreme—is the kind you find in editorials, leaflets, advertisements, short spoken interchanges, and, of course, in letters to the editor in newspapers. It's usually shorter than formal argument, settling for making a couple of the best points—perhaps giving a reason and some information and some personal experience all wrapped up together. Often this kind of argument doesn't try to *change* someone's thinking but rather just to plant a seed. This is the kind of piece you need to write if you are trying to reach readers who have no special reason or commitment to read what you've written.

Brevity is the most common solution to the problem of readers who are liable to wander away at any moment. Whatever you want to say to such an audience, you have to say it fast. You can't take it as your goal to completely change their thinking. Planting a seed or opening a door is probably the best you can hope for.

But informal arguments aren't always short. The crucial thing that marks informal argument is a decision to forgo full argument and instead to *reach* or *interest* readers—perhaps by getting them to experience something or telling a story. For example, *Uncle Tom's Cabin* is a story—a novel—but it functions as a piece of persuasion, and it had a powerful effect on national sentiment about slavery before the Civil War. Informal persuasion may make "points," but more often it succeeds by conveying *experience* or affecting feelings. We will wait till the next unit, "Analyzing Arguments," to concentrate on formal arguments.

READINGS

LETTER TO THE EDITOR

To the Editor:

For the past year I worked as a mental health counselor in a psychiatric unit in a community hospital. Counselors and nurses compose the "frontline staff"—those who work the longest and most closely with the patients. When I hear of nursing schools closing I'm not surprised, but I am concerned.

I talked with one of the psychiatrists about the crisis facing the medical profession. We felt that people don't have the same sense of commitment as they did years ago. This is not startling in a society where the emphasis is on "making it," where people commit themselves to earning money.

People who pursue high incomes have an illusion of happiness. A study conducted by a Duke University professor predicts that as a group the baby-boomer generation will have a higher incidence of suicide in later life because of an already high prevalence of depression.

Pick up the classifieds and count the number of positions advertised for nurses and mental health professionals; jobs where weekends lose their meaning, emotional expense is big, hours are long and the pay is low. It is probably unfair to say that people aren't committed to helping others because commitment simply does not pay the bills.

The reality is college graduates have the weight of loans hanging over their heads and positions as mental health counselors start at or around $12,000. The bottom line is this: the longer we continue to refuse to pay those willing to help, the less likely somebody will be there to help us in the future.

—Richard Fahey, *Boston Globe,* September 8, 1987

TRUST
Lisa Muir

As I went up the stairs, I looked to my right and there he was, sitting on the wall as still as a statue. His gray fur stood out against the color of the wall. His tiny front feet were held up in the air. I just had to try and touch him. As I got closer, with my hand out, he came to sniff my finger. When he got about one-quarter of an inch away, I pulled my hand back. I was afraid he was going to bite me. This made him jump up and run half-way down the wall. When I got my courage back, I put my hand out again and he walked slowly back towards me. We repeated this process three times. Suddenly there was a soft noise behind me. I turned to see a boy walking up the stairs behind me. When I turned back to the wall, the squirrel was gone.

Why did he stay so long? Every other squirrel I have run into has hidden as soon as a human comes along. What made us sit there and try to touch each other? Was he curious, or did he trust me not to hurt him? I stayed because I love wild animals and always attempt to touch them. I was afraid of this tiny squirrel, though. I didn't want him to bite me. Does this mean I didn't trust him?

Trust is a belief in and reliance on the integrity and ability of a person or thing. It also involves hope. It is a feeling of relying on someone. It is not one of those silly games you played as a kid like "catch me," where you test your trust in your friend to catch you. Trust is a real thing. The feeling gets stronger and stronger as the days go by.

Trusting someone is very healthy. It shows that you care and that you're alive. There is a sense of accomplishment in trusting someone. You can't do anything all by yourself. You need a trustworthy person to help. You can't survive without it. But there is one catch: in order to be trusted, you have to be trustworthy. You have to earn the trust you receive and return it. You must keep that trust alive. Not everyone, I'm afraid, has the ability to trust.

This lack of trust bothers me. Not many people are willing to put their trust in anything or anyone. There is evidence of distrust everywhere. On the highway, a hitch-hiker tries to thumb a ride but you don't stop because you don't trust him or her. As you leave your house on your way to the store, you lock your doors and windows so no one can get in. When you reach the store, you lock your car so it will be there when you get back. One day my grandmother had a flat tire on the way home from her friend's house. She was miles from home with no one to help her. She walked to the nearest house to call my godfather, Charlie. The woman who owned the house did not trust my grandmother enough to let her into the house to call. This was her right, of course, but my grandmother needed help. The lady took Charlie's phone number and called for her while grandma stood on the front steps. What was she afraid of? My grandmother is 78 years old! What did she think my grandma was going to do?

Are people *afraid* to trust? I think so. I also think fear is a part of mistrust. Fear may hurt trust, but it also might help it. If you are afraid to have one of your possessions stolen, you are forced to trust someone to protect it. Fear and trust are inseparable.

What is at stake if you give in and trust someone? You may get hurt, but you will never know until you try. If you do get hurt, just start over again, because life goes on.

What causes distrust? There are a number of things that could cause it. As I said, you might have been hurt at one time, and you do not want to get hurt again. Or your parents could, without knowing it, have caused this feeling of mistrust by telling you not to talk to strangers or open the door without knowing who it is. This mistrust will grow inside you and when you are on your own you might become paranoid. Or maybe you just don't *want* to trust anyone. If that's true then I feel sorry for you.

There should be more trust in the world. It would help everyone all over the world, not just in our personal lives but in our political and social lives as well. Think of what it would be like to trust our country's enemies, like Russia. If we trusted them, we could become friends and there would be no more need of weapons or name calling. But trust can't be one-sided. They also have to trust us. Who will make the first move? Socially speaking, I bet everyone would have more friends and get along better if we didn't have to worry about who was saying what behind our backs. Marriages would last longer with a little more trust in them.

As you can see, trust is important to our lives. It makes us stronger. I believe that people would be nervous wrecks if they didn't trust.

FROM THE GOSPEL OF MATTHEW

Pharisees and scribes from Jerusalem then came to Jesus and said, "Why do your disciples break away from the tradition of the elders? They do not wash their hands when they eat food." "And why do you," he answered, "break away from the commandment of God for the sake of your tradition? For God said: *Do your duty to your father and mother* and: *Anyone who curses father or mother must be put to death.* But you say, 'If anyone says to his father or mother: Anything I have that I might have used to help you is dedicated to God,' he is rid of his duty to father or mother. In this way you have made God's word null and void by means of your tradition. Hypocrites! It was you Isaiah meant when he so rightly prophesied:

> This people honors me only with lip service,
> while their hearts are far from me.

The worship they offer me is worthless;
the doctrines they teach are only human regulations."

He called the people to him and said, "Listen, and understand. What goes into the mouth does not make a man unclean; it is what comes out of the mouth that makes him unclean."

Then the disciples came to him and said, "Do you know that the Pharisees were shocked when they heard what you said?" He replied, "Any plant my heavenly Father has not planted will be pulled up by the roots. Leave them alone. They are blind men leading blind men; and if one blind man leads another, both will fall into a pit."

At this, Peter said to him, "Explain the parable for us." Jesus replied, "Do even you not yet understand? Can you not see that whatever goes into the mouth passes through the stomach and is discharged into the sewer? But the things that come out of the mouth come from the heart, and it is these that make a man unclean. For from the heart come evil intentions: murder, adultery, fornication, theft, perjury, slander. These are the things that make a man unclean. But to eat with unwashed hands does not make a man unclean."

THE GREAT PERSON-HOLE COVER DEBATE
A Modest Proposal for Anyone Who Thinks the Word "He"
Is Just Plain Easier . . .
Lindsy Van Gelder

I wasn't looking for trouble. What I was looking for, actually, was a little tourist information to help me plan a camping trip to New England.

But there it was, on the first page of the 1979 edition of the State of Vermont *Digest of Fish and Game Laws and Regulations:* a special message of welcome from one Edward F. Kehoe, commissioner of the Vermont Fish and Game Department, to the reader and would-be camper, *i.e.,* me.

This person (*i.e.,* me) is called "the sportsman." refers to all?

"We have no 'sportswomen, sportspersons, sportsboys, or sportsgirls,'" Commissioner Kehoe hastened to explain, obviously anticipating that some of us sportsfeminists might feel a bit overlooked. "But," he added, "we are pleased to report that we do have many great sportsmen who are women, as well as young people of both sexes."

It's just that the Fish and Game Department is trying to keep things "simple and forthright" and to respect "long-standing tradition." And anyway, we really ought to be flattered, "sportsman" being "a meaningful title being earned by a special kind of dedicated man, woman, or young person, as opposed to just any hunter, fisherman, or trapper."

I have heard this particular line of reasoning before. In fact, I've heard it so often that I've come to think of it as The Great Person-Hole Cover Debate, since gender-neutral manholes are invariably brought into the argument as evidence of the lengths to which humorless, Newspeak-spouting feminists will go to destroy their mother tongue.

Consternation about woman-handling the language comes from all sides. Sexual conservatives who see the feminist movement as a unisex plot and who long for the good olde days of *vive la différence,* when men were men and women were women, nonetheless do not rally behind the notion that the term "mankind" excludes women.

But most of the people who choke on expressions like "spokesperson" aren't right-wing misogynists, and this is what troubles me. Like the undoubtedly well-meaning folks at the Vermont Fish and Game Department, they tend to reassure you right up front that they're only trying to keep things "simple" and to follow "tradition," and that some of their best men are women, anyway.

Usually they wind up warning you, with great sincerity, that you're jeopardizing the worthy cause of women's rights by focusing on "trivial" side issues. I would like to know how anything that gets people so defensive and resistant can possibly be called "trivial," whatever else it might be.

The English language is alive and constantly changing. Progress—both scientific and social—is reflected in our language, or should be.

Not too long ago, there was a product called "flesh-colored" Band-Aids. The flesh in question was colored Caucasian. Once the civil rights movement pointed out the racism inherent in the name, it was dropped. I cannot imagine reading a thoughtful, well-intentioned company policy statement explaining that while the Band-Aids would continue to be called "flesh-colored" for old time's sake, black and brown people would now be considered honorary whites and were perfectly welcome to use them.

Most sensitive people manage to describe our national religious traditions as "Judeo-Christian," even though it takes a few seconds longer to say than "Christian." So why is it such a hardship to say "he or she" instead of "he"?

I have a modest proposal for anyone who maintains that "he" is just plain easier: since "he" has been the style for several centuries now—and since it really includes everybody anyway, right?—it seems only fair to give "she" a turn. Instead of having to ponder over the intricacies of, say, "Congressman" versus "Congressperson" versus "Representative," we can simplify things by calling them all "Congresswomen."

Other clarifications will follow: "a woman's home is her castle . . . " "a giant step for all womankind" . . . "all women are created equal" . . . "Fisherwoman's Wharf." . . .

And don't be upset by the business letter that begins "Dear Madam," fellas. It means you, too.

Analyzing Arguments

In the previous unit on persuasion we celebrated short, informal pieces. We emphasized the central skill in persuasion as getting someone to *listen*—to open the door of his mind. We downplayed longer, formal, carefully reasoned arguments, talking about readers who won't sit still long enough to listen or who simply resist even careful arguments because their minds are closed.

But obviously there are certain situations where it *is* valuable to use a long, careful argument. That is what we turn to in this unit. Our goal is to help you see through any essay to the skeleton of reasoning at its heart in order to evaluate better the arguments of others and to construct better arguments of your own.

We have another goal here too, namely, for you to become more sophisticated about the *nature* of argument. That is, even though argument is a subject complex enough for a whole book—indeed for a whole discipline (called logic or rhetoric)—we can help you be less afraid of it and more able to jump in boldly and do good work. Many people feel they cannot "mess with argument" till they master the principles of logic; yet most of us are intimidated by the jargon associated with logic (for example, "the principle of the excluded middle" and lists of fallacies with Latin names). In this unit we will try to show you that even though the field of logic is complex and important (well worth studying), there are two important things to keep in mind:

1. There is no single, magic *right* way to argue with all other ways being wrong. In fact, the nature of argument differs from field to field.

2. There are powerful procedures for working on argument that don't

depend on the formal study of logic. We show you some of these practical procedures in this unit. If you are interested in the nature of argument, you can turn to "Ruminations and Theory" at the end of the unit where we talk more about this ages-old subject.

The assignment for this unit will be either to *analyze* or to revise one of your previous papers based on an analysis of its argument, or to write a new argumentative essay.

Arguing for Argument

Here are some reasons why carefully built argument is important.

1. Sometimes you are lucky enough to be writing to readers who *are* ready to listen. Some readers have opened the doors of their minds. A few people are open-minded in general, and many people are open-minded about issues where they don't have a personal stake. But they won't accept your view unless you can give a good argument—for they are also listening to people who disagree with you.

2. When you write essays for most teachers—especially essays in subject-matter courses—they won't buy a short informal burst of persuasion: they're usually asking for a full, careful argument. And teachers are not the only people you'll have write to whose job is to look carefully at both sides of an argument. Perhaps you need to argue something that matters to you to a person or committee that has nothing against you but nothing for you either. Certainly in the world of work, one often has to write a report or position paper or memo that carefully marshalls the best argument. We might generalize (recognizing there are important exceptions) that for friends and general readers we need to write short informal pieces of persuasion, but as *professionals* we need to analyze and write more formal and explicit arguments.

3. You might not care at all about persuading others, but just need to figure out some issue for yourself. Persuasive "seeds" are not what you need; you need the best reasons and evidence to help you make up your own mind.

4. We pointed out in the last unit that experience and feelings tend to influence us more than words, but for that very reason, we need careful argument as an *antidote*. Experience and feelings can fool us: a powerful story, letter, essay, or editorial may win our hearts, capture our feelings, and thus lead us to do exactly the wrong thing. One of the glories of language, especially written language, is that it permits us to consider things more carefully—to help us see whether we *should* follow our feelings and experience where they lead us. Writing, in particular, permits us to figure out reasons carefully and fully—to stand back from them and consider them one by one. In short we need to be able to analyze and build arguments in order to make our *own* minds work well and not be bamboozled.

We don't mean to make it an either/or choice between what we emphasized in the last unit and what we emphasize here. The sequence is cumulative. Even though you will now be working on longer, more careful argument, that's no reason to forget the skills you worked on in Unit 10 to get readers to listen and to try to make your position human.

ANALYZING AN ARGUMENT

Summaries of the rules of reasoning are common and easily available, but they (like summaries of the rules of grammar) tend to be wrong unless they are very long and complex. Pamphlets or short books on reasoning—or on grammar—can be handy and can even give useful rules of thumb, but they cannot be trustworthy. Reasoning is too complicated; the effectiveness of reasons in *particular* arguments depends on too many variables. For this unit, then, instead of trying to give you brief rules, we'll help you to harness and extend your *tacit knowledge* (which is enormous and complex): that shrewd common sense you have built up over years of practical reasoning. We'll also help you harness the knowledge of others by working collaboratively. This approach is both more pleasant and more sophisticated.

We present here a simple but powerful method for working on reasoning or arguments. You can learn to use it best if you practice it first on a piece of someone else's writing. It is a tool for standing back and seeing writing with detachment—which is harder with your own writing since you are so close to it. After learning to use this method with the writing of others, you'll be able to apply it to your own writing.

You might practice this procedure on: one of the arguments in the readings at the end of this unit; a piece of persuasive writing by a classmate from the previous unit; the list of reasons we just gave for why careful argument is important; a piece your teacher will give you. By the way, make sure the argument you practice on is written, not just spoken. On paper, you can see reasoning better—with more perspective or detachment—especially if it is not your own.

There are really two different tasks implied by the word *analysis:*

- *Breaking down* an argument into its parts. This is a *descriptive* task of learning how to identify and isolate the main elements of an argument: the claim, the reasons, the support for those reasons, the assumptions, and the implications about audience.

- *Assessing* the effectiveness of an argument. This is an *evaluative* task of deciding how much weight the reasons, evidence, and assumptions will carry with various audiences.

It helps to realize that the first task—seeing what the elements of an argument are—is more important than the second task of trying to evaluate the effectiveness of those elements. If you get bogged down arguing about the effectiveness of an argument—or even of a single reason or piece of evidence—you can easily be distracted from the main job of seeing the argument clearly. Assessing the argument is always a matter of messy dispute—whereas seeing it clearly is something you can manage. You can often get agreement among readers about what the reason *is* and what supports that reason, even though they can't agree on how persuasive the reason is. This tells you something about the nature of argument.

The Main Task: Seeing the Elements of the Argument

1. Look at Reasons and Support

a. Main claim. Read through the argument or persuasive piece, decide what the main claim is, and summarize it in one sentence. Perhaps it is obvious right from the start ("I wish to argue in favor of bicycle paths on campus"). If you're analyzing a draft, the main claim may be unclear (and we hope you will have discovered by now the *value* of doing extensive exploratory writing before making up your mind exactly what you are trying to claim). Even in a finished piece, there may be slippage between an early statement of the claim or thesis and the final summary statement.

Take care to summarize the main claim in the simplest sentence you can manage; wording counts for a lot. For example, there's a crucial difference between saying, "I'm in favor of bicycle paths" and "I'm against bicycles and pedestrians having to use the same paths." Make a note if you find a problem here: if, for example, the writer changes claims or if you think the real claim is different from what the writer says it is. You might end up deciding there are actually the "makings" for two slightly different arguments in the piece you're analyzing. (If it's hard to decide on the main claim, go on to the next step and then come back.)

b. Reasons. Read through the piece again and decide what you think are the main reasons that argue for the main claim you have identified. Summarize each reason in a *simple short sentence.* (A word or phrase won't do because a word or phrase doesn't *say* anything; it only points to a concept. You need a sentence because the sentence forces you to decide what you are saying about this concept.)

Don't be surprised if it's hard to decide just what is a "reason." In truth there's no exact answer; it's a matter of choice. For a three-page essay, you could choose three main reasons or ten. It's a question of how *closely* you want to examine the thinking. Use your judgment; try it out different ways.

Don't worry at this point about the order of these reasons. Just summarize them in the order you find them (or even out of order if you suddenly notice one you missed on a previous page)—even if it seems a jumble. (You can reorder them later if you want to examine the reasoning even more carefully or if you are actually wanting to revise this argument.)

c. Support. For each reason, what support is given? Support might take the form of evidence, illustrative examples, even other "smaller" sub-reasons that you didn't list as major reasons. (Here's an example of supporting evidence: "The average income of divorced women has gone down since the new divorce law took effect.")

2. Look at Assumptions

What assumptions or unstated reasons does the argument seem to make? You may have noticed some of the assumptions as you looked at reasons and support, but to find important assumptions you need to read through the argument once more with only this subtle question in mind: what did the writer seem to take for granted? Assumptions are slippery and often insidious because the writer gets them into the reader's head without *saying* them. For example, the following assumptions might function as unstated reasons in an argument: "What is modern is better than what is old fashioned"; "Saving time is always a good thing." To find assumptions it sometimes helps to imagine what *kind* of person is making the argument—perhaps even make an exaggerated picture of him or her in your mind—and try to think of what that kind of person takes for granted.

3. Think about Readers or Audience

What is the implied audience? Who does the writer seem to be talking to? to people who already agree or don't agree? to peers? professionals? teachers? to a large or a small audience?

And also, how does the writer *treat* the audience? What's his voice or stance? Is he respectful? talking down? distant? hesitant?

The Secondary Task: Judging or Assessing

This step involves looking back at what you have figured out in the previous steps: the reasons, the supports, the assumptions, and the audience implications. For each one simply try to decide on its effectiveness. As we said, this is the messy and arguable part. There are no rules for what works and what doesn't. Different arguments and supports work for different readers. But at least you are looking at smaller elements, and so judgments are a bit more manageable. There are a few techniques that might help:

- Look for counter arguments, counter evidence, or attacks that could be made against this support. That is, play the "doubting game" with each element.

- About each reason, support, or assumption, ask what kind of person would agree and what kind of person would disagree. This is a "humanizing" kind of approach that sometimes opens doors.

(See Section IIIA in *Sharing and Responding,* "Skeleton Feedback," for an example of this procedure used on a sample essay.)

The Power of Collaboration

Analyzing arguments is an ideal job for a pair or a group. You can learn to use this process quicker, better, and more enjoyably if you do it with others. There are various ways to collaborate. You can just work through the argument together, discussing each step as you go. Or each of you can do it on his or her own and then compare notes together. Or you can even divide up the target essay, have each person work on one part, and then put your analysis together. You may think of yet other methods.

Even though logic is a huge subject and even though the analysis of specific arguments is complex and messy, you should not be timid about wading into this process. If you do a careful job with the main task of *summarizing*—and that is feasible—then the secondary task of *evaluating* will not be such a problem.

REVISING YOUR OWN ARGUMENT

We advised you to practice this analytic procedure on the writing of others, but of course one of the main uses is in revising your own writing: to strengthen the argument in some exploratory writing or in an informal persuasive piece. If you are revising, you can't just stop with deciding what's strong and weak in your piece; you need to figure out how to improve it.

Here are a few suggestions:

- When you list main reasons (step 1b), write each one on a 3×5 card or a half sheet of paper. That way you will find it easier to play with a different order of points or even to restructure the whole piece.

- Define your main claim. If you are not sure, it may take a bit more exploratory writing.

- Figure out, finally, the best order for your argument. If you still find this difficult, it helps to realize that even though an argument operates in the realm of "reasoning," that doesn't mean that there's some perfect order you have to find—and if you don't you are lost. There are always a host of possible organizations or sequences that could be effective.

It's an important psychological fact that arguments are not necessarily more effective if they present reasons step by step in the most logical sequence, as in a geometry textbook. It's not just a matter of trying to hide the logic in a poor argument; even a strong argument is sometimes clearer and more persuasive if presented differently from how a logician or geometry text would present it. So try different orders; you can start with the most powerful reason, end with it, give reasons in the order you thought of them (with a kind of narrative thread), or clump them by resemblance.

In short, don't feel you have to have mastered logic to be good at this

PROCESS BOX

Often my rough exploratory writing is too loose, wordy, wandering: to revise it is to tighten it. But recently I've been noticing how it sometimes works the other way: my revising makes something soggy, wordy, heavy. When I get dissatisfied and look back at the draft writing I started with, I see it had punch. My efforts to clarify, explain, and spell out have killed the spunk.

I just noticed this happening again. Here is the passage that made me notice it—a passage I found myself coming up with through my efforts to revise (it's for a paper which I will soon have to read at a meeting):

> I don't experience myself as brave—indeed I tend to feel myself as easily frightened and having copped-out many times in my life—yet somehow I seem to let myself drift into situations which it would have taken courage to have chosen on purpose. Scary teaching situations where I wandered off into the unknown as to group functioning; embarking on decisions to teach things I didn't know about; teaching situations where students are unhappy with me because I don't know where we are going or don't seem to know enough about what we are studying; or because I cannot keep myself from being either less authoritative or sometimes more authoritative than they feel is right.

When I woke up to how soggy this had become, I turned back to the original passage in my exploratory writing. (It was no longer in front of me because I was revising a revision.) And here's what I found.

> I have a kind of hunger/vision of how things could be—and though I don't *experience* myself as brave, I do in fact always let myself drift into situations which it would take courage to choose: scary teaching situations in which students are dissatisfied with me or [in] which I have to reveal more of myself than I am comfortable doing.

It's not great, but the question is, how can I improve it without losing the energy and directness?

PETER ELBOW

process. Use your intuition; follow hunches. Our *nose* for reasoning is usually more acute than our conscious knowledge of reasoning, just as our ear for grammar is usually more acute than our conscious knowledge of grammar. Of course intuition alone can be wrong. That's why you need the two powerful tools we suggest here: an x-ray of the skeleton of reasons in the argument and an assessment of the effectiveness of these reasons. And don't forget the value of collaboration in doing all of this.

MAIN ASSIGNMENT

For your main assignment, choose one of the following:

1. Revise a persuasive essay you've already written, with particular emphasis on strengthening the argument for a particular audience. The most likely essay to revise is the persuasive essay you wrote for Unit 10. But you could revise an earlier essay if you prefer, since a number of them could be called persuasive. That is, they are attempts at argument or making a case.

2. Write a new essay in which you try to build the best argument you can.

3. Write an essay that analyzes the argument in an essay or that compares the nature of the arguments in two essays. You could analyze one or more of your own essays. Or analyze one or more of the essays in the Readings at the end of this unit or other units; the Emig article in Unit 14 or "Cleaning Up the Environment" in the *Sharing and Responding* booklet are particularly apt pieces for analysis of argument. Perhaps your teacher will choose essays from different disciplines or discourse communities (e.g., natural science, social science, and humanities) and ask you to compare the way practitioners seem to argue or give reasons in those different fields.

4. Collaborative option. Two of you could write two versions of the same essay, directing each version to a *different* audience—with particular attention to building the most effective argument for each audience. You could choose an essay that one of you has already written and make two versions of it or start from scratch on a new topic.

ABOUT SHARING AND RESPONDING

If you write an argument of your own, skeleton feedback (see Section IIIA in the *Sharing and Responding* booklet) will give you the best information on the reasoning itself. That's the process we've been using in this unit. The descriptive outline (Section IIIC) will give you the best information on the structure. But perhaps—after all this emphasis on reasoning—you should get feedback on factors like voice or stance toward readers. As always, movies of the reader's mind (Section IV) tend to tell you the most.

PROCESS JOURNAL QUESTIONS

- Do you find yourself more comfortable working with short, informal arguments or longer, more careful arguments?

- Which parts of *you* does this unit bring out that others have not?

- What happened for you as you worked on the various features of an argument: finding the main claim, finding reasons, finding evidence, finding assumptions? Do you notice differences?

- What happens to you when this process is used on your *own* writing: does it make you nervous or defensive? Do you find yourself grateful and pleased? Do you get numb?

- Write about the difference for you between analyzing an argument and building an argument.

RUMINATIONS AND THEORY

Reasoning and Grammar

To figure out what makes good argument is interestingly like the task of figuring out what makes good grammar. Indeed reasoning and grammar are deeply similar: grammar is a picture of the regularities in how people use *language;* reasoning is a picture of the regularities in how people use *thought.*

Take grammar. Though there are certain universals of grammar—certain regularities in how people use language whether they speak English or Chinese—for the most part grammar is a story of local peculiarities: different languages and different dialects are constituted by different regularities. Grammar is largely an empirical business; there is almost nothing but "what native speakers do." That is because at its most basic level, grammar is what makes language possible; consequently, any native speaker inevitably has the potential to speak correctly whenever she opens her mouth. Mistakes are either momentary lapses or—what is more likely—not mistakes in grammar but mistakes in *usage.*

If we let grammar include matters of usage (such as whether you may split infinitives or begin sentences with "And" or "Hopefully"), grammar then becomes defined more narrowly: "what *prestige* native speakers *approve of* or call *appropriate for writing.*" At the level of usage, dictionaries may tempt you to think there are right answers, but dictionaries do nothing but record what natives do or approve of. Thus dictionaries continually change their minds as the years go by and as people change their habits. At any given moment (now, for instance), dictionaries disagree about the usage and even spelling of certain words.

But although there may be no such thing as "correct grammar" built into the universe (or at least very little of it, and it won't help you choose between "who" and "whom"), if you want to avoid being considered a dummy—or if you want to get a good grade, get certain kinds of jobs, or persuade your readers, you have to get rid of what *your* readers call "mistakes." (If you're interested in these matters, you'll find some of the readings in Unit 18 interesting.)

The same situation holds for logic or reasoning. Here too there are few universals. In *The Meno,* Plato stresses the universals, concluding that all humans seem to agree about the rules of geometry or mathematics. But most of our reasoning is *not* about geometry and mathematics, and it turns out that good reasoning in most realms (like good grammar at the level of usage) depends on what different groups of people *call* good reasoning—that is, upon conventions that are different in different cultures and contexts. To reason well is to learn the conventions of a particular community of writers within a particular area of knowledge or practical functioning.

Are we saying that grammar and reasoning are nothing but a set of random rules to memorize—like batting averages or the capitals of the states? No. There is a rational and orderly science of grammar that you can study and master. It's a lovely science—in a sense the science of the human mind. The same goes for reasoning. But fortunately we don't *have* to study and master the science of grammar to make our language strong (or to get rid of most of what others call "mistakes"). And so our point in this unit is that we don't need to study the science of logic to get our reasoning strong (and get rid of our worst mistakes in thinking).

The reason why we can do well without study is that we've done so much talking, listening, discussing, and writing that we already have an enormous amount of *tacit* or *unconscious* knowledge of grammar and reasoning. Can we get good grammar and good reasoning just by putting pen to paper and writing? Don't we all wish! No. We can only benefit from all our tacit knowledge if we go about using it the right way. In this unit we suggest tools to harness our tacit knowledge of reasoning effectively—and in doing so, to gain more control and conscious awareness of that tacit knowledge.

Here are steps to help you make the best use of your tacit knowledge of *grammar* in the process of writing.

1. Start off writing as naturally and comfortably as possible: *don't* think about grammar or about any minor matters of phrasing or spelling; think only about what you want to say. *Talk* onto the paper. In this way you are making the most use of your intuitive knowledge of grammar. The most tangled and mistake-riddled writing almost always results from slow and careful writing. You stop after every three or four words and worry about whether something's wrong—and then think about how to finish the sentence. Or you search a thesaurus for a different word or search the dictionary for a spelling. You lose track of the natural syntax in your head. If instead you can get yourself to *talk on paper* naturally and comfortably, you will have mostly clear and correct syntax to start with. You can clean up minor irregularities later.

2. Next, by whatever revising process you find best, get your text to say *exactly* what you want it to say—but still without worrying about minor matters of phrasing, grammar, and spelling. Thinking about these things will just distract you from paying attention to what you are trying to *say*. And why fix up the grammar and spelling in a sentence you may well throw away or rewrite anyway?

3. Now turn your attention to phrasing, spelling, and grammar. Read over your draft slowly and carefully to yourself and see what improvements you can make and what mistakes you can eliminate. If you read it *out loud*

239

to yourself—slowly and with expression—you will find even more ways to improve it.

4. Read your draft out loud to one or two listeners—for *their* help, yes, but also because their presence as audience will help you find more problems and think of more improvements.

5. Give your final, typed version to another person to copyedit. In Mini-unit K we set out a structured method for getting this sort of help from others.

Thus we do *not* in this book summarize the rules of language or grammar or usage for you. You can easily find other books—handbooks—which attempt to do so. (Unfortunately, however, such handbooks tend to be wrong unless they are enormously long and complex. Any simple rule will have too many exceptions that depend on the context.) You will do a better job of strengthening your language and "fixing your writing" if you work in the more empirical (and more enjoyable) fashion already spelled out. The strength of our approach comes from (1) using language unself-consciously in order to tap your tacit knowledge; (2) examining and revising, in a self-conscious, systematic, and controlled frame of mind, what you've produced; and (3) collaborating with others.*

These same three steps can make your reasoning effective too: (1) write out your argument and its support by talking naturally and unself-consciously on paper; (2) examine and revise what you've written, in the self-conscious, systematic way we've outlined in this unit; (3) get help from others. By going about writing an argument this way, you use both intuitive and systematic modes of thinking; exploiting them together leads to powerful argumentative writing.

READINGS

TO A CONCERNED STUDENT: A PARENT'S REPLY†
Nis Kildegaard

Dear Concerned High School Student:

Please excuse the clumsy salutation, but you didn't sign your name to the letter in last Friday's Gazette, on a page devoted to the recent deaths on Island roads. I'm writing you a tough letter in return—perhaps you will think too tough. I'm writing as a concerned parent, and my words are born of love, tough love, and worry.

---

*You will have a harder time at this task if you are not a native speaker—or even if you seldom read. Your success here depends a lot on what kind of training your *ear* has had. But don't underestimate your ear. If you've heard a lot of radio and television, you've heard plenty of standard English and developed a keen sense of the differences between levels of formality.

†This is a response to a letter to the editor included in Unit 10.

Adolescence is one of the most difficult times of life, and it's no easier on the Vineyard than anywhere else. There are so many changes, and through them all runs the challenge of reaching for new freedoms while coming to grips with the responsibilities they bring. Let me suggest that in this vital area, you have some hard thinking to do.

"On the whole," you write, "we teenagers do not have anything to do for social activities." And you continue, "My fellow students and I would rather stroll along in our cars. It is inexpensive and 'the thing to do.'

"All we need is a place we can call our own. And the sooner the adults on this Island realize this, the less tragic accidents like Kenny Wangler's and Jeff Hayden's will happen. We are not bad kids, just bored and taking risks to make life exciting."

You are raising two separate issues here, and your first mistake is in tangling them. One issue is drinking and driving. The second is the problem of boredom.

In our culture, a car is more than a means of transportation; it is an emblem of freedom; the driver's license a badge of adulthood. The automobile is, for most of us, the most powerful and deadly machine we'll ever control. And the car is used in a public setting, where our irresponsibility endangers not only our own lives, but the lives of our passengers and of others on the road.

At the heart of your argument is a dangerous cop-out. First you claim the privilege of driving a car. Never forget that it is a privilege and not a right: each week, our courts revoke the licenses of those who abuse that privilege by driving while under the influence of alcohol.

So you say you're mature enough to sit behind the wheel of a potentially deadly machine, and in the very next breath, you say it's our fault—the fault of the adults in this community—that your classmates are killing themselves on drunken joyrides and for lack of anything more entertaining to do.

Let me say this to you straight: Until you're adult enough to take responsibility for your own actions as a driver, you have no business behind the wheel. As long as you blame others for your choices, you are acting as a child and should be treated as such.

And on this subject of responsibility, another thought. You complain that you are bored. You ask, "Please give us something to look forward to on the weekends and to keep us entertained."

Just look around, and I think you'll find an immense reservoir of love and concern for your generation on the part of the parents in this community. If you, as Island teenagers, came forward with a clear description of any one program or facility you feel is missing, you might be surprised at how quickly Vineyard parents and the rest of a concerned community would react.

But you are copping out again. We get no proposals from you in your letter, only complaints and the plea: "Give us something . . . to keep us entertained."

Whether you blame your boredom on others or take responsibility for it is your choice. All around you are young people so involved in their world that no day is long enough. These young adults aren't waiting around for somebody to entertain them: They're setting goals and going after them. They're taking responsibility for their lives, just as you must for yours.

If you think you have to risk your life to make it exciting, you're not being very creative. And if you blame others for the sort of choice that cost Jeff Hayden and Kenny Wangler their lives, you're wrong again—maybe dead wrong.

Life is precious and all too short. Two of your friends threw their lives away this summer. Whether you do the same is your decision, and yours alone.

WITH ALL DELIBERATE SPEED:
WHAT'S SO BAD ABOUT WRITING FAST?
William F. Buckley Jr.

If, during spring term at Yale University in 1949 you wandered diagonally across the campus noticing here and there an undergraduate with impacted sleeplessness under his eyes and coarse yellow touches of fear on his cheeks, you were looking at members of a masochistic set who had enrolled in a course called Daily Themes. No Carthusian novitiate embarked on a bout of mortification of the flesh suffered more than the students of Daily Themes, whose single assignment, in addition to attending two lectures per week, was to write a 500-to-600-word piece of descriptive prose every day, and to submit it before midnight (into a large box outside a classroom). Sundays were the only exception (this was before the Warren Court outlawed Sunday).

For anyone graduated from Daily Themes who went on to write, in journalism or in fiction or wherever, the notion that a burden of 500 words per day is the stuff of nightmares is laughable. But caution: 500 words a day is what Graham Greene writes, and Nabokov wrote 180 words per day, devoting to their composition (he told me) four or five hours. But at that rate, Graham Greene and Nabokov couldn't qualify for a job as reporters on The New York Times. Theirs is high-quality stuff, to speak lightly of great writing. But Georges Simenon is also considered a great writer, at least by those who elected him to the French Academy, and he writes books in a week or so. Dr. Johnson wrote "Rasselas," his philosophical romance, in nine days. And Trollope . . . we'll save Trollope.

ooooo

I am fired up on the subject because, to use a familiar formulation, they have been kicking me around a lot; it has got out that I write fast, which is qualifiedly true. In this august journal, on Jan. 5, Morton Kondracke of Newsweek took it all the way: "He [me—W.F.B.] reportedly knocks out his column in 20 minutes flat—three times a week for 260 newspapers. That is too little time for serious contemplation of difficult subjects."

Now that is a declaration of war, and I respond massively.

To begin with: it is axiomatic, in cognitive science, that there is no necessary correlation between profundity of thought and length of time spent on thought. J.F.K. is reported to have spent 15 hours per day for six days before deciding exactly how to respond to the missile crisis, but it can still be argued that his initial impulse on being informed that the Soviet Union had deployed nuclear missiles in Cuba (bomb the hell out of them?) might have been the strategically sounder course. This is not an argument against deliberation, merely against the suggestion that to think longer (endlessly?) about a subject is necessarily to probe it more fruitfully.

Mr. Kondracke, for reasons that would require more than 20 minutes to fathom, refers to composing columns in 20 minutes "flat." Does he mean to suggest that I have a stopwatch which rings on the 20th minute? Or did he perhaps mean to say that I have been known to write a column in 20 minutes? Very different. He then goes on, in quite another connection, to cite "one of the best columns" in my new book—without thinking to ask: How long did it take him to write that particular column?

The chronological criterion, you see, is without validity. Every few years, I bring out a collection of previously published work, and this of course requires me to reread everything I have done in order to make that season's selections. It transpires that it is impossible to distinguish a column written very quickly from a column written very slowly. Perhaps that is because none is written very slowly. A column that requires two hours to write is one which was interrupted by phone calls or the need to check a fact. I write fast—but not, I'd maintain, remarkably fast. If Mr. Kondracke thinks it intellectually risky to write 750 words in 20 minutes, what must he think about people who speak 750 words in five minutes, as he often does on television?

The subject comes up now so regularly in reviews of my work that I did a little methodical research on my upcoming novel. I began my writing (in Switzerland, removed from routine interruption) at about 5 P.M., and wrote usually for two hours. I did that for 45 working days (the stretch was interrupted by a week in the United States, catching up on editorial and television obligations). I then devoted the first 10 days in July to revising the manuscript. On these days I worked on the manuscript an average of six hours per day, including retyping. We have now a grand total: 90 plus 60, or 150 hours. My novels are about 70,000 words, so that averaged out to roughly 500 words per hour.

Anthony Trollope rose at 5 every morning, drank his tea, performed his toilette and looked at the work done the preceding day. He would then begin to write at 6. He set himself the task of writing 250 words every 15 minutes for three and one-half hours. Indeed it is somewhere recorded that if he had not, at the end of 15 minutes, written the required 250 words he would simply "speed up" the next quarter-hour, because he was most emphatic in his insistence on his personally imposed daily quota: 3,500 words.

Now the advantages Trollope enjoys over me are enumerable and nonenumerable. I write only about the former, and oddly enough they are negative advantages. He needed to write by hand, having no alternative. I use a word processor. Before beginning this article, I tested my speed on this instrument and discovered that I type more slowly than I had imagined. Still, it comes out at 80 words per minute. So that if Trollope had had a Kaypro or an I.B.M., he'd have written, in three and one-half hours at my typing speed, not 3,500 words but 16,800 words per day.

Ah, you say, but could anyone think that fast? The answer is, sure people can think that fast. How did you suppose extemporaneous speeches get made? Erle Stanley Gardner dictated his detective novels nonstop to a series of secretaries, having previously pasted about in his studio 3-by-5 cards reminding him at exactly what hour the dog barked, the telephone rang, the murderer coughed. He knew where he was going, the plot was framed in his mind, and it became now only an act of extrusion. Margaret Coit wrote in her biography of John C. Calhoun that his memorable speeches were composed not in his study but while he was outdoors, plowing the fields on his plantation. He would return then to his study and write out what he had framed in his mind. His writing was an act of transcription. I own the holograph of Albert Jay Nock's marvelous book on Jefferson, and there are fewer corrections on an average page than I write into a typical column. Clearly Nock knew exactly what he wished to say and how to say it; prodigious rewriting was, accordingly, unnecessary.

Having said this, I acknowledge that I do not know exactly what I am going to say, or exactly how I am going to say it. And in my novels, I can say flatly, as Mr. Kondracke would have me say it, that I really do not have any idea where they are going—which ought not to surprise anyone familiar with the nonstop exigencies of soap opera writing or of comic strip writing or, for that matter, of regular Sunday sermons. It is not necessary to know how your protagonist will get out of a jam into which you put him. It requires only that you have confidence that you will be able to get him out of that jam. When you begin to write a column on, let us say, the reaction of Western Europe to President Reagan's call for a boycott of Libya it is not necessary that you should know *exactly* how you will say what you will end up saying. You are, while writing, drawing on huge reserves: of opinion, prejudice, priorities, presumptions, data, ironies, drama, histrionics. And these reserves you enhance during practically the entire course of the day, and it doesn't matter all that much if a particular hour is not devoted to considering problems of foreign policy. You can spend an hour playing the piano and develop your capacity to think, even to create; and certainly you can grasp more keenly, while doing so, your feel for priorities.

The matter of music flushes out an interesting point: Why is it that critics who find it arresting that a column can be written in 20 minutes, a book in 150 hours, do not appear to find it remarkable that a typical graduate of Juilliard can memorize a prelude and fugue from "The Well-Tempered Clavier" in an hour or two? It would take me six months to memorize one of those *numeros*. And mind, we're not talking here about the "Guinness Book of World Records" types. Isaac Asimov belongs in "Guinness," and perhaps Erle Stanley Gardner, but surely not an author who averages a mere 500 words per hour, or who occasionally writes a column at one-third his typing speed.

There are phenomenal memories in the world. Claudio Arrau is said to hold in his memory music for 40 recitals, two and a half hours each. *That* is phenomenal. Ralph Kirkpatrick, the late harpsichordist, actually told me that he had not played the "Goldberg" Variations for 20 years before playing it to a full house in New Haven in the spring of 1950. *That* is phenomenal. Winston Churchill is said to have memorized all of "Paradise Lost" in a week, and throughout his life he is reported to have been able to memorize his speeches after a couple of readings. (I have a speech I have delivered 50 times and could not recite one paragraph of it by heart.)

So cut it out, Kondracke. I am, I fully grant, a phenomenon, but not because of any speed in composition. I asked myself the other day, Who else, on so many issues, has been so right so much of the time? I couldn't think of anyone. And I devoted to the exercise 20 minutes. Flat.

✶   WHAT'S IN A GRADE?*
Jonathan Waxler

What is a grade? According to *Webster's New World Dictionary,* a grade is "a degree or rating in a scale classifying according to quality, rank, worth, intensity, etc." To many college students grades are the main purpose of their existence. This is most evident around exam time when people start getting extremely <u>stressed</u> out, worrying about how they're going to do. They lock themselves in their rooms for hours on end, coming out only occasionally to go to the bathroom or to blow off some steam. Then when they get to their exam they are so nervous that they can't recall what they have studied or—even worse—they find out that they have studied all the wrong

*You'll find an analysis of this paper in the readings for Unit 13.

information. They then get a bad grade even though they have put much time and effort into their studies.

Grades are in my opinion a deterrent to the learning process. They cause stress, 1 as shown in the preceding example. They also cause competition among students, 2 which in turn just adds to the stress of school. When the teacher passes back an exam or a paper the sound of people saying "What did you get?" always seems to fill the room. There is always that one person in the class who manages to get an "A" without doing any work, while other people who are always working their asses off seldom get better than a "C."

One of the worst things about grades, however, is that they are usually based 3 not only on how well you do your work but also on whether things are passed in on time and whether you show up for class. Who cares if you show up to class? If you don't show up to class, an "A" paper is still just as good as it was before! We are not here to be graded on our ability to get out of bed to get to class nor are we here to be judged on whether or not the teacher enjoys the subject we choose to write about. The purpose of attending the university is to get an education and to be judged on the amount of knowledge we retain and the amount of progress we make from the start of the semester to the end of it.

If it were up to me, I would turn to a system like that of Hampshire College, where evaluations are given rather than grades. Students in such a system don't learn 1 from a grade but instead from the comments and corrections that are written by the teacher and also by having the teacher go over things that are unclear in the students' minds. Tests are not multiple choice and such; instead, the teacher poses a general question such as, "What have you learned from this class up to this point in time?" The student then writes an essay talking about what he or she has learned and the 2 teacher evaluates that essay, pointing out to the student areas in which the student has not learned the material.

At the end of the semester students receive a final evaluation based on the 3 amount of knowledge they have gained over the course of the semester. The teacher then decides whether this student has shown progress and learned enough of the material to receive credits for the class. Students could then be admitted to other schools, i.e., law school, graduate school, etc., through their file of evaluations and recommendations by their professors.

By turning to this system of evaluating rather than grading, the life of the student would greatly change. There would no longer be that competition to get a better grade 4 than your classmate, since there would only be two grades—pass or fail. Much of the pressure facing the students would also be alleviated since they would be learning for 5 the sake of retaining knowledge as opposed to learning for a test and then forgetting what they have learned three days later. As I've stated before, grades are evil, and I feel that without them learning would be a much more enjoyable process.

TRACKING
Rosemary Merhige

The tracking system used in school districts across the country is detrimental because it labels children and produces critical problems. Tracking is the homogeneous grouping of the students in any course of study according to their intelligence or level of ability. It influences his or her academic standing and attitudes toward him in the classroom, in his peer group and in the community. Different schools have various names for the tracks. In my district it was A-track for honor students, B-track for average students, and C-track for slower children. Originally, this system was set up as a way of helping the slower learners and challenging the gifted.

According to most educators, teaching brighter students is much more rewarding than teaching slower children. Both the students and the teachers show greater enthusiasm. Why keep children who are really interested in learning with students who don't care and don't want to be in school? Most of the lower track students have behavioral problems, are lazy and can't sit still in a classroom. These children will hold back their intelligent peers. This is a common belief.

We are conditioned to think the B-track and the C-track children are not as interested in learning. What would happen if B-track students were placed in an A-track class? In one particular experiment, students who would ordinarily be put in a B- or C-track class were placed in an A-track class. Neither the teachers nor the students were aware of this. The teachers expected more from their students thinking they were capable of better work. Surprisingly, these children actually functioned like other A-track students.

What difference does it make if we label a child an honor student? Children are put in A-track because of their ability to produce work on that level. It is human nature to label and categorize. All through our lives we figure out who is smart, simple, rich, poor, honest, reliable, etc. In my class, we predicted early on who would be the future valedictorian and who wouldn't even make it to graduation.

While being labeled an honor student is encouraging for a child, when labeled as "stupid" or below average, the student finds it extremely difficult to believe that he is capable of more. Although he is not confined to that particular track and does have the opportunity to improve and move up, rarely does this happen. Tracking is a self-fulfilling prophesy. In order for slower children to improve in school, first they must change their self-image and not have their creative impulses stifled by a derogatory label.

By tracking students we are creating a broader gap between rich, poor, and even black and white. It is unusual to find many blacks or other minorities in an A-track class. In my high school, my A-track class was predominantly white as compared to B- or C-track students' classes, which were more integrated. Children from poorer families with uneducated parents do not show what they can achieve. They come from impoverished environments. Their homes do not provide them with the stimulation and encouragement to learn and excel. The hours spent in school surroundings have to make up for this deficit. Unfortunately, they are placed in lower tracks with no personal ambition to go further. These children have only one intent: to get out as quickly and easily as possible. They are victims of their socio-economic class and the school system.

The faculty shouldn't give preference to either "gifted" or "slow" pupils. Each student should be pushed harder with equal expectancy levels. It is only with the implementation of forward-thinking propositions such as these that the true potential of each student can be reached.

ORALITY, LITERACY, AND STAR WARS
Eric A. Havelock

Having been myself a scholar with a background in Greek and Latin, most of what I have had to say during the last thirty years of research about orality and literacy has naturally focused on the ancient Greeks and the alphabet they invented. As a teacher I have been able to enjoy a privileged position. My pupils, men and women, have had no trouble with literacy. If they had, they would not have taken on the task of learning Greek, a formidable challenge. Your job, on the other hand, as teachers of composition forces you to grapple with the basics of the educational process. I have profound respect for your task—what you have to do. Without your work— the teaching of college composition—my work would be impossible.

The Greek alphabet is the one we use every day to express ourselves in writing, and to teach our pupils to express themselves. That is a common bond between us, though most people, including classicists, are not aware of it. They have not taken it into their consciousness. It is this instrument that has created the literature we read, whether in Greek, Latin, English, or any contemporary European tongue, including Russian (despite variation in shapes of characters used). . . .

The objective of literacy is commonly defined as the mastery of the kind of language that deals in concepts, the ability to express oneself abstractly, and so to think logically and clearly. I have myself stressed this as a capacity in ourselves created by what I have called the alphabetic revolution, which had occurred in Greece by the time Plato was born. It can be perceived as the means that enabled him to write as he did. Although we classify him as a philosopher, and do not expect our pupils to be able to write as he did, the prose he created was a prose of ideas, the first of its kind. When we propose that one aim of teaching English composition is to teach pupils how to think abstractly and express themselves conceptually and clearly, we are taking our lesson from him. . . .

I want to get behind the question of literacy, of conceptualism, before returning to it. I want to go back in time, and I want to get below the surface of the written message, to ask what is the oral message lying underneath it.

I assume we take the teachings of Charles Darwin seriously. We are all the children of our evolutionary ancestors. The way we behave today—including our speech behavior—is governed by programs that have been put into our brains through the evolutionary process. This applies no less to the way we communicate than to anything else we do. When we teach composition, we are addressing ourselves to a pupil's brain. That brain, from the time that our species began to leave its apelike ancestors behind, over the span of perhaps a million years, enormously increased its cubic capacity. Evolutionists agree that this capacity was needed to handle language, to be able to talk. The pressures of natural selection gave an advantage to those brains that showed signs of improved ability to communicate through language, to talk to each other. It made us into human beings; it constitutes our humanity.

From the standpoint of the teacher, the basic fact about the brain is that it is programmed to speak, not to write. Writing, along with reading, was a trick to be learned at the very end of the evolutionary process.

Consequently, the brain of a child as it develops is programmed to pick up automatically the elements of whatever language is spoken by surrounding adults. But here there is a catch. It can pick up the basics of a vocabulary. But experience shows that beyond this stage the child always needs help of some sort if he or she is to get further. Evolution seems to have created and fixed in us not only an automatic program but a learning program, a receptivity to a learning process that is not automatic, one that calls for instruction. You can leave the child with a child's vocabulary. It will serve the child, but at a fairly simplified level of communication. A child's brain is ready for more, if instruction can be provided.

This matter is further complicated by an additional fact of evolutionary history, which belongs to the history of culture. At some point in the story, our species became aware of the need to remember not just the basic grammar that you had to share with another in order to communicate with another (the sort of grammar Professor Chomsky talks about), but also whole sentences and statements in order to be able to repeat them. This kind of language was needed and used to store up cultural information, which generation after generation could hand on and reuse, that is, by remembering it and repeating it.

Why was this so? The answer lies in the need for any kind of society above the most elementary level to be guided by some body of custom or law that is stable and can become what we call a tradition. The language used is framed to give this tradition historical and religious dignity. Without it, a given society could not keep coherence.

But how could such a tradition prove effective through survival if it was not written down? The method devised—and I suspect evolutionary pressure played a part here, too—was to arrange language rhythmically, in patterns of sounds that repeated themselves, while at the same time saying new things—what we today call poetry. These had to be taught in their turn. The need for them created a fresh level of linguistic instruction that must have been typical of all human societies worth the name for tens of thousands of years, before reading and writing became effective enough to replace it.

This is a brief and inadequate summary of a very complex story. I put it forward now in order to bring it to bear upon our own problems as teachers of composition. I propose several questions:

First, if the child's brain is initially programmed to master oral language and only oral language, why do we lay such stress on acquiring literacy as early as possible? Why, when we test intelligence even at the primary level, do we tend to give preference to what a pupil sees, in the form of letters or building blocks or whatever, over what he can hear and say?

Second, if the child's brain is programmed to expect and enjoy rhythmic language—the nursery rhyme, for example—and while enjoying it to memorize it, why do we not give more instruction in the recitation and memorization of poetry to children of all ages? Why cannot such a program be continued at the adolescent level, even as the adolescent is simultaneously learning the skills of reading and writing? For that matter, why should training in poetic recitation not be supplemented by training in the rhetorical delivery of rhythmic prose?

Third, may it be true that the teaching of college composition at the freshman level would be greatly assisted if the program included some oral performance of what is being written or read? Might not speech training, elocution, in short, accompany the writing and correction of essays?

These are only questions. Even if they are good questions, the answers may be deemed impractical: There is not enough time or money. One conclusion these questions point to is that in teaching literacy, let alone English composition, our troubles begin in the primary school, not the secondary. That is where too little attention is focused, too little theory thought out, too little money spent. You and I both have to deal in our different ways with opportunities missed at the primary level.

A footnote can be added: The oral rhythmic word, as it has played its part historically in support of cultural evolution, has regularly been associated with the practice of music and dance. In education, as formally conducted and institutionalized, these are treated wholly as fringe benefits, as extracurricular. This attitude may also be flawed.

I now return to the problem facing us at the other end of the spectrum, the teaching of a fully literate speech, meaning conceptualist speech that conveys the ability to think abstractly. It is my contention that if we skip over the oral stage in the educational process too hurriedly, if we slight its importance, we do damage to those very conceptual powers we aim to develop. We impair the quality of the very abstractions we are teaching ourselves and others to use. Let me explain why.

Oral language has this fundamental quality: It is realistic. It deals with the specifics of what one senses and feels. It has a habit of calling a spade a spade. It expresses the realities of our experience in down-to-earth terms. You may think this is not characteristic of rhythmic or poetic language, but this is incorrect. Take the language of the nursery rhyme: Jack fell down and broke his crown and Jill came tumbling after. Nothing could be more sensuous and also unsparing in its fidelity to the hard facts.

If you want a realistic report of what military combat may mean in its effects upon the body of a combatant, read a few passages from Homer. They will tell you in detail what it is like to die while your spleen is torn out by a spear, or your guts disemboweled, or an eye pierced through, or your brain smashed and scattered. If some of our own veterans had been previously conditioned in Homeric Greek, they might have had a better psychological preparation for what they might encounter in Vietnam.

Aside from physical details, which children can sometimes manage better than adults, poetic language, if it is to be poetic, has to operate with images geared to what is actually happening. It is a language of action and reaction, of sharp poignant emotion, not an exercise in logic.

As we learn to use abstractions, we also learn to distance ourselves from this level of experience, and so learn to distance ourselves from physical and emotional reality. I think the supporters of black English have seen this, but it is not simply a black-white problem. To some extent, the creation of this distance is inevitable; otherwise we could not conceptualize trends and place human behavior within patterns that we find useful to grasp. In short, we have to be able to form theories.

But I would argue that this conceptual power should always be held in contact with its close neighbor, the orally expressed reactive language and the lively imagery that it favors. Abstract language should never be allowed to run riot, never be allowed to slide completely into a habit of compulsive generalization. If we do this, we create a screen for ourselves that protects us from reality, and, in time, we lose our capacity to manage reality. That is why I propose that oral and poetic training should be coupled with training in reading and writing and composition at all levels of the educational process.

Let me close by drawing some illustrations of what I am getting at from a recent national event of harrowing proportions and by noting some of the ways we were told about it, some of the ways we were allowed to hear about it, the kind of understanding we were offered of it. The examples I select provide an essay on the theme of abstraction run wild, of conceptualism mismanaged, and of reality disguised, through a habit of avoiding orality and common sense.

On the morning of January 28, 1986, those watching the ascent of the Challenger space shuttle at the Kennedy Space Center saw it suddenly explode. A friend called me up a minute or less later, horrified. I had not been watching it; he had. The immediate reaction, natural and sincere, of perhaps millions of people as the explosion occurred was something like "My God!" Oral language, instinctively expressed, registered instantaneously the reality of what had happened. The language of the media spokesman (I think it was CBS) was very different. First a brief pause, perhaps to swallow, while the clouds of the explosion hovered in the air. Then the pronouncement, "A major malfunction has occurred."

He was not able to exclaim "My God, a total disaster!" He was not even able to say "They are all killed"—a fact immediately obvious to anyone watching. For most of the day, NASA would not allow such an admission of reality to be made—better to disguise it as long as possible, reduce its impact, denature it. You can do that sort of thing more easily if you change what has actually happened into a conceptual formula, applying an abstract term like malfunction and add the attribute major, giving it a category. This avoids expressing the real shock of the truth, because malfunction describes in generic terms any kind of mechanical difficulty, a choked carburetor or a faulty television set. We were encouraged to feel that that was all that had happened. The extraordinary was brought down to the level of the ordinary and, so disguised.

This represents a misuse of conceptual thinking and a degrading of language that only oralism and live oral utterance can correct. When one writes, this kind of misuse can be corrected by sticking as closely as possible to oral idiom, infusing it with whatever conceptual scheme one is constructing. . . .

Interpreting a Text: How Meaning Emerges

Humans are meaning-making creatures. We can't help trying to make sense out of all our experiences—including our reading experiences. So while we are in the process of reading something, we are always engaged in creating meaning from the words. We often remain unaware of this *emerging meaning* as we read, particularly if we're just reading for pleasure. But if a friend stops us while we're in the middle of reading something and asks us what it means, we can usually make explicit the tentative emerging meaning we have been building in our minds.

In this chapter we hope to make clearer for you the whole process of reading and interpreting so that you can become better at what you already do. We want to show you in detail how active and exploratory the process of reading really is—how the meaning of a text is something that is gradually built up in the process of reading. It emerges through fits and starts of *guesses about the future* based on *expectations from the past* (your past experiences with these words and these areas of meaning). In short, reading (like writing) is a messy, imprecise process—but an interesting one. If you understand it better, you can use it better. People have difficulties in reading when they misunderstand the process and try to make it neat, precise, and mechanical.

We have two other goals in exploring the reading or interpreting process: improving your success with hard texts and helping you see and use the collaborative dimension of reading.

MAIN ACTIVITY OF THE UNIT: A MINI-LABORATORY IN THE READING PROCESS

We ask you now to do an exercise to help you become more aware of your conscious and unconscious reactions *as* you read. The exercise will interrupt you and break your reading of a poem into many steps or stages. It may feel artificial as you try it out for the first time, but go along with it as an exercise. The text we're going to use for this practice is given below. Your teacher may read it aloud or may ask you to read it silently to yourself. If you read it to yourself, read it in a slow, relaxed way: let yourself *hear* the words in your head.

First step: Reading and pausing to note what's happening in you. Read or listen now to this poem—in chunks—pausing intermittently to see what's going on in your head. That is, whenever you get to a line of circles (or when the reading voice stops), immediately start freewriting to get down on paper as much as you can of whatever is going on in your mind as a result of what you have heard or read up to that point.

Here are some questions to help your exploratory writing, but don't let them get in your way. That is, at each pause start by writing down as much as you can about what is going on in your mind. *Then* try out the questions as a way to fish out any *more* that might be going on in your mind that you aren't conscious of.

- Thoughts/feelings. If you've been writing mostly about thoughts or interpretations, what feelings were occurring in you? If you've written mostly about feelings, what thoughts or interpretations have been occurring?

- Memory triggers. What are you reminded of by what you have read? How do these words relate to what you have already experienced?

- Hunches or expectations. What do you suspect will come next? What do you sense this whole poem is going to be about?

- Questions. What questions will you be trying to answer as you read further?

- Resonant words or phrases. Which ones stick in your mind or strike you as important? Write a bit about what these words or phrases make you think of.

Then continue reading (or listening) until the next row of circles and repeat the same process of exploratory writing about what was going on in your mind. This might seem an odd exercise at first, but quickly it should seem familiar to you: it is exactly like "process writing," but in this case you are writing about your reading process rather than your writing process. (By

the way, you might find some interesting parallels between what goes on in
your mind as you write and what goes on in your mind as you read.)

THE WRITER
Richard Wilbur

In her room at the prow of the house
Where light breaks, and the windows are tossed with linden,
My daughter is writing a story.
ooooooooooooooooooooooooooooooooooooooooooooooooooooooooo
I pause in the stairwell, hearing
From her shut door a commotion of typewriter-keys
Like a chain hauled over a gunwale.

Young as she is, the stuff
Of her life is a great cargo, and some of it heavy:
I wish her a lucky passage.
ooooooooooooooooooooooooooooooooooooooooooooooooooooooooo
But now it is she who pauses,
As if to reject my thought and its easy figure.
A stillness greatens, in which

The whole house seems to be thinking,
And then she is at it again with a bunched clamor
Of strokes, and again is silent.
ooooooooooooooooooooooooooooooooooooooooooooooooooooooooo
I remember the dazed starling
Which was trapped in that very room, two years ago;
How we stole in, lifted a sash

And retreated, not to affright it;
And how for a helpless hour, through the crack of the door,
We watched the sleek, wild, dark

And iridescent creature
Batter against the brilliance, drop like a glove
To the hard floor, or the desk-top,

And wait then, humped and bloody,
For the wits to try it again; and how our spirits
Rose when, suddenly sure,

It lifted off from a chair-back,
Beating a smooth course for the right window
And clearing the sill of the world.
ooooooooooooooooooooooooooooooooooooooooooooooooooooooooo
It is always a matter, my darling
Of life or death, as I had forgotten. I wish
What I wished you before, but harder.

After you have gone through the poem once in this way, your teacher will probably ask you to move into pairs or groups for the next steps. We want to emphasize the collaborative dimension that is inherent in the making of meaning. It's not that we usually read in groups—we usually read alone. But the meanings of words which we carry around in our solitary heads have really been *negotiated* with others in the process of talking and listening. All meaning has a foundation in society and groups.

Second step: Reading or listening to the whole poem and writing about the emerging meaning. Read or listen to the poem again—this time the whole poem from start to finish. Perhaps someone in your group will read it out loud. Notice, by the way, that if you hear it read by someone different from the person who read it the first time, you are already getting another *interpretation* of the poem—just from the way they read it out loud.

Now freewrite about what is going on in your mind as you hear it again. You will probably have new thoughts about what it means, new feelings, new expectations. Hearing it all at once, you can grasp it better whole. You may see some new connections or meanings. Or you may simply become more convinced of what you saw before. But even your "becoming more convinced" is "something going on in your mind"—and should be noted. Look back at the questions again to see if they help you fish out any more of what was going on in your mind as you read.

Third step: Reading over your notations of emerging meaning. Now read over silently what you've written and find passages that you are willing to share with others in your pair or small group. Perhaps these will be the passages that are most interesting to you, or that best suggest your "reading" of the poem, or that best express your perplexities and uncertainties about the poem. The more you can share with others, the better.

Fourth step: Sharing your notations. Now share those bits of writing with your partner or group. We would encourage you sometimes to quote the lines or sections of the poem that your writing refers to—especially if there is any chance that the listeners might not be sure which lines you mean. One of our goals is to get everyone to see the poem better—get it more into people's ears—and so lots of repetition is useful. It also helps to hear many different readings of the lines.

Fifth step: Writing out new meanings that result from sharing. Now having heard about the emerging meaning that other readers have been creating while listening to the poem—now that you've had a chance to see the poem through *their* eyes—do more freewriting about what this does for *your* reading of the poem. What new meanings, reactions, feelings, or thoughts come to you on the basis of hearing what others wrote? You may now experience

PROCESS BOX

Oh, that's a terrible question! I don't know. Sometimes you get a line, a phrase, sometimes you're crying, or it's the curve of a chair that hurts you and you don't know why, or sometimes you just want to write a poem, and you don't know what it's about. I will fool around on the typewriter. It might take me ten pages of nothing, of terrible writing, and then I'll get a line, and I'll think, "That's what I mean!" What you're doing is hunting for what you mean, what you're trying to say. You don't know when you start.

ANNE SEXTON

large changes in your interpretation of the poem or only small readjustments. For example, you might say, "I never would have read the 'prow' image that way, but now that I try it out, I read the whole poem differently." Or "What an unusual memory to have about 'chair-back,' but now it will stick in my mind whenever I see the phrase."

We're not saying you should try to *agree* with other readers (though agreement may indeed emerge). Just *use* other readers; *try out* their readings to see if they are any help to you. They may help you find a meaning or interpretation of the poem that satisfies you better. The goal is simply to see and understand the poem more fully.

Reading Out Loud or Text Rendering

Critics have often noted that the best interpretation of a text may be a rendition or reading of that text. Figuring out how you want to read a text out loud is a quick and insightful way to figure out an interpretation. Just by trial and error—using your ear—you can decide how a line or stanza or whole poem should *sound*. (The same goes for a short story.) Once you work that out, you *have* interpreted it. You only need to explain "in other words" the interpretation you have already enacted in sound. Most important, the interpretation you work out intuitively because of decisions about how lines and passages should *sound* is usually more sophisticated than the interpretation you come up with if you go straight to "interpretation talk." In reading, as in writing, our ears are very smart. (For more extensive exercises in reading aloud, see Mini-unit C, "Breathing Life into Words.")

Your teacher may ask you to work out how you would read the whole poem—and then to read it either to the class or your group. Or perhaps the assignment will be to pick out that passage of the poem which seems most interesting, pivotal, vexing—or whatever—and share your reading of it.

MAIN ASSIGNMENT

Write a paper about your emerging reading of the poem. Alternatively, you may go through the process we've outlined using one of the other poems in the readings for this unit or Unit 19. Your teacher may suggest other readings. The paper should tell both *what* your interpretation is—what sense or meaning you make of all those words—and *how* you came to see or interpret it this way.

A paper with two elements can sometimes present organizational options. You could tell the story of what happened in your reading and thereby naturally lead up to your interpretation. You could start with your interpretation of the meanings you've arrived at—going on to explain how you got there. Or you may discover other ways to handle it. Just make sure your paper contains both elements: your final interpretation and your process of getting there. And make sure that the latter (the account of your reading process) shows how your thoughts and reactions changed over time and how the thoughts and reactions of other people affected yours.

Before we leave this unit, we want to reassure you that we're not trying to persuade you to go through this long process every time you read something. If you are reading quickly for pleasure, you should read quickly for pleasure. But the process we are demonstrating here, once learned, may *enrich* that fast casual reading. And if you have an assignment to interpret a piece of literature—or any hard text—you might find it helpful to use all the steps we've set up. One of the useful definitions of a poem is a crudely functional one: any piece of writing where the language and meanings are so rich and well put together that they bear extensive *re*reading; the meanings don't get "used up." Indeed the more the words are read again, the more interesting the meanings that emerge.

SHARING AND RESPONDING

You'll probably find Section IIIB, "Believing and Doubting," in the *Sharing and Responding* booklet the most helpful, but Sections IIIC, "Descriptive Outline," and IIB, "Pointing," will also provide you with useful feedback. Here are a few additional questions:

- "Sayback" to me what my interpretation is.

- Is it clear how I got to my interpretation?

- Do you have a sense of how my interpretation changed as I worked on my text?

- Have I made clear how the thoughts and reactions of others affected my thinking?

PROCESS WRITING QUESTIONS

- Reflect on the *kind* of things you noticed in the pauses in your reading. Did you get mostly images, feelings, thoughts, memories?

- Reflect on the differences for you between hearing the piece in parts and then hearing it all at once.

- How did you respond to the readings and interpretations of others? And they to yours? Are you more of a believer or doubter of what others say?

- You've already written extensively about your writing process, but in the main exercise of this unit, we asked you to write about your *reading* process. What similarities and differences do you notice between what happens when you write and when you read (and what happens when you *write about* the two processes)?

- How did you choose to organize this paper—or did the organization choose itself?

- What have your prior school experiences been in literature or English classes? Have these experiences influenced how you feel about literature or how you read it?

RUMINATIONS AND THEORY

A. The Reading Process

B. About the Artificiality of this Unit's Reading Exercise

A. The Reading Process

Reading may *look* passive: we sit quietly and let the image of the words print itself on our retina and thus pass inward to our brain. But the point we want to stress in this unit is that reading—indeed all meaning-making—is a deeply *active* process of exploration. In fact, when we have trouble reading it's often because we've been mistakenly *trying* to be passive—trying to make ourselves like good cameras, that is, trying to become perfect photographic plates on which the meanings on the page *print* themselves with photographic accuracy. But since reading doesn't work that way, our performance suffers when we try to operate on that model.

Even the "simple" act of seeing is exploratory and active. Admittedly the eye *is* a little camera with a clear lens that projects a precise (though inverted) image upon our retina of anything we're looking at. Nevertheless, seeing is not at all like a camera taking into itself an image of what is outside.

257

The mind or brain cannot "take in" retinal images. It can only take in electrical impulses that are nothing like an image, and it must *construct* from these electrical impulses our *sense* of what we see. Thus seeing is more nearly like drawing or sculpting—*constructing* something from fragments of a view. (Or indeed fragments of many views, since our eyes jump around all the time—so that the retina actually receives a jumble of constantly changing images.) In short, "Seeing, hearing, and remembering are all acts of construction which may make more or less use of stimulus information depending on circumstances" (Neisser 10).

Given this more complex process of active exploration, the important thing to realize is that seeing or "making sense" of what is around us is always a process that occurs in stages—through the passage of time— not instantaneously like an image passing through a lens.

In the first stage, our mind takes in the first pieces of information—the first trickles of electrical impulses—and quickly makes a guess, a hypothesis, or a "schema" about what we might be looking at. Then the mind repeatedly checks this guess against further information that comes in. Often we have to change our guess or hypothesis to conform to the new information. Only then do we "see what's really there."

Because perception occurs so quickly, we seldom realize that this process of guessing-and-then-checking is going on, especially since we don't think of vision in these terms. But if you keep this explanation in mind in the days and weeks ahead and watch yourself in the act of seeing—particularly when you are trying to see something obscure or something you've never seen before—you'll catch yourself in the act of making these visual guesses or hypotheses: "Oh yes, that's a yellow car way down the highway," but then in a second, "Oh no, it's a yellow tractor." In short, we tend to see what we *expect* to see—till evidence forces us to revise our expectation.

If seeing and hearing are such active exploratory processes, so much the more is reading: it's exactly the same process. When we read words (or hear them) we understand what we *expect* to understand—till evidence forces us to revise our expectation. Even in the process of reading individual words, research shows that as soon as we see a few letters (or the shape of the whole word or the phrase it's part of) we *guess* what the word is and then, as we get more data—or as our guess doesn't seem to fit—we revise our guess. And so the same constructive process goes on in all reading—whether for words, phrases, sentences, paragraphs, chapters, or whole books.

It's interesting to note that guessing is so central to the perceiving and thinking process—though we can make guessing sound more high-toned by calling it "hypothesis generating." When teachers say, "Never guess," they don't realize how indispensable and central it is for seeing or knowing. Perhaps they mean, "Keep your guesses to yourself till you're sure of them," but in fact it's enormously helpful to share your guesses with others to help you read or understand more accurately. Keeping your guesses to yourself often locks you into wrong perceptions or wrong ideas.

B. *About the Artificiality of this Unit's Reading Exercise*

This exercise in the reading process might seem odd and artificial to you, so we want to spell out now why we are asking you to use it. Our goal is to illustrate both what you *already* do when you read—and also help you a bit with what you *should* do in the future.

A picture of what you already do. Because we keep interrupting you in the middle of your reading and asking you questions to write about, we are clearly producing an artificial reading process. We may cause you to think of things that you never would have thought of just reading quietly on your own.

But reflect a moment about the things "we made you think of " as you were reading. Usually these thoughts or memories were already in your mind anyway: we didn't add anything, and we didn't put anything in your mind. We merely interrupted you and made you pause so that more of what was in your mind came to conscious awareness. We would argue that these things probably influence your reading in ways that are below the level of your awareness—*even if you read quickly without any interruptions.* What's new are not the thoughts and memories, but our making you pause and write long enough to articulate them.

For example, our "artificial" reading may have triggered a memory about a trapped bird, even if just a memory of hearing or thinking about a trapped bird. That memory might not have come to mind during a fast reading, but it might well have *influenced* that fast reading without your noticing it. Research on reading gives more and more evidence of how quick, active, and complicated the process is—how much goes on below the level of awareness. Since we don't "take in meaning," but rather "make meaning," we do that making on the basis of all the thoughts, feelings, and experiences already inside us—not just on the basis of words on the page.

Think about where meaning comes from. There are no meanings in words, only in people. Meaning is what people *bring* to words, and the meanings people bring are their own—amalgams of their own individual experiences. When readers see the word *chat,* for example, they will bring variant memories and associations—all having to do with informal conversation. Someone, for example, might find the word irrevocably colored by an occasion when his boss invited him into his office with the words, "I think we'd better have a little chat," and then during that "chat" scolded him, demoted him, or perhaps even fired him. Another person may associate the word only with talking with friends. And yet a French reader will bring to those same four letters, c-h-a-t, meanings having to do with cats. We are not, of course, born knowing the meanings of words in our native language; we come to know the meanings of words by listening to and observing others. We cannot make the word *chat* mean whatever we want it to mean, but at the point when we use or read the word, we are determining its meaning on the basis of prior personal experiences.

The exercise as a picture of what you should do in the future. If you engage now and then in this exercise with slow, recursive, looking-inside reading, you will learn to be more active and imaginative in your faster, more normal reading. You will learn to pay more attention to the words on the page and their relationships with each other and more attention to the richness—the meanings, reactions, and associations—that *you* already bring to words. By being more skilled at the active and exploratory process of *making meaning,* you will simply understand more: you will be better at seeing the meaning even in very difficult pieces of writing.

READINGS

ON EUGENE GENDLIN'S "FELT SENSE"*
Michelle Snow

Eugene Gendlin's piece on "felt sense" causes us to reflect deeply into ourselves to find the true meaning of our feelings. He is telling us that the first impression of what a feeling means cannot be accepted quite so freely; the true meaning only emerges after a period of self-questioning.

Gendlin is writing about how feeling gets mislabeled—perhaps to hide something? He says he's tired. After prodding and questioning he changes his mind: "Well maybe I am not tired, just weary." And further on, "Maybe I am not even tired or weary physically. I am just 'weary' of my job." He finally states that his reason for being weary of his job is that he is uncertain about his capabilities of handling a project.

Gendlin is not alone when it comes to this mislabeling technique. A lot of us have had a feeling that we wished to ignore, and we "bury" these feelings deep inside of us. This is a natural act. We do not like to face hurt, self-doubt, fear, or grief, and our subconscious tries to protect us by "camouflaging" these feelings. Although these feelings may be buried they are retrievable, as Mr. Gendlin has shown us, but first we must be ready to accept or deal with what we are hiding and that takes time.

I myself have done this "burying and camouflaging" numerous times. Sometimes when I am trying to ignore the fact that I really care what another person thinks of me, I act very confident and indifferent towards them. Acting this way may make me feel and look confident, but deep inside that fear still lurks. If I stop to think about how I am acting, I can come in touch with this fear.

I dealt with one of the most difficult times in my life in this very manner, by trying to escape from it and by not facing what I was feeling and why I was feeling that way. I had just resigned from West Point. I was leaving a place where I had always wanted to go and never thought I would leave, and I was leaving at the very first chance offered. My resignation papers said I was resigning because I had realized that the Academy was just not for me and that I didn't want a life in the military. I gave them this statement and I accepted it.

*Gendlin's essay is included in the readings for Unit 6.

When I was home something kept haunting me, nagging me, but I tried to ignore it. I entered U. Mass and even joined ROTC—so much for not wanting a military career. It was through ROTC that I came to realize that I missed West Point and that this had been one of the nagging elements. It was then that I decided to get to the bottom of my feelings. I had the help of a counselor who made me talk, and it was through this talking that my true feelings started to emerge.

I first realized that my subconscious did not accept my stated reasons for resigning. My feelings didn't fit my words. I knew that I loved the military life. I forced myself to realize that maybe it just wasn't the right time to enter the Academy, maybe I was too "set" for it or had too many expectations. I also made myself come to grips with the fact that I had been scared that I wouldn't succeed. I had set such high expectations for myself that I couldn't possibly reach them, and this made me feel incompetent. The hardest and consequently last feeling I had to accept was that I had quit on myself too early. I hadn't given myself a fair shot.

Making myself face all these feelings was very difficult and painful. It took a long time. Sometimes I still like to pull the camouflage over them, but I now realize that while I may hide them from others, I can't hide them from myself any more. Being honest to myself was something like putting first-aid spray on a cut: it stung like hell at first, but in the long run it made the cut feel better and heal faster.

I have proven to myself that Gendlin's statement is true: that a feeling, though once falsely stated, can be corrected. What I feel he leaves out is that by facing up to the feeling and dealing with it, a person can feel better about that repressed feeling. They may even free themselves from some painful feelings this way.

ABOUT GENDLIN'S "FELT SENSE"*
Thy Oeur

After reading "Felt Sense" by Eugene Gendlin several times, I came up with the idea that he first has some problems identifying whether or not he is tired. However, as he keeps on talking about being tired, he brings up a new word, "weary," to describe what tiredness really is. Eventually he solves his problem by questioning more about why he becomes tired. He seems to think that sometimes something goes wrong with us, but we really do not know what it is until later on when we ask ourselves some questions about it. Then, the problem is solved. The other times, we know what the problem is, but we still can't explain our behavior.

At the beginning of "Felt Sense," Gendlin is not sure if he is tired, because he can not tell by examining the way he looks or how long he has worked. This statement is related to the problem that I had with my father after three years of separation under the Communist regime in Cambodia. I remember the first time I saw him; I couldn't talk to him and kept on crying. I had no idea what was really bothering me at that time. I did not dare look him in the face and of course I had some thought that we were different. I sort of knew that I missed him very much, but I could not express that feeling to him. Instead I walked out on him because I couldn't deal with him asking me to come to visit the rest of the family. Seeing him did not satisfy me a bit and upset me a lot because I never thought that we were that different. I noticed

*Gendlin's essay is included in the readings for Unit 6.

that he was so disappointed and uncomfortable with me because I was acting like I did not recognize him as my father.

Yet when I come to the conclusion of "Felt Sense," I begin to realize that I was wrong in the way I treated my father at that particular time. Now, I understand mostly why I acted so stupidly towards him—the man loved and cared about me. First of all, since I was so young, I was influenced by Communist ideas. I had been taught to forget about my original parents and to think that Communist leaders were my good and true parents. Secondly, being different from my father had scared me out of being close to him because my friends never thought that we were related to each other. He looked healthy and dressed well, indicating that he was a lot better off than I was. For my part, I was having a hard time trying to stay alive because of the hard work and lack of food to eat. Also it caused a lot of pressure for me to see my father again after three years without any information about him. I felt a little bit awkward because my feelings of love for him that I used to have were not there anymore. That is why I could not show that I loved him the moment I saw him. Lastly, my reaction was partly due to the fact that I was not raised by him for three years and because he was not like my old father anymore.

If I were to meet him now, knowing all these things, I probably would not be able to treat him right still, because it has been a long time for me since I last saw him. The treatment that I would give to him would be different. It would be better or worse according to what he'd like to hear from me as an adult. I would probably treat him with a lot of understanding and respect as my father, which is not how I treated him when I was a child. Instead of ignoring him, I'd talk to him face to face, intelligently, with a lot of courage.

In conclusion, Eugene Gendlin's "Felt Sense" talks about how he can not say at the beginning whether or not he is tired until he questions himself deeply about why he becomes tired. Then he discovers the meaning of the tiredness that he had before. His solution has been truthful to my experience with my father. Going to school, I am learning about problems that people have in different parts of the world. I am beginning to understand more about the relationship between me and my father and why I could not talk to him and kept on crying when I met him after three years.

DIGGING
Seamus Heaney

Between my finger and my thumb
The squat pen rests; snug as a <u>gun.</u>

Under my window, a clean rasping sound
When the spade sinks into gravelly ground:
My father, digging. I look down

Till his straining rump among the flowerbeds
Bends low, comes up <u>twenty years away</u>
Stooping in rhythm through potato drills   *memory*
Where he <u>was</u> digging.

The coarse boot nestled on the lug, the shaft
Against the inside knee was levered firmly.
He rooted out tall tops, buried the bright edge deep

To scatter new potatoes that we picked
Loving their cool hardness in our hands.

By God, the old man could handle a spade. *back more*
Just like his old man. *into past*

My <u>grandfather</u> cut more turf in a day
Than any other man on Toner's bog.
Once I carried him milk in a bottle
Corked sloppily with paper. He straightened up
To drink it, then fell to right away *endurance*

Nicking and slicing neatly, heaving sods
Over his shoulder, going down and down
For the good turf. Digging. *weapon → core of things?*
to find meaning?
The cold smell of potato mould, the squelch and slap
Of soggy peat, the curt cuts of an edge
Through living roots <u>awaken in my head.</u>
But I've no spade to follow men like them.

Between my finger and my thumb
The squat <u>pen</u> rests.
I'll dig with it.

Purpose: compare, writing imp.

ROUGH EXPLORATORY WRITING ON "DIGGING"
Mike Donals

Squat pen. Why squat? Like a gun. Snug. The gun is comfortable in some way. The thing rests in his fingers, so it's controllable. The "s" and "q" and "t" sounds make the thing sound not-so-comfortable. Is this ironic? Thumb and gun. Near-rhyming—must be a kind of equivalence here—fingers like a weapon?

○ ○ ○ ○ ○

He's looking out the window at his father, digging potatoes. He's "straining," coming up 20 years away. So maybe he's going back to his youth 20 years ago? The rasping sound is the shovel on the dirt? Or is it an uncomfortableness that has to do with the going back? The words "rump" and "rasping" are crude, like dirt. What's going on here? Digging, and a pen, and a gun. We'll see the similarities here, I think. (But this rasping sound is *clear*. There's a neatness to this.)

○ ○ ○ ○ ○

More description of the act of digging. There's more of a love here in the description of the digging—the picture of the product of those potato tops dislodged, loving the coolness with our hands. Real tough earthy images, lug of the boot, words describing the shovel. I can really see the grime, the disembodied boot, this ol' shovel the man wields, the dirt spraying, the loving with which he does this. *And,* it is his father that does so. We will get, I hope, an exploration of this relationship, that pulls together the writing and the earlier generations' digging.

○ ○ ○ ○ ○

More description of this act of digging, and the sloppiness of it. We also get an exploration, backwards, of the generations of men that have done this digging, of the skill and prowess. The handling of a spade, here, could be like the snug fitting of a pen earlier? Not sure just yet, no explicit link. But my guess is that's it. The father and grandfather go *down, down,* for the *good turf.* The better stuff is down there farther. Like a writer somehow, but as yet no explicit link. Nicking and slicing *neatly,* a sound like the clean one earlier.

○○○○○

Squelch and slap. Curt cuts. These are nastily earthy sounds, like the shovel. And there is remorse that the speaker has "no shovel" with which to do the same, to get to the good turf down, down. Now we *do* have an exploration of the relationship, though now it's one of a *not-having,* a discontinuity. The 3rd and 4th lines are full of smoother "l" sounds, a languid, pondering sound, not like the harder sounds in the first 2 lines.

○○○○○

The pen is squat, and resting, again, as in the first stanza, same image (gun is gone). Though he cannot dig like his father and grandfather, with their shovels on inside of legs, he can go "down, down" to the "good turf" with a pen.

Language is earthy, he suggests. Then he *does* dig.

○○○○○

Neat. This time I saw the bottle of milk corked with paper that I didn't see before. Also, Esther [reader] emphasized the words *digging* throughout the poem a bit more than I had (or at least slowed more noticeably), making them more evident. Also, I heard the word awaken more clearly. That made a whole new thing happen for me. The persona here is watching his father, I'm understanding, digging, and yet the wounds awaken in him, like a dream or a reverie (of which there are a couple here, the milk-bottle, the grandfather, the slinging of sods over the shoulder). Why this should awaken him is maybe to awaken the implicit connection between digging and writing and make it explicit. Maybe it's the "awaken the muse" (though here there isn't much justification in the text—but maybe yes, as it is the *opening* poem of the collection). So maybe all subsequent poems in the book are awakened memories, the "good turf."

○○○○○

What stuck out in my mind right through this whole process is that the ideas of digging and writing are very similar for Heaney, but I know about how deeply he dug and also that he pretty much comes out in China. I respect this kind of metaphorical connection, but I just don't think, past a few layers, it works too well. But here I'm getting into critical theory, and that's bunk, for the most part. So, I guess that's an idea that *changed,* though I haven't given any real good reason.

Something I did feel strongly about keeping was the idea of awakening that I heard in Esther's reading of the thing, the idea that, though the digging was going on right outside the author's window, he was "awakened" to the sound. This sound isn't even necessarily that of the shovel rasping earth, but of the 20 years. That kind of thing is neat, and I think it also *could* contradict my doubts above.

What I hear more and more in each reading, though I didn't hear it in Esther's so much, was the hard, almost Germanic sounds of Heaney's language, that really made the "earthen sods" of the piece visible. Dirt there is like the makings of language.

○○○○○

What I can't wait to see is the paper Keith is busy working on with the sexual imagery in it. I'm curious to see if I can find things in there that I could pick out as valid, as real Freudian points. I mean, critics have lately said there *are* sexual images in Heaney, though I'd really been naive to some of the more blatant things. (And me with my dirty mind.) I want to see if there is anything to the phalloi, the images that look like the sexual act, and all that other stuff. The paper cork in the bottle looks like it could be something too.

I didn't agree completely with Tony's idea about the persona in the poem being physically debilitated. There may be, but I don't think there's anything in the text that really backs that up—but I *do* think there is ample evidence that the writer *is* crippled in some way. He is heart- or mind-sick of the farm, the country, the life of physical toil ("digging") that his forebears did; and also, there are those in the North of Ireland who might consider writers sick. So, maybe there is something to that reading, though not how he saw it.

—Milk as strength symbol.

—Feeling of inadequacy, can't follow.

POEM
H.D.

There is a spell, for instance,
in every sea-shell:

continuous, the seathrust
is powerless against coral,

bone, stone, marble
hewn from within by that craftsman,

the shell-fish:
oyster, clam, mollusc

is master-mason planning
the stone marvel:

yet that flabby, amorphous hermit
within, like the planet

senses the finite,
it limits its orbit

of being, its house,
temple, fane, shrine:

it unlocks the portals
at stated intervals:

Prompted by hunger,
it opens to the tide-flow:

but infinity? no,
of nothing-too-much

I sense my own limit,
my shell-jaws snap shut

at invasion of the limitless,
ocean-weight; infinite water

can not crack me, egg in egg-shell;
closed in, complete, immortal

full-circle, I know the pull
of the tide, the lull

as well as the moon;
the octopus-darkness

is powerless against
her cold immortality;

so I in my own way know
that the whale

can not digest me:
be firm in your own small, static, limited

orbit and the shark-jaws
of outer circumstance

will spit you forth:
be indigestible, hard, ungiving,

so that, living within,
you beget, self-out-of-self,

selfless,
that pearl-of-great-price.

ANALYSIS OF POEM BY H.D.
Norman Holland

If I simply recount my feelings toward the poem and the associations it evokes, I find that I like those sections of the poem that link the shellfish to larger, cosmic beings. I enjoy the internal rhymes and echoes in the poem, particularly "spell" and "shell" in the opening stanza, "bone" and "stone" in the third, and "self-out-of-self/ selfless," near the end. The poem's lists have for me a kind of stately, procession-al quality, "coral, bone, stone, marble," or "oyster, clam, mollusc." In the "for instance" of the first line, I feel the resonance of a human being reciting to me or presenting a formal argument.

Much of what pleases me in the poem, though, is simply the talk about seashells, which never fail to delight me. Although I am no collector, I have often bought shells at seaside shops, to use as a paperweight or simply to leave around on a coffee table to be looked at and handled. I am fascinated by the cellular but mineral hardness and the pattern of annular growth like tree rings, the slow accretion of an exotic and improbable splash of color or (especially) a severely geometric shape. I half-remem-ber articles I have read, linking the shapes of seashells to logarithmic spirals and Fibonacci series, and H.D. reminds me here that it is a senseless, shapeless blob of an animal who achieves such a "stone marvel" as a chambered nautilus. I delight in her conceit that he is a "craftsman" and "master-mason." If only the repairmen my house keeps needing were as docile, skillful, inexpensive, and quiet as oyster, clam, or mollusc.

I find myself drawn most strongly to those parts of this poem where the smaller geometry of the shell is echoed in larger geometric or even cosmic forces. I relish words like "planet," "orbit," "finite," "ocean-weight," "moon," and "darkness." Conversely, I do not enjoy phrases that take that larger geometry and turn it into a threatening, bestial environment. I find myself strongly objecting (like Saul) to the moralizing in the phrase "shark-jaws of outer circumstances" and questioning if it is anatomically possible for whales to swallow molluscs and spit them up again. In general, I resent the last section with its counsel to be firm and ungiving, and I find the last phrase, "pearl-of-great-price," evasive of both the moral and poetic responsibility to come to a precise conclusion.

If I try to systematize my reaction, I find myself approving those sections of the poem that evoke in me a sense of geometric intelligence and a participation in the larger geometry of the cosmos, particularly as a reaction against something "flabby, amorphous," fleshly, and human. I find myself disliking eggs, whales, sharks, and octopus, as against planets, orbits, or circles. I like the points of relatedness in the poem, and dislike unrelatedness. I distinctly react against the shift in the last section from a grammatical third person relating to large cosmic forces and holding his own, to a first person counseling a second in a smarmy scoutmasterish way to "be firm."

Still more generally, as I look back over what I have written, I see that I have repeatedly substituted the abstract, general, cosmic, or universal for the organic, eat-ing-and-being-eaten, personal, and human (even, or especially, the mason who has so repeatedly and expensively failed to repair my front steps!). Thus, in reading the poem, I have also read myself. I am, I believe, a person who would like to master the inside relationships of things by knowledge or vision but who, at the same time, feels his identity preserved in staying on the outside. Thus, I like the parts of this poem that I can interpret in terms of knowledge and vision—the geometry and growth associated with the outsides of molluscs, their stone shells. I like the trans-mutation of the flabby inside to the generalized and abstracted outside. I find myself preferring images to which I can have an external, abstract relation over images which threaten to involve me in an inside where identities are engulfed or eaten.

In general, my style is to seek greater and greater generality, but the poem con-verges into a smaller and smaller radius. Thus, I like the first section most: it seems to generalize and expand the situation of the shellfish. I interpret the second part as arguing that the mollusc should be complete in itself, and I find that mode less pleas-ing. Finally, the last section argues that one should turn inward, and I find this least satisfactory because it urges a position which is not powerful and not outside. I can accept it to the extent it refers to "you," not me, but I still don't like it. . . .

Holland continues his analysis in another mode. See the "Readings" section of Unit 19.

UNIT
13

Purpose and Audience: Writing as Doing Things to People

The goal of this unit is to help you learn to shape your writing better by thinking more pointedly about *what* you want your words to *do* and to *whom*—that is, about purpose and audience. The main assignment is to write an analysis of a piece of your own writing in which you explore the purposes and audience you had in mind and the effects your words actually achieve on readers.

We almost always have a *purpose* in mind when we speak. We may be just expressing ourselves ("Ouch!"), making contact ("Hello, how are you?"), conveying information ("It's ten o'clock"), or persuading ("It's much too hot to work. Come to the beach with us."). Even when we talk to ourselves, we probably have some purpose: to buoy our spirits ("C'mon, you can do it"), to keep from being frightened ("It's only the cat"), or to get something off our chest ("I hate him, hate him, hate him!").

In addition we almost always have an *audience* in mind when we speak. Maybe just anyone ("Help! I'm drowning!"), a good friend ("I've missed you"), a parent ("I've studied all week; can I use the car?"), a teacher ("Do you take off for misspelling?"), peers ("That was a dumb movie")—and, of course, we sometimes just speak to ourselves. Since writing usually takes more time and effort than speaking, we're even more likely to have a purpose in mind when we write compared to when we speak—even if the purpose is mostly to fulfill an assignment for a teacher.

Purpose and audience interact to influence what you say. In all likelihood, if you want to borrow a friend's car, you wouldn't persuade him by saying you had studied all week. You'd be more likely to say, "Are you really my friend?" If you're writing to convey information about the popular music scene to your teacher, you'd probably include more background information than if you were writing to give this information to your peers. When we write only for ourselves, though, we can use whatever language and approach we please—and say whatever we want—since there's no fear of hurting or annoying someone or getting a baffled look.

AUDIENCE IN WRITING

Let's work up to purpose by way of audience. Sometimes you know who your audience is, for example, your parents or a particular committee or group of friends. Perhaps your audience is your classroom partner or group.

But sometimes you don't know who your readers will be. You may have to write a letter to an organization or an application to a bureaucracy and not have a clue about who will actually read it. Sometimes you know *who* your readers are but not what they're *like*. That is, you may write something for a particular newspaper or magazine that gets all sorts of readers with all sorts of views and feelings. Or perhaps you have nobody-and-everybody in mind as your audience: you're writing about an issue for people in general or just for yourself.

There's nothing wrong with writing when you are unclear about your audience. Very good writing can be produced in that frame of mind. In fact, even if you are very clear about your audience but you get confused when you think about them, it pays to forget about them and write your first draft to no one in particular or to a friendly audience. But if your audience is not a problem, you can usually focus your thoughts and language better if you keep them in mind.

Two Kinds of Audience Analysis

The obvious kind of audience analysis is to think about who your readers are and where they stand on the topic you are writing about. If you are writing something persuasive or argumentative, you will probably think most about where they *disagree* with you: after all, that's why you're writing—to change their minds.

But watch out. Yes, you need to understand the points of disagreement, but your best hope of persuasion is usually to build from a platform of agreement or shared assumptions. Your audience analysis needs to focus on figuring out some of those points of agreement. Even if your disagreement is very large—even if you feel you are trying to persuade people who are deeply different from yourself—there are probably crucial *assumptions* that you share. (For example, die-hard pacifists and hawks in this country often agree about the desirability of democracy and individual freedom.) To put it another way, if you cannot find any shared agreement or feel some *kinship* with the "enemy," it's probably a waste of time writing to persuade them.

269

Often it's difficult and even boring to try to decide before you write what your audience is like and where it stands on a particular matter. You'll often discover much more about them if you get a draft written first—and then pretend to be your audience while you read it over: try to read through their eyes. You'll discover some of their feelings, ideas, and assumptions you wouldn't otherwise have noticed. It also helps enormously to enlist other readers to help you read like your audience.

But even when you don't know who your audience is—or what they're like—there's a second kind of audience analysis that helps in revising. That is, you can analyze the audience that your writing *implies.* For if you look closely at any piece of your writing, you can find cues about who you were *unconsciously assuming* as reader. For example, does your piece have little cues that imply your readers are smart or dumb? informed or uninformed about the topic? likely to agree or likely to fight you? frivolous or serious?

The "implied reader" is a subtle dimension of a text (and an important critical concept in the field of literature as well as composition). Most of us need the help of responders to discover the implied reader in what we write. For example, sometimes a responder will show you that your text gives off contradictory audience cues. Perhaps at one point your writing implies that the readers are already interested in your topic, and at another point that they are uninvolved. Perhaps you can carry this off (somehow making it clear that you are writing to all readers), but the contradiction may undermine your writing by alienating *all* readers: everyone feels, "He's not talking to me."

One of the most common kinds of implied reader is what you might call a "reader in the head"—that is, some past reader who has been very powerful in her influence on us. For example, responders may show you that your letter to a newspaper is full of confusing qualifications because you are still unconsciously writing for a teacher who told you never to make a broad generalization when writing about a controversial subject. It's probably not suitable advice for this audience. Or your essay for an economics teacher is full of impressive verbal fanciness that had always won praise from English teachers, but it's inappropriate for this audience. We carry around audiences from the past in our heads, and we need readers to help us notice when we continue to write to them. (See the short essay about our dilemmas with conflicting purposes for this textbook in the "Readings" section at the end of this unit.)

Digression on Teacher as Audience

Teachers read differently from most readers. They read not for pleasure or information, but because it's their job. They read as coach or director. Think about how a director watches a play she's directing—as opposed to how the audience watches it. The director is certainly a *real* audience; she is "really" watching the play, probably more carefully than the "real" audience. Yet, of course, the performance is not for her but for those who bought the tickets.

They paid to see the play; she's being paid to watch it. She's not so much trying to tell the actors how *she* reacts to the play (she may be tired of it by now), but rather how she imagines the audience will react.

School writing situations are often comparable. For example, your writing teacher may explicitly specify an audience other than herself for a writing assignment (for example, the readers of the editorial page of the local newspaper). Or she may simply assume that the writing is not *only* for her but also for general readers or other students in the class. In either case you have some kind of *double-audience* situation—especially if you are graded on the piece. (It is rare that we write something *only* for the teacher. Notice the difference if you write a letter to her arguing for a change in your grade.) On the one hand, your teacher will probably try to read as your coach or editor, telling you not so much how *she* reacts but how she thinks your real audience will react. But, of course, her own reactions will tend to be expressed too.

A "coach" or "editor" is a nice image for the writing teacher. For a coach or editor is an ally rather than an adversary. A coach may be tough on you, but she is not trying to be the enemy; she's trying to help you beat the real "enemy" (the other team). There's no point in fighting the coach or being mad at her, nor for the coach to fight you. The better you and the coach work together, the better chance you both have of achieving your common goal of "winning" against a common adversary.

PROCESS BOX

Writing comments on students' papers always appears more difficult than it becomes once I start. Just finished doing that—when I finished reading one of the papers, I felt I had absolutely nothing to say and yet I feel it's important to respond—so I have to find something. The wonder is that once I found something—I was off and went on writing and writing as though I too were writing a paper instead of just a response to a student's paper. And, inevitably, having written such a long comment, the student's paper began to look better and better. I feared for a moment that I had said something too negative and went back to try to make it more tactful—but I had written in ink and couldn't. But I rationalized my comments by convincing myself that they had grown out of a long response and the student should see them in that light. Strange, students wonder what our responses will be to their writing—and we worry equally about how they'll react to what we say. Writing responses almost always turns out to be a pleasure once I get going. Much more of a pleasure than grading!

PAT BELANOFF

But you may have noticed that teachers can easily fall into being *grumpy* coaches. Sometimes it seems as though all we do is criticize your writing. One reason is because of the conditions under which we have to read student papers. As writing teachers, we always read student writing in stacks of 25, 50, or 75 papers at a time. Have you ever thought about what a peculiar (and not very pleasant) way of reading this is? Teachers naturally fall into what you might call "schematic" reading. After the tenth or fifteenth paper (especially if all the papers are on the same topic or in the same genre), we often develop a kind of "ideal paper" in our heads. Instead of just reading the paper to see what it has, we read it "up against" that model—looking for certain points that need to be made or certain features that this assignment calls for. We fall into looking at each paper in terms of how well it fits or doesn't fit "what we are looking for." (Notice how we teachers easily talk in terms of what we are "looking for," and how you students ask us, "What are you looking for?") In "normal" reading conditions, the reader isn't checking what he reads for the presence of something he *already* knows, he's looking to find things he *doesn't* know.

We're not trying to blame teachers. This kind of reading is an inevitable consequence of the *role* of teacher and the conditions in which we read. A director can't enjoy a play in the way a paying audience can. Frankly, we think most writing teachers are overworked and underpaid. But the role and these reading conditions can lead teachers to be grumpy or to emphasize mistakes. That's why we urge you so much in this book to use *fellow students* (in pairs or small groups) as another audience for your writing. Fellow students may not be as skilled in reading as your teacher, but they can read your writing like a "real person"—take it on its own terms and simply look for pleasure or usefulness—and not feel they are reading as a job or duty or to "teach" you.

In short, we want you to get the best of both audiences: use your teacher for her professional expertise in diagnosis and advice; use your fellow students for their ability to tell you what actually happens when real readers read your words. You get the *worst* of both worlds if you try to get your fellow students to give you professional diagnosis and advice and ask your teachers not to be critical. It is worth having some frank discussions about this tricky double-audience situation in school writing: for students to say honestly what they sense as audience situations when they *write* school assignments, and for teachers to talk honestly about what the audience dimension is like when they *read* school assignments. It is a painful area, but not one for blaming: there are no right answers here. It's a question of gradually seeing clearly something that, as far as we know, no one yet understands well.

PURPOSE IN WRITING

We can highlight *purpose* in writing if we consider for a moment the situation where writing itself undermines its very purpose. That is, in some situations you can persuade better by *not* writing: by sitting down with your audience and *talking.* If you write to him, that written document may put him off with its formality and distance. Indeed, sometimes the most persuasive thing you can do is not so much even to talk but to *listen.* Often your only hope of persuading someone is to show him that you respect his thinking and are in fact willing to adjust yours on the basis of what he's saying.

But, of course, writing is sometimes a better mode of persuasion than speaking. For in some situations and with some people, speaking just leads to useless arguments. A piece of writing can be less disputatious, less intrusive, calmer. Writing can give you a chance to express something quietly to the person without the need for him to answer back to you: a chance to plant a seed and avoid all arguing.

Does this sound like an odd digression—to question *whether* to write at all? Well, the digression highlights the practical and, as it were, nitty-gritty approach you need to take to purpose if you want to make an actual difference in your writing. If you really think about who your audience is and what you want to do to them, you may have to rethink a lot of things you took for granted. Most of us tend to stress what words *mean,* not what they *do.* But, of course, some of the best and most highly paid writers in our society—writers of advertisements—think very much in terms of what words do. There are a number of things that will help you at articulating your purposes more clearly in this concrete and specific way:

- Practice *responding* to writing by telling what the words actually *do* to you—that is by giving movies of your mind as a reader. (See Section IV of the *Sharing and Responding* booklet.)

- Hear movies of the minds of readers as they read what *you've* written. (You'll get more chance for this during the unit.)

- Look at advertisements in print and on radio and TV and analyze them for their purpose: what was the writer trying to make *happen* in us?

- Consider examples of specific statements of purpose—such as the following—and force yourself to come up with comparably specific statements for your own writing:
  —To make readers *act* in a certain way (buy something, vote for someone, give a contribution, write a letter to their representative, and so forth).
  —To make them feel a certain way (for instance, to feel sympathy for a particular person). Or to give them a vicarious experience—that is, to make them feel as though they've actually been there (to "show" them, not just "tell" them).
  —To make them trust you. Or make them laugh.
  —To impress readers (teachers?) that you've really learned a lot of material and thought things through.
  —To convince readers that you are right.

—To make readers feel you understand how they see or feel things.

—To bowl readers over.

—Instead of wanting to bowl readers over (with the danger of making them feel threatened or making them want to fight against you), just to plant the seed of a difficult or alien view.

—To give readers information. (But notice that this is falling short of the task. No advertising writer would let herself stop there. *Why* are you giving readers information? What do you want the information to make them feel or do?)

An Extended Example: Our Purposes in Writing this Textbook

By way of further example, let us list here some of the specific purposes we've had in mind in writing the textbook you hold in your hands. Our audience is students. However, students will never read a course-oriented textbook unless it is chosen and assigned by their teacher. So it turns out we have the same tricky, double-audience situation that you often have: teachers aren't our "real" audience, but they "really" are our audience.*

Our purpose is to make things happen in the world, to change behavior. We take our book as a very practical enterprise. Suppose, for example, that some reader should come up to us and say, "I just *love* reading your book. It's so interesting and entertaining. Of course, I never do any of those funny activities you describe; I just continue to write the way I always have." We might feel a glint of pleasure that this reader "loves" our book, but we'd have to admit that we'd *failed* in our main purpose of affecting behavior.

But we can't affect people's behavior unless we can affect their attitudes. We want to make teachers and students trust us. We want to make them think that we know a lot about writing and teaching and that we understand their problems. We want teachers to feel, "This is a smart, sensible book; it will make my teaching easier and more effective."

In the end our major purpose is to *help students become better writers.* Notice, however, that such a broad, pious statement of purpose is not specific enough to be of much use—for revising or helping readers give us feedback, for instance. Here are more down-to-earth statements of what we are trying to do to you to make you better writers:

- To get you over any nervousness or fear of writing you might have.

- To make you trust that you always have lots of words and thoughts available—and thereby make you more confident about writing.

---

*Double audiences aren't as odd as you might think: you can't get an article or even a letter into the newspaper unless the editor thinks it's suitable. A children's book must appeal to grownups before it gets a chance to be read by children. *Every* book must appeal to an editor before it can be published and be read by an audience. Indeed most books, even after they are published, won't get into many readers' hands unless they succeed at appealing to reviewers.

- To get you to *like* writing and thus write a great deal. For we believe that you'll learn more in the end from writing a great deal than from advice or suggestions. And you won't write lots unless you like writing.

- To make you realize that when you have to write something you have a number of different ways to go about writing it: to feel a sense of choices, options, power.

- To get you to be much more aware of your writing process, to *notice* the different gears you use and the funny tricks your mind and feelings play—and thereby help you end up with more conscious control over yourself as you write. (Students sometimes think process writing is odd or "merely theoretical" at first, but we want you to feel that it is practical: a method that can help you get unstuck and figure out the best way to tackle the writing task at hand.)

- To help you move comfortably back and forth between being loose and accepting in exploratory writing, and tough-minded and critical in assessing and revising.

- To help you work more independently without always having to have directions from the teacher or the book.

- To help you collaborate better with each other—in writing and responding to writing.

(We talk more about our dilemmas of purpose in one of the readings of this unit.)

MAIN ASSIGNMENT

The assignment for this unit is to write an essay that analyzes audience and purpose in a piece you have *already written,* perhaps without considering audience and purpose at all. You can choose any piece of writing to work on—from a collage to a descriptive piece to an argument (though your teacher may ask you to work on one particular kind of writing). Here are the main questions to address in your analysis:

- *Audience.* Whom did you see then as your audience and whom do you see now? Perhaps you weren't thinking about audience as you wrote; or perhaps you would now change your mind about who should read your words. Be sure to relate what you say about audience to *specific* words or features in the writing. That is, what words and method of organization did your sense of audience lead you to use?

- *Purpose.* Were you consciously trying to do something to readers when you were writing your piece? Can you now see any unconscious purpose you had? (For example, you might have been trying politely to persuade, but now you can see that unconsciously you were trying to *jab* your readers and make them look silly.) Again don't forget to tell what specific words or features your purposes lead you to use.

—There's an interesting "sub-question" about purpose: what effects did you want—consciously or not—your writing to have on *yourself.* For example, perhaps you were trying to figure something out for yourself or get something off your chest in addition to having some effect on readers.

- *Actual effects.* What actual effects does your writing seem to have on the readers in your group? What specific words or features seem to cause their reactions?

- If your group members are the "wrong" audience for this piece, what differences do you think there would be between their reactions and those of your "right" audience?

- *Advice for revising.* Finally, make sure your paper includes some advice to yourself for revising. On the basis of what you have learned about audience, purpose, and effects, what changes would you make if you were to revise? This might make a separate section at the end, or these thoughts might be scattered through your analysis.

The goal of this analysis paper is not to *judge* but to *describe.* That is, we're not trying to get you to congratulate or criticize yourself ("I tried to make them laugh, but they sat there stony faced!"), but rather to write a paper that describes *purposes* in writers and *effects* on readers—relating those purposes and effects to *specific* words and features on the page. (In writing this essay, you might find it helpful to make references and comparisons to other pieces you heard and discussed in your group.)

Variations on the Assignment

1. Compare your writing with the writing of someone else in your group: the audience, purposes, and effects of *two* pieces of writing. (Sometimes analysis is easier when you have two pieces to compare.)

2. Write an essay about purposes and audience in *three or four* papers in the group. Obviously you can't write a full analysis of that many papers. Your analysis would have to center on one or two key, common issues of purpose (for example, trying to get hostile readers on your side or trying to make readers experience a certain emotion), and explore that issue in terms of examples and illustrations from all the papers.

3. Write a collaborative essay with two or three people in your group whose writing is also being analyzed. In the readings at the end of this unit, there is a collaboratively written essay that analyzes essays in Units 4 and 5.

MAIN ACTIVITY FOR THE UNIT

There are many ways you could go about writing the essay for this unit, but here is a sequence of steps you will probably find helpful.

- Pick out the piece of writing you want to analyze—something you've already done. If your teacher gives you free choice, pick whatever piece intrigues you. Perhaps it's interesting because you are pleased with it and want to look more closely at something that worked for you. More likely, it's a piece that still troubles you and you think you might want to revise it.

- Do some fast exploratory writing about the audience and purpose you had in mind in your original writing. Try to put yourself back into that situation. Do you have any different feelings now about audience and purpose for this piece?

- Look at any response you got from your teacher on this paper and see what you can learn about the effects your words had on her.

- Share your piece with your partner or group and ask them to tell you in detail about the *effects* the writing had on them. Ask them to give you careful movies of their minds. It will help a lot if you make them stop periodically and report specifically what is happening to them as readers.

- Then, changing to a more analytic mode, ask them to relate these effects to specific features of the text. If a reader got bored or hostile, can you figure out what words or tone or structural feature in the writing caused it? You can join in on this analysis.

- Then ask your partner or group to talk about who they see as being the audience and what your text implies about audience. Does the text imply that readers are professional or amateur? emotional or cool? Can they see any old "audiences in your head" which lead you to shape your writing inappropriately? Again, you can join in.

- Finally, if your group is the wrong audience for your piece, ask them to speculate on any differences between their reactions and those of your intended reader. In this discussion, don't overestimate *differences* between readers. That is, if your intended audience is your teacher or a newspaper editor, your classmates are admittedly different; many of their reactions will be different from those of your teacher or the editor. But you can learn a great deal from seeing what your words did to the wrong readers. For example, your group might say they felt intimidated by your tone. Probably your teacher would not feel exactly intimidated, but there may well be something problematic about your tone. Perhaps it is smug.

SHARING AND RESPONDING

In order to get material for your essay you'll need to get feedback from class-mates on the paper(s) you're analyzing. "Movies of the Reader's Mind" (Section IV of the *Sharing and Responding* booklet) is probably the best technique for this. If you are doing this unit's assignment collaboratively, make sure that you enlist others outside your group to give you feedback both on the paper(s) you're analyzing and on the essay you produce as a result of the analysis. But you should already have some feedback on the paper you're analyzing if it's a paper you wrote for an earlier unit in the textbook. See if you can locate that feedback.

For feedback on the paper you're writing for this unit, you'll find the following sections of the *Sharing and Responding* booklet particularly use-ful: "Sayback" (IIA), "Descriptive Outline" (IIIC), "Skeleton Feedback" (IIIA), and "Criterion-Based or Judgment-Based Responding" (V), espe-cially the criteria traditionally applied to expository writing.

In addition, be sure to ask your readers or listeners to give you respon-ses to the following:

- whether you've identified the audience of the paper(s) and based that identification on specific words or features

- whether you've stated clearly both the conscious and the unconscious (if you had any) purposes you see in the works being analyzed and if you've based your statements solidly on words and features of the text(s)

- whether you've included a presentation of the actual effects of the writ-ing on an actual audience

- whether you've made it clear what you would do if you were going to revise the paper(s) you've analyzed

PROCESS JOURNAL QUESTIONS

- How did you react reading over the piece you chose—thinking about your original audience and purpose?

- What differences were there between the reactions of your readers and how you'd originally wanted readers to react? Did they see in it the same audience and purpose you did?

- Did your analysis lead you to audiences or purposes you hadn't been aware of?

- Did you find problems or satisfactions writing this paper that you hadn't encountered with previous papers? (After all, this is a somewhat theoretical analysis as well as an analysis of your *own* work.)

- Do you usually have a definite audience in mind when you start to write? How do various audiences affect your writing? teachers? your writing group? Which audiences do you find most helpful and most problematic? Do you find it difficult to ignore audience?

- How do you see and experience the teacher as audience?

- Do you usually have some definite purpose in mind when you start to write? Or do you discover purposes after starting? How does purpose function for you as you write?

RUMINATIONS AND THEORY: SOME OF OUR THINKING BEHIND THIS UNIT

A. Purpose, Genre, and an Overview of Rhetorical Terrain

B. Global Goals: Expressive, Transactional, and Poetic

C. Can We Forget about Purpose and Audience?

A. Purpose, Genre, and an Overview of Rhetorical Terrain

In Unit 7 we emphasized genre; in this unit we emphasize purpose. It's worth exploring how genre and purpose are similar and how they differ.

It seems as though certain genres are designed to accomplish certain purposes. If you want to persuade someone, you're likely to assume you should write a persuasive essay—not a poem or a story. (In this case the genre's name even carries the name of the purpose—to persuade.) And yet if you take it for granted that you shouldn't write a poem or story, you should think again. You would be putting too much stock in genre and not thinking concretely enough about purpose.

For really there is no *necessary* connection between genres and purposes. Poetry, for example, may seem to express personal emotion more often than informational essays do, but that's just a matter of how poetry has tended to develop since the romantic period in the nineteenth century. Essays can express personal emotion, and poems can convey information. (Till the romantic period, poetry was treated as an appropriate genre for conveying information—even scientific information. The first version of atomic theory came in a long Greek poem, "On the Nature of Things," by Lucretius. Alexander Pope wrote an important poem called "An Essay On Man"—which is, indeed, an essay.) The important practical point here is that the persuasive essay is not the only way to persuade. Stories, novels, poems, and letters can sometimes persuade better than essays. (We've mentioned the persuasive power of *Uncle Tom's Cabin* before the Civil War. See Levensky's use of a published letter to persuade [Unit 7].) And the essay can be a form of lyric or autobiography.

It turns out that the grading of writing is often linked to assumptions about genre. If someone says, "This is a poor persuasive essay," he may well mean that the piece violates what he expects of the persuasive essay genre—yet it may in fact persuade many readers. Or a teacher may say, "This is an excellent persuasive essay" (and even give it an A)—and yet not actually be persuaded by it.

Some writers don't care whether their pieces fit the forms and conventions in which people have traditionally written. That is, some story writers don't care if some readers say, "This is a very peculiar story; there's no denouement" or "I can't figure out whether this is a story or an essay." Some business writers don't care if readers say, "This writer doesn't seem to know the rules for proper memos." Those writers simply want to have a certain *effect* on readers, and they have decided they can do it better by breaking certain "rules" or "conventions" about genres. (Of course, they must recognize the risk in this approach: they will annoy those readers who don't like departures from genre.) It is through this process that genres change. For example, it's no longer clear that the story genre demands a climax or denouement.

Another way to say this is that there isn't a perfect genre for each purpose. You can do many things with any one genre—for example, you can use a story to amuse, to persuade, or even to convey information. (Think about the purely informational qualities of novels like Arthur Hailey's *Airport* and James Michener's *Hawaii.*) The point is that you need to think concretely and realistically about purpose—and not take things for granted.

○○○○○

Let's look at this rhetorical territory with more theoretical perspective. We emphasized finding your topic in Unit 6 ("Private Writing"); we emphasized genre and audience in Unit 7 ("From Private to Public Writing"). Now we emphasize purpose and audience. It is a good time to stand back and see how purpose, audience, genre, and topic are distinct yet intertwined.

There is a traditional diagram called the communications triangle that sets out a schematic overview of what we might call the rhetorical terrain:

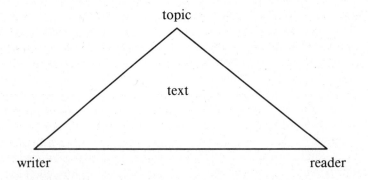

- To focus on purpose is to focus on people—what the writer intended and what happens to readers as they read.

- To focus on the topic is to focus on the world or message.

- To focus on genre is to focus on the text—the form and the conventions used. (To think about conventions is also to think about the history of texts—for example, whether stories need to have denouements.)

When you focus on one dimension, you may leave other dimensions vague or ambiguous for a while. For example:

- We may get quite far in writing a poem about something (thus knowing genre and topic) but not be sure of audience or purpose. There's nothing wrong with proceeding in that manner.

- We may be engaged in writing a letter to someone (knowing genre and audience) but not be sure of the topic or purpose: we just know we want to write to them. Fine.

- We may start to write something entertaining about something (purpose and topic) but not be sure of the audience or genre.

- Indeed, we may know only that we want to write about a particular *topic* (e.g., an issue or a frightening experience) and remain vague about all three other dimensions: audience, genre, and purpose. We simply need to write in an exploratory way and see where it takes us.

Each rhetorical dimension is related to the other. Any change in one is likely to cause a change in the other. But as we have seen, the lines of connection are a bit rubbery. But *before you are finished* with any piece of writing, you should be sure of all four dimensions. Indeed, one way to check over a piece of writing, if it is very important to you, is to make sure you are clear and consistent about audience, purpose, genre, and topic (or message).

B. Global Goals: Expressive, Transactional, and Poetic

In this unit we've emphasized small, nitty-gritty goals: What specific effects do you want your words to have on specific people? What observable changes would occur if your words worked? We've warned you against large global aims because they are fuzzy. But we don't mean to dismiss the value of talking in larger terms.

James Britton provides perhaps the most useful (and influential) statement of three *global* concepts for describing purposes in writing: "expressive," "transactional," and "poetic."

1. *Expressive writing* is writing that somehow expresses or pictures the writer. Expressive writing may be the pure "venting" of words which no one but the writer would ever understand—words which merely get what was inside outside, with no concern for the reader. Or they may be perfectly clear to readers: a clear and careful expressing of something in the writer.

2. *Transactional writing* is writing that makes something happen in the

world. It informs, persuades, or—to give a crass but concrete example—it produces a refund by return mail. When your aim is transactional, you are jumping into events and using words as a *participant* or as a way of *acting* on the world—trying to have an *effect*.

3. *Poetic writing* is writing that remains valuable for itself—apart from any expressive or transactional purpose. That is, poetic writing (in Britton's sense of the term) is worth saving and reading not because it expresses you or gets anything done (though it may do one or both these things), but because it is pleasing for itself as language. Thus a "poem" (in the conventional sense of the term) is usually "poetic writing" in Britton's sense. That is, the poet is trying to make the language and the form so pleasing that you will value the poem even if you hate what it says. But, of course, a novel or an essay or any form of writing can be pleasing in itself, as language, and thus be an instance of poetic writing in Britton's sense.

These three terms are slippery since a piece of writing can have all three purposes: we may write a *poem* to *express ourselves* and thereby to *make something happen* in the world. An example is a poem to express how you feel that's designed to get someone to marry you. Nevertheless we can often clarify our goals for a piece of writing if we ask ourselves which of the three purposes, if we *had* to choose, is our main priority. Thus, if you *had* to choose, which do you care more about: succeeding in expressing how you really feel? ending up with a good poem? or getting the person to marry you? Or if you had to choose between getting a refund or having a splendid letter which magnificently pulverizes the store for incompetence, which would you choose? If your goal were transactional, you would take the refund and be willing to throw away the writing—or ruin the writing by making it dull or even servile—if that's what it took to get the refund. If your goal were poetic, you would be willing to skip the refund so long as you could make a wonderfully witty or acerbic letter which perhaps you would save—even publish; but no refund.

It is helpful to bring the communications triangle to bear (pictured in the previous section). Expressive writing can be said to focus more on the writer, poetic writing more on the text and language, transactional writing more either on the reader (persuading) or on the topic and the world (explaining).

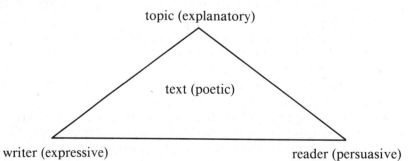

topic (explanatory)

text (poetic)

writer (expressive)　　　　　　　　　reader (persuasive)

But it doesn't pay to put too much faith in these neat schema. If anything is neat, it probably doesn't fit the messy realities of language and communication very well. For instance, transactional writing may very well be expressive and put the focus on the writer: that is, we sometimes get our refund by expressing how we feel—not by cajoling the reader or explaining events. The same goes for poetic writing: sometimes our poem about a tree represents the tree by telling how things are with us.

It helps to think of expressive writing as coming first or being a foundation for the others (and this is Britton's point). That is, often we cannot find impersonal arguments for a refund or create an accurate picture of the tree until we first find words for our personal reactions concerning the refund or the tree. Britton argues that expressive writing (where you don't usually worry about audience, accuracy, or effect) underlies transactional and poetic writing even if all it does is help people *get going* on a piece of writing—even if it never makes any appearance in the finished piece.

C. Can We Forget about Purpose and Audience?

We have spoken of the value of thinking about audience and purpose; then we turn around and say it is sometimes useful to forget about audience and purpose if your hands are full just trying to figure out what *you* think (rather than worrying about how to convey what you think to others).

Does it sound as though we think you can just turn on and turn off all orientation toward audience and purpose—as with a mental faucet? It's important to acknowledge that in a sense one can never *avoid* orientation toward audience and purpose in any use of language: to open our mouths is to have the impulse to say something to someone for some reason. Our language is often shaped quite well by audience and purpose without our having any conscious awareness of who the audience is and what our purposes are.

But even if we can't get away from audience and purpose (or putting this in its most general form: even if human intelligence is deeply social and human behavior is deeply purposive), there's still a big difference between *being* conscious of audience and purpose and *not* being conscious of them. There's also a big difference between trying to make your writing *fit* audience and purpose and consciously allowing your writing *not* to fit audience and purpose (for example, in exploring a topic). Thus, even if we can't get away from orientation toward audience and purpose, we *can* get away from trying to think about them and plan for them. In short, there are advantages in trying to plan and know and control what we are doing, but also advantages in leaving quite a lot to intuition or the tacit dimension.

We recognized this same issue when we spoke of organization versus messiness in freewriting. Does doing fast and furious freewriting and not worrying at all about organization mean you are getting away from organization? No, for it's impossible to get away from organization—everything has organization. But it does mean three important things:

- You are getting away from *thinking* about organization.

- You are inviting messy organization.

- You are inviting your *intuitive* or *tacit* power of organizing—your imagination. For we can often make a more interesting organization by intuition than by careful planning.

Thus, when we forget about audience and purpose, we invite writing that doesn't fit an audience or purpose. But we also invite writing that suits an audience and purpose more cleverly than we could have planned. So what it all boils down to is trying to learn to take the best advantages of *both* dimensions of the mind: careful conscious planning and intuition. For even though we are often more intelligent in our unconscious intentions than in our conscious ones, intuition can also lead us down the garden path. Therefore, *before we are finished with a piece of writing,* we do well to try to invoke the careful and conscious side of our minds: to become clear about audience and purpose and organization. For example, we may have to wrestle with a decision between conflicting aims that our intuition had allowed into our text. "Let's see. Now that I'm finishing this piece, who am I really writing to? What do I really want to do to them? Persuade, yes, but what things do I need to do to them to persuade them? Out of everything I've written so far, what would work best to achieve this purpose? What do I need to discard?"

READINGS

WRITING "MONICA'S BARREL"*
Madeleine Blais

"Monica's Barrel" is a small bit of writing, barely more than what Henry James and his crowd like to call a pensée. But it was a great pleasure to compose, and I wonder why. One reason may be that throughout the research and the writing, I had a clear vision of an audience, not just one person, but many. First of all, I imagined what Monica would think when she read the piece. Surely it would please her to be described as radiant, trim, with an easy smile and a face that is a sculpture, all planes and angles. But more than that, I admired her generosity and her thrift, the thoughtfulness that caused her to save this scrap of soap and that trinket and to take the

---

*These are Madeleine Blais' own comments on "Monica's Barrel," which is included in the readings for Unit 4.

time to package them and send them to people she had left behind. I thought of the many women in Miami like her, blacks, from islands, now in this country, often wearing the uniforms of maids, riding public buses or walking at the end of the day, tired, on swollen feet, having spent the day in the service of richer women most people would also call more lucky. I felt the piece was a tribute to all of them.

Before I used Monica's name, I made certain her immigration status was aboveboard. I could imagine the Immigration and Naturalization Service using such a piece to pick up someone like Monica and force her to leave the country if she had been an "illegal alien," a term with Martian overtones used by our government to keep us from acknowledging the humanity of some of the people who have fled to this country, a term worthy of Orwell's worst dreams about bureaucratic language. I hoped that Monica's boss would read this, would see her generosity. I imagined a reader might think $200 a week was small change for the services supplied by someone of Monica's diligence and might contact Monica and offer her more. I thought it would be fun to know what a psychoanalyst would think of Monica, all her scurrying and squirrelling. The barrel could also be seen as a bribe, something to keep the evil eye of others, of those who have stayed behind, from gazing unfavorably on Monica in her new life. Fear of the envy of others can be a powerful motive in many human transactions. I could even imagine this piece read by a minister or rabbi or priest, from the pulpit or altar, particularly during those holidays in which we are called upon to give and often feel too empty to share, too depleted ourselves. I am not very religious myself, so this thought surprised me, but I guess journalism sometimes contains an element of the sermon, so I should not be that taken aback.

I wanted my husband to like this piece. He writes fiction, and I am always fascinated by the fiction in journalism, the lifelike details in an account that are not (as in fiction) *like* life, but life itself. It is one of the most powerful forces in journalism, the power of what is real. The writer of fiction whom I would like to have seen write about Monica is Gabriel García Márquez. He often documents the heroism and the poetry in ordinary lives. Of course I wanted the audience to think of me as perceptive and not ungifted, to acclaim the thin thread of talent it took to begin the piece using the second person, so as to snare the audience's attention inescapably, and to enjoy, as I did, the delicious doubleness of things which can make a little article that seems to be about canned tuna and Brillo pads and codfish also address larger subjects, such as racial inequities, envy, and religion.

When the piece was published, I heard through Velma, a friend of Monica's and my initial contact for the story, that she liked the article, everything except the part where it says she doesn't like getting on a ladder to dust the dust on paddle fans.

Just a week ago, I spoke to Velma and I asked "How's Monica doing?" and she said, "Just fine. Still packing up her barrels."

LET'S DO IT!*
Lisa Muir and Jonathan Waxler

What is it about writing that allows one assignment to be addressed in many different ways? The answer is style. Writing is quite an individualistic exercise, and therefore style varies from person to person. This variation in style allows for many audiences

*This piece analyzes essays included in the readings for Units 10 and 11.

and purposes to stem from one topic. For example, both papers that have been chosen to be evaluated in this essay stem from the same assignment, yet as we will show they have completely different audiences and purposes.

While Jon's paper on grades has a specific audience in mind, Lisa's is addressed to no one in particular; rather it is addressed to anyone who will read it. At the time that Jon wrote his paper he saw the students as his general audience. Upon reading the final draft, however, it became apparent to him that he would have much more success in attaining his purpose if he instead addressed the administration.

Lisa's paper on trust is aimed at the whole world. This is apparent in her use of the words "you" and "your" throughout her paper. She also uses words and phrases such as "many people," "anything," and "anyone" to show how the world is her audience. She assumes that her audience doesn't really know what trust is. In order to give her audience a better understanding of trust she gives examples of distrust and her own interpretation of what trust is.

When Jon decided to change his audience from students to administrators, he also saw that it would be necessary to change his purpose. When he originally wrote his paper Jon was trying to instill anger in the students by using words such as "working their asses off," "stressed out," "who cares," and "the life of the student would greatly change." His voice, however, is not personal enough for this to work. He separates himself from his fellow students by using "they" when referring to fellow students rather than using "we." His purpose also seems to fail due to the fact that the paper doesn't have that get-up-and-fight feeling necessary to get the students to rebel.

On the other hand, Lisa's paper is aimed at informing people about the lack of trust in the world. She uses a story about a little squirrel at the beginning of her paper to grab the reader's attention. Besides using this story as an attention-getter, Lisa is also trying to get the reader to trust more, which is sort of the moral of the story. In her fourth paragraph, in order to try to get the reader to trust more, she points out the benefits of trusting someone and shows that we can't do everything by ourselves.

Another purpose of her paper is to shame the reader into trusting more. She thought that if readers felt bad about not trusting or felt that they let her down, they would attempt to trust. Her fifth paragraph was written for this purpose. It uses examples of mistrust in an attempt to shame the reader into trust. To illustrate her point further, she uses a real-life example of her grandmother: 78 years old with a flat tire, not trusted enough to be let in a stranger's house to use the phone.

Although the introduction drew the reader into the essay, it soon became boring and therefore the reader loses interest. When the paper has the audience's attention, it makes them think about trust and why people are naturally distrustful. However, her purpose of shaming the reader into trusting more didn't work. It isn't that the paper is poorly written but rather that the purpose is too far-fetched to work.

In order to make her purpose work, she must use more examples of distrust. These examples should serve to get the reader thinking about trust more, realizing its importance. A key part of the paper is the mistrust of strangers, which she only hints at. She should state this in the paper instead of relying only on subtle hints. Another trick to get the audience to think about trust is to use examples of what could be at stake if you don't trust. Trust is too important not to have a lot at stake. If she gives the audience ways to begin to trust, they might be convinced of its importance. Lastly, she should adopt a more convincing tone, somewhere in between formal and informal.

Jon's paper is written in a very angry tone and works in terms of getting the student angry. It makes the students wish that things were different yet doesn't succeed in getting them to rebel. He runs into a wall of apathy and might therefore be better off addressing the trustees, who would look at the matter through less apathetic eyes.

In order to make the administration his new audience, it is necessary to make a few changes in Jon's paper. He would be much better off taking a more straightforward, adult-like attitude rather than calling the administration a bunch of idiots. He should also use "we" when presenting the case of the students. By using strong adult words Jon would be able to show that the students care about their education and are mature. Perhaps by doing these things he will be able to persuade some of the administrators to take his side.

As you can see, both Lisa's and Jon's papers take on quite different styles—yet they both originated from the same assignment. Audience and purpose are quite important in both. As was shown in both papers, the style of writing is important in getting the purpose to work. If the audience is made to feel left out or the paper is not able to hold the reader's attention, then the purpose will fail. This failure can become success, however, through the revision process. Style also plays a big role in determining the audience, which is not always clearly defined in the paper. Since style varies from person to person, so do audience and purpose, even if the papers are on the same topic.

IS PHOENIX JACKSON'S GRANDSON REALLY DEAD?*
Eudora Welty

A story writer is more than happy to be read by students; the fact that these serious readers think and feel something in response to his work he finds life-giving. At the same time he may not always be able to reply to their specific questions in kind. I wondered if it might clarify something, for both the questioners and myself, if I set down a general reply to the question that comes to me most often in the mail, from both students and their teachers, after some classroom discussion. The unrivaled favorite is this: "Is Phoenix Jackson's grandson really *dead?*"

It refers to a short story I wrote years ago called "A Worn Path," which tells of a day's journey an old woman makes on foot from deep in the country into town and into a doctor's office on behalf of her little grandson; he is at home, periodically ill, and periodically she comes for his medicine; they give it to her as usual, she receives it and starts the journey back.

I had not meant to mystify readers by withholding any fact; it is not a writer's business to tease. The story is told through Phoenix's mind as she undertakes her errand. As the author at one with the character as I tell it, I must assume that the boy is alive. As the reader, you are free to think as you like, of course: The story invites you to believe that no matter what happens, Phoenix for as long as she is able to walk and can hold to her purpose will make her journey. The *possibility* that she would keep on even if he were dead is there in her devotion and its single-minded,

*This is Eudora Welty's analysis of "The Worn Path," included in the readings for Unit 5.

287

single-track errand. Certainly the *artistic* truth, which should be good enough for the fact, lies in Phoenix's own answer to that question. When the nurse asks, "He isn't dead, is he?" she speaks for herself: "He still the same. He going to last."

The grandchild is the incentive. But it is the journey, the going of the errand, that is the story, and the question is not whether the grandchild is in reality alive or dead. It doesn't affect the outcome of the story or its meaning from start to finish. But it is not the question itself that has struck me as much as the idea, almost without exception implied in the asking, that for Phoenix's grandson to be dead would somehow make the story "better."

It's *all right,* I want to say to the students who write to me, for things to be what they appear to be, and for words to mean what they say. It's all right, too, for words and appearances to mean more than one thing—ambiguity is a fact of life. A fiction writer's responsibility covers not only what he presents as the facts of a given story but what he chooses to stir up as their implications; in the end, these implications, too, become facts, in the larger fictional sense. But it is not all right, not in good faith, for things *not* to mean what they say.

The grandson's plight was real and it made the truth of the story, which is the story of an errand of love carried out. If the child no longer lived, the truth would persist in the "wornness" of the path. But his being dead can't increase the truth of the story, can't affect it one way or the other. I think I signal this, because the end of the story has been reached before old Phoenix gets home again: she simply starts back. To the question "Is the grandson really dead?" I could reply that it doesn't make any difference. I could also say that I did not make him up in order to let him play a trick on Phoenix. But my best answer would be: "*Phoenix* is alive."

The origin of a story is sometimes a trustworthy clue to the author—or can provide him with the clue—to its key image; maybe in this case it will do the same for the reader. One day I saw a solitary old woman like Phoenix. She was walking; I saw her, at middle distance, in a winter country landscape, and watched her slowly make her way across my line of vision. That sight of her made me write the story. I invented an errand for her, but that only seemed a living part of the figure she was herself. What errand other than for someone else could be making her go? And her going was the first thing, her persisting in her landscape was the real thing, and the first and the real were what I wanted and worked to keep. I brought her up close enough, by imagination, to describe her face, make her present to the eyes, but the full-length figure moving across the winter fields was the indelible one and the image to keep, and the perspective extending into the vanishing distance the true one to hold in mind.

I invented for my character, as I wrote, some passing adventures—some dreams and harassments and a small triumph or two, some jolts to her pride, some flights of fancy to console her, one or two encounters to scare her, a moment that gave her cause to feel ashamed, a moment to dance and preen—for it had to be a *journey,* and all these things belonged to that, parts of life's uncertainty.

A narrative line is in its deeper sense, of course, the tracing out of a meaning, and the real continuity of a story lies in this probing forward. The real dramatic force of a story depends on the strength of the emotion that has set it going. The emotional value is the measure of the reach of the story. What gives any such content to "A Worn Path" is not its circumstances but its *subject:* the deep-grained habit of love.

What I hoped would come clear was that in the whole surround of this story, the world it threads through, the only certain thing at all is the worn path. The habit of love cuts through confusion and stumbles or contrives its way out of difficulty, it remembers the way even when it forgets, for a dumfounded moment, its reason for being. The path is the thing that matters.

Her victory—old Phoenix's—is when she sees the diploma in the doctor's office, when she finds "nailed up on the wall the document that had been stamped with the gold seal and framed in the gold frame, which matched the dream that was hung up in her head." The return with the medicine is just a matter of retracing her own footsteps. It is the part of the journey, and of the story, that can now go without saying.

In the matter of function, old Phoenix's way might even do as a sort of parallel to your way of work if you are a writer of stories. The way to get there is the all-important, all-absorbing problem, and this problem is your reason for undertaking the story. Your only guide, too, is your sureness about your subject, about what this subject is. Like Phoenix, you work all your life to find your way, through all the obstructions and the false appearances and the upsets you may have brought on yourself, to reach a meaning—using inventions of your imagination, perhaps helped out by your dreams and bits of good luck. And finally too, like Phoenix, you have to assume that what you are working in aid of is life, not death.

But you would make the trip anyway—wouldn't you?—just on hope.

TWO DILEMMAS OF PURPOSE IN WRITING THIS TEXTBOOK
Peter Elbow and Pat Belanoff

Let us describe how we tried to deal with two dilemmas we discovered as we thought more about our purposes for this textbook.

1. A structural dilemma. We want to create a good structure or sequence of units so that lots of teachers will want to build their course around our sequence. Nevertheless we also want a book for those teachers who don't like our structure and want to make a very different order for their course. For we realize that there's really no "right" or "ideal" structure for teaching writing: teachers differ from each other; students differ from each other. (And we can't help but recognize that this is part of a deeper dilemma of purpose for our text: we want to give teachers freedom to teach the way they want; yet we also want to influence how they teach—encouraging them to emphasize the writing process and collaboration.)

We've wrestled with ourselves about this conflict of purposes. We know theoretically that we can't really have it both ways (and some of our feedback has emphasized this problem). But in the end we can't resist trying to see how far we can get with both goals.

You could take a kind of cynical view and say that it's really just a matter of audience: teachers who agree with us feel comfortable with our structure and those who disagree will feel hemmed in. But it's not so simple. For lots of teachers who agree with us don't *like* textbooks and hate the idea of a book's determining the structure of a course.

Our solution has been to use the kind of messy structural compromise you see. In effect we are trying to avoid two extremes: on the one hand, a book that is so closed in structure that all users must proceed in exactly the same order; and on the other hand a book that is so open in structure that *every* teacher has to go to the trouble of creating her own course from scratch. So as you see, we ended up putting the units in as good a sequence as we could—a sequence where they build on each other. Yet we tried to write the units in such a way that they *could* go in any order.

This compromise led to another compromise: putting all our *Sharing and Responding* material into a completely separate booklet. Originally this material was distributed among the units themselves: users would get the units in our order and the responding activities in our order. But when we decided we would invite teachers to shuffle the order of the units, we realized we were *not* comfortable inviting them to shuffle the order of responding activities. And so we finally saw that we could create a book for the units and a booklet for sharing and responding.

Once we made that decision—feeling it a messy compromise—we were pleasantly surprised with one of the side effects. A separate and self-contained booklet on sharing and responding means that *after* you have practiced all the responding techniques, you can quickly and easily refer to the booklet on its own when you want feedback on some piece of writing—perhaps even after the course is over. If the responding activities were blended into the units as originally planned, they'd be harder to find and use later. So this serendipitous idea helps our major goal: leaving the writer finally more in control of how she wants to get feedback.

2. A dilemma about voice, stance, or *ethos*—that is, how we want to present ourselves in our writing. The real test of our book is whether the activities and assignments improve your writing and your understanding of writing. But those activities and assignments won't have a chance to work unless we somehow get you to—well, if not *like* them, then at least do them with some investment and commitment: to *try*. A student who is too grudging and skeptical can sabotage even the best teaching or textbook in the world. In short, we have to get you to trust us.

We might have tried to impress you by sounding enormously authoritative and learned. But we don't like books where the writer does that; it doesn't make us trust him or her. And we don't like the impersonal tone of most textbooks. We decided early that we would allow ourselves to sound informal, down to earth, like ourselves. Thus we decided to speak in the first and second persons: to refer to ourselves as "we" and to you as "you"—instead of leaving ourselves out and just talking about "the student" the way most textbooks do. And we decided to include in our process boxes glimpses of our struggles with writing in more or less unrevised exploratory writing.

But this approach creates a danger. By taking an informal and even personal stance and celebrating the personal and messy dimension of writing, we may lead some readers to think that we are not *professional* and that we don't know what we're talking about. Occasionally some of our students and colleagues get that opinion of us. Will the book be too "unbuttoned" to be trustworthy—especially for some teachers?

We hoped that our interest in theoretical issues about writing would offset any danger of our sounding too unprofessional or folksy. In effect we felt it would be all right to be ourselves because in addition to being naturally informal, we are also smart and interested in professional and theoretical issues. So in our first draft we had no "Ruminations and Theory" sections: everything was piled into the main sections of the units themselves. We often put the theoretical material near the beginning of the units to *introduce* the central issues of the unit. But we got lots of feedback on our first draft that convinced us that the units were much too long and clogged with this theoretical matter.

Thus again we were alerted to a conflict or contradiction in purposes—being informal and being professional—and again we decided to try to solve it with what felt like a crude "compromise": we put most of the theoretical material in the separate, optional "Ruminations and Theory" sections at the end of each unit. Again we found ourselves surprised and pleased: the compromise had advantages we had been unable to come up with on our own. We love the idea of having all this material *in* the units—but in there in such a way that only those who like it will read it, and those who hate it will not be alienated by having to wade through it. (And even when they don't read it, they get a glimpse from a distance of our "professional" side.)

It seems to us that our experiences with our dilemmas of purpose are typical of those fortunate times when writing works as it ought to work. We started out by trusting ourselves. We wrote things that didn't work. We discovered the problems and got readers to help us discover them. We admitted the problems to ourselves rather than trying to deny them. We waded in to try to figure out solutions. And thereby we were led to *new* ideas we'd never have thought of if we'd tried to plan everything *right* from the start.

UNIT
14

Library Research as Revising

We've heard students say that there are two kinds of writing: writing that you "make up out of your head" and writing that you "summarize out of books." We don't like that way of categorizing writing, but it is understandable, since students so often make up most "regular" papers out of their head and summarize most "research" papers out of books and articles. In this text we are trying to break down that crude dichotomy.

In most units we have been trying to legitimize the social dimension of writing—telling you that it's fine, indeed normal, to let "your own writing" grow not just out of your own head but out of dialogue with others. Now in this unit we are working from the other end. We are asking you to create a research paper that grows as much out of your *head* as out of library books. That is, the task is to write a research paper by means of revising something you've already written—without any contact so far with a library. You should end up with a paper that represents your own thinking, but one in which your thinking is *supported, carried farther,* or *adjusted* by means of searching out information and ideas that others have published about your topic.

We're trying to get away from the old "research paper mentality" that makes you say, "Let's see, this is a research paper. Therefore, none of my own thinking belongs here. My job is to find a topic that lets me quote and summarize from the assigned number of books and articles. This is library work: filling out cards, making outlines, pasting it all together, and getting footnotes right." We're asking for a paper that grows out of your own thinking, but that joins your thinking to that of others. In a sense your job is to carry forward a conversation that has already been going on—a conversation you can hear when you listen hard in the library.

In this unit we want you to learn to have comfortable traffic back and forth between your own thinking and the thinking and information that others have published. In most units we emphasize collaboration with fellow students. Here we want you to understand that you can also collaborate with people you know only through their published works.*

Deciding Which Paper You Want to Carry Further

Your first job, then, is to find something you've already written—something that you find sufficiently interesting or perplexing that you could get satisfaction from investigating it further by looking into books, articles or documents in the library. An obvious choice would be a piece of expository writing about some topic that continues to interest you. (Thus, for example, you might use the essay you wrote for Unit 3, "Loop Writing," or Unit 9, "The Expository Essay.") Another obvious candidate is a piece of persuasive or argumentative writing (for example, in Units 10 and 11) whose topic you might enjoy researching to find background information on or further arguments for or against. You might also use your process writing in Unit 6, "Private Writing," as a stimulus for research into some aspect of the writing process.

Don't neglect less obvious choices. If you got interested in the poem you wrote about in Unit 12, you might enjoy some research on the poet—making your account of *your* reading of the poem part of a larger paper that also treats the poet's life or treats what other critics have said about the poem or about that poem and related poems.

You might even be able to do research relating to a piece of your narrative or descriptive writing. It couldn't so easily be a *part* of your piece, but you might write an accompanying or background piece: perhaps a piece about the history of a region or town you have written about—even about a particular street or building. (A librarian can help you find records and other documents. James Joyce used to do a kind of research while abroad and engaged in writing *Ulysses:* he would write back to Dublin and ask for specific details about some particular house or fence or view.) Even if your story is purely fictional, there might be something in it that you would like to explore more fully (e.g., supermarkets, jealousy, elevators, children's play). Of course, if your piece has a science-fiction dimension, the opportunities for research on the technology are obvious.

These last suggestions may seem a bit fanciful, but we mention them to encourage you to open the doors wide in looking for a research question that

---

*We are are grateful to Charles Moran, director of the Writing Program at the University of Massachusetts at Amherst, from whom we first learned of this sensible approach to library research.

can be truly rewarding for *you*. (Also you *may* use this unit on the heels of Unit 16 and thus be all set with a paper you've already started by means of personal research—and now can continue with library research.)

Figuring Out Which Questions You Can Try to Answer in a Library

Not every question can be feasibly answered by library research—especially in a short time. So your job will be to think about lots of questions you might try to answer—lots of "angles" or "handles" on your topic—and then see which of them are most feasible given your resources of time, library facilities, and library skills.

Again, you can generate a list of possible questions by yourself, but you can also get help through sharing and discussion with others. On your own do some exploratory freewriting to brainstorm as many questions about your paper as you can think of or that you might try to answer by searching in a library. The important thing is to do this in a spirit of accepting all ideas—a brainstorming mentality of not rejecting anything; write down everything that comes and wait till later to decide whether it's possible. Read over what you've written and underline the ones that seem most interesting or fruitful. Then share these with others in your group (or with a partner) and see if they have any further suggestions.

Suppose, for example, that you'd written the "Ice Cream Man" story (see the readings for Units 4 and 5) and wanted to do some research about these traveling ice cream salesmen. Here are some questions that might come to you in your own brainstorming and in your discussions with others:

- What would it take to be a driver—to run or even own my own truck? set up my own business? How are these businesses regulated? Who determines "territory"?

- What is the licensing process—for this in particular and traveling sellers in general?

- When did this business start? Who started it? Could I sketch in a history of it?

- Where did the name "Good Humor" come from?

- Who are the people that drive these trucks? What statistics or case studies are available about them?

- What poetry, stories, and novels are there where ice cream—or even these shops on wheels—play an important role?

- When was ice cream invented? soft ice cream?

- How does the business work? Are the drivers paid by the hour, by the week, by commission? Have there been changes?

- Can I find any case studies of one of these businesses?

- How does it compare to other franchises, such as McDonald's.

- What's the relation between these seemingly shoestring businesses and more settled, non-mobile ice cream franchises like Friendly's or Baskin-Robbins? What is the reason for a sudden spurt of new, chic, expensive ice cream businesses now? Are they causing a decline in "ice cream men," or have they resulted from a decline?

- How has this business changed over time? Are there more franchises and fewer independent trucks now? How does it look for the future?

- What does this business tell about how business works: franchises, markup, profits, etc.?

- What does this business tell about the history of free enterprise or capitalism?

- What safeguards are there against cheating?

- How bad for you is ice cream?

- Do sweets really make kids hyper? How?

- What's ice cream made of? What are the different kinds and different ingredients?

- How can you tell that ice cream is sanitary? When it goes bad, what happens chemically?

- What safeguards are there about standards?

- How do you measure standards in ice cream?

Half the battle is in getting a really rich and full list of possible topics. For this the brainstorming help of your partner or group is a godsend. Then it's not so hard to find two or three topics that interest you. It is best to have more than one since finding library resources is harder for some than others.

Before you do *any* research, freewrite about the topic you've given yourself. Write down everything you know about it and whatever questions you come up with. This will help you "own" the topic. Also, when you do this writing prior to research, your reading or research on the topic almost always becomes more interesting and meaningful. You'll find you have ideas of your own and therefore begin reading in a more active and less passive stance.

Using the Library

It takes time to feel comfortable finding your way around libraries. Obviously you cannot "master" a college library on the basis of this one task, but the trick is not to feel intimidated. Few people who use libraries *ever* master

PROCESS BOX

Discouraging. To work and work on something and think you've got something good going—a really good idea which you haven't gotten the parts of quite together, but know you can. And then read something using essentially the same data which comes to an almost diametrically opposed conclusion which seems valid. It isn't that I don't believe the opposing conclusion—I do—and yet still think there's validity in my own and now there's even more work to do to make some sort of higher synthesis. And then, too, I have another idea about all the stuff which doesn't rely too much on conclusions I've drawn which contrast to the conclusions I just read—an idea which is somewhat outside what I've been doing—but good, I think. But that requires starting almost totally over again. Contemplating that is depressing.

PAT BELANOFF

them. Realize that it's legitimate to ask librarians for help; don't be afraid to ask "dumb" questions. Most librarians are happy to help as long as you treat your own questions as occasions for learning—not just as requests for them to do the work for you. Also, libraries are ideal places for wandering and browsing; people who like libraries let themselves pause and glance at books or documents that they are passing—read a few titles, pick up a book, look at the table of contents, and read a page. Libraries are good for serendipitous finds. Don't give in to the feeling that many people have: "I don't belong here if I don't know where to find what I want." Check to see whether your library has a handout or some other introduction to the library. It might also provide special guided tours.

Here are some of the most promising places to look for information in a library:

- General encyclopedias (e.g., *Encyclopedia Americana* or *Encyclopaedia Britannica*)

- Specialized encyclopedias (e.g., *McGraw-Hill Encyclopedia of Science and Technology, International Encyclopedia of Higher Education,* or *The New Grove Dictionary of Music and Musicians*). There are specialized encyclopedias in many areas. Ask the librarian about your interest.

- Almanacs (e.g., *World Almanac* or *Facts on File*)

- Biographical dictionaries (e.g., *Dictionary of American Biography* or *International Who's Who*)

- General periodical indexes to short articles (e.g., *Reader's Guide to Periodical Literature* or *Book Review Digest*)

- Specialized periodical indexes (e.g., *Education Index* or *United States Government Publications*). There are many such specialized indexes.

- The subject index in the card catalogue.

This list of reference books is, of course, only illustrative. There are far too many to list here. (A full writing handbook or a textbook devoted to research papers will give more.) To see what's available—and you can often find a reference book that is just what you need—consult a guide like Eugene P. Sheehy's *A Guide to Reference Books* or ask the help of a librarian. The value of reference books is that they give you an overview of your topic and a range of books and articles you can track down.

The essential skill for doing library research is to learn a *different relationship with the printed word*. We tend to feel we have to *read* articles and books; but in research you need to learn to *glance, browse,* and *leaf* through print. If you learn to tell in a few seconds from a title or an abstract* whether something is worth tracking down, then tell in a minute or two whether an article is worth reading—and in two or three minutes whether a book is worth spending an hour trying to "mine" (not necessarily read)—you have learned the main thing. To do this makes you feel insecure at first, but give yourself permission to keep on till you feel more comfortable. Instead of feeling intimidated by the *weight* or *mass* of what might seem like everything that's ever been written, try to change gears and think of it as a vast collection of meeting rooms. In each room people are talking about a topic. Imagine that you have an invitation to poke your head into as many rooms as you want just for a moment or two: no one will be disturbed by your coming in for a few moments or by your leaving in the middle of the discussion.

Of course, you have to do some *careful* reading too. Think of it this way: you don't have so much time for this research assignment, so you want to end up having browsed and dipped into a number of books and articles— and found fifty to one hundred pages that are worth reading carefully for the light they throw on your topic. The procedure should make you more skilled and comfortable when you have something you want to investigate further. Our goal is that you should feel that from now on you can wade in and make use of a library whenever you have something that merits the search— whether a school assignment or something you need to know in your life.

---

*An abstract is a summary of a scholarly work. Abstracts are included in some kinds of reference books.

Remember too that you cannot say *everything* about any topic. You always need to limit what you say in some way. Your research is always more convincing and valid to the degree that you realize—and you show your reader that you realize—that you are not claiming to have read everything on the subject. This means that you can feel fine about acknowledging what you *haven't* done (instead of trying to hide it or be defensive about it). One of the most interesting parts of a research paper can be a section that talks about questions or material you *would* pursue if you were able to carry on with more research—or what you suggest for others who might want to carry the question further. Good researchers almost always do this.

Revising and Reshaping Your Paper

In taking a paper you wrote earlier and revising and reshaping it on the basis of research, you may find yourself simply trying to *bolster* the thinking you've already done. That's fine. But please also allow your research and reading to lead you to *amplify* or *change* your thinking—even change your mind. Give yourself permission to write a paper with a completely different slant. That's usually more *interesting* than just bolstering your thinking. Either way, you will probably have to reorganize your paper to find a way to put together your own thinking with the information and thinking you've found in the library. You are creating a more complex creature here, and it can be a struggle to figure out how to put it all together. Try to avoid a situation where references to external information and thinking are just tacked on. Think of your paper as brand new in its overall conception, even though it will have much from the paper you chose to use as a starting point.

In a sense you can think of yourself as doing first-level revision as we define it in Unit 8. As in all revising, there are no magic tricks or formulas: it always boils down to looking at everything that seems valuable and then struggling to find an organization for it. You will have quite a bit of material to sort through and organize: your original paper, notes taken on whatever you located in the library, additional writing you've done based on feedback from your partner or group. Finding some way to put this all together so it comes out as a coherent whole will probably not be easy. Some people use an outline; some people do freewriting to help them get straight for themselves what their focus will be and how that focus will help them organize all the pieces. You can read or describe your bits to others and ask them for suggestions about what they see as central and organizing. There are no "right answers" as to how a paper should be organized: it's a question of what works best for readers.* You may want to try out two or three organizations.

---

*There are some important exceptions here: if you write a research paper for a particular discipline such as chemistry or sociology, there *are* some formats and customs for how it should be put together—just as there is a standard form for scientific articles in certain fields. But we assume that you will not be writing that kind of paper now.

Quotations

It is possible to do lots of research and learn from the information and opinions of many published works and just write a terrific paper of your own—without a single quotation or footnote. (Joyce has no footnotes in *Ulysses* for all the details he checked up on.) But for this assignment we are asking for some quotations and footnotes. You should integrate and internalize what you learn into your own thinking, but this is also an assignment in showing to readers that *others* have said things about your topic. Your reader should not feel he is in a closet with you having a dialogue, but rather that he is in a large room with a number of people—other voices—involved in the issue.

For the format and use of quotations in your text, see the mini-unit on that topic.

Footnotes Aren't Footnotes Any More

"Footnote" is the word that probably springs to mind when you think of how to document your sources: a "note" at the "foot" of the page. But we are following the recent Modern Language Association (MLA) guidelines for citing sources *without* footnotes. The new MLA citation system makes life easier for both writers and readers and is now standard for academic writing in most of the humanities. (You can still use footnotes for an aside to the reader—as here*—but try not to use too many since they can make a reader feel bumped around.)

The documentation procedure has two elements: the *parenthetical citation* in your text as you go along, and the *list of works cited* at the end. When you want to document a source—that is, to tell readers what article or book you are quoting from or referring to—add a small parenthetical citation. Parentheses show readers where to look for the full information about the article or book in the final list of works cited without distracting your reader as much as old-style footnotes do.

Parenthetical Citations

Put in the parentheses only the information that readers need for finding the article or book in your list of works cited. Thus:

- Give *only* the page number(s) in your parentheses if you mention the author in your text. For example your text might read as follows:

  `Murray writes of a pregnant waiting and silence`
  `that come before starting to write (377).`

*If you need to use a citation system that fits the social or natural sciences, you will probably want the American Psychological Association (APA) system, which is explained in most handbooks. A number of the essays in the readings in this book, as you've probably noticed, use the APA documentation style.

Note that the parenthesis is *inside* the sentence's punctuation.

- If the author's name is not in your sentence, then add the name to the parenthesis. For example:

  ```
  Some writers speak of the need for waiting and
  silence before writing (Murray 377).
  ```

  Note that there's no comma after the author. The last name alone is sufficient unless you are using two authors with the same name.

- If you cite more than one work by Murray in your essay, add the title (or shortened title) to your parenthesis, e.g., (Murray, *Learning by Teaching* 377–8). But you can skip the title if you mention it in your sentence. Note the comma after the author but not after the title.

Other conventions:

- Titles of articles or chapters are in quotation marks; book titles are underlined—with no quotation marks.

- If the work has more than one volume, specify which one you are citing, followed by page number, e.g., (1:179).

- If citing a passage from a poem, give line numbers. If citing a passage from a play, give act, scene, line, e.g., (4.5.11–14).

- If there are two or three authors, give their names; for more than three, give first author and "et al."

Works Cited

This is a list that comes at the end of your paper on a separate sheet. The items are alphabetized by author and follow this general sequence: author, then title, then publisher. Here's the order in more detail:

- author (last name first)
- title of the work you're citing
- the title of larger work, magazine, or journal—if the work you're citing is contained in it
- editor or translator
- edition
- number of volumes
- city of publication
- publisher
- year of publication

- page numbers (if the work you're citing is only a portion of the larger publication)

Here is a list of the most common kinds of citations:

- Book:

> Aitchison, Jean. The Articulate Mammal: An
>   Introduction to Psycholinguistics. New
>   York: McGraw-Hill, 1976.

> Note that if Aitchison had been the editor rather than the author, her name would be followed by a comma and "ed."

- Essay from a professional journal:

> Flower, Linda, and John R. Hayes. "A Cognitive
>   Process Theory of Writing." College
>   Composition and Communication 32 (1981):
>   365-86.

> Note that the second author's name is not reversed. Because the pages of this journal are continuously numbered throughout the year, we have "32 (1981): 365-86." If it were a journal where each issue started with page 1, the note would read "32.4 (1981): 17-38." (The "4" here means the fourth issue of that year.)

- Poem or essay in a collection edited by someone else:

> Friebert, Stuart. "The Apron." 50 Contemporary
>   Poets: The Creative Process. Ed. Alberta T.
>   Turner. New York: David McKay, 1977. 102.

- Book review:

> Nilsen, Don L. F. Rev. of American Tongue and
>   Cheek: A Populist Guide to Our Language,
>   by Jim Quinn. College Composition and
>   Communication 37 (1986): 107-8.

- A personal letter [or interview]:

> Trimbur, John. Letter to the author [or Telephone
>   interview]. 17 Nov. 1984.

- If it is an unsigned work (e.g., in an encyclopedia or newspaper), begin with the title. (Thus its place in your alphabetized list would be determined by the first letters of the title.) If it is an unsigned U.S. Government publication, however, begin with "United States" then the agency that puts it out and then the title of the piece—as though the government were the author.

The punctuation in these citations is a bit sparse and counterintuitive—hard to remember: we ourselves have to look it up again and again. You could make a xerox of these pages to keep handy. And we've printed this information inside the back cover for ready reference.

Note how citations have "hung margins." That is, the first line of each citation is "flush left" (all the way left), and succeeding lines of each citation are indented five spaces—as we have shown them. However ours are single spaced (as they usually are in published or printed matter), but on manuscripts like yours they should be typed double spaced.

We have given here only the most common kinds of citations. You will have to consult a good handbook for more complicated ones, especially for using works from unusual sources (such as a television advertisement, record jacket, or map). On the other hand, few readers will care too much about deviations from correct form when it comes to seldom-cited kinds of sources.

SHARING AND RESPONDING

For this unit, you'll find "Analytic Responding" (*Sharing and Responding* booklet, Section III) particularly useful when you're working with your group to come up with questions to use as a basis for your research. After you have a draft of your revised paper, you'll find "Sayback," "Descriptive Outline," and "Criterion-Based or Judgment-Centered Responding" (*Sharing and Responding* booklet, sections IIA, IIIC, and V, respectively) helpful. You may also want to ask your classmates the following questions:

- Does my paper seem to be a unifed whole?

- Are there too many quotations? Not enough?

- Have I made clear the limits of my subject?

- Are the conclusions *I* draw evident and separate from the information derived from my research.

QUESTIONS FOR YOUR PROCESS JOURNAL

What did you notice and what can you learn from:

- Your process of choosing a paper to develop further?

- Your process of finding further questions to answer with the help of a library? Which *kinds* of questions seem to lend themselves to library research and which not? Did you by any chance fall into thinking that "research questions" mean "boring" or factual questions?

- Your first efforts in the library—especially if you had not used a library much before? What were your *feelings* when first starting to use the library? How did your feelings change over the course of this assignment? What aspects of library work are you best at or do you find most congenial? Which parts do you have the most trouble with or find most frustrating?

- Your success (or difficulties) with trying to integrate your thinking and the thinking or information you found in the library? Did your thinking change much or not at all on the basis of library work? Do you draw any conclusions from that?

- Your use of documentation techniques? What were you good at and bad at? What would help you with this kind of work in the future?

READINGS

ANOREXIA NERVOSA
Pamela Ellis

anorexia nervosa—a personality disorder chiefly in young women, characterized by aversion to food, obsession with weight loss.

—Webster's Dictionary

This is a very simplistic way of looking at anorexia nervosa. It certainly is a personality disorder, but what the definition fails to make clear is the seriousness of the disease. Not only can this "personality disorder" physically harm your body for life, but it can also end in death. There are endless stories of young women who permanently damage their bodies as a result of anorexia. It is primarily due to a lack of self-confidence and an abundance of insecurities. These relate back to our society's obsession with being thin. Much emphasis is placed on the exercise craze and the fact that "thin is in."

From my experience with the disease, I have learned that anorexia is not the type of thing that develops overnight. There is much more behind it than most people realize. Much thought and calculation goes into planning it. It is a desperate cry out for attention and help. My experience with the disease is proof of this. I watched my lifelong friend waste away in front of my eyes, and for a long time had no idea what was happening to her. I wish now that I had been educated in this area so perhaps I could have detected that my friend Lynn was in serious trouble.

In second grade I moved down the street from Lynn. Since then we have been the best of friends. As far as appearance goes, Lynn and I could not have looked more different. Lynn developed much earlier than everyone else our age. This made that period very difficult for her because she was the one who looked different. I, on the other hand, was on the short side and very skinny, making it difficult to relate to the way Lynn felt about her size. She was very insecure about the way she looked. Being the largest kid in the sixth grade, Lynn felt very awkward. Soon everyone began to catch up with her, and she wasn't as self-conscious. But the next thing that happened was that she began to put on weight. Again this started a chain reaction of new insecurities. She hated things like getting her picture taken, especially with other people, or walking on the beach in a bathing suit. Upon meeting Lynn she seems to be a confident, outgoing person. In reality, she looked down on herself because of some severe hang-ups which she had developed.

The hang-ups Lynn had developed were not due solely to her size. She also tended to feel insufficient at home. Dr. Philip C. Wilson, a New York psychoanalyst, made these comments about over 100 families of anorexics he has worked with: "The parents are perfectionists and overly conscientious. They emphasize good behavior and social conformity. Usually they are hardworking, achieving, and mor-alistic—but too moralistic. Not only are they successful, but they are active in their communities" (Brown 160). Lynn comes from a family of high achievers. Her father holds an important position in a nationally known computer company. Her mother has become a well-known artist in the area. At our hometown high school, her sister Carol had acquired the label of borderline genius, which is a hard act to follow. Tommy, her brother, aside from achieving high marks, was wanted by many top colleges to play football. Because of all this Lynn began to feel like an underachiever. The truth of the matter is that this is absolutely untrue. Lynn was a very ambitious girl, which is typical of anorexics. What she didn't realize is that she did not have to compete with her sister and brother to achieve the same status. It was not necessary to be a superachiever. She had many other things going for her. Because of her flam-boyant personality, Lynn was a very popular girl. She brought a lot of smiles to everyone's face. In addition, she was always in the top twenty of our class, which is something to be proud of.

These things always seemed to go unnoticed by Lynn. She always seemed to focus on the things that she didn't have. During our sophomore year in high school, Lynn applied to go on an exchange to another country for a year. She claimed she wanted to achieve something that no one she knew had achieved, or so she thought. She needed to get away for a while because she was unhappy with herself. She was accepted into this program and informed that she would be going to Japan. The real-ity of what she had gotten herself into began to sink in. She would be living in a culture which she knew nothing about, nor spoke the language, for a year. I think that this type of exchange program is a great opportunity for high school kids. It would have been a great opportunity for Lynn if she had done it for the right reasons. Basically, she was going away to try to make herself a better person, someone who could compete with those she felt inferior to. Only at the time she would not admit this. She was going away to try and amend her own insecurities, and to do this she would start her "super diet." This is an example of the thought and calculation which goes into the planning of anorexia nervosa.

This whole experience turned out to be dangerously disastrous. She found her-self in a country where communication was near to impossible. The family that she lived with did next to nothing to help her adjust, and to make things worse, they were all under 5'2" and very thin. This did nothing for her insecure feelings about her size. At this time in her life, Lynn was 5'7" and about 145 lbs. The whole point of the trip in Lynn's eyes was blown. She had gone away to avoid feeling inadequate, but there it was intensified. Now she felt very stupid because she couldn't communicate and very big because she lived in a house and country of small people. This is when she started the starvation bit. She was fed up with feeling so inadequate.

Later, Lynn told me that she thought that this would be the perfect place to lose a lot of weight. There would be no one around to give her a hard time about eating. I received letters from her frequently informing me that she was unhappy and very homesick. Usually at the end she would mention casually that she had dropped a few pounds and that she was exercising regularly. What she neglected to tell me was that losing weight had become an obsession. A typical anorexic loses her perspective of the way she appears physically and is drawn toward obsessive isolation (Leven-kron 11). Lynn could not have been more isolated than by being in Japan. An anorexic's thoughts become nearly all food/weight/exercise related as the disease progresses. Rigorous exercise and meal planning become a major preoccupation throughout the day (Levenkron 5).

Lynn began sending pictures of herself to her close friends and her parents. This was her way of showing everyone that she was achieving something. The preoccu-pation with weight is such that most patients can give a detailed history of their weight changes. In the pictures she looked frighteningly unhealthy and gaunt. Her parents grew instantly worried. When I expressed my concern to Lynn in letters she only insisted that the pictures must have been deceiving because she had not lost that much weight. What I didn't realize was that she was doing what most anorexics do, denying anything was wrong. She knew exactly what she was doing to her body. Yet she assured me that she was smarter than that and that I had no reason to worry. This assurance satisfied me until the next batch of pictures came in. These showed very clearly the physical state that Lynn was in. The clothing which used to fit her perfectly looked about ten sizes too big. It looked as though she had invaded her father's wardrobe. Her face looked distorted because she was so thin, and hair loss was evident. This is a very typical symptom which anorexics acquire. Other symp-toms include constipation, loss of scalp hair, insomnia, hyperactivity, complaints of coldness, and growth of fine body hair due to a hormonal imbalance possibly caused by malnutrition. About three days after we received these her parents were told that Lynn was in a hospital in Tokyo. She was severely malnourished and dehydrated.

This occurred about three weeks before Christmas. A few days before Christmas Lynn was sent home. This was more than six months earlier than scheduled. When she arrived home the only thing that she could put in her system was small amounts of liquids. Her appearance was shocking at first. When I went to visit her for the first time she could barely stand up. I went to go hug her, and she felt like a bundle of bones which I was crushing. I was speechless. My outgoing best friend was so weak that she was having difficulty speaking. From here it was a long and difficult road to recovery. Her body had been without solid food for so long that it refused to digest it. Lynn still refused to eat, especially in front of others. Anorexics don't like to be seen eating, and it becomes an extremely private activity. A sense of vulnerability, shame, and competition for thinness becomes attached to food (Levenkron 5).

Lynn had dropped down to 85 lbs yet thought she was overweight. This is another striking feature of anorexics. Their perceptions of their body size are totally distorted. They are convinced they are still overweight and think they look terrific when others are revolted by their skeleton-like figure. Most of the time anorexics see the appearance of others accurately but distort their own appearance.

Under close watch by her family, friends, and doctors, Lynn slowly began to recover. For a while she was very difficult to live with because she would deny that there was anything wrong and resented the fact that she was being watched. She followed the typical route of becoming defiant and secretive in the area of weight control. She disregarded others' perceptions of her appearance and nutritional needs. It took close to a year for her to physically recover, although she still does not menstruate. This is a very common feature of most descriptions of anorexia nervosa. The medical term for loss of menstruation is amenorrheia (Abraham and Llewellyn-Jones 14). This is something that she may never regain. She has damaged her body so severely that it may never fully recover. Lynn is now a vegetarian and has gained back a good portion of the weight she lost. It took a while for her to realize how horrible she looked. She needed a lot of support and understanding from her close friends and her family. Most of this period was very difficult for both Lynn and me, but well worth it to see her healthy again.

Whatever forms of therapy prove most helpful for women with eating disorders, it is clear that this is only half the battle. What is important is that the disease is caught in an early stage and treated immediately through both physical and psychological therapy. My friend Lynn was lucky, although this is a strange word to call what she went through. She survived through all of the psychological, physical, and reproductive dangers of dieting and excessive thinness. Many women don't recover from anorexia nervosa for years, and sadly enough for some it results in death.

WORKS CITED

ABRAHAM, SUZANNE, and DEREK LLEWELLYN-JONES. *Eating Disorders: The Facts.* New York: Oxford UP, 1964.
BROWN, KIM. "When Dieting Goes Berserk." *Parents* Apr. 1985: 160, 162, 165.
ERENS, PAMELA. "Bodily Harm." *Ms* Oct. 1985: 62, 63, 66, 82.
LEVENKRON, STEVEN. *Treating and Overcoming Anorexia Nervosa.* New York: Warner, 1983.

NON-MAGICAL THINKING:
PRESENTING WRITING DEVELOPMENTALLY IN SCHOOLS
Janet Emig

" . . . the freedom to act upon the world and to construct reality is both the aim and the process of education." If we accept this bedrock developmental proposition, what are the implications for the ways in which writing is presented in schools? Writing represents, of course, powerful, if not unique, ways of constructing reality and of acting upon the world. Consequently, writing can itself serve as both an aim and a major process of education.

Presenting writing developmentally means that from the outset we put aside a belief that the cognitive psychologist Howard Gruber calls "magical thinking":

> We wish the child to grow up and in fact he does: we therefore attribute his growth to our own desires and our efforts (Piaget, 1930). This questionable causal attribution provides the main justification for adult efforts to educate children.
>
> In recent years we have become increasingly aware that adults do not teach children some of the most fundamental ideas; at best, we help to provide circumstances in which children discover what they must know.

That teachers teach and children learn no one will deny. But to believe that children learn *because* teachers teach and only what teachers explicitly teach is to engage in magical thinking, from a developmental point of view.

Most North American schools are temples to magical thinking, with the focus not only on explicit teaching but on a specific form of explicit teaching—adults performing before large groups of learners. As evidence: I recently heard of a note an evaluating administrator slipped a teacher who was helping small groups of writers actively construct their reality through imaginative sequences of experiences and activities. The note read: "I'll come back when you're teaching."

Where matters of language like writing are concerned, the evidence from research is particularly compelling that, as Courtney Cazden of Harvard has observed, " . . . it is not certain that teaching knowledge *about* language helps us in any way." (italics mine) She continues: " . . . One reason, therefore, why language is such a difficult subject for curriculum planners is that we do not understand the relationship between what is in some way learned and what can be *taught*."

Perhaps the greatest irony in the back-to-basics movement is that current relentless and expensive efforts to teach writing, and reading, are so undeniably cases of magical thinking on the part of all the adults involved. (Another irony is that the success of explicit teaching, in this era of accountability, is measured by indexes of explicit learning by children on standardized tests.)

Teachers of writing, for many reasons, have come to believe that children's learning to write is the direct outcome of their explicit teaching. Perhaps, because of massive public pressure, they have been forced to become the most magical thinkers of all. But what if, as evidence from many disciplines now suggests, writing is developmentally a *natural* process? What if "it is just as natural . . . to write books and to read them as it is natural to die or be born?"

Natural for this context must be quickly defined: As humans we seem to have a genetic predisposition to write as well as to speak; and, if we meet an enabling environment, one that possesses certain characteristics and presents us with certain opportunities, we will learn.

Since the late fifties and early sixties we have heard from such linguists as Chomsky and such biologists of language as Lenneberg strong arguments for the innatist position that humans have a propensity for creating language, that such special, even unique, capacities are "wired-in." . . .

Vygotsky makes the further case that the gesture is developmentally a requisite to the development of written language. In *A Prehistory of Written Language* (1934, trans. 1978), Vygotsky claims that the gesture is "the initial visual sign that contains the child's future writing as an acorn contains a future oak."

Gestures are writing in air, and written signs frequently are simply gestures that have been fixed.

Early on, children shuttle between actual gestures and scribbles on paper that "supplement this gestural representation." In fact, Vygotsky regards the child's first marks on paper developmentally as recorded gestures rather than as drawing in the true sense of the word. One thinks as well, of course, of Piaget, who posits that sensorimotor activity is the source of schemes that transform into subsequent modes of representation.

These marks on the paper go through a series of evolutionary changes, from undifferentiated marks through indicatory signs and symbolizing marks and scribbles to the drawing of little figures and pictures to the moment when the child realizes that "one can draw not only things but speech." This recognition makes possible the transformaton of writing from a first-order symbolic act, to a second-order symbolic act, from the "mnemotechnic" stage to the stage where one can deal with disembodied signs and symbols—to the stage, that is, of symbolic maturity.

Children's games represent the second realm that "links gestures and written language." In play children use objects in their representational gestures: a piece of wood can serve as a baby or a wand, for example:

> . . .therefore, children's symbolic play can be understood as a very complex system of "speech" through gestures that communicate and indicate the meaning of playthings. It is only on the basis of these indicatory gestures that playthings themselves gradually acquire their meaning—just as drawing, while initially supported by gesture, becomes an independent sign.

He concludes:

> symbolic representation in play is essentially a particular form of speech at an earlier stage, one which leads directly to written language.

These two transformations can be represented by the following sketch:

Vygotsky's statements about the requisites of symbolic play to the development of writing in the life of the child are corroborated and extended by studies that examine the roots in childhood of gifted and creative performances in adults, particularly studies by Gardner (1973) and Singer (1973).

Benjamin Singer draws from his research into the fantasy lives of children five conditions "which are conducive to nurturing a predisposition to fantasy play":

1. An opportunity for privacy and for practice in a relatively protected setting where the external environment is reasonably redundant so that greater attention can be focused on internal activity. Naturally, such a situation exists also at the time of preparation for sleep and during sleep itself.
2. Availability of a variety of materials in the form of stories told, books, and playthings which increase the likelihood that the material presented to the child in the course of the reprocessing activity or in the course of a set toward elaboration of this material will be interesting and sufficiently novel so that the child will experience positive affect while playing make-believe games.
3. Freedom from interference by peers or adults who make demands for immediate motor or perceptual reactions. . . .
4. The availability of adult models or older peers who encourage make-believe activity and provide examples of how this is done or provide basic story material which can be incorporated in privacy into the child's limited schemata.
5. Cultural acceptance of privacy and make-believe activities as a reasonably worthwhile form of play.

In *From Two to Five,* the Russian poet Kornei Chukovsky charmingly illustrates his hypothesis that between the ages of two and five all children are linguistic geniuses. Chukovsky confined his examples to the oral utterances of children. But in his recent study of metaphoric development in children, Howard Gardner extends the ages and range of art forms for the manifestation of creative genius in children. Gardner's conclusions:

> Perhaps the chief mystery confronting the student of artistic development is the relationship between the mature adult practitioner—the skilled poet, the painting master, the virtuoso instrumentalist or composer—and the young child playing with words, humming and inventing melodies, effortlessly producing sketches and paintings while engaging in many other activities that have only a tenuous relationship to the arts. Clearly there are important differences in skill, acquaintance with the artistic tradition, sensitivity to nuance between the child and the adult participants in the artistic process. But a more fundamental question for the psychologist is whether the schoolchild must pass through further, qualitatively different stages in order to become an artist (as it has been argued that he must pass through qualitatively different stages en route to becoming a practicing scientist). On this question I have arrived at an unexpected conclusion: the child of 7 or 8 has, in most respects, become a participant in the artistic process and he need not pass through any further qualitative reorganization. . . .

What are the possible implications of these research findings for the presentation of writing in schools?

1. Although writing is natural, it is activated by enabling environments.
2. These environments have the following characteristics: they are safe, structured, private, unobtrusive, and literate.
3. Adults in these environments have two especial roles: they are fellow practitioners, and they are providers of possible content, experiences and feedback.
4. Children need frequent opportunities to practice writing, many of these playful.

None of these conditions is met in our current schools; indeed, to honor them would require nothing less than a paradigm shift in the ways we present not only writing but also other major cognitive processes as well. Shifting paradigms is no easy task; in fact, developmentally, there is probably no more complex cognitive process.

As Gruber points out in a remarkable essay comparing children and scientists, notably Darwin, making a paradigm shift requires not only cognitive change but the courage to make the change. To give up one paradigm about the nature of learning and teaching for another requires that teachers undergo a particularly powerful conversion.

. . .The change in thinking means moving away from an established and perhaps hard-won set of relations with other human beings. This may be more important in the case of children than has been realized. When the child, for example, shifts his way of thought so that he restrains himself from making a judgment based on purely perceptual criteria, he is also making a serious change in life-style. He is increasing his independence from the stimulus. In that sense,

309

he is increasing his independence more generally, and any increase in independence carries with it both a promise and a threat. We would probably discover, if we looked a little more closely at those moments when the child's thinking really seems to move, that the child experiences a sense of exhilaration. When we speak of "insight" or the "Aha Experience," it is not just seeing something new. It is feeling. And what the person is feeling is both the promise and the threat of this unknown that is just opening up. When we think new thoughts we really are changing our relations with the world around us, including our social moorings. . . .

Before specifying what in my opinion such a conversion requires, how can the two paradigms be characterized? What, first, are the tenets of the magical thinking paradigm about writing that currently dominates the schools? Here is its credo:

1. Writing is predominantly taught rather than learned.
2. Children must be taught to write atomistically, from parts to wholes. The commonplace is that children must be taught to write sentences before they can be allowed to write paragraphs before they can be permitted to attempt "whole" pieces of discourse.
3. There is essentially one process of writing that serves all writers for all their aims, modes, intents, and audiences.
4. That process is linear: all planning precedes all writing (often described in the paradigm as transcribing), as all writing precedes all revising.
5. The process of writing is also almost exclusively conscious: as evidence, a full plan or outline can be drawn up and adhered to for any piece of writing: the outline also assumes that writing is transcribing, since it can be so totally prefigured; thought exists prior to its linguistic formulation.
6. Perhaps because writing is conscious, it can be done swiftly and on order.
7. There is no community or collaboration in writing: it is exclusively a silent and solitary activity.

What, in contrast, are the findings from the developmental research into writing:

1. Writing is predominantly learned rather than taught.
2. Writers of all ages as frequently work from wholes to parts as from parts to wholes: in writing, there is a complex interplay between focal and global concerns: from an interest in what word should come next, to the shape of the total piece.
3. There is no monolithic process of writing: there are processes of writing that differ because of aim, intent, mode, and audience: although there are shared features in the ways we write, there are as well individual, even idiosyncratic, features in our processes of writing.
4. The processes of writing do not proceed in a linear sequence: rather they are recursive—we not only plan, then write, then revise; but we also revise, then plan, then write.
5. Writing is as often a pre-conscious or unconscious roaming as it is a planned and conscious rendering of information and events.
6. The rhythms of writing are uneven—more, erratic. The pace of writing can be very slow, particularly if the writing represents significant learning. Writing is also slow since it involves what Vygotsky calls "elaborating the web of mean-

ing," supplying the specific and explicit links to render lexical, syntactic, semantic, and rhetorical pieces into organic wholes.

7. The processes of writing can be enhanced by working in, and with, a group of other writers, perhaps especially a teacher, who give vital response, including advice.

What constitutes a conversion experience for those who present writing in schools, from the magical thinking paradigm to a developmental view? Obviously, since the shift is so great, so dramatic (and, at times, traumatic), the evidence and the experiences must be extremely powerful and, indeed, they must be developmental.

To undergo such a conversion, teachers of writing, our research strongly suggests, must:

1. write themselves in many modes, poetic and imaginative, as well as transactional and extensive, and introspect upon their own histories and processes as writers;

2. observe directly, and through such media as videotape, female and male writers of many ages and backgrounds engaging in the processes of writing; and speculate systematically with other teacher-writers about these observations and their implications for presenting writing in schools;

3. ascertain attitudes, constructs, and paradigms of those learning to write because the evidence grows stronger that, as with any learning process, set affects, perhaps even determines, both process and performance;

4. assess growth in writing against its developmental dimensions, with perhaps the most important accomplishment a growing ability to distinguish between a *mistake* and what can be termed a *developmental* error. . . .

Developmental errors contrast readily with mistakes in that developmental errors forward learning while mistakes impede it. Developmental errors have two characteristics that mistakes do not: 1) they are bold, chance-taking; 2) and they are rational, intelligent.

While the making of mistakes marks a retreat into the familiar, the result of fear and anxiety, developmental errors represent a student's venturing out and taking chances as a writer, from trying a new spelling, or tying together two sentences with a fresh transition, to a first step into a mode previously unexplored.

A second characteristic of developmental errors is that they are rational and logical; unfortunately, they often happen also to be wrong. In *Errors and Expectations,* our most thorough account of errors among a given segment of writers, those she calls BW writers (Basic Writers), Mina Shaughnessy notes the "most damaging aspect" of the BW's experiences with writing:

they have lost all confidence in the very faculties that serve all language learners: their ability to distinguish between essential and redundant features of a language left them logical but wrong; their abilities to draw analogies between what they knew of language when they began school and what they learned produced mistakes; and such was the quality of their instruction that no one saw the intelligence of their mistakes or thought to harness that intelligence in the service of learning. . . .

Assessing growth in writing is a far larger, more complex, more individual and more interesting matter than testing. Too many testing programs, particularly those devised and given by state and national agencies, public and private, use evidence divorced from the linguistic and human histories of the students involved, and evidence divorced from the only sensible developmental requirement that students write organic, sustained pieces of discourse, like the students themselves, with histories and with futures.

Presenting writing developmentally in schools will require major transformations: transformations from the traditional school paradigm that promulgates magical thinking; and consequently, transformations of teacher learning and development. It is quite as demanding as the ways of teaching writing traditionally—perhaps more demanding—requiring no less than that adults admit that the only way they can help others learn to write is that they themselves become learners and writers.

REFERENCES

BETTELHEIM, B. *Paul & Mary: Two Case Histories of Truants from Life.* New York: Doubleday, Anchor, 1961.

CAZDEN, C. B. "Problems for Education: Language as Curriculum Content and Learning Environment," in "Language as a Human Problem." *Daedalus* (Summer, 1973), CII, 3, 135.

CHOMSKY, N. *Language and Mind.* New York: Harcourt Brace Jovanovich, 1972.

CHUKOVSKY, K. *From Two to Five.* M. Morton (Ed. & Tr.). Berkeley, CA: University of California Press, 1963.

CONDON, W., & SANDER, L. "Neonate Movement Is Synchronized with Adult Speech: Interactional Participation and Language Acquisition." *Science,* 183 (4120), 1974, 99–101.

DUCKWORTH, E. "The Having of Wonderful Ideas." M. Schwebel & J. Raph (Eds.), *Piaget in the Classroom.* New York: Basic Books, 1973, 21–22.

FELDENKRAIS, M. *Body and Mature Behavior,* New York: International Universities Press, 1949, 132. Ken Macrorie brought this reference to my attention.

GARDNER, H. *The Arts & Human Development: A Psychological Study of the Artistic Process.* New York: Wiley, 1973.

GRUBER, H. "Courage and Cognitive Growth in Children and Scientists," in M. Schwebel & J. Raph (Eds.), *Piaget in the Classroom.* New York: Basic Books, 1973, 74.

LENNEBERG, E. *Biological Foundations of Language,* New York: Wiley, 1967.

PIANKO, S. "A Description of the Composing Processes of College Freshman Writers," *Research in the Teaching of English* (February, 1979), XIII, 1, 5–22.

POLANYI, M. *Personal Knowlege: Towards a Post-critical Philosophy.* Chicago: University of Chicago Press, 1958.

REDINGER, R. V. *George Eliot: The Emergent Self.* New York: Knopf, 1975.

Report of the New Jersey Writing Project to the National Dissemination Panel, Washington, D.C.: (May, 1979).

SCHWEBEL, M. & RAPH, J. "Before and Beyond the Three R's," in M. Schwebel & J. Raph (Eds.), *Piaget in the Classroom.* New York: Basic Books, 1973, 21–22.

SHAUGHNESSY, M. *Errors and Expectations: A Guide for the Teacher of Basic Writing.* New York: Oxford University Press, 1977, 10–11.

VYGOTSKY, L. "The Prehistory of Written Language" (1934), in S. Scribner *et al.*

(Eds.), *Mind in Society: The Development of Higher Psychological Processes.* Cambridge, MA: Harvard University Press, 1978, pp. 105–111.
YOUNG, J. Z. *Programs of the Brain.* New York: Oxford University Press, 1978, 10.

WHEN A CHILD HAS CANCER
Kymberly Saganski

When a child is afflicted by cancer, the family members react differently as a result of the initial shock. In the case of my family, my parents experienced a typical preoccupation with the trivial things, a fear of death and worries about finances. My own reactions included fear, disorganization and even selfishness. These are all common among families dealing with a profoundly ill member.

The ultimate determination that a family member has cancer is never easy to accept, but it seems more difficult when the ill member is a child. At the age of fifteen, my younger brother was diagnosed as having acute lymphoblastic leukemia and lymphoma. In its advanced stages, "leukemic blood cells rapidly glut the bone marrow, pour over into the bloodstream, and invade the lymph nodes, the spleen, and such vital organs of the body as the liver, brain and kidneys (Levitt and Guralnick 72). It seemed ironic that my father's first thoughts were of his son's high school sports career and the soon to be arriving hospital bills. My mother, having watched my grandfather die of the same rare combination of diseases, thought only of my brother's fifty percent chance for survival. In order to avoid the entire situation, I worried about the fact that I was getting behind in work at my Massachusetts school since my mother and I had joined my father and brother in New Jersey where they were living. Peter, my brother, was hospitalized immediately, and the bills started to accumulate from that moment forward.

After this initial hospitalization, the patient often feels lost, helpless and scared. Parents become frantic as they watch their son's or daughter's dreams for the future become unstable and begin to topple. The remaining children fight for their position in the reshuffled family. Although they are not decision makers, their needs are often considered when decisions are being made. Many times, even though there is nothing concrete that they can do to help the situation, the presence of other children is soothing in and of itself.

The patients, themselves, may react in a variety of ways. Sometimes they withdraw from everyone else, repressing their thoughts and emotions. Other times, they become bitter and resentful, blaming everyone and everything for their predicament. Barbara Rabkin, a scientific journalist for *Macleans* magazine, contends that the entire process of "coping with leukemia itself . . . is complicated by the lack of public understanding and acceptance of the disease" (54–5). There are a few patients who seem to accept their condition from the beginning and maintain an open mind and a positive attitude. These cases, however, are few and far between. According to Rabkin, this is the time when the support of other families is the most important. The family members dealing with the cancer need to have contact with unafflicted families in order to maintain their grasp on "real life" (55). I don't happen to agree with this rationalization.

My family dealt with the cancer as individuals. We each reacted in our own separate ways to my little brother's illness. My parents tried to be supportive, as I did, but Pete had decided that his best defense was anger. He was angry at his doctors for misdiagnosing his cancer as an allergy when he had first become sick eleven months earlier. He was angry at himself for not knowing his own body better, and he was angry at all of his friends and relatives for showing him sympathy, which he interpreted as pity. He decided then and there that he was going to hate this cancer until it left him alone.

I had no idea as to what I should do with myself. My brother seemed to resent the fact that I was up and around while he was hooked up to machines and lying flat on his back in a hospital bed. John Spinetta, writing for *Human Behavior,* contends that this resentment is a natural phase of the cancer acceptance cycle by the patient (49), but I couldn't deal with the rejection of my sympathy for my brother. Because I seemed so uncomfortable at the hospital, I was given the choice of missing school for a month and staying in New Jersey or returning to Cape Cod and living alone for an indefinite period of time. That was the least of the decisions that I was asked to assist in making. I delayed my return home in case I could be some help to my parents.

My brother had the option of three different kinds of chemotherapy. He refused to have any input whatsoever, so my parents asked me to put myself in my brother's position and try to imagine living with the various side effects of the different drugs. I had a lot of difficulty with this task, but I tried my best in order to take some of the pressure off my parents. I decided then that even though I seemed to be a comfort to my mother, her worries about my falling behind in school were just added troubles to her already heavy heart, so I returned to school. This return to an almost normal life helped me to deal with the situation, and the fact that I had the added responsibility of living by myself kept my mind from wandering back to Peter constantly.

I was surprised at the amount of time that the social workers on Peter's case spent with my entire family. I had never before realized that an illness such as cancer affects the whole family in such a complete way. Ann Brierly, a social worker at my brother's hospital, believes that the best way to ease the pain of a family illness is to educate all members about the nature of the illness. Once my parents were adequately informed concerning Peter's cancer, they were able to deal with it from a clinical point of view. When people inquire as to Peter's condition, I say that after all we have been through, he is what is so far considered cured. In my heart I feel like I should answer, "We survived," and I hope we will never have to live through such an ordeal again.

WORKS CITED

BRIERLY, ANN. Telephone interview. 6 May 1985.

LEVITT, PAUL M., and ELISSA S. GURALNICK. *The Cancer Reference Book.* New York: Paddington Press, 1979.

RABKIN, BARBARA. "Childhood Leukemia." *Macleans* 23 Apr. 1979: 54–5.

SPINETTA, JOHN. "Childhood Cancer: Study of a Family Coping." *Human Behavior* May 1979: 49.

Case Study:
Yourself as a Writer

Our experience has taught us that if you want to make your writing easier and better, you will probably learn the most by becoming a student of your own writing process. Thus, our major aim in this unit is to get you to learn something about yourself and your writing process that will be useful when you are doing future writing tasks in school. But we also hope the work of this unit will help you see some role for writing in your life outside of school assignments. Along the way you should discover for yourself that writing leads to learning.

Your major assignment will be to produce a case study of yourself as a writer. And since you will be using writing you've done throughout the semester as a basis for your case study, this unit will encourage you to look back on the term and assess honestly what happened to you and to your writing.

For most of you, this may be your final assignment of the term. It will help you solidify and benefit from what you have been learning all semester. Some of what you've learned you've been explicitly aware you were learning; but you have learned many other things in an intuitive, unconscious way. This case study will help you see and consolidate *all* you have learned. It needn't be too much work, yet you can discover much about your own learning and how it has affected the way you write.

The theme of your case study is the theme of the course: *the writing process.* The case study will help you see the writing process in detail and empirically—not just settle for generalizations. The *facts* about what you actually do when you write are probably somewhat different from what you *think* you do. Discovering these facts almost always makes your writing easier and better.

POSSIBLE INGREDIENTS, ISSUES, OR THEMES

Following are topics to help you collect materials for your case study. Some of these topics you've already written about in your process journal throughout the term. You should look back through your journal and mark such passages. Other topics that we suggest in the list that follows you will not have written on. You should begin writing on any or all of these and see what happens; you probably won't be able to write much on a lot of them. The important thing to remember is that—for right now—you're not trying to draw conclusions: you're still in the data-collection stage.

Moments. What important incidents do you remember from past writing experiences?

Stages. Intuitively divide your life as a writer into a few stages or periods; then ask yourself what characterizes each of those stages.

Kinds. What kinds of writing have you done in the past and what kinds do you do now? Remember that there are many more kinds of writing than those you've done in school: making lists is writing; so is graffiti. What is different about your experience with different kinds of writing?

In-school versus out-of-school writing. Do you go about both of these the same way? Differently? Do you feel the same way about both? Why or why not?

Audience. Who are the important people you have written for? (Not just teachers.) What effects have these different audiences had? on your feelings? on your writing? Which audiences helped you most or held you back? How often do you feel yourself to be the only audience of what you are writing? (Don't forget "ghost audiences" or audiences we carry around in our heads and unconsciously try to please—usually left over from experiences with past audiences.) Many people remember bad audiences more than good ones. Is that true of you? Why?

Physical. Where do you write? When? How fast or slow? What are the effects of using pen, pencil, typewriter, or word processor? How do you hold and move your body? Tell everything that could be figured out from a *complete video recording* of your writing from start to finish.

Process. Can you isolate specific ingredients in your writing process: that is, generating words and responses, copyediting, publishing? Non-writing counts too: sitting and thinking, talking to people. Which of these give you the most trouble? least? the most satisfaction? least? Why?

Intervention. In what ways have others intervened in your writing? ("Here, let me show you!" "Do it this way." "You must start by making an outline." "You must start by freewriting"—and so forth.) How has intervention affected your writing?

Response and feedback. What kinds of response and feedback have you gotten—and not just from teachers? What effects did this feedback have on you? (Don't forget no response and nonverbal response—silence and laughter.)

Writing for other classes versus writing for this class. If you've written papers for other classes this term, what's different about how you went about it? Did you do any freewriting, produce a draft which your teacher responded to either verbally or in writing, revise one or more times, copyedit? Compare the total effort involved in that project and the total effort involved in writing a piece for this class. Pay attention too to any differences in feelings or attitudes toward the two pieces of writing. If you did not use the techniques we've been stressing in this book, do you think you could have or should have? Why or why not?

Problems. Stuck points and breakthroughs. What's hardest for you or what gets in the way most? How have you made or not made progress? Where have you made greatest progress?

Myths. What are some of the feelings or ideas that you've had about your writing (or that most people seem to have) that you now see are *false?* Where did these myths come from? What purposes did they serve and what effect have they had on you? What follows from abandoning them?

The word **writer.** Who do you think of as a writer? What are the characteristics of a writer? Can you think of yourself as a writer? If not, why not?

Temperament or character. Do you see any relation between your writing process and your temperament, character, or feelings? Does your writing process show you to be "loose" or "tight," vulnerable or confident? In general, do you think that someone's writing process reflects her character?

MAKING A DRAFT

You should now have much raw material—some developed, some just bits. Read through all of this *and* through all your process writing from the semester. (You probably have more than you realize; some of your assign-

317

ments have been process writing or include bits of it. You'll find other bits here and there. Some will be in notebooks for other subjects.) Mark the bits that are interesting and useful. You can probably use some of this process writing as part of your paper if you choose and cut well.

Next, consider what all this process writing is telling you. Do some free-writing or outlining or note jotting to figure out what your paper might focus on.

Two additional things we consider particularly important in any case study: one is a mini-study or close look at *one* specific piece of writing, and the second is an analysis of how your present writing process differs from the way you used to write. We could have included both of these in our earlier list, but we wanted to give them special emphasis.

1. For your mini-study, choose something that you wrote this semester. Choose that piece which—as the psychologists say—you "cathect" most: that piece you have the strongest feelings about or feel the strongest connection with. You can learn most from looking honestly and in detail at such a piece. You might also, however, simply pick the piece which you happen to have the most process writing for—the most evidence as to what actually was going on as you wrote. Evidence maximizes learning. Spend some time reconstructing how you wrote this piece from beginning to end in as much detail as possible; look at the writing itself, the various drafts, and see what they tell you. Select specific passages which you can quote and comment on. Do some freewriting, outlining, and jotting about what you figure out as you study this piece.

2. Think back on the writing you did *before* this course. (Some of your process writing will be about that too. You might have included it in the collage you did early in the semester about your writing history.) What does that early writing tell you? Many of you have probably saved copies of papers written in high school. You might want to look at these and see how much you can remember about writing them. This should lead you to some conclusions about the similarities and differences between how you used to write and how you write now. This, in turn, should make clearer the effects of this semester's work on your writing.

Now you have the ingredients for producing a draft. You can do some cutting and pasting and arranging, but make sure to let this draft making be a process of *new discovery*—not just an assembling of what you already have. Look at all this material that you now suspect belongs in your draft. What does it mean? What does it add up to? What emphasis, claim, focus, shape, approach, spirit, do you want your case study to have? If you keep these questions in mind, you will find new answers as you write and paste.

In making your draft, you are finally ready to ask the practical question: what useful advice or suggestions can you give yourself for future writing?

What are the *dangers* for you as a writer? What do you wish someone would whisper in your ear as you undertake writing tasks in the future?

A good case study can be structured like a story or like an essay. That is, you can build it around *either* of the two major structural impulses for writing:

- Narrative, temporal. ("And then, and then, and then . . ."—with scattered "so what's" that tell the *point* of the story.)

- Expository, conceptual. ("Here's what I'm trying to tell you, and here's what it means or why it's important.")

If you choose the story mode, make sure there is enough "so what." Don't let it be *just* a story. If you are clever, you can make *some* of the "so what"—the significance—be implied or unstated. But some of it has to be explicit too. There's nothing wrong with "just a story"—*as* a story—but *as* a case study this assignment asks you to spell out some of the meaning or significance. (For more about case studies as a genre, you can read the "Ruminations and Theory" section at the end of the unit.) If you choose the essay or expository mode, don't let it get too dry, abstract, or generalized. Keep the life in it by using specific examples, telling mini-stories, and incorporating descriptions—including particulars and quotations from writing you did, feedback you got, and so forth.

Try to emphasize for yourself that this task can be fun, not just work. Remember:

- You are the authority on you.

- You've done lots of writing and thinking this semester about yourself as a writer. What has been most interesting and useful to *you?*

- Your audience is not just your teacher but also yourself: what you can figure out for yourself is really more important than what you can figure out for your teacher. Your classmates are an additional audience. Your teacher will probably give you a chance to share your case study, but if not, find a way; case studies are almost always a treat to read and hear.

MINIMAL GUIDELINES

Make certain your case study includes at *least* the following. Undoubtedly you'll want to do more; this is just a foundation for you to check your draft against.

1. Examination of your writing both *before* taking this course and *during* this course. That is, the study should function somewhat as a way of talking about how this course affected or did not affect how you write.

319

PROCESS BOX

What's going on here? Something about my official professional writing. I wrote a paper. [About ignoring audience!] Important. Working on and off a couple of years. Rejected two times for publication.

I was really hungry to get it in front of an audience of people interested in writing. Worked hard—feeling sure it's an important piece. Yet it seems to be turning off readers too. (I'm seeing irritation in the pieces of feedback from official "readers" who write a report on the piece for the journals where I submit it.) Lots of revising over many months. Finally accepted. Hooray! More revising—it's even better, I say to myself, and send it in. Done at last.

Today I discover I've screwed up on it. I've just heard from the journal that the only two things they asked me to do I didn't do. (They had to do with footnotes and references.) "Thud. Uh oh, I screwed up."

How did I do this? In the case of references I thought I was doing exactly what they wanted. In the case of footnotes I knew I was making an "adjustment" in their request, but I thought my adjustment fit with something else they had requested in their letter. But when I looked today for that something else in their letter, it did not exist. I must have imagined it. (I think now that I remembered it from a different letter from a different journal.)

Can it be I have an instinctive desire to refuse to do what "they"

★ (ex.) 2. Examination of one piece or episode of writing in some detail. That is, make a bit of a mini–case-within-a-case. (Indeed, you could center the *whole* case study around your examination of one piece of writing, bringing in the other parts of your case study in *relation* to this mini-study.)

★ details 3. Quotations from your writing. Show how these examples of words-on-the-page illustrate (or do not illustrate) what you are saying about your writing process. That is, explain the relationship between your process and your product—between *what*'s on the page and *how* it got there.

★ 4. Examination of comments or feedback by others. Comments can be from teachers, friends, or classmates, from this course or other courses. helpfullness from feedback

★ 5. A bit of advice for yourself: on the basis of all this exploration, what suggestions can you give yourself to make your writing go better in the future? Give your case study a *practical* dimension. Make it something

want—what "the teacher" wants? I was such a good student—dutiful and eager. Then I had trouble. I wasn't a bad boy, but I found myself *incapable* of doing assignments—unable to do what they wanted me to do—no matter how hard I tried. I thought I was done with that. Is it rearing its head again?

It makes me think about how often writing—and especially writing in school—is a matter of giving them what they want—or at least doing what they want you to do. One is always writing for someone who has authority or power over you. ("They" "own" the journal, and I can't get my words out to the public unless they accept them. Makes me feel powerless.)

I've thought a lot before about "writing as giving": you often can't get your meaning clear unless you are willing to *give* of yourself—and sometimes we don't want to. But I hadn't thought till now about writing as *giving in*.

It simply happens that difficulties in writing get all mixed up with difficulties in *authority* and *obedience*. Yes. Whether students solve *writing difficulties* often depends on whether they can solve authority and obedience difficulties. I'm not good at giving in.

And yet there are complications here. It seems as though people can't get something written unless they do some real *giving in*. Yet on the other hand, it also seems as though people don't write really well unless they are people who *don't give in*.

PETER ELBOW, 10/86

that you will find useful to read over in the future when you are engaged in writing.

SUGGESTIONS FOR SHARING AND RESPONDING

The most useful feedback is probably what's produced by using the techniques in Section IIA, "Sayback," and Section IIB, "Pointing; Summarizing," in the *Sharing and Responding* booklet. But you may also want to get some comments on how your structure is coming across—especially when you've gotten to the final-draft stage. To get some feedback on this, you can use the *Sharing and Responding* units grouped under structural responses. You might also find "Movies of the Mind" useful.

Here are some more specific questions to use, but the important thing is for you to ask for the kind of feedback *you* feel most useful.

- What changes do you see in me as a writer? What do you think I've learned during this term? What do you think I need to work on most?

321

- What do I seem to feel most confident about? least confident about?
- Inconsistencies? That is, do you think some of what I've recorded contradicts any conclusions I've drawn? Do you feel gaps—something missing that would make the picture of me as a writer more complete?
- What do you find the most surprising or unique about my case study?
- What did you find helpful for *yourself* as a writer from my case study. What did you learn from me that *you* find most valuable?

QUESTIONS TO HELP WITH PROCESS WRITING

As always, these are merely suggestions. In fact, you may even want the last segment of your case study to consist of comment on and analysis of what it was like writing it.

- How did you feel about this assignment *before* you started it? Did you think you would enjoy doing it? find it a bore? feel unable to come up with enough material? What were your feelings when you were finished?
- What did you find most surprising about writing this paper?
- Were you able to come up with genuine advice for yourself—advice that you think will be truly useful?
- In what ways did others help you discover things about your own writing process?
- If you had a chance to hear or read the case studies of others, what were your reactions? Did you sense mainly similarities or differences between theirs and yours?
- Do you think *how* you write makes a difference? Why or why not?
- Do you think writing is or will be important to you? What evidence do you have for your answer?

RUMINATIONS AND THEORY: THE CASE STUDY

"Case study" is a phrase we usually associate with social scientists, particularly those who need to work with specific situations in real-world settings. For example, professionals in the field of social work are often dealing with one individual; in order to best help that individual, they need to collect as much information as possible about that person and his background. Social workers get most of that information from the person himself. They ask him about important parts of his life: his relationships with family, friends, and lovers; his physical health; his history (where he has lived, worked, gone to school, and so forth); significant special events—exactly what happened; his goals for himself; something about what he considers past successes and failures.

In addition social workers also try to interview others who know the person (particularly family members) and try to observe the environments in which the person spends his time and how he acts within those environments.

Only when the social worker has collected as much of this information as possible, studied it, and usually talked it through with other professionals, is she ready to draw conclusions about how best to help her client. The social worker draws conclusions from this wealth of material and also helps the client draw conclusions.

There are, of course, other kinds of case studies: case studies of a neighborhood in decline, case studies of race relations in a particular area, case studies of the ups and downs of a particular business or industry, case studies of the effects of pollution on a lake or river, and so forth. The value of case studies is that they force the researcher to collect as much specific information as possible, since she can often not tell what's significant and important from the beginning. What's important emerges from the material itself. The researcher begins to see certain patterns developing which help her understand a given situation. She can either use this understanding to help others in similar situations or use it to draw conclusions about how to improve the situation she has been studying (to reverse a neighborhood's decline, better race relations, and so forth).

Those who do case studies may thus be interested in generalizing, abstracting, and constructing theories, but they are usually primarily interested in doing something about the particular situation they have been studying. Many of us resent outsiders who come in and tell us how to improve our lives or our neighborhoods based on generalizations derived from what those outsiders consider to be similar situations. We usually feel (rightly) that our situation is unique and needs to be studied *before* suggestions for improvement are implemented.

Thus we think that you can best come to conclusions about ways to improve *your* writing process by studying *your* writing process—by collecting as much information as you can about it and drawing conclusions about it *only* as a result of discovering patterns in it. We use our students' case studies as guides to helping us design our courses and assignments. Obviously we cannot design a course for one individual, so we seek common elements in the case studies we read. In other words, we generalize in an effort to come to conclusions which are valid for many student writers. Despite this, however, we recognize that each student's writing process is slightly different. We recognize, that is, the importance of specific data even as we make attempts at generalizations. But your task (at least right now) is different from ours. Your concern is to improve *your* writing. Thus your case study needs to focus solely on you and to draw conclusions solely from your personal experiences.

READINGS

CASE STUDY OF MYSELF AS A WRITER
Barbara Smith

It is only recently that I have come to think of myself as a writer. As a student, of course, I have done a lot of writing, but I would think of this only as a method of communication, that is, to make the teacher aware of my grasp of the material. I have often used writing as therapy. Once a disturbing thought is recorded, it seems I can put it aside with the assurance that I can always retrieve it if the disturbing thought or once-repressed declaration should ever become an immediate, pressing issue. Even then, though, I didn't see myself in terms of a "writer" any more than I considered myself a "phone caller" or a recording secretary. Writing was one of many activities which I employed as a tool in my role as student and in my life as a functioning human being.

When I think of my writing as it was before I began my graduate work three years ago, I understand how my perception of myself as a writer has changed. In my previous academic writing experiences, I was carefully molded; I allowed this to happen because the path of least resistance seemed to be that of a teacher pleaser. I did well in high school and as an undergraduate because of this attitude. I was eager to share my papers with whoever was interested enough to want to read them, and was pleased when some of my pieces were displayed or presented in school publications. I never experienced the "highs and lows," the fears and passions that I sometimes do now. I realize now that this was because while I was given the satisfaction of external validation of my work, my own standards were held off, somewhere distant, and undeveloped. I was successful according to other people's standards. I now realize that it made little difference whether those standards were high or low; they simply were not mine. Writing was a game more than it was an intensely personal experience. The better I got at playing it, the more comfortable I felt. Any negative feelings that I can now recall, were, at the time, suppressed. Finally, I became aware that insensitivity and passionless writing was too high a price for the comfort and security of teacher pleasing. I am now able to find value in game playing, but I have to be master of the game—harness the rules to work for me as an exercise or an adventure into new experiences.

The major events which eventually led to my identity as a writer were spread out over a long period of time. The first significant event was as an undergraduate. I had one instructor who eased the transition from learning to write for teachers to learning to write for myself as well. He made this a painless process by stressing that pleasing myself was an important element in pleasing him. For the first time, feedback was actually helpful. I learned how to say what I wanted to say better. I reached a new plateau in that class, but I still didn't feel like a writer.

Soon after graduation, I stopped writing anything. It was a dark period for me. I was living in Connecticut then, and could feel something strange happening to me. For years I felt a vague uneasiness that defied identification. My self-esteem had plummeted to new lows. I now believe that this is why I stopped writing. Nothing I had to say would be important enough to commit to paper. And, now that I was out of school, there was no one to please. I tried to analyze what this new world of mine was like, what the cause of this ineffable lack of self-awareness was. The answer came through writing.

One Sunday while reading the theater section of the *Times,* I came upon a review of a new play in which a woman was victimized by perpetrators who committed a "series of little murders." There was nothing subtle about the effect that phrase had on me. It struck me as a lightning bolt, and I began to write. This frenetic writing session lasted for weeks. I would allow very few interruptions as I enumerated and expanded on what I for the first time perceived as the victim of a "series of little murders." I began to feel as though my brain had been invaded. As I thought and wrote about my writing experiences, I began to see them as a microcosm of my larger world. My extreme compliance and submissiveness led me to become dependent on other people's acceptance of my writing (and myself). Rather than face the tension that was caused between pleasing others and pleasing myself, I simply stopped writing, and for all intents and purposes, stopped being; I had never felt less alive. I saw myself as a victim, and finally realized that I alone allowed it to happen. The spark of self-recognition generated by that phrase ignited an untapped source of power and self-awareness; if I permitted it, I could also forbid it, and for the first time I felt great control—over myself, my writing, my life.

For a long time I would not show any of this writing to anyone. I came to understand that this atypical behavior (insistence on privacy) was the result of producing a piece of writing that was mine. Showing it was revealing myself. I was not yet prepared to do that. But here was writing that was important, articulate, precious, and mine.

Soon after, I could articulate precisely what I perceived a few short weeks ago as merely vague and disturbing, and I knew what I needed to do about it. I truly believed that my survival was at stake. We moved back to New York (my roots), away from a stifling environment, and I began my graduate work at Stony Brook.

I attacked writing projects with vigor, and refused to be "thrown." Once I discovered the power in writing, I wanted to explore every facet of it. I wanted to study literature, to understand the power and skill of great writers. And I wanted to develop my own skills and style.

As I continue to understand myself better, and become more at peace with who I am, I try to harness my bitter reactions to a formerly repressive writing (and living) atmosphere. The wildness and abandon which was so productive for me during that frenetic burst of writing and explosion of truth sometimes must be tamed in later revisions. But I try to keep the life there, and the power.

If the subject of a paper I am writing excites me, I can infuse even term papers with life and power. I usually generate the best of this kind of writing early on, when I'm just writing to get started, to state the thesis as best as I can, and to support it based on what is already in my head. The paper then gets drier, more "scholarly" as I refer to the text I am studying or to critical material. I must channel my thoughts and discipline myself to focus on goals set by professors. But the processes involved in meeting those goals have been ones of my own devising. I think of myself as a writer now. I try to "sprinkle" those sentences that reflect my excitement throughout the paper when I revise, so that I as the writer come through, and so that I don't wind up with a paper that is separated into halves by tone.

When I'm not engaged with the topic, the paper is usually a disaster. I feel that old "forced" feeling, the need to write for teachers only, to write the "right" things, to guess at what they want, because what I want has no meaning or relevance if I can't muster up some feeling for the subject. In these cases I don't think of myself as a writer (well, perhaps some kind of diminutive one). I feel more like a secretary who has been instructed to write a letter in regard to some specific matter. I can do it, but I remain detached, and the paper suffers. What I've learned from all this is that choosing a topic that fascinates me is a crucial first step that could lead to my best writing. Unlike my earlier writing stages, I am now cautious about sharing my writing; first I must trust the reader. I take this as a good sign—I am in that piece, this is me that is being perused, not an inanimate response to an assignment. It is a stage to be worked through, although I suspect the apprehension will never completely subside. I have developed a strong resistance to writing to please others and yet am still a bit anxious about saying, in effect, "Here I am." It is a concern that I'm pleased finally to be able to recognize, and one which I hope one day to celebrate as the beginning of a healthy self-consciousness as a writer.

I suppose that writing, like any art form, is best when it is a mode of unadulterated self-expression. But there seems to be a problem of inconsistency in how we value self-expression. The problem involves great risk; if the artist is good, self-expression is celebrated. If she is merely adequate, it is tolerated; and if poor, it is ridiculed. Writing, like life, can be kept "safe" from public scrutiny. But I have learned that being "safe" may be dull and boring, and for me, boredom is far more destructive than risk taking. Sharing this paper is a risk, but it is also a thrill—a dangerous, exhilarating exposition. I know too, that the reason for my positive attitude is that I trust my audience. What I haven't figured out yet, is how to write with this degree of investment—vulnerability, actually—for an audience I don't trust or even know—how to put what I am into my writing, and not what I think I should be. Of course, it's easier to walk a tightrope when you know there is a net beneath you. Taking risks is safer then. No net, less tricky stuff. Less tricky stuff, less risk—less risk, more safety—more safety, more boring. Boring = no growth, and no growth = no life. I guess what I'm saying is that risks are crucial. And writing which is powerful because of the assurance that it will remain private, often (ironically) is the very writing that ought to be shared. This is the paradox that I am in the process of working out.

CASE STUDY
Mitchell Shack

I hate to start out on a negative comment, but I feel I must say that I don't like to think of this as a case study. It makes me feel as if I am preparing a report for a doctor or psychiatrist. Actually I would like to think of it as simply an expression of my feelings about my accomplishments and struggles of being a writer.

In order to write such a paper, I must remember not only works I have written this semester, but also ones that I have written in the past years. Remembering the latter bunch is not such an easy task; not just because of the time difference between now and when they were written, but because I would rather not remember some of the papers. The papers were not actually bad, but I have bad memories of my writings in those days. What I mean is that those papers were written because I was forced to write them; not because I wanted to write them. The papers accomplished the task that they were supposed to do, but they did little more. They were quite boring and uninspired works. Actually the word "works" is an accurate description of those writings because that's exactly what I thought of them—as doing work.

Most of my writings—correction—all of my writings, were assignments in high school, usually English essays. These papers were usually about a book we read in class, or an essay on a test. My style of writing was simple. I just stated the facts, one right after another, and somehow linked all these facts together to form an essay. There was little creativity at all and it was amazing that the teacher didn't dose off before reaching my closing paragraph.

Well, that's how I stood coming into this class, and I anticipated little change in my attitude upon completion of this class. As a matter of fact, I thought that I was going to hate writing even more than I already did, if that was even possible. Much to my surprise my attitude took a complete reversal during the span of this course. "What brought about that change?" you may ask. I think it is because I began to write about things that I wanted to write, not things that other people wanted me to write. I began to even enjoy my writing; something that was previously all too painful just to think about. My writings have drastically improved because of this change in attitude. My papers have become more creative and not just a list of facts anymore. My style of writing has become more natural. It has become smoother and I have "opened up" more so that I can get what I'm thinking in my head down on the paper. That may not seem like a big task to some people, but it would have seemed almost impossible to me just a few months ago. My papers have changed from simply stating what happened to explaining how I felt when it happened. I have also learned new techniques and methods of writing which I will pick up on later.

So far I have been telling you about changes that have come as a result from taking this course, so I think I should give some examples of these changes to prove my point. The paper that I like the best was a descriptive narrative about my favorite person of my childhood, the ice-cream man, so I think it's only fair to talk about that piece. I enjoyed this piece because I was able to open up and explain how I felt and what I was thinking at that time and not just give a plot summary. For example one line from the story says, "The truck from far away looked like an old bread truck, but it would not have mattered one bit if it looked like a garbage truck, just as long as it sold ice cream." The same line written before this class would have probably looked more like "The truck was white and looked like a bread truck." I changed from just putting down facts to putting down feelings along with those facts. This brightens up my papers greatly, gives a more personal feel to it, and makes it much more interesting and entertaining to read. I accomplished this task in an "Image of an Ice-Cream Man," and that is why I feel this paper is a representative of not only one of my better papers, but also of my improvements in writing over previous years.

There are many techniques that I learned which I can attribute to my change in writing. One such thing is the use of freewriting. I have never before used freewriting, and early in the semester I just thought it was a waste of time. In looking back over my papers and some of the freewriting I did that led to those papers I realized I was mistaken. Many of my ideas came as a result of freewriting; some of which I may not have thought of if I just sat down and wrote the paper. I used freewriting in the "Image of an Ice-Cream Man," and the paper benefited from its use. For example I wrote, "I watched him as he was making it, and my mouth watered just looking at all the ice cream, lollipops, bubble gum, chocolate bars, Italian ices, and other candy I saw inside the truck." This line and many of the others were taken right out of my freewriting. The freewriting allowed me to open up and "look back" in my mind and remember things that I have forgotten over the years. In the line above, using free-writing allowed me to remember in my mind exactly what the truck looked like and what I saw when I looked in it. Another thing that I like about freewriting is that I am not restricted to a topic or an idea. I can let my mind wander and go where it wants to go. I don't even have to worry about punctuation, grammar, or anything else that can inhibit my thinking. The result is usually writing that "flows" and seems natural, and this type of writing can enhance any paper.

Another useful technique which I learned is the loop writing process. I only used this process for one paper, and I must admit that what resulted was one of my weakest papers. This was not because of the loop writing process, but it's because of what I did in actually writing the paper after using the loop writing process. To tell you the truth, the loop writing process worked too well. The process consisted of using all different ways of thinking about a topic to get ideas on that topic. This included my first thoughts, prejudices, dialogues, lies, stories, and portraits about the topic. I used this process in writing "How Death Motivates Us in Life," and my problem was that I came up with too many ideas about the topic. The loop writing process allowed me to think of so many different aspects of the topic and for each aspect come up with several ideas pertaining to it. The problem came when I tried to write an essay which incorporated all these ideas in them. I mentioned all these ideas, but because of the great number of them, I didn't go into any single one in great detail. This resulted in a lot of superficial ideas, but no depth to my paper. What I should have done was pick out the ideas that proved my point the best and go into depth with those items. What I am trying to get across is that the loop writing process is very helpful, especially with topics that you seem short on ideas to pursue. But I have to be careful and not get carried away with myself and try to fit every single idea that I come up with into my paper.

So far I have been talking about methods I learned which aided me in my writings, but I haven't really talked about how I go about using these methods in actually creating a piece. Believe it or not, my favorite way of writing is to compose my paper directly on my computer. This may seem odd or difficult to some people, but to me it works fine. Actually I usually start by freewriting on the topic, or using the loop writing technique if I'm short on ideas. Next I usually make a rough outline of what I am going to say. I try to think about how I want my paper organized and in what order each point should go, and then I create the basic form of an outline. I then go back and jot down a few examples under each argument to prove it. I don't write in sentence form; I just scribble down a few key words and later on when I actually write my paper I look over these key words and then write about them.

This is the part when my computer comes into play. I load up my word processor, set my margins, and start writing. I like using the computer rather than a typewriter or pen and paper because I can edit directly as I go along. I can switch sentences around, delete words, add phrases, and do many other operations immediately. The words look on screen as they will on paper so I can see the structure forming and know how the finished product will look. I can go back and change my paper three weeks or three months later without having to retype it since it is saved on disk. Also my word processing program contains a spelling checker which I find very useful since I am far from being the world champion in spelling bees, and it contains a thesaurus so I can have some place to turn to if I get stuck. . . .

One thing that I haven't already mentioned and I feel is a major reason why I enjoyed taking this course is that I was actually able to tell a story. I was able to relate an experience that over the years didn't seem important enough to tell anybody. This year I got the chance and just being able to do that has made this course worthwhile for me.

From HUNGER OF MEMORY
Richard Rodriguez

At school, in sixth grade, my teacher suggested that I start keeping a diary. ('You should write down your personal experiences and reflections.') But I shied away from the idea. It was the one suggestion that the scholarship boy couldn't follow. I would not have wanted to write about the *minor* daily events of my life; I would never have been able to write about what most deeply, daily, concerned me during those years: I was growing away from my parents. Even if I could have been certain that no one would find my diary, even if I could have destroyed each page after I had written it, I would have felt uncomfortable writing about my home life. There seemed to me something intrinsically public about written words.

Writing, at any rate, was a skill I didn't regard highly. It was a grammar school skill I acquired with comparative ease. I do not remember struggling to write the way I struggled to learn how to read. The nuns would praise student papers for being neat—the handwritten letters easy for others to read; they promised that my writing style would improve as I read more and more. But that wasn't the reason I became a reader. Reading was for me the key to 'knowledge'; I swallowed facts and dates and names and themes. Writing, by contrast, was an activity I thought of as a kind of report, evidence of learning. I wrote down what I heard teachers say. I wrote down things from my books. I wrote down all I knew when I was examined at the end of the school year. Writing was performed after the fact; it was not the exciting experience of learning itself. In eighth grade I read several hundred books, the titles of which I still can recall. But I cannot remember a single essay I wrote. I only remember that the most frequent kind of essay I wrote was the book report.

In high school there were more 'creative' writing assignments. English teachers assigned the composition of short stories and poems. One sophomore story I wrote was a romance set in the Civil War South. I remember that it earned me a good enough grade, but my teacher suggested with quiet tact that next time I try writing about 'something you know more about—something closer to home.' Home? I wrote a short story about an old man who lived all by himself in a house down the block. That was as close as my writing ever got to my house. Still, I won prizes. When teachers suggested I contribute articles to the school literary magazine, I did so. And when I was asked to join the school newspaper, I said yes. I did not feel any great pride in my writings, however. (My mother was the one who collected my prize-winning essays in a box she kept in her closet.) Though I remember seeing my by-line in print for the first time, and dwelling on the printing press letters with fascination: RICHARD RODRIGUEZ. The letters furnished evidence of a vast public identity writing made possible.

When I was a freshman in college, I began typing all my assignments. My writing speed decreased. Writing became a struggle. In high school I had been able to hand-write ten- and twenty-page papers in little more than an hour—and I never revised what I wrote. A college essay took me several nights to prepare. Suddenly everything

I wrote seemed in need of revision. I became a self-conscious writer. A stylist. The change, I suspect, was the result of seeing my words ordered by the even, impersonal, anonymous typewriter print. As arranged by a machine, the words that I typed no longer seemed mine. I was able to see them with a new appreciation for how my reader would see them.

From grammar school to graduate school I could always name my reader. I wrote for my teacher. I could consult him or her before writing, and after. I suppose that I knew other readers could make sense of what I wrote—that, therefore, I addressed a general reader. But I didn't think very much about it. Only toward the end of my schooling and only because political issues pressed upon me did I write, and have published in magazines, essays intended for readers I never expected to meet. Now I am struck by the opportunity. I write today for a reader who exists in my mind only phantasmagorically. Someone with a face erased; someone of no particular race or sex or age or weather. A gray presence. Unknown, unfamiliar. All that I know about him is that he has had a long education and that his society, like mine, is often public *(un gringo)*.

'What is psychiatry?' my mother asks. She is standing in her kitchen at the ironing board. We have been talking about nothing very important. ('Visiting.') As a result of nothing we have been saying, her question has come. But I am not surprised by it. My mother and father ask me such things. Now that they are retired they seem to think about subjects they never considered before. My father sits for hours in an armchair, wide-eyed. After my mother and I have finished discussing obligatory family news, he will approach me and wonder: When was Christianity introduced to the Asian continent? How does the brain learn things? Where is the Garden of Eden?

Perhaps because they consider me the family academic, my mother and father expect me to know. They do not, in any case, ask my brother and sisters the questions wild curiosity shapes. (That curiosity beats, unbeaten by age.)

Psychiatry? I shrug my shoulders to start with, to tell my mother that it is very hard to explain. I go on to say something about Freud. And analysis. Something about the function of a clinically trained listener. (I study my mother's face as I speak, to see if she follows.) I compare a psychiatrist to a Catholic priest hearing Confession. But the analogy is inexact. My mother can easily speak to a priest in a darkened confessional; can easily make an act of self-revelation using the impersonal formula of ritual contrition: 'Bless me, father, for I have sinned. . . .' It would be altogether different for her to address a psychiatrist in unstructured conversation, revealing those events and feelings that burn close to the heart.

'You mean that people tell a psychiatrist about their personal lives?'

Even as I begin to respond, I realize that she cannot imagine ever doing such a thing. She shakes her head sadly, bending over the ironing board to inspect a shirt with the tip of the iron she holds in her hand. Then she changes the subject. She is talking to me about one of her sisters, my aunt, who is seriously ill. Whatever it is that prompted her question about psychiatry has passed. . . .

What did my father—who had dreamed of Australia—think of his children once they forced him to change plans and remain in America? What contrary feelings did he have about our early success? How does he regard the adults his sons and daughters have become? And my mother. At what moments has she hated me? On what occasions has she been embarrassed by me? What does she recall feeling during those difficult, sullen years of my childhood? What would be her version of this book? What are my parents unable to tell me today? What things are too personal? What feelings so unruly they dare not reveal to other intimates? Or even to each other? Or to themselves?

Some people have told me how wonderful it is that I am the first in my family to write a book. I stand on the edge of a long silence. But I do not give voice to my parents by writing about their lives. I distinguish myself from them by writing about the life we once shared. Even when I quote them accurately, I profoundly distort my parents' words. (They were never intended to be read by the public.) So my parents do not truly speak on my pages. I may force their words to stand between quotation marks. With every word, however, I change what was said only to me.

'What is new with you?' My mother looks up from her ironing to ask me. (In recent years she has taken to calling me Mr. Secrets, because I tell her so little about my work in San Francisco—this book she must suspect I am writing.)

Nothing much, I respond.

I write very slowly because I write under the obligation to make myself clear to some-one who knows nothing about me. It is a lonely adventure. Each morning I make my way along a narrowing precipice of written words. I hear an echoing voice—my own resembling another's. Silent! The reader's voice silently trails every word I put down. I reread my words, and again it is the reader's voice I hear in my mind, sound-ing my prose.

When I wrote my first autobiographical essay, it was no coincidence that, from the first page, I expected to publish what I wrote. I didn't consciously determine the issue. Somehow I knew, however, that my words were meant for a public reader. Only because of that reader did the words come to the page. The reader became my excuse, my reason for writing.

It had taken me a long time to come to this address. There are remarkable chil-dren who very early are able to write publicly about their personal lives. Some chil-dren confide to a diary those things—like the first shuddering of sexual desire—too private to tell a parent or brother. The youthful writer addresses a stranger, the Other, with 'Dear Diary' and tries to give public expression to what is intensely, privately felt. In so doing, he attempts to evade the guilt of repression. And the embarrassment of solitary feeling. For by rendering feelings in words that a stranger can understand—words that belong to the public, this Other—the young diarist no longer need feel all alone or eccentric. His feelings are capable of public intelligibility. In turn, the act of revelation helps the writer better understand his own feelings. Such is the benefit of language: By finding public words to describe one's feelings, one can describe oneself to oneself. One names what was previously only darkly felt.

I have come to think of myself as engaged in writing graffiti. Encouraged by physical isolation to reveal what is most personal; determined at the same time to have my words seen by strangers. I have come to understand better why works of literature—while never intimate, never individually addressed to the reader—are so often among the most personal statements we hear in our lives. Writing, I have come to value written words as never before. One can use *spoken* words to reveal one's personal self to strangers. But *written* words heighten the feeling of privacy. They permit the most thorough and careful exploration. (In the silent room, I prey upon that which is most private. Behind the closed door, I am least reticent about giving those memories expression.) The writer is freed from the obligation of finding an auditor in public. (As I use words that someone far from home can understand, I create my listener. I imagine her listening.)

My teachers gave me a great deal more than I knew when they taught me to write public English. I was unable then to use the skill for deeply personal purposes. I insisted upon writing impersonal essays. And I wrote always with a specific reader in mind. Nevertheless, the skill of public writing was gradually developed by the many classroom papers I had to compose. Today I *can* address an anonymous reader. And this seems to me important to say. Somehow the inclination to write about my private life in public is related to the ability to do so. It is not enough to say that my mother and father do not want to write their autobiographies. It needs also to be said that they are unable to write to a public reader. They lack the skill. Though both of them can write in Spanish and English, they write in a hesitant manner. Their syntax is uncertain. Their vocabulary limited. They write well enough to communicate 'news' to relatives in letters. And they can handle written transactions in institutional America. But the man who sits in his chair so many hours, and the woman at the ironing board—'keeping busy because I don't want to get old'—will never be able to believe that any description of their personal lives could be understood by a stranger far from home.

From A CASE STUDY OF MYSELF AS A WRITER
Jean Shepherd

When I begin writing, I compose the first sentence in my head. As I put pen to paper, words begin to rush into my mind. For a few seconds, I can hardly write fast enough to get them all down, but after a brief period, maybe after several sentences, I pause and read what I have written. Possible revisions of words and phrases occur to me, and I write them anywhere I can—to the side, above, or below appropriate sections of the text, often with arrows pointing to their future positions. I reread once more to get the sound of my writing in my head, and then I'm off again in a frantic race with my mind to get the words on paper before they are gone. I use this write, stop, read, revise, read, start again process until I am through writing or until I come to a good stopping place.

At this point, my paper looks like a plate with words and arrows spilled over it in different directions. No one else could ever read this draft, and if I wait a day, I won't be able to read it either. Therefore, I must begin immediately to copy over, selecting words and phrases out of the choices I have given myself on the previous writing. Sometimes new word options and ideas occur to me as I rewrite; during this stage I seem to be more aware of sentence rhythms, and I try to write more slowly this time so I will put the endings on my words. The result of this stage is what I call my rough draft. If I get too caught up in rewriting and again write too fast, I may have to copy it over a second time.

The rough draft often contains ideas that never occurred to me before I wrote. It is obvious that during the first stages of writing I move pen on paper, think of words, spell words, punctuate, see relationships between ideas, invent new ideas, hear the sound of my words, read, and revise all at the same time. The pen becomes an extension of my mind, and unfortunately, my fingers can never move as quickly as my thoughts come, so I am always in a race to the end of a sentence. While producing this rough draft, I am unaware of anything around me. My body is tense with concentration as I rush to record my ideas. During this stage, my thinking is almost unconscious.

The next step of writing, the first revision, is a more conscious stage, and I am more relaxed as I progress. At this point, I correct sentences and sometimes continue to add ideas. I may mark out phrases or entire sentences to avoid wordiness. I change forms of subordination, usually making dependent clauses into phrases, and check coordination to see if it should remain as it is or if it should become subordination. At this point, I am very aware of sentence rhythms and variety, and I try to avoid awkward repetitions of words. I have the poor speller's habit of avoiding words I can't spell, so at this stage, I make a conscious effort to use whatever word I really want. Sometimes, when I get toward the end of the paper, I will think of words to add at the beginning, so I go back and put them in the margin. When I have gone over my paper once this way, I read again, making a few more minor adjustments, and then my first revision is complete.

For the next revision, I am calm and quite relaxed. This is the mechanical stage. I go through the paper and check all punctuation. Then I go back for my most hated task, checking spelling. I underline every word that may not be spelled correctly. Then I look up each one in a word book or dictionary. Oddly enough, I still may change some words or add a phrase even at this stage; I always seem to be aware of the sound of my writing. When this stage is complete, I am ready for the last step, typing.

My evaluation of what I've written is constantly changing as I go through all of these stages. During the first two steps of my rough draft, I feel excited. I'm sure that everything I am saying is clever and imaginative. I am convinced that I've written something that everyone will enjoy and admire. If I am writing for a class, I am sure that I will make an A and that my paper will be the best in the class. When I begin the first revision, my heart sinks. I am embarrassed by my own words and feel confident that anyone else who reads it will laugh and think me a fool. If I am writing for a class, I am sure that I will fail. I have to force myself to go on and not throw the paper out, telling myself that I have to turn in something and that I don't have time to begin again.

After I type a paper, it seems very separate from me. When I read it over, I find words and ideas that surprise me. I can't remember having written such words or having conceived of such thoughts. At this point, I become pleased with parts of my writing, but I have no idea how it will seem to someone else. I have never turned in an assignment with any notion of what grade it may earn.

UNIT
16

Personal Research

Research results from the desire to know something. What that "something" is determines the kind of research the researcher undertakes. In Unit 14 you worked with research questions which led you to seek information mainly from print sources: books, periodicals, and newspapers. In this unit our aim is to guide you toward a more personal sort of research: research which requires you mainly to <u>observe</u> and <u>interview</u>. As you work through the activities outlined in this unit, we hope you'll begin to believe as we do that personal research and library research are equally valid. It's what we want to know that determines how we do research. Sometimes we need to talk and observe; sometimes we need to go to the library. Often we need to do both.

Your assignment in this unit is to do personal research on some question or questions that interest you and then write up and appropriately document that research and the conclusions you draw from it.

You'll find this unit more rewarding if you're working with some subject that grows out of a personal need to know. Questions come into our minds every day and leave as quickly as they come. A good way to preserve some of these questions for further investigation is to keep a "need-to-know" journal for a few days. Preferably this should be a small note pad which you can carry around comfortably. Use it to jot down whatever questions come into your mind—no matter how trivial the questions may seem to be. Perhaps as you get up in the morning you wonder how much sleep you really need to function well or how much sleep others need. If you were to continue this line of reasoning, you might begin to wonder if there are definable characteristics of "morning people" and "evening people." Per-

334

haps as you walk to class, your arm begins to itch and you wonder what causes itching or you see some graffiti and wonder about who did it and about differences in graffiti in different buildings and on different campuses. You see a male maintenance worker and a female secretary and you wonder which gets paid more and how their salaries compare to those of your teacher—and why some professions get paid more than others. You think about a possible profession for yourself and wonder what it's like to work in that profession. Even if you only keep such a journal for a day, you'll be surprised at the number of questions about your own life and environment you come up with.

FIRST ROUND OF FREEWRITING

One way to start discovering what you'd like to know more about is to do some exploratory writing about the items you've jotted down in your need-to-know journal. As you write, let your thoughts go wherever the writing takes you. Deliberately seek questions, but also let the questions find you. This may seem odd but it can happen if you let it.

But there are other ways to come up with areas to explore. You can sit down and do exploratory writing even without a need-to-know notebook. Just start freewriting. Your focus should be on moments or areas in your life where you feel perplexity or dis-ease or problems. Explore those areas: what would it help you to *know about?* If you've been keeping a personal journal, skimming through it will undoubtedly provide a number of subjects for you.

At any point during the process we've been outlining, you may come up with something that you *know* is the thing you want to follow up on. If this happens, you can skip what follows and move directly to the second round of freewriting.

But if you have difficulty getting started on exploratory writing and don't have a topic already, use one of the following suggestions to start your thinking. Don't worry about staying on a topic; the point of this is to get you to reach back into your memories and down through your surface concerns to underlying questions and issues.

- What do you see as your major problem at the moment? How is that problem affecting you? Do others you know have this same problem? How does it seem to affect them? Is there something you could do to resolve the problem? If you're unsure, write out possible solutions.

- Which people in your life are currently causing you difficulties? friends? parents? girlfriend/boyfriend? other family members? How does this difficulty make itself known? Is this difficult relationship a long-standing one? a recent one? What caused it?

- Is there someone you would like to understand better? perhaps someone who causes you difficulty? perhaps someone you admire? or per-

335

haps someone you love: for example, someone who is elderly whom you want to know better while you still can.

- Look around the immediate environment in your classroom. Are there more women or more men in your class? a preponderance of certain racial or ethnic groups? Does the make-up of your classes change substantially from one subject to another? Which students participate the most? Do women or men tend to be called on most often? Does this seem to have any connection to whether the teacher is male or female? What happens in large lecture classes? What are most students doing: listening, sleeping, taking notes, talking, passing notes to friends? At what point or points in a lecture class do students seem to pay the most attention? Do your teachers have different teaching styles? Describe them.

- What was the most interesting conversation you've had recently? Who was it with? What was the topic? What made it interesting? If you had a chance to revive this conversation, how would you start it off?

- What would you like to be doing in five years? Do you think you'll be married? have children? be working close by or somewhere else in the country? maybe in a foreign country? in a city, the suburbs, or the country?

- What troubles you most in the society around you? How does what is troubling you affect your actions? your thoughts?

After you've done this freewriting, set it aside for a while. Then come back to it, look it over, and decide what you'd most like to follow up on. Make a list of possible topics. Don't worry about whether others might consider your choices trivial; that's not important. What *is* important is your interest in knowing more about them. Maybe you're thinking of buying a used car and need to know how best to go about it. Maybe your concern is a summer job and how to get the most interesting, best-paying one. Or perhaps you'd like to know more about a career that seems attractive to you. Perhaps you're interested in transferring to another school. Or maybe something has happened in your life that makes you want to understand divorce better or attitudes toward death and caring for an elderly relative. Maybe you'd like to know how foreigners learn English or how people react to certain kinds of advertisements. Perhaps it's interracial marriage or taking care of begonias you're interested in.

As you decide what to follow up on, keep in mind that it isn't the subject that matters: it's your interest in the subject.

SECOND ROUND OF FREEWRITING

Once you have a list, look it over and decide which items could best be addressed by doing most of the work in the library. Set these aside since this unit focuses on personal research. This may seem arbitrary to you (in fact, it is), but in this unit we want you to do research which can't be done by using traditional print resources in a library. This doesn't mean you won't have to go to the library; it just means the heart of the research will not be there. After you've eliminated what seem to be library-research items, pick out the one or two remaining ones which appeal to you most. Do more free-writing on each one.

In this second round of freewriting, you may want to focus at first on why you're interested in this particular subject, when you first remember being interested in it, and what you already know about it. (If you decide that one of the subjects you're writing about is the most interesting to you, go on with it and forget the other.)

As you do this writing, push yourself as much as you can to get down on paper what you already know and what your opinions on the subject are. Don't worry about whether what you write is "right" or not. The point is to make clear to yourself exactly where you're starting from. You may be sur-prised to discover that you actually know more than you think you do and have more opinions about your subject than you're aware of. After you do all this writing, you'll be a position to make a list of questions which aim at what you don't know or what you're unsure about.

For the sake of an example, let's say you choose to find out something about attitudes toward advertisements. After having written out what you already know or think is valid, perhaps you might come up with the follow-ing questions:

- How much do advertisements affect people's buying habits?

- Which advertisements influence people most: those on TV, in maga-zines, in newspapers, in flyers left on people's front steps?

- What kinds of people usually show up in advertisements? upper class? middle class? rich people? men? women?

- How are men and women portrayed in advertisements? Are there noticeable differences?

- Do men and women react differently to advertisements?

- Are certain kinds of advertisements more evident in certain kinds of magazines?

- What do advertisements tell us about the media they're in or the tele-vision program they're in the middle of? the magazines or newspapers that feature them?

Once you have your list, discard questions which can best be answered by using library resources. Go through this same procedure with the other topic you narrowed your original list down to. Now you'll have exploratory writing and questions on both topics. If you can't make up your mind which is the most interesting to you, discuss what you've written about them in class. Perhaps during that discussion you'll come to a decision.

If you think you've decided what subject you'd like to pursue and what question (or questions) you'd like to seek an answer to, you can share with your group what you've written so far. During the discussion you may find yourself revising your question. Many researchers discover that the question they end up answering is not exactly the one they started with. This is as it should be. As researchers uncover information, that information leads them to reformulate questions.

Once you've decided on a question to begin with, you'll need to do some thinking and planning about how and where to seek an answer. If there's time during your group discussion, others can probably give you suggestions about what to do. Going back to our example, let's say you decide you'd like to know more about how young people react to the portrayal of men and women in magazine advertisements. In order to do this, you'll probably want to interview young men and women. You'll need to plan how to do this and what questions to ask. When you reach this stage of your project, you may or may not need to do some reading, depending upon your topic and your knowledge of it.

ooooo

A note of caution: students often think that research papers have to prove something. But (one of the lessons we stressed in Unit 10), we can't often prove things—all we can do is get people to listen. Except in rare cases, you're not going to be able to get a definite answer to whatever question you pose for yourself. The best you can do is gather data which give you insight into a possible answer. But that doesn't mean you aren't producing something with force; what you uncover should be valid within the limits you set for yourself. Researchers usually need to pool their work in order to begin

---

PROCESS BOX

I sail a lot by the vaguest of markers, discovering as I go just what it is that I am traveling toward. It's not automatic writing, not with my two words forward—three words back—attention to the words. But I often feel myself following a step or two behind my characters, full of curiosity about what they're going to do next. . . . I keep coming back to hearing people speak, which is more interesting to me than watching the art of writing unfold. That "otherness" is deep and prevailing, yet I wish to pursue it because I still write for the same reason I wrote when I was nine years old: to speak more perfectly than I really can, to a listener more perfect than any I know.

ROSELLEN BROWN, *ANYTHING CAN HAPPEN*

---

to think about definitive answers. In fact your small group may decide to focus on one topic, which you can each do research on. You can then integrate what you've done and turn this unit into a collaborative writing project.

THIRD ROUND OF FREEWRITING

Before you actually begin to do whatever research you've laid out for yourself, we suggest that you write a quick version of what you think or hope your research will uncover. This may seem odd to you, but it often makes your research more exciting if you've already got some possible conclusions in mind. This quick version can be very sketchy. Just fantasize that you're someone who already knows all there is to know about your topic. Having your preconceptions more consciously in mind will make the research more interesting and help you be more aware of your biases.

INTERVIEWING AND OBSERVING

Your subject may be quite different from the one we've been using as our example. Strategies for research are as varied as the questions that can be asked. But you should be able to lay out a plan of action for yourself—with the help of your teacher and your classmates. The important thing is to keep your task manageable, to make it into something you can handle within the time you have. Your teacher will let you know how much time you can devote to this unit.

In general we can think of two main activities you'll use in doing your research: one is interviewing; the other is observing. For the topic we've been using as an example, you'd be doing mostly interviewing. But if you've come up with a slightly different topic, say, finding out more about the interaction of various racial groups on your campus, you'll be mostly observing. For many topics you might use both.

If you decide to do interviewing, we suggest you go back and review Unit 2. Much of what we talk about there should be helpful to you. You may realize that you'd like to interview each person twice—despite the added time and effort. If you do have two interviews, you can write up a preliminary report after the first interview and, during the second interview, check it with your interviewees and follow up on what was unclear to you or not as fully developed as you'd like. Perhaps you'll decide that the best way to get at what you're interested in is to interview everyone in your dorm or everyone in a club you belong to. That may make it possible for you to go around your dorm again or attend another club meeting and follow up on each of the interviews.

If your research is best done through observing, you should map out where to observe and what sorts of interaction you'll want to look for. The questions you draw up to further your research will be mainly questions you'll be addressing to yourself while you're observing. You may also need to do some preliminary investigation to discover where students are most likely to congregate. Others in your class should be able to make suggestions to help you.

And, of course, you may decide you need to do some interviewing along with your observations. Then you'll have to draw up questions both for yourself and for others.

EXPLORATORY DRAFT

Once you've done whatever tasks you set for yourself as a means to find out what you want to know, you're ready to write an exploratory draft. Before beginning though, we recommend that you lay out all the notes and writing you've done so far and read through everything. After this perusal do some freewriting to record what you've learned and how you react to seeing all the material. Think particularly about whether you've discovered any patterns or recurrent themes in your writing and notes. Think about what parts of your research have been most helpful.

You may discover at this point that you really haven't answered the question you started with or discovered what you originally wanted to discover. In that case you'll need to do more research if you're still anxious to answer your original question. But you may decide that you have, in fact, answered a more interesting question or discovered something more thought provoking than what you started out to discover.

What you need to do then before you start writing a draft is to write out clearly for yourself what you have discovered. This will help you decide whether you've finished your research and can start writing or if you need to do more research. You'll probably be able to include some of this writing in your paper.

Whenever you decide you have done as much research as you need to do, you are ready to write a first draft of your paper. If your teacher has asked for a paper longer than five or six pages, you may want to make an outline before you start writing. Or you may decide instead to make an outline *after* you've written your first draft. We find that this actually works better for us. If you decide to do this, your outline can be something like the kind we describe in Section IIIC of *Sharing and Responding,* "Descriptive Outline," or it can just be a skeletal outlining of your structure as described in Section IIIA, "Skeleton Feedback."

If you decide to make an outline before your first draft, remember not to agonize so long over your outline that you have too little time and energy to write the paper itself. You don't need to spend a lot of time on an outline. It can be as simple as this:

> I'll start by stating why I was interested in my subject, move to how I went about doing the research, lay out some of what I found, and end with my conclusions.

Or you may want something as detailed as this:

1. Statement of question

2. Statement of methods of research and questions asked

3. Recounting of interviews
   a. Interviews of residents of my dorm
   b. Interviews of members of film club

4. Conclusions in reference to differences between men and women interviewees

5. Possible explanations of my conclusions

6. What I learned and what it means to me

7. What I'd still like to know

An important thing to remember about outlines—whether generalized or specific—is that they're only outlines: you need not follow them like a robot. As you begin to write, you may discover some better structure. That may cause you to go back and revise your outline—although you needn't do that if you feel that the structure you're working with is satisfactory.

A little aside: One of the best ways to structure your final paper is to present the story of your search. Tell how you started—including false starts, early hypotheses, what was going on in your head as you worked through the series of steps we've included below, the order in which you discovered things, what you did, partial conclusions you drew, and what you finally concluded. In other words, your paper could end up being a mixture of process writing and the results of that process. But in order to do this, you'll need to do process writing throughout. So we suggest that at the end of each piece of your search, you do some writing in your process journal. Even if you don't decide to use it in your paper, it will be a valuable record for you. (See the end of this unit for two sample personal research papers. The first is on the subject we've been using as an example.)

You'll also need to make sure that you know how to document the information you've used in your paper. If you've used mainly interviews (as would be true in the sample we've given), you must document these interviews. Your teacher will tell you what style of documentation she wishes you to use. She may also want to go over some of that technical information in class.

If your research consisted mostly of observing, you won't need to do much documenting—although, of course, you may decide to interview some of the people you've been observing. If you did some reading in the course of your research, you'll need to document those sources. You can look back to Unit 14 for help with the technical aspects of this. We've also printed examples of the most common kinds of footnotes on the inside back cover.

Documentation of sources is particularly important in research papers. This is a lesson we stressed in Unit 14, but it's just as important for personal research as for library research. None of us has the right to claim credit for the ideas and words of others regardless of whether we read them or heard them in an interview. And, from a pragmatic point of view, documentation lends authority to your research paper. If people know that you feel secure about revealing your sources and thus giving readers the opportunity to check their validity, they're far more likely to give your words credit. In all likelihood documentation for the sort of research paper required in this unit will be far less complex than for the library-research paper required in Unit 14. That doesn't make it any less important though.

SUGGESTIONS FOR SHARING AND RESPONDING

You might use "Sayback" (*Sharing and Responding,* Section IIA) when sharing your first exploratory writing and freewriting in this unit. This sort of feedback will help you figure out where you are going or want to go. Ask listeners to concentrate particularly on what they see as the implications of what you've written. In addition to "Sayback," here are some questions you may find helpful:

- What do you think I'm primarily interested in finding out?

- Do you think that the task I'm setting for myself is feasible? If not, how can I alter it?

- How do you think I can go about answering my question or finding out what I want to know?

- If I wanted to use library and print materials to supplement what I have, how might I do so? What questions could I answer that way?

When doing sharing and responding for drafts of your research paper, you'll find "Sayback" valuable again. But you might also ask your readers to do "Skeleton Feedback" in Section IIIA of *Sharing and Responding.*

We suggest too that you write out some questions you specifically want listeners and readers to give you feedback on. In addition to these specific questions, here are some general questions you may find helpful at this stage of your project:

- Have I accomplished what I led you to expect I was going to accomplish?

- Have I given you sufficient evidence to justify whatever conclusions I've drawn?

- Do you think I've interpreted my data correctly?

- Is there more I could do?

- Does my organization work?

Since these papers are likely to be longer than those you've been sharing in class, it may be difficult for your teacher to provide class time for everyone to read his paper. If you and your group members exchange papers and take them home for commenting, the questions of each writer will be particularly valuable. After you've gotten written comments from one or more of your classmates, you'll probably want to talk them over with whoever made them. Perhaps your teacher will provide time for this in class, perhaps not. But you can still—and we highly recommend that you do—talk to whoever has made comments on your paper.

THEORY AND RUMINATIONS: THE ONGOING CONVERSATION

The usual thing we do when we need to know something is ask questions. Often what we need to know is very simple: What time is it? How do I get to the zoo? In these cases we ask someone and that's usually the end of our research. (The fact that we may get the wrong answer is irrelevant since we won't realize that until later.) But once we've gotten an answer, we're in the position of passing it along to others. We can now, for instance, direct someone else to the zoo—and that person can direct another and on and on. And perhaps the person who gave us directions originally got them from someone else. So we're in the midst of a conversation the beginning of which we were not present for and the ending of which we're unlikely to be present for either.

But just as often what we need to know may be more complex: How have digital watches affected people's sense of time? Why do people go to the zoo? What do we get out of looking at animals? To get answers to these questions, we need to do more than ask one question of one person. We need to figure out how to ask questions, observe reactions, and draw conclusions. And often what we want to know may require us to seek out information in books and periodicals.

Just as often, though, we can't state precisely what we want or need to know. It may be so fuzzy in our minds that we don't know what questions to ask to start off our research. So we have to do a fair amount of thinking, talking, writing, and reflecting in order to pinpoint and focus our purpose. We, in effect, put ourselves into conversation with ourselves and with others. In a sense this too is research. More than one philosopher has noted that asking the right questions is often more meaningful than getting the right answers.

However we come to decide what our research will be and how best to do it, when we finally do report it to others, we continue the conversation we had joined when we began our research. In fact, whenever we use language, whether written or oral, we are joining an ongoing conversation—either with ourselves or with others. Oral conversations tend to move steadily forward since it's difficult for us to have access to what was spoken a year ago much less centuries ago. But written conversations can span centuries, continents, and even languages. Almost as far back as we have written records, writers have been addressing issues of human relationships, power struggles, the meaning of life, proper behavior, and so forth. Not one of us can read and digest all that has been written on subjects which interest us. But printed materials at least give us access to some portion of all that's available. Teachers and other experts can point us to what our culture and traditions see as the most significant prior writings on any given subject. Even received opinions change over time as scholars uncover new documents or understand better the true significance of documents once considered unimportant.

When you do print-based research in a library, you are entering into a conversation with those who wrote centuries ago or thousands of miles away. But in order to situate yourself within that conversation and to make valid contributions to it, you need to know what has been said in it. This is the basic purpose of most education: to help you find your place in the ongoing flow of history. Unless you show your familiarity with this conversation, most people will not give much weight to your contribution to it. If, for example, you want to write about the role of economics in society, you should probably be familiar with canonical works on the subject: Malthus and Marx and others whom your economics teachers will identify for you. You'll also need to become familiar with what is currently being written on the subject. Knowing both what has been and is being written on the subject will enable you to make valuable contributions to this particular ongoing conversation. And if you want to make some permanent impact on that conversation, you'll write your words down so they'll be available for future study. Writing thus allows all of us to talk both to the past and to the future as well as to the present.

But you can have an ongoing conversation with yourself also. That conversation will obviously draw part of its substance from what you've read and what you've heard from others. Yet a large part of its substance will come from interaction with what you've previously thought and said. This conversation may concern the same subjects as the historical conversations: the meaning of life, human relationships, and so forth. For instance, you probably often find yourself saying something like: "I used to think x about the difference between Republicans and Democrats, but I now think y." Or, "I used to want to be an engineer, but now I think I'd rather be a teacher." What we say to ourselves changes as we experience more of the world around us. For most of us the conversation with ourselves is unrecorded. One of our aims in this book is to push you to record some of this personal conversation in your freewriting and exploratory writing. If you've done this, you've discovered how often such personal conversation can be interesting to others as well as to yourself. So often we've had students who moan that they have nothing to say. We think that they believe this because they haven't yet realized that their personal ruminations can be engrossing for others. A large part of the appeal of essays is that they foreground the workings of one mind as it treats a particular subject. We talk more about this in Unit 17.

Why are we writing about this here in Unit 16? Because we believe that research is often a way of integrating our personal conversations with ourselves into our conversations with others across history and geography. Most research becomes both. In articles reporting scientific research, for instance, authors often begin with a review of the literature. Such a review is merely a summing-up of the most important writing on a subject. Having done that, the authors move on to report their particular, personal research on that subject. In their conclusions they often integrate what they've uncovered and what previous researchers have uncovered. These articles, in turn, will be used by future researchers who desire to join the conversation.

These sweeping conclusions may seem grandiose considering that we got to them from simple questions such as "What time is it?" and "How do I get to the zoo?" But we contend that all research begins simply and that all research is a combination of personal insights and an awareness of what others have contributed. This is what makes it a conversation.

READINGS

WOMEN AND ADVERTISEMENTS ☆
Gail Hopus

Most advertisements which have women in them make me angry—whether the advertisements are in newspapers or magazines or on television. Sometimes I would share my reactions with my friends, but not all of them agreed with me. I decided I'd like to find out more systematically how people my age react to certain kinds of *goal* advertisements. At first I wanted to see people's reactions to television ads, but that would have meant sitting in front of the set for a long time with a group of people. That didn't seem possible, so instead I made copies of all the advertisements in *Good Housekeeping* for a three-month period in 1985, gave them to people to look at, and then interviewed them about what they noticed. After that I asked each person I *strategy* interviewed a set of questions. These are attached to the end of this paper. This paper reports what I found out from doing this personal research.

One of the things people commented on was that most of the advertisements *1* didn't show women making important decisions. They weren't shown buying cars or major household appliances. Usually they were shown buying cosmetics and cleaning products. Nor were women portrayed as selling important things like insurance; they were usually shown selling something like perfume. About 40 percent of the women I interviewed were annoyed by this. As one of my friends said: "You'd think the only thing women cared about was how they smell. I myself hate the strong smell of perfume."[1] Over 60 percent of the men didn't think it was important. About 20 percent of the women and 30 percent of the men thought that this was the way society is and therefore advertisers had to show it this way.

Another thing people commented on was the sexiness or non-sexiness of the women in the advertisements. In fact, this was the aspect of the ads most people commented on first. They noticed that in the small number of ads where women were shown as bank officers or selling house insurance, the women were dressed as business people and were not particularly sexy, though they were usually fairly pretty. But in advertisements for home products, women were often portrayed as sex objects. This was, of course, even more obvious in the ads for perfume and jewelry. Three of the women I interviewed thought this was only natural since women who stayed at home or women who were interested in jewelry would naturally be more feminine and that when women worked in office jobs they had to play down their feminineness. Quite a few of the men agreed with this conclusion. But a majority of the women said that they didn't see any reason why business women couldn't be feminine and that feminine was not the same as sexy. 90 percent of the women resented the emphasis on sex appeal in the ads. Only 10 percent of the men did. One of the boys in my dorm just laughed and said: "Sex is here to stay—why shouldn't it be in ads?"[2]

What bothered the women I interviewed the most (other than the obvious over-use of sex appeal) was that most of the women in the advertisements were depicted either as housewives or without any connection to a working profession outside the home. Eighty-five percent of the women I talked to and 55 percent of the men felt that this was unfair to today's women. Even more of the men, about 65 percent, said the advertisements didn't portray the kind of women they knew, but they didn't feel very connected to the men in some of the advertisements either.

Both men and women noted that most of the people in the advertisements looked high-class and wealthy. But this was not surprising to any of them because they said they were used to people in ads looking like this. Several noted that people on television ads tended to look more middle class and ordinary than people in magazine and newspaper ads. Advertisers usually try to connect their products to the good life. The people I interviewed simply said they had seen this so much they didn't believe it anyway but just thought of it as the way advertisements are. Even my roommate commented: "Who wants to see ordinary people in ads? We can see them every day. Rich, pretty people make magazines more attractive."[3]

Very few men noticed that a high number of the ads showed women dependent upon men in some way. But many of the women did notice it. But again about 40 percent of the women felt that this is the way it is in the real world. But quite a few of the women were angered by this feeling that the advertisements reinforced the stereotypes of society. They also felt that when women see themselves portrayed this way so often they begin not to think it significant when they see it in the real world. "I often wonder," said one of my club members, "whether any of these ads are drawn by women."[4]

A few of the women I interviewed noticed that housewives were often shown as having interests other than housework. For example, they might be shown in the kitchen (which was always sparkling clean) talking to someone about going to dance class or a PTA meeting. These women felt that the advertisers were making some kind of concession to the women's movement by developing such ads, but they also felt that this suggested that being a full-time housewife left lots of time for other things or that being a full-time housewife was not a good thing. A student who lives down the hall from me said that she didn't think it was right for motherhood to be viewed as unimportant by feminists.[5]

The ad that made the women maddest was one showing a woman who wanted to "commit murder" because a dinner guest criticized her clogged saltcellars. How can anyone have any respect for someone who criticizes something as trivial as saltcellars? Furthermore, in the ad the man is seen in a positive light, since he tells his wife not to be so critical of his sister. *specific 1 ads*

The next most irritating ad to both men and women was one showing a woman with the caption, "This dress and hat doesn't cost me a cent!" As you read the ad, you realize that the woman had purchased a General Electric vacuum cleaner which because it was such a good buy left her enough money to buy a dress and hat. This ad annoyed the women because it suggests that women are stupid and don't have enough sense to realize that the dress and hat aren't free, and it annoyed the men because they saw the woman as spending their money and of course it was always free to her. "Who do you think makes that money?" asked one of them.[6] *2*

I drew several conclusions from my observations and interviews. First is that most people don't pay very much attention to advertisements—at least that's what they say. They say that advertisements are never truthful about products, and the fact that the people in them look rich and beautiful just adds to the non-truthful quality. Second I concluded that women pay most attention to women in advertisements and men also pay most attention to women. Third women are more likely than men to blame advertisements for portraying people as they do; men didn't think that was too important. Very few men were angered by the ads, but quite a few women were. And finally, my last conclusion was that both men and women think that women do most of the buying in our society and that ads are mostly directed to them. *Concl.*

What I found out then by doing this little bit of personal research is that only about 20 to 30 percent of the 50 women I interviewed and only 5 percent of the men get as angry about ads as I do. Someday I'd like to do a more extensive survey of this sort and focus on whether ads have changed during the last 50 years or so and whether there are differences in reactions between generations. But for now, I figured out something I wanted to know and since I think the people I questioned are pretty representative of my school, I feel that my conclusions have some validity at least here. *future?*

NOTES

[1] Interview, Peggy Jones, April 8, 1986.
[2] Interview, Vincenzo Corso, April 8, 1986.
[3] Interview, Joyce Atkins, April 8, 1986.
[4] Interview, Janet Moresco, April 9, 1986.
[5] Interview, Karen O'Leary, April 7, 1986.
[6] Interview, Joe Brown, April 6, 1986.

Questions for Interviews

1. What's your main impression about the people in these ads?
2. Do you see differences between the way men and women are portrayed in the ads?
3. What do you note about male-female relationships from these ads?

4. Do any of these ads make you angry? Why?
5. If you were from Mars, what conclusions would you draw about what men and
     women do in our society?
6. Who do you think most of these ads are directed to?
7. Which of these ads would be most likely to sell you something?

PREACHER GRANDMOTHER
Lorraine Mitchell

What I Knew

It wasn't until last year when a very close friend—who is considered an aunt to the
family—married my cousin that I found out she and my grandmother were both
ordained ministers.

What I Want to Know

Ten years have passed since my grandmother passed away and now I would like to
know more about her. I'm interested in her life and how she got into ministry. Did
she have any problems getting into ministry? What kind of person was she like, and
what were some of her views she stood by firmly?

In writing this paper I got most of my information from my mother, along with
my Aunt Faith and Rita Miller, the close friend spoken of earlier.

This paper was not written in an interview form, but as a life story. I was given
facts about my grandmother's life from my mother, the only child out of six who
was left living with her, where the others were out on their own. Other bits of information were added by my Aunt Faith and Rita when possible.

While talking with Aunt Faith and Rita, I found out there was much information about grandmother they did not know themselves. I hope I've put all the pieces
of her life together in a way that, for whoever reads this paper, they get a true picture
of how she was.

Part I

It was a miracle with all the strength of this woman,
to serve the Lord like she had.

Grandmother Finley, Juanita Anas Foster, was born in Allegan county in 1893. She
lived and went to school in Pearl, Michigan, where she graduated from the 8th grade.

After graduation, Grandmother Finley went to work as an apprentice to a beau-
tician. She established the first beauty shop owned by a black in the South Bend area.
The shop catered to only whites. A few specialties of her shop were rain water for
shampooing, human hair to make her own hair pieces, and her own cold creams.

As years went on, Grandmother Finley became a nurse, studying under a German doctor. She became noticed when she took care of a very distinguished woman
named Mrs. Pugh, who was burned in the Great Chicago Theater fire. Mrs. Pugh's
hands were so badly burned that she lost the tips of her fingers. Besides nursing Mrs.
Pugh, Grandmother made all of her gloves to properly fit her fingers.

348

In the following years, Grandmother Finley took advantage of any training and education she could obtain. For her time, she was a highly self-taught educated woman. She felt you should learn everything you could, and would encourage you to do so.

Shortly after Grandmother's marriage to Herman Finley, she became a Christian and a member of the Morgan Park Pentecostal Church.

Mom was an unexpected arrival when Grandmother was at the age of forty. The family then moved to Bangor, Michigan.

In 1941 while Grandmother was critically ill and not expected to live, Grandfather unexpectedly passed of a heart attack.

Not expected to live, Grandmother made a promise to the Lord, that if he would heal her so she could raise Mom, she would dedicate the balance of her life to him.

The Lord did answer Grandmother's prayer; though not completely healed, she was able to start her work for him after Grandfather's death.

While serving the Lord as a State-side Missionary, Grandmother and my mom traveled around the states, going to Chicago, Kentucky, Cincinnati, Indiana, back to Chicago again, and then settling in Allegan, Michigan.

While on her mission of serving the Lord, Grandmother and Mom lived in faith homes, rented rooms, over and behind churches, and in a remodeled chicken coop. Running water and other facilities were not always available. Often times Grandmother did not know where the next meal was coming from, and the Lord would provide. Throughout her lifetime, she lived the life of Faith, and was never paid a salary, but managed to get Mom through school and pay the bills.

This great woman of Faith was called to Allegan back in the forties from Chicago, a faithful worker in the Morgan Park Pentecostal Church. She and her daughter, Erma, established residence in Allegan and began working and digging out souls for the Lord in this pioneer field. (1:15)

When Grandmother Finley first came to Allegan, she was involved with the Missionary Band sanctioned by the United Pentecostal Council of the Assemblies of God, Inc. She was ordained about ten years before her death by Bishop R. W. Sunday of the Church Council. There were no problems getting into the Pentecostal Church; or if there were any, they were never discussed by Grandmother.

Grandmother never made it known to too many she was an ordained minister. She opposed the idea of female ministers wearing man tailored suits and things like that. She maintained herself as being a woman, by dressing in a feminine way.

A Bible in her hand and Faith in her heart, she labored faithfully, paying a tremendous sacrifice in country fields and the city's bright lights. At times her daughters would provide transportation so door to door visitation and prayer for the sick could be possible. Her labor of love was sometime met with embittered opposition, but nothing darkened her Faith in God. She was the finest example of a leader, teacher, pastor and Mother in the Gospel. Working up north in Holland, Michigan, she pastored the All Nation Full Gospel Church for a period of time. She loved the saints and pressed her way in all sorts of storms and weather.

Sister Finley was very ambitious, fasted, prayed for a 32 mile radius around Allegan. Her vision was to build a House of Worship. Among her visions she desired to do missionary work in Africa, God didn't grant her crossing the seas, but laid heavy burdens upon her for the missionaries that were already laboring in the field. She and her daughters prepared boxes and great efforts were performed through this burden for Africa. (1:15)

As stated, Grandmother's vision was to have a House of Worship and also a home somewhere on a lake. To do Baptising in the water and provide a place where saints (members of the church) could come for a period of time and rest.

Grandmother wanted a Full Gospel Church in Allegan. A small group of people banded together to collect money for a building fund for the church, and money today is still being collected.

Because of Grandmother's promise to the Lord, she visited the sick and took care of cancer patients. She had a contact in getting hospital beds, wheel chairs, bandages, and any other needed materials for her cancer patients.

She spent her life working with unfortunate people and preached the Bible.

Part II

Grandmother Finley was a "determined headstrong woman"; the Bible was her "Sword of life."

She believed in the King James Version of the Bible (English translation of the Bible published in 1611). Her views on the Bible were you shouldn't take one part and reject the other. During her lifetime Grandmother always lived and studied by the Bible. Whatever she taught or preached to others, she did herself.

Grandmother believed there was a God who had a son named Jesus, who died on the cross. She believed there was a "Heaven to gain, and a Hell to shun," and strongly believed in the Ten Commandments.

It was in Grandmother's faith, that once you became a Christian, you should live a visible life to others, separating yourself from things that would be considered sinful to the Lord, such as drinking, dating, dancing, theater, smoking, makeup of any kind, card playing, and some types of fund raising projects. These were only a few beliefs she stood by. It was also in Grandmother's faith that when once "saved," your life had to be different than before. That being "saved" you were actually "born again," to live a new life and put aside worldly things.

Grandmother didn't believe in those ministers, regardless of being black or white, who manipulated and used minorities, taking advantage of the congregation and stripping it of its money. She didn't believe in those churches that weren't based on "sound religious beliefs" or those that were of a "store front makeup."

It was Grandmother's faith to believe in Divine Healing (healing of physical ills by God's direct intervention or the practice of seeking this healing through prayers and other expressions of faith; faith cured). Divine Healing isn't something where you lay your hands on a person and he is healed, it is soul-healing. If Grandmother were alive today, she would be very dissatisfied with some of today's Divine Healing on television.

Even though Grandmother believed in soul-healing for herself, she did believe in others going to doctors. When it came to death, she didn't believe life should be maintained by artificial means, such as some shots or intravenous feeding, given in many cases to keep life support systems going.

At the time Grandmother knew that she was going to die, she chose not to be put into the hospital, but to lay at rest in her own home until she passed on.

For people who are sick for a long period of time in their home and die there, it is sometimes difficult to obtain a death certificate with a medical doctor's signature. In Grandmother's case, Mom was able to make arrangements before she died with Mr. N————, a funeral director in town. He contacted Doctor B————, a local doctor, [who] then came out to the house after Grandmother died and signed the death certificate.

Grandmother spent her life working for the Lord, most of which she sacrificed to help others. When her help was needed, she would always go, and many of these times she was put into difficult situations. Never would Grandmother refuse anything given to her; she would eat food passed to her, knowing that later she would be sick. Grandmother would always give up what she had to give to those in need.

It was well known that Grandmother lived a very private life, and never liked to live with anyone. But a young woman in Allegan named Rita Miller desired to live with her right after three years' training from a Bible Institute on the East Coast. The desire must have stemmed from practical training under this great Woman of Faith. Many a prayer was answered, various kinds in many walks of life. Grandmother was not only a great source of faith and encouragement, but a qualified Bible instructor. She knew her Bible well.

Up until the last two months before Grandmother died, she led a very active life, and was not one for boasting or making a great display of herself. After her husband died in 1941, she never remarried.

August 3, 1966, Juanita Anas Finley went home to be with the Lord. It was out of pain and sorrow that it took a "miracle" for her to take care of the sick, work for the Lord, and go through all the hardships that she had after 1936.

Conclusion

In writing this paper, I found out a lot about my grandmother that was never known to me or other relatives before. She was a great leader and influence to those she came in contact with and I wish I could have gotten to know her better.

I plan on making copies of this paper to send to various relatives, for the benefit of their own use.

Source of Information

1. Pamphlet: Fifty-Seventh Annual Convocation & Youth Congress for the United Pentecostal Council of the Assemblies of God, Inc. July 12–19, 1976.

Interviews (March 1977)

2. ERMA MITCHELL—mother
3. FAITH PORTRUM—aunt (mother's sister)
4. RITA MILLER—ordained minister (close friend)

The Essay

Our aim in this unit is to introduce you to the essay as a literary form and to help you understand the difference between personal and impersonal essays. We hope too to impress upon you something we believe strongly: that personal writing is not less valuable than impersonal writing; it's just different and serves different purposes. Aspects of your own life and culture can serve as a basis for various kinds of writing; it's not necessarily the topic that determines the degree of formality of a piece of writing.

The modern essay is a slithery form; perhaps (notice we only say *perhaps*) we all recognize an essay when we see one, but few of us could actually define the form. That may well be its strength: it permits much; its outlines are pliable. To help you understand the essay better, see the readings at the end of this unit.

We haven't used the word *essay* much in this textbook; we usually call what you're asked to do "papers" or "writing." "Composition" is a word we tend to avoid because it tends to be used for writing done only in school—or only in English classes. We're hoping we can get you to see that writing is writing: it isn't something you do just for English classes or just for school. Nor are we teaching a way of going about writing which is applicable only to school writing.

Your assignment for this unit will be to try your hand at writing both a personal and an impersonal essay on the same subject. Once you've made drafts of each type, you can either finish off both of them or just one. (Perhaps your teacher will decide.)

We've sequenced this unit by first asking you to do some writing to develop your essay and then giving you suggestions to think about when reading the three published essays at the end of the unit. You or your teacher may want to reverse these activities and analyze the published essays before beginning your own. We chose this sequence in order to minimize the possibility that your exploratory writing would be too much influenced by your analysis of the readings. From our own experience, we know that a certain amount of modeling—of using a published work as a model—can be useful, provided you don't consider the model as the only acceptable or even the best one of its kind. The essay is such a flexible form that no one manifestation of it can be considered an ideal representation.

WAYS TO BEGIN

It isn't subject matter that determines whether an essay is personal or impersonal—it's the way the writer approaches that subject matter that counts. Thus we are going to ask you first to work out what you have to say on your topic and only then to direct your efforts to revising toward the personal, impersonal, or both.

Perhaps you already have a topic in mind that you'd like to explore. Perhaps this topic may be something you've already done some writing on in this course but never had the chance to follow up on. But if not, the best way for you to discover a topic is to do some exploratory writing—in effect letting your topic choose you. You might want to use some of the methods we've already introduced (for example, the Perl guidelines or the open-ended process, both in Unit 6). Don't worry at this point about whether the emerging topic is based in personal experience and feelings or in abstract thinking of some kind.

If you have difficulties coming up with a topic, we'll suggest a few. We've chosen these for a particular reason. You'll notice that they all have something to do with your own culture. Most of your school tasks will ask you to write impersonally; yet most of these school tasks will also benefit from your thinking about them in a personal way.

We're also pointing you in this direction because your culture is one you're an expert on in ways others are not: you're living it. Because you're inside that culture, you see it in ways others cannot. This makes what you have to say about it valuable—both to yourself and to others. And we also want you to begin to realize that you can bring to bear what you learn in school upon an analysis and understanding of your culture. What you learn in school affects how you see that culture—just as the culture itself affects how and what you learn in school.

Our suggested topics tend to overlap, and so you may want to draw on more than one. (However, you should probably check with your teacher if you want to deal with more than two because of the danger of being too superficial.) You may want to adapt one of our topics and focus it on your *ethnic, geographical,* or *gender* identity. Also, we talk here of your culture in terms of your age—as though you are all adolescents. We recognize that some of you are older.

- What do you consider your generation's chief areas of interest and non-interest (soap operas, music, clothes, sports, politics, government, world affairs)? What do you think such interests or noninterests reveal about your generation?

- How do you see the value system of your generation as being different from that of your parents' or grandparents' generation? in religion, sexual mores, gender roles, ethnic identification?

- In what ways do you feel comfortable with your generation? In what ways do you feel you don't fit in, that you're different? Do you think your generation is fairly homogeneous? How do you react to such stereotypes as "jocks," "preppies," "yuppies," "punks," and other terms that are sometimes applied to some members of your generation?

- Do you think your friends and peers are basically *conservative:* interested in finding a good job, getting married, having children, fitting into society as it's currently structured? Or do you think your friends and peers are basically *liberal* in their outlooks: mainly concerned to change certain aspects of society to make it better for themselves and others? Or do you consider these two terms inapplicable to your generation?

- What do you consider to be your generation's chief fears in life? Are you mostly worried about nuclear war, drug addiction, career choice, or something else?

- What does your generation most want from education? knowledge? a job? culture? How large a role does education play in the life of your generation?

- What upsets you the most about your generation: drugs? alcoholism? musical interests? something else?

- Commentators on the current youth scene often talk and write about young people being less intelligent, poorer writers and thinkers, and less prepared for college work than before. How do you react to such characterizations?

ooooo

If you have already done a lot of exploratory writing in the process of finding what you want to write your essay about, you have already begun. If you decided on a topic without doing exploratory writing, start now by just jumping in and writing as much as you can in a half or three-quarters of an hour. (Use one of our exploratory techniques if you think it would help.) Don't think yet about what *kind* of essay you are writing—just see what comes as you deal with the topic.

Once you've done some writing, look back over it and decide what its basic orientation is: does it mainly tend to give information, or does it tend more to focus on your own thoughts and reactions about that information? Try to separate these two kinds of discourse. There's no way you can separate them totally: the information you select is always a personal selection. But once you've selected that information, you can present it more as *information* or more as your personal *attitudes* toward information.

Now write a bit more. This time, however, work on two separate pieces: one which presents information as though you're trying to inform people, the other which presents information as a way of conveying your personal thinking and reacting.

Each of these two pieces can serve as the basis of an essay: one personal and one impersonal. Which you want to develop first depends on you, but we suggest that you make a draft of an essay out of both pieces of writing. At the conclusion of this unit, you'll find two such drafts.

SUGGESTIONS FOR SHARING AND RESPONDING

As you share your exploratory rough writing, you'll find the techniques in Section IIA of *Sharing and Responding,* "Sayback," and Section IIB, "Pointing; Summarizing," particularly productive. Additionally here are some questions you'll find helpful:

- What comes across most: me or the information? my mind and the way it works or my subject?

- Point to specific spots where the way I think and the kind of person I am is most evident. Least evident.

- What do you think I haven't included in my thinking which needs including?

- What would I need to do to this rough writing to make it more personal? more impersonal?

When sharing and responding to draft(s) of your essay(s), you'll find these sections of *Sharing and Responding* most useful: "Descriptive Responding," Section IIC; "Descriptive Outline," Section IIIC; "Skeleton Feedback," Section IIIA; and "Criterion-Based Feedback," Section V. But you may also want to consider the following questions:

- For each essay draft, am I emphasizing facts or the way I think about facts?

- Are there spots where my essay drifts too far from its basic orientation: either personal or impersonal?

- What is the purpose of my essay(s)?

PROCESS BOX

I'm revising *Sharing and Responding.* Almost done with final revising for our textbook. It feels as though I'm making it much simpler and that's making me pleased—even excited. (If you think it's too long or complicated now, you should have seen it before!) I've just succeeded in figuring out a simpler structure—an overview. I have a sense of a complicated crowd of trees resolving itself down into some clear *clumps.* And with it a simpler labeling system.

Suddenly it strikes me (and this is what moved me to stop and write a process note) that perhaps we've been sending the wrong message about revising. We've tended to stress how hard it is—and how it's the least enjoyable part of writing. That generating is more lively and fun. (I was forgetting, when I wrote this, that our unit on revising *did* avoid too much emphasis on struggle and agony—thanks to Pat.)

Maybe that's all wrong. It needn't be a struggle. It's just a matter of setting the draft aside for enough time—getting distant. (Without that time it *is* a struggle.) I've had a chance to forget all about this part of the book for quite a few months. Coming back fresh.

But you may also want to ask the questions about your essay(s) which we list in the next section for you to use when reading the three published essays at the end of this unit.

READING ESSAYS

Essays range from personal to impersonal and can have a full range of purposes: expressive, transactional—either communicative or persuasive—or poetic. (See Unit 13 for more on these purposes for writing.) Furthermore, there is no necessary connection between purpose and level of personalness or impersonalness: an expressive essay, for example, can be personal or impersonal, even though it usually tends toward the personal.

We selected the three essays at the end of this unit because they represent a mix of styles and purposes. Another factor in our choice, which will become obvious as soon as you start reading them, is their subject matter.

As you read these essays, do some writing. You may want to use the writing-while-reading strategies we've set out in other units (10, 12, 13, and the mini-units on dialectical notebooks and text rendering). You can, of course, use some combination of these. After you've done some writing on all three essays, draw some conclusions about the following:

- In which essay does the author seem to speak to you most directly? Which essay do you feel least like an audience for? Why?

With this distance and perspective, it was just a matter of looking back over it—and back over it—with a certain attitude:

- That this really *does* need to be changed: it's too complicated and unclear.
- But that *of course* I'll find a way to do it. I simply won't settle for not doing so.

With this attitude of *demand* yet *confidence*—and with some real effort and patience—the new view and new structure just came. It'll take time and effort to work out the changes I've come to, but it doesn't feel at all like struggle.

Another thought, however. I'll bet my upbeat mood is also coming from the fact that we're almost done revising this book. It's uplifting to be nearing the end of any writing project you care about—all the more so when it's a long one. I am buoyed by the feeling of, "Yes I really *can* do it. I can let go of those nagging, discouraged feelings of 'Oh no, this is *too* hard, we'll never make it.' "

PETER ELBOW, 9/87

- Which would you describe as the most personal? the most impersonal? Point to specific features which lead you to these conclusions.

- Which essay seems to you most like literature? Why? Again, point to specific features.

- If you wanted to recommend these essays to a friend, what would you give as the reason why she might want to read each?

- Look for expressive, communicative, persuasive, and poetic elements in each of the essays. Having done this, what do you see as the *chief* purpose of each one?

- From which essay did you learn the most? the least?

- As you were reading, which essay made you feel most like you were inside the author's mind?

- For each essay, was the emphasis on the facts presented or on the author's thinking about the facts?

- Which essay was the most interesting to you? the least? Why? How do your answers to these questions relate to the questions you've already answered?

After you've answered the preceding questions, pretend that each of the essays is the only true representative of the essay form and write three separate, brief definitions of the genre. Then write one definition which covers all three essays. Think about this definition: What's in it that surprises you? What's not there that you think is important? Or do you think your definition is adequate as a general definition of the genre?

THEORY AND RUMINATIONS

The Essay

Historically the essay as an individual form was born in the sixteenth century. Its birth occurred during the Renaissance, during a time we think of as an age of individualism and new discovery. Thus it is a true child of its times. The Frenchman Michel de Montaigne, who initiated the form, named it *essai,* a French word that means "try"—and which has its roots in the Latin words *exagium,* meaning a weighing or balancing, and *exigere,* meaning to examine. For Montaigne, the *essai* was "a try" or a kind of "go at" something. In writing about this new form he was developing, Montaigne says that its purposes are essentially private.

> I desire therein to be delineated in mine own genuine, simple and ordinary fashion, without contention, art or study; for it is myself I portray. . . . Myself am the groundwork of my book.

Francis Bacon was the first English writer of essays. His essays are quite different from Montaigne's; the first ones, in fact, are more like notes. It is probably Abraham Cowley who should be considered the father of the English essay, but it wasn't until the eighteenth century that the essay became a dominant form in English literature. We're not going to go on with this history here because you can find it in Gosse's "The Essay," one of the selections in our "Readings" section. But we do hope you noticed that in our last sentence we spoke of the essay as "literature."

We invite you also to read the essay in the "Readings" section entitled "What I Think, What I Am," by Edward Hoagland. In it he notes that "essays . . . hang somewhere on a line between two sturdy poles: this is what I think, and this is what I am." The conclusion of his essay merits repetition.

> A personal essay frequently is not autobiographical at all, but what it does keep in common with autobiography is that, through its tone and tumbling progression, it conveys the quality of the author's mind. Nothing gets in the way. Because essays are directly concerned with the mind and its idiosyncrasy, the very freedom the mind possesses is bestowed on this branch of literature that does honor to it, and the fascination of the mind is the fascination of the essay.

What's so fascinating about the personal essay is that we can find it engaging even when the subject doesn't interest us at all. What engages us

358

is the workings of a human mind. When an essayist gives us that, the subject takes a back seat: it is merely the way of getting into another's mind.

You'll notice that the preceding quotation begins with the words "a personal essay." But there is also something known as the "impersonal essay," an essay which is focused more on *what* is said than on the qualitites of the writer's mind. Yet even that is only a relative alteration of the form. Perhaps it's best to think of essays along a continuum from personal to impersonal: each essay blends these two in its own way.

As you have already realized by reading this far, the essay is not usually a school-assigned form. Most teachers are mainly interested in what you know and tend to judge your writing on that basis. There are, of course, classes in which teachers want you to assess the information you present and come to conclusions of your own; but this usually means they're interested in seeing how intelligently you can think about your material. Seldom is their primary interest in your mind as it engages the task of thinking about the material. Consequently you may well write impersonal essays to fulfill school assignments, but you'll not often write a personal essay to do so. The one place where you're likely to be asked to write personal essays (other than in a course like this one) is in an advanced composition course. Such courses are often rightly grouped with courses in writing fiction and poetry—because the essay is a literary genre.

Another way we can talk about the essay is to go back to the terms we used in Unit 13, where we briefly presented James Britten's taxonomy of types of writing: expressive, transactional, and poetic. The personal essay lies in the expressive camp, moving perhaps toward the poetic; the impersonal essay lies within the transactional field with some nods toward the expressive. (The transactional includes both communication and persuasion as purposes.)

The impersonal essay moves toward the "article." We often speak of "newspaper articles" or "professional articles": articles which usually appear in the periodicals of a particular discipline and manifest the language features of that discipline. But professionals also write articles directed toward a general public; such articles or "essays" are often more personal than purely professional articles.

In a recent essay in the *New York Times Book Review,* Elizabeth Hardwick writes:

William Gass, in what must be called an essay, a brilliant one, about Emerson, an essayist destined from the cradle, makes a distinction between the article and the essay. Having been employed by the university and having heard so many of his colleagues "doing an article on," Mr. Gass has come to think of the article as "that awful object" because it is under the command of defensiveness in footnote, reference, coverage, and would also pretend that all must be useful and certain, even if it is "very likely a veritable Michelin of misdirections." If the article has a certain sheen and professional polish, it is the polish of "the scrubbed step"— practical economy and neatness. The essay, in Mr. Gass's view, is a great meadow of style and personal manner, freed from the need for defense except that provided by an individual intelligence and sparkle. We consent to watch a mind at work, without agreement often, but only for pleasure. Knowledge hereby attained, great indeed, is again wanted for the pleasure of itself. (44)

And one more quote. In a recent review of a collection of essays by Italo Calvino, the reviewer, Christopher Lehmann-Haupt concludes:

These essays are instructive and often arresting, but it is the responsive play of Mr. Calvino's mind that seduces us. We are invited into a circle that includes the work, its creators and Mr. Calvino as observer. (C24)

READINGS

UNTITLED 1
Eleanor Klinko

I had an inkling of what was going on but when the words were stated to my face it was like an earthquake shattering my world into tiny pieces. My very close friend, the one with whom I have shared so many wonderful times, just told me she was gay.

It was a balmy Wednesday afternoon and my friend and I were driving down my street headed for an exotic boutique. Sitting next to me she seemed jumpy, her hands moving as she talked. I only remember jumbles of what she said about girls and feelings. These words led up to one word that I do remember. I only heard it after I daringly asked, "Are you gay?" I choked on my words.

She replied, "Yes." We were looking at each other face to face. My mind was not controlling my foot on the brake. Realizing this I quickly pressed the pedal to the floor, jerking the car to a stop before hitting the car in front of mine.

I was stunned. The words were a slap across my face. My cheek stung as my mind was bombarded with flashbacks of our days spent together. We would play the guitar, play basketball, go to concerts, listen to music, study history, shuffle through leaves, and shoot coconuts at each other in the snow. These are the activities of two energetic high school girls.

She talked about a young English teacher she liked in school. She had seen her at a gay bar and they danced together. This conversation was awkward, probably because I never had one like it before and never expected to. Weren't two girls supposed to be talking about guys? But I didn't go against her; I actually tried to help her figure a strategy to be with this woman. I don't know why I didn't start yelling and bombard her with questions. I was stunned, a little scared, confused, and really didn't want to accept what she was saying.

There she sat, my friend, in the passenger seat of my car. Her soft pale skin and long thin blonde hair did not coincide with her tall muscular body. She really didn't have any feminine features except for her fair complexion and soft hair. She dressed in faded jeans and ripped concert T-shirts. Studded black leather dressed her waist and wrists. Maybe I should have known from her appearance but I didn't. She had masculine features. She used a trucker's wallet which attached to her pants by a chain, sewed a Harley Davidson patch on her leather jacket, wore black leather motorcycle boots, and had four tattoos on her body. She smoked cigarettes and drank beer like a guy. She did not hold and puff on a cigarette the way a woman does.

What do I do now? I loved her and would do almost anything for her, but how could I feel this way now? She might think that I wanted to be more than a friend. But I didn't want to lose her friendship because I didn't want to lose the good times we shared.

I couldn't tell anyone about my situation. I was embarrassed to talk to my father about the subject. He would not tell me to stop my friendship with her because he allows me to choose my own friends. But he would prefer I spent less time with her so my feelings wouldn't be influenced by hers. I didn't tell any other people, partly because it wouldn't be fair to my friend and partly because I feared the rumors that might start about her and me being more than just friends. People in high school love to start rumors especially if they're not true. People who knew that she and I were close friends might assume that I was like her. And if guys thought I was gay then I would never get asked for a date by a male.

I was in a state of confusion. I wanted to continue with our regular friendship but it felt as if a cloud hung over us. I needed time to think about the situation. Although I liked her for what she was and for being open with me, I didn't like her any more than a friend, and I knew I could never have a relationship with a girl. I told her all this. She accepted. I didn't hold anything against her because I had no right to. She didn't hurt me; she just made me think about a reality of life.

UNTITLED 2
Eleanor Klinko

Three years ago my best friend told me she was gay. We had been friends for over ten years and I had never even suspected it. Perhaps I should have because her soft pale skin and long thin blonde hair did not coincide with her tall muscular body. She really didn't have any feminine features except for her fair complexion and soft hair. She dressed in faded jeans and ripped concert T-shirts. Studded black leather dressed her waist and wrists. Maybe I should have known from her appearance but I didn't. She had masculine features. She used a trucker's wallet which attached to her pants by a chain, sewed a Harley Davidson patch on her leather jacket, wore black leather motorcycle boots, and had four tattoos on her body. She smoked cigarettes and drank beer like a guy. She did not hold and puff on a cigarette the way a woman does.

Certainly others have faced this situation, but I didn't know personally anyone who had. I can remember seeing a segment of "Love Boat," where one of the crew member's friends had had a sex change. Part of the story was how the crew member adjusted to that. I also remember that on one of the soap operas there was a family who had to deal with the discovery that the son was gay. I had known about homosexuals for years; in fact, I remember when I thought I could recognize gay men as I walked around the streets of the Village. But later I realized from some reading I did that gays are not identifiable according to some stereotypical image. Gay men can be short or tall, fat or thin, muscular or not. They can be construction workers, truckers, or ballet dancers. They can prefer baseball to cooking. I now know one cannot tell if a man is gay by looking at him. But I didn't know that at the time my friend confided in me.

I knew far less about gay women. My experience suggests that gay women are less likely to "come out of the closet" than gay men. Many of my male friends are sure that they know what a gay woman looks like—and their descriptions are not very flattering. And even though my friend, I now realize, has masculine traits, I suspect that gay women can look as feminine in the traditional sense as straight women. And, also, I know many women who wear just as much leather as my friend does and are *not* gay.

I now realize that when my friend told me about herself, I had three choices. I could accept her and continue our friendship. I could reject her, which I suspect is what my father would have wanted me to do had he known. Or I could simply act as though I didn't know and continue our friendship just as it was. I knew the latter was not really possible since I suspected the lack of honesty between us would kill our relationship. I couldn't reject her because she had been and still was my friend. So I accepted her and was able to tell her how I felt. She, in turn, was able to accept that.

One thing I have learned from this experience is that gay people are more like the rest of us than unlike us. My girlfriend loves her parents, curses her car when it won't start, values honest relationships, wants to do well in school, get a good job, and make a fair amount of money. The biggest difference between us, I guess, is that I want to get married and have a family. Even so, my friend and I still have enough in common to spend hours talking.

THE ESSAY*
Edmund Gosse

ESSAY, ESSAYIST (Fr. *essai,* Late Lat. *exagium,* a weighing or balance; *exigere,* to examine; the term in general meaning any trial or effort). As a form of literature, the essay is a composition of moderate length, usually in prose, which deals in an easy, cursory way with the external conditions of a subject, and, in strictness, with that subject only as it affects the writer. Dr Johnson, himself an eminent essayist, defines an essay as "an irregular, undigested piece"; the irregularity may perhaps be admitted, but want of thought, that is to say lack of proper mental digestion, is certainly not characteristic of a fine example. It should, on the contrary, always be the brief and light result of experience and profound meditation, while "undigested" is the last epithet to be applied to the essays of Montaigne, Addison or Lamb. Bacon said that the Epistles of Seneca were "essays," but this can hardly be allowed. Bacon himself goes on to admit that "the word is late, though the thing is ancient." The word, in fact, was invented for this species of writing by Montaigne, who merely meant that these were experiments in a new kind of literature. This original meaning, namely that these pieces were attempts or endeavours, feeling their way towards the expression of what would need a far wider space to exhaust, was lost in England in the course of the eighteenth century. This is seen by the various attempts made in the nineteenth century to coin a word which should express a still smaller work, as distinctive in comparison with the essay as the essay is by the side of the monograph;

---

* From an entry in the famous eleventh edition of the *Encyclopaedia Britannica,* 1910.

none of these linguistic experiments, such as *essayette, essaykin* (Thackeray) and *essaylet* (Helps) have taken hold of the language. As a matter of fact, the journalistic word *article* covers the lesser form of essay, although not exhaustively, since the essays in the monthly and quarterly reviews, which are fully as extended as an essay should ever be, are frequently termed "articles," while many "articles" in newspapers, dictionaries and encyclopaedias are in no sense essays. It may be said that the idea of a detached work is combined with the word "essay," which should be neither a section of a disquisition nor a chapter in a book which aims at the systematic development of a story. Locke's *Essay on the Human Understanding* is not an essay at all, or cluster of essays, in this technical sense, but refers to the experimental and tentative nature of the inquiry which the philosopher was undertaking. Of the curious use of the word so repeatedly made by Pope mention will be made below.

The essay, as a species of literature, was invented by Montaigne, who had probably little suspicion of the far-reaching importance of what he had created. In his dejected moments, he turned to rail at what he had written, and to call his essays "inepties" and "sottises." But in his own heart he must have been well satisfied with the new and beautiful form which he had added to literary tradition. He was perfectly aware that he had devised a new thing; that he had invented a way of communicating himself to the world as a type of human nature. He designed it to carry out his peculiar object, which was to produce an accurate portrait of his own soul, not as it was yesterday or will be to-morrow, but as it is to-day. It is not often that we can date with any approach to accuracy the arrival of a new class of literature into the world, but it was in the month of March 1571 that the essay was invented. It was started in the second story of the old tower of the castle of Montaigne, in a study to which the philosopher withdrew for that purpose, surrounded by his books, close to his chapel, sheltered from the excesses of a fatiguing world. He wrote slowly, not systematically; it took nine years to finish the two first books of the essays. In 1574 the manuscript of the work, so far as it was then completed, was nearly lost, for it was confiscated by the pontifical police in Rome, where Montaigne was residing, and was not returned to the author for four months. The earliest imprint saw the light in 1580, at Bordeaux, and the Paris edition of 1588, which is the fifth, contains the final text of the great author. These dates are not negligible in the briefest history of the essay, for they are those of its revelation to the world of readers. It was in the delightful chapters of his new, strange book that Montaigne introduced the fashion of writing briefly, irregularly, with constant digressions and interruptions, about the world as it appears to the individual who writes. The *Essais* were instantly welcomed, and few writers of the Renaissance had so instant and so vast a popularity as Montaigne. But while the philosophy, and above all the graceful stoicism, of the great master were admired and copied in France, the exact shape in which he had put down his thoughts, in the exquisite negligence of a series of essays, was too delicate to tempt an imitator. It is to be noted that neither Charron, nor Mlle de Gournay, his most immediate disciples, tried to write essays. But Montaigne, who liked to fancy that the Eyquem family was of English extraction, had spoken affably of the English people as his "cousins," and it has always been admitted that his genius has an affinity with the English. He was early read in England, and certainly by Bacon, whose is the second great name connected with this form of literature. It was in 1597, only five years after the death of Montaigne, that Bacon published in a small octavo the first ten of his essays. These he increased to 38 in 1612 and to 68 in 1625. In their first form, the essays of Bacon had nothing of the fulness or grace of Montaigne's; they are meagre notes; scarcely more than the headings for discourses. It is possible that when he wrote them he was not yet familiar with the style of his predecessor, which was first made popular in England, in 1603, when Florio published that translation of the *Essais* which Shakespeare unquestionably read. In the later editions Bacon greatly expanded his theme, but he never reached, or but seldom, the freedom and ease, the seeming formlessness held in by an invisible chain, which are the glory of Montaigne, and distinguish the typical essayist. It would seem that at first, in England, as in France, no lesser writer was willing to adopt a title which belonged to so great a presence as that of Bacon or Montaigne. The one exception was Sir William Cornwallis (d. 1631), who published essays in 1600 and 1617, of slight merit, but popular in their day. No other English essayist of any importance appeared until the Restoration, when Abraham Cowley wrote eleven "Several Discourses by way of Essays," which did not see the light until 1668. He interspersed with his prose, translations and original pieces in verse, but in other respects Cowley keeps much nearer than Bacon to the form of Montaigne. Cowley's essay "Of Myself" is a model of what these little compositions should be. The name of Bacon inspires awe, but it is really not he, but Cowley, who is the father of the English essay; and it is remarkable that he has had no warmer panegyrists than his great successors, Charles Lamb and Macaulay. Towards the end of the century, Sir George Mackenzie (1636–1691) wrote witty moral discourses, which were, however, essays rather in name than form. Whenever, however, we reach the eighteenth century, we find the essay suddenly became a dominant force in English literature. It made its appearance almost as a new thing, and in combination with the earliest developments of journalism. On the 12th of April 1709 appeared the first number of a penny newspaper, entitled the *Tatler,* a main feature of which was to amuse and instruct fashionable readers by a series of short papers dealing with the manifold occurrences of life, *quicquid agunt homines.* But it was not until Steele, the founder of the *Tatler,* was joined by Addison that the eighteenth-century essay really started upon its course. It displayed at first, and indeed it long retained, a mixture of the manner of Montaigne with that of La Bruyère, combining the form of the pure essay with that of the character study, as modelled on Theophrastus, which had been so popular in England throughout the seventeenth century. Addison's early *Tatler* portraits, in particular such as those of "Tom Folio" and "Ned Softly," are hardly essays. But Steele's "Recollections of Childhood" is, and here we may observe the type on which Goldsmith, Lamb and R. L. Stevenson afterwards worked. In January 1711 the *Tatler* came to an end, and was almost immediately followed by the *Spectator,* and in 1713 by the *Guardian.* These three newspapers are storehouses of admirable and typical essays, the majority of them written by Steele and Addison, who are the most celebrated eighteenth-century essayists in England. Later in the century, after the publication of other less successful experiments, appeared Fielding's essays in the *Covent Garden Journal* (1752) and Johnson's in the *Rambler* (1750), the *Adventurer* (1752) and the *Idler* (1759). There followed a great number of polite journals, in which the essay was treated as "the bow of Ulysses in which it was the fashion for men of rank and genius to try their strength." Goldsmith reached a higher level than the Chesterfields and Bonnel Thorntons had dreamed of, in the delicious sections of his *Citizen of the World* (1760). After Goldsmith, the eighteenth-century essay declined into tamer hands, and passed into final feebleness with the pedantic Richard Cumberland and the sentimental Henry Mackenzie. The *corpus* of eighteenth-century essayists is extremely voluminous, and their reprinted works fill some fifty volumes. There is, however, a great sameness about all but the very best of them, and in no case do they surpass Addison in freshness, or have they ventured to modify the form he adopted for his lucubrations. What has survived of them all is the lightest portion, but it should not be forgotten that a very large section of the essays of that age were deliberately didactic and "moral." A great revival of the essay took place during the first quarter of the nineteenth century, and foremost in the history of this movement must always be placed the name of Charles Lamb. He perceived that the real business of the essay, as Montaigne had conceived it, was to be largely personal. The famous *Essays of Elia* began to appear in the *London Magazine* for August 1820, and proceeded at fairly regular intervals until December 1822; early in 1823 the first series of them were collected in a volume. The peculiarity of Lamb's style as an essayist was that he threw off the Addisonian and still more the Johnsonian tradition, which had become a burden that crushed the life out of each conventional essay, and that he boldly went back to the rich verbiage and brilliant imagery of the seventeenth century for his inspiration. It is true that Lamb had a great ductility of style, and that, when he pleases, he can write so like Steele that Steele himself might scarcely know the difference, yet in his freer flights we are conscious of more exalted masters, of Milton, Thomas Browne and Jeremy Taylor. He succeeded, moreover, in reaching a poignant note of personal feeling, such as none of his predecessors had ever aimed at; the essays called "Dream Children" and "Blakesmoor" are examples of this, and they display a degree of harmony and perfection in the writing of the pure essay such as had never been attempted before, and has never since been reached. Leigh Hunt, clearing away all the didactic and pompous elements which had overgrown the essay, restored it to its old *Spectator* grace, and was the most easy nondescript writer of his generation in periodicals such as the *Indicator* (1819) and the *Companion* (1828). The sermons, letters and pamphlets of Sydney Smith were really essays of an extended order. In Hazlitt and Francis Jeffrey we see the form and method of the essay beginning to be applied to literary criticism. The writings of De Quincey are almost exclusively essays, although many of the most notable of them, under his vehement pen, have far outgrown the limits of the length laid down by the most indulgent formalist. His biographical and critical essays are interesting, but they are far from being trustworthy models in form or substance. In a sketch, however rapid, of the essay in the nineteenth century, prominence must be given to the name of Macaulay. His earliest essay, that on Milton, appeared in the *Edinburgh Review* in 1825, very shortly after the revelation of Lamb's genius in "Elia." No two products cast in the same mould could, however, be more unlike in substance. In the hands of Macaulay the essay ceases to be a confession or an autobiography; it is strictly impersonal, it is literary, historical or controversial, vigorous, trenchant and full of party prejudice. The periodical publication of Macaulay's Essays in the *Edinburgh Review* went on until 1844; when we cast our eyes over this mass of brilliant writing we observe with surprise that it is almost wholly contentious. Nothing can be more remarkable than the difference in this respect between Lamb and Macaulay, the former for ever demanding, even cajoling, the sympathy of the reader, the latter scanning the horizon for an enemy to controvert. In later times the essay in England has been cultivated in each of these ways, by a thousand journalists and authors. The "leaders" of a daily newspaper are examples of the popularization of the essay, and they point to the danger which now attacks it, that of producing a purely ephemeral or even momentary species of effect. The essay, in its best days, was intended to be as lasting as a poem or a historical monograph; it aimed at being one of the most durable and precious departments of literature. . . .

ON ESSAYING
James Moffett

While doing summer institutes on writing I have frequently encountered teachers who will call every kind of writing that is not book-report, term-paper, essay-question stuff "personal" or "creative" writing (the two terms being interchangeable) and hence put it in a big bag that goes up on the shelf. Priority goes of course to "exposition," which is equated with "essay," which is equated in turn with forced writing on given topics from books, lectures, or "current issues." In these institutes with teachers I break a class into trios in which members help each other, over several weeks, to develop subjects and techniques by hearing or reading partners' writing ideas at various stages of working up the material. Some of this material is gleaned from memory, some is information obtained fresh by interviewing or observing, and some is feeling, thought, or imagination elicited suddenly by a stimulus such as a tune or other in-class presentation. The material may take the form of stories, dialogs, essays, or songs and poems. It soon becomes obvious that ideas stem from all kinds of material and take all kinds of forms and that the very limited sort of exposition used for testing enjoys no monopoly on intellectual activity; participants can see, often with astonishment, how loaded with ideas is this rich variety of writing they have produced.

When schools narrow the notion of essay to fit it to editing, they are violating the whole tradition of the genre from its very inception to the present. College composition instructors and anthologists of essays have doted for years on George Orwell's "Shooting an Elephant," which they hold up to students as a model of essay or "expository writing." Please look closely at it even if you think you know it well; if a student wrote it, it would be called "personal writing," that is, soft and non-intellectual. Orwell narrated in first person how as a British civil servant in Burma he was intimidated by villagers into shooting an elephant against his will. But so effectively does he say what happens by telling what happened that the force of his theme—the individual's moral choice whether or not to conform to the group— leaves us with the impression that the memoir is "expository,"—that is chiefly cast in the present tense of generalization and in third person. What we really want to help youngsters learn is how to express ideas of universal value in a personal voice. Fables, parables, poems and songs, fiction and memoir may convey ideas as well as or better than editorials and critiques. Orwell does indeed provide a fine model, but teachers should not let prejudice fool them into misunderstanding the actual kind of discourse in which he wrote "Shooting an Elephant" and other excellent essays, for this leads to a confusing double standard whereby we ask students to emulate a great writer but to do it in another form.

The Essay: An Attempt

Orwell wrote deep in a tradition of English letters, honoring the essay as a candid blend of personal and universal. It was resurrected if not invented during the Renaissance by Montaigne, who coined the term essai from essayer, to attempt. From his position of philosophical skepticism ("What do I know?") he saw his writing as personal attempts to discover truth, what he thought and what could be thought, in exactly the same sense that Donald Murray or Janet Emig or I myself might speak of writing as discovery. From Burton's *Anatomy of Melancholy* and Browne's *Urn Burial;* Addison's and Steele's *Spectator* articles; through the essays of Swift, Lamb,

Hazlitt, and DeQuincey to those of Orwell, Virginia Woolf, Joan Didion, and Norman Mailer, English literature has maintained a marvelous tradition, fusing personal experience, private vision, and downright eccentricity, with intellectual vigor and verbal objectification. In color, depth, and stylistic originality it rivals some of our best poetry. Look back over Hazlitt's "The Fight" and compare it with Mailer's intellectual reportage of the Ali-Frazier fight in *King of the Hill* or "On the Feeling of Immortality in Youth" or "On Familiar Style"; DeQuincey's "Confessions of an Opium Eater" or "On the Knocking at the Gate in *Macbeth*," which begins: "From my boyish days I had always felt a great perplexity on one point in *Macbeth*"; or Lamb's "The Two Races of Men," "Poor Relations," or "On Sanity of True Genius." Consider too a book like Henry Adams's *Education of Henry Adams* for its simultaneous treatment of personal and national or historical.

Some essayists, like Montaigne and Emerson, tend toward generality, as reflected in titles like "Friendship" or "Self-Reliance," but tone and source are personal, and we cannot doubt the clear kinship between essays featuring memoir or eyewitness reportage and those of generality, for the same writers do both, sometimes in a single essay, sometimes in separate pieces; and Lamb and Thoreau stand in the same relation to Montaigne and Emerson as fable to moral or parable to proverb. The difference lies not in the fundamental approach, which is in any case personal, but in the degree of explicitness of the theme. "I bear within me the exemplar of the human condition," said Montaigne. Descending deep enough within, the essayist links up personal with universal, self with self.

Writing and Reading

These essayists frequently write about their reading, and they love reading. They set, in fact, a model for writing about reading that is very different from writing-as-testing, because they have selected what to read according to their own ongoing pursuits, and, because they cite ideas and instances from books in mixture with ideas and instances drawn from everyday experience, thus fusing life with literature. Many openly framed assignments that I have long advocated will elicit from students exactly the kinds of essays that constitute our fine heritage in this flexible form. They call for the writer to crystallize memories, capture places, "write a narrative of any sort that makes a general point applying beyond the particular material," "put together three or four incidents drawn from life or reading that all seem to show the same thing, that are connected in your mind by some idea," or "make a general statement about something you have observed to be true, illustrating that truth by referring to events and situations you know or have read of." The point is to leave subject matter to the writer, including reading selections. Any student who has done such assignments will be better able, strictly as a bonus, to cough up some prose to show he has done his homework than if he has been especially trained to write about reading.

Transpersonal, Not Impersonal

Schools mistreat writing because the society suffers at the moment from drastic misunderstandings about the nature of knowledge. Applying "scientific" criteria that would be unacceptable to most real scientists making the breakthroughs out there on the frontier, many people have come to think that subtracting the self makes for

367

objectivity and validity. But depersonalization is not impartiality. It is, quite literally, madness. Einstein said, "The observer is the essence of the situation." It is not
by abandoning the self but by developing it that we achieve impartiality and validity.
The deeper we go consciously into ourselves, the better chance we have of reaching
universality, as Montaigne knew so well. Transpersonal, not impersonal. It is an
undeterred faith in this that makes a great writer cultivate his individuality until
others feel he speaks for them better than they do themselves. Teachers should be
the first to understand this misunderstanding and to start undoing it, so that schooling in general and writing in particular can offset rather than reinforce the problem.

Here are two examples of what we're up against—one from a famous current
encyclopedia and one from a leading publisher, typical and telling symptoms. Most
English majors probably sampled or at least heard of Sir Thomas Browne, a very
individualistic seventeenth-century master of an original prose style, a writer's writer
much admired by successors. Of his *Pseudodoxia Epidemica* Funk and Wagnalls
Standard Reference Encyclopedia says, "Its unscientific approach and odd assemblage of obscure facts typify his haphazard erudition," and then concludes the entry:
"Despite Browne's deficiencies as a thinker his style entitles him to high rank among
the masters of English prose." What this verdict tells me is that the writer of that
entry felt overwhelmed by all the books Browne had read that he had not and that
he knew far less than he should have known about the enormously important and
complex networks of thought and knowledge, called esoteric, that after several mil-
lenia of evolution still had great influence on Newton, Bacon, and Descartes (who
displayed at times equally "irrational" intellectual behavior). The encyclopediast's
judgment on such a writer as Browne is nothing but smart-ass chauvinism: permitted
to poison basic information sources, it makes "science" as deadly a censor as ever
the Church was during its Inquisition.

We can avoid producing Brownes in our school system by having all youngsters
read and write the same things—a goal we have closely approximated—and then
their approach will not be unscientific, their assemblage odd, their facts obscure, nor
their erudition haphazard. And we will have ensured that no one will be able to
emulate the great essayists we hold up as models (or even read them with any comprehension). Real essaying cannot thrive without cultivation of the individual. Who
would have any reason to read anyone else? (And I want to know how Browne's style
could be worth so much if he were merely raving.)

The second example is personal. When I received the edited manuscript of the
original edition of *Student-Centered Language Arts and Reading, K-13* back from the
publisher, I was aghast. "My" editor had rewritten sentences throughout the whole
book to eliminate first-person references and other elements of the author's presence
and voice. This included altering diction and sentence structure at times to get a
more anonymous or distanced effect. Faced with the appalling labor of restoring all
those sentences, I called the editor, furious. She said righteously, "But we always do
that—it's policy." It never occurred to her to exempt, or even to warn, an author
who wouldn't be publishing the book in the first place if he weren't regarded as some
kind of expert in writing.

Remove the Double Standard

You can't trust your encyclopedia, your publisher, your school administration. And
you can't trust yourself until you learn to spot how you too may be spreading the
plague, as Camus calls it. The double standard in "Look at the greats, but don't do

what they did" naturally goes along with our era of Scientific Inquisition, which is really technocratic plague. Teachers stand in a fine position to spread infection. If you let yourself be convinced that "personal" or "creative" writing is merely narcissistic, self-indulgent, and weak-minded, then you have just removed your own first person.

ESSAY: WHAT I THINK, WHAT I AM
Edward Hoagland

Our loneliness makes us avid column readers these days. The personalities in The New York Post, Chicago Daily News, San Francisco Chronicle constitute our neighbors now, some of them local characters but also the opinionated national stars. And movie reviewers thrive on our need for somebody emotional who is willing to pay attention to us and return week after week, year after year, through all the to-and-fro of other friends to flatter us by pouring out his (her) heart. They are essayists, as Elizabeth Hardwick is, James Baldwin was. We sometimes hear that essays are an old-fashioned form, that so-and-so is the "last essayist," but the facts of the marketplace argue quite otherwise. Essays of almost any kind are so much easier for a writer to sell now than short stories, so many more see print, it's odd that though two fine anthologies remain which publish the year's best stories, no comparable collection exists for essays. Such changes in the reading public's taste aren't always to the good, needless to say. The art of telling stories predated even cave-painting, surely; and if we ever find ourselves living in caves again, it (with painting) will be the only art left, after movies, novels, essays, photography, biography and all the rest have gone down the drain—the art to build from.

One has the sense with the short story form that while everything may have been done, nothing has been overdone: it has a permanence. Essays, if a comparison is to be made, although they go back 400 years to Montaigne, seem a newfangled, mercurial, sometimes hokey sort of affair which has lent itself to many of the excesses of the age from spurious autobiography to spurious hallucination, as well as the shabby careerism of traditional journalism. It's a greased pig. Essays are associated with the way young writers fashion a name—on plain crowded newsprint in hybrid vehicles like The Village Voice, Rolling Stone, The Soho Weekly News (also Fiction magazine), instead of the thick paper stock and thin readership of Partisan Review.

Essays, however, hang somewhere on a line between two sturdy poles: this is what I think, and this is what I am. Autobiographies which aren't novels are generally extended essays, indeed. A personal essay is like the human voice talking, its order the mind's natural flow, instead of a systematized outline of ideas. Though more wayward or informal than an article or treatise, somewhere it contains a point which is its real center, even if the point couldn't be expressed in fewer words than the essayist has employed. Essays don't usually "boil down" to a summary, as articles do, but on the other hand they have fewer "levels" than first-rate fiction—a flatter surface—because we aren't supposed to argue about their meaning. In the old distinction between teaching versus story-telling—however cleverly the author muddles it up—an essay is intended to convey the same point to each of us.

This emphasis upon mind speaking to mind is what makes essays less universal in their appeal than stories. They are addressed to an educated, perhaps a middle-class, reader, with certain presuppositions shared, a frame of reference, even a commitment to civility—not the grand and golden empathy inherent in every man which

369

the story-teller has a chance to tap. At the same time, of course, the artful "I" of an essay can be as chameleon as any narrator in fiction; and essays do tell a story just as often as a short story stakes a claim to a particular viewpoint.

Mark Twain's piece called "Corn-pone Opinions," for example, which is about public opinion, begins with a vignette as vivid as any in "Huckleberry Finn." When he was a boy of 15, Twain says, he used to hang out a back window and listen to the sermons preached by a neighbor's slave standing on top of a woodpile. The fellow "imitated the pulpit style of the several clergymen of the village, and did it well and with fine passion and energy. To me he was a wonder. I believed he was the greatest orator in the United States and would some day be heard from. But it did not happen; in the distribution of rewards he was overlooked. . . . He interrupted his preaching now and then to saw a stick of wood, but the sawing was a pretense—he did it with his mouth, exactly imitating the sound the bucksaw makes in shrieking its way through the wood. But it served its purpose, it kept his master from coming out to see how the work was getting along."

The extraordinary flexibility of essays is what has enabled them to ride out rough weather and hybridize into forms to suit the times. And just as one of the first things a fiction writer learns is that he needn't actually be writing fiction to write a short story—he can tell his own history or anyone else's as exactly as he remembers it and it will still be "fiction" if it remains primarily a story—an essayist soon discovers that he doesn't have to tell the whole truth and nothing but the truth, he can shape or shave his memories as long as the purpose is served of elucidating a truthful point. A personal essay frequently is not autobiographical at all, but what it does keep in common with autobiography is that, through its tone and tumbling progression, it conveys the quality of the author's mind. Nothing gets in the way. Because essays are directly concerned with the mind and its idiosyncrasy, the very freedom the mind possesses is bestowed on this branch of literature that does honor to it, and the fascination of the mind is the fascination of the essay.

Writing in the Disciplines

Our aim in this unit is to get you to do some thinking about the *differences* between the kinds of writing done in various disciplines and to help you understand the importance of learning to write within your chosen discipline. But we also want you to think about how all writing is alike: much of what makes for good sociological writing also makes for good natural-science writing. Nor can we say that a particular discipline has only one form of writing associated with it. Within each discipline there is a formal and an informal style (at the very least) and a style used for those in the field and for those out of the field. After all, it is important for specialists in any field to be able to talk to nonspecialists too. Yet common to those different styles (or "registers," to use a piece of jargon from linguistics) within each discipline is a *way of thinking* that is characteristic of that discipline: a way of arguing or an agreement about what counts as reasons and evidence. If you're interested in the theory behind our aims, you can turn to the "Ruminations and Theory" section of this unit.

We also have two important subsidiary aims in this unit: to help you become a better and more critical reader of texts in various disciplines and to help you make connections between what you learn in a writing class and what you learn in other classes.

Your assignment is to write a paper that analyzes and discusses the differences and similarities in the writing of various disciplines.

GETTING STARTED

A good way to begin to understand differences in the discourses of various disciplines is to look at several pieces of writing on the same subject.

371

Included in the "Readings" section of this unit are three articles about language acquisition. The first one is written by a linguist, Breyne Arlene Moskowitz; the second one by a psychologist, Roger Brown; and the third by Eric Lenneberg, a neurobiologist. As you read through these articles, record your reactions in your process journal. Don't edit these reactions; put down whatever comes into your head as you read, just as you do when you give a "movies of the mind" response to a classmate's paper (see *Sharing and Responding,* Section IV). Another way to analyze each piece is to put down in a semi-outline form what each paragraph or small section *says* and *does,* a strategy we describe in Section IIIC of *Sharing and Responding.* Using the thinking and writing generated by these two ways of responding, do some freewriting about all three essays. (If you want to see what this might look like, see the sample—based on a different piece—at the conclusion of this unit). Focus your freewriting on the following topics:

- Vocabulary. Every discipline has a specialized vocabulary composed both of discipline-specific words and words used in special ways. Can you pick out such words in the piece? Is there a large percentage of such words? How would you characterize the language in general? Does it tend more to the abstract or the concrete?

- Reasoning or thinking. What kinds of reasons or arguments does the author use?

- Evidence. What sort of information does the author give to back up what she or he is saying? Or does the author not feel the need to back it up?

- Assumptions. All writers make certain assumptions about what their audience knows. What assumptions is this author making? Point to specific segments which rely on unstated assumptions. Do you think these assumptions are specific to this piece, or do they seem to be assumptions which underlie the discipline itself?

- Structure. How does the writer organize material? Does she or he rely on logic as the structuring device? Does she or he tend to use partial summaries at the end of segments of the writing?

- Purpose. Why is the author writing this piece? to explain? to persuade?

- Relationship set up between the writer and you. You'll want to think about whether you feel like an audience for the piece. If so, is the author addressing you as a colleague, as a friend, as an educated lay person? And if not, who do you think the piece is written for? Do you think the writer is thinking of her or his audience as knowledgeable in the field? Or do you have a sense that the writer isn't making any attempt to establish contact with any audience at all?

- Personal and impersonal. How personal is the writer in the presentation of material? Is the writing completely impersonal, or can you identify spots where the writer becomes more personal—and figure out why? How does the personal or impersonal quality of the writing affect your response?

- Writer. What kind of person do you think the writer is? This question doesn't mean that you should go out and try to find out something about the author. What we're asking is that you try to characterize the writer on the basis of the piece of writing itself.

- Language. Are sentences complex in structure? Do they tend to be long or short? Does the author use straightforward language? Or does the author make use of figurative language at times? Point to specific spots.

- Evaluation. How would you describe the strengths and weaknesses of this piece of writing? Would people in all fields call these strengths and weaknesses?

- Comprehension. What is particularly puzzling for you: the language and vocabulary, your lack of background knowledge, an inability to understand the underlying assumptions or the purpose?

If there's time, either in class or out, you can share this preliminary writing with others who can help you come up with more raw material before you move to the next step, which requires you to draw conclusions from this raw material.

MOVING TO A DRAFT

Once you've done all this, you're ready to write up your conclusions. Remember the assignment: to figure out the differences and similarities between the writing and thinking in these three essays. To do this you can compare the various dimensions of the essays.

(But first we need to make a qualification. We've picked the three essays to be analyzed and have specified the fields in which they're written. The three authors are well respected in their disciplines, but we ourselves are not professionals in those fields and so cannot judge with authority that the essays are truly representative of all work in those disciplines. Even professionals would probably argue about the question of whether they were. Without having a description of the text features of the writing in a particular discipline, we cannot pick representative texts—if indeed, there are such. Students need to realize that, on the basis of these selections alone, they cannot make blanket statements about the discourses of linguistics, neurobiology, and psychology.)

As you write up your conclusions, consider the following:

- Language. Which of the essays uses language in the most specialized way?

- Thinking. Reasoning and arguing: what's different and similar about what each writer seems to value as the best kind of reasons or arguments? Evidence: what sorts of evidence does each essay use to put forth its ideas—very factual and numerical evidence or appeals to an audience's understanding of human nature?

- Assumptions. Which of the essays most (and least) seems to rely on unsaid assumptions? How do these assumptions differ from essay to essay?

- Writer-audience relationship. Audience stance: do the authors seem to be addressing you as an individual, or do they seem to be writing impersonally? Voice: which of the essays seems to have the most individualized personality? Personal responses: which of the essays do you respond to with the most appreciation and/or understanding and why?

- Structure. Do the essays seem to be structured in much the same way or in noticeably different ways?

- Strengths and weaknesses. Are they the same or different? How do they relate to the strengths and weaknesses of writing in other fields?

What we're asking you to do is difficult; it will require time and considerable thought. Because any task which asks you to do something new will puzzle you at first, we suggest that after you complete each part of this task, you set aside what you've done for a day if possible to get a break from it. When you come back to it, you'll probably understand more fully what your task is. In fact, you may want to reread one or more of the essays and do some more writing. But, whether you decide to do more writing or not, you should pull together what you've done and decide what parts of it you can benefit from sharing with your writing group. Because this is such an intense project, your teacher may have you work in pairs in class so there will be time for in-depth discussion of each person's project.

While you're doing all this writing and thinking and talking, you'll probably discover what you'd most like to use to fulfill the assignment for this unit. Basically, there are four general approaches you might use.

1. You can pick two of the essays and compare them.

2. You can pick one feature—reasoning and arguing and use of evidence, for example—and analyze the similarities and differences in all three essays.

3. You can practice writing within a particular discipline—something short, maybe three or four paragraphs—and then discuss what you've done. In other words, you'll be analyzing a piece of your own writing in light of what you can learn about the characteristics of writing in the discipline you've chosen. If you select this option, you'll need to analyze also at least

one piece of writing (but not a textbook) in the field you select—unless you choose one of the fields of the pieces we've asked you to analyze. You'll then have a basis for your piece, something to model it on. You may decide, for instance, to analyze a piece of art criticism and then write a short piece yourself. Your essay will focus on the traits of art-criticism writing as demonstrated in the short piece you wrote and in at least one other piece in the field.

4. A variation on this assignment is to write collaboratively with one or two other members of your class. You can pool your information and decide among yourselves which of the approaches just listed you'd like to take to the assignment.

Whichever approach you choose, you'll want to isolate whatever aspect or aspects seem specific to a particular discipline and whatever aspect or aspects seem similar to those of the other disciplines.

SUGGESTIONS FOR SHARING AND RESPONDING

As you share your writing with your partner or group, you'll want particularly to ask them to focus on whether you've attended carefully enough to features of discourse—*ways of thinking and writing.* Your focus should not be on *what* each essay says, but on *how* it says it and how it *reasons* about what it says. Your teacher may not be able to provide you with in-class time for feedback at all stages of this unit: after your initial freewriting, after your rough draft, and after your next-to-final draft. If not, try to get feedback outside class from a friend, family member, or writing-center tutor. The complexity of the assignment demands intense feedback. You can be sure that your professors who write for publication seek feedback at many stages during their work on important articles in their fields. You'll find Section IIB of *Sharing and Responding* helpful for this unit, particularly the parts which ask responders to tell you what the center of gravity is, what the piece *almost* says. In addition, you may find the following questions useful, both when you're sharing your earliest freewriting and your later first rough draft:

- What aspect of discourse do I seem to be most interested in? What aspect of discourse do I say the least about? Do I need to say more about it?

- Which essay do I give most attention to? Does this detract from what I'm doing? Do I need to give more attention to another or other essays?

- Have I given sufficient attention to the ways the writing is both different from and similar to all other kinds of writing?

- Do you see any structure latent within what I've written?

If there's time for oral or written response to a second draft, ask your readers to focus particularly on these questions:

- Is my piece coherent, that is, am I linking my assertions to one another or do they seem like scattered observations undirected to some common purpose?

- Have I used sufficient examples to demonstrate what I am saying? Or have I overdone examples and thus obscured my assertions?

- Do you think I have overlooked something relevant to my topic?

- Have I included a look at how the writing I'm analyzing shows features in common with all writing?

RUMINATIONS AND THEORY

Knowledge and Writing within Discipline Communities

One of the most important things you learn while you're in college is to speak and write in new ways. You've undoubtedly noticed yourself that the way people write about poems and stories is usually different from the way they write about atomic particles. It isn't just that the subject matter of the writing is different or even that the style is different. It's that the *kind* of writing and thinking is different; how the writer presents material differs from one subject to the next.

You need to learn to write in ways acceptable within various fields—particularly within the field of your chosen major. Learning to do this requires, of course, that you learn the subject matter: if you're majoring in physics, you have to learn a lot of physics. But in the process of doing that learning, you'll be learning the method; you'll absorb almost unconsciously the language and ways of thinking of physicists. You'll begin to use that language and thinking when you're talking about subjects within the field. You'll also begin to use them when you write about such subjects. A large part of being a good physicist is being comfortable with the *way* physicists

---

PROCESS BOX

Got my seminar paper back—professor said it was publishable, but I'd have to make the style "more academic." Gee, I thought my style was academic—what to do and how to get it more academic—haven't the slightest clue. The comment did make me feel a bit inferior.

PAT BELANOFF

talk and write about their subject. If this seems like a strange idea to you, we hope this unit helps you begin to understand what we're saying.

All this doesn't mean that you'll write *exactly* like other physicists; some of your personal ways of putting words and ideas together will stay with you. What happens is that you bring your own language to your major field; what you learn alters that language in certain ways, but your language also modifies the language of the discipline in certain ways. Even within physics—often considered one of the least subjective of sciences—writers have individual styles.

Most of your learning to use the methods of different academic disciplines may not occur till after your freshman year. But all of you will be taking courses in some of these disciplines during your first year in college; perhaps now you're taking a math course or an introductory psychology or sociology course. If so, you're already absorbing the language and thinking of these disciplines along with the knowledge. The real and essential "knowledge" *is* the language and thinking—not just some list of facts. If you write papers for the course, your professor will probably expect you to demonstrate that you have developed some skill in the ways of writing in that discipline.

You needn't actually worry about acquiring the language of a particular field: that happens gradually and usually imperceptibly. But you do need practice at it. That's why it's important for writing and speaking to be a part of all disciplines—from mathematics to philosophy.

As you begin to ingest the knowledge of a particular discipline, you're also and inevitably ingesting an understanding of how that discipline *creates knowledge* through the use of language. As you recreate that knowledge in your writing, you'll use the language and ways of thinking of that discipline. If, when you reach your senior year, you were to compare papers written in an advanced course in your major with papers you wrote in an introductory course in the same discipline, you'd probably be startled at the differences, differences which have been produced by small changes throughout your college years. You'll realize that you now sound more "academic" than you used to. But, even as a senior in your major—a "member" of the field—you will still find yourself making adjustments in your writing (after you've clarified ideas for yourself on paper): one set of adjustments for people in your field and another set of adjustments for nonacademics or academics not in your field. Given the increasing isolation of specialties in our society, we believe strongly that academics need to develop language that is accessible and comfortable for those not in their fields. Some of the very *best* scholars in a discipline often write in the most accessible way.

Within our field (the teaching of composition), we have a special language too—our own jargon. We've tried not to use too much of it in this book because it requires explanation. Also, if you're like us, you find it annoying when people in a particular field—one you're *not* in—use the language of that field in conversations with you. But in this unit, we do need to rely on one word which is often heard within our field: *discourse.* One of the ways this word is used is to designate the language of a particular discipline; you'll hear us and our cohorts talking about "the discourse features of sociological writing" or more succinctly, "the discourse of sociology." Discourse means both writing and speaking—both language and thinking.

So another way to say what we've been talking about is to say that you need, during your college days, to learn to use or enter into the discourses of a number of disciplines. That won't happen immediately, but it will happen if you spend a fair amount of time talking, writing, reading, listening, and learning within a particular discipline.

It may sound as though we're saying that first you get facts or ideas (about some subject, economics, for example), and then you make them conform to some artificial form deemed acceptable by economists. But this is far too simple a conclusion. In a very important sense, the way economists talk and write *creates* economic knowledge. Just as we saw in Unit 7 that a genre can lead you to see *new* facts and ideas, not just shape ideas you already have, so too a discipline can lead you to see *new* facts and ideas, not just shape ones you already have. Think of it this way: economists, psychologists, and mathematicians can all look at the same phenomena—for example, a space-shuttle disaster—and derive different knowledge. That knowledge is a product of their particular angle of vision, their kind of language and thinking, and their kind of questions. Consequently you can never truly write appropriately within a discipline until you have become immersed in its ways of perceiving, thinking, and constructing knowledge.

One further caveat. The modern university or college with its various departments is a fairly recent creation—at least viewed against hundreds of previous years of formalized education. Dividing knowledge up into segments—calling some physics, some philosophy, and so forth—is a human act. Since that's so, we need to leave room for the possibility of segmenting knowledge into different categories from the ones we now use. If all of us get locked into the language of our own fields, we're not so likely to see possibilities in the interaction of disciplines or for the creation of new disciplines.

Another problem with this strict departmentalization is one you may be experiencing: it's often difficult for you to integrate the pieces of your education. What you learn in one class often seems to have little relevance to what you learn in another class. This realization has led many universities and colleges to set up interdisciplinary courses where the interaction of science, art, religion, and history, for example, becomes evident.

The Other Side

Because of the close marriage between language and knowledge in any discourse field, many experts in the teaching of writing advocate abolishing freshman composition and having all writing occur within disciplinary or subject-matter classes. We don't agree. We think that there are certain things common to all writing. Chief among these is the process of writing things out for oneself—for one's *own* purposes—before adjusting that writing to others. How you go about doing this constitutes your personal writing process. But no matter what you're writing and for whom, you'll benefit from going through both these steps. It's too difficult to work things out for yourself and for others at the same time.

Thus attention to your writing process as *process* is essential. Perhaps you work things out best for yourself by freewriting (we do); but perhaps you find list-making more productive or drawing diagrams or meditating. Perhaps you use several of these on the same task. Perhaps you alter your ways of working out ideas according to what you're writing. Maybe you always do it the same way no matter what your subject. But there is one solid fact here: when you actually sit down to make something clear for yourself, it doesn't matter much if the stuff in your head comes from your personal experience, from reading in a textbook or professional magazine, or from lectures by your professor.

Once you've worked out something for yourself by whatever process you have discovered, you need to have processes for moving your writing toward an audience. Maybe you cut-and-paste, maybe you put aside what you've done for hours or days, maybe you read it or give it to someone for feedback, maybe you make one draft, maybe you make three or more. Again, whatever you do may be invariable—not dependent at all on your subject or audience. Or maybe you vary this part of your process according to what you're writing and for whom. As you become a better observer of your own writing and revising processes, you'll probably be fairly certain about some things you need to do: make sentences and paragraphs longer or shorter, keep an eagle eye for repetitiousness and slips in logic, check to see if you have too many or not enough examples, and so forth. How much of each of these you do may depend on whether your way of writing for yourself is closer to an academic style or closer to a casual style. Thus, depending on your audience, you may need to "academize" your writing or "unacademize" it. Our point is that attention to process is important. (If you've gotten this far in our textbook, we really didn't have to tell you that!)

This is what we believe to be common to all writing. Whether all writing shares certain features such as clarity, logic, voice, and so forth is a debate we're not entering at this point (though we think that there are certain common features in all good writing). The existence of language universals—truths which underlie *all* languages—has been debated for centuries. (Do all languages have ways of expressing subjects or agents of action? Do all languages have ways of expressing action apart from the agents of action? Do all languages have expressive, communicative, and persuasive capabilities?) That's another debate we hardly have room for. Here we're arguing something much less broad: that underlying any writing one does is a process for getting that writing done. Our aim in this book is to help you find *your* process.

Preliminary Analysis of "Dialect"

In writing the following responses to "Dialect" (the first selection in the "Readings" for this unit), we first wrote whatever came into our heads as we read and reread the selection. Afterwards we rearranged our thoughts to fit the questions we had set up earlier in the unit.

Vocabulary. Important for authors—want words to be used appropriately—spend lots of time on being sure "dialect" is understood. Start out not being very discipline specific—but later move into using things like "articulatory and acoustic and macro-linguistic." Also want to be sure "accent" is properly understood. "Accessible" in quotes, suggesting they want it to have special meaning. Don't know what "diatypes" are. "Interference" seems used in a discipline-specific way. Also "intermediate rules." Return to more generalized language at end.

Reasoning or Thinking. In first paragraph method of argument is to define—positively and negatively. Assertions supported by references to other authorities. Recognition that there's a community of thinkers on topic. Bring in examples. Return to authorities again in stuff about bilingual. Define ideolect and talk about how things affect that and cause change—most interested in getting rid of misconceptions. For example, they say what ideolect is and then qualify it by saying it changes over time and even within purposes and such. Define quite a bit by what something is not. Why? A way of isolating and delimiting their topic?

Evidence. Authorities in citations. Example from Appendix—makes it sound like there's scientific tables or some such—shows need to make evidence available. Appeals to personal experience of reader—makes that valid. For many of assertions, no evidence. Studies count as evidence. Words properly used can become evidence.

Assumptions. That readers think "dialect" is negative term. That assumption probably underlies linguistics in general—not just this piece. Assume that I know that some people have ranked dialects according to aesthetic or psychological traits (how could someone do the latter?) Assume that I might think ideolects don't change. Assume that someone has shown that there is no such thing as linguistic "goodness." Main assumption that "dialect" is often not used the way authors want it to be used. Assume that it's necessary first to dispel wrong notions before putting forth right ones.

Structure. General introduction to dialect—clear away what it isn't. Describe different categories of dialect and end up with "ideolect" which has traits of all other kinds of dialects. [We cut the central portions of the essay.] Structure builds up to this and thus seems to give it added importance in some way.

Purpose. To explain, although right at the end—the last sentence—there's a feel of persuasion.

Relationship Set Up between the Writer and You. Don't particularly feel like an audience for this piece. Authors are addressing us as colleagues—they think of audience as knowledgeable in the field. Have a sense that the writers are trying to establish contact with an audience; they want to make it possible for the audience to understand them—for what they say to be clear. They could have just started out, after all, by not bothering to explain at all the ways they use "dialect." Beyond the first paragraphs, they become more personal, appealing to personal experience and to my desire to have a linguistic identity. We feel that they know that would make us sympathetic. So relationship changes—at first, they're cold and impersonal, and when they get to end of talking about ideolect, they—appropriately we suppose—become more personal, more human sounding.

Personal and Impersonal. Don't see any slips into personal in first paragraphs. Impersonal comes through in such phrases as "So it is not the custom in linguistics." Makes us feel as though we're dealing with something very scientific—very measurable and categorizable. First paragraph holds us back from considering language and dialect as we usually think of them—not as precise as they wish it would be. Authors make language seem quite precise. We wonder about nonspecialized public—is that us? Poor country cousin—a bit folksier. Become more personal in "Most of us"—awareness of personal element in lives of people. It feels more human at the end then at the beginning. Does scientific beginning lure us into accepting everything after as equally scientific?

Writer. Authors are middle-aged or older—they've done a fair amount of writing in the field—probably teachers because of the care they take in explaining terms. They consider themselves scientists—we've read impassioned pleas about dialect and reasons not to belittle it, which are humanly, socially based. This is more "objective" sounding. But they're smart people. As read further, begin to sense some personal commitment to their concepts which is more than scientific. Don't like sneer about feminism.

Language. At the beginning sentences are complex in structure: see particularly the last sentence of the first paragraph and the second sentence of that paragraph. Sentences mainly long. Language is pretty straightforward—nothing figurative here. But becomes less formal and scientific sounding later. Notice paragraph beginning "Variation within an idiolect"; authors seem quite scientific in way they say this, but then they restate it in language which is more everyday sounding: "The things we do and the activities we indulge in will influence the choice of words we use." Somehow this doesn't seem necessary for an audience of colleagues—so maybe they're addressing a wider audience than that. As language gets less scientific, it becomes more directed to lay people. Perhaps "poor country cousin" brings up certain connotations that most of the language doesn't. We get a picture of a country boy, a rube, a hick, standing in the middle of a corn field, holding a rake. Appeals to my ear—maybe it's the alliteration? Basically doesn't want the magic that comes from metaphor—although last sentence uses something which may still have metaphoric force: mirror.

Evaluation. Strengths of the language: clear introduction to what is going to be included in what follows. Makes us feel that they really know what they're talking about. Language is mostly abstract—specificity only in citing articles—we guess that's a kind of specificity. Get the feeling that they're using terms like "culturally non-biased" with precision—that they've worked with these terms for some time and have adopted certain ways of saying things as being the most precise and concise. Another strength is that language becomes less scientific whenever authors appeal to experience of audience—style and content work well together in this way. Weaknesses of language in that the sentences at the beginning are long and there's that one vague place: what does "speaker's place on dimensions" mean—does this phrase go with language habits or with what follows? Language at the beginning turns us off a bit—don't particularly want to read on: it's cold and impersonal—we feel alienated—that's straightened out a bit by the end. Another strength: makes just about every word count—possible exception is "or enlightening" and the sentence before where they seem to be repeating themselves for a lay audience. How often does that occur? Should check it.

Comprehension. Main problem in accepting this would be in knowing whether or not authors have interpreted their authorities correctly. Since we don't know these pieces, we can't judge that. If authors are misinterpreting (or if other interpretations are possible), this would rather undermine the whole piece since they seem to be establishing a foundation. Puzzled by some of the vocabulary—things like "diatypes." Bigger puzzle is to work out cold scientific tone at beginning and more personal, somewhat persuasive, tone at the end. Is it because they're discussing personal language and it's important for them that there be such a thing? Other than stuff about citations, we seem to have enough background to understand most of this.

READINGS

DIALECT
Michael Gregory and Susanne Carroll

Cornwall: What mean'st by this?
Kent: To go out of my dialect, which you discommend so much.
                                                            King Lear

Those characteristic features of language which we relate to different users of a language are categorized as dialectal. By this term we make no reference to the 'quality' of a variety; a dialect is not necessarily less complete, less logical, less 'language' than a language. Ranking varieties in terms of aesthetic or psychological traits has not proved to be productive or enlightening, for the notion of linguistic 'goodness' has been shown to be nebulous. There seems to be no objective, culturally non-biased way of measuring it (Martinet, 1965). So it is not the custom in linguistics to use the term dialect as a pejorative term for 'lesser' types of language (cf. Haugen, 1966); we will be using it to refer to the relationships of language habits with the speaker's place on dimensions of individuality, time, place, social class and speech community.

If the non-specialist public have a tendency to think of dialect as language's poor country cousin, they also tend to confuse dialect and accent. Accent normally refers to articulatory and acoustic features of language while dialect refers to the totality of lexical, grammatical and phonological features. Dialect therefore incorporates accent but remains distinct from it. It can be thought of as the user's macro-linguistic identity defining him in terms of birthplace, class, education and age. So while a person's accent may initially be the most striking aspect of his language, that of which we are consciously and immediately aware, it comprises only a part of the variation possible.

Temporal Dialects

The categorization of language into temporal dialects is a traditional, and seemingly natural, part of linguistic study. When we read *Sir Gawain and the Green Knight,* or a play by G. B. Shaw, we are aware of varying differences between our own language and that of both the authors; differences which cannot be attributed entirely to *genre* or to the peculiarities of the authors' styles. The indexical markers may be subtle differences in meaning or they may be quite glaring grammatical distinctions. The following passage from Shakespeare's *Romeo and Juliet* may illustrate (Act I, sc. 1):

SAMPSON: Gregory, o' my word, we'll not carry coals.

GREGORY: No, for then we should be colliers.

SAMPSON: I mean, an we be in choler we'll draw.

GREGORY: Ay, while you live, draw your neck out o' the collar.

SAMPSON: I strike quickly, being mov'd.

GREGORY: But thou art not quickly mov'd to strike.

SAMPSON: A dog of the house of Montague moves me.

GREGORY: To move is to stir, and to be valiant is to stand, therefore if thou art mov'd, thou runn'st away.

The distinction of second-person polite and second-person informal as realized in the pronominal contrast 'thou'/'you' and its corresponding verb forms 'art'/ 'runn'st' and 'are'/'run' no longer exists in modern English. Where these forms are used distinctively today they are related to a stylistic decision for or against archaism. Less obvious perhaps is the use of the word 'house' for 'family' and the prepositional phrase 'of Montague' for the pre-placed possessive form 'Montague's house'. The punning centring on the various meanings of 'move' also seems a little dated. The meaning of the passage is, however, reasonably transparent in spite of features such as 'an' (modern English 'if'). The same could not be said for the following text from Old English (Early English Text Society, 1891, pp. 220–1):

Þissum tidum Middlengle Peadan Pendan sunu Þæs cyniges Cristes geleafan 7 sodfæstnisse geryne enfengen. Waes he Peada ging ædeling good 7 cyninges nomon 7 hada welwyrde; 7 se fæder him fordon rice fesealde Þære Þeode.

The Germanic origins of English are perhaps more evident in this second text, a fact which unfortunately does not render the text more comprehensible for most contemporary users of English. It needs translating:

At this time the Middle Angles, with Peada, son of King Penda, received the faith of Christ and the mysteries of the truth. Paeda was an excellent young prince, well worthy of the name and rank of king; and for this reason his father made over to him the government of that people.

Both these texts are written, and much of our understanding of temporal dialects comes from an examination of the written word. This technique has its limitations since we can gain only limited information about the sound systems of earlier periods (from such features as variation in spellings, and spelling 'errors') and since we do not have available for study those language activities which were not deemed worthy of written record. Naturally the study of pre-literate language remains speculative. Linguistics has therefore greatly benefited from the development of tape-recording techniques which capture what is said as it is spoken. Such techniques have made for more accurate articulatory and prosodic phonetics and have permitted a more rapid development of the study of language variation, intra- and inter-individual.

Language forms a continuum in time so that when we look back at a given period it is not possible to determine precisely when one temporal dialect begins and another ends. Diachronic variation, the variable use of features from two different temporal dialects, must occur as change spreads. Traditionally, linguists have maintained that such change could not be directly observed. At best, it was felt, only the successive stages of the progression could be observed, much in the way we note that the hands of a clock have moved without seeing the movement. However, recent work on pidgins and creoles (and what has been called by some 'the post-creole continuum') has led to the development of dynamic models of language. Instead of relegating variables to a 'free variation' waste-basket, specific features are now being described in terms of the trends they typify, particularly as features spread from age group to age group, or class to class (cf. Bickerton, 1973; Smith, 1973). By looking at the differences in dialects of different periods and at the differences in the speech of successive generations the linguist can determine whether a variable is spreading or receding in the community.

Descriptive terms like 'Old', 'Modern' or 'Contemporary' English do not, then, refer to exact periods of time but rather to progressive stages of development. These epithets are used as well to categorize temporal varieties of other languages at quite different dates. Old English is reputed to have ended at about 1150 but Old French was still spoken in the 1300s. Because the impetus for linguistic change is embedded in the social matrix, change will be dependent on the kinds of social pressures exerted upon various sub-groups. The evolutionary timetables for different languages will therefore be culturally determined and not coterminous.

Change may be sudden and abrupt, like the generalization of aeronautic jargon in American English: 'take-off', 'blast-off', 'spacewalk', and so on. It may also be gradual—the anglicization of some minority groups in the northern parts of Canada or its West has taken several generations because of their relative isolation and the institutional independence of their anglophone neighbours. Change may originate in the upper echelons or in the lower: 'franglais' in France, the borrowing of English lexical items and pronunciations, is largely a middle-class phenomenon, but in Canada it begins largely in the lower class.

Change affects us all as individuals and as members of social groups. Our language develops as we do; we do not speak at fifty as we did at five. The ageing politician trying to impress his younger constituents with his capacity to understand their problems may pepper his discourse with expressions and slang from a succeeding generation. His attempts at 'image-building' testify to associations of language and philosophy, language and behaviour. Differences in language will reflect increased knowledge (learning about baseball or *haute cuisine* involves learning how to talk about them), or greater experience, personal ambitions, and individual mobility (so that if we want to fit into a group we will model our language, consciously or unconsciously, along appropriate lines).

If language change is viewed as a type of evolutionary process it cannot be interpreted as being determined entirely by 'natural', universal laws. On the contrary, we have suggested that change is rooted in social processes. This is illustrated by the development of pidgins and creoles. Pidgins are structurally simplified, functionally undifferentiated languages which develop in contact situations between linguistically disparate groups. This contact situation is different from other kinds (immigration, conquest, etc.) in that individual bilingual intermediaries are lacking, so that intergroup communication depends upon the use of a simplified 'mixed' language. In certain situations the pidgin can become the mother tongue of some element of the groups involved. This necessitates lexical expansion and functional differentiation of the pidgin. The new language resulting from this process is the creole (cf. Todd, 1974). Pidgins and creoles have often been looked upon as only marginally interesting but are now evoking great interest among linguists because they indicate some of the processes by which change occurs at the individual level and at the level of the community. They provide excellent examples of diachronic, or temporal, and synchronic variation (regional or social variation within a given temporal framework) (cf. Smith, 1973). . . .

Idiolect

Idiolect differs from other categories in that it reflects all of them at once. The uniqueness of an individual's speech comes not by abstracting features of temporal, geographical, social and standard or non-standard dialect but rather from the configuration of these features.

Idiolect is a more 'accessible' variety than the others since abstractions made are characteristic of a single speaker and not those features shared by many. This 'accessibility', however, does not make idiolect easier to isolate and describe. On the contrary, linguistic individuality may be more difficult to isolate simply because it is the consequence of the inter-relationships of the other dialects and of the range of diatypes controlled by the individual.

Most of us will recognize favourite expressions that we use habitually or that we hear others using. But we may also have preferences or tendencies to use specific syntactic forms and typical pronunciations. Looking at an isolated segment from the Appendix, we note that while both speakers are asking questions and requesting information, D seems to prefer interrogatives using modals and rising intonation, Wh- constructions, or inversion and rising intonation:

D: do you want any more ↗

D: do you want me to hand you the thing Gilles ↗

D: what can I do for you ↗

D: can I help you ↗

S, on the other hand, seems to prefer structurally simplified utterances where interrogation is marked only by intonation:

S: two ↗

S: coffee ↗

S: oui, Marie ↗

These examples are cited merely to illustrate how speech can vary between individuals. The isolation and description of an idiolect would naturally require a detailed examination of a much larger corpus.

Variation in individual speech can also be part and parcel of learning another language. Since most of us know our mother tongue better than a second language, we are likely to borrow structures, words and meanings from our first language as we learn the second (L_2). At the same time bilinguals may be less likely to naturalize elements borrowed from other languages and may introduce foreign lexical items into their discourse.

When a person attempts to become bilingual he must learn new rules which constitute the L_2 (rules encoding and organizing meaning into sound). When interference occurs it indicates that the learning process is incomplete. The learner may also produce utterances which are aberrant but which cannot be said to be interference. These may be produced because the learner has developed intermediate rules, what Selinker (1974) has called 'interlanguage' and Nemser (1974) has termed 'approximate systems'. As a speaker becomes more fluent in the L_2 his rule-governed output, his interlanguage, will replicate to an increasing degree what the native speaker would use.

Variation within an idiolect will also reflect developmental processes of the individual as he 'learns' his own language. It will reflect personal experience certainly and also changes in values and ideology. The things we do and the activities we indulge in will influence the choice of words we use. The *vendeuse* whose sales pitch includes epithets like 'fabulous', 'stunning' or 'superb', expects those words to produce a specific effect on a client. But the choice between those words and saying, 'Oh, isn't that nice!' will undoubtedly reflect the personality of the individual implicated.

As change occurs at the social level it will be reflected in the way the individual chooses to express himself. The 'four-letter word' is no longer restricted to back rooms or to the boys who inhabit them. Nice ladies are no longer defined by their avoidance of 'foul' language. In a similar vein minority groups and 'libbers', aware of the psychological power of denigratory terms like 'nigger', 'wop', or 'Mick' approach the problem of changing attitudes at the level of individual speech. Hence the activity of anti-defamation leagues and those who would rid us of the word 'man'.

It would be difficult to describe an idiolect on the basis of a single text or even from texts taken from a single period of a person's life. In a sense we possess several styles over the course of a lifetime, each one a typical reflection of our individuality.

Normally an unconscious reflection of experience, idiolect can also be manipulated, like other variables, for creative, humorous purposes. The mimic selects and often exaggerates those features we associate with a famous celebrity, and for the writer, the conscious perfection of literary style is a necessary part of the craft. The conscious style can take on an existence in addition to idiolect when the latter becomes parody or caricature. Lillian Ross (1961, pp. 57–8), in her biography of Ernest Hemingway, may have done more to perpetuate the myth than to expose the reality, notably the public image of Hemingway as the tough novelist emanating *machismo:*

> I began to learn to read French by reading the A.P. story in the French paper after reading the American A.P. story, and finally learned to read it by reading accounts of things I had seen—les événements sportifs—and from that and les

crimes it was only a jump to Dr. de Maupassant, who wrote about things I had seen or could understand. Dumas, Daudet, Stendhal, who when I read him I knew that was the way I wanted to be able to write. Mr. Flaubert who always threw them perfectly straight, hard, high and inside. Then Mr. Baudelaire, that I learned my knuckle ball from, and Mr. Rimbaud, who never threw a fast ball in his life. Mr. Gide and Mr. Valéry I couldn't learn from. I think Mr. Valéry was too smart for me. Like Jack Britton and Benny Leonard.

Variation is a natural part of everyday linguistic intercourse. We change our habits to accommodate the people who surround us and to meet the circumstances in which we find ourselves. This is the type of variation which will concern us in the rest of this book—diatypic variation; language-in-situation. But let us not forget that what we say is an indication of who we are as individuals, although even as unique persons our habits are neither fixed nor stable but mirror the constant variability of environment and attitude which makes up our lives.

NOTES FOR ESSAY ON *SPORTS ILLUSTRATED* AND *PSYCHOLOGY TODAY* ARTICLES
Paul Ivanisin

Sports Illustrated Article

Vocabulary. Simple, down-to-earth. A few "catch phrases" related to sports. "Kick the Bat"—"Turn 1 at Indy"—"on the mound"—"Never mention a no-hitter in the dug-out"—"slump"—"Take Grounder"—"Do windsprints"—"Arrange pine tar, weighted doughnut and resin," etc.

Reasoning/Thinking. Doesn't really make an argument one way or the other. States facts, infers coincidences, relates stories. Doesn't really assert an opinion, but from the way the piece is written, it sounds as though he's making fun of the superstitions. Takes extreme cases of superstition to exaggerate.

Evidence. Since author is not making an overt point, he doesn't really use evidence. Relates extreme stories to imply how silly superstition is but doesn't overtly say it.

Assumptions. Author assumes that audience is mainly sports fans—that they have moderate knowledge of players and teams and sports references. Most sports writers assume same thing unless they know they're writing for non-sports-lovers.

Structure. First few paragraphs start with "The next time . . ." Presents a general view of superstition. Then a few more examples. Then background information. A few more examples and then a summary interview.

Purpose. Author wrote article to show lengths some athletes go to for superstition. Tries to show how silly some are but doesn't necessarily argue against them. More of an explanatory/satirical piece.

Personal/Impersonal. Author personal in beginning—"The next time you're . . . " Not much more personal in the rest of the piece.

Writer. Sounds like Bob Uecker, "Hey, sports-fans! I love ya!"

Language. Not really long sentences, more quick-to-the-punch. Mostly straightforward language but some figurative language as listed above in vocabulary.

Comprehension. I don't understand the author's main point. He's making fun of superstitions but not in a negative way. He doesn't say whether he thinks they work or not.

Psychology Today Article

Vocabulary. "observed," "fetishes," "fatalistic," "deity to intercede," "carrel," "pre-literate," "alleviate," "empirically." Words like this occur often. Definitely more "educated" than *SI* article. Directed toward people with some background in education as opposed to sports.

Reasoning/Thinking. Because magic has never been proven to exist, the authors explain it as giving a sense of control and boosted confidence—which may have improved their performance.

Evidence. The evidence used doesn't necessarily prove point. Surveys just proved that a lot of college students use magic and that it makes most of them feel better. The authors don't address the problem of whether magic works or not. They don't discuss the success ratio of the people who used magic.

Assumptions. Authors assume that audience knows implications of things like ESP and supernatural. Also that the audience "realizes" that magic doesn't work. Also assume that audience understands how anxiety works. Not all these assumptions specific to psychology.

Structure. Starts out with an introduction about a certain group of people who believed in magic and continues this train of thought throughout the piece. Does tend to use partial summary after getting into main body of piece. Summaries include some background information.

Purpose. To persuade that magic only helps in so far as it relieves stress in order to make people perform more efficiently.

Relationship. I don't feel like an audience for this piece because the article sounds like it was written for someone who's interested in psychology—possibly for someone interested in becoming a psychologist—or just for someone interested in magic.

Personal/Impersonal. The closest these authors come to being personal is when they say "we" ("We call it magic"). Other than that they are completely impersonal.

Writers. Analytical and a little bit arrogant.

Language. Straightforward sentences, not extremely long, semi-complex.

COMPARING ESSAYS IN *SPORTS ILLUSTRATED* AND *PSYCHOLOGY TODAY*
Paul Ivanisin

When I first thought about writing a paper comparing *Sports Illustrated* to *Psychology Today*, I was hard pressed to think of any similarities. Now that I've read the two articles "Green Cars, Black Cats, and Lady Luck" and "Can a Lucky Charm Get You Through Organic Chemistry," I've discovered that they're not that different. Sure, the subject matter and styles of writing might be a little different but there are more similarities than I would've expected. The structure and assumptions made by the articles are very similar in some respects and the differences between the two are based more on the type of audience they're addressing.

I expected the *Sports Illustrated* article to be written for an avid sports fan. No foot-long words. No intricate, paragraph-filling sentences. And that's just what I found. The article is easy to understand, although some of the references to sports-figures and sports-terms are somewhat obscure. The language is simple and slightly figurative. The writer spiced up his article with catch-phrases like " . . . superstition isn't all rabbits-feet and four-leaf-clovers." Although the writer is trying to reach a wide range of readers, his use of sports lingo like "kick the bag," "Turn 1 at Indy," "on the mound," and especially "Arrange the pine tar, weighted doughnut and resin" severely limits his audience.

The *Psychology Today* article, on the other hand, started out with a very limited audience. While the article doesn't use any extremely long words, it is much less personal and didn't make any attempt at spicing up the information. I expected this also. Psychology magazines like *Psychology Today* are not known for their satire. This article presented its information in the form of charts and figures based on those charts, while the *Sports Illustrated* article uses anecdotes. This is logical considering the audiences each article is addressing. The *Psychology Today* article is addressing professional people like other psychologists, and the *Sports Illustrated* article is addressing amateurs and even those who don't participate in the sports field at all. Words like "fetishes," "fatalistic," and "empirically" are not the kind of words you would find in a sports article to spice it up. They are, however, used in the psychology article. The audience for psychology magazines would be more interested in facts and figures than sports fans would, unless the sports fan was looking for statistics on his favorite sports hero—and even then, the facts would probably be embellished by a story or two.

The only other way that the two articles differ is in the type of evidence presented. The *Sports Illustrated* article appeals more to human nature than the psychology paper. The sports article uses amusing anecdotes to convince the readers that superstition is silly at times, whereas the *Psychology Today* article uses its statistics and charts to draw a direct conclusion. Instead of trying to convince the reader outright, the *Sports Illustrated* article gives extreme examples of rituals and leads the reader to the conclusion indirectly. The psychology article is more direct in its linking of evidence to conclusion.

As for the other features of writing, the two articles don't differ very much. Both articles make the same assumption that magic and superstition have no scientific basis for belief and superstition only helps to alleviate stress under extreme situations. The structures of both articles are basically the same. Each one gives examples of certain kinds of rituals and then gives reasons for the rituals. They also give background on certain types of rituals, their origins and how they came to be practiced today. In fact, most of the differences between the articles arise from the need to address two different audiences. These two articles say basically the same thing: Superstition and magic only help in so far as they give people a sense of control. The only difference is that the articles state this in different terms.

WRITER-AUDIENCE RELATIONSHIPS IN THREE ESSAYS ON SUPERSTITION
Maura Foley

I found the essay from *Sports Illustrated* ("Green Cars, Black Cats, and Lady Luck") to be the most loose and free-flowing of the three essays about superstition and luck. Athletes and sports enthusiasts will be the ones to find this article most appealing because they can relate their own experiences with those of a few well-known sports personalities. I found myself responding to this article more than to the others because I play competitive tennis and I have many superstitions when I play.

The writer of this article made an immediate effort to establish contact with the reader. We see this in the very first line, "The next time you're at a baseball game, watch the first base coach. . . ." The writer goes through this article much as though he were telling stories to a friend. His voice is relaxed and conversational, especially compared to the article from *Current Anthropology* ("Uncertainty and the Use of Magic"). Reading the *Sports Illustrated* piece, I felt as though I were attending a sports event with the writer, with him telling me background stories and even gossip about the superstitions of various athletes. The writer-audience relationship here is very direct and, as it were, one-on-one. I feel as though I know the writer well, so his personal style of writing proved to be effective. As I was reading I could see the writer joking with me at certain points, then being serious at other times. His voice was also so personal that I was able to imagine how he would sound. I heard him putting emphasis on certain words as he spoke.

The other two articles (from *Current Anthropology* and *Psychology Today*) also used superstition as their topic. However, they examined superstition in general rather than just in sports. Although these two articles use the same factual material (after all the articles were written by the same authors and based on the same research), they differ in terms of the voice used and the audience implied.

In the *Psychology Today* article ("Can a Lucky Charm Get You Through Organic Chemistry"), Felson and Gmelch occasionally include themselves in the audience. For example they say, "How do *we* handle. . . ." In speaking this way, they are not only speaking to the audience but at the same time associating themselves as part of it. This is effective in bringing an audience closer to the writer. People are going to pay attention and be more responsive to a writer if they can relate to him.

This piece seems to be directed at college students, but it seems clear to me that the writers are speaking to more than one person (especially from the use of the first-person plural throughout the article). I envision a man at a podium speaking to a medium-sized group. He is quite knowledgeable on his topic and does a nice job of relating to his audience on a personal level.

When Felson and Gmelch write for *Current Anthropology,* we see a change in the voice they use. They take an impersonal approach and come across to the reader as abrupt and to the point. It sounds as though they are making a technical presentation on the subject of luck and superstition to their professional colleagues. The voice makes me see a person at the head of a long table with his charts and notes, talking carefully about his findings in his study. Although the writing is clear and well organized here, the general public will be less interested in this piece because it lacks the personal quality of the other two articles.

THE ACQUISITION OF LANGUAGE
Breyne Arlene Moskowitz

An adult who finds herself in a group of people speaking an unfamiliar foreign language may feel quite uncomfortable. The strange language sounds like gibberish: mysterious strings of sound, rising and falling in unpredictable patterns. Each person speaking the language knows when to speak, how to construct strings and how to interpret other people's strings, but the individual who does not know anything about the language cannot pick out separate words or sounds, let alone discern meanings. She may feel overwhelmed, ignorant and even childlike. It is possible that she is returning to a vague memory from her very early childhood, because the the experience of an adult listening to a foreign language comes close to duplicating the experience of an infant listening to the "foreign" language spoken by everyone around her. Like the adult, the child is confronted with the task of learning a language about which she knows nothing.

The task of acquiring language is one for which the adult has lost most of her aptitude but one the child will perform with remarkable skill. Within a short span of time and with almost no direct instruction the child will analyze the language completely. In fact, although many subtle refinements are added between the ages of five and 10, most children have completed the greater part of the basic language-acquisition process by the age of five. By that time a child will have dissected the language into its minimal separable units of sound and meaning; she will have discovered the rules for recombining sounds into words, the meanings of individual words and the rules for recombining words into meaningful sentences, and she will have internalized the intricate patterns of taking turns in dialogue. All in all she will have established herself linguistically as a full-fledged member of a social community, informed about the most subtle details of her native language as it is spoken in a wide variety of situations.

The speed with which children accomplish the complex process of language acquisition is particularly impressive. Ten linguists working full time for 10 years to analyze the structure of the English language could not program a computer with the ability for language acquired by an average child in the first 10 or even five years of life. In spite of the scale of the task and even in spite of adverse conditions—emotional instability, physical disability and so on—children learn to speak. How do they go about it? By what process does a child learn language?

What Is Language?

In order to understand how language is learned it is necessary to understand what language is. The issue is confused by two factors. First, language is learned in early childhood and adults have few memories of the intense effort that went into the learning process, just as they do not remember the process of learning to walk. Second, adults do have conscious memories of being taught the few grammatical rules that are prescribed as "correct" usage, or the norms of "standard" language. It is difficult for adults to dissociate their memories of school lessons from those of true language learning, but the rules learned in school are only the conventions of an educated society. They are arbitrary finishing touches of embroidery on a thick fabric of language that each child weaves for herself before arriving in the English teacher's classroom. The fabric is grammar: the set of rules that describe how to structure language.

The grammar of language includes rules of phonology, which describe how to put sounds together to form words; rules of syntax, which describe how to put words together to form sentences; rules of semantics which describe how to interpret the meaning of words and sentences, and rules of pragmatics, which describe how to participate in a conversation, how to sequence sentences and how to anticipate the information needed by an interlocutor. The internal grammar each adult has constructed is identical with that of every other adult in all but a few superficial details. Therefore each adult can create or understand an infinite number of sentences she has never heard before. She knows what is acceptable as a word or a sentence and what is not acceptable, and her judgments on these issues concur with those of other adults. For example, speakers of English generally agree that the sentence "Ideas green sleep colorless furiously" is ungrammatical and the sentence "Colorless green ideas sleep furiously" is grammatical but makes no sense semantically. There is similar agreement on the grammatical relations represented by word order. For example, it is clear that the sentences "John hit Mary" and "Mary hit John" have different meanings although they consist of the same words, and that the sentence "Flying planes can be dangerous" has two possible meanings. At the level of individual words all adult speakers can agree that "brick" is an English word, that "blick" is not an English word but could be one (that is, there is an accidental gap in the adult lexicon, or internal vocabulary) and that "bnick" is not an English word and could not be one. . . .

An event that revolutionized linguistics was the publication in 1957 of Noam Chomsky's *Syntactic Structures.* Chomsky's investigation of the structure of grammars revealed that language systems were far deeper and more complex than had been suspected. And of course if linguistics was more complicated, then language learning had to be more complicated. In the 21 years since the publication of *Syntactic Structures* the disciplines of linguistics and child language have come of age. The study of the acquisition of language has benefited not only from the increasingly sophisticated understanding of linguistics but also from the improved understanding of cognitive development as it is related to language. The improvements in recording technology have made experimentation in this area more reliable and more detailed, so that investigators framing new and deeper questions are able to accurately capture both rare occurrences and developing structures.

The picture that is emerging from the more sophisticated investigations reveals the child as an active language learner, continually analyzing what she hears and proceeding in a methodical, predictable way to put together the jigsaw puzzle of language. Different children learn language in similar ways. It is not known how many processes are involved in language learning, but the few that have been observed appear repeatedly, from child to child and from language to language. All the examples I shall discuss here concern children who are learning English, but identical processes have been observed in children learning French, Russian, Finnish, Chinese, Zulu and many other languages.

Children learn the systems of grammar—phonology, syntax, semantics, lexicon and pragmatics—by breaking each system down into its smallest combinable parts and then developing rules for combining the parts. In the first two years of life a child spends much time working on one part of the task, disassembling the language to find the separate sounds that can be put together to form words and the separate words that can be put together to form sentences. After the age of two the basic process continues to be refined, and many more sounds and words are produced. The other part of language acquisition—developing rules for combining the basic elements of language—is carried out in a very methodical way: the most general rules are hypothesized first, and as time passes they are successively narrowed down by the addition of more precise rules applying to a more restricted set of sentences. The procedure is the same in any area of language learning, whether the child is acquiring syntax or phonology or semantics. For example, at the earliest stage of acquiring negatives a child does not have at her command the same range of negative structures that an adult does. She has constructed only a single very general rule: Attach "no" to the beginning of any sentence constructed by the other rules of grammar. At this stage all negative sentences will be formed according to that rule.

Throughout the acquisition process a child continually revises and refines the rules of her internal grammar, learning increasingly detailed subrules until she achieves a set of rules that enables her to create the full array of complex, adult sentences. The process of refinement continues at least until the age of 10 and probably considerably longer for most children. By the time a child is six or seven, however, the changes in her grammar may be so subtle and sophisticated that they go unnoticed. In general children approach language learning economically, devoting their energy to broad issues before dealing with specific ones. They cope with clear-cut questions first and sort out the details later, and they may adopt any one of a variety of methods for circumventing details of a language system they have not yet dealt with.

Prerequisites for Language

Although some children verbalize much more than others and some increase the length of their utterances much faster than others, all children overgeneralize a single rule before learning to apply it more narrowly and before constructing other less widely applicable rules, and all children speak in one-word sentences before they speak in two-word sentences. The similarities in language learning for different children and different languages are so great that many linguists have believed at one time or another that the human brain is preprogrammed for language learning. Some linguists continue to believe language is innate and only the surface details of the particular language spoken in a child's environment need to be learned. The speed with which children learn language gives this view much appeal. As more parallels between language and other areas of cognition are revealed, however, there is greater reason to believe any language specialization that exists in the child is only one aspect of more general cognitive abilities of the brain.

Whatever the built-in properties the brain brings to the task of language learning may be, it is now known that a child who hears no language learns no language, and that a child learns only the language spoken in her environment. Most infants coo and babble during the first six months of life, but congenitally deaf children have been observed to cease babbling after six months, whereas normal infants continue to babble. A child does not learn language, however, simply by hearing it spoken. A boy with normal hearing but with deaf parents who communicated by the American Sign Language was exposed to television every day so that he would learn English. Because the child was asthmatic and was confined to his home he interacted only with people at home, where his family and all their visitors communicated in sign language. By the age of three he was fluent in sign language but neither understood nor spoke English. It appears that in order to learn a language a child must also be able to interact with real people in that language. A television set does not suffice as the sole medium for language learning because, even though it can ask questions, it cannot respond to a child's answers. A child, then, can develop language only if there is language in her environment and if she can employ that language to communicate with other people in her immediate environment. . . .

It seems to be virtually impossible to speed up the language-learning process. Experiments conducted by Russian investigators show that it is extremely difficult to teach children a detail of language more than a few days before they would learn it themselves. Adults sometimes do, of course, attempt to teach children rules of language, expecting them to learn by imitation, but Courtney B. Cazden of Harvard University found that children benefit less from frequent adult correction of their errors than from true conversational interaction. Indeed, correcting errors can interrupt that interaction, which is, after all, the function of language. (One way children may try to secure such interaction is by asking "Why?" Children go through a stage of asking a question repeatedly. It serves to keep the conversation going, which may be the child's real aim. For example, a two-and-a-half-year-old named Stanford asked "Why?" and was given the nonsense answer: "Because the moon is made of green cheese." Although the response was not at all germane to the conversation. Stanford was happy with it and again asked "Why?" Many silly answers later the adult had tired of the conversation but Stanford had not. He was clearly not seeking information. What he needed was to practice the form of social conversation before dealing with its function. Asking "Why?" served that purpose well.)

In point of fact adults rarely correct children's ungrammatical sentences. For example, one mother, on hearing "Tommy fall my truck down," turned to Tommy with "Did you fall Stevie's truck down?" Since imitation seems to have little role in the language-acquisition process, however, it is probably just as well that most adults are either too charmed by children's errors or too busy to correct them.

Practice does appear to have an important function in the child's language-learning process. Many children have been observed purposefully practicing language when they are alone, for example in a crib or a playpen. Ruth H. Weir of Stanford University hid a tape recorder in her son's bedroom and recorded his talk after he was put to bed. She found that he played with words and phrases, stringing together sequences of similar sounds and of variations on a phrase or on the use of a word: "What color . . . what color blanket . . . what color mop . . . what color glass . . . what color TV . . . red ant . . . fire . . . like lipstick . . . blanket . . . now the blue blanket . . . what color TV . . . what color horse . . . then what color table . . . then what color fire . . . here yellow spoon." Children who do not have much opportunity to be alone may use dialogue in a similar fashion. When Weir tried to record the bedtime monologues of her second child, whose room adjoined that of the first, she obtained through-the-wall conversations instead.

From DEVELOPMENT OF THE FIRST LANGUAGE IN THE HUMAN SPECIES
Roger Brown

Of course, the question about the mother tongue that we should really like answered is, How is it possible to learn a first language at all? On that question, which ultimately motivates the whole research enterprise, I have nothing to offer that is not negative. But perhaps it is worth while making these negatives explicit since they are still widely supposed to be affirmatives, and indeed to provide a large part of the answer to the question. What I have to say is not primarily addressed to the question. How does the child come to talk at all? since there seem to be fairly obvious utilities in saying a few words in order to express more exactly what he wants, does not want, wonders about, or wishes to share with others. The more exact question on which we have a little information that serves only to make the question more puzzling is, How does the child come to *improve* upon his language, moving steadily in the direction of the adult model? It probably seems surprising that there should be any mystery about the forces impelling improvement, since it is just this aspect of the process that most people imagine that they understand. Surely the improvement is a response to selective social pressures of various kinds; ill-formed or incomplete utterances must be less effective than well-formed and complete utterances in accomplishing the child's intent; parents probably approve of well-formed utterances and disapprove or correct the ill-formed. These ideas sound sensible and may be correct, but the still scant evidence available does not support them.

At the end of Stage I, the child's constructions are characterized by, in addition to the things we have mentioned, a seemingly lawless oscillating omission of every sort of major constituent including sometimes subjects, objects, verbs, locatives, and so on. The important point about these oscillating omissions is that they seldom seem to impede communication; the other person, usually the mother, being in the same situation and familiar with the child's stock of knowledge, usually understands, so far as one can judge, even the incomplete utterance. Brown (1973) has suggested the Stage I child's speech is well adapted to his purpose, but that, as a speaker, he is very *narrowly* adapted. We may suppose that in speaking to strangers or of new experiences he will have to learn to express obligatory constituents if he wants to get his message across. And that may be the answer: The social pressures to communicate may chiefly operate outside the usual sampling situation, which is that of the child at home with family members.

In Stage II, Brown (1973) found that all of the 14 grammatical morphemes were at first missing, then occasionally present in obligatory contexts, and after varying and often long periods of time, always present in such contexts. What makes the probability of supplying the requisite morpheme rise with time? It is surprisingly difficult to find cases in which omission results in incomprehension or misunderstanding. With respect to the definite and nondefinite articles, it even looks as if listeners almost never really need them, and yet child speakers learn to operate with the exceedingly intricate rules governing their usage. Adult Japanese, speaking English as a second language, do not seem to learn how to operate with the articles as we might expect they would if listeners needed them. Perhaps it is the case that the child automatically does this kind of learning but that adults do not. Second-language learning may be responsive to familiar sorts of learning variables, and first-language learning may not. The two, often thought to be similar processes, may be profoundly and ineradicably different.

Consider the Stage I child's invariably uninflected generic verbs, In Stage II, American parents regularly gloss these verbs in one of the four ways: as imperatives, past tense forms, present progressives, or imminent-intentional futures. It is an interesting fact, of course, that these are just the four modulations of the verb that the child then goes on, first, to learn to express. For years we have thought it possible that glosses or expansions of this type might be a major force impelling the child to improve his speech. However, all the evidence available, both naturalistic and experimental (it is summarized in Brown, Cazden, & Bellugi, 1969), offers no support at all for this notion. Cazden (1965), for instance, carried out an experiment testing for the effect on young children's speech of deliberately interpolated "expansions" (the supplying of obligatory functional morphemes), introduced for a period on every preschool day for three months. She obtained no significant effect whatever. It is possible, I think that such an experiment done now, with the information Stage II makes available, and expanding only by providing morphemes of a complexity for which the child was "ready," rather than as in Cazden's original experiment expanding in all possible ways, would show an effect. But no such experiment has been done, and so no impelling effect of expansion has been demonstrated.

Suppose we look at the facts of the parental glossing of Stage I generic verbs not, as we have done above, as a possible tutorial device but rather, as Slobin (1971) has done, as evidence that the children already intended the meanings their parents attributed to them. In short, think of the parental glosses as veridical readings of the child's thought. From this point of view, the child has been understood correctly, even though his utterances are incomplete. In that case there is no selection pressure. Why does he learn to say more if what he already knows how to say works quite well?

To these observations of the seeming efficacy of the child's incomplete utterances, at least at home with the family, we should add the results of a study reported in Brown and Hanlon (1970). Here it was not primarily a question of the omission of obligatory forms but of the contrast between ill-formed primitive constructions and well-formed mature versions. For certain constructions, *yes-no* questions, tag questions, negatives, and *wh-* questions, Brown and Hanlon (1970) identified periods when Adam, Eve, and Sarah were producing both primitive and mature versions, sometimes the one, sometimes the other. The question was, Did the mature version communicate more successfully than the primitive version? They first identified all instances of primitive and mature versions, and then coded the adult responses for comprehending follow-up, calling comprehending responses "sequiturs" and uncomprehending or irrelevant responses "nonsequiturs." They found no evidence whatever of a difference in communicative efficacy, and so once again, no selection pressure. Why, one asks oneself, should the child learn the complex apparatus of tag questions when "right?" or "huh?" seems to do just the same job? Again one notes that adults learning English as a second language often do not learn tag questions, and the possibility again comes to mind that children operate on language in a way that adults do not.

Brown and Hanlon (1970) have done one other study that bears on the search for selection pressures. Once again it was syntactic well-formedness versus ill-formedness that was in question rather than completeness or incompleteness. This time Brown and Hanlon started with two kinds of adult responses to child utterances: "approval," directed at an antecedent child utterance, and "disapproval," directed at such an antecedent. The question then was, did the two sets of antecedents differ in syntactic correctness? Approving and disapproving responses are, certainly, very reasonable candidates for the respective roles "positive reinforcer" and "punishment." Of course, they do not necessarily qualify as such because reinforcers and punishments are defined by their effects on performance (Skinner, 1953); they have no necessary, independent, nonfunctional properties. Still, of course, they often are put forward as plausible determinants of performance and are thought, generally, to function as such. In order differentially to affect the child's syntax, approval and disapproval must, at a minimum, be governed selectively by correct and incorrect syntax. If they should be so governed, further data still would be needed to show that they affect performance. If they are not so governed, they cannot be a selective force working for correct speech. And Brown and Hanlon found that they are not. In general, the parents seemed to pay no attention to bad syntax nor did they even seem to be aware of it. They approved or disapproved an utterance usually on the grounds of the truth value of the proposition which the parents supposed the child intended to assert. This is a surprising outcome to most middle-class parents, since they are generally under the impression that they do correct the child's speech. From inquiry and observation I find that what parents generally correct is pronunciation, "naughty" words, and regularized irregular allomorphs liked *digged* or *goed.* These facts of the child's speech seem to penetrate parental awareness. But syntax—the child saying, for instance, "Why the dog won't eat?" instead of "Why won't the dog eat?"—seems to be set right automatically in the parent's mind, with the mistake never registering as such.

In sum, then, we presently do not have evidence that there are selective social pressures of any kind operating on children to impel them to bring their speech into line with adult models. It is, however, entirely possible that such pressures do operate in situations unlike the situations we have sampled, for instance, away from home or with strangers. A radically different possibility is that children work out rules for the speech they hear, passing from levels of lesser to greater complexity, simply because the human species is programmed at a certain period in its life to operate in this fashion on linguistic input. Linguistic input would be defined by the universal properties of language. And the period of progressive rule extraction would correspond to Lenneberg's (1967 and elsewhere) proposed "critical period." It may be chiefly adults who learn a new, a second, language in terms of selective social pressures. Comparison of the kinds of errors made by adult second-language learners of English with the kinds made by child first-language learners of English should be enlightening.

If automatic internal programs of structure extraction provide the generally correct sort of answer to how a first language is learned, then, of course, our inquiries into external communication pressures simply are misguided. They look for the answer in the wrong place. That, of course, does not mean that we are anywhere close to having the right answer. It only remains to specify the kinds of programs that would produce the result regularly obtained.

WORKS CITED

BROWN, R. (1973). *A first language: The early stages.* Cambridge: Harvard University Press.

BROWN, R., CAZDEN, C., & BELLUGI, U. (1969). The child's grammar from 1 to 3. In J. P. Hill (Ed.), *Minnesota Symposium on Child Psychology, 2.* Minneapolis: University of Minnesota Press.

BROWN, R., & HANLON, C. (1970). Derivational complexity and order of acquisition in child speech. In J. R. Hayes (Ed.), *Cognition and the development of language.* New York: Wiley.

CAZDEN, C. B. (1965). *Environmental assistance to the child's acquisition of grammar.* Unpublished doctoral dissertation, Harvard University.

LENNEBERG, E. H. (1967). *Biological foundations of language.* New York: Wiley.

SKINNER, B. F. (1953). *Science and human behavior.* New York: Macmillan.

SLOBIN, D. I. (1971). Developmental psycholinguistics. In W. O. Dingwall (Ed.), *A survey of linguistic science.* College Park: University of Maryland.

PRELIMINARIES TO THEORIES ON BRAIN MECHANISMS OF LANGUAGE
Eric H. Lenneberg

The neurophysiology of behavior comprises three realms of mechanisms: those concerned with input, those with central integration, and those with output. The first realm includes reception, transduction, and transformation of exogenous stimuli; the third deals with control, regulation, and coordination of muscular activity. The nature of the second realm can be inferred only from the imperfect correlation that exists between input and output. There are many types of input that produce no overt motor output, and many an output (verbal or motor) does not seem to be correlated with any specific environmental input. Registration in our minds of some event need not lead to any immediate or even future predictable motor act. On the other hand, a motor act, or an utterance such as "A black scorpion is not dropping on my plate" (which B. F. Skinner told his students was said to him by A. N. White- head during a discussion of verbal behavior) need not be evoked by any closely related physical event in the environment.

Up to the present, experimental neurophysiological research and the interpre- tation of the respective data have been almost exclusively focused on the first and, to a lesser extent, on the third realms. However, the biology of *knowing language* is essentially a problem of the second realm. Knowing a language means relating, com- puting, and operating on specific aspects of the environment. Learning language means doing these things in very specific ways. Theorizing about the brain mecha- nisms of language made extremely difficult by our nearly complete ignorance of how any of the processes of the second realm function. The difficulty is not merely the absence of specific facts that may shortly become available. The difficulty is the pres- ent lack of even a general or abstract *theoretical model* of how this second realm might work—how behavior and cognition might be related to brain function. The theoretical models that enjoy greatest popularity among neurophysiologists today try to explain how physical patterns (such as the configuration of a chair) might be trans- formed into "the language of the brain," but they do not face the problem of what happens to the transformed data—of what goes on in the second realm.

The map-making aphasiologists endeavor to tell us where the neurally encoded speech signal first arrives in the cortex, where it is shunted next, and where it "exists" to produce speech acts. Quite apart from the innumerable questions that surround such functional maps, they would not actually explain what the physiology of lan- guage knowledge is, even were the anatomical locations by now firmly established. A nervous system is not like a trumpet into which the environment can blow and produce a tune. Brains are not passive conveyors of information; they are very active objects, and their activity states are highly unstable, easily perturbed, and subject to modulation from the outside. That is why treating the brain as a communication channel or viewing behavior simply as a function of the input to the system is mis- leading. It tends to ignore the fact that behavior is in many ways autonomous activ- ity, in the sense that it derives its energy *not* from the stimuli that are behaviorally significant, but from energy stores that are supplied through the body's metabolic activities. Psychologically important stimuli trigger and shape behavior, but the stimuli are not the architects of the principles by which behavior operates; nor is behavior a transform of the brain's input. The relevance of these observations to language is obvious.

The acquisition and maintenance of the language function is a particular exam- ple of the general biological problem of how patterns come about and are main- tained. It is a special problem within the general problem of biological specificity. We are faced with quite similar problems in the contexts of both evolution and ontogeny. And the problem extends to the field of structure as well as to the field of function and of behavior. Thus, our ability to "explain" language biologically is inex- tricably tied up with our ability to explain the organism's ontogenesis.

The clinical data, especially the relationship between lesioning and age and the importance of the rate at which cortex is destroyed, emphasize the role of morphogenetic processes during the establishment of language capacities. It is only by bringing the notions of embryological regulation, differentiation, and determination to bear upon the functional organization of the human brain during the critical years of language development that we can hope to understand the occurrence and nonoccurrence of language disturbances. Piaget and his colleagues are the only psychologists who have clearly seen the intimate relationship between embryological processes and the unfolding of cognition. Nothing could illustrate better the direct connections between developmental biology and developmental psychology than the neurology of language. As the behavioral capacities become differentiated during growth, the human brain is undergoing its final structural and functional differentiation as well. It is especially the functional differentiation that should be of interest to the student of behavior and language. Functions do not suddenly start when the "machine has been assembled," as in a computer that is suddenly ready to be used. Cognitive functions and the capacity for language knowledge have an epigenetic history; they are transforms of earlier, less specialized functions and their correlated physiological processes. The family of cerebral activity patterns that constitute the use and knowledge of language have gradually developed characteristics (their modes of functioning, the nature of their perturbability, the types of transitions between their states), and these, in turn, depend in part on the system's anatomical differentiation history and in part on the history of perturbations that the developing system has incurred. . . .

Text Analysis through Examining Figurative Language

Since there are a number of units on analyzing texts in this book, you've probably tried at least one approach already. Our aim in presenting these various approaches is to help you find more to say when you're asked to analyze a text. In this unit we specifically want to help you see the value of attention to figurative language in the analysis of discourse. To do this, you'll need to understand the main kinds of figurative language: metaphor, simile, image, and symbol. Metaphors and these other figures of speech are often the centers of intensified energy and meaning in discourse. And they are often spots that best reveal what is *implied* rather than what is *said.* You've undoubtedly focused on figures of speech in your English classes as a way of getting closer to the meaning of fiction or poetry. But we want to convince you here that attention to figurative language can also help you as you analyze expository writing such as essays and editorials. All this close looking at texts should make you more consciously aware of language as specific words and phrases that can carry secondary as well as primary meaning. Your assignment for this unit is to write an analysis of a text based on its figurative language. Before we describe more specifically how to do that though, we're going to talk a bit about figurative language itself to give you background for your analysis.

FIGURATIVE LANGUAGE

Metaphor

Metaphor is the most basic or universal "figure"—the paradigm of figurative language. A metaphor is a word or phrase used in something other than its normal or usual fashion—used not literally but figuratively. If we say, "The farmer *plowed* the field," "plowed" is literal. But if we say, "The student *plowed* through his homework," "plowed" is figurative. To put it crassly, a metaphor always involves a kind of *wrong* or *mistaken* use of a word, a use which awakens us to new possibilities of meaning. By saying that the student "plowed" through homework, the speaker forces us to realize that "plowing" cannot mean what farmers do to fields. Therefore we are forced to create or remember a sense of plow that fits the sentence. ("Oh, I see; he went through his homework methodically and persistently.") We have probably heard the word *plow* in this metaphorical sense before so that we don't have to ask ourselves directly, "Let's see; what can you do to homework that is like what a farmer does to a field?"

When we hear a metaphor we've never heard before, however, we are forced to forge new meaning. "In her room at the prow of the house . . ." (writes Richard Wilber in his poem "The Writer"). Most of us have probably not heard this metaphor before. This use of "prow" asks us to see a house in a new way—as a ship—and to sense one room as somehow forging forward. But the usage is not *so* odd—the meaning not so new—because we have probably heard "prow" used metaphorically of various things besides ships, if not of houses. We are more obliged to *make new meaning* in these lines by Dylan Thomas in "Poem in October" about his thirtieth birthday:

> I rose
> In rainy autumn
> And walked abroad in a shower of all my days.

The "shower of all my days" metaphor invites us to experience an October shower falling on us as making us feel also a birthday awareness of all the past days of our life falling about us.

If we keep talking about people "plowing through" things, we will someday cease to experience that use of "plow" as a metaphor. We will call it literal. (Just as we probably experience "She *upset* me by being late for dinner," as equally literal with "He *upset* the glass of wine at dinner.") When that time comes, we will say that "plow" means something like "to cut methodically and persistently through something" just as literally as it means what farmers do to fields.

Though we can usually tell the difference between what is literal and metaphorical, there is no hard and fast way to decide in a fuzzy case—in the case of a metaphor that is so common that we can't decide whether to call it literal. Many of our literal meanings started out metaphorical. In an argument there may be no definite answer. Whether a word is metaphorical depends on whether people experience that usage as literal or not—whether there is any "wrongness" or "blockage of meaning" in the usage. Thus consider "leg of a table": is "leg" a metaphor or not? Probably not for most of us, but if you feel "leg" as a word that only fits animals, not tables, then you will feel a "wrongness" that gives the word a metaphorical force. (In the nineteenth century, people sometimes put skirts on tables to cover their legs—showing perhaps that they experienced legs as primarily animal.) Some people might even argue that "plow" is now literal in our "plowed through the homework" sentence.

Simile

We move from metaphor to simile when we use "like," "as," "seems,"— or some such word—to *signal* a comparison. Thus we can change Wilbur's metaphor to a simile by saying, "Her room, *like* the prow of a ship. . . ." In one sense the difference between metaphors and similes is trivial, just a matter of sticking in a "like" or an "as." But it's interesting to note that deep down, metaphors and similes represent different orientations to reality. Metaphors insist on bending reality or telling lies—and thus in a sense represent magical thinking: houses have no prow. Similes refuse to bend reality; they insist on being literal. They say only that the room is *like* a prow. Metaphors can thus be said to represent a different and more metaphysical view of reality. When we meet them in the flesh, however, metaphors and similes often don't function so very differently; similes can be just as startling or resonant, even magical, as metaphors: "I was like a tree in which there are three blackbirds." In fact the full sentence as Wallace Stevens wrote it grafts a metaphor onto the first element of the simile or comparison:

PROCESS BOX

Stories tend to appear to me, not as formal ideas, but as metaphors, and these metaphors seem to demand structures of their own: they seem to have an internal need for a certain form. [Questioner: Can you say something more about these metaphors that your fiction grows out of?] They're the germ, the thought, the image, the idea, out of which all the rest grows. They're always a bit elusive, involving thoughts, feelings, abstractions, visual material, all at once. I suppose they're a little like dream fragments, in that such fragments always contain, if you analyze them, so much more than at first you suspect. But they're not literally that—I never write from dreams. All these ideas come to me in the full light of day. Some, when you pry them open, have too little inside to work with. Others are unexpectedly fat and rich. Novels typically begin for me as very tiny stories or little one-act play ideas which I think at the time aren't going to fill three pages. Then slowly the hidden complexities reveal themselves.

ROBERT COOVER, *ANYTHING CAN HAPPEN*

> I was of three minds,
> Like a tree
> In which there are three blackbirds.
> > —from "Thirteen Ways of Looking at a Blackbird"

Image

Images need not be metaphors or similes at all; they need not involve any comparison or anything figurative. Images are simply picture-words —words which *set something before our eyes.* However, images are often *involved* in metaphors and similes. So much so that people often use the word *imagery* when they mean "metaphors, similes, and images." Critics say, "Let's look at the imagery of this poem" and they mean all the figures. Thus if we take the second half of the comparison in the passage just quoted—"a tree in which there are three blackbirds"—we see that it is nothing but an *image,* nothing *but* a picture. But once Stevens says something is "*like* a tree in which there are three blackbirds," he makes it a simile. Thus he gives us a simile in which the first term, a metaphor, is said to be "like" the second term, an image.

Another image:

> A pleasant apron with flowers and teacups all over. The kettle was singing. And steaming.
> > —Stuart Friebert

This is just an image with no simile or comparison (though it contains the common metaphor of a kettle "singing"). Notice that the image is not just visual; it presents to us a kitchen scene which appeals to our ears and perhaps even to our tactile sense of the steam.

The distinguishing mark of an image then is that it appeals to our *senses,* not just our minds. It's a *showing* not just a *telling*—a re-creating of something palpable, not just a naming or explaining. Here too, of course, there is no firm dividing line between when something is shown versus told. Thus the following three phrases would probably not count as images for most people because they are scarcely more than naming:

> the notes of bells, the sounds of musical instruments, the noises of wind, sea, and rain. . . .

But you could argue that they are small images. Dylan Thomas continues his list, however, with three more items which, though short, are so artfully phrased as to bring a sound to almost any reader and thus make us count them as strong images:

> the rattle of milkcarts, the clopping of hooves on cobbles, the fingering of branches on a window pane. . . .

403

Let's look at Thomas's *whole* sentence—a long singing one—and notice how it combines the three figures we've talked about: image, simile, and metaphor. That is, the whole thing is an extended simile or comparison. Many of the compared items are images; and one of those images contains a metaphor "fingering of branches." (He is speaking of his childhood experiences while reading.)

> And these words were, to me, as the notes of bells, the sounds of musical instruments, the noises of wind, sea, and rain, the rattle of milkcarts, the clopping of hooves on cobbles, the fingering of branches on a window pane, might be to someone, deaf from birth, who has miraculously found his hearing.

Symbol

The symbol is a word or phrase that *stands for* ("symbolizes") something. It presents a comparison but only an *implied* one, not a stated one: a comparison between x and y when only x is stated. The symbol symbolizes by virtue of *resembling* or *partaking of* what it stands for. Thus the circle has often been a symbol of infinity or perfection, the rose a symbol of beauty or of the Virgin Mary, the sun a symbol of reason. The symbol is inherently more magical or mystical than the metaphor or simile: it resonates with the life and significance of what it symbolizes.

Thus if we have a piece of writing where circles turn up frequently—not in metaphors or similes but just in literal description (for example, a dream poem where birds fly in perfect circles), and if we feel that the way the writer *uses* these circling birds is somehow a bit *loaded* or *resonant*—such that the writing seems to point *beyond* mere birds flying in circles, then we could say that these descriptions are functioning as symbols and ask ourselves what their symbolic meaning might be. Perhaps we would conclude that they symbolize perfection. Remember, however, that symbols do not carry automatic symbolic meanings that you can look up in a dictionary. (Admittedly there *are* dictionaries of symbols or of dream symbols, but you shouldn't trust them. They tell only what some alleged authority *thinks* or *pronounces* to be symbol-with-translation—for example, that whenever you dream of bread or houses you are dreaming of your mother. Sometimes yes, sometimes no. It depends on how symbols are used.)

The Wallace Stevens poem we just quoted opens with what one could call a symbol:

> Among twenty snowy mountains,
> The only moving thing
> Was the eye of the blackbird.

Or later in the poem:

> The river is moving.
> The blackbird must be flying.

Some might say there are no symbols here, merely evocative literal statements. One cannot settle arguments about whether something is a symbol or is functioning as a symbol; the key is whether we sense a word or phrase *standing for* or *symbolizing* something—and doing so not arbitrarily but by virtue of its own nature and the way it relates to its linguistic context. Once we sense that, we try to find out *what* the word or phrase stands for or symbolizes; that is, we try to "translate" the symbol. Our attempt to find a translation demonstrates what symbolism is all about; as we "translate" we are working toward meaning. The moving eye of the blackbird among twenty white mountains may stand for or symbolize a "piercing awareness at the heart of no awareness." And the moving river linked to the flying blackbird might stand for or symbolize "change being everywhere and all changes somehow linked to each other." But notice that there is no metaphor or simile in either case.

To pinpoint a symbol we need to sense first that the language is heavy with meaning; the language itself draws our attention. Needless to say, not all readers are going to be drawn to the same language. And even where readers agree on the presence of a symbol, they will often disagree about what the symbol means.

A PROCESS FOR WRITING AN ANALYSIS BY EXAMINING FIGURATIVE LANGUAGE

What follows is a somewhat schematized procedure for writing an analysis of a text. We suggest these steps because writing analysis is hard, and there is a particular danger of jumping too soon into conclusions without examining enough evidence from the text. The power of the following steps for exploratory writing is that they force you to do the bulk of your writing *before* figuring out what your main points are or how you will organize your final essay. When you do this noticing-and-exploring before you stop and work out what it all means, that working out is almost invariably more interesting and intelligent. It builds on richer thinking. (Be sure to do your exploratory writing on only one side of the paper so that you can cut and paste later.)*

Reading the Text

Read the text you want to analyze at least a couple of times. Try to read it with pleasure—but also with care. Don't worry about analyzing it, just try to *immerse* yourself in it as much as you can. The goal is not "figuring out" but *noticing*. Best of all is to read it out loud—trying out a few variations

---

*We are indebted to the Bard Institute for Writing and Thinking for help in working out this method for analyzing a text.

and hearing others try a few different readings. (See the mini-unit on "Text Rendering.")

Writing a Draft

1. Put the text aside and list the figurative words, phrases, or passages that come to you as somehow memorable or important or intriguing. Don't worry about whether things are really figurative or about distinctions between various kinds of figurative language. Just list words or passages that seem especially alive or important—more often than not they will have figurative language.

2. Circle the three or four words or passages that somehow seem most important or intriguing.

3. Choose one—the one that seems most interesting to you. Briefly describe it and go on writing about it—as much as you can—associating freely with other memories of the piece, and with whatever thoughts and feelings you find. (You might want to look at the text again to see it freshly.)

4. To end this piece of writing, figure out the main thing you want to say.

5. Do the same two steps now for the two or three more phrases you circled.

6. Reread the whole text and then write about what these three phrases or passages have in common. What do they tell you about the text? How might they be characteristic of it?

7. What *doesn't* fit here: what have you written in your separate segments that doesn't fit easily with what you wrote in other segments? What aspects of the text are neglected by what you have been saying? What's puzzling about what you've just written? What other phrases or parts of the essay need comment?

8. Now read or think back over what you have written and do some "So what?" writing. Work on figuring out what you want to say about how this text works—in itself or on readers. Force yourself to come up with some *assertions* or *ideas* about this text. (Note that your assertion itself need not pertain to figurative language: it might be simply something about the meaning or form of the piece or how it works on readers. Analysis of figurative language would simply be your *evidence* for supporting what you are saying.)

If possible, it helps to go through these activities in a class or workshop with others—not just for the encouragement and company but so that at various points you can share some of what you've written and hear some of what others have written.

Revising

You now have already produced the makings or ingredients of a draft of an analytic essay. To revise, we suggest these steps:

- Look back over the text. Read it aloud again to see if you hear it any differently now.

- Look back over what you have written.

- Make up your mind now about what you really want to have for your main point. (Perhaps you've already done this in step 8.) In truth, there are good published works of literary analysis that consist of just a succession of many good small observations or insights. But many teachers feel that you don't have a critical essay unless you reach some conclusion that ties together those smaller points.

- In the light of your main point, cut and paste what you've already written into the order that makes the most sense.

- Now read over your cut-and-paste draft and wrestle with it to get it the way you want. Perhaps you'll have to make major structural changes—even change your mind about what you are saying; perhaps you'll just make smaller changes. (We discussed this in detail, of course, in the unit about revising.)

SUGGESTIONS FOR SHARING AND RESPONDING

If people share pieces of first-stage writing—as in the eight steps—look for feedback that simply carries the writing forward: "Sayback" and "Pointing, Summarizing" in *Sharing and Responding,* Sections IIA and IIB, may help. These will encourage the writer to say more by telling him what you hear implied and almost said.

About step 8, the "So what?" writing:

- Check to see whether there really is an assertion and if not, ask the writer to keep talking to find one. Suggest any you hear implied. Check also to see whether the assertion is supported by the writing.

About a draft:

- Does the draft actually say something or reach a conclusion, or is it just a collection of insights?

- Does the writer manage to make you see the text as she does? Is her analysis convincing to you? What parts or aspects of the text do you

PROCESS BOX

Reflections on two "naughty feelings" I discover in myself. First, not wanting to copyedit or revise. I have some other notes to myself about this.

Second, not wanting writing to be clear; not wanting to "give it"—"give" my meaning. When I was a student I was mad at my teachers—but didn't know it. I wanted my writing to hide what I was saying so that they wouldn't appreciate it unless they really could see how smart and good I was. It was a trick. To see if they were smart enough to know that I was smart and good. If I got a bad mark on my writing, *they* failed.

Not so much that it was a conscious trick of a smart-ass boy. I wish I'd been confident enough to be smart-ass. No, it was unconscious. For in fact when I would get a bad grade—which I often did—I would feel crushed, awful: "What's the matter with me?" Only later in my life did I realize that I'd been mad at these teachers all along and that I was secretly in some sense giving them the finger, telling them, "If you won't appreciate me the way I am, then the hell with you; I refuse to do it your way; I refuse to do what you want me to do to be liked."

It's hard to explain how it really was—I guess it shows there's such a thing as an unconscious. For it's absolutely clear to me that *at the time* I desperately wanted to please them and get good grades: I often succeeded, but often couldn't. And as the years of schooling went on I somehow found it harder and harder to write the way teachers wanted me to write—and I really was trying my heart out. But it's just as clear to me *now* that these opposite feelings were also going on—and indeed determining my behavior; the *reason* I found myself unable to write

feel she doesn't pay enough attention to? Do you have suggestions for how to make her point stronger? Would you try to talk her into a different perspective?

QUESTIONS FOR YOUR PROCESS JOURNAL

- What was it like for you to read through your chosen text? Were you able to do it just as a reader, or was your reading changed in some way because analysis was on your mind?

the way my teachers wanted me to write was because—underneath it all—I was *refusing*.

I don't especially recommend doing things as I did them. That is, I don't recommend being unconscious of it all. It would have been much better if I had realized what I was feeling. Then I could have thought about it and made a real decision: either, "Okay, I hate this, but I'm going to do what they want!" Or, "Damn it, I'm so mad at them, I refuse to do what they want and I'll take the consequences. To hell with getting a good grade." Instead of that I trapped myself in the middle. I *thought* I was trying as hard as I could; worse yet I thought there was something the matter with me—that I was dumb or incapable of writing.

Perhaps it was that I couldn't stand to have to *prove* myself or *urge my case*. I wanted to be *appreciated*. I wanted people to *see* that I'm good, nice, smart—whatever. (And I guess I persist in that—in my professional work. I'm damned if I'm going to have to fit myself into the modes or standards that are conventional; I want to be myself and be appreciated for being myself. But the result is that a lot of people think I'm nutty or dumb and won't listen to me—who otherwise would think that I'm smart and would believe me if I were willing to "do it their way.")

This relates to the other thing about proofreading. A refusal to try to pretty up my "product." "These are my words, this is what I wrote down, this is the real me. If you don't like it the way it came out of me, then it's tough luck; it just shows that you're not my friend. I don't want you to be my friend unless you'll take it as it came. I don't want your help and admiration unless you give it to me without my having to put on cosmetics for you." A childish feeling, unhelpful. But not quite so damaging now that I see it's there.

PETER ELBOW, 11/86

- Did you follow our sequence of steps for writing? Did it help or get in your way?

- Did the words and phrases that came to your attention seem to be figurative language? If not, what kinds of things made the language memorable or interesting?

- Did the three or four pieces you chose seem to hang together or to point in different directions?

- How about assertions? Were they obvious to you, or did you have to struggle to find them? Was it equally difficult or easy to find some single assertion to link your ideas together?

THEORY AND RUMINATIONS

Figurative Language as a Window on the Mind

It might help to stand back for a bit of perspective on the whole process of text analysis. There are various things people do when they analyze a text— or indeed analyze any discourse, spoken or written. There are two main traditions:

- Exploring what *effect the text has on the reader* and explaining how it achieves that effect.

- Exploring the relationship between *what is said* and *how it's said*— between the meaning and the form.

The first approach with its focus on effect on audience reflects the tradition of *rhetoric*—a strong tradition since Aristotle; this way of viewing analysis has tended to be applied more to essays and other expository writing than to literature and poetry. The second approach with emphasis on close analysis of the text reflects the more recent tradition of *poetics* and has tended to be applied more to poems and other imaginative writing. In recent years both approaches have been applied to all kinds of texts. We maintain that both approaches are valid for any text.

There are various *dimensions of discourse* that you can emphasize when analyzing a text.

- An analysis of the *reasoning:* what is the main assertion, the reasons given, and the backing and assumptions that support those reasons? What are strengths and weaknesses of the reasoning? (This is the emphasis of Unit 11, on argument.)

- An analysis of persuasive strategies other than reasoning. (This is the emphasis of Unit 10, on persuasion.)

- An analysis of the voice, tone, diction, and the stance of the writer toward the reader.

- An analysis of the form, structure, organization, division into parts— and how they relate to the meaning.

- An analysis of the figurative language, which is the approach we are introducing in this unit.

Why Emphasize Figurative Language?

If you think that figurative language occurs only in literature, you've been misled by the fact that it is *talked* about most in the study of literature. Figurative language is universal. Listen closely to any extended conversation. Better yet, record it so you can really examine the language. You'll find plenty of metaphors, similes, and images in the words people just speak as they go about their life. You'll probably find even more in sports writing and political speeches. Slang is peppered (note the metaphor) with figurative language.

It's not easy to give a good answer as to why figurative language appeals to the mind at such a deep level. Perhaps there are many reasons. For one thing it's simply in the nature of our mind to see things as like other things or standing for other things. That's how we *do* see. It's virtually impossible to see any chair or person exactly in its uniqueness; we tend to see it as an instance of a type. Thinking could be defined as nothing but seeing things as like and unlike other things. To put it bluntly, there is a deep human impulse to call things by the "wrong" name.

But it's not just a mistake. Language is like a lens for looking at things. Literal language is a lens, and it distorts—like any lens. But we are so used to literal language that we think it is clear glass. (That's all "literal" means: the word or lens that we are used to which therefore seems "regular.") But though we are *used to* literal language, most of us realize deep down that distortion is going on. We know there are things we aren't seeing—or saying—with the common lens, and that if we tried out other lenses, we'd see some new things. Most of us feel that we can't say things *just as they are* with our literal or regular language. Words don't ever seem to get quite accurately at what they stand for; there is always some slippage. So we all have the impulse to find other words (or other media) to capture things we cannot quite say right—in short to call things by the wrong name.

We cannot make up *new* words—no one will understand them. But we can use the old words in new ways, and *that* does indeed bring out aspects of our experience that we cannot capture otherwise. A new lens brings new distortions, but it helps us notice what we didn't notice with the accustomed lens. Thus we all use metaphor to make sense of things that are hard to make sense of.

And why images? If we see something that is really powerful or important (or hear it or touch it), we seem to have the impulse to put our experience in words—for ourselves and to tell others. We see this phenomenon most clearly when someone has been in a terrible accident or has experienced something very frightening: he has an impulse to tell about it again and again. The same is true if something wonderful happens:

> "Did I tell you about what happened at third base? The ball bounced out of Schmitt's mitt and into the catcher's? You should have seen the look. . . ."
> "Yes, you've already told me three times."

The truth is we all *need* to talk about what is important—and tell it again and again. The telling helps us digest and make sense of our experience.

Thus if we find the metaphors in the conversation of a friend, we'll usually find the most interesting places, the places where his mind *reveals itself* most. If these are *new* metaphors—metaphors he made up (and people do it all the time)—they will represent the *making of new meaning:* places where he wasn't satisfied with the implications of literal language. These are usually places where his mind is most in touch with the action he's describing.

If they are *used* metaphors—metaphors he found handy—they will represent places where you usually get the quickest and surest picture of the attitudes that he lives inside of. For example, if someone says he "scored a touchdown on the physics exam," he is showing that at some level he thinks of school as a competitive game where the object is to win. To find the metaphors in someone's language is to find the keys to how he understands the world.

If you find the places where someone lingers for a moment over a detail and gives a bit of an image for it—where he doesn't just say he went to a restaurant but tells how the candles looked or how the waiter spoke—you can find some of the experience that is probably most felt and most important to the person.

Figurative language is not just important for the speaker or writer but also for the audience. Passages of figurative language often have the strongest effect on listeners. If someone tells you, "For me, playing music is like flying over a spectacular landscape," this probably gets more of your attention and slips more things into your mind and feelings than something literal like, "I love playing music," or "I am utterly involved in the excitement of playing music." Suppose the person goes on to say, "To play music is to take your audience on a trip; they ride the waves with you. Your highs and lows are their highs and lows. Their emotional landscape becomes yours for a small piece of time. They participate in your movements; you move in unison." This puts the notion before your senses—and somehow things that touch our senses seem to get into our minds quicker and deeper than things that just touch our minds.

We are taking here a *cognitive* and *functional* approach to figurative language—not a *decorative* approach. That is, some critics talk as though figurative language is important because it "beautifies" thought. Some venerable theories of poetry say that the poet first finds her idea and then "clothes it" in "rich fabric" or in the "colors of rhetoric"—meaning figurative language. But though some writers work that way—and all of us sometimes stop and search for a fancy word when we want to dress up something we are saying—figurative language is much better understood as reflecting the way the mind works. This approach makes the examination of figurative language more interesting and fruitful.

Therefore the quickest way to get to the heart of what's interesting and important in a conversation—or in a political speech, an advertisement, a story, novel, or poem—is to look at the figurative language. If we examine the metaphors, similes, images, and symbols that seem most alive, we can often see how the mind of the author is working—and how the piece of writing works.

READINGS

MY MOTHER, THAT FEAST OF LIGHT
Kate Barnes

My mother, that feast of light, has always sat down,
Composed herself, and written poetry, hardly
Reworking any, just the way she used to
Tell us that Chinese painters painted; first they
Sat for days on the hillside watching the rabbits,
Then they went home, they set out ink and paper,
Meditated; and only then picked up their brushes
To catch the lift of a rabbit in mid-hop.

"If it didn't come out I would throw it away."
                                      Oh, she
Is still a bird that fills a bush with singing.
The way that she lifts her tea cup, the look she gives you
As you sit across from her, it is all a kind
Of essential music.
                   I also remember my father
Alone at the dining-room table, the ink bottle safe
In a bowl, his orange-red fountain pen in his big
Hand. The hand moved slowly back and forth
And the floor below was white with sheets of paper
Each carrying a rejected phrase or two
As he struggled all morning to finish just one sentence—
Like a smith hammering thick and glowing iron,
Like Jacob wrestling with the wonderful angel.

MY MOTHER, THAT BEAST OF BLIGHT
Amber Moltenbrey

The three pieces that I have picked out from the poem "My Mother, That Feast of Light" all relate together in the image of a story. The story begins to unravel with the line "If it didn't come out I would throw it away." This sentence brings the introduction of the mother, that beast of blight. I imagine the mother in the poem as a bottomless well of words, which she forms together to produce a feast of interesting phrases—only, at the completion of a piece, to cast it aside as a reject of her own senses, a work that she has no desire to keep.

The sentence "I also remember my father/Alone at the dining room table . . ." brings to me a feeling of sorrow or pity, and leads me to side with the father in this tale of literary unrest. The father in the story is what starts my mind rolling. I do not see the father as a poet, or anything close to one, for that matter. I see him as a struggling businessman, trying to manage the farm efficiently, as he writes a letter to the local bank explaining a late payment.

413

In the line "As he struggled all morning to finish just one sentence . . . ," the father seems to be performing a chore rather than a pleasant ritual. It is here that I see the father resenting the mother for her writing ability; and her, a blight to all of his efforts. This becomes the plot-thickening ingredient in the poem.

In the story I see the mother as very well respected by her children, writing poetry when the mood strikes her, only to abandon it as something she had never written. I see the father as a one-man-band in the family. The piece of the poem that states "the look she gives you/As you sit across from her . . ." makes me wonder why no one sits across from the father as he writes. Maybe a boost of confidence is all that is needed for the father to complete a piece of writing successfully. It seems it is a wondrous occasion when the mother writes (and only then to throw it away), but when the father writes it is a thankless task "to finish just one sentence. . . ." It is as though the father has no one to stand by him, no one to share his problem with, no one there to offer help. I feel that the father has been left out of a family secret, or something special that the whole family should share.

The story in my mind leads me to think about the literary unrest that occurs in the poem. The mother, having seemingly no problems producing a piece of writing, and the father struggling to construct a respectable sentence, create a symbolic contrast that gives the poem an added feature. This twist makes the story more intriguing and leads the reader to dig deeper into the meaning of the poem.

The aspects that have been neglected by my story are the ones that might prove that the mother has any sensitivity. The story of the Chinese painters gives a hint of sentimentality that I don't care to relate in my story, although it may very well be an important part of someone else's interpretation. Jacob wrestling the "wonderful" angel is not incorporated in my story either because of the "wonderfulness" of it. I don't see the children of the family ever relating their father to something "wonderful."

The effect of this piece of poetry has hit me like few others. I find it difficult to read and comprehend an average poem. This poem worked because of the many images that focused in my mind. Not only the ones I have written about, but other images that I didn't have time to develop. The figurative language in the poem adds color to the story. I also believe that the author leaves room for many interpretations in the poem by using the different methods of figurative language.

WRITING STYLES IN "MY MOTHER, THAT FEAST OF LIGHT"
Karen Daley

The poem "My Mother, That Feast of Light" by Kate Barnes is a comparison between two very different writing styles. Barnes poetically describes her parents while illustrating their unique methods for writing. Her mother is presented as a natural writer who has the ability to transform her thoughts and images onto paper. She spends a great deal of time just thinking through what she wants to write before she actually picks up her pen, allowing her words to flow freely onto her paper, not revising a single word. Her father has a much more tedious writing style. He knows what he wants to write, but the words that come out of his pen are much different, often awkward and unclear. He struggles with every word until his thoughts and images are presented in a creative manner.

As the poem begins you can see how Barnes illustrates her mother possessing such a creative and natural writing ability. "My mother, that feast of light" is a phrase that stands out, creating a positive view of her mother. A light is something that shows you the way in the dark, it is warm, bright, and alive. When it is used to describe her mother, the reader tends to develop a favorable opinion of her because the word "light" is associated with many positive images. Another phrase that eloquently presents her mother as a talented writer is "To catch the lift of a rabbit in mid-hop." The mother possesses the special ability to refer back to her own memory and create a vivid picture of a rabbit hopping, through the use of her carefully chosen words. The mother has this special ability due to the fact that she spends a great deal of time reflecting upon her vivid memories before she actually begins to write.

"I also remember my father alone at the dining-room table." The word *alone* stands out from the rest of the sentence. It conjures up negative feelings, forcing the reader to sympathize with the father. The phrase is written in common, everyday language lacking the imagination and creativity that was present in the first sentence describing the mother. Barnes seems to change her own style of writing when describing each parent. She describes her parents the way they might describe themselves: the mother who is very confident and expressive as opposed to the father who is unsure and always struggling with his words. Barnes writes with great detail and imagination, reinforcing the image of her mother as a talented poet. Her style changes when she describes her father. Her images become plain and uncreative, presenting her father as a struggling writer.

The idea that her father is a hard-working writer is reinforced once again. "The ink bottle safe in a bowl, his orange-red fountain pen in his big hand." Why is her father so persistent? It must be because he has ideas in his head that he wants to express on paper. Unfortunately he has a great deal of difficulty doing so. "The ink bottle is safe in a bowl" symbolizes the thoughts and images that are trapped in his head; he must struggle with them to get his ideas onto paper. Often the way he writes is awkward, which seems due to his large hand. We assume that the word *big* represents the difficulty he has with writing his thoughts down clearly. Fortunately, he does not allow his big hand to keep him from writing, although writing is much more of a struggle for him than for his wife.

Both of these writers are equally gifted, but go about writing in two totally different ways. Their thoughts are dreamlike (vivid but unreal) and until they reach paper their readers cannot see and feel the thoughts that they are trying so hard to share. The mother's method appears very carefree and simple, making her come across as a confident writer whom many readers may envy. The father struggles through his writing. His frustrations dealing with poetry are very common and familiar emotions that cause the reader to empathize with him. As you can see, Barnes uses her words not only to illustrate the two different writing styles but to force the reader to feel the same emotions that she, as a writer, is trying so hard to get across.

ANALYSIS OF POEM BY H.D.
Norman Holland

As my treating the poem in three sections shows, however, I am not responding to it in a completely subjective, intuitive way.* I also respond to it as a professional

---

* For the earlier section of Holland's essay about this poem, see p. 266. H.D.'s poem appears on p. 265.

reader, a critic and teacher using what discipline, skill, and experience I have. As a professional, the first and most basic question I ask myself is, How can I interrelate all the different details of the poem? This, to me, is the fundamental task of the literary critic, and it is one that all readers almost automatically set themselves. Certainly Saul and Sandra did.

For me, a great deal of this poem comes together around the theme of boundaries. In a literal way, the whole poem says, "if you create an outer boundary, you achieve security against outer forces so that you can create within." That "you," however, masks over one of the boundaries within the poem. That is, as I argued to Sandra, I see it in three discrete sections: lines 1–22 which are written in the third person about the shellfish; lines 23–37 which speak in the first person—"I sense my own limit," "I in my own way know"; and lines 38–46 which address "you."

To my abstracting eye, size also marks off these three sections. The last part deals with things inside, smaller than the shellfish. The middle section deals with animal-sized things. True, they vary from mollusc and egg to whale and octopus and even on to "limitless ocean-weight; infinite water" (although this is surely hyperbole—the distance is the depth of the ocean, not infinity). Even so, these are distances that have to do with life on earth, unlike the distances in the first part of the poem which go beyond "the planet" which "senses the finite" and "limits its orbit," distances astronomical in size, approaching the "infinity" which would be "too much" compared to the earthly "tide-flow." Associated with this first, largest section are words like "spell," "marvel," "temple, fane, shrine," or "hermit," with religious dimensions. Scallop-shell, egg, and pearl can all serve as symbols for the Virgin (although I do not know if I would have noticed this in the poem if I were not already aware of H.D.'s interest in mythological and religious signs).

I sense the importance of boundaries in still another way, by lists like "coral, / bone, stone, marble," or "house, / temple, fane, shrine." The beginning or end of such a list constitutes a boundary, and I would expect those boundaries to coincide with the stanza or line boundaries within the poem. Here they do not coincide, and I find myself made more sharply aware of the whole question of where one stanza leaves off and another begins. Consider the sequence of phrases in the sentences which says the water

> can not crack me, egg in egg-shell;
> closed in, complete, immortal
>
> full circle, I know the pull
> of the tide . . .

Although a semicolon marks off the egg from the "full circle," they could equally well be appositives connected by commas. The sentences run into one another in sense (if not punctuation) with no clear semantic boundary, especially none that coincides with line or stanza divisions.

As against these fluid boundaries, the plain sense of the poem urges "you" to set boundaries up, and many words and phrases, like "be firm" or "unlocks," presuppose the existence of definite limits. This is a poem that lets me find plenty of boundaries in its form—a boundary every two lines, in fact. Yet the poem sloshes over these boundaries with run-on sentences, phrases carrying across from one stanza or line to the next, and overlapping lists, until the last half-dozen lines. Then it firmly imposes limits, even within lines, as it tells us to do. Read aloud, those last lines sound this way to my ear: Be indigestible . . . hard . . . ungiving . . . so that . . . living within . . . You beget . . . self-out-of-self . . . selfless . . . that pearl-of-great-price.

In its larger, structural form, I find each of the poem's three phases starts small, opens up, and then closes down again. The first begins with "it," the tiny animal inside a seashell, but enlarges it to a planet in its orbit, and then closes down again at line 22 with "nothing-too-much." The second begins there, in the first person now ("*I* sense *my* own limit"), but compares that tiny me to the moon in the octopus-darkness and then clamps down again with the reassurance that "the whale cannot digest me" at line 37. Finally, the third section deals with "you," tells *you* to be firm so you will be safe against the vast, abstract "outer circumstance," and then it clamps down again with the tight phrasings of the last half-dozen lines. In form, then, as well as content, the poem, as I re-create it for myself, lets the boundaries down and sets them up again.

In short, in my experience of it, the poem comes together around twinned themes of creation and dependency, both comprised in the single idea of boundaries. Dependency makes one vulnerable to threats from outside. Against them one sets up a definition of self created from within like a seashell, but outside the self. Then that first act of creation permits another, a still more beautiful creation, like a pearl, inside. In other words, if you set up barriers to hold off threats from outside, you achieve both an inner security and a magical power to create a double beauty, a beautiful boundary outside like a seashell or inside like a pearl. And, of course, the poem (read this way) matches H.D.'s general pattern: to perceive the relation between oneself and the world as a gap; then, isolated, to create—or even be—the beautiful thing that fills the gap. Further, this central theme brings into a coherent whole even such oddities in the poem as the "for instance" of the first stanza and the "pearl-of-great-price" of the last. Each reaches out beyond this poem to something else, either the poem before this in the cycle of *The Walls Do Not Fall* or the riches of reference and symbolism in the Biblical echo. Thus each calls attention to a boundary while it breaches it—as indeed the whole poem does and the act of creation must always do.

WEN-FU
Lu Chi (A.D. 261–303)

Taking his position at the hub of things, [the writer] contemplates
the mystery of the universe; he feeds his emotions and his
mind on the great works of the past.

Moving along with the four seasons, he sighs at the passing of
time; gazing at the myriad objects, he thinks of the complexity
of the world.

He sorrows over the falling leaves in virile autumn; he takes joy in
the delicate bud of fragrant spring.

With awe at heart, he experiences chill; his spirit solemn, he
turns his gaze to the clouds.

He declaims the superb works of his predecessors; he croons the
clean fragrance of past worthies.

He roams in the Forest of Literature, and praises the symmetry of
great art.

Moved, he pushes his books away and takes the writing-brush,
that he may express himself in letters.

At first he withholds his sight and turns his hearing inward; he is
    lost in thought, questioning everywhere.
His spirit gallops to the eight ends of the universe; his mind
    wanders along vast distances.
In the end, as his mood dawns clearer and clearer, objects, clean-
    cut now in outline, shove one another forward.
He sips the essence of letters; he rinses his mouth with the extract
    of the Six Arts.
Floating on the heavenly lake, he swims along; plunging into the
    nether spring, he immerses himself.
Thereupon, submerged words wriggle up, as when a darting fish,
    with the hook in its gills, leaps from a deep lake; floating
    beauties flutter down, as when a high-flying bird, with the har-
    poon-string around its wing, drops from a crest of cloud.
He gathers words never used in a hundred generations; he picks
    rhythms never sung in a thousand years.
He spurns the morning blossom, now full blown; he plucks the
    evening bud, which has yet to open.
He sees past and present in a moment; he touches the four seas in
    a twinkling of an eye.
Now he selects ideas and fixes them in order; he examines words
    and puts them in their places.
He taps at the door of all that is colorful; he chooses from among
    everything that rings.
Now he shakes the foliage by tugging the twig; now he follows
    back along the waves to the fountainhead of the stream.
Sometimes he brings out what was hidden; sometimes, looking for
    an easy prey, he bags a hard one.
Now, the tiger puts in new stripes, to the consternation of other
    beasts; now, the dragon emerges, and terrifies all the birds.
Sometimes things fit together, are easy to manage; sometimes
    they jar each other, are awkward to manipulate.
He empties his mind completely, to concentrate his thoughts; he
    collects his wits before he puts words together.
He traps heaven and earth in the cage of form; he crushes the
    myriad objects against the tip of his brush.
At first they hesitate upon his parched lips; finally they flow
    through the well-moistened brush.
Reason, supporting the matter [of the poem], stiffens the trunk;
    style, depending from it, spreads luxuriance around.
Emotion and expression never disagree; all changes [in his mood]
    are betrayed on his face.
If the thought touches on joy, a smile is inevitable; no sooner is
    sorrow spoken of than a sigh escapes. . . .

THE BOOK OF THE GROTESQUE
Sherwood Anderson

The writer, an old man with a white mustache, had some difficulty in getting into
bed. The windows of the house in which he lived were high and he wanted to look

at the trees when he awoke in the morning. A carpenter came to fix the bed so that it would be on a level with the window.

Quite a fuss was made about the matter. The carpenter, who had been a soldier in the Civil War, came into the writer's room and sat down to talk of building a platform for the purpose of raising the bed. The writer had cigars lying about and the carpenter smoked.

For a time the two men talked of the raising of the bed and then they talked of other things. The soldier got on the subject of the war. The writer, in fact, led him to that subject. The carpenter had once been a prisoner in Andersonville prison and had lost a brother. The brother had died of starvation, and whenever the carpenter got upon that subject he cried. He, like the old writer, had a white mustache, and when he cried he puckered up his lips and the mustache bobbed up and down. The weeping old man with the cigar in his mouth was ludicrous. The plan the writer had for the raising of his bed was forgotten and later the carpenter did it in his own way and the writer, who was past sixty, had to help himself with a chair when he went to bed at night.

In his bed the writer rolled over on his side and lay quite still. For years he had been beset with notions concerning his heart. He was a hard smoker and his heart fluttered. The idea had got into his mind that he would some time die unexpectedly and always when he got into bed he thought of that. It did not alarm him. The effect in fact was quite a special thing and not easily explained. It made him more alive, there in bed, than at any other time. Perfectly still he lay and his body was old and not of much use any more, but something inside him was altogether young. He was like a pregnant woman, only that the thing inside him was not a baby but a youth. No, it wasn't a youth, it was a woman, young, and wearing a coat of mail like a knight. It is absurd, you see, to try to tell what was inside the old writer as he lay on his high bed and listened to the fluttering of his heart. The thing to get at is what the writer, or the young thing within the writer, was thinking about.

The old writer, like all of the people in the world, had got, during his long life, a great many notions in his head. He had once been quite handsome and a number of women had been in love with him. And then, of course, he had known people, many people, known them in a peculiarly intimate way that was different from the way in which you and I know people. At least that is what the writer thought and the thought pleased him. Why quarrel with an old man concerning his thoughts?

In the bed the writer had a dream that was not a dream. As he grew somewhat sleepy but was still conscious, figures began to appear before his eyes. He imagined the young indescribable thing within himself was driving a long procession of figures before his eyes.

You see the interest in all this lies in the figures that went before the eyes of the writer. They were all grotesques. All of the men and women the writer had ever known had become grotesques.

The grotesques were not all horrible. Some were amusing, some almost beautiful, and one, a woman all drawn out of shape, hurt the old man by her grotesqueness. When she passed he made a noise like a small dog whimpering. Had you come into the room you might have supposed the old man had unpleasant dreams or perhaps indigestion.

For an hour the procession of grotesques passed before the eyes of the old man, and then, although it was a painful thing to do, he crept out of bed and began to write. Some one of the grotesques had made a deep impression on his mind and he wanted to describe it.

At his desk the writer worked for an hour. In the end he wrote a book which he called "The Book of the Grotesque." It was never published, but I saw it once and it made an indelible impression on my mind. The book had one central thought that is very strange and has always remained with me. By remembering it I have been able to understand many people and things that I was never able to understand before. The thought was involved but a simple statement of it would be something like this:

That in the beginning when the world was young there were a great many thoughts but no such thing as a truth. Man made the truths himself and each truth was a composite of a great many vague thoughts. All about in the world were the truths and they were all beautiful.

The old man had listed hundreds of the truths in his book. I will not try to tell you of all of them. There was the truth of virginity and the truth of passion, the truth of wealth and of poverty, of thrift and of profligacy, of carelessness and abandon. Hundreds and hundreds were the truths and they were all beautiful.

And then the people came along. Each as he appeared snatched up one of the truths and some who were quite strong snatched up a dozen of them.

It was the truths that made the people grotesques. The old man had quite an elaborate theory concerning the matter. It was his notion that the moment one of the people took one of the truths to himself, called it his truth, and tried to live his life by it, he became a grotesque and the truth he embraced became a falsehood.

You can see for yourself how the old man, who had spent all of his life writing and was filled with words, would write hundreds of pages concerning this matter. The subject would become so big in his mind that he himself would be in danger of becoming a grotesque. He didn't, I suppose, for the same reason that he never published the book. It was the young thing inside him that saved the old man.

Concerning the old carpenter who fixed the bed for the writer, I only mentioned him because he, like many of what are called very common people, became the nearest thing to what is understandable and lovable of all the grotesques in the writer's book.

MINI-
UNITS

Writing Skills Questionnaire

In order to help you get more out of our text and take more control over your own learning, we've made a list of specific skills we are attempting to teach. Filling out the questionnaire will help you notice better what you are learning and not learning—and help us teach you better.

You will benefit most from this questionnaire if you fill it out three times—at the beginning, middle, and end of the course. This way you'll be able to see more about what changes are taking place. (The second and third times you use this form, you may want to cover your previous answers.)

When you complete the questionnaire at the beginning of the course, fill in the *left-hand* column of blanks. In the middle of the course, use the *middle* column of blanks. At the end use the *right-hand* column of blanks.

Use *Y, N,* and *S,* for "Yes," "No," and "Sometimes." If you don't know the answer—which may often happen at the start of the course—use a question mark.

ATTITUDES TOWARD WRITING

— — — Do you enjoy writing?

— — — In general do you trust yourself as a person who can find good words and ideas and perceptions?

— — — Do you think of yourself as a writer?

GENERATING

— — — On a *topic of interest to you,* can you generate lots of words fairly quickly and freely—not be stuck?

— — — Again on a topic of interest to you, can you come up with ideas or insights you'd not thought of before?

— — — On a topic that *doesn't* much interest you (perhaps an assigned topic), can you generate lots of words fairly quickly and freely— not be stuck?

— — — On a topic not of interest, can you come up with ideas or insights you'd not thought of before?

— — — On a topic where you start out not knowing what you think, can you write or think your way through to a conclusion?

— — — On a topic where you start out with your mind made up, can you write or think your way into actually *changing* your mind?

REVISING

— — — Can you revise in the literal sense of "resee"—thus rethink and change your mind about major things you have said?

— — — Can you find a main point in a mess of your disorganized writing?

— — — Can you find a *new* shape in a piece of your writing which you had previously organized?

— — — Can you find problems in your reasoning or logic and straighten them out?

— — — Can you make your sentences clear—so they are clear to readers on first reading?

— — — Can you get your sentences lively? Can you give them a human voice?

— — — Can you get rid of *most* mistakes in grammar, spelling, punctuation, and so on. Can you clean your writing up enough so most readers would not be put off?

— — — Can you get rid of virtually *all* such mistakes?

PROCESS BOX

People will not realize how little conscious one is of these things [technical cleverness]; how one flounders about. They want us to be better than we are. . . .

E. M. FORSTER, *PARIS REVIEW*

— — — Can you guess how most readers will react to something you've written?

— — — Can you adjust something you've written to fit the needs of particular readers?

FEEDBACK

— — — Can you enjoy sharing with friends a draft of what you've written?

— — — Can you read out loud to listeners a draft of your writing so it is really clear and "given," that is, not mumbled and "held back"?

— — — Can you openly listen to the reactions of a reader to your writing and try to see it as she sees it, even if you think her reactions are all wrong?

— — — Can you give noncritical feedback—telling the writer what you like and summarizing or reflecting what you hear the words saying?

— — — Can you give "movies of your mind" as a reader—a clear story of what was happening in your mind as you were reading someone's writing?

— — — Can you give "criterion-based feedback"—telling the writer how the draft matches up against the most common criteria of good writing?

COLLABORATION

— — — Can you work on a task collaboratively with a small group: pitch in, share the work, help the group cooperate, keep the group on the task?

AWARENESS AND CONTROL OF WRITING PROCESS

— — — Can you give a *detailed* account of what was going on when you were writing: the thoughts and feelings that go through your mind and the things that happen in the text?

— — — Do you notice problems or "stuck points" in your writing and figure out what the causes are?

— — — Can you make changes in the way you go about writing based on those things you noticed?

— — — Can you vary the way you go about writing depending on the situation: the topic, audience, type of writing, and so on.

Double-Entry or Dialectical Notebooks

> *All there is to thinking ... is seeing something*
> *noticeable which makes you see something you*
> *weren't noticing which makes you see something*
> *that isn't even visible.*
> —Norman Maclean, *A River Runs Through It*

One of the goals of this book is to help you pay more attention to the *way* you write—what actually goes on as you put words down—how you make meaning and change meaning. Thus all the process writing.

It turns out to be just as useful to pay attention to the way you *read*— and interestingly enough the central activities are the same: making meaning and changing meaning. In this unit we will show you a simple and practical way to take notes on what you are reading. In the short term, a double-entry notebook helps you understand better the particular piece you are reading: in the long term it improves your skill in reading. More about the theory in the "Ruminations and Theory" section.

KEEPING A DIALECTICAL OR DOUBLE-ENTRY NOTEBOOK

Let us quote Ann Berthoff, who devised this procedure:

I ask my students (all of them: freshmen, upperclassmen, teachers in graduate seminars) to furnish themselves with a notebook, spiral bound at the side, small enough to be easily carried around but not so small that writing is cramped. . . . What makes this notebook different from most, perhaps, is the notion of the double-entry: on the right side reading notes, direct quotations, observational notes, fragments, lists, images—verbal and visual—are recorded; on the other (facing) side, *notes about those notes,* summaries, formulations, aphorisms, editorial suggestions, revisions, comments on comments are written. The reason for the double-entry format is that it provides a way for the student to conduct that "continuing audit of meaning" that is at the heart of learning to read and write critically. The facing pages are in dialogue with each other (44).

That's all there is to it. But if you do this regularly, you will notice how that dialogue—that continuing audit of meaning—gradually helps you read more accurately and more creatively and thus helps you get more out of your reading.

Try it (1) on a piece of reading, then (2) on a piece of your experience.

1. Choose a piece of reading that you can learn from and reflect on—not just something you read to pass the time. Start reading it, and as you do, pause to write down (on the right side of your notebook) words, details, images, or thoughts that strike you. You're not "taking notes." Don't clench and try to capture or summarize everything; just encourage yourself to note words and ideas and reactions that draw your attention—to muse and speculate about your reading. If you find yourself reading more than a few pages without any notations, stop and ask yourself what you noticed in those pages you just read—or how you were reacting. At the end make a few more notations to capture quickly what's in your head as you finish reading.

Now read these entries back slowly. As you do, jot down on the left side of your notebook whatever comes into your mind as you read the right side. There is no "right" way to do this, but here are some suggestions of entries you could make:

- Summary. What's the most important thing you notice about your notes as you read them over? What kinds of connections can you find in your notes? What conclusions about your reading do your notes make possible? What parts now seem particularly important or unimportant. (It's wise to consider carefully what *seems* unimportant: something about it attracted your attention.)

- Second thoughts. What further ideas do your recorded notes suggest?

- How do your notes relate to other parts of your life—to your deepest concerns or interests?

- Reactions to your reactions. What do your notes tell you about how your mind works or what you are interested in?

- Dialogue with the author. What do *you* have to say? How would he or she reply?

- Who do you want to talk to about these things? What would you tell or ask them?

Don't worry about the exact difference between what to write on the right and on the left. There's no rigid difference. Mainly it boils down to time: as you are reading something for the first time, whatever you write goes on the right side. As you read this over, whatever additional thoughts you have go on the left. Thus the important thing about this process is to get your *thoughts to be in dialogue with each other.* The dialectical notebook makes it possible for you to exploit the advantages of being two people at once—having two different viewpoints or having discussions with yourself. (Thus it is like our exercises in writing dialogues.)

2. Try the same thing with a recent experience: an important conversation, argument, or interchange with someone; a walk that was important to you (perhaps in a beautiful place or at a time when you needed to think something over); an activity that was important to you (such as being in a deciding game, taking a crucial exam, surviving a harrowing ordeal, or being invited to a party with new friends). On the right side, put down first-stage notes: what you can remember, what you notice. Then go on to write second-stage reflexive *notes on those notes* on the left side of your notebook.

If possible, share both sides of your notebook with others and listen as they read theirs. This will give you some hints about the ways others read, ways you may want to try out. Others will learn from you in the same way.

RUMINATIONS AND THEORY

Dialectical Notebooks and the Parallel between Reading and Writing

The dialectical or double-entry notebook reinforces the *parallel* between reading and writing. The central activity in both is the *making of meaning.* We tend to think that "meaning" is "out there," that our task in reading and writing is to discover it—not to make it. But even though it *looks as though* writers "have" meanings which they "put into the words"—and then readers "take the meaning out" at the other end—this is an illusion. We don't have a meaning till we have words for it. But even this does not encompass the complexity: words cannot "have" or "contain" meanings—only people can; words are only meaningful insofar as people *attribute* meanings to them. In short, words cannot transport a writer's meanings into our heads; they can only give us a set of directions for creating our own meanings in our own heads—meanings which, *if all goes well,* will resemble what the writer had in mind.

It's as though the writer has movies in her mind and she wants to *give* us her movies. But in truth she cannot. She has to hope that she has been clever enough to create a set of directions that leads us to create movies in our minds that are like the ones in hers. Needless to say, that's hard. This little allegory explains something we all know about language: that it's hard to make people truly understand what we have in mind.

This view of language and communications as *complex* shows us something important about reading (or listening): reading is not finding meaning but *making meaning*—not hunting for messages that are already there, but building messages. If you have the wrong idea of reading, you tend to feel (if things go well), "Oh goody, I found it"—as in an Easter egg hunt. And if things don't go well you feel, "Oh dear, where did they hide it?" When you are having difficulty in reading, it's counterproductive to think of it as a problem in finding a pesky little hidden packet; it's better to think of it as a problem in building or creating.

We're not going so far as to say (as Humpty Dumpty did to Alice) that words can mean anything—that we can build any meaning we want out of a set of someone else's words. There are *rules* for doing this building which people have to obey, or they build all wrong. We all know the difference between being involved in successful communication and unsuccessful communication, though most of us would be hard put to articulate *how* we know this. The trouble is that the rules for building meanings out of words are *unstated,* and they are *continually in the process of negotiation.* For that's a picture of a natural language (such as English): a game played by a large number of people where they follow unspoken rules which (because they are unspoken) are continually in the process of slight change. Can you remember games like "Pass the Scissors" where you join in and play before you know the rules—and the process of playing is the process of trying to learn the rules? That's how it is with language. And that's why critics and ordinary readers are able to find new meanings even in much-studied classics such as *Hamlet.*

Therefore to help us read better—particularly when we are reading something difficult or our reading is not going well—we need to pay more attention to the *process by which we build meanings out of other people's words.* A dialectical notebook helps us do that. It can help you assess what happens when you engage in *making meaning* from a text. Do you have strong feelings about the subject matter? or about the writer? Are you bored by it? What associations jump to mind as you read? How does this writing relate to other things you know and other things in your life? Do you tend to create mental images as you read or relate what you're reading to other things you have read? Do you attend mainly to ideas or to the way something is written? What things impress you? What things do you tend to overlook? We cannot know the *rules* for building meaning—almost no one does—but we can watch more closely as we go about building meaning. We can learn to be more sensitive and insightful as we read—and perhaps learn to detect what doesn't fit the meaning we're gradually building up. (What doesn't fit often provides clues to the need for us to shift our sights a bit.) We *can* learn something about *how* and *why* we construct the meanings we do construct. All this we can do instead of just saying, "Where is the meaning? Where did the writer hide it?"

○○○○○

This mini-unit draws heavily on Ann Berthoff's "A Curious Triangle and the Double-Entry Notebook; or How Theory Can Help Us Teach Reading and Writing." The notebook is her idea. But see also Peter Elbow's "Methodological Doubting and Believing" in *Embracing Contraries* (151–53).

Breathing Life into Words: Text Rendering or Reading Out Loud

It's an old principle that the best *interpretation* of a text is a good *performance* of it: a good reading of it out loud. Whether your goal is the enjoyment of a text or the practical goal of having to work out a full interpretation (perhaps for an essay assignment), the fastest and most satisfying way to learn what a text means and how it works is to read it out loud.

But first, we want to speak for a moment to any misgivings you may have about reading out loud. It may be that you *hate* it. Many students do: when we make them do it, they feel we are punishing them. There are many reasons you may feel this way:

- You may feel self-conscious when you read out loud: as though you are "making a spectacle of yourself" or "sticking out"—or even "making a fool of yourself."

- You may be bad at it.

- It may in fact have been "punishment" in school when everyone had to take a turn reading aloud from the book—and if you were bad, you had to read more.

- You may even hate having someone read aloud *to* you, feeling as though the enjoyment is "babyish" (even though you undoubtedly loved it as a child).

But we find that once we give students practice in reading aloud, most of them appreciate it: partly for the practical benefits that we stress here, but also for the pure pleasure of making words alive instead of dead. There are some important guidelines we've learned, however, for overcoming bad feelings about it.

- If you're not used to reading out loud, it's best to start with your *own* writing. Then you have the best reason to read out loud: your text is probably handwritten, perhaps marked up with corrections and revisions, so that others would have a hard time reading it. But you know how it should sound, and you have a reason to want to get it across to others. (We hope you've already done lots of this reading in sharing sessions.)

- When we push someone to render something he didn't write, we always give him some time to practice reading it aloud to himself: to whisper privately or speak it out loud in his head. This gives him a chance to stumble and experiment, to check out the pronunciation of unfamiliar words, and to figure out what the piece means and how to express it. It's not fair either to the reader or to the listeners to push someone to read something out loud they can't read decently. (After someone has practiced, we help him with his shyness by insisting that he come out with it forcefully.)

TRYING IT OUT

The main thing is practice. Following are four slightly different ways of practicing text rendering as interpretation.

1. Text rendering or interpretation as figuring out the *literal meaning*. Suppose you are faced with a text that is difficult to understand. You look at it and it looks odd; you start reading it over silently and can't figure out what it's saying (even if you know most of the words and phrases). Perhaps it is a modern poem—perhaps one without any punctuation—or an experimental short story or novel, or something with older language like Chaucer or Shakespeare used.

Try reading it out loud. Force yourself to *say* the words—trying to feel out the best way to phrase them. If the language seems odd or difficult, sound it out tentatively and listen for how it "goes": where the words seem to speed up, pause, or stop; where the stresses appear; where your voice rises and falls in pitch. Your instinct can guide you as you proceed. Of course you may stumble a bit and need to try a line one way and then another. You may find yourself repeating a particularly difficult spot. But you'll be surprised at how often your *voice* and your *ear* find sense in a passage of words where your eye was lost. Your voice and ear have better instincts than your eye about rhythm, intonation, and syntax.

Here is a poem that seems difficult when read silently, but becomes clearer (if not completely clear) when you read it out loud. You need to give yourself a chance to stumble and experiment as you try it out. Don't just go through it once and give up; don't allow yourself to get bogged down by trying to interpret it as you read. Give your voice and ear freedom. Read it through five, six, seven times—however many times it takes to go from beginning to end fluidly.

SPRING AND FALL:
To a Young Child

Márgarét, are you gríeving
Over Goldengrove unleaving?
Leáves, líke the things of man, you
With your fresh thoughts care for, can you?
Áh! ás the heart grows older
It will come to such sights colder
By and by, nor spare a sigh
Though worlds of wanwood leafmeal lie;
And yet you wíll weep and know why.
Now no matter, child, the name:
Sórrow's spríngs áre the same.
Nor mouth had, no nor mind, expressed
What heart heard of, ghost guessed:
It ís the blight man was born for,
It is Margaret you mourn for.

—Gerard Manley Hopkins

2. Text rendering or making the meaning *live*. Reading is no fun, however, if it's only figuring out the plain meaning—as though it were a puzzle. What makes reading worthwhile is when the meaning seems alive and jumps from the page to your mind—and lives in your mind. Text rendering helps here too more than anything else. When language works at its best, the "inner dimension" (meaning) and the "outer dimension" (sound, rhythm, emphasis, and tone) all work together. This is what it means for words to have life or breath. Try reading the Hopkins poem again—but this time make your task not just to figure out the literal meaning; try to read the text aloud in a way that can help *make the meaning clear to a listener who has never heard the words before and has no text to look at.* In fact, when you first read it to someone, she should *not* have the text before her.

Or try the activity with this poem by William Carlos Williams:

A SORT OF SONG

Let the snake wait under
his weed
and the writing
be of words, slow and quick, sharp
to strike, quiet to wait,
sleepless.

—through metaphor to reconcile
the people and the stones.
Compose. (No ideas
but in things) Invent!
Saxifrage is my flower that splits
the rocks.

We're not trying to imply that text rendering is only for poetic or creative texts. You can take any text—or passage from a text—that you simply want to understand better. Practice saying the text till you can say it so that listeners *hear* or *experience* the meaning. That's all. But it's not easy. The process will make you not just understand the text but get inside it so that you can *mean* the words as you say them. For that's the central act in reading something out loud so it works: *you* have to succeed in feeling or experiencing the meaning in the words. Listeners can tell when you are asleep at the switch, when you are just going through motions and reciting something you haven't gotten inside of. This is just as necessary when reading expository prose as when reading fiction or poetry. If you are reading a physics textbook and having trouble, you can solve much of the problem (perhaps not all) by forcing yourself to read it out loud.

Try working out a reading of the following passage from William James till you can really experience what he is saying, till you can say it so that a listener will get the meaning.

The Empirical Self of each of us is all that he is tempted to call by the name of *me*. But it is clear that between what a man calls *me* and what he simply calls *mine* the line is difficult to draw. We feel and act about certain things that are ours very much as we feel and act about ourselves. Our fame, our children, the work of our hands, may be as dear to us as our bodies are, and arouse the same feelings and the same acts of reprisal if attacked. And our bodies themselves, are they simply ours, or are they *us?* Certainly men have been ready to disown their very bodies and to regard them as mere vestures, or even as prisons of clay from which they should some day be glad to escape.

You will sometimes feel a kind of click when you get something to sound right—and when you do, you will immediately understand better what the piece is about and how it works.

It is helpful to hear different readings of the same passage by two or more people (and the readings will differ even if the passage is a plain and straightforward piece of prose). Listeners can simply tell which parts of which readings *came through* most clearly. If you then discuss individual reactions, the discussion will inevitably lead you to the relationship of the form and the meaning and to questions of how words work on readers— and thus lead you right to the heart of the most important questions for interpretation.

Notice that you are trying to *act* or *perform* or *dramatize* here: you are trying to let the meaning find its way into sound. Have you noticed that good readers of poetry often don't act at all? Sometimes there is no "personality" in their readings. Sometimes they sort of chant or intone the words, searching *not* for performance but for the *sound* of the meaning-in-language.

3. Text rendering or interpretation as *finding the right voice, tone, stance.* When we discuss the interpretation of a story, essay, or poem, or when we are writing an essay of interpretation, one of the main doorways

---

PROCESS BOX

[*I had been writing in a workshop and now for 15 minutes the assignment was to do some process writing—and perhaps consider the question, "What do you want or need to work on?" Here is part of what I wrote.*]

Also I need to work on more "connected" writing—like I did this morning—where I pretend it's a letter and I'm *not* to revise. In much of my at-home-on-a-word-processor writing, I make too much of a mess. I don't enough proceed somewhat slowly as I do now in this by-hand writing, and *speak* the words deliberately onto the paper. I think there is sometimes more voice and energy in some of the writing I do by hand in workshops like this than the drafting I do on the computer. On the computer I go so fast and make rushes of words—and then change them and change them—sometimes in mid phrase. Here I create more genuine and full *sentences*—not exactly *craft* them—but I pause and give some deliberation. I guess there's a bit of the indelible quality to my by-hand writing—which is after all in ink. I realize I can't so easily undo it, so I give a bit more *weight* to what I write. Do I pause first? Maybe. And when I'm embarked on a sentence I somehow force myself to push my way through it instead of just throwing down words and being able to recast or change them.

PETER ELBOW

---

in is through voice, tone, or stance. We may argue, for example, about whether words are ironic or sarcastic or straight. To answer such questions is central to interpretation—yet difficult. And arguments about such questions are notoriously hard to settle. Probably the best way to deal with these issues is to work out your own reading and then compare alternate readings by others. Again, your voice and ear often *tell* you the tone before you even need to think about the question in theoretical terms. And instead of letting two people argue on and on, have them each *read* the text as they think it should sound. That sometimes settles things, and when it does not (after all, texts do invite different readings) it usually makes the discussion much more fruitful and down to earth.

By the way, don't assume that you can use this approach only on short poems or short pieces—just because we have used such pieces here for convenience. If you are working on a long essay or story, even a novel, you can pick out passages that seem most interesting or perplexing or passages that seem to illustrate the main voices or tones in the piece—and work out readings. Once you can say and hear an important passage right, you can often hear the interpretation of the whole piece.

For example, if you are trying to discuss how *The Adventures of Huckleberry Finn* works, you could center the whole discussion on the task of figuring out how its opening passage should *sound*—how it should be read. Try out different readings and talk about which attempts *sound* right. The discussion will probably boil down to figuring out what kind of person Huck is and how he relates to Twain. The best way to deal with that slippery theoretical discussion is with the ear as you try out different voices.

> You don't know about me, without you have read a book by the name of "The Adventures of Tom Sawyer," but that ain't no matter. That book was made by Mr. Mark Twain, and he told the truth, mainly. There was things which he stretched, but mainly he told the truth. That is nothing. I never seen anybody but lied, one time or another, without it was Aunt Polly, or the widow, or maybe Mary. Aunt Polly—Tom's Aunt Polly, she is—and Mary, and the Widow Douglas, is all told about in that book—which is mostly a true book; with some stretchers, as I said before.

4. Text rendering or interpretation as *hearing other voices:* play, distortion, exaggeration, parody, deconstruction. Sometimes the best way to discover what's in a text is by a process of elimination; see what's not there and what's almost, sort of, marginally there: try out distorting lenses. Read a text aloud in a way that deliberately exaggerates or parodies it. Obviously you'll discover what's not in the text, but the striking thing about this playing around is how it surprises you: you keep discovering that what you assumed was all wrong and a complete violation of the text manages in fact to capture a subtle note that's really there. When you do a hysterical reading of some staid essay, you'll catch a glimpse of some below-the-surface hysteria; or a tragic reading of a comic piece may show you a bit of darkness

lurking there. There is often a bit of rightness in that "wrong" voice, tone, or stance.

You can try this playfully "foolish" approach on any of the preceding examples. Or try it on the opening passage of *Pride and Prejudice.*

It is a truth universally acknowledged that a single man in possession of a good fortune must be in want of a wife.

However little known the feelings or views of such a man may be on his first entering a neighborhood, this truth is so well fixed in the minds of the surrounding families, that he is considered as the rightful property of someone or other of their daughters.

Try it on an advertisement or a political speech.

Try it on the essay or story you are currently writing: you'll discover some rich hints and possibilities you didn't know were in your own text. Sometimes you'll decide to get rid of this underlying tone or voice: maybe you uncover a hint of whining or self-pity which you know undercuts your meaning. But sometimes you'll decide to emphasize one of these faint notes, bring it more to the foreground and out of obscurity. For example, you may uncover in your serious essay a humorous strand that is worth bringing out. It's not so uncommon to uncover a tone of uncertainty and doubt you didn't know was there. You'll feel the impulse to get rid of it; maybe it undermines your position. But think again. More often than not your piece will be stronger if it *acknowledges* that doubt better and allows itself to be somewhat *about* the uncertainty you were hiding from yourself.

Here then is a way to find the richness of implications in almost any set of words. All these exercises in breathing life into words are ways of learning to read better.

Writing with a Word Processor

ADVANTAGES OF USING A WORD PROCESSOR

The two main cognitive skills needed for writing well are the ability to *make* a mess and to *clean up* that mess. That is, you can't have *good* words unless you have more to choose from than you can use—which means a mess. Yet in order to write well, you also need the opposite mental skill: the ability to doubt, reject, and change, that is, to clean up that fertile mess. It turns out that the word processor is ideal for both these mental operations.

The word processor helps you get more down quicker. When you're trying to get started—which is usually the hardest part of writing—you can start anywhere, often in the middle. You just start with an idea that you feel confident of, one you know you will want in there somewhere. This gets you going. You can add other ideas later—before, after, or in the middle of what you've already written. It's much easier to find those missing ideas once you've gotten rolling.

When you are writing on a word processor and your mind jumps to something new (a problem about what you're writing, or a different idea, or an idea about how to organize the piece), you can get it down before you forget. You don't have to try to remember it or jot it on a different piece of paper. You can zip to the beginning or the end of the file and put it there. Or you can write it right where you are: just start a new line or write in caps or indent the whole passage—so it's obvious later that it's an interruption. You don't have to worry about finding the right place for it now; you can move it later. Or if you run out of energy on a particular topic or phase of your project, you can drop it and go on to another idea without worrying about a transition or about effective sequencing of your ideas. You can figure out the structure later—and good ideas for structure often pop into your head when you are steaming along. *Because* you know you can correct and rearrange later, you have more permission to make a mess—but a fruitful, creative mess.

Most of all, the word processor makes it easy to revise. You suddenly see a new idea or new arrangement when you're almost done, and you can wade in and try it. Or you've finished and you're reading it over and you discover something awkward or problematic. Before you would have had to retype the whole thing; now you can quickly make the change and print it again.

The processor even encourages you to experiment with multiple possibilities that you wouldn't have been able to compare using pen or typewriter. You can save a file of what you have and then start revising. Meanwhile you have the original for comparison just in case the experiment makes it worse or—what's more likely—it makes part better and part worse. Being able to revise this way makes it easier for revising to be what it ought to be: movement back and forth between generating and refining, between creating a mess and cleaning up.

We've stressed how word processors help you make a mess, but they turn out paradoxically to be just as useful in cleaning up messes. They make it easy to come up with neat copy: to throw away what you don't want, change and rearrange bits, and fix words and spellings.

Spelling and grammar have always been superficials of writing, but they've always unduly influenced readers and unduly weighed on writers. Snobbery enters in: just as some people look down on others and ignore what they say on the basis of *accent,* even more people do the same thing on the basis of *spelling* and *grammar.* This may be unfair but there is a level of deviation from accepted norms which becomes intolerable to almost everyone. Word processing programs with spelling checkers and so-called grammar checkers can detect many (but not all) mistakes for us.

The word processor also makes it easier to share with readers—sometimes for feedback and sometimes just for the sense of audience. You can quickly print out a copy to try on readers. Even if your piece is at an early stage, you can still have it neat and easy to read. Indeed you can give them a disk and let them comment on the document—or even revise for you. Thus the processor is great for collaborative writing: one person writes a very rough draft and gives a copy of the disk to the other person to revise it through to the next stage; and then the first person revises it again. This is the procedure we've used in writing this book. Before long we couldn't remember who started, who put in what: neither of us feels it as *his* or *her* piece—it feels like *ours.*

NEW ATTITUDE, NEW POWER

The most important effect of using a word processor is probably on one's *attitude* toward writing. It often leads to a subtle but deep change: it can

438

make writing feel more like play, experimentation, even fooling around—less sacred and "heavy." Once you see how easy it is to do away with words on the screen, you no longer think of ideas as permanent just because they've been put into words. Though good writers are often reverent about writing, they are equally adamant about the necessity to play and juggle. Writing with a word processor can get rid of that feeling of anxiety and indelibility about writing—the fear of "putting it down in black and white."

Paradoxically the word processor has a way of convincing you of the power of writing too. You type something and think, "I don't want anyone to read that." You erase it immediately. But somehow it stays with you and affects you as you continue to write—even though it no longer exists anywhere in print. Suddenly you realize that anything you take the trouble to shape into writing assumes a certain independence or power it didn't have before.

An even subtler matter of attitude: it's as though the word processor is a kind of bridge or intermediary between our minds and the paper. Our minds are fluid—and usually messy; writing is static—and supposed to be well organized. The difficulty in writing is trying to bridge this gulf between what is fluid and what is static—what is messy and what is coherent. The word processor can serve as a bridge: it's both mind-like and paper-like. When you get used to writing on a computer, you come to feel as though the words you are writing are half in your mind and half on paper. The computer functions as a second mind and as a second piece of paper.

Like your mind, it is easily changed, fluid, easily emptied; and you can't look at all of it at once. Admittedly you have more distance from what's on the screen than you do from what's in your mind. The computer gives you a bit of leverage, but not as much as you get when you see something on paper. Thus it gives you a second mind that you have more control over.

But when you print out something you are writing, you've moved that "sort of in-mind" document to something that's "sort of on-paper." It's *on* paper—still and quiet—no longer fluid and changeable; you can get a mind scan. Yet it's nevertheless so easily changeable; it's still "wet," and you are never *stuck* with it.

DANGERS

Losing what you've written. When people start using a computer they often proceed very gingerly for fear of hurting this delicate machine by pressing the wrong button. Though you can easily hurt it by dirt, smoke, or spilling something on it, it's hard to do harm by pressing wrong buttons. *But you can harm what you've written*—harm it out of existence. It's fine to start in writing before you have much mastery over your computer or your word processing program, but don't write anything that *matters* till you're good at saving what you've written. Make sure you save onto a backup file every ten to twenty minutes—and onto a backup disk every time you end a spell of work.

I'm writing the little introduction to the anthology of student writing (on returning from a week's vacation). I keep getting stuck. The same thing happened when I had been working on it before vacation and I put it aside. It suddenly strikes me that it might have to do with writing on the word processor. It's the first time I've ever really "composed" on the machine. Trying to write something serious and for an audience; not transcribing a draft of something I have already written; nor just making notes for Middlebury teaching (two tasks which had given me no trouble on the machine).

What's the problem? I keep getting stuck in sentences; millions of options. It's such a short piece; not very complicated. (But I am aware of loaded audience dimension: it will go to all 101 students—and very much from me in my administrative role. Important document. I've never written something to ALL students before. "NOW HEAR THIS.")

It suddenly struck me that perhaps the word processor gives me an overdose of the very thing that I celebrate—and that's driving me crazy: the capability to do SO MUCH editing kept stopping me in mid sentence or mid paragraph and making me think of a different way of saying it; different arrangement. And that was the form of my writing; constantly stopping in mid whatever and starting new sentence, new paragraph.

I suddenly felt that it would have been a relief to be plunged back into the old technology: writing in ink on expensive paper (or talking from a stage): there would have been the necessity to make up my mind and *say* it—say it somehow, and go on—even if not perfect. Thus, I was feeling the pressure or the suction of the possibility of changes and editing and options. It kept preventing me from making up my mind and *saying* what I want to say and not worrying or changing it if it's not right.

Thus, there seems to be a need for the old consciousness that I work against: making up one's mind a bit beforehand.

But there's complexity here: two issues—two kinds of stopping and changing my mind. For the changes I've been making tend to be at a small level: sentences and arrangement. That is, I *wasn't* using the technology for pure exploratory draft writing. I already had more or less made up my mind to some extent as to what I was saying. I kept being driven crazy by the possibilities of different *ways* of saying it.

What would it have been like if I'd been revising on paper: if I'd printed out a draft? I've been trying to train myself to edit on screen. I think that may confuse me. Some very quick changes and additions that I could have done with a pencil were slightly complicated when I had to do them all with keys and cursor.

PETER ELBOW, 8/83

Premature editing. It's so easy to fix mistakes or make changes with a word processor—indeed it seems like fun—that you may find yourself tempted to stop and go back and make a correction every time you mistype, misspell, or change your mind about a word. Learn to block that impulse. Learn to keep on writing and leave the mistakes there. If you think of a better word or phrase, write it where you are, but don't go back and remove the old one. (You may find later that the old one is better or that you want to scrap the whole section—why waste all that time and trouble on something you may later reject?) You may even be tempted to spend lots of time playing for-matting games—on a paragraph or section you later decide to discard. All this can disrupt what may be a productive spurt of idea generation.

If you find you have trouble keeping yourself steaming along—too dis-tracted perhaps by your environment, problems with other things you have to do, or anxiety about word choice, grammar, and spelling—try "invisible writing": turn your screen down. When you can't see what you write, you are *forced* to keep steaming ahead—forced to concentrate intensely on what you are trying to say. Invisible writing becomes easy if you just try it a few times. At first you may be disoriented not to see your words; but if you keep at it, you may find it exhilarating to be almost totally free from words as graphic symbols and totally caught up in words as carriers of meaning.

Too much fluidity. Sometimes you can be tempted into *over-utilizing* the computer's potential for change: you write it this way, then change it to that, then try it a different way, then a fourth. (This can happen from the word level to the section level.) Suddenly your head starts to swim, and you feel you are sinking into quicksand. Some people even get addicted to small-scale *fiddling* with the text and end up spending *more* time than if they were writing with a quill on parchment. The cure shows how this problem is related to that of premature editing: sometimes you have to just force your-self to keep writing and writing in the direction you're going, forbidding yourself to make any changes—pretending you are writing in ink. Once you have a whole draft—or more or less the makings of a draft—then the play-ing with changes doesn't do so much harm. The danger is when you let it interrupt you at early stages.

Wordiness. The "kitchen sink" syndrome. It's good that word processors make people write more (and research shows that they do), but it's not so good that word processors tempt people to leave too much in the final doc-ument. It's so tempting to keep everything you've written. You can just clean it up, find the most logical place in the document, and electronically paste it right in there. If you had to copy the whole piece over again you'd think twice about keeping that extra word, phrase, paragraph, or section! Perhaps the best cure is to force yourself to read the whole thing over *out loud*—so you are forced to experience it as a reader experiences it. Another possible cure is to make one paper into two or even three. This may well have the benefit of making each paper effectively focused.

The seduction of neatness. No matter what you write, you can print it out in lovely neat letters, paragraphs, and pages—perhaps even with all the words spelled right (thanks to a spelling checker). Yet it may be awkward to read, repetitive, and incoherently organized. (And those correctly spelled words may be the wrong ones.) Nothing makes readers feel better treated than to give them a neat document; yet when that neatness serves to cover up messy or careless thinking, those same readers are sometimes even madder at you than if you had handed them something that honestly revealed itself as work in progress. The best cure is the same as before: to force yourself to read over out loud what you have written before giving it to someone. Of course, you can also warn your readers—orally or in writing—that, even though the piece *looks* neat, it is really quite an early draft.

Trying to revise or edit on screen. It may seem as though it's a waste of time to print out a "hard" copy and edit on paper: it takes time to print it out and you have to make changes on paper and then transfer those changes to the file. It's tempting to think you can save time if you just read your piece off the screen and make any editing changes there. But the truth is that you cannot revise well on screen because you can't see enough of the document on the screen. Since you can't get a picture of the whole thing, you lack perspective on the structure and shape of your thinking.

Trying to revise on screen leads to an overload in your own head— makes you slow, tired, and confused. With printed copy, you'll find you can proceed much more crisply and quickly—and with a clearer head. If you worry about consistency of thought, for instance, you can put three passages side by side and work on all three at once. You can't do this on the computer. Thus it's always worth printing a copy to revise from unless you are making *only* tiny changes at the word level—and even here most people find it easier to spot misspellings, typos, and other small mistakes on paper than on screen. (Frequent printing for the sake of revising is also insurance against *losing* what you've written through a mistake or disk error.)

LEARNING TO MASTER YOUR WORD PROCESSOR

Word processing programs can be cheap or expensive, limited or powerful in what they can do, simple or complex to use, poorly explained or well explained. And those factors don't always correlate. We're not experts on this, but we know that you don't have to pay top money to get one that is powerful, well explained, and relatively simple to use. If you are in the position to buy one, take plenty of time and get *lots* of expert advice. And, if possible, devote some time to trying each one out.

More often than not, unfortunately, the instructions are not clear. They tend to be written by technicians and to be "COIK": "Clear Only If Known" already. And they are often aimed at editors more than at real writers. You can negotiate the instructions better if you have a sense of what you *need* to know. Here's our experience of what's important.

Most important. Naming, renaming, copying, and saving files; moving the cursor quickly and comfortably all around the file (it's worth learning any tricks early); efficient deleting (by word, line, sentence, paragraph—or however your program lets you); printing.

Also important. (Some programs won't do all these things.) Working with blocks of text (moving, copying, temporarily hiding them, turning them into a different file); using place markers so you can move quickly here and there in a file; using "windows" (if that's a capability) so you can consult notes or a different file; playing with formatting and reformatting (such as using different margins and page lengths); "hang paragraphing" where you indent a whole paragraph 5 or 10 spaces; and creating and having easy access to footnotes.

Midterm and End-Term Responses to a Writing Course

As teachers we don't benefit much from students' telling us we are terrific or awful teachers. But when a student can give us a specific picture of what she's learned and noticed and of what our various teaching activities have made her think and feel, that's pure gold. You may not realize how much in the dark we teachers are about the effects of our teaching. The essential principle in responding to teaching is the same as that in responding to writing: instead of trying to *judge* or to give objective evaluations or God-like verdicts, it's much more helpful to give *honest and accurate information about what happened,* that is, to tell about the effects of the teaching on you.

Another essential principle from writing also fits teaching: the person *giving* feedback learns as much as the person *getting* it. Think of the responses you write for this mini-unit, therefore, as being for your benefit as much as for the benefit of your teacher. People don't usually learn unless they are reflective and thoughtful about their experiences. Thus the best way to increase learning in school work is to reflect back on *what* you've learned, *how* you've learned it, and what it *means.*

As teachers we always try to build into our courses some quiet retrospective moments to help students pause and reflect on their learning. We find that these moments help students get in the habit of being more reflective about their learning in all areas. And it turns out that our students' reflections on their learning are usually the most useful kind of feedback for us as teachers.

NOT JUST AT THE END OF A COURSE BUT IN THE MIDDLE TOO

Traditionally teachers ask for these kinds of responses at the end of a course. But we've found that they are also helpful—in some ways more so—at the middle point in a course. Of course, you cannot judge the whole course when it's only half over, but at the midpoint there's still time to *talk* to students about something in our teaching that may be confusing and time to make adjustments in our teaching. Many issues come out in mid-semester responses, and they need talking about. Sometimes they can lead to a change of procedure; sometimes they show us that we need to discuss and clarify something we had been taking for granted. Almost always they help.

Turning from the teacher's benefit to your benefit, if you pause at mid-semester for some retrospective reflections on the weeks that have gone by, you may notice a habit of yours that is getting in your way. Perhaps you realize that you tend to be preoccupied while writing with whether you will please the teacher. As you reflect on those feelings, you will probably see more clearly how much they get in the way of doing your best writing. Or perhaps this mid-course writing will help you reflect on your dissatisfaction with the course. You may realize that your dissatisfaction is indeed justified. But your reflections may also help you realize that you only have two choices: learning something despite the dissatisfaction or not learning anything. It all depends on how you deal with your dissatisfaction. Your mid-course explorations may show you how to get the best out of a bad situation instead of just letting *yourself* pay the penalty because someone else isn't meeting your needs or expectations.

Here then are questions to help you write responses that will be useful both for yourself and for your teacher. We've given far more questions than you can use for a short document. Perhaps your teacher will specify certain ones you should answer—or leave the choice up to you. Probably your teacher would like to see some of these responses, but it is helpful to write them with utter honesty for yourself first—leaving till later the question of which ones you will show to others.

QUESTIONS FOR RESPONSE

1a. Which *moments* come to mind when you think back over the class? good moments? bad moments? perplexing moments? Quickly sketch in a small handful of such moments. Two or three sentences can easily sketch a moment; often one sentence will do (indeed you can

PROCESS BOX

I'm glad you asked me Thursday night how my paper was going. Once I told you openly about my disappointment at the criticism you'd written—about my disappointment at not being done after all—and once you said I didn't have to *use* your criticisms, then the authority I felt in your written response dissipated. Somehow I didn't believe you when you "said" in writing that I could ignore your criticism, but I did when you spoke it out loud. Once nothing mattered but what I wanted, then I was freed up to rewrite using your suggestions, and it was fun. I didn't exactly freewrite because the freewriting kept turning into good stuff that I wanted to keep.

FROM A STUDENT TO ELBOW ABOUT HIS FEEDBACK

sometimes point with just a phrase to a moment that your reader will obviously remember—e.g., "That morning you lost your temper about people coming in late"). Just take the moments that come to mind.

1b. What do these moments tell about you as a student, about the teacher, and about the course?

2. What are you most proud of about your own effort or accomplishment in the course? What are you not satisfied with, or what do you want to work on improving?

3. What are the most important strengths or skills you brought to this course?

4. What's been the greatest challenge for you?

5. Tell about the effects of the course on your writing. Talk about:
   - changes or lack of change in the quality of *what* you write
   - changes or lack of change in *how* you write
   - changes or lack of change in your attitudes and feelings about writing.

6. What have you learned other than about writing—perhaps about yourself or about people or about learning?

7. What has been the most important thing you've learned? If you wish, you can just circle something you've already written.

8. What do you most need to learn next?

9. What was most and least helpful about:

- in-class activities
- homework assignments
- group work
- comments on papers
- readings
- conferences
- grading procedures
- how the course is structured
- how the teacher operates.

10. What aspects of you has the course brought out? What aspects did it leave untapped or unnoticed?

11. Imagine this course as a journey: where is it taking you?

12. Imagine it as a detour or setback in some larger journey: explain.

13. Describe the climate and weather of the course. Has it remained the same or gone through cycles?

14. Describe the course as a machine, as a living organism, as a slow-acting poison, as a *Mission: Impossible* script.

15. If you could start over again, what would you do differently? What have you learned about how to learn better?

16. Do you have any suggestions about how the course could be made more helpful?

OTHER FORMAT FOR WRITING RESPONSES

A letter to your teacher. The questions are helpful because they pinpoint many important issues and permit relatively short answers. But you may find it more helpful to *read through* the questions slowly and then write a letter to your teacher. There's something powerful about starting off on a blank piece of paper with "Dear ————." To write a letter is to be faced with the best question of all: "What do *I* need to *say* to this person?" Because it's a letter and because you are writing very much *to* her, you cannot help treating your teacher as a person (not just a role or an authority figure), and this awareness may lead you to certain insights you wouldn't get from "answering a questionnaire."

F

The Sentence and End-Stop Punctuation

Look at the following groups of words and decide whether or not each one is a sentence. Don't agonize over the decision; just read each one quickly *out loud* and let your instincts tell you yes or no.

Sitting on the doorstep.

Go.

With careful analysis and painstaking research.

Stupid!

To the door.

The people at the end of the block who have been living there for years.

Jane and John were the kind of people who remained good friends even if you hadn't seen them for ten years.

Jennifer and her mother.

Come and visit with us whenever you can find the time.

John lost.

Let's go.

All the way around the block, into the building, up the stairs, and into the apartment.

Because it's dark.

But only if you have finished your work.

While all of us were sitting on the beach, watching the sun sprinkle sparkling lights on the calm waters of the inlet and feeling far away from everyday cares.

And then there were none.

After you've decided which of these are sentences, check to see if others agree.

We started off this unit asking you to do this exercise because linguists tell us that native speakers of a language recognize complete sentences in their language. In fact, many linguists believe that children as young as two have intuitive knowledge of what a sentence is. Our beginning exercise is a way of testing this premise. We suspect that you and your classmates agreed on almost all your responses. In other words, we believe that linguists are right: native speakers of a language do "know" what a sentence is. They "know" in the sense that they can intuitively produce and recognize sentences.

If what we're saying is true, why do so many native speakers have problems with incomplete and run-on sentences? We can think of two important reasons.

First, knowing what a sentence is doesn't mean we know how to demonstrate that information when we write. This is one way in which spoken and written language differ greatly. Our voice punctuates our speech so that others can understand it; on paper we have to use punctuation marks. That is, we often need to turn intuitive knowledge into conscious knowledge. That may sound easy; it usually isn't. Second, no sentence exists in a vacuum; sentences always have a context. In speech that context includes the words we have already spoken, but it also includes our physical surroundings and our own gestures. If you're sitting on a beach, watching a beautiful sunset, you can gesture toward the setting sun and say "Beautiful!" Anyone listening will consider that a complete sentence because of the context which allows them to fill in the missing words: "The sunset is beautiful." Or in conversation, if someone says, "Why are you leaving?" and you answer "Because I'm hungry," anyone listening will consider your words a complete sentence because they can fill in the missing words: "I'm leaving because I'm hungry."

These are called fragments—understood words are missing—and in writing they are often called *wrong,* even though they are fine in speech. That's what causes trouble. Most teachers and editors would consider the following wrong:

The senators refused to withdraw their proposal to ship wheat to the drought-stricken countries. A proposal unpopular with the president.

Even though most of us would agree on mentally inserting the words *which they knew was* after *proposal,* this agreement isn't enough in a piece of writing; most of us probably want the words to be there on the page.

Maybe you think this is being picky, but it really isn't. We think everyone who reads our piece will automatically insert the intended words, but sometimes we're wrong. In speaking we can see our audience and tell whether they "get" our omitted words, but in writing we don't know how our reader is doing. If we're wrong, our reader may either find our writing incoherent or—what may be worse—misconstrue our meaning.

Nonetheless, good writers use fragments, and you can too, provided you don't confuse your readers. If you want to make sure that none of your fragments are confusing or awkward to readers, always ask a couple of people to read what you write before you hand it in. Ask them to let you know if they're confused. If it's a fragment that's causing the confusion, you'll probably want to fix it. Keep in mind, however, that your friends may not notice fragments that are *not* confusing—fragments that *function* as complete sentences even though they're missing a subject or a verb. It's a good idea to find out how your teacher feels about fragments such as these.

Let's reconsider the "test" we started with. When linguists say that all native speakers know what a sentence is, they mean that native speakers can recognize sentences when *spoken* and in *context*. You may have had some disagreement on the "test"—and perhaps even some downright "mistakes"—because (1) it's harder to tell what's a sentence if it's not spoken, and (2) it's difficult to deal with any set of words which have no context since such a condition doesn't match our own experience. (In extended pieces of writing, the issue is even more complicated. The sentences are in a context, but for the sake of punctuation we have to act as if they are not—act as if the sentences stand alone even though they don't. This runs counter to our intuition.) Still, it needn't take much for you to learn to *adapt* the sentence-knowing skills you have to these harder conditions.

Fragments earn their name because they lack words that complete them. Run-ons display the opposite fault: they contain too many words, enough words, in fact, for two sentences. Run-ons are never a feature of the spoken language of native-born speakers. We all indicate sentence division in speech by pitches and pauses. This being true, we can correct written run-ons by reading aloud. The only problem is to decide what mark of punctuation to use at the point of sentence division: an end mark, a semicolon, a colon, or a conjunction with a comma. Thus you can use your intuition to avoid run-ons only up to a certain point. Beyond that, you're going to have to know some of the rules.

SOME PRACTICE AND SOME RULES

Grammar books usually define a sentence as a group of words which contain a subject and a verb and a complete idea. The problem with "complete idea" is that it's often difficult in practice to decide what a complete idea is, where it starts, and where it ends. "A sentence is a group of words that can stand alone" probably works better as a definition because it allows you to rely on your implicit knowledge of what a sentence is. Thus once you decide that a group of words can stand alone, you need look only at whether it has an explicit subject and verb. The only kind of English sentence that doesn't need a subject is an order ("Come here, please") since the understood subject of all orders is "you," and our grammar doesn't require us to make this "you" explicit.

Here are a few exercises you can do to make you think explicitly about the use of end marks in written prose.

1. Read through the following paragraph and decide where end marks should go; that is, decide which groups of words make complete sentences.

The essayist does not usually appear early in the literary history of a country he comes naturally after the poet and the chronicler his habit of mind is leisurely he does not write from any special stress of passionate impulse he does not create material so much as he comments upon material already existing it is essential for him that books should have been written, and that they should, at least to some extent, have been read and digested he is usually full of allusions and references, and these his reader must be able to follow and understand and in this literary walk, as in most others, the giants came first: Montaigne and Lord Bacon were our earliest essayists, and, as yet, they are our best.

After you've completed this exercise, compare the way you did it with the way others in your group did it and arrive at a consensus about each punctuation mark. If there's class time for more comparisons, all the groups in the class can compare results and work toward a class consensus.

2. Pick out a paragraph from a piece you're currently working on and give an unpunctuated copy of it to someone else. Ask him or her to follow along as you read the passage aloud, and insert appropriate punctuation marks. When you've finished reading, you and your listener can compare the two copies and work out whatever discrepancies exist. But don't argue if you disagree.

When you and your partner have made your decisions about what to agree and disagree about, bring your paper to your entire group for possible resolution of differences. What your group cannot resolve to the satisfaction of everyone, you can save for a full-class discussion. At this point you may also want to consult a grammar book or handbook for help.

Remember that—in disputed cases—you are the author and should make the choice that seems best to you. Not everything is hard and fast, even in the world of grammar. There are exceptions to many usage rules, and choices can depend on context.

One of the most important things you'll discover from doing this exercise is that your voice can help you make decisions about punctuation. As you listened to others read, you undoubtedly heard their voices drop in pitch at the ends of sentences and then pause briefly before continuing.

3. Decide whether you think the following groups of words, all punc-

tuated as sentences, are in fact sentences. One way to do this is to read the passage aloud and force your voice to take its cues from the punctuation. That is, let your voice drop off in pitch whenever you see a period and then pause before continuing with the next sentence.

> I knew I couldn't think. All I knew then was what I couldn't do. All I knew then was what I wasn't, and it took me some years to discover what I was.
>
> Which was a writer.
>
> By which I mean not a "good" writer or a "bad" writer but simply a writer, a person whose most absorbed and passionate hours are spent arranging words on pieces of paper. Had my credentials been in order I would never have become a writer. Had I been blessed with even limited access to my own mind there would have been no reason to write. I write entirely to find out what I'm thinking, what I'm looking at, what I see and what it means. What I want and what I fear. Why did the oil refineries around Carquinez Straits seem sinister to me in the summer of 1956? Why have the night lights in the bevatron burned in my mind for twenty years? *What is going on in these pictures in my mind?*

After you've made decisions about the end marks in the excerpt, talk with your group members about their decisions. There are fragments in this passage. Did you have problems with them? Did others?

SUGGESTIONS

If you have trouble marking sentence endings in writing, you're going to have to do a fair amount of extra work. We suggest the following approach:

1. Read your piece of writing backward (that is, read what you take to be the last sentence, then the preceding one, and so on). That sounds strange, we know. But sentences in a piece of writing often sound complete to us because we are in possession of whatever information prior sentences have given us. Thus we read individual sentences in the context of what precedes them. This is, of course, exactly what we should be doing, but it can blind us to the grammatical incompleteness of a particular sentence. Reading backward makes it impossible for us to apply previously given information to a sentence.

Start by reading the last sentence of your piece. When you've made a decision about that, go to the second-to-final sentence and read that, and so on. If certain sentences are problematic for you, write them out on a separate piece of paper and give them to someone else to read. This way they'll have to deal with the sentence in isolation—and for this purpose, that's exactly what you want them to do.

2. Check a good handbook for the rules on punctuation. We think the following rules are crucial:

- Complete sentences can end with a period, a semicolon, a colon, a question mark, or an exclamation point.

- If you use a semicolon after a complete sentence, make sure that a complete sentence follows the semicolon also.

- Do not use a comma to separate complete sentences. Most teachers will not approve. This error is usually called a "comma splice" or a "run-on." (Such creatures regularly appear in published prose, but they are often considered unacceptable in academic writing.)

Commas

Commas rules are the hardest of all. We'll give you some rules, but almost all commas rules have exceptions. Effective use of commas requires you not only to know the requisite rules but also—at least some of the time—to make decisions.

Rule 1. Use a comma before the conjunction in a compound sentence:

> This is the first clause in a compound sentence, and this is the second clause.

There are two exceptions:

- If the clauses in a compound sentence are short, you can omit the comma:

  > That is short and this is too.

- If both clauses in a compound sentence have the same subject—and there is no chance for misreading—you can omit the comma.

  > This clause is independent and it's short too.

Rule 2. Use a comma after introductory words, phrases, and clauses:

> After these introductory words, you should use a comma.
> Second, you need a comma here also.
> When a sentence begins with a dependent clause, put a comma after the clause.

There is an exception:

- If the introductory segment is short—and there is no chance of misreading—you can omit the comma:

    After this you don't always need a comma.

    But beware of skipping the comma and ending up with a sentence that leads the reader to say it wrong:

    After this writing will never be the same.

Rule 3. Use a comma to separate items in a series:

> A series can be made up of any items that are parallel: sentences, clauses, phrases, or words.

Note that the final comma—the one after *phrases*—is optional, but you should be consistent.

Rule 4. Use a comma to separate nonrestrictive or nonessential parts of a sentence from the main part of the sentence.

> An embedded clause, which is what this is, can be either restrictive or nonrestrictive.
> An embedded clause which is restrictive should not be set off by commas.

Commas and Pausing

These rules don't quite cover all comma use because sometimes we sense the need for a comma in a certain spot just because we "feel" a pause in the structure or rhythm of a sentence. This usually means that if we read our piece aloud, we'd pause at this spot. The pause we make as we *speak* helps our listeners understand our words. The comma performs the same function in written language. Even when we're reading silently and not physically hearing words, we often "feel" pauses, and it's reassuring to see commas in these spots. Conversely, when we see a comma at a spot where neither structure nor meaning requires a pause and where a pause would disrupt meaning, we're confused. Our comprehension of what we're reading then suffers.

So the best advice we can give you about commas is to read what you've written aloud and notice where there are pauses. You can then examine each spot to see if a comma is advisable. Another way to do this is to give someone else a copy of your writing and let them mark the text wherever you pause. In this way you won't break the flow of your words by stopping to mark pauses. Still another way to do this is to read your piece into a tape recorder and then mark the pauses yourself as you listen to the playback. These are particularly good exercises to use if you tend not to use enough commas.

PROCESS BOX

As I wrote out the grammatical rules for using commas, I kept thinking, "This is too complicated. Why can't I just say that there are four uses of the comma, give the uses, and let it go at that?" But exceptions keep coming into my mind even as I'm writing a rule: "Use a comma after an introductory phrase." But as I wrote that I was thinking, not about the rule, but about the exceptions. Still, I've always been pretty good at explaining grammatical things in common-sense terms. And, yet. Maybe I want to give too much linguistic background—I think it's interesting and so think students will find it interesting—but. I don't know. I don't think I can curb my desire for as full an explanation as possible. Maybe I just fear sounding too much like a prescriptive grammarian and want students to realize that I'm describing, not prescribing, language. It's like the old joke about the kid who asked his mother where he came from, and the mother gave him a whole lesson in the birds and the bees, after which the kid says: "Oh, I asked because Johnny next door came from Topeka." Maybe I do that with grammar.

PAT BELANOFF

Another tactic is to read aloud your writing and pause slightly at each comma (or ask someone else to read it aloud this way). This is probably the best tactic if you tend to overdo comma use. If commas (and periods and semicolons, for that matter) match the speaking voice and sentence structure, your readers (even a diligent teacher!) will probably find no fault. In fact, research studies have shown that teachers are unlikely to notice mechanical errors of any kind if what they read truly engages their interest. So that's the main advice we can give you: make your writing interesting to your readers.

A Historical Note

Historically commas (and other punctuation marks) developed to mirror certain qualities of oral language which convey meaning but are not represented by recording the sounds of words. These qualities include pauses and variations of pitch and stress. At the end of a sentence, for instance, we usually pause and slightly lower the pitch of our voice. Periods in written language are the equivalent of these speech features. At the spots where commas appear, we often pause (although this pause is usually shorter than that at the end of a sentence), but pitch usually stays the same. Read the following excerpt aloud, and you'll probably get some sense of how this works:

Of course we're here an hour before the game starts. I don't mind, though. Now I can see all the other crazy Syracuse Orangemen basketball fans beside me! My brother and I sit down, taking the whole scene in. The Carrier Dome is a massive building with a white, balloon-like roof. It can hold a 100-yard football field, but today there is a blue curtain cutting the area into two parts. One half has vendors selling refreshments and Syracuse University paraphernalia. There is also a stage with two men singing, tables with important patrons clad in orange, and a giant-sized screen which will show the game for the unfortunate fans sitting behind the blue curtain.

When written language began to be considered as important as spoken language (or more important), punctuation began to have quite a different function: *to show the grammatical structure of sentences.* Quite a few rules came into existence to do this, but through the years this list has usually been reduced to the four we listed at the beginning of this mini-unit.

These two systems of punctuation now exist side by side: to guide us in pausing and to show the grammatical structure of sentences. But usually they do not conflict. It's easy to see why since the structure of sentences has a great deal to do with where a speaker pauses. In fact, the two systems often work harmoniously together. We often decide whether to use a comma after introductory words on the basis of whether we "hear" a pause:

In August, I'll go.
In August I'll go.

There really is no right or wrong here, but the two sentences shouldn't sound alike when read aloud.

Here's a paragraph (from the essay just used). See if you can put in commas and give a reason for each one. You can then check what you've done against the writer's punctuation. (The essay is included at the beginning of the *Sharing and Responding* booklet.)

The score is now tied with two minutes left in the first half. Two minutes in a basketball game is quite a long time. Everyone is anxious wondering who will have the lead at half-time. The odors of hot dogs mustard sweat beer and stale air-conditioned ventilation combine as the temperature in the Carrier Dome rises. With thirty seconds to go stocky pivot guard Pearl Washington of Syracuse dribbles the ball intending to have the last shot of the first half. After what seems like a lifetime with ten seconds left he takes an outside shot and . . . it's good! Syracuse leads by two. Hysteria breaks out in the Dome.

Once you've practiced on this paragraph, you can select one of your own and do the same thing. Perhaps your teacher will give you a chance to do this in class so you can work with others. If all the members of your group punctuate at least one paragraph written by each group member, you'll have the basis for a lively and profitable discussion about commas.

Note. There are a number of fine points about commas—tiny rules and exceptions which we have chosen not to include in this short treatment. You need to check a comprehensive handbook for difficult cases. But if you really master the main things we treat here, you will seldom get in trouble.

H

Apostrophes

The apostrophe is a peculiar punctuation mark. No language except English uses it. Basically it performs two functions in written language: it takes the place of deleted letters, and it shows possession. The first of these functions usually causes no problems for most writers:

> she [i]s = she's
> I [ha]ve = I've
> can[no]t = can't

But the use of the apostrophe to show possession causes problems for most inexperienced and even for some experienced writers. Speech is no help at all: we can't *hear* the difference between *boys, boy's,* and *boys'.* We use *context* to tell us what the sounds mean.

> The boys left early.
> The boys left hand is stronger than his right.
> The boys left hands were tied behind their backs.

Speech thus trains us to use context to determine the meaning of the *s* sound at the end of words. Having learned this, we tend to transfer this strategy to written language and allow the context to guide us here also.

But, standard written English requires that we use apostrophes even though they may be unnecessary for meaning. That's probably why apostrophes are so hard. You *do* need to get them right though, because whether we like it or not, teachers and most other people regard someone who makes mistakes with apostrophes as a dummy.

Apostrophes to Show Possession

The basic rules seem simple. An apostrophe indicates that the preceding word possesses something: *boy's* indicates that *a boy* possesses something: *boys'* indicates that *boys* possess something. One way to help yourself is to use an *of* phrase to test whether the apostrophe is appropriate:

> The boy's left hand is stronger than his right.

The "left hand of the boy" is what "boy's left hand" means, so the apostrophe is appropriately placed.

> The boys' left hands are tied behind their backs.

"The left hands of the boys" is what "the boys' left hands" means, so again the apostrophe is correctly placed.

Look at the following paragraph and see if you can get apostrophes into it where they belong:

> I wholeheartedly believe in the value of education, but sometimes it seems to be more trouble than its worth. I transferred to this school from a small college upstate in order to get a better education and to extricate myself from a situation I felt I had to reassess. (That, however, is a different story!) Since my parents home is an hour and fifteen minute drive from Stony Brook, the logical thing for me to have done was to get some form of housing nearer to school. This I proceeded to do, by moving into an apartment that was way beyond my means, and glibly signing a years lease in the bargain. My roommate was a good friend from high school who was dying to get out of her mothers house. We received countless warnings on the dangers of friends living together, but we brushed off those of little faith, knowing it would be different for us.
>
> ○○○○○
>
> As it turned out, there *had* been a mistake, and I would get the loan, but only after reapplying for it, as the computer had erased me. "It will only take eight to ten weeks to process," the polite voice informed me sweetly.
>
> "Oh, no, thats not possible," I laughed airily. "You see, my rents due next week, and theres nothing in the house to eat, and. . . ."
>
> Im sorry," she interrupted firmly, "That is the length of time is takes to process a loan."
>
> "But I havent even bought my books yet!" I said desperately.
>
> "Im sorry," she replied crisply, and hung up.
>
> ○○○○○
>
> Our friendship definitely benefited from the situation. Since weve been home, theres no tension over who *always* has to clean the bathroom, and over who used up the last of the mayonnaise and didn't get more. Were almost on the same footing as when we moved in together, which makes us both very happy. The commuting isnt too bad either, as I enjoy driving. Who knows? Maybe next year Ill live at home and use my loan for updating my wardrobe.

You can check what you did against what the writer did by turning to the end of the section on apostrophes.

Apostrophes for Other Uses

It's only fair to warn you that apostrophes do appear in other sorts of places also. Some handbooks advise using them for plurals of letters and numbers:

> I cannot read her 7's.
>
> The 1960's are both praised and maligned.
>
> I particularly like the A's on that sign.

Other handbooks, however, prefer no apostrophes in these sentences:

> I can read her 7s.
>
> The 1960s are both praised and maligned.
>
> I particularly like the As on that sign.

We also want to warn you that the apostrophe is not always an indicator of true possession. *An hour's stay* doesn't really mean the hour possesses the stay, but the test we suggested above still works: *an hour's stay* equals *a stay of an hour.*

If you have real problems with apostrophes, you're going to have to do some hard, rather tedious proofreading which will require you to check every *s* that comes at the end of a word. We do think, though, that if you do this conscientiously for a while, you'll find yourself beginning to put the apostrophe in with greater regularity *as* you're writing.

Note. We haven't done a survey, but we bet most apostrophe errors occur with *its* and *it's.* Just remember that *it's* equals *it (i)s* and *its* is a possessive. That last one seems contradictory—since we associate the apostrophe with possessives—but *hers* and *theirs* and *his* don't have apostrophes either. The it's/its conundrum is similar to two others:

> *who's* (*who* plus *is*) and *whose*
>
> *they're* (*they* + *are*) and *their*

Apostrophes as the Writer Used Them

> I wholeheartedly believe in the value of education, but sometimes it seems to be more trouble than it's worth. I transferred to this school from a small college upstate in order to get a better education and to extricate myself from a situation I felt I had to reassess. (That, however, is a different story!) Since my parents' home is an hour and fifteen minute drive from Stony Brook, the logical thing for me to have done was to get some form of housing nearer to school. This I proceeded to do, by moving into an apartment that was way beyond my means, and glibly signing a year's lease in the bargain. My roommate was a good friend from high school who was dying to get out of her mother's house. We received countless warnings on the dangers of friends living together, but we brushed off those of little faith, knowing it would be different for us.
>
> ○○○○○
>
> As it turned out, there *had* been a mistake, and I would get the loan, but only after reapplying for it, as the computer had erased me. "It will only take eight to ten weeks to process," the polite voice informed me sweetly.

"Oh, no, that's not possible," I laughed airily. "You see, my rent's due next week, and there's nothing in the house to eat, and. . . ."

"I'm sorry," she interrupted firmly, "That is the length of time it takes to process a loan."

"But I haven't even bought my books yet!" I said desperately.

"I'm sorry," she replied crisply, and hung up.

ooooo

Our friendship definitely benefited from the situation. Since we've been home, there's no tension over who *always* has to clean the bathroom, and over who used up the last of the mayonnaise and didn't get more. We're almost on the same footing as when we moved in together, which makes us both very happy. The commuting isn't too bad either, as I enjoy driving. Who knows? Maybe next year I'll live at home and use my loan for updating my wardrobe.

Quotation and the Punctuation of Reported Speech

Quotation marks are the primary way to show in writing *exactly* which words were said or written by someone other than you.

Notice how this works:

> Elizabeth Kinney, a student who read an earlier draft of our book, said about it, "I think the idea of considering all of us as writers is absurd, and I don't think any student really takes that notion seriously."

The quotation marks tell you exactly which words are Elizabeth Kinney's and which are ours.

THE CONVENTIONS FOR USING QUOTATION MARKS

The conventions for using quotation marks can be tricky, but if you master them and end-stopping (getting periods where they are needed and keeping your reader from shouting "sentence fragment!" or "run-on sentence!"), you have mastered 95 percent of what you need to know about punctuation. (Colons and semicolons are infrequent and easy; commas are hopelessly arguable.)

    1. *Periods and commas go* INSIDE *quotation marks.* If the *quoted* sentence doesn't end where you end your quotation, you should include four

dots with spaces between them to show that you stopped quoting before the person finished her sentence:

> Elizabeth Kinney, a student who read an earlier draft of our book, said, "I think the idea of considering all of us as writers is absurd. . . ."

(Notice that the first dot has no space before it. Note also that many British editors use an alternate style: they put periods and commas outside quotation marks. Perhaps you've observed this practice in some books. We think it best to follow the style used by American editors, since that is probably what your teacher will prefer—though, of course, you can ask her.)

If you omit words in the middle of a sentence you're quoting, use only three dots, with a space before the first dot and after the last one:

> I think . . . considering all of us as writers is absurd. . . ."

2. *Semicolons and colons belong* OUTSIDE *quotation marks.* To show what this looks like, we've rewritten our original excerpt slightly.

> Elizabeth Kinney, a student who read an earlier draft of our book said, "I think the idea of considering all of us as writers is absurd"; then she went on to disagree with us further.

3. *Question marks, exclamation points, and dashes sometimes go inside and sometimes outside.* They go *inside* the quotation marks if they're part of the quotation and *outside* if they're not.

> Do you think she was right when she said, "[C]onsidering all of us as writers is absurd"?

The question is ours, not Kinney's, so the question mark belongs outside the quotation marks. (The *C* is in brackets because it wasn't capitalized in the original.)

> We had to think about our position again when Kinney asked, "Do you really want all students to think of themselves as writers?"

This time the question was hers, and so the question mark belongs inside.

4. *Quoted material which blends directly into your words needs no extra punctuation mark.*

> Elizabeth Kinney said our idea of treating students as writers "is absurd."

5. *When you use a phrase of attribution ("she said" or "John insisted on announcing" etc.), you need a colon or comma after the phrase of attribution.* Generally colons appear before formal statements and commas

463

before informal ones. Levels of formality are difficult to assess though. What you should keep in mind is that using a comma before a quotation suggests less formality to your readers. If that's what you want, the comma is probably correct. In other words, the choice is mostly a stylistic one. Thus both of these are correct; the comma in the first passage keeps the tone slightly informal:

> A student reader of our text said, "I think the idea of considering all of us as writers is absurd, and I don't think any student really takes that notion seriously."

> She went on to say: "Even if you define a writer as anyone who writes, the public thinks of a writer as a professional who is capable of writing and doing a good job of it."

6. *If the phrase of attribution follows the quotation, a comma is needed*—unless, of course, the quotation ends with an exclamation point or a question mark.

> "When you propose that all students can think of themselves as writers, it sounds patronizing," said Elizabeth Kinney.

> "When you propose that all students can think of themselves as writers, it sounds patronizing!" said Elizabeth Kinney.

7. *If you have a quotation-within-a-quotation, use regular quotation marks for the main quotation and single quotation marks for the inner quotation.*

> She went on to say: "Even if you say 'a writer is anyone who writes,' the public thinks of a writer as a professional who is capable of writing and doing a good job of it."

8. *If you quote a long passage—three lines or more—it's usually clearer if you indent ten spaces from your left margin and* OMIT *the quotation marks.* Precede the quotation with a colon. Thus:

```
Here is a comment from a student who used an
earlier draft of our book:

        Even if you say a "writer is anyone who
        writes," the public thinks of a writer as
        a professional who is capable of writing
        and doing a good job of it. When you
        propose that all students can think of
        themselves as writers, it sounds
        patronizing.
```

Now that you've read over these conventions, we suggest that you look closely at the student and professional interviews in Unit 2 and analyze these writers' use of punctuation relative to quotations. Have they followed the conventions?

Practice

Bring in a paragraph you're working on (even if it isn't from a final draft) which contains a fair quantity of quoted words. Put in punctuation and then read through the paragraph with a classmate or two explaining to them why you used each mark. Since class time may be limited and your teacher will want to use most of it for substantive matters (like discussing content, organization, tone, etc.), you may not have time for in-class work on these conventions. But you can still get feedback—from a friend, classmate, family member, or tutor in your school's writing center. If something's particularly problematic, you may want to check it with your teacher.

Spelling

Spelling, like punctuation, is solely a feature of the written language. And for many it's a very important feature. Many people—not just teachers—will think you are not just illiterate but stupid if your spelling is poor. In fact, research studies have demonstrated that spelling has little to do with intelligence. But it's also true that spelling is highly tied to reading; we get our sense of correct spelling from *seeing* words, not from hearing them. Thus if you do a lot of reading, you're more likely to spell more words correctly. Consequently readers tend to think that anyone whose spelling is poor has not read much; that is, he's illiterate.

Nor do we want you to think we're minimizing the importance of spelling. If each of us spelled our own way, writing would become totally chaotic. Misspelled words can block communication. And most readers—including us—get annoyed by misspellings. Our annoyance causes us to get mad at the writer, and this hostility blocks our intent to focus on meaning. We react this way because we feel that if someone really wanted to communicate with us, he or she would take the trouble to spell correctly.

English is basically a phonetic language. What that means is that written English words represent sounds, not things. For example, *house* represents the spoken word "house," which in turn represents a building or structure people live in. The symbol ⌂ on the other hand, would represent the building or structure directly. (Despite this phonetic base, most of us probably do not need to hear the word *house* when we read it in order to know what it means: we probably go directly from the marks on the page to the idea of "house.") In some languages of the world, like Chinese, written words are not a record of the spoken language. Chinese characters represent things without reference to the way a speaker would represent them.

Even though English is phonetically based, it is not *purely* phonetic. The letter *A* in English represents *various* sounds. And conversely the sound that in the International Phonetic Alphabet is represented as /e/ and pronounced like the vowel sound in *say* is represented in a number of different ways in written English.

Why has English slipped from being fully phonetic? Evidence suggests that our writing was once totally phonetic. Old English scribes probably recorded, or tried to record, the sounds of the language directly. We know this because scribes from different regions spelled words differently—depending on the accent or dialect of that region. When printing was introduced in England during the fourteenth century, printers began to feel the need for standardization of spelling. The *sounds* of the spoken language continued to change, but the *spelling* of words did not. And so, today, for example, the word *says* is pronounced more like *sez,* but you don't see it written like that except in special circumstances.

All this explains why our spelling can cause difficulty, but it is of no help at all as you seek to deal with that difficulty. Some people seem to be chronically poor spellers (even if they do read a lot), and others seem to be good spellers without much effort. Most of us fall somewhere in between. Certain words give us trouble and other words—usually those we use all the time—give us no trouble at all. Consequently all we need to do is to look up new words when we want to use them.

But for those of you who are poor spellers, dictionaries are often not much help because you just don't know which words to look up. And, needless to say, looking up all the words you use would be enormously onerous. Some handbooks and secretarial manuals give lists of frequently misspelled words, and there are some special spelling dictionaries which help you find words even if you look them up under the wrong spelling. But these do not solve all one's problems. So what do you do?

Our best suggestion is to learn to use a word processing program on a computer and equip your computer with a spelling checker. (Or use a typewriter with a built-in spelling checker.)

Nevertheless you'll still need to check for "correctly spelled mistakes" such as using *effect* for *affect* or *except* for *accept.* You'll want to gradually compile a list of these homophones (sound-alikes) that trip you up, and make your spelling checker flag them for you—along with those special words that you have difficulty with which may not be built into the spelling checker itself. Also, beginning to appear on the market now are credit-card sized spelling checkers which look like small calculators and can contain up to eighty thousand words. Buying one of these may be a good investment for anyone who is a chronically poor speller.

Our second best suggestion is to enlist the aid of a friend, roommate, or family member who is a good speller and ask him to read through whatever you plan to submit for grading. All he needs to do is mark the misspelled words. It is your job to look them up. This may be a lot to ask of someone, particularly if you are a really bad speller. But perhaps there's something you can do for this person to return the favor. Even if you just read through whatever he writes and give him your reactions to it, you'll be doing something important for him.

There's something sociable and communal about getting help from a friend, but there's also something attractive about *not* getting help from a friend. That means spending money. *Some* typists are skilled spellers and will simply fix all your spelling. You may have to pay a bit extra. But look long and hard enough—perhaps insist on references—till you find one who really *is* expert.

Frankly, other than that, we can't give you much help. We do believe that the more you write and the more you look up words, the better speller you'll become. But you may never become good enough to give up relying on help.

Finally, we *may* be able to help you somewhat with the following account of the major spelling problems. We suggest that you keep a special spot in your notebook and see if you can group your spelling errors according to the following list. Undoubtedly you'll also need to set up some personal categories—plus a list which gathers together the uncategorizable words. This may help you gain some control over the problem even if you can't eliminate it. Furthermore, such lists may also prove to you that you're not making a lot of errors, just some of the same errors over and over.

Here are special areas of difficulty for most poor spellers:

1. Doubling Letters

This causes the most difficulty when you're adding endings to words. The basic rule is to double the final letter of a word before adding a suffix if it meets the following three conditions:

  a. The ending to be added to the main word must begin with a vowel: *-ing, -es, -ed, -y.*

  b. The word must either be a one-syllable word (such as *sit, tap, slip*) *or* end with an accented syllable (such as *admit, begin,* and *prefer*).

  c. The word must end with a single consonant that is preceded by a single vowel. (For example, *occur* ends in a single consonant that is preceded by a single vowel, so we get *occurred* and *occurring.* The word *creep,* on the other hand, ends in a single consonant, but that consonant is not preceded by a single vowel, so we get *creeping.)*

  Exceptions:

  • *qu* is considered one consonant sound, so *equip + ing = equipping.*

- *x* is a double consonant sound since *x* is really the two sounds *k* and *s*, so *fox* + *es* = *foxes.*

- Think of both *y* and *w* as vowels, so *toy* + *ing* = *toying.*

Test yourself: add *-ing* to *forget* and *compel;* add *-ed* to *shop* and *drape;* add *-y* to *cat;* add *-er* to *plan;* add *-ance* to *remit;* add *-ent* to *repel.* (Answers are at the end of this mini-unit.)

2. Dropping the Silent *E* before Adding Endings

The basic rule is to *drop* a silent *e* when adding a suffix that begins with a vowel: *bite* + *ing* = *biting.*

Exception: Keep the silent *e* which occurs after *c* or *g* if the added ending begins with an *a* or *o: change* + *able* = *changeable.* (This exception grows out of the pronunciation rules of English. Most of the time we pronounce the *g* or *c* before *a, o,* and *u* differently from the way we pronounce it before *i* or *e: gin* and *gone; necessary* and *case.*)

Other exceptions are *dyeing* (meaning to change color), *acreage, mileage, truly, judgment, acknowledgment, ninth, wholly.*

Try some: *outrage* + *ous; manage* + *able; love* + *able; race* + *ed.* (Answers are at the end of this mini-unit.)

3. Adding *ify/efy*

Verbs are formed by adding *ify: classify, justify, amplify.* There are only four exceptions: *liquefy, stupefy, rarefy, putrefy.*

4. Words Ending in *sede/ceed/cede*

a. Only one word ends in *sede: supersede.*

b. Only three words end in *ceed: exceed, succeed, proceed.*

c. All other words ending with the "seed" sound, end in *cede:* for example, *concede, precede, recede.*

5. *ie/ei.*

The old jingle is probably the most helpful:

I before *e* except after *c* or when sounded like *ay* as in *neighbor* or *weigh.*

Thus *priest* and *niece,* but *ceiling* and *perceive.*

Exceptions: *neither, either, leisure, seize, weird, sheik, financier, foreign,* and *conscience.*

Try these: *theif* or *thief, deceit* or *deciet, piece* or *peice, consceince* or *conscience, frieght* or *freight.* (Answers are at the end of this mini-unit.)

6. Adding *able* or *ible*

The rules here are so complex that they're more confusing than helpful. Your best tactic is simply to keep a list. In general, common words add *able: eatable, readable, comfortable.* Less common words usually use *ible: admissible, ineligible, accessible.* There are many exceptions though, such as *possible.* Here are a few common ones:

abominable, accountable, avoidable, commendable, considerable, creditable, demonstrable, dependable; favorable, incorrigible, inevitable, intelligible, invincible, irritable, laughable, legible, notable; perishable, permissible, reducible, seasonable, unthinkable.

7. Adding *ance* or *ence*

Again, just keep two separate lists.

ANCE: abundance, acquaintance, appearance, brilliance, endurance, guidance, ignorance, importance, maintenance, reassurance, remembrance, repentance, significance, tolerance.

ENCE: absence, audience, coincidence, conference, confidence, consequence, competence, convenience, correspondence, dependence, difference, essence, excellence, existence, experience, inference, influence, intelligence, magnificence, occurrence, patience, permanence, preference, presence, reference, severence, residence, sentence, violence.

8. Words Ending in *ary* or *ery*

Only two commonly used words end in *ery: cemetery* and *stationery* (meaning the stuff you write letters on).

9. Changing *y* to *i* before Adding Endings

a. Change *y* to *i* before adding to any ending *not* beginning with *i.* Thus *happy + ly = happily; jolly + er = jollier; pity + ful = pitiful;* but *pity + ing = pitying.*

b. Keep the final *y* if it is preceded by a vowel: *play* + *er* = *player.*

c. Exceptions occur when adding *ness, ship, like,* or *ly: shyness, citylike, ladyship, slyly.*

Try some: *beauty* + *ful*; *marry* + *ing*; *fly* + *er*; *history* + *cal*; *ninety* + *eth*; *lonely* + *ness*; *copy* + *ing*; *victory* + *ous*; *delay* + *ed*; *dry* + *ness.* (Answers are at the end of this mini-unit.)

10. Learn to Look for Homonyms—Words that Sound Alike but Have Different Meanings or Use, Such as *berth* or *birth*

Any good grammar book or handbook will have lists of these words, usually under some heading like "Words commonly confused."

Final word. Spelling can psychologically discombobulate some people more than any other dimension of writing. The thing to keep in mind if you are troubled by spelling is that it is *not* necessary to know spelling. It is only necessary that for certain important pieces of writing *you must—by hook or by crook—get the spelling right.*

Think of it like typing. When you submit writing to someone, often it *must* be typed. That doesn't mean *you* must type it. There's nothing morally wrong with hiring a typist to do it for you. However it's nicer and cheaper if you can type; you don't feel dependent on others. This is exactly how it is with spelling.

Answers to Examples

1. forgetting, compelling, shopped, draped, catty, planner, remittance, repellent.

2. outrageous, manageable, lovable, raced.

5. thief, deceit, piece, conscience, freight.

9. beautiful, marrying, flier, historical, ninetieth, loneliness, copying, victorious, delayed, dryness.

MINI-UNIT
K

Copyediting and Proofreading

Bring to class a typed copy, or copies, of the final draft of a paper you plan to hand in. Another student will copyedit and proofread your paper, and you will do the same for her. If there's time, you will want to exchange papers with at least two people. Your teacher may allow time for this in class, or she may ask you to do this work at home.

Read your classmate's paper *very carefully,* and pencil in any corrections you think appropriate. You are looking for *all* errors in mechanics or typing (capitalization, underlining, abbreviations, and so forth) and *all* violations of the rules of Standard Written English. What you'll want to check particularly are spelling, punctuation, sentence structure, subject-verb agreement, and pronoun reference. If you aren't sure about a change you've made, put a question mark by it. If a sentence doesn't sound right to you, but you can't pinpoint exactly what's bothering you, just draw wiggly lines under it. Be sure to sign your name to the paper as editor. Your teacher may want to collect all edited copies of each paper in order to pinpoint particular students' problems.

When you're finished, select two of the corrections you've made and write a rule for each. Don't look up the rule in a handbook; just state the rule in a way that explains why you made the correction. Here's more of the essay we quoted from in Unit 8, with copyediting changes added, as well as two rules written by the student-editor:

```
    Upon entering, the bar is to the person's

  immediate left and a few steps below is the dance

  floor.  By the way, the steps are notorious killers
```

since many, under the influence of alcohol, forget they exist. On the other side, there is the seating area consisting of dozens of tables and black velvety, cushiony, recliner-type chairs. They are the type of chairs you~~r~~ *one* lose you~~r~~self *one* in.

There's a lower level which is reached by descending a flight of wooden stairs. This staircase is actually wooden slate/s bound together, which allows heels to get caught. Many-a-times, there ~~'s~~ *are* men standing below it waiting for damsels to decend, preferably those wearing skirts. This lower level is a very quite *sp* and intimate dwelling (designated) for those couples who want to leave their inhibitions behind.

Rule: Don't use you in an essay.
Rule: Use commas after introductory words.

Once you get the copies of your paper back, you'll need to make a decision about each correction or comment made by your editor(s). If you're sure they're right (perhaps your mistake was carelessness or poor typing), make the correction neatly in ink on your good copy. If you're sure they're wrong, don't erase the change; leave it, so your teacher will know what you've made a decision about. If you're not sure one way or the other, you'll have to check in a handbook. If your teacher hasn't recommended one for you to buy, you should ask her for a recommendation.* If you can't find what you need in your book, you'll need to find some other authority: a classmate, your roommate, a family member, your teacher, or a tutor in the Writing Center.

Sometimes the best strategy for dealing with problems you can't clearly define is to rewrite the problem sentence in a different way. Try to think yourself back into the idea you had when you wrote the sentence, and see if

---

*For help with understanding how grammatical and usage rules work, see *The Right Handbook,* by Pat Belanoff, Betsy Rorschach, Mia Rakijas, and Chris Millis (Montclair, N.J.: Boynton/ Cook, 1986).

you can write it in a way that matches your idea more clearly. Say what you mean aloud to yourself, talk it through—then try writing it again. You may want to rewrite the sentence several ways. You'll probably recognize which one is the best one. If you do rewrite an entire sentence, you should reread the paragraph it's in to make sure you haven't disrupted the flow of the ideas and language. If, when you've made decisions about all suggested changes, you discover you've made so many that it's hard to read your paper, ask your teacher if she'd like you to retype it. If you do retype it, remember it needs proofreading again. (This is one advantage of writing on a computer.)

If your teacher gives you additional class time, you can share your findings and problems with others in the class. All of us store rules about language in our heads, even though we may not be consciously aware of them. If we didn't have such rules, we couldn't talk or write at all. If you can become consciously aware of the rules you use, you can discard or alter those that are unacceptable (as defined by your teacher or the grammar book you are using) and sharpen those that are valid. Class discussion will make you aware of which you should keep and which you should discard.

If you make a relatively high number of usage errors, you'll need to do some extra work. Set aside several pages in your journal or notebook to list the errors you make. In this way, you can discover which errors recur and concentrate on avoiding them. What you'll probably discover is that you're not making many different errors, but the same errors over and over. Your teacher may, of course, expect you to do some extra work to begin clearing up your particular set of errors.

Your teacher probably won't be able to provide time in class for you to proofread and copyedit every paper you hand in. But *you* should find the time for it. You may be able to make arrangements with classmates to do this outside of class. Otherwise, you can ask your roommate, a friend, or a family member. You can even hire a tutor to help. Very few of us are able to edit ourselves, but most of us can do a better job on someone else's paper than on our own. (Every published writer gets help copyediting from editors—as we did on this book.) Typographical and usage errors can destroy the best piece of writing; once you've spent a lot of time getting your thoughts straight and in good order, it's foolish not to take a little extra time to make them readable. Surface flubs can make readers decide not to read at all—or to read in a hostile mood.

Table of Readings

Table of Short Essays in "Ruminations and Theory" Sections

Works Cited

See Acknowledgments for bibliographical information on the readings and the process boxes.

Austen, Jane. *Pride and Prejudice.* New York: Penguin, 1981.

Balaban, John. "South of Pompeii the Helmsman Balked." *College English* 39 (Dec. 1977): 437–41.

Bashō. *A Haiku Journey: Bashō's "The Narrow Road to the Far North" and Selected Haiku.* Trans. Dorothy Britton. New York: Harper and Row, 1974.

Belanoff, Pat, et al. *The Right Handbook.* Upper Montclair, NJ: Boynton/Cook, 1986.

Berthoff, Ann. "A Curious Triangle and the Double-Entry Notebook; or How Theory Can Help Us Teach Reading and Writing." *The Making of Meaning: Metaphors, Models, and Maxims for Writing Teachers.* Upper Montclair, NJ: Boynton/Cook, 1981. 41–47.

Blau, Sheridan. "Invisible Writing: Investigating Cognitive Process in Composition." *College Composition and Communication* 34 (1983): 297–312.

Britton, James, et al. *The Development of Writing Abilities (11–18).* Urbana, IL: NCTE, 1975.

Bruffee, Kenneth. *A Short Course in Writing.* Boston: Little, Brown, 1985.

Chaucer, Geoffrey. "The Nun's Priest's Tale." *Works of Geoffrey Chaucer.* Ed. F. N. Robinson. 2nd ed. Boston: Houghton Mifflin, 1957.

Clemens, Samuel. *Adventures of Huckleberry Finn.* New York: Dodd, 1984.

Conrad, Joseph. Preface. *The Nigger of the Narcissus.* New York: Doubleday, 1954.

Cowley, Abraham. *The Essays and Other Prose Writings of Abraham Cowley.* Ed. Alfred B. Gough. Oxford: Clarendon Press, 1915.

Daily News. Unsigned Letter to the Editor. 20 Mar. 1986.

Darwin, Charles. *Autobiography of Charles Darwin.* Ed. Nora Barlow. New York: Norton, 1969.

Dickens, Charles. *A Tale of Two Cities.* New York: Bantam, 1981.

Durso, Joseph. "Knight Has a Whirlwind Week." *New York Times* 1 June 1986: 53.

Elbow, Peter. "Methodological Doubting and Believing: Contraries in Inquiry." *Embracing Contraries: Explorations in Learning and Teaching.* New York: Oxford UP, 1986. 254–300.

———. *Writing with Power.* New York: Oxford UP, 1973.

———. *Writing without Teachers.* New York: Oxford UP, 1981.

Gendlin, Eugene. "Experimental Phenomenology." *Phenomenology and the Social Sciences.* Ed. M. Natanson. Chicago, Northwestern UP. 1973.

———. *Focusing.* 2nd ed. New York: Bantam, 1981.

Gray, Francine du Plessix. "I Write for Revenge against Reality." *New York Times Book Review* 12 Sept. 1982: 3.

Hailey, Arthur. *Airport.* New York: Doubleday, 1968.

Hardwick, Elizabeth. "Its Only Defense: Intelligence and Sparkle." *New York Times Book Review* 14 Sept. 1986: 1.

Hopkins, Gerard Manley. "Spring and Fall: To a Young Child." *Poems of Gerard Manley Hopkins.* London: Oxford UP, 1930.

James, William. *The Variety of Reli-*

gious Experience. New York: Penguin, 1982.

Joyce, James. *Portrait of the Artist as a Young Man.* New York: Penguin, 1977.

———. *Ulysses.* New York: Random, 1967.

Lucretius. *The Nature of Things.* Trans. F. O. Copley. New York: Norton, 1977.

Lurie, Pauline. Letter to the Editor. *New York Times* 19 Aug. 1987.

Maclean, Norman. *A River Runs through It.* Chicago: Chicago UP, 1976.

Macrorie, Ken. *Searching Writing.* Rochelle Park, NJ: Hayden, 1980.

———. *A Vulnerable Teacher.* Rochelle Park, NJ: Hayden, 1974.

———. *Writing To Be Read.* Rochelle Park, NJ: Hayden, 1968.

Michener, James A. *Hawaii.* New York: Random, 1959.

Montaigne, Michel de. *Montaigne: Essays.* Trans. J. M. Cohen. New York: Penguin, 1959.

Neisser, Ulrich. *Cognitive Psychology.* New York: Appleton-Century, 1967.

New York Times, Unsigned Letter to the Editor. 20 Mar. 1986.

Odell, Lee. "The Process of Writing and the Process of Learning." *College Composition and Communication* 31 (1980): 42–50.

Perl, Sondra, and Nancy Wilson.

"Guidelines for Composing." Appendix A. *Through Teachers' Eyes: Portraits of Writing Teachers at Work.* Portsmouth, NH: Heinemann, 1986. 165–69.

Pope, Alexander. "An Essay on Man." *Pope: Poems and Prose.* New York: Penguin, 1985.

Schultz, John. *Writing from Start to Finish.* Upper Montclair, NJ: Boynton/Cook, 1982.

Sheehy, Eugene P. *Guide to Reference Books.* Chicago: American Library Assn., 1986.

Stafford, William. "A Way of Writing." *Writing the Australian Crawl.* Ann Arbor, MI: U of Michigan P, 1978. 17–20.

Stevens, Wallace. "Thirteen Ways of Looking at a Blackbird." *Harmonium.* New York: Knopf, 1950. 158.

Stowe, Harriet Beecher. *Uncle Tom's Cabin.* New York: Bantam, 1981.

Swift, Jonathan. *Gulliver's Travels. The Portable Swift.* Ed. Carl Van Doren. New York: Viking, 1977.

———. *A Modest Proposal. The Portable Swift.* Ed. Carl Van Doren. New York: Viking, 1977.

Wilbur, Richard. "The Writer." *New and Collected Poems.* New York: Harcourt Brace Jovanovich, 1988.

Williams, William Carlos. "A Sort of Song." *Collected Later Poems.* New York: New Directions, 1944.

Acknowledgments

Page 10: Excerpt from *The Autobiography of Charles Darwin,* edited by Nora Barlow. Reprinted by permission of Harcourt Brace Jovanovich, Inc. and A. D. Peters & Co., Ltd.

Page 24: "Robert Bingham (1925–82)," *The New Yorker,* July 5, 1952. Reprinted by permission; © 1982 The New Yorker Magazine, Inc.

Page 27: Excerpted from Donald Murray, "The Feel of Writing—And Teaching Writing," in *Reinventing the Rhetorical Tradition,* edited by Aviva Freedman and Ian Pringle (Conway, AR: L&S Books, for the Canadian Council of Teachers of English, 1980). Copyright © by the Canadian Council of Teachers of English. Reprinted by permission.

Page 46: Excerpted by permission from Robert Parker and Vera Goodkin, "Kathy's Writing," *The Consequences of Writing: Enhancing Learning in the Disciplines,* Boynton/Cook Publishers, A Division of Heinemann Educational Books, Inc.

Page 57: Excerpted by permission from Raymond Federman, in *Anything Can Happen,* edited by Tom LeClair and Larry McCaffery, University of Illinois Press.

Page 81: Preface to *The Nigger of the Narcissus* by Joseph Conrad. Copyright 1914 by Doubleday, a division of Bantam, Doubleday, Dell Publishing Group, Inc. Reprinted by permission of the publisher.

Page 89: Excerpt copyright 1941, 1969 by Eudora Welty, reprinted from "A Worn Path" in her volume *A Curtain of Green and Other Stories* by permission of Harcourt Brace Jovanovich, Inc.

Page 91: From Madeleine Blais, "Monica's Barrel," *Tropic* Magazine, Sunday Magazine of *The Miami Herald,* August 9, 1987, pp. 15–16.

Page 108: Eudora Welty, "A Worn Path," copyright 1941 and renewed 1969 by Eudora Welty, reprinted from *A Curtain of Green and Other Stories* by permission of Harcourt Brace Jovanovich, Inc.

Page 115: "The Story of Caedmon's Hymn," in *The Whole Works of King Alfred the Great,* trans. J. A. Giles, vol. 2, pp. 348–51. Reprinted from the AMS Press edition of 1969.

Page 118: Reprinted by permission from "Guidelines for Composing," in Sondra Perl and Nancy Wilson, *Through Teachers' Eyes,* Heinemann Educational Books, Inc.

Page 123: From Virginia Woolf, "Sunday (Easter) 20 April," from *The Diary of Virginia Woolf,* Vol. I: 1915–1919, edited by Anne Olivier Bell, copyright © 1977 by Quentin Bell and Angelica Garnett, reprinted by permission of Harcourt Brace Jovanovich, Inc.

Page 125: From Joseph Durso, "Knight Has a Whirlwind Week," *New York Times.* June 1, 1986. Copyright © 1986 by The New York Times Company. Reprinted by permission.

Page 126: From William Stafford, "A Way of Writing." First appeared in *Field.* Reprinted by permission.

Page 134: From Eugene Gendlin, "Experiential Phenomenology," in *Phenomenology in the Social Sciences,* vol. 1, edited by Maurice Natanson. Copyright © 1973 by Northwestern University Press. All rights reserved. Reprinted by permission of the publisher.

Page 156: From Mark Levensky, "A Letter," *Elementary English* Jan.

York Times Company. Reprinted by permission.

Page 247: From Eric Havelock, "Orality, Literacy, and Star Wars," *Written Communication* Oct. 1986: 411–20. Copyright © 1986 by Sage Publications, Inc. Reprinted by permission of Sage Publications, Inc.

Page 253: Richard Wilbur, "The Writer," from *The Mind-Reader*. Copyright © 1971 by Richard Wilbur, reprinted from his volume *The Mind-Reader* by permission of Harcourt Brace Jovanovich, Inc.

Page 255: From Anne Sexton, "Noted with Pleasure," *New York Times Book Review* Oct. 13, 1985. Copyright © 1985 by The New York Times Company. Reprinted by permission.

Page 262: Seamus Heaney, "Digging," from *Poems 1965–1975* by Seamus Heaney. Copyright © 1966, 1969, 1972, 1975, 1980 by Seamus Heaney. Reprinted by permission of Farrar, Straus and Giroux, Inc. and Faber and Faber, Ltd.

Page 265: H.D., "Poem," from *Collected Poems, 1912–1944*. Copyright © 1982 by The Estate of Hilda Doolittle. Reprinted by permission of New Directions Publishing Corporation.

Page 266: Excerpted from Norman Holland, *Poems in Persons*. Reprinted by permission of Sterling Lord Literistic, Inc. Copyright © 1973 by Norman Holland.

Page 287: Eudora Welty, "Is Phoenix Jackson's Grandson Really Dead?" From *The Eye of the Story: Selected Essays and Reviews by Eudora Welty*. Copyright © 1978 by Eudora Welty. Reprinted by permission of Random House, Inc.

Page 306: Excerpted from Janet Emig, "Non-Magical Thinking: Presenting Writing Developmentally in Schools," *The Web of Meaning,* 1983, by permission of Lawrence Erlbaum Associates, Inc., Publishers.

Page 329: From *Hunger of Memory* by Richard Rodriguez. Copyright © 1981 by Richard Rodriguez. Reprinted by permission of David R. Godine, Publisher.

Page 338: Excerpted by permission from Rosellen Brown, in *Anything Can Happen,* edited by Tom LeClair and Larry McCaffery, University of Illinois Press.

Page 348: Reprinted by permission from Lorraine Mitchell, "Preacher Grandmother," in *Searching Writing* by Ken Macrorie, Boynton/Cook Publishers, A Division of Heinemann Educational Books, Inc.

Page 359: From Elizabeth Hardwick, "Its Only Defense: Intelligence and Sparkle," *New York Times* Sept. 14, 1986. Copyright © 1986 by The New York Times Company. Reprinted by permission.

Page 362: From Edmund Gosse, "The Essay." Reprinted with permission from *Encyclopaedia Britannica,* 11th edition (1910–11).

Page 366: Reprinted by permission from James Moffett, "On Essaying," in *Fforum: Essays on Theory and Practice in the Teaching of Writing,* edited by Patricia L. Stock, Boynton/Cook Publishers, A Division of Heinemann Educational Books, Inc.

Page 369: From Edward Hoagland, "Essay: What I Think, What I Am," *New York Times* June 27, 1976. Copyright © 1976 by The New York Times Company. Reprinted by permission.

Page 382: Excerpt from Michael Gregory and Susanne Carroll, *Language and Situation: Language Varieties and Their Social Context.* Reprinted by permission of Routledge & Kegan Paul.

Page 390: From Breyne Arlene Moskowitz, "The Acquisition of Language," *Scientific American* Nov. 1978: 92–95. Copyright © 1978 by Scientific American, Inc. All rights reserved.

Page 394: From Roger Brown, "Development of the First Language in the Human Species," *American Psychologist* 27 (1973): 79–106.

Page 397: "Preliminaries to Theories on Brain Mechanisms of Language" from "The Neurology of Language" by Eric H. Lenneberg is reprinted from *Language as a Human Problem,* edited by Einar Haugen and Morton Bloomfield, by permission of W. W. Norton & Company, Inc. Copyright © 1973, 1974 by the American Academy of Arts and Sciences.

Page 401: From Dylan Thomas, "Poem in October," *The Poems of Dylan Thomas.* Copyright 1945 by the Trustees for the Copyrights of Dylan Thomas. First published in *Poetry.* Reprinted by permission of New Directions Publishing Corporation and David Higham Associates, Ltd.

Page 402: Excerpted by permission from Robert Coover in *Anything Can Happen,* edited by Tom LeClair and Larry McCaffery, University of Illinois Press.

Pages 403, 404: Excerpts from Wallace Stevens, "Thirteen Ways of Looking at a Blackbird." Copyright 1923 and renewed 1951 by Wallace Stevens. Reprinted from *The Collected Poems of Wallace Stevens* by permission of Alfred A. Knopf, Inc.

Page 413: Kate Barnes, "My Mother, That Feast of Light," *Blair and Ketchum's Country Journal* (Brattleboro, VT: Country Journal Publishing Co., 1984).

Page 415: Excerpt from Norman Holland, *Poems in Persons.* Reprinted by permission of Sterling Lord Literistic, Inc. Copyright © 1973 by Norman Holland.

Page 417: Excerpted by permission from Lu Chi, "Rhymeprose on Literature: The *Wen-Fu* of Lu Chi," translated by Achilles Fang, *Harvard Journal of Asiatic Studies* 14 (1951): 527–66.

Page 418: Sherwood Anderson, "The Book of the Grotesque," from *Winesburg, Ohio* by Sherwood Anderson. Copyright 1919 by B. W. Heubsch, Inc., renewed 1947 by Eleanor Oppenhaver Anderson. All rights reserved. Reprinted by permission of Viking Penguin, Inc.

Page 423: Excerpt from E. M. Forster from *Writers at Work, Fourth Series,* edited by George Plimpton. Copyright © 1974, 1976 by The Paris Review, Inc. All rights reserved. Reprinted by permission of Viking Penguin, Inc.

Page 433: William Carlos Williams, "A Sort of Song," from William Carlos Williams, *Collected Later Poems.* Copyright 1944 by William Carlos Williams. Reprinted by permission of New Directions Publishing Corporation.

About the Authors

Peter Elbow is Professor of English at the University of Massachusetts at Amherst. He is author of *Writing without Teachers, Writing with Power, Embracing Contraries: Explorations in Learning and Teaching,* and *Oppositions in Chaucer.* He has published numerous articles about writing, teaching and literature and has given talks and conducted workshops at many schools and colleges across the country. He was formerly Director of Writing Programs at the State University of New York at Stony Brook and in his twenty-five years of teaching has also taught at the Massachusetts Institute of Technology, Franconia College, Evergreen State College, and Wesleyan University. He received a B.A. from Williams College, a B.A. and an M.A. from Exeter College, Oxford University, and a Ph.D. from Brandeis University.

Pat Belanoff is Director of Writing Programs and Assistant Professor of English at the State University of New York at Stony Brook. She was previously Assistant Director of the Expository Writing Program at New York University and has taught at the Borough of Manhattan Community College, a branch of the City University of New York, and at Kean College in New Jersey. She is a co-author of *The Right Handbook* and the author of numerous articles on writing, teaching writing, teaching literature, and the women of Old English poetry.